“In an era in which misinformation and “alternative facts” abound, it is difficult to know what to believe anymore. The resulting uncertainty has seeped into all corners of human consciousness, including the self. The second edition of the *Handbook of the Uncertain Self* brings together a distinguished group of scientists who grapple with the key issues within this domain. Their insights crystalize what is known and lay out the agenda for future work on this topic, making this volume essential reading for anyone interested in this topic.”

William Swann, *Professor of Psychology, University of Texas, Austin*

“Uncertainty is the ubiquitous feature of the fast-changing world we live in. It is about the only thing one can be certain about. This important volume illuminates the varied ways in which uncertainty affects people’s lives for good or ill, and offers useful insights about coping with uncertainty’s inevitable reality.”

Arie Kruglanski, *Distinguished University Professor of Psychology, University of Maryland, College Park*

“The book takes on a major challenge of our time—uncertainty about who we are and who we want to be in a rapidly changing world. A stellar lineup of authors take on this challenge through a wide range of lenses, including cognitive, intergroup, and relationship processes. For those who want to understand self-doubt and self-uncertainty, this book is a must read.”

Jennifer Crocker, *Emeritus Professor and Ohio Eminent Scholar in Psychology, The Ohio State University*

THE ROUTLEDGE HANDBOOK OF THE UNCERTAIN SELF

The second edition of this handbook explores the social, cognitive, motivational, interpersonal, clinical, and applied aspects of personal uncertainty. It showcases both the diversity and the unity that defines contemporary perspectives on uncertainty in self within social and personality psychology.

Featuring chapters written by distinguished scholars from a range of disciplines in psychology, this book explores the similarities and differences between personal uncertainty and other psychological experiences in terms of their nature and relationship with human thought, emotion, motivation, and behavior. It takes an interactionist perspective to examine what social and personality psychology knows about the experience of self-uncertainty in its various forms, exploring its determinants and consequences within and across individuals and groups. The new edition has been extensively revised and updated and includes new material on self-uncertainty within intimate relationships, in groups, and within spiritual and educational contexts. There is also new content on conspiratorial thinking as well as on the uncertain self within the broader context of uncertainty associated with the COVID-19 pandemic. Throughout, strategies specifically designed to assist others in confronting the unique challenges posed by self-uncertainty in ways that emphasize healthy psychological functioning and growth are promoted.

Featuring cutting-edge theory and research on the determinants, experiences, and consequences of uncertainty in the self, the handbook is an invaluable resource for researchers, practitioners, and senior undergraduate and graduate students in social and personality psychology, clinical and counseling psychology, educational psychology, and developmental psychology.

Patrick J. Carroll is Professor of Psychology at The Ohio State University-Lima, USA.

Kimberly Rios is Professor of Psychology at the University of Illinois-Urbana Champaign, USA.

Kathryn C. Oleson is Professor of Psychology at Reed College, USA.

ROUTLEDGE INTERNATIONAL HANDBOOKS

THE ROUTLEDGE INTERNATIONAL HANDBOOK OF CRITICAL DISABILITY STUDIES
Edited by Katie Ellis, Mike Kent and Kim Cousins

THE ROUTLEDGE INTERNATIONAL HANDBOOK OF SIGNIFICANCE AND MATTERING
Edited by Arie Kruglanski, Isaac Prilleltensky and Amiram Raviv

THE HANDBOOK FOR THE FUTURE OF WORK
Edited by Julie MacLeavy and Frederick Harry Pitts

THE ROUTLEDGE INTERNATIONAL HANDBOOK OF HIMALAYAN ENVIRONMENTS, DEVELOPMENT AND WELLBEING
Edited by Ben Campbell, Mary Cameron and Tanka Subba

THE ROUTLEDGE HANDBOOK OF ACCOUNTING FOR THE SUSTAINABLE DEVELOPMENT GOALS
Edited By Andrea Venturelli and Chiara Mio

THE ROUTLEDGE HANDBOOK OF THE UNCERTAIN SELF, 2ND EDITION
Edited by Patrick J. Caroll, Kimberly Rios and Kathryn C. Oleson

THE HANDBOOK OF CULTURAL ECOSYSTEM SERVICES
Edited by Pamela McElwee, Karen Allen, Rachelle K. Gould, Minna Hsu and Jun He

ROUTLEDGE HANDBOOK ON TRANSNATIONAL COMMERCIAL LAW
Edited by Bruno Zeller and Camilla Baasch Andersen

THE ROUTLEDGE HANDBOOK OF THE UNCERTAIN SELF

Second Edition

Edited by
Patrick J. Carroll, Kimberly Rios, and Kathryn C. Oleson

Routledge
Taylor & Francis Group
NEW YORK AND LONDON

Designed cover image: gremlin via Getty Images

Second edition published 2025
by Routledge
605 Third Avenue, New York, NY 10158

and by Routledge
4 Park Square, Milton Park, Abingdon, Oxon, OX14 4RN

Routledge is an imprint of the Taylor & Francis Group, an informa business

First edition published by Psychology Press 2010

Library of Congress Cataloging-in-Publication Data
Names: Carroll, Patrick J. (Patrick James), editor. | Rios, Kimberly (College teacher), editor. | Oleson, Kathryn Carman, editor.
Title: The Routledge handbook of the uncertain self / edited by Patrick J. Carroll, Kimberly Rios, and Kathryn C. Oleson.
Description: Second edition. | New York, NY : Routledge, 2025. | Series: Routledge international handbooks | Includes bibliographical references and index.
Identifiers: LCCN 2024040591 | ISBN 9781032425917 (hardback) | ISBN 9781032420233 (paperback) | ISBN 9781003363385 (ebook)
Subjects: LCSH: Uncertainty. | Social psychology.
Classification: LCC BF463.U5 R68 2025 | DDC 153.4—dc23/eng/20241023
LC record available at https://lccn.loc.gov/2024040591

ISBN: 9781032425917 (hbk)
ISBN: 9781032420233 (pbk)
ISBN: 9781003363385 (ebk)

DOI: 10.4324/9781003363385

Typeset in Times New Roman
by codeMantra

***Kathy**: To Gordon, Sydney, and Jackson, with much love and certainty.*
***Kim**: To my late colleague and mentor Mark Alicke. I miss your insights about self-concept research, your random (hilarious) emails, and most of all your friendship.*
***Pat**: I would like to dedicate this to my parents.*
***Collective dedication**: In addition to our individual dedications, we would like to collectively dedicate this handbook to the memory of Robert (Bob) Arkin. Bob was a wonderful colleague, mentor, and friend, in addition to being a loving father and husband. His interest in self-uncertainty was an ongoing theme of his many collaborations with students and colleagues. He was the guiding force behind the first edition of this handbook and continues to be an inspiration to those studying the uncertain self. He will be sorely missed but his intellectual influence along with his generosity of spirit lives on in the hearts and minds of those who knew him.*

CONTENTS

ABOUT THE EDITORS

Patrick J. Carroll, PhD, is currently a Professor of Psychology at The Ohio State University-Lima. After receiving his PhD from the University of Florida, he was a National Institute of Mental Health Postdoctoral Fellow in the Social Psychology program at The Ohio State University from 2004 to 2007. His research focuses on the social revision of identity and the ultimate consequences of those identity revisions for mental health and well-being. His work has been featured in several leading journals within social and personality psychology, including the *Journal of Experimental Social Psychology and Social Psychological and Personality Science*. He is a fellow of both the Society of Experimental Social Psychology and the Society of Personality and Social Psychologists and has served as co-associate editor for a special issue of *Basic and Applied Social Psychology*. He currently serves on the editorial board of the journal of *Self and Identity, Imagination, Cognition, and Personality, Frontiers in Psychology*, and the *Journal of Social Psychological Research*. Carroll also served as co-editor of the 2010 *Handbook of the Uncertain Self* and the 2015 *Handbook of Personal Security* through Taylor & Francis press.

Dr. Kimberly Rios is Professor of Psychology at the University of Illinois Urbana-Champaign. The overarching goal of her work is to better understand how individuals respond to threats to their social and personal identities, with a particular focus on majority versus minority identity. Her work has been published in several different leading journals within social and personality psychology, including *Personality and Social Psychology Review*, *Personality and Social Psychology Bulletin*, *Social Psychological and Personality Science*, and the *Journal of Experimental Social Psychology*. She was awarded the 2019 Outstanding Early Career Award by the International Society for Self and Identity, as well as the 2024 Society for Experimental Social Psychology Diversity Science Award. She has also earned several extramural grants from organizations such as the Russell Sage Foundation, the John Templeton Foundation, and the Society for the Psychological Study of Social Issues to support her work. Finally, she serves as Editor-in-Chief for the journal *Self and Identity*, Specialty Chief Editor for the groups and intergroup relations section of the brand-new journal *Frontiers in Social Psychology,* and Associate Editor for *Group Processes and Intergroup Relations* and the *International Journal for the Psychology of Religion.*

Dr. Kathryn (Kathy) Oleson is Dean of the Faculty and Patricia and Clifford Lunneborg Professor of Psychology at Reed College. She joined the Reed faculty in 1995 as a professor of psychology before becoming the dean of the faculty in July 2020. She served as the founding director of the Center for Teaching and Learning at Reed from 2014 to 2016. She earned an MA and PhD in Social Psychology from Princeton University, funded by a National Science Foundation Graduate Fellowship, and a BA in Psychology from the University of Kansas. She served as a National Institute of Mental Health Postdoctoral Fellow at Ohio State University from 1993 to 1995. She has been Associate Editor of the journal *Basic and Applied Social Psychology* and co-editor (with Robert Arkin and Patrick J. Carroll) of the *Handbook of the Uncertain Self.* Her research primarily explores ways to make the college classroom more inclusive, with a particular focus on productive and unproductive discomfort. In 2021, she published a resource for faculty to facilitate creating an inclusive college classroom: *Promoting Inclusive Classroom Dynamics in Higher Education: A Research-Based Pedagogical Guide for Faculty* (Stylus Publishing).

CONTRIBUTORS

Marios Biskas is a Postdoctoral Researcher at the University of Bradford, UK. His research focuses on self-regulation, with a particular emphasis on how emotions impact well-being.

Shannon T. Brady is an Assistant Professor of Psychology at Wake Forest University. Her research examines how people make meaning of themselves and their environments, how various practices and messages affect this meaning-making, and the consequences thereof for diverse outcomes including well-being, achievement, relationships, and inequality.

Pablo Briñol is a Professor of Psychology at Universidad Autónoma de Madrid (Spain). His research on attitudes and persuasion focuses on understanding fundamental processes of psychological change.

Patrick J. Carroll is a Professor of Psychology at The Ohio State University-Lima, USA. His research examines the determinants and consequences of self-change.

Nathan N. Cheek is an Assistant Professor at the University of Maryland, College Park, USA. His research explores how people reason about their own and others' experiences, including how people make sense of their choices and how people understand the effects of hardship and adversity.

Zhansheng Chen is a Professor of Psychology at The University of Hong Kong. His research focuses on social influence. In particular, he investigates the consequences of ostracism and objectification. He is also interested in positive psychology.

Marcus Chur is a Graduate Student in Clinical Psychology at the University of Colorado Springs. His work focuses on PTSD and other responses to trauma.

David Dunning is the Walgreen Professor of the Study of Human Understanding, and of Psychology, at the University of Michigan. He focuses on the psychology underlying misbeliefs about the self and the surrounding social world.

Molly Ellenberg is a PhD Candidate in Social Psychology at the University of Maryland (USA). She holds an MA in Forensic Psychology from The George Washington University and a BS in Psychology with a Specialization in Clinical Psychology from UC San Diego. Her research focuses on terrorism, radicalization, and deradicalization, and the quest for significance. Her research has been cited over 400 times and has been published in numerous peer-reviewed journals.

Julie J. Exline is a Professor in the Department of Psychological Sciences at Case Western Reserve University. She does research on spiritual struggles and supernatural beliefs and experiences.

Rebecca Getu graduated with an undergraduate degree in Psychology from Wake Forest University. She has a keen interest in psychological research and mental health advocacy.

Jeff Greenberg is a Regents Professor Emeritus of Psychology at the University of Arizona. His theories and research focus on understanding how the knowledge of mortality and other existential concerns affect a wide range of attitudes, beliefs, and behaviors.

Yingchi Guo is a Doctoral Student in Psychology at the University of British Columbia, Canada. Her research focuses on the experiences of self-environment fit and state feelings of authenticity.

Andrew Hales is an Assistant Professor of Psychology at the University of Mississippi, USA. His research focuses on the causes and consequences of social ostracism, and how it can be used to influence others.

Rease Haley is a Psychology student at The Ohio State University-Lima. His research focuses on the link between naïve beliefs about mental health conditions and treatment-seeking behavior.

Marlone D. Henderson is a Professor of Psychology at the University of Texas at Austin. His research examines the role basic cognitive processes play in promoting social harmony.

Michael Hogg is Professor of Social Psychology at Claremont Graduate University, Los Angeles, USA, and an Honorary Professor of Psychology at the University of Kent, UK. His research focuses on social identity dynamics within and between groups, with a specific focus on influence and leadership and on self-uncertainty and extremism.

Zachary P. Hohman is an Associate Professor of Psychology at Texas Tech University, USA. Dr. Hohman's research examines (1) the role that self-uncertainty and attitude ambivalence play in risk-taking, attitude change, and persuasion, (2) influence processes within and between groups, and (3) the structure of self-conception and identity in group and intergroup contexts.

Jennifer L. Howell is an Associate Professor of Psychological Sciences at the University of California, Merced, USA. Her research occurs at the intersection of social and health psychology, with a particular focus on psychological-threat management and health decision-making.

Jacob Juhl is Associate Professor of Psychology at the University of Southampton, UK. His research focuses on existential psychology.

Radhika Kothari is a Psychology Graduate from Mumbai University and a Behavioural Researcher. Her research focuses on self-persuasion, compliance among other forms of social influence.

Allan Lam is a Graduate Student in the Department of Psychology at the University of California, San Diego, USA. His research investigates how the size of a police lineup affects eyewitness identification performance.

Mark Landau is a Professor of Psychology at the University of Kansas, USA. He studies the motivational and cognitive processes behind meaning-making, identity, and self-esteem.

E. Allan Lind is a Professor Emeritus at Duke University. Much of his research investigates perceptions of fairness and how fair treatment affects feelings of inclusion and cooperative behavior.

Denise Marigold is an Associate Professor in Social Development Studies at Renison University College, affiliated with the University of Waterloo, Waterloo, Canada. Her research focuses on self-esteem and close relationship processes.

Ian McGregor is a Professor of Psychology at the University of Waterloo, Canada. His research probes basic motivational dynamics of reactive hostility, extremism, self-transcendence, and meaning in life.

Yehudis Keller is a Clinical Psychology PhD student at Case Western Reserve University, where she researches psychological adjustment in exit from high-cost religion.

Olivia R. Kuljian is an Assistant Professor of Psychology at Eastern Oregon University, USA. Her research investigates how group-level attributes, such as prototypes and leadership, inform self-identity and shape consequences for uncertainty, intergroup relations, and extreme intergroup behavior.

Andrew C. Moffitt is a Clinical Psychology PhD student at Case Western Reserve University. His research focuses on spiritual struggles and their relationship to mental health among sexual and gender minorities.

Erica Molinario, PhD, is an Assistant Professor of Social Psychology at Florida Gulf Coast University (USA) and a Visiting Assistant Professor at the Center for Social Cognitive Studies at Jagiellonian University (Poland). Her research focuses on understanding pro-environmental behaviors, political activism, extremism and radicalization, migration intentions, and intergroup conflicts. Her work has been supported by the US Department of Defense, the Polish National Center of Research, and the European Commission.

Alexis T. Morales is a Graduate Student at the University of Illinois Urbana-Champaign. Her research focuses on identity conflict.

Steffen Moritz is a Professor of Psychology at the University Medical Center Hamburg, Germany. His research focuses on the understanding and treatment of cognitive biases in psychological disorders.

Gregg A. Muragishi is a Postdoctoral Scholar in the Psychology Department at the University of Washington. His research focuses on identifying and mitigating the effects of cultural biases and stereotypes on marginalized group members' belonging, motivation, retention, and performance in organizational and educational settings.

Sandra L. Murray is a Professor of Psychology at the University at Buffalo, State University of New York. Her research examines motivated cognition in the context of close relationships.

Jae-Eun Namkoong is an Associate Professor of Marketing at the University of Nevada, Reno. Her research focuses on social cognition and causal judgment.

Kathryn C. Oleson is the Dean of the Faculty and Patricia and Clifford Lunneborg Professor of Psychology at Reed College,USA. Her research primarily explores ways to make the college classroom more inclusive, with a particular focus on productive and unproductive discomfort.

Borja Paredes is a Professor of Psychology at Universidad Autónoma de Madrid, Spain. His research focuses on identity, meta-cognition, and their impact on behavior.

Kenneth I. Pargament is a Professor Emeritus at Bowling Green State University. He studies spiritual struggles and efforts to catalyze spiritual competency training across the mental health disciplines.

Richard E. Petty is a Distinguished University Professor of Psychology at The Ohio State University, USA. His research focuses broadly on the situational and individual difference factors responsible for changes in beliefs, attitudes, and behaviors.

Laura Prislei is a PhD Candidate in Social Psychology at Sapienza University of Rome (Italy), where she obtained her MA in Communication and Marketing Psychology and a BS in Psychology and Health. Her research focuses on youth political participation and susceptibility to radicalization particularly in the context of social crises. During her doctoral studies, she undertook research visits to the Jagiellonian University in Krakow and Claremont Graduate University in California, collaborating with leading experts in the field of Social Psychology.

Tom Pyszczynski is Emeritus Distinguished Professor of Psychology at the University of Colorado Springs. His research focuses on the role that awareness of the inevitability of death plays in diverse aspects of life, especially the role it plays in motivating the pursuit of meaning, self-esteem, and close relationships.

Kimberly Rios is a Professor of Psychology at the University of Illinois Urbana-Champaign. Her research focuses on the causes and consequences of perceived threats to personal and group identities.

Young Ju Ryu is a Graduate Student at the University of Kansas, USA. Her research focuses on the motivational basis for both defensive and non-defensive reactions to perceived threat.

Carmen Sanchez is an Assistant Professor at the University of Illinois at Urbana-Champaign, USA. She studies how people misjudge their abilities as they are learning, how to overcome overconfidence and decision-making.

Toni Schmader is a Professor and Head of Psychology at the University of British Columbia, Canada. Her research examines how people are affected by their membership in negatively stereotyped groups.

Barry Schwartz is an Emeritus Professor of Psychology at Swarthmore College and a Visiting Professor at the Haas School of Business at Berkeley. He has written *The Paradox of Choice* and studies choice and the self in collaboration with Nathan N. Cheek.

Constantine Sedikides is Professor of Social-Personality Psychology at the University of Southampton. His research focuses on self-evaluation, narcissism, mental time travel (e.g., nostalgia), and authenticity.

Kyros Shen is a Graduate Student in the Department of Psychology at the University of California, San Diego, USA. His research investigates how the similarity of faces in a police lineup affects eyewitness identification performance.

Kate Sweeny is a Professor of Psychology at the University of California, Riverside. Her research takes an affective science approach to the question of how to wait well, with a focus on worry and impatience.

Yunqian (Fiona) Tian is a PhD Candidate at The University of Hong Kong, HKSAR, China. Her research focuses on the process of social inclusion and rejection.

Stephanie J. Tobin is a Senior Lecturer in the School of Psychology and Counselling at Queensland University of Technology, Australia. Her research focuses on the social aspects of technology and media use and how they relate to belonging and well-being.

Kees van den Bos is a Professor of Social Psychology and a Professor of Empirical Legal Science at Utrecht University, The Netherlands. He studies fairness judgments, uncertainty feelings, radicalization, and trust in social institutions.

Tim Wildschut is a Professor of Psychology at the University of Southampton, UK. His research focuses on nostalgia.

Kipling Williams is a Distinguished Emeritus Professor of Psychological Sciences at Purdue University. He has published extensively in the areas of ostracism, silent treatment, and social exclusion.

John Wixted is a Professor of Psychology at the University of California, San Diego, USA. His research focuses on the cognitive and brain mechanisms of recognition memory and on the practical use of recognition memory procedures for eyewitness identification.

PREFACE

These days change represents a constant of life. From the pandemic and the economic instability it has fostered to the increasingly polarized and divided political climate, people must adapt to rapid and dramatic changes in the world around them. One adaptation is that individuals have become increasingly dynamic or open to change themselves. Indeed, more than ever in human history, people routinely make voluntary and dramatic changes, ranging from changing careers (including "the great resignation" of the pandemic), to moving from one city to another, through to marrying and divorcing only to remarry again. In his book *The World is Flat*, Tom Friedman tells how exciting this new world is, but he also cautions readers that people can be trampled if they can't keep up with the change. Whether introduced by the person or the environment, change introduces uncertainty into modern life. This uncertainty shrouds the self, the world, and the interrelation between the self and the world. Ironically, then, self-uncertainty, or self-doubt, may be one of the few certainties left in modern life.

This challenge of uncertainty has sprung to the forefront of modern consciousness. It can be seen reflected in contemporary culture, the arts, the business world, politics, consumer behavior, and other arenas. In the arts, the hit Broadway play "Doubt" by the celebrated playwright John Patrick Shanley (e.g., the Oscar-winning screenplay "Moonstruck") is focused on people's certainty of death and the ambiguity of everything else in their lives. Doubt is said to be the norm in life, the "universal condition of man." In the business world, with management models that are to inspire success, confidence has been characterized as the channel through which management decisions are translated into positive results (Rosabeth Moss Kanter, Confidence, 2004). "Consumer confidence" is the common index of the United States and global concerns about the economy and job security. In the global political arena, the role of terrorism in inspiring fear and doubt, anger, and vengeance tends to determine political points of view and, in turn, is influenced by them. The interest in self-doubt can also be seen in the recent proliferation of self-help books, programs, and conferences focusing on how to effectively cope with self-uncertainty within an increasingly uncertain world. In his book, *Disrupt! Think Epic! Be Epic!*, author Bill Jensen outlines how "trusting your gut and values" along with 25 successful habits of 100 contemporary heroes can pave your way through nagging self-doubt arising from an increasingly complex and unstable world to extraordinary accomplishments you too can enjoy.

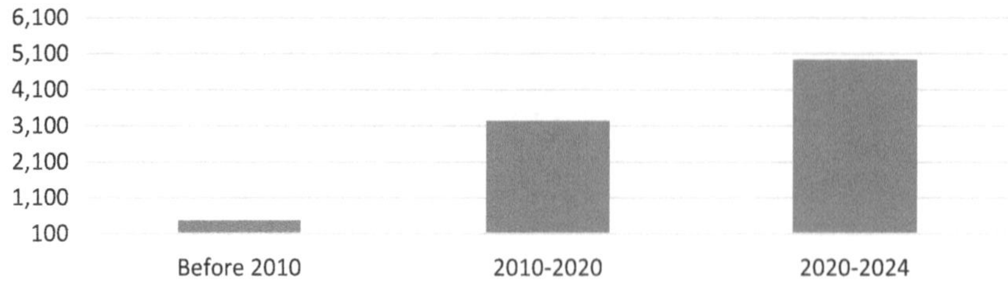

The public interest in the topic is only matched by the continuing scientific interest of self-uncertainty or doubt. In 2010, Taylor and Francis published the *Handbook of the Uncertain Self.* At that time, we defined self-uncertainty or, self-doubt, as uncertainty regarding oneself, the world, and the interrelation among the two. The first edition featured chapters from leading experts on the topic up to that point. Since the publication of the first edition, the scientific appetite for and insights on the topic of self-uncertainty has exploded. To illustrate, Figure 1 displays the historical trend of citation counts per year on self-uncertainty. For example, a quick Google Scholar search using the key terms "self-uncertainty" or "self-doubt" reveals 461 citations/year (total 46,121 citations) from January 1st, 1910 through January 1st, 2010. However, a restricted search reveals that 3,228 citations/year (total 32,280 citations) appeared after the publication of the first edition in 2010 through January 1st, 2020 and, thus, do not include any citations before 2010 or after January 1st, 2020. Since the pandemic hit, the number of such citations per year has continued to skyrocket even higher to 4932 citations/year (total 19,730 citations) within the past four years. That is, rather than fading into obscurity, the topic of self-uncertainty or self-doubt has catapulted into the forefront of public consciousness like never before. As the figure illustrates, the second edition of this handbook could not have come at a better time. The time seems ideal for social and personality psychologists to gather forces once again and confront the issue of personal uncertainty in the social world in this second edition. It will provide the necessary supply of new scholarship on self-uncertainty required to meet the rising demand for additional conceptual and practical knowledge on this topic.

Of course, it should come as no surprise that social and personality psychologists have much to contribute to a better understanding of how people experience and cope with uncertainty in their personal lives. As it turns out, uncertainty or doubt has been an essential ingredient in the core pursuits of social and personality psychology for a long time. In the 1930s, work on conformity by Jenness and Sherif showed that a prevailing accuracy motive would drive people to conform to others when uncertain how to respond in a given situation. In the 1950s, Leon Festinger's theory of informal social communication noted that a pressure toward uniformity in group judgments stemmed from the uncertainty inspired by *dis*unity. Social comparison theory, later in the 1950s, set the stage for a longstanding tradition in which the search for clarity and certainty about one's opinions, emotions, and abilities would guide theory and research for decades. Fritz Heider also distinguished between "persons" and "things" in understanding the world. Whereas the behavior of "things" was predictable based upon natural laws, the behavior of "persons" was only partly predictable, being governed by rules that were inherently uncertain. Today, "understanding" is still a central, guiding motive that organizes many people's thinking about social behavior (e.g., Fiske's BUCET formula).

In the 1960s and 1970s, theory and research on the basis of emotional life and attributions drew on these foundations to show how people would seek information, organize it, and strive to reach a conclusion about the causes of events. Attribution approaches preceded the so-called cognitive revolution in social psychology and became linked with the "warmer" and rich tradition of exploring how people strive to establish prediction and control in their lives, and to deflect feelings of uncertainty, unclarity, and self-doubt. Too, the research on self-deception, self-handicapping, overachievement, causal uncertainty, and many other domains of research all explore the role of motivation in social cognition, sometimes showing that people surprisingly strive to *sustain their uncertainty* rather than confront reality squarely and seek always to be clear, certain, and correct, as Festinger would have had it.

Overall Organization. Apart from substantive quality, we used several criteria to select our ultimate organizational framework for this edited volume. First, like the first edition, we wanted to select an organizational framework that defined the parameters of primary focus and level of analyses at the interface of person and environment. This perspective reflects the true perspective of social and personality psychology that permits the examination of uncertainty within the individual but also embraces analyses that reside in the interface of two, or more, people (e.g., Kuljian and Hohman's work on motivated ingroup behavior). Second, like the first edition, we wanted to use a framework that captures core themes that cut across each of our individual selections without compromising the substantive diversity that separates each unique contribution. In addition to these selection criteria, we have asked second-time contributors to update their chapters considering new theories and research that have emerged in the past fifteen years since the publication of the first edition. We have also added several chapters to cover topics missing from the first edition. Among other new topics, we have added chapters on self-uncertainty within close relationships, groups, spirituality, and educational contexts as well as within the broader context of pandemics like COVID-19.

We separated the 20 individual contributions into three major parts according to distinct themes that unify the individual research programs: (1) Meta-Cognition and Uncertainty (2) Motivation and Uncertainty, and (3) Clinical and Applied Implications of the Uncertain Self. In addition to the thematically organized individual contributions, the edited volume begins with an introduction by the editors which considers historical developments within the study of self-uncertainty and foreshadows the current contributions to the study of self-uncertainty (Chapter 1). The volume closes with a general commentary provided by a leading expert (Michael Hogg) on the general topic of self-uncertainty. This unique combination of broad and specialized expertise provides the ideal perspective within which to both highlight and assimilate those contributions within the broader context of core themes that run throughout the handbook.

Part I Organization. Part I surveys a diverse range of perspectives that emphasize the importance of meta-cognitive processes in the cause and consequences of uncertainty. In Chapter 2, Briñol and Petty review their work on Self-Validation Theory showing how doubt can attenuate, eliminate, or even reverse the impact of thoughts on attitudes and behavior. In Chapter 3, Shen, Lam, and Wixted discuss the complicated relationship between confidence and accuracy in eyewitness testimony, emphasizing the conditions that strengthen the link. In Chapter 4, Cheek and Schwarz discuss how unlimited personal freedom can overwhelm the human decision-maker with numbing uncertainty. In Chapter 5, Paredes, Briñol, and Petty thoughtfully examine how doubt influences the usage of antecedents to identity and the consequences of identity as well as the conditions under which (when) meta-cognitive doubt assessments are more likely to be taken into consideration. In Chapter 6, Carroll, Kothari, & Haley discuss how self-uncertainty ties together processes of identity revision and stability over time. In Chapter 7, Van den Bos and Lind further unpack their general theory of how people manage uncertainty through fairness judgments, detailing (among other things) the role that trust plays in the process. In Chapter 8, Sedikides, Biskas, Juhl, & Wildschut then consider how nostalgia can provide a psychological antidote to self-uncertainty. In Chapter 9, Sanchez, Moritz, and Dunning neatly integrate the literature from clinical and social psychology to illuminate why people in general may be prone to types of errors, including overconfidence, in everyday decision-making and judgment when they jump to conclusions. In Chapter 10, Guo and Schmader present their modified SAFE model to consider how and when states of person-environment misfit are experienced as self-uncertainty.

Part II Organization. Part II includes contributions that consider the role of intrapsychic and interpersonal motivations in the development, maintenance, and consequences of uncertainty in self. In Chapter 11, Landau, Ryu, Greenberg, Chur, & Pyszczynski then discuss the role of death denial in quelling uncertainty over human specialness, belonging, shared reality, and self-esteem that collectively contribute to numbing existential uncertainty. In Chapter 12, Namkoong, Henderson, & Tobin discuss how automatic (automatic abstraction) as well as deliberate mechanisms work together to resolve activated causal uncertainty. In Chapter 13, McGregor and Marigold review a wide range of different intellectual traditions that converge on the problem of anxious uncertainties in life, the reflex for hostile and self-serving reactions to them, and on the power of self-transcendent-value commitment to help overcome anxious-uncertainties and the maladaptive reactions to them. In Chapter 14, Kuljian and Hohman present a compelling theoretical and empirical case for how self-uncertainty mediates the link between prototypicality threats and motivated ingroup behavior. Finally, in Chapter 15, Chen, Law, and Williams examine how uncertainty in one's relational security can be conceptualized as the immediate symptom of painful social exclusions. In Chapter 16, Sandra Murray discusses her fascinating work on how people manage and respond to doubts about relationship security in daily life.

Part III Organization. Part III moves beyond the antecedents and process of uncertainty in self to examine the effects of self-uncertainty within applied and clinical settings. In Chapter 17, Molinario and colleagues thoughtfully examine how pandemic-related uncertainty and angst may be countered by addressing the enhanced certainty of negative outcomes that arise during pandemics like COVID-19 and discuss their work examining how people manage and resolve social identity uncertainty during pandemics like COVID-19. In Chapter 18, Rios and Morales present their fascinating work on the antecedents of belief-based conflicts and their consequences for self-uncertainty. In Chapter 19, Sweeny and Howell present their exciting work on the management of acute uncertainty in daily life. In Chapter 20, Brady and colleagues then discuss her exciting translational work to help underrepresented students overcome lingering doubts about belongingness in university settings. Finally, in Chapter 21, Julie Exline and colleagues conclude by discussing sources, processes, and consequences of religious doubt.

The edited volume closes with a general commentary provided by a leading expert (Michael Hogg) on uncertainty in self. Collectively, these individual contributions as well as the commentaries highlight the diversity and the unity that defines contemporary perspectives on uncertainty in self within social and personality psychology. We are confident that the present handbook will provide readers with a comprehensive, yet accessible, survey of recent advancements in the study of self-uncertainty. Our objective with this Handbook is to help to generate future insights by formally organizing past insights and exploring in the greatest depth thus far this timely topic of personal uncertainty in social life. Although the Uncertain Self has often been an afterthought, it is now front and center under the spotlight of public and scientific interest—and there are compelling reasons for this shift. This volume gathers what is now known while, at the same time, setting the stage for the next wave of research and theory on this critical topic.

1

INTRODUCTION

The Uncertain Self

Kimberly Rios, Kathryn C. Oleson and Patrick J. Carroll

Introduction

People face sweeping changes in the world around them. From the terror and uncertainty stemming from *9/11* and the pandemic, to the globalization of the workplace, to the digital revolution that Tom Friedman portrays in *The World is Flat*, people must adapt themselves to these changes as they emerge. One likely adaptation is that people embrace rather than resist the tides of change in themselves. Perhaps more than ever, people *voluntarily* institute dramatic changes in their professional, personal, and interpersonal lives. People routinely change careers, marry and divorce, and move from one city to the next for a fresh start. Perhaps, nothing exemplified this more than "The Great Resignation" of 2021 in the wake of the pandemic, when the numbers of people voluntarily quitting their jobs skyrocketed to nearly 4 million a month.

Friedman tells how exciting this new world is, but he also cautions that people will be trampled underfoot if they don't keep up with the change. Whether introduced by the individual or the environment, change introduces a measure of uncertainty into modern life. This uncertainty shrouds the self, the world, and the interrelation between the self and the world. For some, this is problematic, whereas for others, it is promising. Rebecca Solnit writes how hope is more intimately connected to uncertainty than certainty (July 2016, The Guardian). For her, the embrace of uncertainty actually offers a refreshing alternative to the certainty of both optimists and pessimists. Indeed, she argues that *only* in this "spaciousness of uncertainty" can we find the opportunities to act to improve the world. Whatever your personal perspective, one certainty is that *un*certainty is a defining quality of today's world. As social and cultural environments have continued to shift at an ever-increasing pace, the issue of uncertainty has become one of the defining struggles of modern human existence.

This struggle with uncertainty is by no means personal either. Rather, it has sprung beyond the individual to all levels of modern life, from family, society, culture, and world stage. For example, at the cultural level, it has been expressed in contemporary movements within the arts, business, consumer behavior, politics, and other arenas. In the arts, the hit Broadway play "Doubt" by the celebrated playwright John Patrick Shanley (e.g., the Oscar-winning screenplay "Moonstruck") is focused on people's certainty of death and the ambiguity of everything else in their lives. In the business world, "consumer confidence" is the common index of concerns about the economy and

DOI: 10.4324/9781003363385-1

job security. In the global political arena, the role of terrorism in inspiring fear and doubt, anger and vengeance, tends to determine political points of view and, in turn, is influenced by them. The interest in self-doubt can also be seen in the recent proliferation of self-help books, programs, and conferences focusing on how to effectively cope with self-uncertainty within an increasingly uncertain world. In *Disrupt! Think Epic! Be Epic!*, author Bill Jensen outlines how "trusting your gut and values," along with 25 successful habits of 100 contemporary heroes, can pave your way through nagging self-doubt to extraordinary accomplishments.

The public interest in self-uncertainty has risen in parallel to the continuing scientific interest in self-uncertainty or doubt. In 2010, Taylor and Francis published the first edition of the *Handbook of the Uncertain Self.* Since the publication of the first edition, the scientific appetite for and insights on the topic of self-uncertainty has exploded (see Figure in Preface). In 2021 (Vol 52, No. 8), there was even an article in the Monitor magazine on the "Science of Uncertainty" (https://www.apa.org/monitor/2021/11/lab-science-uncertainty).

As these examples illustrate, the human struggle with personal uncertainty is a grand and epic battle that continues to increase with the ever-increasing forces of change that inspired it. As a consequence, rather than fading into obscurity, the topic of self-uncertainty has catapulted further into the forefront of public and scientific consciousness.

The History of Self-Uncertainty in Social and Personality Psychology

Thus, the present time seems ideal for social and personality psychologists to gather forces once again in this second edition and confront the issue of personal uncertainty head-on in the social world. And, why not? Across its history, social and personality psychology has exalted the study of personal uncertainty as a core intellectual pursuit.

In the 1930s, work on conformity showed that a prevailing accuracy motive would drive people to conform to others when uncertain about how to respond in a given situation (Jenness, 1932; Sherif, 1935 autokinetic effect). In the 1950s, Leon Festinger in his theory of informal social communication noted that a pressure toward uniformity in group judgments stemmed from the uncertainty inspired by *dis*unity. Later in the 1950s, Social Comparison Theory (Festinger, 1954) suggested that, when people felt uncertain about their own attitudes, opinions, or abilities, they would seek out similar others in order to make comparisons that confirmed the accuracy of those attitudes, opinions, and abilities. In so doing, it set the stage for a longstanding tradition in which the search for clarity and certainty about one's opinions, emotions, and abilities would guide theory and research for decades. Fritz Heider also distinguished between "persons" and "things" in understanding the world (Heider, 1958). In this view, whereas the behavior of "things" was predictable based upon natural laws, the behavior of "persons" was only partly predictable, being governed by rules that were inherently uncertain. Today, "understanding" is still a central, guiding motive that organizes many people's thinking about the social world and their place within it (see Susan Fiske's BUCET model, 2004).

Throughout the 1960s and 1970s, new theories and research on emotion and motivation as well as attributional processes (Schacter & Singer's Misattribution paradigms, 1962; or Jones & Gerard's concept of Unequivocal Behavioral Orientation-UBO, 1967) built from these early foundations laid down by Festinger and Heider to show how people seek information, organize it, and strive to come to a conclusion about the causes of events. Attribution approaches preceded the so-called cognitive revolution in social psychology and became linked with the "warmer" tradition of exploring how people strive to establish prediction and control in their lives, and to deflect feelings of uncertainty, unclarity, and self-doubt. The work on the self-assessment motive assumed that we were driven to reduce uncertainty and attain accurate self-appraisals (see Sedikides & Strube, 1997; Trope, 1979). Reducing uncertainty and achieving a sense of self-certainty was considered an important motivational priority because the self is a major organizing structure or frame of reference for diverse thoughts, feelings, and perceptions.

Other work began to focus on the developmental underpinnings and consequences of self-doubt. For example, Berglas and Jones (1978) discussed how self-doubt arose from early "conditional love experiments," wherein the child received mixed messages regarding the exact antecedent conditions that produced parental love and approval. Too, the research on self-deception, motivated reasoning, self-handicapping, subjective overachievement, causal uncertainty, and many other domains of inquiry have all explored the role of motivation in social cognition, sometimes showing that people surprisingly respond in ways to *sustain* their self-uncertainty and illusions rather than to confront reality head-on and always seek to be certain and correct, as Festinger would have had it.

Although past social and personality psychologists have already made enormous contributions to the study of this topic, their intellectual bloodline also runs thick through the cutting-edge contributions of *today's* generation of self-uncertainty scholars. Indeed, from Van den Bos's Uncertainty Management Model, to Hogg's Uncertainty Identity Theory, and Sweeny's Uncertainty Navigation Model, the study of personal uncertainty remains alive and well. And, as these newer contributions continue to proliferate, the need to organize them into a single centralized sourcebook has grown too.

To that end, we set out 15 years ago to chart the theoretical and empirical landscape of the Uncertain Self in the first edition. As then, this edition of the handbook presents a theoretically organized and representative sample of 21 leading perspectives (excluding introductory chapter and commentary) on personal uncertainty within today's social and personality psychology. Before diving into the guiding goals, focal concept, and prevailing perspective, we first step back to note the points of similarity as well as the distinction between the current and prior edition of this handbook.

Similarities and Differences between Second and First Volume

The current volume has points of both overlap with and distinction from the first volume. In many ways, this is designed to strike that delicate balance between maintaining continuity in the narrative of personal uncertainty while, at the same time, pushing it further to include new storylines. In terms of similarities, beyond the obvious inclusion of some of the same authors, we discuss below how the current edition adopts the same definition of personal uncertainty, the same guiding goals, and the same "interactionist" perspective. Moreover, the current volume retains the same three-part thematic organization (see below) as well as a relative focus on the antecedents, processes, and consequences of personal uncertainty.

Despite these points of similarity, however, points of distinction exist as well. There are new features and elements of the current volume that were not present in the original version. First and foremost, the current volume has benefitted from 15 additional years of theory and evidence on the topic of personal uncertainty. Thus, setting aside the new contributors, even the return contributors bring to bear over a decade more of additional conceptual and empirical insights.

Second, this edition includes a greater representation of chapters focusing on how uncertainty relates to specific key issues in modern society. For example, the second section now includes a contribution that examines how uncertainty operates in the context of significant relationships. The third section includes contributions that examine how uncertainty operates in the aftermath of

COVID-19 and belief conflict as well as in the context of religious beliefs. The third section also includes a contribution that unpacks a fascinating new Emotion-Motivation-Obstruction model of how people manage the experience of acute uncertainty in stressful waiting periods and another contribution that surveys how theoretical models can inform practical interventions to reduce feelings of belongingness uncertainty among marginalized groups within educational or even work contexts. These contributions are not only grounded in sound theory but, in addition, illustrate how theory can be applied to better understand and manage important issues in modern society.

Third, this edition features a greater representation of chapters focused on self-uncertainty within group contexts. From the extension of the SAFE model in the chapter by Schmader and colleagues to Kuljian and Hohman's chapter on prototypicality threat and self-uncertainty to the work of Paredes and colleagues on the role of self-uncertainty (certainty) in group identification, these chapters exemplify the social psychological emphasis on situating and understanding self-uncertainty at the individual level within the context of prevailing groups. Although not exhaustive, these represent just a few of the key points of distinction as well as overlap between this new and the previous edition of the *Handbook of the Uncertain Self.*

The Guiding Goals, Focal Concept, & Prevailing Perspective of This Handbook

We begin by defining the central goals that guide the different contributions to the study of self-uncertainty featured in this handbook. As with any scientific production, this edited volume can be understood with reference to the goals that guide it. More specifically, it strives to improve the human condition by ultimately translating epistemic advancements in understanding and prediction into the practical control of pressing social problems. We briefly expand on these goals, their interrelation, and our vision of how the present volume can contribute to their collective advancement.

Our first goal of epistemic advancement is the desire to enhance knowledge regarding the nature of uncertainty, including the subtle distinctions and commonalities among the conceptual models of self-uncertainty. In so doing, we hope to provide a comprehensive digest for identifying the essential as well as peripheral features of this focal concept. Prior to the first edition, the lack of any single volume created a conceptual tower of Babel devoid of any strong definitional foundation as to what self-uncertainty was. Under its long shadow, dialogue on self-uncertainty became constrained by the definitional particulars that each participant imposed on the variable. That is, people were talking about "self-uncertainty," but the conversation was distorted by idiosyncratic differences in the exact definition(s) used. Thus, one objective of this volume is to feature a set of leading experts whose work establishes such distinctions between various specific forms of self-uncertainty (e.g., existential versus belongingness uncertainty) as well as carves away clear distinctions between the category of self-uncertainty variables and other variables, defining *what is not* as well as *what is* "self-uncertainty."

We do not view the first goal as independent of the second. That is, epistemic advancement should be considered an instrumental goal that supports the related goal of practical control. In particular, the individual contributions featured in the final section of this volume attempt to illustrate the ways in which epistemic advancement can be translated into practical gains such as the enhancement of positive well-being, exemplifying Kurt Lewin's (1935) illustrious idea that there is nothing so practical as a good theory. In this same spirit, it is fitting that the last section features contributors (e.g., Brady and colleagues) who have actively applied advances in basic knowledge on self-uncertainty to optimize psychological functioning in important applied contexts. Now that we have defined the goals that will guide this handbook, we turn to defining the concept of interest itself—Self-Uncertainty.

That is, what *exactly* do we mean by "self-uncertainty"? Is it a state or trait? Is it a process, an attribute, or an experience? These are questions that continually resurface as the reader moves across the different chapters. Although many definitions exist, we draw from the first edition to define self-uncertainty as a subjective sense of doubt in self-views, worldviews, and the interrelation between the two. Rather than reduce it to either the person or the environment, this definition carries the advantage of allowing self-uncertainty to operate at the interface of the person *and* the environment. This definition provides the ideal point of departure given the essential "interactionist" focus of social and personality psychology that unites each of the individual contributions to this handbook.

Having said that, it is worth noting that this definition varies in the degree to which it fits the conceptualization of self-uncertainty preferred within each individual chapter. This variance does not seem problematic so long as limitations to the applicability of our definition (or any other) for any given chapter are clearly pointed out and explained to the reader. As the reader will soon see, the explicit effort of individual authors to identify the points of consensus and departure between their own consideration of self-uncertainty and other contributions (including our own) adds conceptual resolution to discussions of self-uncertainty. As noted above, it is our hope that this collective of individual contributions will not only (a) flesh out the distinctions among different variables within the category of self-uncertainty (within-variable differentiation) but go further to (b) carve away clear distinctions between the category of self-uncertainty variables and other constructs (between-variable differentiation). With respect to this between-variable differentiation, epistemic advancement in the study of self-uncertainty depends not only on defining what self-uncertainty is but, as (or more) importantly, what *it is not* (Schlenker, 1992).

Applying this logic to self-uncertainty, the goal of epistemic advancement requires conceptual boundaries on what can reasonably be considered a form of self-uncertainty. For example, it becomes clear that variables such as worry, anxiety, low self-esteem, ambivalence, self-complexity, need for cognitive closure, and personal need for structure are distinct from the concept of self-uncertainty. In addition, specific chapters (e.g., Van den Bos & Lind) define important differences between self-uncertainty and other uncertainty-related constructs (e.g., informational uncertainty). Although these can be considered related forms of uncertainty, these theorists point out that the antecedents, processes, and ultimate implications for these various forms may be very different.

We now turn to address the broader perspective that unifies the various contributions to this edited handbook. As the founder of social and personality psychology, Kurt Lewin, so eloquently noted, a complete understanding of human action cannot be found by focusing on the factors residing solely in the person or the environment. Rather, the complete understanding of human action requires knowledge of how the two—person and environment—dynamically interact. In the spirit of Kurt Lewin, this edited volume provides a range of perspectives united by their common adherence to the contextual perspective that defines the essence of social and personality psychology.

Overall Organization

Apart from substantive quality, we used two criteria to select our ultimate organizational framework for this edited volume. First, we wanted to select an organizational framework that mirrored our broader perspective and focus on the interaction between person and environment. As noted earlier, this perspective reflects the social psychological viewpoint that permits the examination of uncertainty within the individual but also embraces analyses that reside in the interface of two, or more, people (e.g., Sandra Murray's work on certainty through social connection). Second, we wanted to use a framework that captured core themes cutting across these chapters without compromising the substantive diversity that separated each one.

Ultimately, we separated the 21 individual contributions into three major parts according to distinct themes that unify the individual research programs: (1) Meta-Cognition and Uncertainty, (2) Motivation and Uncertainty, and (3) Clinical and Applied Implications of the Uncertain Self. In addition to the individual contributions, the edited volume begins with a preface along with this opening chapter and closes with a general commentary provided by a leading expert on the topic of self-uncertainty (Michael Hogg). This unique combination of broad and specialized expertise provides the ideal context within which to situate as well as highlight those contributions under the broader context of core themes that run throughout the handbook.

Part I Organization. Part I surveys a diverse range of perspectives that emphasize the importance of meta-cognitive processes in the causes and consequences of uncertainty. In Chapter 2, Briñol and Petty review their work on Self-Validation Theory, showing how doubt can attenuate, eliminate, or even reverse the impact of thoughts on attitudes and behavior. In Chapter 3, Shen, Lam, and Wixted discuss the complicated relationship between confidence and accuracy in eyewitness testimony, emphasizing the conditions that strengthen the link. In Chapter 4, Cheek and Schwarz discuss how unlimited personal freedom can overwhelm the human decision-maker with numbing uncertainty. In Chapter 5, Paredes, Briñol, and Petty examine how doubt influences the usage of antecedents to and consequences of identity as well as the conditions under which (when) doubt assessments are more likely to be taken into consideration.

In Chapter 6, Carroll, Kothari, and Haley discuss how self-uncertainty ties together processes of identity revision over time. In Chapter 7, Van den Bos and Lind further unpack their general theory of how people manage personal uncertainty through fairness judgments, detailing the role that trust plays in the process. In Chapter 8, Sedikides and colleagues then consider how nostalgia can provide a psychological antidote to self-uncertainty. In Chapter 9, Sanchez, Moritz, and Dunning integrate the literature from clinical and social psychology to illuminate why people in general may be prone to types of errors, including overconfidence, in everyday decision-making and judgment when they jump to conclusions. In Chapter 10, Guo and Schmader present their modified SAFE model to consider how and when states of person-environment misfit are experienced as self-uncertainty.

Part II Organization. Part II includes contributions that consider the role of intrapsychic and interpersonal motivations in the development, maintenance, and consequences of uncertainty in self. In Chapter 11, Landau, Ryu, Greenberg, Chur, and Pyszczynski then discuss the role of death denial in quelling uncertainty over human specialness, belonging, shared reality, and self-esteem that collectively contribute to numbing existential uncertainty. In Chapter 12, Namkoong, Henderson, and Tobin discuss how automatic (automatic abstraction) as well as deliberate mechanisms work together to resolve activated causal uncertainty. In Chapter 13, McGregor and Marigold review a wide range of different intellectual traditions that converge on the problem of anxious uncertainties in life, the reflex for hostile and self-serving reactions to them, and on the power of self-transcendent-value commitment to help overcome anxious uncertainties and the maladaptive reactions to them. In Chapter 14, Kuljian and Hohman present a compelling theoretical and empirical case for how self-uncertainty mediates the link between prototypicality threats and motivated ingroup behavior. Finally, in Chapter 15, Chen, Tian, Hales, and Williams examine how uncertainty in one's relational security can be conceptualized as the immediate symptom of painful social exclusions. In Chapter 16, Sandra Murray discusses her fascinating work on how people manage and respond to doubts about relationship security in daily life.

Part III Organization. Part III moves beyond the antecedents and processes of uncertainty in self to examine the clinical and applied effects of chronic personal uncertainty on mental health. In Chapter 17, Molinario and Ellenberg thoughtfully examine how pandemic related uncertainty and angst may be countered by addressing the enhanced certainty of negative outcomes that arise during pandemics like COVID-19. In Chapter 18, Rios and Morales present their fascinating work on the antecedents of belief-based conflicts and their consequences for self-uncertainty. In Chapter 19, Sweeny and Howell present their exciting work on the management of acute uncertainty in daily life. In Chapter 20, Brady and colleagues then discuss their exciting translational work to help underrepresented and marginalized individuals overcome lingering doubts about belongingness in educational and other organizational settings. Finally, in Chapter 21, Julie Exline and colleagues conclude by discussing the religious struggles and potential growth that come from feelings of doubt.

The edited volume closes with one general commentary by a leading expert on the study of uncertainty in self: Michael Hogg. The commentary attempts to summarize the contributions of the handbook as well as set the stage for future research by identifying unresolved issues on the topic of uncertainty in self. Collectively, the goal of the individual contributions as well as the general commentary is to showcase the diversity and the unity that defines contemporary perspectives on uncertainty in self within social and personality psychology.

The antecedents, Processes, and Consequences of Self-Uncertainty

Of course, as with most handbooks, the diverse range of contributions featured in this volume address self-uncertainty from a range of possible conceptual and methodological angles. Although we have categorized the chapters according to one of three major themes, the chapters can also be distinguished according to their relative focus on the antecedents, processes, or consequences of self-uncertainty. To some extent, each chapter provides a diverse mixture of progressive research programs that represent theory and evidence across each of the three components of self-uncertainty we have defined—antecedents, processes, and consequences. Collectively, however, these chapters provide the reader with a balanced survey of contemporary work on the antecedents, processes, as well as consequences of self-uncertainty across a wide range of general and specific life domains.

With respect to the antecedents of self-uncertainty, several featured chapters identify a variety of factors that cause the experience of self-uncertainty to arise and persist in the first place. For example, Landau and his colleagues review the extensive body of research on Terror Management Theory suggesting that overwhelming existential uncertainty arises from uncertainty over human specialness, belonging, shared reality, and self-esteem. In turn, these theorists discuss how these different sources of uncertainty (and the existential uncertainty they give rise to) can be quelled by death denial. In addition, Sanchez, Moritz, and Dunning discuss how certain types of errors, including overconfidence, stem from jumping to conclusions. These authors draw from extensive theory and research in both social and clinical psychology showing that the process of jumping to conclusions enhances overconfidence.

Beyond the antecedents, several chapters focus on explicitly unpacking the processes that regulate the experience of self-uncertainty. For example, Namkoong, Henderson, and Tobin discuss how automatic (automatic abstraction) and controlled processes work together to resolve the experience of causal uncertainty. In addition, Guo and Schmader extend their State Authenticity as Fit to Environment (SAFE) model to suggest that, when the self is perceived as malleable (vs. stable), state self-uncertainty (vs. inauthenticity) arises from instances of person-environment misfit to signal that one is currently redefining themselves in that context, with the end result being that one is less motivated to avoid or leave those contexts that cue state self-uncertainty (vs. inauthenticity). With respect to the consequences, several chapters provide new insights regarding the ultimate consequences of self-uncertainty (good and bad) for psychological functioning. In many ways, the value of these contributions cannot be overstated given that the true significance of any construct must be measured against the practical yardstick of its ultimate implications for psychological health and well-being. After all, no one writes (let alone reads) extensive handbooks devoted to the unpleasant experiences of hangnails or dropped cell phone calls because, however painful, neither (at least not to our knowledge) have lasting implications for mental or behavioral health.

Thus, we feel that these chapters extend the focus beyond why and how self-uncertainty arises to exactly why anyone should care. In particular, chapters featured within the final section focus explicitly on the implications of self-uncertainty for mental and behavioral health. For example, Sweeny and Howell discuss how people manage (to both reduce and sustain) the consequences of acute uncertainty over time. Many of these chapters even go beyond reviewing the consequences of these various experiences related to self-uncertainty to suggest interventions designed to influence these consequences to enhance mental and behavioral health. For example, Brady and colleagues discuss a range of cost-effective, scalable interventions proven effective in reducing feelings of belongingness uncertainty among marginalized groups within various contexts, including school settings. Although the last section explicitly focuses on the consequences of self-uncertainty, several chapters that appear in the first two sections also address the implications of self-uncertainty for psychological health. For example, Nathan Cheek and Barry Schwartz make a compelling argument that limiting choice options may actually enhance rather than diminish well-being and satisfaction at times. Sandra Murray discusses how interventions that affirm the safety of social connection through significant relationships can mitigate uncertainty about one's place in the social world.

Furthermore, although many chapters focus on the implications of uncertainty across broader topic domains, there are several chapters that link the consequences of self-uncertainty to domains at more specific levels of interest. For example, Shen, Lam, and Wixted discuss the complex link between eyewitness confidence and accuracy in the legal domain. In addition, Van den Bos and Lind illuminate the link between self-uncertainty and fairness perceptions and subsequent judgments, with a particular eye on the role of trust.

It is worth noting that our own characterization of the foregoing chapters as focusing on antecedents, processes, or consequences of self-uncertainty should not be taken as a statement that any one of these chapters focuses *exclusively* on one or even two such elements. As readers will soon learn, the scholars featured within this volume have research programs that are not easily encapsulated under an exclusive focus on any of these aspects of self-uncertainty. Rather, each of these chapters touches to some degree on the determinants (antecedents and processes) as well as consequences associated with self-uncertainty.

Conclusion

The Uncertain Self has often been an afterthought. However, times have changed. In the contemporary literature, the Uncertain Self is now the front and center, of focal interest, and there are compelling reasons for this shift in theory and research. Our objective is to help generate future insights by formally organizing new insights on this topic. The present handbook serves as a comprehensive sourcebook of recent advancements in the study of personal uncertainty. This volume brings together what is now known and sets the stage for the next wave of research and theory on this timely topic of personal uncertainty in social life.

References

Berglas, S., & Jones, E. E. (1978). Drug choice as a self-handicapping strategy in response to noncontingent success. *Journal of Personality and Social Psychology*, *36*(4), 405–417.

Festinger, L. (1954). A theory of social comparison processes. *Human Relations*, *7*(2), 117–140.

Fiske, S. T. (2004). *Social Beings: A Core Motives Approach to Social Psychology*. John Wiley. Hoboken, NJ

Heider, F. (1958). *The psychology of interpersonal relations*. New York: Wiley.

Jenness, A. (1932). The role of discussion in changing opinion regarding a matter of fact. *The Journal of Abnormal and Social Psychology*, *27*, 279–296.

Jones, E. E., & Gerard, H. B. (1967). *Foundations of social psychology*. New York: John Wiley.

Lewin, K. (1935). *A dynamic theory of personality*. New York: McGraw-Hill.

Schacter, S., & Singer, J. E. (1962). Cognitive, social, and physiological determinants of emotional state, *Psychological Review*, *69*, 379–399.

Schlenker, B. (1992). On shape-shifters and theories, *Psychological Inquiry*, *3*, 342–344.

Sedikides, C., & Strube, M. J. (1997). Self evaluation: To thine own self be good, to thine own self be sure, to thine own self be true, and to thine own self be better. In M. P. Zanna (Ed.), *Advances in experimental social psychology* (Vol. 29, pp. 209–269). Academic Press.

Sherif, M. (1935). A study of some social factors in perception. *Archives of Psychology*, *27*(187), 1–60.

Solnit, R. (2016). Hope is an embrace of the unknown: Rebecca Solnit on living in dark times. *The Guardian*, July, 2016.

Trope, Y. (1979). Uncertainty-reducing properties of achievement tasks. *Journal of Personality and Social Psychology*, *37*(9), 1505–1518.

PART I

Meta-Cognition & Uncertainty in Self

2

MULTIPLE EFFECTS OF DISCARDING THOUGHTS THROUGH INVALIDATION

Attenuation, Elimination, Reversals, and Compensation

Pablo Briñol and Richard E. Petty

This chapter explores the role of doubting one's thoughts on judgments and behaviors based on the principles of Self-Validation Theory (SVT; Briñol & Petty, 2022). SVT argues that any mental contents (thoughts, attitudes, goals, and traits) generally become less consequential for judgment and action as the perceived validity of the thoughts is decreased. For example, two people might have the very *same* initial thought, but one person might believe that it is less valid than the other person and thus is less likely to form a judgment based on it and act upon it.

As this example suggests, SVT is a metacognitive theory based on the distinction between having cognitions (initial thoughts) and subsequently taking into consideration the validity of those thoughts (i.e., thoughts about thoughts) to guide judgments and behaviors. Primary thoughts are those that occur at a direct level of cognition and involve people's initial associations of an object with some attribute, such as "This vaccine policy is not beneficial," or "I like you." In addition to generating primary thoughts, people can also generate subsequent thoughts that involve reflections on the initial thoughts (e.g., "I am not sure if the new vaccine policy is beneficial"). These reflections on initial thoughts are referred to as metacognitions and they involve thinking about one's own thinking (e.g., Goupil & Kouider, 2019). As we describe shortly, metacognition is consequential in determining the extent to which initial thoughts are used to guide further thinking, judgment, and action.

SVT focuses on a subjective sense that one's thoughts are appropriate (valid) to use, and this assessment is influenced by thought-relevant as well as incidental factors (e.g., one's emotions) completely unrelated to the content of the initial thoughts. SVT proposes that thoughts that are perceived as relatively invalid are mentally discarded which can lead to different outcomes compared to the normal impact of one's thoughts, which typically involves some default degree of validation. Specifically, invalidation can attenuate, eliminate, or even reverse the impact of one's thoughts. As described next, both doubt in the correctness of thoughts (cognitive invalidation) and feeling bad about the thoughts (affective invalidation) can lead people to discard their thoughts leading to those three different outcomes.

DOI: 10.4324/9781003363385-3

Invalidation Can Attenuate Thought Use

Research on SVT has typically found that experiencing relative uncertainty and/or unpleasantness regarding one's thoughts can lead those thoughts to have a reduced impact on judgments compared to relative certainty and/or pleasantness. This predicted pattern of results is represented in the first panel of Figure 2.1. As will be the case throughout the chapter, the figure shows the predicted, prototypical patterns expected for each of the proposed invalidation effects. In this first category, inductions of doubt or unpleasantness can lead to an attenuated impact of valenced thoughts on judgment, and that is represented in the figure, Panel 1.

In an early SVT study that is consistent with the pattern shown in Figure 2.1, Panel 1, Briñol and Petty (2003) asked participants to generate either positive or negative thoughts about a new campus policy (thought valence manipulation) while moving their heads vertically or horizontally (manipulation of perceived validity). It was found that merely having participants shake their heads horizontally from side to side (as if saying no) was sufficient for them to think that there was something wrong with their thoughts, thus undermining the impact of those thoughts in forming judgments compared to conditions of moving their heads vertically up and down (as if saying yes; cf. Wells & Petty, 1980). The feeling of doubt stemming from head shaking was misattributed to the thoughts generated thereby reducing the impact of those thoughts on judgment.

The induction of the valence of one's thoughts (positive or negative) still had a significant impact on judgment under the low validity conditions (head shaking), but it was reduced in magnitude compared to the validation conditions. In persuasion paradigms, reducing the use of positive thoughts reduces persuasion (i.e., less agreement with the message) but reducing the use of negative thoughts increases persuasion (Petty et al., 1976). In other paradigms beyond persuasion, mental constructs (e.g., goals, traits) held with doubt or associated with unpleasantness were also less predictive of judgments and behaviors than when they were associated with certainty and pleasantness (see, e.g., Díaz et al., in press; Santos et al., in press for recent examples).

In another study showing that invalidation can attenuate the impact of thoughts, Paredes and colleagues (2013) asked participants to generate either positive or negative thoughts about another person (thought valence manipulation) while holding a pen between their teeth (i.e., facilitating the emergence of a facial pose of smiling associated with pleasure and confidence) or while holding a pen between their upper lip and the nose (i.e., facial expression of frowning associated with unpleasantness and doubt; Strack et al., 1988). Then, participants evaluated the person for whom they generated their initial thoughts (dependent variable). The results showed that thoughts generated affected the evaluation of the person in all cases, but the effect of those thoughts was less pronounced for the invalidating condition (frowning) than for the validating condition (smiling). This pattern of results in which doubt attenuates the impact of thoughts is also illustrated conceptually in panel 1 of the figure.

Taken together, it appears that inductions of doubt (from head shaking) or unpleasantness (from frowning) can lead to an attenuated impact of thoughts on judgment. We argue that this attenuation effect is especially likely to occur when doubt is informative of or associated with perceptions of low validity. Importantly, invalidation processes can not only attenuate thought usage, but they can also lead to other outcomes that are described next.

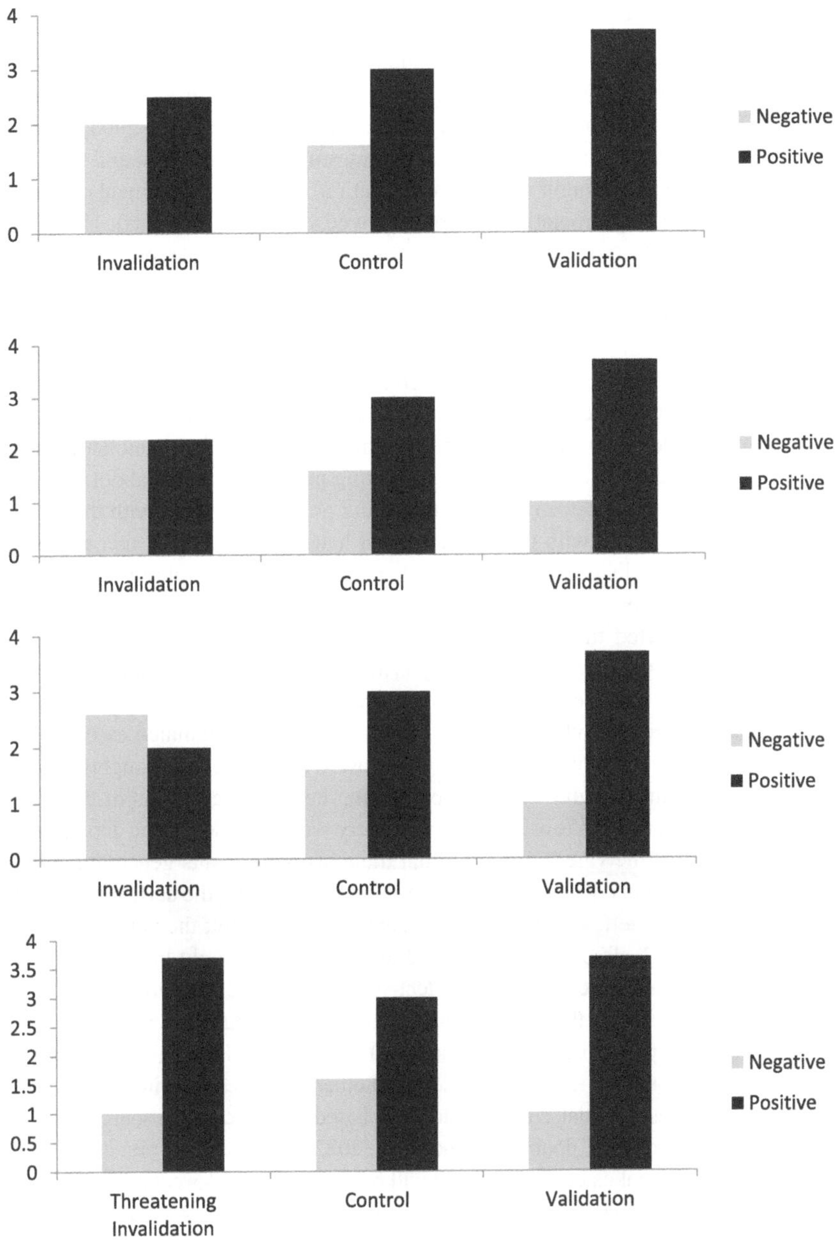

Figure 2.1 Conceptual figure illustrating that any potential induction of doubt or unpleasantness can lead to an attenuated impact of valenced thoughts on judgment (e.g., when informative of low validity; Panel 1), to null effects of valenced thoughts (e.g., when doubt is high; panel 2), to reversed effects of valenced thoughts (e.g., when the induction is extreme or people are engaged in categorical thinking; panel 3) or to compensatory effects (when invalidation is threatening; panel 4).

Invalidation Can Eliminate Thought Use

The attenuation of thought use can be complete such that the invalidation induction entirely eliminates reliance on thoughts. This pattern of predicted results is represented in the second panel of the figure. For example, in another early SVT experiment (Briñol & Petty, 2003, Experiment 4), we asked participants, as part of a presumed graphology study, to think about and write down their best or worse qualities (i.e., thought valence manipulation) using their dominant or non-dominant hands (i.e., overt behavior manipulation to vary perceived validity of thoughts). Then, participants rated their confidence in the thoughts they listed (proposed mediator) and reported their self-esteem (dependent measure). Since writing with the non-dominant hand happens infrequently and is very difficult, and because whatever is written with the non-dominant may appear "shaky," we expected and found that using the non-dominant hand decreased the confidence with which people held the thoughts they had listed. As a consequence, the effect of the initial valence of thoughts (i.e., positive vs. negative) on state self-esteem was significant only when participants wrote their thoughts with their dominant hand. When thoughts were written with the non-dominant hand, the effects of the thoughts on self-esteem disappeared. That is, writing positive thoughts about oneself with the dominant hand increased self-esteem relative to writing positive thoughts with the non-dominant hand. However, when writing with the non-dominant hand people did not feel any worse about themselves when they just listed negative rather than positive self-relevant thoughts.

In a more recent example of invalidation eliminating the impact of thoughts, Gascó and colleagues (2018) manipulated the perceived origin of participants' thoughts following a task in which they generated positive or negative thoughts about modifying their bodies using plastic surgery. That is, after being assigned to generate either positive or negative thoughts about bariatric surgery, participants were led to believe either that their thoughts originated externally (i.e., they arose from societal views) or internally (i.e., they arose from the self). Thoughts about bariatric surgery served as the initial cognition in this paradigm, the perceived origin of thoughts was the validating variable, and attitudes toward bariatric surgery were assessed as the dependent measure. The results revealed that the valence of the initial thoughts participants generated only impacted their attitudes toward surgery when their origin was perceived to be the self. When the perceived origin was external to the self, and the thoughts seemed less pleasant, the valence of the thoughts did not matter. These SVT effects were meditated by changes in thought liking.

These two examples are conceptually consistent with the proposed pattern of results graphed in panel 2 of the figure, revealing that inductions of doubt (from using one's non-dominant hand) or unpleasantness (external perceived origin of thoughts) can totally eliminate the impact of thoughts on judgment and behavior. SVT research has identified other examples showing that invalidation can also make thoughts inconsequential, such as inductions based on low credible sources (Requero et al., 2020), recalling past episodes of doubt (Moreno et al., 2022), and recalling previous experiences of feeling powerless (Lamprinakos et al., 2024). As will be discussed, we speculate that this elimination effect is especially likely to occur when doubt is moderately high, though not extreme. Overall, whether doubt reduces or eliminates the impact of thoughts is likely due to the magnitude of the doubt manipulation, though sometimes this difference could simply be due to the power of studies to detect an effect under low validation conditions. Importantly, at the conceptual level, these two impacts are similar.

Invalidation Can Reverse the Impact of Thoughts

Third, invalidation can not only reduce or eliminate but can also reverse the impact of initial thoughts. In one study showing reverse effects, Briñol and colleagues (2013) asked participants to write down either positive or negative thoughts about a healthy diet on a piece of paper. Then, participants were randomly assigned to either: (a) take the paper on which they had written their ideas and place it in a trash can (invalidation), (b) take the paper and keep it in a safe place such as their pocket or purse (validation), or (c) merely fold the corners of the paper and leave it on the table (control). After performing one of these actions, participants rated their attitudes toward the diet. As expected, attitudes reflected the valence of participants' thoughts in the control condition. Also as predicted, participants in the validation condition showed a more pronounced effect of thought valence on attitudes than in the control condition. In contrast, the effect of thought valence on attitudes was reversed for those in the thought invalidation condition (a prototypical pattern illustrated in the third panel of the figure). That is, participants asked to generate positive thoughts about the diet showed significantly less favorable attitudes than those asked to generate negative thoughts, the opposite pattern of results obtained in the control, and validation conditions.

In a more recent demonstration of invalidation leading to reversals, Kim et al. (2021) examined whether variations in the meaning associated with the specific action taken with thoughts would make a difference. Participants in this experiment were first asked to write positive or negative thoughts about increasing their level of physical exercise (initial thought valence induction). Then, all participants were asked to move what they wrote to a box in front of them labeled either as a "trash can" (low validity condition) or as a "safety box" (high validity condition). Results showed that physically moving thoughts to the trash led them to have a reversed impact on judgment compared to when the thoughts were physically moved to a safety box. Even though the physical action was the same in both conditions (moving thoughts to a box), the meaning of the action (trash vs. safety) made a difference. Consistent with SVT, these results reveal that it is the meaning of the action and not the action per se that is critical in producing invalidation effects.

Taken together, these two examples illustrate cases in which invalidation inductions have been shown to *reverse* the effects of one's valenced thoughts (e.g., see Briñol et al., 2007, for an additional example using sadness as the invalidation induction). There are at least two aspects associated with invalidation that we hypothesize could lead to reversals in judgment rather than attenuation or elimination, though neither has been investigated explicitly. The first is the *extremity* of the perception of invalidity. If people have so much doubt about the correctness of their thoughts or hate what they have in mind so much, they might want to do the opposite of what their thoughts imply (e.g., if my thoughts are favorable toward this new job, but I think those thoughts are very wrong, the new job must be bad). As noted, the prediction is that the more extreme the perception of incorrectness or dislike of one's thoughts, the greater the likelihood of a reversal. Placing one's thoughts in the trash is plausibly a relatively extreme form of invalidation, but to date, no research has explicitly varied the extremity of an invalidation induction. In this explanation, as the extremity of the invalidation induction increases, the judgmental outcome goes from attenuation to elimination to reversal.

In addition to the extremity of the doubt, we propose that a second factor that could produce reversals is whether the thoughts or the judgment are represented or framed as leading to one of two categorical outcomes (e.g., winner vs. loser, smart vs. dumb, young vs. old) rather than when those thoughts are seen as implying a more continuous decision (e.g., relative success, intelligence, or age). In such cases of categorical thinking, we suggest that invalidation might be more likely to produce a reversed impact, perhaps even if the induction is only moderate rather than extreme. For example, if a person driving to a new destination reaches a fork in the road and initially thinks that going left is warranted, because there are only two opposite options, having even moderate doubt about turning left would likely lead to turning right.

Summary

The research described so far illustrates how some variables (ranging from bodily movements to the perceived origin of thoughts) can attenuate, eliminate, and even reverse the impact of initial cognition on judgment. A critical issue to study is what determines when each of those three outcomes is more likely to occur. For example, although speculative at this point, we have suggested that reversals could be linked to the extremity of the perception of invalidity and/or when thoughts or the relevant judgment are framed in categorical terms (Briñol & Petty, 2022).

Taking these ideas together, the research described so far suggests that inductions of doubt or unpleasantness can lead to an attenuated impact of thoughts on judgment (e.g., when informative of low validity), to null effects (e.g., when doubt is higher), to reversed effects (e.g., when the induction is extreme or people are engaged in categorical thinking). These hypotheses about the specific conditions in which each of those invalidation outcomes is more likely to appear to remain fully tested. Next, we describe a fourth possible outcome emerging from invalidation. That is, instead of the effects just reviewed, invalidation might sometimes *enhance* thought use relative to a control.

Some prior research suggests that the enhanced impact of thoughts under doubt is most likely to occur when the prospect of invalidation is highly threatening. When experiencing a threatening uncertainty (or threatening dislike of one's thoughts), individuals can be motivated to behave in ways that restore their sense of confidence (to mitigate the threat) such as by adopting more extreme attitudes (*compensatory conviction*; McGregor et al., 2001) or by using any other mental content more. Under these conditions, inductions of doubt can potentially result in an increased (rather decreased) impact of current thoughts (see also, Siev et al., 2022). Next, we describe a few illustrative cases of this category.

Invalidation Magnifying the Impact of Unrelated Thoughts

People can respond to perceived threats by either seeking out or by developing compensatory confidence when such opportunities are available (e.g., Hart, 2014). For example, people often cope with mortality-related inductions (e.g., thinking about one's death) by validating (i.e., affirming confidence in) their cultural worldviews (e.g., Burke et al., 2010; Greenberg & Kosloff, 2008). Given that the polarizing effects of mortality salience are similar to those proposed for compensatory confidence, it is plausible that the salience of one's mortality could lead people to become more confident in, and thus rely more on the thoughts they have already generated toward an attitude object that is completely independent of the threat.

Recent research by Horcajo and colleagues (2022) examined this possibility by testing whether compensatory confidence in reaction to death reminders can be misattributed to primary thoughts, even if those initial thoughts are unrelated to the mortality threat. Participants in this paradigm were first asked to read either a strong or a weak resume of a job applicant. This induction was designed to manipulate the valence of initial thoughts, with participants generating positive thoughts in response to the strong vita and negative thoughts to the weak one (Petty et al., 1976). Then, participants were asked to think about their own death (i.e., mortality salience condition) versus about being cold (i.e., control condition; adopted from Lambert et al., 2014). Finally, participants reported confidence in their thoughts about the applicant (proposed mediator), as well as their attitudes toward the applicant (dependent measure). Participants who were assigned to the mortality salience (vs. control) condition showed a greater impact of their previously generated thoughts on their subsequent attitudes toward the job candidate. Furthermore, this effect of attitude polarization was mediated by changes in thought confidence. These results revealed that attitudes unrelated to mortality can be polarized by death reminders, and that this effect can operate through a compensatory process of thought validation. This possible pattern of results is illustrated in the fourth panel of the figure.

The same compensatory effect described above can be relevant for understanding how people respond to other threat inductions. For example, during the COVID-19 pandemic, when faced with the threat of the possibility of being infected, people defensively looked for ways to alleviate the associated unpleasantness, sometimes by either seeking or expressing compensatory *confidence* in domains unrelated to the perceived threat (e.g., Randles et al., 2017; Simchon et al., 2021). In line with this prior work, a recent set of studies examined how compensatory processes stemming from COVID-19-related threats can increase confidence in *any* accessible thought, again, even if those initial thoughts are unrelated to the threat.

In one study, Moreno and colleagues (2023, Experiment 3) had participants first read either a strong or a weak version of the curriculum vitae of a job candidate and then list their thoughts about it. Thoughts about the job candidate served as the initial cognition to be validated or invalidated. Next, participants were randomly assigned to complete a task designed to increase the salience of the COVID-19 pandemic or received a low-threat induction. Specifically, in the high perceived COVID-19 threat condition, participants were asked to describe *what thoughts or emotions they experienced about the possibility of being infected by COVID-19*. In the low-threat condition, participants had to write about a mildly aversive topic that served as a control (i.e., "being cold"). Finally, participants reported their thought confidence and their attitudes toward the job candidate. As predicted, participants in the COVID-19 condition showed a greater impact of their previously generated thoughts on attitudes toward the job applicant (for a conceptual illustration of this pattern, see Panel 4 of Figure 2.1). Importantly, this study also provided evidence for the proposed compensatory mechanism by showing that the obtained results on attitudes were mediated by the impact of the COVID-19 threat on thought confidence (i.e., more threat producing more confidence).

As noted, it is important to understand when invalidation inductions (in this case coming from death or COVID-19 threats) lead to more rather than less confidence. In general, one would expect threats to be associated with initial doubt rather than confidence. For example, threats are often associated with anxiety and anxiety is an affective state associated with uncertainty (Keltner & Lerner, 2010). If individuals respond to threats with uncertainty, then threats would be expected to attenuate the use of thoughts as illustrated in the first studies of this chapter (conceptually represented in panels 1–3 in Figure 2.1). However, instead of attenuating the use of thoughts, the research just described revealed that thought use could be enhanced relative to a control, and we argue that this compensatory effect is more likely to appear when the doubt is highly threatening to the person as is likely to be the case for the threats related to death and COVID-19. When experiencing a threatening uncertainty (Haas & Cunningham, 2014), the SVT studies described in this section suggest that individuals can be motivated to behave in ways that restore their sense of confidence (to mitigate the threat) such as by using one's thoughts more, even if those thoughts are unrelated to the threat.

Finally, we suggest that future research in this context can benefit from specifying further what the essential features of uncertainty are that trigger compensatory rather than direct behavioral effects. For example, some analyses suggest that only certainty that feels threatening to the person matters such as when the uncertainty involves an important issue or when the self-uncertainty involves thoughts of one's own mortality (see Hogg, 2021; Simchon et al., 2021).

Invalidation Magnifying the Impact of Relevant Attitudes

The research described in the previous section shows that uncertainty can make attitudes more extreme, and we propose that this effect occurs through a "fluid compensation," when the response occurs outside the threatened domain. In line with previous research (McGregor et al., 2010), we call this fluid compensation because people relied on their initial thoughts following threats even if those primary cognitions were unrelated to the threats (cf., Siev et al., 2024). In contrast to fluid compensation, in this section, we describe research showing that uncertainty about specific attitudes can provoke "attitude-specific compensation," when the response targets the threatened attitude directly. This parallels the distinction made previously between "across-domain" and "within-domain" forms of threat compensation (Mandel et al., 2016).

The idea behind this recent research on attitude-specific compensation is that, although highly confident attitudes are usually more impactful in guiding behavior (Petty & Krosnick, 1995; Rucker et al., 2014), doubtful attitudes can sometimes have more impact. This occurs because when people want more certainty, they often engage in efforts to bolster or secure their weak position (Cheatham & Tormala, 2017; Sawicki & Wegener, 2018). Additionally, complementary work on uncertainty management suggests that self-uncertainty leads people to seek clarity about the self through alignment with extreme groups and beliefs (e.g., Hogg, 2007).

Following a similar logic, Siev and colleagues (2023) reasoned that attitude uncertainty can lead people to seek certainty about their position through alignment with extreme attitude-consistent behaviors. Extreme behaviors are especially likely to be involved in belief defense efforts because they are viewed as diagnostic of a person's beliefs and strongly signal a commitment to one's position (Fiske, 1980; Skowronski & Carlston, 1989). Extreme behaviors are conceptualized here as those that increasingly deviate from the norm (e.g., Kruglanski et al., 2021; Siev et al., 2022). According to this view, people are expected to express openness to extreme behaviors only when they need to defend and secure beliefs that feel vulnerable.

Across six samples, Siev and colleagues (2023) assessed participants' attitudes toward COVID-19 mitigation policies, certainty about those attitudes, perceived threat from COVID-19 and willingness to engage in mitigation-related behaviors varying in extremity. Furthermore, 20 behaviors were rated by external judges for the behaviors' extremity, using these normative extremity ratings as an additional predictor in the analyses. It was predicted and found that external ratings of the behaviors' extremity moderated the relationship between attitude certainty and the willingness to act on one's attitudinal position. Whereas greater certainty was associated with increased willingness to engage in moderate behaviors such as washing one's hands (the typical certainty result; Rucker et al., 2014), lower certainty was associated with increased willingness to engage in extreme behaviors such as committing violence against those opposed to COVID-19 mitigation. The latter effect was especially strong among participants who were worried about becoming ill from COVID-19.

In sum, although SVT research has shown individuals tend to act more on thoughts and attitudes about which they have greater certainty, this new research showed that this relationship does not always hold. Instead, this work revealed that being more uncertain about COVID-19 mitigation policies was associated with a greater willingness to support extreme mitigation-related behaviors. Additionally, the negative associations between certainty and extreme behaviors were strongest when the topic was highly threatening, consistent with the notion that the relationship reflects defensive motivation producing efforts among those with doubts to bolster their position. As noted, we argue that this compensatory effect of invalidation leading to extremism is more likely to occur when strength is challenged or when strength is especially desired (e.g., when under threat).

Among other implications, this research makes contributions to certainty, extremism, and compensation. Regarding certainty, these results join a small but growing body of work showing that doubtful (vs. confident) attitudes sometimes have more impact (e.g., Sawicki & Wegener, 2018; see Petty et al., 2023 for a review). Regarding extremism, our findings align with perspectives which posit that people can go to extremes to manage uncertainty (McGregor et al., 2010) and to defend attitudes they perceive as vulnerable (Oettingen et al., 2022), whether due to being challenged by others (Gollwitzer et al., 2022) or, as here, because they seem too weak to meet the demands of a threatening situation. Finally, these results also contribute to research on psychological compensation for self-threats, suggesting extreme actions like risky and aggressive behavior might serve a defensive function in relation to threats like the pandemic (Bartusevičius et al., 2021).

In closing this section, it is important to note that subsequent ongoing research has extended this idea of compensation by endorsing more extreme behaviors from the domain of attitudes to the domain of identity. This recent work by Paredes and colleagues (this volume) shows that people can compensate for the doubt they have with regard to their group identity by engaging in extreme pro-group behaviors typically associated with confidence. Importantly, this research also shows that this compensatory effect is especially likely to occur when having doubts about group identity is threatening (e.g., in this case, when doubts are about identity with relevant groups but not for irrelevant groups).

Direct vs. Compensatory Validation

The SVT research described in the first part of the chapter showed how variables associated with high validity (e.g., nodding, smiling, ease, internal origin of thoughts) can polarize judgments by having a direct impact on thought confidence. Unlike this direct link to thought confidence, the research described in the second part of this chapter showed that attitudes and behaviors can also change through a self-validation mechanism that is produced through a compensatory (rather than direct) route. For example, as explained earlier, uncertainty can make attitudes more extreme through "fluid compensation" when the response occurs outside the threatened domain (Horcajo et al., 2022; Moreno et al., 2023).

Although on the surface these two routes to confidence (direct vs. compensatory) lead to apparently similar outcomes—increased thought use and attitude polarization compared to a control condition–a critical question to examine is whether there are any differences in long-term consequences between the direct and compensatory routes. Recent research conducted by Gandarillas and colleagues (2024) has examined this question using an SVT paradigm based on attachment theory (Mikulincer & Shaver, 2020). In one study, participants were asked to generate either positive or negative thoughts about a new topic—working from home after the pandemic. This induction served to manipulate the valence of primary cognitions. Next, participants were randomly assigned to one of four different attachment style conditions. Specifically, participants were asked to write about a time their parental figures responded (1) sensitively and appropriately to their needs making them feel protected (secure attachment), (2) did not understand their needs and made them feel insecure (disorganized attachment), (3) ignored them by minimizing their experiences (avoidant attachment), or (4) reacted in different and unexpected ways without a reason (anxious attachment; see Green & Campbell, 2000). Following the thought valence and attachment inductions, participants reported their attitudes and behavioral intentions toward the remote working proposal (dependent measures).

Consistent with SVT, the results showed that the impact of the initial thought induction on attitudes toward remote working was greater for the validation condition (secure attachment) compared to the invalidation conditions (avoidant and anxious attachment). Interestingly, thought usage was also *greater* for the disorganized attachment condition compared to the invalidation conditions. The disorganized attachment plausibly led to a compensatory process because it is more threatening than the others and it has been associated with several defense mechanisms in prior research (Gillath et al., 2010), including more extreme behavior (Lyons-Ruth et al., 1993). In fact, secure and disorganized conditions looked similar to each other (as illustrated in the figure, panel 4).

At first glance, these two routes to confidence (direct confidence from secure attachment and compensatory confidence from disorganized attachment) led to similar degrees of attitude polarization. However, we hypothesized that those conditions could plausibly differ in terms of *attitude strength* (Petty & Krosnick, 1995) with secure attachment producing stronger attitudes than disorganized attachment. Importantly, stronger attitudes should lead to greater attitude-behavior correspondence. The results revealed that attitudes resulting from the direct route to validation (secure attachment) guided behavioral intentions significantly better than the attitudes emerging from the compensatory route (disorganized attachment). Thus, although secure and disorganized conditions were both capable of polarizing attitudes relative to invalidation conditions to a similar degree, only the attitudes that came from a secure attachment style were subsequently translated into action.

Additional Findings and Future Directions

Before concluding this chapter, we next describe some additional research that demonstrates the breadth of SVT and how it can inspire new research. We first describe research showing that validation and invalidation can even apply when the initial thoughts are about doubt, and that the outcome of this process can vary as a function of the nature of initial thoughts (univalent or ambivalent). We then describe further ongoing research on the meaning of doubts, and beyond.

Doubts about Doubts

As described throughout the chapter, perceived validity can be applied to whatever mental elements are salient at the time, regardless of their specific content, valence, and nature. For example, in the studies reviewed so far, validation and invalidation processes operated for self-relevant thoughts, for thoughts about other people, as well as for beliefs about different topics (e.g., remote working, job candidates) and persuasive proposals (e.g., plastic surgery, increasing physical exercise).

Given that any thought can be susceptible to an SVT analysis, an interesting case examined in SVT research occurs when people have certainty (or doubt) in their own mental certainty or doubt. That is, self-doubt can sometimes be the primary cognition (e.g., when students think about their abilities), and people can then vary in the extent to which they have certainty or doubt in that self-doubt. In one relevant study conducted by Wichman and colleagues (2010), participants were first primed with doubt or certainty (initial thought to be validated) and then were exposed to a head movement manipulation as the induction of validity (Briñol & Petty, 2003). Next, participants read a brief description of another person and rated him on various characteristics, including how confident and certain the target was. As expected, head nodding (vs. shaking) accentuated the impact of the initial doubt (vs. certainty) manipulation on the ratings of the target's certainty. That is, participants rated the target as more certain when they were primed with certainty rather than doubt and were nodding rather than shaking their heads (validation induction). In contrast, participants rated the target as less certain when they were primed with certainty rather than doubt and were shaking rather than nodding their heads (invalidation induction). This line of research demonstrated that a secondary manipulation of certainty or uncertainty can interact with an initial induction of the same construct in the manner specified by SVT rather than in the additive way that might have been expected from prior work on sequential inductions of constructs (Kidder et al., 2018).

The most recent research using this paradigm revealed that validating or invalidating one's own initial doubts with a secondary manipulation of certainty or doubt can have important consequences for information processing and persuasion. In one study, Moreno et al. (2024) began by asking participants to focus either on their attitudes toward a topic (junk food taxation) or to focus on their doubts about that topic. This initial manipulation served to prime two different mental constructs (attitudes vs. doubts) to then be validated or invalidated. Next, participants were randomly assigned to recall past episodes of confidence or doubt. This second induction was designed to validate or invalidate the previously primed constructs (Petty et al., 2002). Following the two inductions, participants were exposed to a persuasive message containing either strong or weak arguments in favor of taxing junk food. In this paradigm, the argument quality manipulation served to assess the amount of thinking in which participants engaged by evaluating the relative impact of strong and weak arguments on subsequent thoughts and attitudes toward the proposal (Petty et al., 1976).

As predicted, the results showed a three-way interaction. Increasing confidence in one's initial attitudes reduced processing as indicated by reduced argument quality effects. This is a conceptual replication of the traditional attitude strength effect in which attitude confidence prior to a message reduces the need to process subsequent information (Rucker et al., 2014). In contrast, when participants were led to focus on their initial doubts (rather than on their initial attitudes), the effect was the opposite. As predicted, in this case, the second induction of confidence validated initial doubts increasing subsequent processing (as indicated by greater argument quality effects). Conversely, the results showed that doubting one's initial doubts reduced the impact of those initial doubts on processing, a paradoxical outcome conceptually consistent with the idea that doubting one's doubt can increase confidence (Wichman et al., 2010), therefore reducing the need to process subsequent information.

Doubts about Ambivalence

In all examples reviewed so far, the initial thoughts that were validated or invalidated had a dominant content (e.g., positive or negative, strengths or weaknesses, attitudes or doubts). As illustrated throughout, validation of univalent thoughts leads to attitudinal and behavioral polarization, whereas invalidation leads to attenuation and reversals (or compensation if the doubt is threatening). But what if thoughts are mixed in direction (e.g., some cooperative, some competitive)? That is, what if people are ambivalent in their thoughts (positive and negative reactions toward becoming a scientist; Kaplan, 1972; Priester & Petty, 1996), and this ambivalence is validated? Consistent with SVT, validating ambivalence should magnify the typical effects of being ambivalent.

To provide a specific SVT example, Durso and colleagues (2016) had participants read information about an employee whose behavior was either consistent (entirely good or entirely bad) or mixed (both good and bad). Subsequently, participants were induced to feel powerful or powerless by having them recall incidents in their lives in which they had power over another person or in which someone else had power over them. This manipulation of power has been found to affect thought confidence (e.g., Briñol et al., 2007, see also, Lamprinakos et al., 2024, for a recent example of validation through power). Then, participants were required to decide whether to promote or fire the employee. The time it took to make the decision was recorded. For the entirely positive or negative employees, feeling powerful was associated with faster decision making, replicating previous research in this domain (e.g., Galinsky et al., 2003). However, in contrast to prior work, for the mixed (ambivalent) employees, feeling powerful led for the first time to *slower* decision making. In sum, when individuals' thoughts were ambivalent, power validated these conflicting reactions, which caused greater power to lead to slower action. Conversely, doubting mixed (ambivalent) reactions served as a formula to undermine the typical consequences associated with ambivalence.

Pathological Doubt

We next consider the potential of SVT for understanding individual differences in pathological styles of thinking. In recent research guided by SVT, Díaz et al. (2024) treated pathological styles of thinking as a primary cognition for which people can vary in their perceived validity. Specifically, this research examined the extent to which confidence (vs. doubt) could improve the predictive validity of one of the most used self-administered instruments to assess persecutory delusions is the Persecutory Ideation Questionnaire (PIQ). Across two studies, participants from the general population and from a clinical sample were first asked to complete the PIQ. Individual differences in PIQ scores are important because they predict the severity of symptoms associated with psychosis-related disorders. Paranoid thinking has been also associated with *pathological confidence* which occurs when people feel highly certain despite contrary input from reality (Hirstein, 2005), jumping to conclusions and engaging in constant confirmatory biases (see Sanchez et al., this volume). Then, participants were asked to report the confidence and doubt associated with their responses to the PIQ inventory.

These two variables (PIQ scores and confidence/doubt) served to predict two new outcomes in this research: Satisfaction with life and a clinically relevant behavior (i.e., therapy length needed for hospital discharge for the clinical sample). As expected, the PIQ significantly predicted satisfaction with life across all participants, and the duration of therapy required to receive hospital discharge for the clinical sample. These main effects confirmed the validity of this PIQ inventory to predict relevant outcomes in both samples. Most importantly, confidence further moderated the extent to which the PIQ's scores predicted these consequences, with greater consistency between the PIQ and the dependent measures obtained for those with high (vs. low) confidence. Described differently, for participants with high levels of doubt in their responses to the questionnaire, the predictive validity of PIQ was significantly attenuated, or even eliminated in one of the studies of this series. Thus, asking a single item about the confidence/doubt associated to the PIQ improves the predictive capacity of this instrument across domains (see also, Paredes et al., 2020; Santos et al., 2019; Santos et al., in press; Shoots-Reinhard et al., 2015).

Future studies could also examine the extent to which confidence vs. doubt can moderate the predictive validity of other inventories typically associated with pathological doubt (rather than with pathological confidence, like PIQ). Pathological doubt occurs when people do not rely on what they should know to be true (Hirstein, 2005). This form of dysfunctional uncertainty is frequently seen in cases of obsessive disorders; where the person needs to triple-check everything as if objective reality cannot provide a proper feeling of knowing (Hermans et al., 2003). Therefore, SVT has the potential to help understand pathological (but not threatening) levels of perceived validity (e.g., paranoid thinking) and invalidity (e.g., obsessive thinking).

Meaning of Doubt

In the examples reviewed so far, validating and invalidating variables had clear meanings. Most personal experiences that people have (e.g., throwing something in a garbage can) have a default or common meaning (e.g., throwing something away means disposal because it is unwanted). However, the meaning of many validating and invalidating variables can depend on the person or the situation. That is, the meaning of variables that affect thought validity is flexible. A relevant SVT postulate is that changing the meaning of any experience (from high to low validity, or vice versa) can change the effect of that experience on thought usage. As described earlier in this chapter for the research inducing people to throw away their thoughts (Briñol et al., 2013; Kim et al., 2021), it is the ultimate meaning of the induction that matters with respect to its impact on thought usage.

It is important to note that even the meaning of confidence and doubt can vary. That is, although in most cases confidence is associated with high validity (e.g., truth) and doubt with low validity (e.g., wrong) sometimes the opposite is true. That is, doubt can on occasion be associated with high validity meanings such as a sign of the need to work harder, to bolster and as a sign of dialectical, complex, expert thinking.

Recent research has emphasized the role of the perceived meaning of doubt in understanding how doubt can decrease or increase thought usage depending on the psychological mindset present at the time. In a series of studies, Toader and colleagues (2024) began by asking participants to complete the Aesthetic Processing Preference Scale (Kopatich et al., 2021). This questionnaire is a standardized instrument designed to measure individual differences in appreciation for art. It includes items such as "*I like art objects that I don't understand immediately*" and "*I like to evaluate art objects as a product of the time in which they are produced.*" The responses to this inventory served as the initial cognition to be validated. Next, confidence was manipulated by asking people to recall either past episodes of confidence or doubt. After completing the art appreciation scale and receiving the manipulation of confidence, participants were randomly assigned to two different types of mindset inductions (epistemic vs. hedonic). In the epistemic mindset induction, participants were told that the goal was to learn and have an informative experience by focusing on artistic understanding. In contrast, in the hedonic mindset, participants were told that the goal was to have fun and enjoy as much as possible with the art experience. This manipulation was equivalent to similar inductions designed to vary epistemic vs. hedonic mindsets in other domains (Briñol et al., 2018; Cancela et al., 2021). The dependent measure was a performance task in which participants were asked to write as many alternative uses for a *pencil* as possible within a three-minute time (a creativity task used in previous research; see Puryear et al., 2017, for a review).

The results were consistent with the idea that mindset can vary the effects of confidence and doubt on thought usage. For the epistemic conditions, higher scores on the art scale were associated with greater performance in the creativity task, especially for those assigned to the confidence (vs. doubt) conditions. That is a conceptual replication of the typical SVT result in which confidence improves the predictive validity of mental constructs, including the predictive validity of diverse inventories (e.g., Santos et al., in press; Toader et al., in press) including also the Persecutory Ideation Questionnaire described earlier (Díaz et al., in press).

For the hedonic mindset, we found the opposite results. That is, when participants were asked to focus on having fun (rather than on learning), higher scores on the art scale were also associated with greater performance on the creativity task, but this time that was especially the case for those assigned to the doubt (vs. confidence) conditions. This is a new finding in which doubt increases (rather than decreases) the impact of initial cognition. Thus, this research is the first to show that doubt can either decrease or increase the use of initial thoughts depending on mindset. Changing the mindset affects the meaning of doubt. Doubt is associated with low validity meanings in the epistemic mindset (e.g., not having enough information, knowledge, etc.), whereas doubt might be associated with high validity meanings in the hedonic mindset (e.g., mystery, potential, novelty, etc.). Although the research described earlier in this chapter showed that doubts can not only decrease but also increase thought usage when uncertainty is threatening, this is the first evidence that doubts can increase the usage of thoughts in non-threatening, hedonic contexts.

Summary

This review offered several insights based on SVT. First, we showed how incidental inductions of doubt and unpleasantness (e.g., head shaking, frowning, throwing thoughts away) can invalidate people's thoughts leading to different outcomes. Invalidation processes can result in attenuation, elimination, and reversal effects, depending on the circumstances. As argued, inductions of doubt or unpleasantness can lead to an attenuated impact of thoughts on judgment (e.g., when informative of low validity), to null effects (e.g., when doubt is higher), to reversed effects (e.g., when the induction is extreme or people are engaged in categorical thinking). Conversely, variables associated with high validity (e.g., nodding, smiling, etc.) increase thought usage and polarize judgments by having a direct impact on thought confidence.

Second, we also noted that sometimes doubt can actually increase (rather than decrease) the use of mental contents through a compensatory (rather than direct) route. Uncertainty can make thoughts used more (and attitudes more extreme) both through "fluid compensation" when the response occurs outside the threatened domain, as well as by a "domain-specific compensation," when the response targets the threatened attitude directly. As noted, we argue that this compensatory effect of invalidation leading to extremism is more likely to occur when strength is challenged or when strength is especially desired (e.g., when under threat), leading people to react to maintain, demonstrate, or enhance their confidence.

Third, although at first glance these two routes to confidence (direct vs. compensatory) can lead to similar outcomes (increased thought usage, polarizing attitudes), the most recent SVT research has shown that there are potential differences in long-term consequences between those two routes. As described, attitudes changed through direct (vs. compensatory) confidence could be more likely to serve as a stronger basis to guide subsequent behavior.

Finally, we concluded with research showing how SVT can inspire new research. First, the final section described studies showing that validation and invalidation can apply to any mental content, including cases in which initial thoughts are about normal (and pathological) levels of confidence and doubt and cases in which initial thoughts are ambivalent. Second, we described how the meaning of variables that affect thought validity is flexible and can vary depending on the person or the situation, in this case as a function of epistemic versus hedonic mindsets.

References

Bartusevičius, H., Bor, A., Jørgensen, F., & Petersen, M. B. (2021). The psychological burden of the COVID-19 pandemic is associated with anti systemic attitudes and political violence. *Psychological Science*, *32*, 1391–1403.

Briñol, P., Gascó, M., Petty, R. E., & Horcajo, J. (2013). Treating thoughts as material objects can increase or decrease their impact on evaluation. *Psychological Science*, *24*, 41–47.

Briñol, P., & Petty, R. E. (2003). Overt head movements and persuasion: A self-validation analysis. *Journal of Personality and Social Psychology*, *84*, 1123–1139.

Briñol, P., Petty, R. E., Valle, C., Rucker, D. D., & Becerra, A. (2007). The effects of message recipients' power before and after persuasion: A self-validation analysis. *Journal of Personality and Social Psychology, 93*, 1040–1053. Briñol, P., Petty, R. E, Stavraki, M., Lamprinakos, G., Wagner, B. C., & Díaz, D. (2018). Affective and cognitive validation of thoughts: An appraisal perspective on anger, disgust, surprise, and awe. *Journal of Personality and Social Psychology, 114*, 693–718.

Briñol, P., & Petty, R. E. (2022). Self-validation theory: An integrative framework for understanding when thoughts become consequential. *Psychological Review, 129*, 340–367.

Burke, B. L., Martens, A., & Faucher, E. H. (2010). Two decades of terror management theory: A meta-analysis of mortality salience research. *Personality and Social Psychology Review, 14*, 155–195.

Cancela, A., Briñol, P., & Petty, R. E. (2021). Hedonic vs. epistemic goals in processing persuasive communications: Revisiting the role of personal involvement. *Motivation and Emotion, 45*, 280–298.

Cheatham, L. B., & Tormala, Z. L. (2017). The curvilinear relationship between attitude certainty and attitudinal advocacy. *Personality and Social Psychology Bulletin, 43*, 3–16.

Díaz, D., Briñol, P., Bajo, M., Stavraki, M., Beato-Fernández, L., & Petty, R. E. (in press). The association of the Persecutory Ideation Questionnaire with clinically-relevant and other outcomes: The moderating role of confidence. Scientific Reports.

Durso, G. R. O., Briñol, P., & Petty, R. E. (2016). From power to inaction: Ambivalence gives pause to the powerful. *Psychological Science, 27*, 1660–1666.

Fiske, S. T. (1980). Attention and weight in person perception: The impact of negative and extreme behavior. *Journal of Personality and Social Psychology, 38*, 889–906.

Galinsky, A. D., Gruenfeld, D. H., & Magee, J. C. (2003). From power to action. *Journal of Personality and Social Psychology, 85*, 453–466.

Gandarillas, B., Moreno, L., Briñol, P., & Petty, R. E. (2024). Attachment styles influence attitudes and persuasion by through metacognitive processes: Implications for direct vs. compensatory validation. *Manuscript in Preparation.*

Gascó, M., Briñol, P., Santos, D., Petty, R. E., & Horcajo, J. (2018). Where did this thought come from? A self-validation analysis of the perceived origin of thoughts. *Personality and Social Psychology Bulletin, 44*, 1615–1628.

Gillath, O., Sesko, A. K., Shaver, P. R., & Chun, D. S. (2010). Attachment, authenticity, and honesty: Dispositional and experimentally induced security can reduce self- and other-deception. *Journal of Personality and Social Psychology, 98*, 841–855.

Gollwitzer, A., Olcaysoy Okten, I., Pizarro, A. O., & Oettingen, G. (2022). Discordant knowing: A social cognitive structure underlying fanaticism. *Journal of Experimental Psychology: General, 151*, 2846–2878.

Goupil, L., & Kouider, S. (2019). Developing a reflective mind: From core metacognition to explicit self-reflection. *Current Directions in Psychological Science, 28*, 403–408.

Green, J. D., & Campbell, W. K. (2000). Attachment and exploration in adults: Chronic and contextual accessibility. *Personality and Social Psychology Bulletin, 26*, 452–461.

Greenberg, J., & Kosloff, S. (2008). Terror management theory: Implications for understanding prejudice, stereotyping, intergroup conflict, and political attitudes. *Social and Personality Psychology Compass, 2*, 1881–1894.

Haas, I., & Cunningham, W. (2014). The uncertainty paradox: Perceived threat moderates the effect of uncertainty on political tolerance. *Political Psychology, 35*, 291–302.

Hart, J. (2014). Toward an integrative theory of psychological defense. *Perspectives on Psychological Science, 9*, 19–39.

Hermans, D., Martens, K., De Cort, K., Pieters, G., & Eelen, P. (2003). Reality monitoring and metacognitive beliefs related to cognitive confidence in obsessive–Compulsive disorder. *Behavior Research and Therapy, 41*, 383–401.

Hirstein, W. (2005). Brain fiction: Self-deception and the riddle of confabulation. MIT Press: Cambridge, Massachusetts.

Hogg, M. A. (2007). Uncertainty-identity theory. In M. P. Zanna (Ed.), *Advances in experimental social psychology* (Vol. 39, pp. 69–126). Academic Press.

Hogg, M. A. (2021). Self-uncertainty and group identification: Consequences for social identity, group behavior, intergroup relations, and society. *Advances in Experimental Social Psychology, 64*, 263–316.

Horcajo, J., Briñol, P., Paredes, B., Petty, R. E., DeMarree, K. G., & See, Y. H. M. (2022). Attitude polarization as a function of mortality salience: A meta-cognitive analysis. *Psicothema, 34*, 226–232.

Kaplan, K. J. (1972). On the ambivalence-indifference problem in attitude theory and measurement: A suggested modification of the semantic differential technique. *Psychological Bulletin, 77*, 361–372.

Keltner, D., & Lerner, J. S. (2010). Emotion. In S. Fiske, D. T., Gilbert, & G. Lindzey (Eds.), *Handbook of social psychology* (5th ed., Vol. 1, pp. 317–352). Wiley & Sons.
Kidder, C. K., White, K. R., Hinojos, M. R., Sandoval, M., & Crites, S. L. (2018). Sequential stereotype priming: A meta-analysis. *Personality and Social Psychology Review*, *22*, 199–227.
Kim, T., Duhachek, A., Briñol, P., & Petty, R. E. (2021). How posting online reviews can influence the poster's evaluations. *Personality and Social Psychology Bulletin*, *47*,1401–1423.
Kopatich, R. D., Steciuch, C. C., Feller, D. P., Millis, K., & Siegesmund, R. (2021). Development and validation of the Aesthetic Processing Preference Scale (APPS). *Psychology of Aesthetics, Creativity, and the Arts, 17(5)*, 645–659.
Kruglanski, A. W., Molinario, E., & Lemay, E. P. (2021). Coping with COVID-19-induced threats to self. *Group Processes & Intergroup Relations*, *24*, 284–289.
Lambert, A., Eadeh, F. R., Peak, S. A., Scherer, L. D., Schott, J. P., & Slochower, J. M. (2014). Toward a greater understanding of the emotional dynamics of the mortality salience manipulation: Revisiting the "affect free" claim of terror management research. *Journal of Personality and Social Psychology*, *106*, 655–678.
Lamprinakos, G., Santos, D., Stavraki, M., Briñol, P., Magrizos, S., & Petty, R. E. (2024). Power can increase but also decrease cheating depending on the thoughts validated. Journal of Experimental Social Psychology, 111. E104578. https://doi.org/10.1016/j.jesp.2023.104578
Lyons-Ruth, K., Alpern, L., & Repacholi, B. (1993). Disorganized infant attachment classification and maternal psychosocial problems as predictors of hostile aggressive behavior in the preschool classroom. *Child Development*, *64*, 572–585.
Mandel, N., Rucker, D. D., Levav, J., & Galinsky, A. D. (2016). The compensatory consumer behavior model: How self-discrepancies drive consumer behavior. *Journal of Consumer Psychology*, *27*, 133–146.
McGregor, I., Nash, K., Mann, N., & Phills, C. E. (2010). Anxious uncertainty and reactive approach motivation (RAM). *Journal of Personality and Social Psychology*, *99*, 133–147.
McGregor, I., Zanna, M. P., Holmes, J. G., & Spencer, S. J. (2001). Compensatory conviction in the face of personal uncertainty: Going to extremes and being oneself. *Journal of Personality and Social Psychology*, *80*, 472–488.
Mikulincer, M., & Shaver, P. R. (2020). Broaden-and-build effects of contextually boosting the sense of attachment security in adulthood. *Current Directions in Psychological Science*, *29*, 22–26.
Moreno, L., Briñol, P., & Petty, R. E. (2022). Metacognitive confidence can increase but also decrease performance in academic settings. *Metacognition and Learning*, *17*, 139–165.
Moreno, L., Briñol, P., Petty, R. E., & Garcia-Marques, T. (2024). Doubting our own doubts: Implications for information processing and persuasion. *Manuscript in Preparation.*
Moreno, L., Paredes, B., Horcajo, J., Briñol, P, See, Y. H., DeMarree, K., & Petty, R. E. (2023). The effects of perceived COVID-19 threat on compensatory conviction, thought reliance, and attitudes. *European Journal of Social Psychology, 53,* 139–1325.
Oettingen, G., Gollwitzer, A., Jung, J., & Okten, I. O. (2022). Misplaced certainty in the context of conspiracy theories. *Current Opinion in Psychology*, *46*, 101393.
Paredes, B., Santos, D., Briñol, P., Gómez, A., & Petty, R. E. (2020). The role of meta-cognitive certainty on the relationship between identity fusion and endorsement of extreme pro-group behavior. *Self and Identity*, *19*, 804–824.
Paredes, B., Stavraki, M., Briñol, P., & Petty, R. E. (2013). Smiling after thinking increases reliance on thoughts. *Social Psychology*, *44*, 349–353.
Petty, R. E., Briñol, P., & Tormala, Z. L. (2002). Thought confidence as a determinant of persuasion: The self-validation hypothesis. *Journal of Personality and Social Psychology*, *82*, 722–741.
Petty, R. E., & Krosnick, J. A. (Eds.) (1995). *Attitude strength: Antecedents and consequences.* Erlbaum Associates.Petty, R. E., Siev, J. J., & Briñol, P. (2023). Attitude strength: What's new? *The Spanish Journal of Psychology*, *26*, e4, 1–13.
Petty, R. E., Wells, G. L., & Brock, T. C. (1976). Distraction can enhance or reduce yielding to propaganda: Thought disruption versus effort justification. *Journal of Personality and Social Psychology*, *34*, 874–884.
Priester, J. R., & Petty, R. E. (1996). The gradual threshold model of ambivalence: Relating the positive and negative bases of attitudes to subjective ambivalence. *Journal of Personality and Social Psychology*, *71*, 431–449.
Puryear, J. S., Kettler, T., & Rinn, A. N. (2017). Relationships of personality to differential conceptions of creativity: A systematic review. *Psychology of Aesthetics, Creativity, and the Arts*, *11*, 59–68.

Randles, D., Heine, S. J., Poulin, M., & Silver, R. C. (2017). Experienced adversity in life is associated with polarized and affirmed political attitudes. *Social Psychological and Personality Science*, *8*, 652–659.

Requero, B., Santos, D., Paredes, B., Briñol, P., & Petty, R. E. (2020). Attitudes toward hiring people with disabilities: A meta-cognitive approach to persuasion. *Journal of Applied Social Psychology*, *50*, 276–288.

Rucker, D. D., Tormala, Z. L., Petty, R. E., & Briñol, P. (2014). Consumer conviction and commitment: An appraisal-based framework for attitude certainty. *Journal of Consumer Psychology*, *24*, 119–136.

Santos, D., Briñol, P., Petty, R. E., Gandarillas, B., & Mateos, R. (2019). Trait aggressiveness predicting aggressive behavior: The moderating role of meta-cognitive certainty. *Aggressive Behavior*, *45*, 255–264.

Santos, D., Requero, B., Moreno, L., Briñol, P., & Petty, R. E., (in press). Certainty in holistic thinking and responses to contradiction: Dialectical proverbs, counter-attitudinal change, and ambivalence. British Journal of Social Psychology.

Sawicki, V., & Wegener, D. T. (2018). Meta-cognitive reflection as a moderator of attitude strength versus attitude bolstering: Implications for attitude similarity and attraction. *Personality and Social Psychology Bulletin*, *44*(5), 638–652.

Shoots-Reinhard, B., Petty, R. E., DeMarree, K. G., & Rucker, D. D. (2015). Personality certainty and politics: Increasing the predictive utility of individual difference inventories. *Political Psychology*, *36*, 415–430.

Siev, J. J., Petty, R. E., & Briñol, P. (2022). Attitudinal extremism. In A. W. Kruglanski, C. Kopetz, & E. Szumowska (Eds.), *The psychology of extremism: A motivational perspective* (pp. 34–65). Routledge.

Siev, J. J., Petty, R. E., Paredes, B., & Briñol, P. (2023). Behavioral extremity moderates the association between certainty in attitudes about COVID and willingness to engage in mitigation-related behaviors. *Social and Personality* Psychology Compass, *17*(8), e12767. https://doi.org/10.1111/spc3.12767

Siev, J. J., Xu, M., Luttrell, A., & Petty, R. E. (2024). The role of attitude strength in addressing the COVID-19 pandemic. In M. Miller (Ed.), *The social science of the COVID-19 pandemic: A call to action for researchers*. Oxford University Press.

Simchon, A., Turkin, C., Svoray, T., Kloog, I., Dorman, M., & Gilead, M. (2021). Beyond doubt in a dangerous world: The effect of existential threats on certainty expressions in societal discourse. Journal of Experimental Social Psychology, 97, a104221. https://doi.org/10.1016/j.jesp.2021.104221

Skowronski, J. J., & Carlston, D. E. (1989). Negativity and extremity biases in impression formation: A review of explanations. *Psychological Bulletin*, *105*, 131–142.

Strack, F., Martin, L. L., & Stepper, S. (1988). Inhibiting and facilitating conditions of the human smile: A non-obtrusive test of the facial feedback hypothesis. *Journal of Personality and Social Psychology*, *54*, 768–777

Toader, I., Moreno, L., Briñol, P., & Petty, R. E. (in press). Power corrupts and being sure of felt power corrupts even more: implications for immoral decisions and cheating. *European Journal of Social Psychology.*Toader, I., Moreno, L., Briñol, P., Petty, R. E., & Garcia-Marques, T. (2024). Beauty appreciation: The moderating role of epistemic vs. hedonic mindsets. *Manuscript in Preparation.*

Wells, G. L., & Petty, R. E. (1980). The effects of overt head movements on persuasion: Compatibility and incompatibility of responses. *Basic and Applied Social Psychology*, *1*, 219–230.

Wichman, A. L., Briñol, P., Petty, R. E., Rucker, D. D., Tormala, Z. L., & Weary, G. (2010). Doubting one's doubt: A formula for confidence? *Journal of Experimental Social Psychology*, *46*, 350–355.

3

THE CASE OF CONFIDENCE IN EYEWITNESS TESTIMONY

Kyros Shen, Allan Lam and John Wixted

Most people, when asked how reliable eyewitness memory is, reply with answers like "not very reliable" or "not reliable at all." This understandable response accords with the large number of wrongful convictions associated with confident eyewitness misidentifications in a court of law. According to the Innocence Project, eyewitness misidentifications played a role in almost 70% of 375 wrongful convictions overturned by DNA evidence since 1989, which is more than any other contributing factor (Innocence Project, 2023).

In addition to these cold statistics, highly publicized real-life cases have further underscored the unreliability of eyewitness memory, even when an eyewitness exhibited the highest level of certainty at the criminal trial. The case of Ronald Cotton is one of the most well-known examples, and his story was eventually published as a compelling memoir called *Picking Cotton* (Thompson-Cannino et al., 2009). In 1984, Jennifer Thompson, a college student at the time, was brutally raped, and Cotton was wrongfully convicted based mainly on her eyewitness identification. Thompson was absolutely certain that she made the correct identification, but, after serving more than ten years in prison, Cotton was eventually exonerated based on DNA evidence that revealed the identity of the true rapist (a man named Bobby Poole).

Although real-life examples like this helped to create the widespread impression that eyewitness memory is unreliable, it was scientific research conducted by experimental psychologists that fully cemented that impression in the minds of many. This research was regarded as being sufficiently conclusive and sufficiently accepted by the field at large that it was described in amicus briefs filed by the American Psychological Association as follows: "The findings drawn from this research are also overwhelmingly accepted within the scientific community" (American Psychological Association, 2014a, p. 4). In this same brief, one of the most widely accepted findings was summarized as follows: "This belief that confidence correlates with accuracy was once shared by some courts. See, e.g., Neil v. Biggers, 409 U.S. 188, 199 (1972). Modern scientific research, however, has called that notion into very serious question" (American Psychological Association, 2014a, p. 6).

If eyewitness memory is error-prone, and if the relationship between confidence and accuracy is weak, then the implication would be that eyewitness memory is inherently unreliable. Indeed, in a subsequent APA amicus brief filed in 2016, the upshot of the overall message from the psychological science of eyewitness identification was characterized this way: "Moreover,

DOI: 10.4324/9781003363385-4

although the unreliability of eyewitness identifications is well known in the scientific community and among many lawyers, it is not understood by lay juries (American Psychological Association, 2016, p. 9)." And as recently as 2019, an amicus brief doubled down on this pessimistic message, emphasizing the fact that "eyewitnesses are frequently mistaken in their identifications" (American Psychological Association, 2019, p. 6).

Fast forward to today, and we can now find statements such as "our understanding of the relation between confidence and accuracy in eyewitness identification has changed... psychological studies increasingly favor the idea that confidence is closely related to accuracy under some conditions and poorly related under others" (Schacter, 2022, p. 452) and "Under those conditions, ... (a) confidence and accuracy are strongly related and (b) high-confidence suspect identifications are remarkably accurate" (Wixted & Wells, 2017, p. 10). In other words, researchers now hold a much more nuanced opinion when discussing the confidence-accuracy relationship in eyewitness memory.

What caused opinion to shift away from the almost universal belief about how unreliable eyewitness memory is to the more nuanced understanding that it is sometimes highly reliable? This chapter will discuss the field's complicated journey to this new understanding and how, counterintuitively, it provides actual evidence of innocence for many prisoners who may have been wrongfully convicted but for whom no DNA evidence will ever be available to exonerate them.

The History of Eyewitness Memory Research

It is important to emphasize that the DNA exonerations occurred in the context of scientific research that was already casting serious doubt on the reliability of eyewitness memory. For example, the 1970s and 1980s saw an upsurge in false memory studies calling into question the intrinsic fidelity of human memory. Loftus and Palmer's (1974) groundbreaking work set the stage by demonstrating the potential malleability of memories as a result of post-event misleading information. Their seminal experiment, which is covered in virtually every psychology textbook, demonstrated how merely tweaking a suggestive word ("smashed" versus "contacted") in a post-event questionnaire could alter eyewitnesses' recollections, leading them to estimate the cars traveling at higher speeds and even falsely remember the existence of broken glass on the ground.

Loftus et al. (1978) further highlighted the susceptibility of visual memories to post-event suggestions by leading participants to mistakenly remember a stop sign instead of the original yield sign from a traffic accident scene. Although there are controversies surrounding this memory phenomenon (McCloskey & Zaragoza, 1985; Zaragoza et al., 1987), the result itself was consistent across a number of different studies. This consistency persisted even as studies ventured into the realm of much more complex fabricated memories, such as the "lost in a shopping mall" scenario (Loftus & Pickrell, 1995), where a false memory of getting lost in the mall as a child was implanted in nearly 30% of the participants tested. Another example is the "hot air balloon ride" (Wade et al., 2002), where the false memory of riding a hot air balloon as a child was induced with a fake photograph. Even emotional false memories involving crimes have been successfully induced (Shaw & Porter, 2015).

The inescapable message from the false memory research conducted by Loftus and her colleagues was that far more than had been previously appreciated, memory is *malleable*. In other words, just as other kinds of forensic evidence can be contaminated (e.g., DNA, fingerprints), so too can an eyewitness's recall of events. A separate line of research suggested that the same might be true of eyewitness identification, which is a recognition test. A recognition test does not require the recall of details but instead asks whether a physically present stimulus (such as a face in a lineup) was seen before. For example, Luus and Wells (1994) found that eyewitnesses to a staged crime became significantly more confident in their identifications when told that a co-eyewitness picked the same suspect, and significantly less confident when told that the co-eyewitness either did not make an ID or picked a different suspect. Wells and Bradfield (1998) later demonstrated that eyewitnesses who received confirming feedback after making the initial identification subsequently reported inflated levels of confidence in their decision.

These revelations about the malleability of memory (and corresponding malleability of confidence) raised two major concerns. First, juries find confident eyewitness identifications to be extremely compelling. Second, there is usually a long gap between the crime and the trial, a period where eyewitness memories are continuously vulnerable to distortion. Thus, for decades, and still to this day, eyewitness memory researchers have cautioned the legal system about placing much weight on the confidence a witness expresses at trial when identifying a defendant in front of a jury. This message has not changed over time.

If eyewitness memory is unreliable after it has been contaminated (just every other form of forensic evidence is when contaminated), it seems natural to wonder about how reliable it is—and whether confidence is related to accuracy—before it is contaminated. In other words, in a test of uncontaminated memory using a proper lineup procedure (e.g., a fair lineup, see next section), is eyewitness confidence in a positive identification strongly related to the accuracy of that identification? If eyewitness memory is unreliable even under those conditions, then, obviously, relying on eyewitness memory in forensically relevant settings would never make sense. In that case, the problem would be that eyewitness memory is simply an inherently unreliable form of evidence, and the job of scientists would be to make this clear to the legal system.

In the early research investigating this issue, scientists took an intuitive approach by computing the correlation between eyewitness confidence and accuracy. After all, if you want to find out if two measures are related (in this case, confidence and accuracy), then computing the correlation between them seems like a reasonable thing to do. When a lineup is used to test memory, the specific correlational measure of interest is called the point-biserial correlation coefficient (r_{pb}). This measure represents the correlation between the dichotomous outcome of accuracy (each participant is either correct or incorrect in their lineup decision) and the continuous measure of self-reported confidence (i.e., each participant also supplies a confidence rating). This approach attempts to boil the confidence-accuracy relationship down to a single number.

Early studies using this method often reported low r_{pb} values of ~.20, (Deffenbacher, 1980; Bothwell, Deffenbacher & Brigham, 1987; Wells & Murray, 1984), though somewhat higher values closer to ~.40 were obtained when the analysis was limited to "choosers," that is, to participants who did not reject the lineup (Sporer et al., 1995). These low point-biserial correlations, which were obtained under ideal testing conditions in the lab, understandably created considerable skepticism toward eyewitness confidence in general. If the correlation is that low even under perfect testing conditions in the lab and even when memory has not yet been contaminated, it seems reasonable to suppose that the correlation is essentially negligible in the real world.

Putting it all together yields a rather damning picture of the confidence-accuracy relationship and of the reliability of eyewitness memory in general. First, the DNA exoneration statistics revealed the outsized role played by eyewitness misidentifications in wrongful convictions. Second, influential scientific research showed how malleable human memory can be. And third, another line of scientific research appeared to show how little an eyewitness's expressed confidence tells us about their accuracy, even under the best of conditions. All of this led to a clear verdict: eyewitness memory is simply unreliable, and the confidence expressed by an eyewitness, although convincing to juries, should be disregarded.

It is perhaps not surprising, then, that in a survey that summarized the opinions of 63 eyewitness experts, more than 80% agreed that confidence is not a good predictor of accuracy (Kassin et al., 1989). In a later survey, Kassin et al. (2001) again found that more than 80% of experts still agreed with the statement that "An eyewitness's confidence is not a good predictor of his or her identification accuracy." A remarkable 87% of experts agreed with that statement, which is even more than the 83% who agreed with a statement summarizing one of the most well-established principles in all of experimental psychology: "The rate of memory loss for an event is greatest right after the event and then levels off over time." The fact that the typical time course of forgetting follows that basic trajectory, now enshrined in the "power law of forgetting," was first established by Ebbinghaus in 1885 and has been extremely well documented in the ensuing years (Anderson & Schooler, 1991; Ebbinghaus, 1885, 1913; Wixted & Ebbesen, 1991; Wixted, 2022).

If more experts believe that eyewitness confidence does not predict accuracy than believe in a well-established principle of forgetting, then it seems fair to say that the issue was considered to be settled science. This, in turn, would explain why this idea made its way into multiple amicus briefs filed by the American Psychological Association. It would also explain why it made its way into textbooks, which is presumably why, as recently as of 2019, a remarkable 82% of surveyed undergraduates agreed with the following statement: "An eyewitness's confidence is never a good predictor of his or her identification accuracy" (Brewin et al., 2019, emphasis added).

The Evolution of Eyewitness Memory Research

Things have changed, and to appreciate why, it is important to first understand the details of a lineup procedure. These days, law enforcement agencies predominantly use photo lineups (not live lineups) to test eyewitness memory. Photo lineups consist of one suspect—whose guilt or innocence is to be determined—alongside a set number of known-to-be-innocent fillers, typically five in the U.S. The eyewitness can either identify an individual from the lineup (the suspect or one of the fillers) or they can reject the lineup altogether if they believe the perpetrator is not present. Longstanding recommendations for administering a fair lineup procedure include using fillers who match the witness's description of the perpetrator, implementing a double-blind procedure (i.e., neither the witness nor the lineup administrator is told who the suspect is), warning the witness that the perpetrator may or may not be in the lineup, and collecting an immediate confidence statement (Wells et al., 1998, 2020).

In actual criminal investigations, it is impossible to know whether a suspect is guilty prior to a lineup. However, this can be easily manipulated in laboratory settings by simply changing the suspect presented to the witness. When the suspect is the actual perpetrator, the lineup is called a "target-present" (TP) lineup. When the suspect is an innocent person who bears a passing resemblance to the actual perpetrator—this is considered a "target-absent" (TA) lineup. In a typical lab study, each participant observes a mock crime and then is tested only once using a TP or TA lineup. Thus, the data consist of suspect IDs, filler IDs, and lineup rejections from TP lineups and suspect IDs, filler IDs, and lineup rejections from TA lineups. Each lineup decision is either correct or incorrect (0 or 1) and is accompanied by a confidence rating. The correlation between confidence and accuracy is computed from these data.

As noted earlier, even using a proper lineup procedure and testing uncontaminated memory, research showed that the correlation between confidence and accuracy was weak. However, Juslin et al. (1996) were the first to explain why using point-biserial correlation as an indicator of confidence-accuracy relationship is problematic. They argued that this measure is not only less than optimal, but it is also potentially misleading (possibly extremely so). Instead, Juslin et al. recommended an alternative method known as calibration analysis, which quantifies the correspondence between confidence measured on a hundred-point scale and percent-correct accuracy, which is also measured on a hundred-point scale. Perfect calibration exists when eyewitnesses who express 100% confidence are 100% accurate, those who express 75% confidence are 75% accurate, and so forth. Critically, the point-biserial correlation coefficient can be misleadingly close to 0 even when confidence is *perfectly* calibrated to accuracy (Juslin et al., 1996). Subsequent studies corroborated the value of calibration analysis. For example, using that approach, Brewer and Wells (2006) reported a high confidence-accuracy relationship, particularly among "choosers" (i.e., those who made a positive ID of the suspect of a filler).

However, even this undeniably improved method for assessing the confidence-accuracy relationship ultimately turned out to be less than optimal as well. The calibration approach is perfectly fine for an identification procedure like a showup, which involves a single suspect (innocent or guilty). In a showup, to compute accuracy for a given level of confidence (e.g., high-confidence decisions made with 90–100% confidence), one simply uses the formula $100\% \times \frac{GS_{high}}{GS_{high} + IS_{high}}$, where GS_{high} represents the number of correct identifications of the guilty suspect made with high confidence (i.e., 90–100%), and IS_{high} represents the number of incorrect identifications of the innocent suspect made with high confidence. Similar values can be computed for the remaining levels of confidence, and the computed accuracy scores can then be plotted as a function of confidence to create a calibration curve.

Unlike a showup, a lineup has fillers, and intuition suggests that filler IDs should somehow be considered in the calibration score as well. Whether a filler ID is made from a TP lineup or a TA lineup, it is incorrect, which raises a question: How should these additional incorrect decisions be factored into the calibration equation?

The calibration curve of most interest is the one that represents the performance of "choosers" (i.e., those who positively identify someone). For a positive ID, the only correct response is an identification of the guilty suspect. Thus, the numerator of the calibration equation consists only of such IDs made with a certain level of confidence, whereas the denominator consists of all identifications (correct or incorrect) made with that same level of confidence. Thus, it might make sense to add incorrect filler identifications (i.e., the number of filler IDs from TP lineups and the number of filler IDs from TA lineups) to the denominator of the equation presented above for the showup. In practice, it is sometimes done that way (e.g., Brewer et al., 2002), but more often errors from TP lineups are excluded on the grounds that they are known to be innocent (e.g., Brewer & Wells, 2006). However, the fillers in TA lineups are also known to be innocent and could be similarly excluded. But they never are.

The fact that TA filler IDs are never excluded from calibration analysis reflects a methodological feature commonly used in lineup studies. Specifically, unlike in real police lineups, in lab studies, TA lineups often have no designated innocent suspect (i.e., the lineup consists only of filler photos) and thus have no predefined set of innocent fillers distinct from the suspect to exclude. It makes sense to create TA lineups in this way because when a real lineup contains an innocent suspect, from the witness's perspective, the lineup consists of nothing but fillers (i.e., nothing but people who match the witness's description of the perpetrator but who did not commit the crime). An innocent suspect is special only from the perspective of the police because they mistakenly believe he might be guilty.

Because of this design feature, should filler IDs from TA lineups be included in the calibration score even while excluding filler IDs from TP lineups? This is not really a sound approach. If one is going to compute calibration, and if TA filler IDs are going to be included in the calculation as errors, then TP filler IDs should also be included as errors. As recently as 2014, an APA amicus brief used this more reasonable approach and cited calibration research as demonstrating the following:

> Importantly, error rates can be high even among the most confident witnesses. Researchers have performed studies that track, in addition to identification accuracy, the subjects' estimates of their confidence in their identifications. In one article reporting results from an empirical study, researchers found that among witnesses who made positive identifications, as many as 40 percent were mistaken, yet they declared themselves to be 90 percent to 100 percent confident in the accuracy of their identifications...This confirms that many witnesses are over-confident in their identification decisions.
>
> (American Psychological Association, 2014b, pp. 17–18)

Thus, even though calibration research made it clear that eyewitness confidence was more informative than previously assumed, the longstanding message from psychological science to the courts remained essentially the same: eyewitness identifications are unreliable even when made from a pristine lineup, even before memory was contaminated, and even when confidence was high. But that message was about to change.

Post-2010 marked a significant shift in the field of eyewitness memory research because it is when basic memory research in the field of cognitive psychology began to cross-pollinate with its applied counterpart in the field of eyewitness identification. Cognitive psychologists took a different approach to studying eyewitness identification by framing as recognition tests as they are often framed in basic research, namely, as a signal detection task (Mickes et al., 2012; Wixted & Mickes, 2014; Wixted, Vul et al., 2018). It is well known that the basic signal detection model of recognition memory inherently predicts a strong confidence–accuracy relationship, so it initially seemed like a poor fit for eyewitness identification research (Wixted, 2020). However, the problem was not with signal detection theory. Instead, the problem was with how the confidence-accuracy relationship was being assessed in terms of correlation or calibration.

Mickes (2015), drawing on Bayesian principles in conjunction with signal detection theory, introduced the Confidence-Accuracy Characteristic (CAC) as an enhancement over calibration analysis methods when a lineup is used. In a legal context, the question of interest is usually how reliable a *suspect* ID is, given that the ID was already made. By contrast, witnesses who initially make filler identifications and lineup rejections should not make it to the witness stand to positively identify the suspect (although, as discussed later, they sometimes do). Those who initially identify the suspect are usually the ones who end up testifying about their positive identification. The CAC approach therefore calculates the accuracy of suspect identifications per se at each level of confidence, providing a more relevant metric. In other words, CAC analysis answers the following question: given that the eyewitness identified a suspect from the lineup with a certain level of confidence, how likely is that identification to be correct? Signal detection theory predicts a strong confidence-accuracy relationship for *this* measure (i.e., the one judges and juries care about).

In CAC analysis, the formula for computing accuracy is the same one presented earlier for computing calibration when a showup procedure is used. In that formula, only correct and incorrect suspect IDs are included (because there are no filler IDs when a showup is used). The same formula should be used even when fillers are present (i.e., even when a lineup is used). In other words, the information value of filler IDs from TA and TP lineups should be assessed by analyzing them separately from suspect IDs. CAC analysis keeps the focus squarely on correct and incorrect suspect IDs made with different levels of confidence. But how does one compute innocent suspect IDs from TA lineups in the common lab design in which these lineups consist of nothing but fillers (i.e., no designated innocent suspect)? In that case, incorrect innocent suspect IDs can be estimated by simply dividing the number of TA filler IDs by lineup size. In essence, one way or another, CAC analysis excludes filler IDs from both TP and TA lineups.

Wixted and Wells (2017) took CAC analysis and retroactively applied it to data from 15 simulated crime studies that previously employed point-biserial correlation and calibration analyses. Their reanalysis showed a new pattern: suspect IDs made with high confidence were highly accurate (well above 90% correct), whereas the ones associated with low confidence were not much better than chance (Wixted et al., 2016). In other words, far from being uninformative, on an initial, properly conducted test of uncontaminated memory, an eyewitness's expressed level of confidence could scarcely be more informative than it is. Critically, this is the very definition of reliability. Thus, the longstanding and almost universal verdict concerned with the unreliability of eyewitness memory was turned on its head.

Remarkably, this strong confidence-accuracy relationship was also present in real-world data involving actual eyewitnesses in investigations conducted by the Houston Police Department (Wixted et al., 2016). This study adhered to recommended pristine lineup procedures, so the findings were unlikely to be artifacts of unfair lineups or police steering witnesses to pick suspects. The key finding was that when witnesses picked a filler, they often did so with low confidence, but when they picked a suspect, they typically did so with high confidence. Given that these photo lineups were conducted early in a police investigation (thereby minimizing the chances that memory had already been contaminated) and in such a way that a witness could only land on a suspect at above-chance levels using their memory of the perpetrator, the results were entirely consistent with the new understanding of eyewitness reliability based on lab studies.

Subsequent research also using real-world lineups confirmed this robust confidence-accuracy relationship (Quigley-McBride & Wells, 2023) and additionally underscored another variable that was found to be associated with accuracy: response time. Basically, as lab-based research has long shown, IDs made quickly tend to also be made with high confidence, and the same is true of real-world identifications from police lineups (Seale-Carlisle et al., 2019). Together, confidence and decision time were dubbed "reflector variables" (i.e., variables that reflect identification accuracy).

With compelling empirical evidence now spanning both simulated and real-world settings, the 2010s emerged as a period that saw cognitive psychologists build a cogent, theoretically grounded case for the predictive value of confidence and the reliability of eyewitness memory. Research in the field is now using detailed signal-detection modeling to dive deeper into the mechanisms that underlie the process of eyewitness identification (Wixted, Vul et al., 2018; Shen et al., 2023; Fitousi, 2023).

It is worth noting that the confidence-accuracy relationship that we have discussed thus far does not conflict with earlier research attesting to the frailties of human memory. For instance, the wrongful convictions overturned by the Innocence Project make it clear that an eyewitness's testimony at trial is often tainted by post-identification misinformation. Precisely because memory is malleable, the strong confidence-accuracy relationship can only be observed in *initial* IDs (prior to memory contamination) obtained under pristine testing conditions. Therefore, rather than being at odds, these two perspectives can be seen as complementary factors of a complex issue, each contributing insight into the broader understanding of eyewitness memory and its role in the legal system.

The Mechanisms of Eyewitness Memory

So far, we have briefly considered the role of signal detection theory in helping to understand the confidence-accuracy relationship in eyewitness identification. However, there is much additional work from the basic science-of-memory literature that needs to be considered in order to fully appreciate why everything we just explained with regard to the impressive confidence-accuracy relationship applies to the *first* test of an eyewitness's memory for a suspect. As a general rule, no later test provides more reliable information than the first because (1) the first test minimizes the chances of testing contaminated memory and (2) the test itself contaminates the witness's memory for the suspect. Thus, from a scientific perspective, the first test is of special importance. By contrast, from a legal perspective, the last test (at trial) is of special importance. The last test is of special importance from a legal perspective because the witness (1) is under oath and (2) can be cross examined by opposing counsel. However, the test that occurs at the criminal trial provides the least reliable information because it maximizes the chances of testing contaminated memory. Placing the witness under oath and allowing the witness to be cross examined cannot change that unfortunate fact. Basically, the choice is between reliable information obtained when the witness is not under oath and cannot be cross examined vs. unreliable information obtained when the witness is under oath and can be cross examined.

In the personal experience of the senior author of this chapter, prosecutors sometimes worry that putting an emphasis on the initial identification test might simply create a loophole for the benefit of the perpetrator. For example, imagine that on the initial test, the witness rejects a lineup containing a recognizable photo of the suspect. However, the police nonetheless remain convinced that the suspect is the perpetrator and proceed to test the witness again, perhaps using a live lineup this time on the theory that it provides a better test of memory. Now, the witness might identify the suspect for the first time, and the police will likely conclude that, on the second test, the witness "found" the memory of the perpetrator that they failed to find on the first test. After all, everyone has had the experience of failing to remember a detail on the first try (e.g., the name of a recent acquaintance) and then successfully remembering it days, weeks, or even months later. Perhaps something similar is happening when the witness finally recognizes the suspect that the police already believe may have committed the crime.

However, that is not what is happening, and believing otherwise reflects an understandable yet catastrophic lack of expertise on the part of judges and jurors. It is certainly true that certain kinds of memory, specifically recollection memory (e.g., recalling someone's name), can initially fail but succeed later—a phenomenon technically known as "reminiscence" (Gilbert & Fisher, 2006). Reminiscence can lead to overall memory performance improving as a function of repeated testing for a single encoding event (e.g., repeatedly testing memory for the once-presented list of words). This overall improvement in performance is known as "hypermnesia." However, it is crucial to understand that this phenomenon applies to the recollection of details but does not ordinarily apply to a recognition test (Payne & Roediger, 1987), and a lineup test is a recognition test. Why not?

Recollection tests ask for information that is not physically present during the test—e.g., "What was the perpetrator wearing?" This retrieval cue prompts the eyewitness to conduct a probabilistic search of memory to retrieve the relevant detail. Because of its probabilistic nature, a failure in the initial test does not distort the stored memory, so if the attempt to find that information on a later try, it is not inherently problematic. Analogously, you can fail to find your keys when first searching for them, but if you find them when you search again later, the keys are still exactly as they were before (having been unaffected by the initial failed search).

By contrast, recognition memory tests ask about a stimulus that is physically present. In a lineup, for example, the question is: "Do you see the face of the person who committed the crime?" The nature of this test involves picking out the option that elicits the strongest familiarity signal (or rejecting the lineup if even that face is not sufficiently familiar). The face familiarity signal is immediately available because it is not the result of a search process. Instead, it is the result of a *matching* process.

To appreciate this key issue, consider Mandler's classic "Butcher on the Bus" anecdote (Mandler, 1980). This anecdote describes an experience of encountering a man on a bus whose face is so familiar that it calls for a search of memory to determine the source of familiarity. The source of the familiarity signal is not physically present and therefore requires a search of memory to find the original encoding context ("Where do I know him from?"). However, the familiarity signal itself—that is, the familiarity signal associated with the physically present face—is not like that. The familiarity signal is experienced promptly upon viewing the face because no search of memory is required.

In a police lineup, the face is physically present (no search required) and so is the relevant context in which the face might have been previously encountered because the police ask the witness who committed the crime (again, no search required to find the relevant context where the face might have been originally encoded). Because everything that one might have to search for in memory is already available, if a face in the lineup is not immediately familiar, no amount of searching memory or analyzing facial features or comparing and contrasting the faces ("it is between these two") will change that fact. Instead, the lack of a strong and promptly experienced familiarity signal upon viewing the faces in the lineup means that none were encoded into the witness's memory. None of the faces are familiar either because they are all innocent (including the suspect) or because the suspect is guilty, but the witness did not get a good look at the perpetrator at the time of the crime.

Unfortunately, witnesses do not understand this principle, and neither do the police. Thus, it is not uncommon for a witness to spend *minutes* searching memory in a hopeless effort to find the face familiarity signal somewhere in their brain. Jennifer Thompson's initial identification of Ronald Cotton, for example, came after almost five minutes of analyzing the faces in the lineup. But 10 or 20 seconds into the lineup, it was already clear that no one matched the memory of the perpetrator encoded in her brain (including Rondald Cotton). Had everyone understood what we know now—namely, that on this crucial initial test of uncontaminated memory, Jennifer Thompson made an ID with very low confidence—Cotton may never have been wrongfully convicted.

Critically, there are no second chances to test a witness's uncontaminated memory for a suspect, and this is true no matter how perfect or how suggestive the initial lineup procedure was and no matter what the outcome of the initial test was (a suspect ID, a filler ID, or no ID). One way to appreciate why this is true is to consider the "memory for foils" paradigm (Jacoby et al., 2005) in which participants' first study of the list of words followed a recognition test in which they are asked to distinguish between words that appear on the list (targets) and words that did not (foils). Later, the participants are given an unexpected recognition test for the foils (now targets), which are intermixed with another set of novel foils. Note that when taking the first recognition test, the participants were only making recognition decisions, not attempting to memorize anything. Moreover, they correctly rejected most of the foils that would appear on the subsequent surprise recognition test. After all, there is nothing suggestive about a memory test like this. Yet on the surprise test that followed (testing memory for the recently seen foils), their memory performance was as good as it was for the targets on the first test. The clear implication is that testing memory by means of recognition creates a memory of the tested items, including the foils.

Somehow, it has not been sufficiently appreciated that the same memory principle applies when memory is tested by recognition using a lineup. In a lineup test, an innocent suspect is a foil. Thus, there are no second chances to test uncontaminated memory for a suspect because the act of taking the test and evaluating the options creates a representation of the faces in the lineup (including the suspect's face). Even worse, these memory records are being created at a time when the witness is thinking about the crime, thereby associating the face with the crime. Thus, if any one of these faces appears in a subsequent test (as only the innocent suspect's face will), it will seem more familiar than would otherwise be the case and the source of that familiarity signal may be attributed to the crime. Pretending that such contamination has not happened and that the witness at trial can instead find an untainted, independent source of their memory for what happened on the day of the crime is a game that results in tragic consequences.

If the witness recognizes a face on a second test after failing to recognize it with high confidence on the first test, it is not an instance of reminiscence but is instead a reflection of memory contamination. *This* is how witnesses come to confidently misidentify an innocent defendant in front of a jury, leading to a wrongful conviction, not because eyewitness memory is unreliable. Witnesses are reliable on the first test, and it is not their fault that no one listens to what they have to say at that time. Instead, the rules of evidence at a criminal trial are such that judges and juries are almost certain to consider what the witness has to say at trial, long after the witness's memory has been contaminated. The contamination begins with the first lineup test and is later exacerbated by many subsequent events, such as confirming feedback from police or prosecutors (Wells & Bradfield, 1998). All the while, as the police keep the focus on the innocent suspect (right up until the criminal trial a year or two later), the memory of the actual once-seen perpetrator in the brain of the eyewitness is gradually fading away.

Prisoners who are now serving long sentences and whose cases illustrate this problem are not hard to find. In fact, this may be the most important implication of the new understanding according to which there is only one chance to a witness's uncontaminated memory for a suspect and on that initial test, eyewitnesses provide reliable information. For a field that has, for decades, emphasized the inherent unreliability of eyewitness memory, the idea that memory actually tends to be reliable on the first test is disconcerting. The fear is that witnesses will do on the first test what they often do on the last test at trial, namely, misidentify an innocent suspect with high confidence. Contrary to that understandable concern, the opposite seems to be true.

Garrett (2011) analyzed trial testimony from 161 DNA exoneration cases and found that in 57% of those cases, there was testimony about what the eyewitness did on the first test (92 cases in all). These 92 witnesses all testified with high confidence at trial, of course, but how many did so on the first test involving the suspect who would later be wrongfully convicted? Not a single one did so. And why would they? That is, why would a witness immediately and confidently misidentify the face of an innocent suspect that does not match their fresh memory of the perpetrator? Instead, and understandably, all of these witnesses identified the suspect with low confidence or picked a filler or rejected the lineup. Some said they did not even see the perpetrator in the first place. Garrett's (2011) findings, perhaps more than any other, underscore the importance of keeping the focus on the first test (i.e., the test that provides reliable information). They also underscore the point from lab studies that on the first test, eyewitnesses are not unreliable. Instead, it is the criminal justice system that is unreliable because it does not listen to what the witness says on the first test and then repeatedly tests the witness's' contaminated memory to win a conviction.

Once the focus is placed on the first test, it becomes clear that there are many cases just like the DNA exoneration cases but for which no DNA evidence is available. Thus, for these unfortunate prisoners, no DNA exoneration will ever happen. In these cases, the apparent evidence of guilt that led to the conviction (namely, the high-confidence testimony of eyewitnesses at the criminal trial), properly understood, actually points in the opposite direction (i.e., on the initial test, the exact same eyewitnesses provided clear evidence of innocence). We end this chapter by considering one case that illustrates the importance of the story we have told here. However, this is by no means the only case.

Case Illustration

In 2009, James Joseph Garner was at a bar in Denver Colorado when a gunman opened fire, injuring brothers Arturo, Christian, and Roberto Adame-Diaz (People of the State of Colorado v. James Joseph Garner, 2015). Immediately after the shooting, witness #1 (Roberto) told police that he had not clearly seen the shooter. Witness #2 (Arturo) did see the shooter described him as a man who was 27 years old and 5 feet, 2 inches tall, but Garner was nine years older and 6 inches taller than that. Witness #3 (Christian) also saw the gunman and provided the most detailed description, telling the police that he was bald, wearing no glasses, with no facial hair, and with a tattoo on his head. Unlike the gunman Christian described, Garner had short black hair, glasses, facial hair, and no such tattoos. Thus, it seems that Christian described a different person. On an initial test of uncontaminated memory (but not on later tests of contaminated memory), witness descriptions tend to be highly reliable (e.g., Wixted et al., 2018). Thus, already at this early stage of the investigation, the witness descriptions would seem to weigh against Garner being the shooter.

The police nevertheless suspected Garner and placed his photo in an array along with five similar fillers. This was the key test, the one that provided the most reliable information because it minimized the chances of testing contaminated memory. On this key test, *none of the three witnesses selected Garner*. Indeed, Christian Adame-Diaz pointed to Garner's photo (number two in the lineup) and said "He was there but he was not the shooter." The fact that all three witnesses looked at Garner's face and did not identify him provides considerable evidence that Garner is innocent. But this first test also contaminated the memories of the three witnesses by creating a memory of Garner's face at the time they were thinking about the crime. Many more opportunities for memory contamination would occur in the subsequent *three years* leading up to Garner's criminal trial.

In contrast to the initial test, at the criminal trial, all three witnesses confidently identified Garner. You might think that, upon hearing that the witnesses were unable to identify Garner on the initial test, the jury would scoff at the high-confidence IDs that occurred at trial and return a verdict of "not guilty." That is, you might think that their prior inconsistent statements would impeach the credibility of the confident IDs made in court. However, it would be a serious mistake to think along these lines. Recall, for example, the 92 DNA exoneration cases analyzed by Garrett (2011) in which the inconclusive ID came up at trial and the jury still found the defendant guilty every time. A fundamental problem is that when a witness's memory changes from the first test early in a police investigation to the last test at trial, a speculative non-science-based explanation for this change will almost always be offered, either by the witness or by the prosecutor, and juries tend to uncritically accept that explanation.

In the Garner trial, the prosecutor argued that the witnesses failed to identify Garner from mere photos but recognized him three years later at trial because now (at trial) the identification procedure was an in-person test. According to this line of reasoning, in-court IDs following an initial failure to identify the suspect from a photo lineup is not a recipe for a wrongful conviction but instead serve the cause of justice. However, the relevant science says it might be the other way around.

Contrary to the prosecutor's assertion, multiple studies have found that live lineups yield no better performance than photo lineups. Fitzgerald et al. (2018) reviewed the relevant literature on the live lineup superiority hypothesis and succinctly summarized their findings as follows: "In spite of our efforts to be as charitable as possible to the live superiority hypothesis, we found little reason to support it" (p. 321). In a subsequent study, Rubínová et al. (2021) conducted a large-scale investigation of this issue, and the title of their paper makes their findings clear: "Live presentation for eyewitness identification is not superior to photo or video presentation."

What other explanation might explain why all three witnesses failed to identify Garner on the all-important first test but did so with ultimate confidence in front of the jury at the criminal trial? The alternative explanation considered at Garner's trial is that the witnesses might be lying, but the prosecutor quite reasonably rejected that theory:

> Is it possible that all three of these guys come in here and lie to you and tell you that they're 100 percent sure he's the shooter and that they're all three willing to send an innocent person to get convicted of this? I would submit to you that its not even possible, but it's certainly not reasonable.
>
> (Colorado Court of Appeals, People of the State of Colorado vs. James Joseph Garner, 2015, p. 27)

Faced with these two possible explanations for why the witnesses were identifying Garner now despite not having done so previously—namely, they had better memory for live faces seen now than for photos seen three years ago vs. they are all simply lying—the jury apparently accepted the former one. Garner was found guilty and sentenced to 32 years in prison.

But there is a third explanation that fits the facts much better than the other two theories, one that was never considered at the criminal trial or during his subsequent appeals. It is a theory that is based on a new scientific consensus that emerged in 2020: testing a witness's memory for a suspect unintentionally contaminates the witness's memory for that suspect (Wells et al., 2020; Wixted et al., 2021). A few exceptions notwithstanding (e.g., when the witnesses were lying not at trial but on the first test), the contaminating effect of the first test renders all later tests less reliable than the first. On the first and only test of uncontaminated memory, conducted early in the police investigation (a time when the memory of the perpetrator would still be strong), the three witnesses excluded James Garner as being the shooter. Thus, the most relevant eyewitness evidence in this case points in the direction of innocence, not guilt.

In many of the DNA exoneration cases, it was not the witnesses who were unreliable. Attributing wrongful convictions to the unreliability of eyewitness memory diverts attention from addressing the primary issue, which is that the legal system inadvertently prioritizes the least reliable test of a witness's memory while neglecting the most reliable one. To solve that problem, the legal system should find a way to keep the focus on the reliable first test of memory and take it off of the unreliable last test at trial.

References

American Psychological Association. (2014a). *Brief for Amicus Curiae, Commonwealth v. Walker*. Retrieved from: https://www.apa.org/about/offices/ogc/amicus/walker.aspx

American Psychological Association. (2014b). *Brief for Amicus Curiae, Commonwealth of Massachusetts v. Gomes*. Retrieved from: https://www.apa.org/about/offices/ogc/amicus/gomes-johnson

American Psychological Association. (2016). *Brief for Amicus Curiae, Payne v. Commonwealth of Virginia*. Retrieved from https://www.apa.org/about/offices/ogc/amicus/payne.pdf

American Psychological Association. (2019). *Brief for Amicus Curiae, Watson v. Commonwealth of Virginia.* Retrieved from https://www.apa.org/about/offices/ogc/amicus/watson-virginia

Anderson, J. R., & Schooler, L. J. (1991). Reflections of the environment in memory. *Psychological Science, 2*(6), 396–408.

Bothwell, R. K., Deffenbacher, K. A., & Brigham, J. C. (1987). Correlation of eyewitness accuracy and confidence: Optimality hypothesis revisited. *Journal of Applied Psychology, 72*(4), 691.

Brewer, N., Keast, A., & Rishworth, A. (2002). The confidence-accuracy relationship in eyewitness identification: The effects of reflection and disconfirmation on correlation and calibration. *Journal of Experimental Psychology: Applied, 8*(1), 44–56. https://doi.org/10.1037/1076-898X.8.1.44

Brewer, N., & Wells, G. L. (2006). The confidence-accuracy relation in eyewitness identification: Effects of lineup instructions, foil similarity, and target-absent base rates. *Journal of Experimental Psychology: Applied, 12*, 11–30.

Brewin, C. R., Li, H., Ntarantana, V., Unsworth, C., & McNeilis, J. (2019). Is the public understanding of memory prone to widespread "myths"? *Journal of Experimental Psychology: General, 148*, 2245–2257.

Deffenbacher, K. (1980). Eyewitness accuracy and confidence: Can we infer anything about their relationship? *Law and Human Behavior, 4*, 243–260.

Ebbinghaus, H. (1885). Über das Gedächtnis: Untersuchungen zur experimentellen Psychologie. Leipzig: Duncker & Humblot.

Ebbinghaus, H. (1913). *Memory: A contribution to experimental psychology.* (H. A. Ruger & C. E. Bussenius, Trans.). Teachers College Press. (Original work published 1885).Eyewitness misidentification. Innocence Project. (2023, May 1). Retrieved from https://innocenceproject.org/eyewitness-misidentification/

Fitousi, D. (2024). A signal detection–based confidence–similarity model of face matching. *Psychological Review, 131*(3), 625.

Fitzgerald, R. J., Price, H. L., & Valentine, T. (2018). Eyewitness identification: Live, photo, and video lineups.*Psychology, Public Policy, and Law, 24*(3), 307–325. https://doi.org/10.1037/law0000164

Garrett, B. L. (2011). *Convicting the Innocent: Where Criminal Prosecutions Go Wrong.* Cambridge, MA: Harvard University Press.

Gilbert, J. A., & Fisher, R. P. (2006). The effects of varied retrieval cues on reminiscence in eyewitness memory. *Applied Cognitive Psychology, 20*(6), 723–739.

Innocence Project. (2023). Retrieved from https://www.innocenceproject.org/exonerate/

Jacoby, L. L., Shimizu, Y., Daniels, K. A., & Rhodes, M. G. (2005). Modes of cognitive control in recognition and source memory: depth of retrieval. *Psychonomic Bulletin & Review, 12*(5), 852–857. https://doi.org/10.3758/bf03196776

Juslin, P., Olsson, N., & Winman, A. (1996). Calibration and diagnosticity of confidence in eyewitness identification: Comments on what can be inferred from the low confidence-accuracy correlation. *Journal of Experimental Psychology: Learning, Memory, and Cognition, 22*, 1304–1316.

Kassin, S. M., Ellsworth, P., & Smith, V. L. (1989). The "general acceptance" of psychological research on eyewitness testimony. *American Psychologist, 44*, 1089–1098.

Kassin, S. M., Tubb, V. A., Hosch, H. M., & Memon, A. (2001). On the "general acceptance" of eyewitness testimony research: A new survey of the experts. *American Psychologist, 56*(5), 405–416. https://doi.org/10.1037/0003-066X.56.5.405

Loftus, E. F., Miller, D. G., & Burns, H. J. (1978). Semantic integration of verbal information into a visual memory. *Journal of Experimental Psychology: Human Learning and Memory, 4*(1), 19.

Loftus, E. F., & Palmer, J. C. (1974). Reconstruction of automobile destruction: An example of the interaction between language and memory. *Journal of Verbal Learning and Verbal Behavior, 13*(5), 585–589.

Loftus, E. F., & Pickrell, J. E. (1995). The formation of false memories. *Psychiatric Annals, 25*(12), 720–725.

Luus, C. A., & Wells, G. L. (1994). The malleability of eyewitness confidence: Co-witness and perseverance effects. *Journal of Applied Psychology, 79*(5), 714.

Mandler, G. (1980). Recognizing: The judgment of previous occurrence. *Psychological Review, 87*, 252– 271.

McCloskey, M., & Zaragoza, M. (1985). Misleading postevent information and memory for events: arguments and evidence against memory impairment hypotheses. *Journal of Experimental Psychology: General, 114*(1), 1.

Mickes, L. (2015). Receiver operating characteristic analysis and confidence–accuracy characteristic analysis in investigations of system variables and estimator variables that affect eyewitness memory. *Journal of Applied Research in Memory and Cognition*, *4*(2), 93.

Mickes, L., Flowe, H. D., & Wixted, J. T. (2012). Receiver operating characteristic analysis of eyewitness memory: Comparing the diagnostic accuracy of simultaneous and sequential lineups. *Journal of Experimental Psychology: Applied*, *18*, 361–376.

Payne, D. G., & Roediger, H. L. (1987). Hypermnesia occurs in recall but not in recognition. *American Journal of Psychology*, *100*, 145–165.

People of the State of Colorado v. James Joseph Garner. (2015). Colo. App. 12CA2540. Retrieved from https://cases.justia.com/colorado/court-of-appeals/2015-12ca2540.pdf?ts=1450368352

Quigley-McBride, A., & Wells, G. L. (2023). Eyewitness confidence and decision time reflect identification accuracy in actual police lineups. *Law and Human Behavior*, *47*(2), 333.

Rubínová, E., Fitzgerald, R. J., Juncu, S., Ribbers, E., Hope, L., & Sauer, J. D. (2021). Live presentation for eyewitness identification is not superior to photo or video presentation. *Journal of Applied Research in Memory and Cognition*, *10*(1), 167–176. https://doi.org/10.1016/j.jarmac.2020.08.009

Schacter, D. L. (2022). Memory sins in applied settings: What kind of progress? *Journal of Applied Research in Memory and Cognition*, *11*(4), 445.

Seale-Carlisle, T. M., Colloff, M. F., Flowe, H. D., Wells, W., Wixted, J. T., & Mickes, L. (2019). Confidence and response time as indicators of eyewitness identification accuracy in the lab and in the real world. *Journal of Applied Research in Memory and Cognition*, *8*(4), 420–428.

Shaw, J., & Porter, S. (2015). Constructing rich false memories of committing crime. *Psychological Science*, *26*(3), 291–301.

Shen, K. J., Colloff, M. F., Vul, E., Wilson, B. M., & Wixted, J. T. (2023). Modeling face similarity in police lineups. *Psychological Review*, *130*(2), 432–461. https://doi.org/10.1037/rev0000408.

Sporer, S. L., Penrod, S., Read, D., & Cutler, B. (1995). Choosing, confidence, and accuracy: A meta-analysis of the confidence-accuracy relation in eyewitness identification studies. *Psychological Bulletin*, *118*(3), 315.

Thompson-Cannino, J., Cotton, R., & Torneo, E. (2009). *Picking cotton: Our memoir of injustice and redemption*. Macmillan.

Wade, K. A., Garry, M., Don Read, J., & Lindsay, D. S. (2002). A picture is worth a thousand lies: Using false photographs to create false childhood memories. Psychonomic Bulletin & Review, *9*(3), 597–603.

Wells, G. L., & Bradfield, A. L. (1998). "Good, you identified the suspect": Feedback to eyewitnesses distorts their reports of the witnessing experience. *Journal of Applied Psychology*, *83*, 360–376.

Wells, G. L., Kovera, M. B., Douglass, A. B., Brewer, N., Meissner, C. A., & Wixted, J. T. (2020). Policy and procedure recommendations for the collection and preservation of eyewitness identification evidence. *Law and Human Behavior*, *44*(1), 3.

Wells, G. L., & Murray, D. M. (1984). Eyewitness confidence. In G. L. Wells & E. F. Loftus (Eds.), *Eyewitness testimony: Psychological perspectives* (pp. 155–170). Cambridge University Press.

Wells, G. L., Small, M., Penrod, S., Malpass, R. S., Fulero, S. M., & Brimacombe, C. E. (1998). Eyewitness identification procedures: Recommendations for lineups and photospreads. *Law and Human Behavior*, *22*(6), 603.

Wixted, J. T. (2020). The forgotten history of signal detection theory. *Journal of Experimental Psychology: Learning, Memory, and Cognition*, *46*(2), 201.

Wixted, J. T. (2022). Absolute vs. relative forgetting. *Journal of Experimental Psychology: Learning, Memory, and Cognition*, *48*, 1775–1786.

Wixted, J. T., & Ebbesen, E. (1991). On the form of forgetting. *Psychological Science*, *2*, 409–415.

Wixted, J. T., & Mickes, L. (2014). A signal-detection-based diagnostic feature-detection model of eyewitness identification. *Psychological Review*, *121*, 262–276.

Wixted, J. T., Mickes, L., Dunn, J. C., Clark, S. E., & Wells, W. (2016). Estimating the reliability of eyewitness identifications from police lineups. *Proceedings of the National Academy of Sciences*, *113*(2), 304–309.

Wixted, J. T., Mickes, L., & Fisher, R. P. (2018). Rethinking the Reliability of Eyewitness Memory. *Perspectives on Psychological Science*, *13*, 324–335.

Wixted, J. T., Vul, E., Mickes, L., & Wilson, B. M. (2018). Models of lineup memory. Cognitive Psychology, *105*, 81–114.

Wixted, J. T., & Wells, G. L. (2017). The relationship between eyewitness confidence and identification accuracy: A new synthesis. *Psychological Science in the Public Interest*, *18*(1), 10–65.

Wixted, J. T., Wells, G. L., Loftus, E. F., & Garrett, B. L. (2021). Test a witness's memory for a suspect only once. *Psychological Science in the Public Interest*, *22*(1_suppl), 1S–18S. https://doi.org/10.1177/15291006211026259

Zaragoza, M. S., McCloskey, M., & Jamis, M. (1987). Misleading postevent information and recall of the original event: Further evidence against the memory impairment hypothesis. *Journal of Experimental Psychology: Learning, Memory, and Cognition*, *13*(1), 36.

4

BE CAREFUL WHAT YOU WISH FOR

The Dark Side of Freedom

Nathan N. Cheek and Barry Schwartz

The amount of choice Americans face every day has exploded (Schwartz, 2016). This should be good news. American society is guided by assumptions about well-being so deeply embedded in most of us that we don't realize either that we make those assumptions, or that there is an alternative. The assumptions can be stated in the form of a rough syllogism (Markus & Schwartz, 2010; Schwartz & Cheek, 2017):

The more freedom and autonomy people have, the greater their well-being.
The more choice people have, the greater their freedom and autonomy.
Therefore, the more choice people have, the greater their well-being.

From the view of contemporary U.S. society, it seems hard to quarrel—logically or psychologically—with this syllogism. The moral importance of freedom and autonomy is built into this nation's founding documents, and the psychological importance of freedom and autonomy is now amply documented (e.g., Deci & Ryan, 2002; Ryan & Deci, 2000; Seligman, 1975). There is also no denying that choice improves the quality of people's lives. It enables people to control their destinies and to come closer to getting exactly what they want out of any situation. Healthy people want and need to direct their own lives, and choice is what enables each person to pursue precisely those objects and activities that best satisfy their own preferences within the limits of their resources. Any time choice is restricted in some way, there is bound to be someone, somewhere, who is deprived of the opportunity to pursue something of personal value.

And as important as the instrumental value of choice may be, choice reflects another value that might be even more important. Freedom to choose has *expressive value*. Choice is what enables people to tell the world who they are and what they care about. Every choice people make is a testament to their autonomy.

When people have no choice, life is almost unbearable (Araki, 2024; Bone et al., 2014; Hill et al., 2016; Reutskaja et al., 2022). As the number of available choices increases, as it has in modern consumer culture, the autonomy, control, and liberation this variety brings is powerful. And because people are, in theory, free to ignore choice possibilities when they don't want them, increasing the amount of choice people have seems to be what economists call a "Pareto efficient" move: it will make some people (those who want increased choice) better off, but make no one

DOI: 10.4324/9781003363385-5

worse off. Said another way, it seems reasonable to assume that the relation between choice and well-being is monotonic.

In this chapter, we will argue that, however reasonable the above syllogism seems, it is false. The relation between choice and well-being is non-monotonic: there can be too much choice, and there can be too much freedom. Having too much choice induces paralysis, makes even trivial choices seem high-stakes and identity-relevant, and reduces satisfaction, happiness, and health. After briefly reviewing the now substantial literature on the negative consequences of abundant choice, based largely on consumer research, we offer a new perspective on how excessive freedom can change the very meaning of choice itself, with consequences for self-uncertainty and goal pursuit. We then consider evidence from a variety of life domains that too much freedom is making people worse rather than better off. In closing, we suggest that, perhaps counterintuitively, the path to self-certainty and to a healthier and happier society may be through embracing some constraints even at the cost of unlimited freedom.

Choice Overload

Compared to having very limited options, having a moderate amount of choice can make people feel more decision freedom (Reibstein et al., 1975), can increase the perceived value of choice (Reutskaja et al., 2018), can increase satisfaction (Cheek et al., 2023), and can increase the likelihood people will actually make a choice (Shah & Wolford, 2007). But the past two and half decades of consumer research has shown that these benefits diminish, and indeed reverse, when the number of options continues to grow, ultimately resulting in "choice overload"—the experience of having too much choice. Building on earlier research on information processing and cognitive conflict (e.g., Malhotra, 1982; Tversky & Shafir, 1992), the literature incited by Iyengar and Lepper (2000) has revealed many negative consequences of very large assortments, including choice paralysis (the failure to make any choice at all); negative subjective outcomes like decreased satisfaction, increased regret, and higher levels of frustration, uncertainty, and self-blame; and negative objective outcomes like choosing normatively worse options (e.g., Botti & Iyengar, 2004; Iyengar & Lepper, 2000; Iyengar et al., 2004; Bhargava et al., 2017; Schwartz, 2016; Shah & Wolford, 2007; for reviews, see Chernev et al., 2015; Misuraca et al., 2020).

Though some criticisms (Scheibehenne et al., 2010) underline the need for further research on moderators of choice overload (Chernev et al., 2015; Misuraca et al., 2020), a large literature now supports these potential costs of unlimited choice. But a focus on the immediate positive and negative consequences of assortment size for cognition and satisfaction might be missing a more fundament effect of proliferating choice—namely, that it can change the core meaning of choice itself. In the following section, we turn to the possibility that a particularly profound "dark side" of choice may be the tendency to render even trivial choices relevant to the self, with implications for decisions, self-uncertainty, relationships, and well-being.

Choice Set Size and Self-Expression

Choices have functions beyond the satisfaction of immediate goals. They are also *acts of meaning* (Bruner, 1990; see also Goffman, 1959) that may reflect information about the choosers' identity to themselves and to the world (e.g., Levy, 1959; Kim & Markus, 1999; Schwartz & Cheek, 2017). Importantly, self-expressiveness can depend on individual factors (e.g., Cheek & Cheek, 2018; Kokkoris, 2020) and contextual factors (e.g., Rozenkrants et al., 2017; Sela et al., 2017). We propose that one contextual factor that influences the perceived expressiveness of choices is the scarcity or abundance of choice itself: larger choice sets should make choices feel more self-expressive.

Indeed, we recently found support for this claim across a series of online experiments (Cheek et al., 2023). In our first study, participants were randomly assigned to choose a drink from either 20 options or a randomly selected subset of three options, after which we asked participants how much their choice expressed their identity. We found that those who chose from a larger set of options thought their choice was more self-expressive, an effect mediated by participants' perceptions that choices from the larger set better matched their preferences. At first glance, this result makes sense and may seem normative or even obvious: if larger choice sets provide additional alternatives that better satisfy choosers' preferences, then it is hardly surprising they feel their choices express more about who they are. After all, at least in terms of preferences, their choices really would be more expressive.

However, our second study added some more complexity to this story. We again randomly assigned participants to choose from either a set of three options or a set of 20 options—this time, the options were Italian restaurants. In this study, however, we composed the large choice set by taking the three options in the small set and adding 17 objectively inferior options that were lower on at least one of several dimensions (price, quality ratings, offering reservations, parking availability). Doing so meant that participants could not better match their preferences in the larger set in this study, because the additional options were all inferior (and therefore less rather than more able to satisfy participants' preferences). Nonetheless, we again found that participants who chose from the larger set of options thought their choice was more self-expressive, and we again found that participants' perception that they had better matched their preferences when choosing from the larger choice set mediated this effect.

It thus seems that abundant choice can create the *illusion* of preference satisfaction even when this is at odds with reality, perhaps because of how closely people's understandings of freedom and of abundant choice are connected to preference satisfaction, at least in individualistic cultural contexts like the U.S. (e.g., Bellah et al., 1985; Markus & Kitayama, 1991; Schwartz & Cheek, 2017). Accordingly, an illusory perception of preference matching may turn choices made from larger sets into expressions of the self regardless of whether such choices actually reflect any more information about choosers. Large assortments may also make choices feel more self-expressive because they offer more variety, which facilitates self-expression (e.g., Sirgy et al., 1986); because they require more effort and investment of the self (e.g., Belk, 1988; though see also Labroo & Pocheptsova, 2016, on disfluency); or because fewer people may choose the same option when assortments are larger, thereby increasing expressiveness of choices (e.g., Kelley, 1973).

In our work, we also identified some boundary conditions on the effect of choice set size on perceived self-expression (Cheek et al., 2023). In one study, we found that participants who chose from a larger array of vacuums did not perceive their choice as more self-expressive than those who chose from a smaller array, even though the larger array did provide participants with a greater sense of preference matching. In another study, in contrast to U.S. participants, Indian participants who chose from a larger assortment did not find their choices more self-expressive than their counterparts who chose from a smaller assortment. Both of these findings show moderation by whether choices *can* be expressive—some domains, such as the utilitarian choice of vacuum (Khan et al., 2005), are rarely expressive, and choices in some cultural contexts, such as India (Savani et al., 2008), are not as closely linked to individual preference matching and self-expression.

The effects of choice domain and cultural context in our studies suggest that choices probably need to have some initial expressive potential for a momentary manipulation of choice set size to influence how choosers interpret the identity relevance of their choices. But over time, even choices that were once far from expressive may eventually take on expressive meaning as variety increases in the marketplace. Mull (2019), for instance, recounts how proliferating options caused reusable water bottles to move beyond their mundane, utilitarian function to become modern symbols of identity and status among younger generations. We suggest that, in the modern marketplace, where a multitude of products can be quickly and cheaply made, reusable water bottles are not unique in taking on identity relevance as product lines expand dramatically. And, of course, companies can help the process along by explicitly marketing their products as self-expressive (as one sock-specific company implores, "Use your socks as a form of self-expression"; Socks n' Socks, 2018) and by connecting their products to entities that already have expressive value (e.g., by having celebrities with aspirational identities advertise their products; McCracken, 1989).

At least in the past few centuries, there has also been a group of people who already had access to fairly abundant options—the highly affluent. People with more money to spend naturally have a wider array of options from which to choose (or to create, if the options they want do not yet exist). Veblen's (1899/2009) early study of conspicuous consumption highlighted the expressive nature of wealthier consumers' choices (e.g., buying and using products purely for expression rather than need) in comparison to the choices of lower-income consumers made primarily to meet basic needs. These social class differences in the perceived expressiveness of choices continue today, with middle-class consumers attending more to and caring more about the individual self-expressive value of their choices than working-class consumers (Snibbe & Markus, 2005; Stephens et al., 2007).

Yet, in some ways, the abundant choice available to modern consumers also reflects an expansion of the conspicuous consumption class, as now even stores that foreground affordability such as superstores or dollar stores feature extensive choice and identity-relevant decision-making (Shrestha, 2016). There are still social class differences to be sure, but even financially constrained consumers may encounter very large assortments, and in our research, we found no evidence to suggest that working-class consumers' perceptions of the expressiveness of their choices were any less affected by choice set size than those of middle-class consumers (Cheek et al., 2023). That choices can express the self is not a 21st-century phenomenon, but expanded freedom and nearly unlimited choice for consumers across the social class spectrum may be, such that both working- and middle-class individuals may start feeling that even their everyday choices say more about who they are.

Is the effect of choice set size on self-expression a good thing? We suspect that, like other choice set size effects, it depends on how large assortments get. When people gain options, moving from limited assortments to more moderate ones, increased self-expression may well be a good thing. As we found, moderate assortments increase satisfaction in part through self-expression (Cheek et al., 2023), and people generally find pleasure in expressing themselves (Tamir & Mitchell, 2012). People have to be able to feel autonomy and control, and in individualistic contexts, expressing the self through choice helps meet these needs. Nonetheless, as choice continues to expand, and as self-expression continues to increase, it may start to hurt people more than help them. One important way too much choice might hurt people is by undermining the stability of, and therefore people's certainty about, the self.

Freedom, Self-Expression, and Uncertainty

Our review has focused primarily on consumer choices, a focus mirrored in the choice overload literature, though overload has been documented in other domains like leisure activities (Thai & Yuksel, 2017) and dating (D'Angelo & Toma, 2017). Given the ubiquity of consumer choices, the importance of seemingly trivial choices can't be dismissed. Yet, even more important than the question of "What should I buy?" are the questions of "What should I do with my life?" and "Who should I be?" (Though our argument is that, as choice set size increases and choices become more self-expressive, the question of what to buy *becomes* the question of who to be.) It is in these latter questions that freedom and autonomy (i.e., choice) loom largest, and there is little doubt that freedom of choice in these self-defining domains has expanded alongside freedom of choice in the world of consumer goods (Jackson et al., 2019; Schwartz, 2000, 2016).

Young people find themselves with much less constrained choices when it comes to where they live, what they study, what kind of work they do, what religion they practice, who, if anyone, they become romantically involved with, what family commitments they will make, what name they will use, and how they will express themselves to the world. As this volume attests, people are free to decide all matters of identity; they are no longer stuck with identities they inherit from family and friends. And having made decisions about who they are, people are also free to change them.

To be sure, much of this freedom is good. It is good that people can marry whom they want; it is good that people can pursue new educational and vocational opportunities; it is good that people can move far away from where they grew up; and it is good that people can change who they are if they are no longer happy. But the benefits of freedom aren't free: they come at a cost for the self. Scholars from philosophy (Taylor, 1989, 1992), sociology (Turner, 1976), and psychology (Baumeister, 1986) have argued that, over the past 500 years, self-understanding in Western cultural contexts has been moving from "outside-in," through membership in larger entities (the divine order, the "great chain of being," nation, caste, community, family, etc.) to "inside-out," with purpose discovered from within each individual and the notion of "authentic" self-expression as the supreme aspiration. This transition in the conceptualization of the self places the burden of self-definition on individuals, who must now navigate the world while also constructing a personal identity from an almost unlimited set of possible selves (Markus & Nurius, 1986).

This task of self-definition amidst unprecedented freedom, we argue, drives self-uncertainty. In a world of uncertain, completely chosen, and easily altered selves, identity may be so malleable as to undermine people's sense of a true, stable self. Half a century ago, Trilling (1972) worried that the threat of modernity is that "the center will not hold," so that people increasingly have no central sense of self and therefore cannot be authentically themselves. If selves are unstable, even fleeting, then how can people achieve a sense of self-certainty? What if there is no self to be certain of?

There is a rich theoretical tradition in social psychology and in consumer research that recognizes that choices can be linked to identity, such that choices teach choosers (and observers) about themselves and making one choice over another can shape people's self-concept (e.g., Bem, 1972; Escalas & Bettman, 2003; Goffman, 1959; Levy, 1959; Sirgy, 1982). Whereas this may previously have been specific to particularly important or identity-linked choices, our suggestion is that abundant choice can make virtually any choices self-diagnostic (though perhaps not to the same degree), raising the stakes of decision-making across everyday life. Indeed, we have found that people who choose from larger assortments think their choice is more important even when it is something as ephemeral as a short YouTube clip, and this is mediated by the perception that their choice is more self-expressive (Cheek et al., 2023). With abundant choice, there may be no choice too trivial to contribute to the instability of self.

Just as abundant choice may create uncertain selves, uncertain selves then shape subsequent choices. People may turn away from more effective paths to happiness like social relationships in search of self-certainty in the form of physical possessions (Rios Morrison & Johnson, 2011) and an embracing of materialism (Shrum et al., 2022). And abundant choice may not only change self-expressiveness, but also *how* people go about making choices. Because any new choice or change might threaten the stability of the self, people may also feel forced to forgo choices they would otherwise make, such as avoiding canceling an unused, financially wasteful subscription service, for fear of disrupting self-concept clarity (Savary & Dhar, 2020). Perhaps most importantly, if any choice can express the self, people might no longer be satisfied with good but imperfect choices. Instead, it might be that only the best will do.

Is Good Enough Good Enough? Maximizing Versus Satisficing

Half a century ago, Simon (1955, 1956, 1957) argued that, in choice situations, individuals will often "satisfice," that is, choose the first option that surpasses some threshold of acceptability, rather than attempt to "maximize" and find the best possible choice. Such a satisficing strategy was thought to make manageable the otherwise overwhelming (and impossible) task of evaluating options in terms of every piece of information that could potentially be known about them. Rather than attempt to engage in an exhaustive and ultimately limitless search for perfect information regarding a particular choice (as often posited by rational choice theorists; von Neumann & Morgenstern, 1944), people would simply end their search as soon as an option was found that exceeded some criterion.

In the past two decades, researchers have turned to studying individual differences in the goals choosers adopt during choice (for a review, see Cheek & Schwartz, 2016). Schwartz et al. (2002) developed the first measure of individual differences in maximizing and introduced the theory that some choosers seek only the very best, whereas others are content to satisfice. Hundreds of studies have since examined the correlates and consequences of maximizing as an individual difference, and as with any literature, debates have arisen about how best to conceptualize and measure maximizing (for some differing perspectives, see Cheek & Goebel, 2020; Cheek & Schwartz, 2016; Dalal et al., 2015; Diab et al., 2008; Lai, 2010). Here, we conceptualize maximizing as a pursuit of the best possible option through extensively searching for and comparing alternatives.

Compared to satisficers, maximizers tend to seek out more options during choice and expend more effort and time comparing them to determine the best (Cheek & Ward, 2019; Dar-Nimrod et al., 2009; Iyengar et al., 2006; Schwartz et al., 2002). This approach is effective in that maximizers often end up with objectively better choices than satisficers (Iyengar et al., 2006; Polman, 2010), but maximizers also report more dissatisfaction and regret after choosing (Moyano-Díaz et al., 2014; Schwartz et al., 2002). Maximizers are perfectionistic (Kokkoris, 2019) and indecisive (Barkley-Levenson & Fox, 2016; Cheek & Goebel, 2020), finding decisions more difficult and stressful than satisficers (Schwartz et al., 2002). Depending on how maximizing is measured, it has also been linked to negative outcomes more generally, including neuroticism, unhappiness, depression, ADHD, and even suicidality (Bruine de Bruin et al., 2016a; Schepman et al., 2012; Schwartz et al., 2002). A focus on the best may also complicate relationships, delaying relationship commitment (Ishiguro, 2022) and undermining relationship satisfaction (French & Meltzer, 2019). Broadly speaking, a general picture emerges whereby individuals who tend to seek the best possible choice often suffer as a result, winding up less satisfied than if they began their searchers hoping simply to satisfy their preferences with a "good enough" option (particularly for more consequential choices; see Belli et al., 2022, for a review of research on maximizing and well-being).

Research has also highlighted maximizers' attention to how others are doing and to their relative social standing. Maximizers engage in more social comparison and counterfactual thinking (e.g., Elembilassery et al., 2024; Ma & Roese, 2014; Schwartz et al., 2002), and are particularly interested in making the best choice *compared to others*—even if it means selecting an option lower on a different dimension (e.g., quality: Weaver et al., 2015). We suggest that maximizers' tendency to compare, and especially to compare with others, is inherent to seeking the best and makes maximizing a recipe for self-uncertainty.

The problem with wanting only the best option is determining what is the best—unlike perfectionists, whose quest for perfection can be evaluated by identifying (or not) any flaws, maximizers must engage in comparison processes to figure out if they have made the best choice (Schwartz et al., 2002). That is, the best is *relative*. As a result, maximizers *must* engage in extensive information search and social comparison. And this comparison continues even after they have made their choice, as they continue to search for confirming evidence that they made the best choice (Kim, 2022). Unlike satisficers, who marshal their psychological resources to reduce any cognitive dissonance, maximizers do not seem to "close" decisions (Sparks et al., 2012). Shiner (2015) even found that extreme maximizers are aware of this tendency, and may be grateful when choices are irreversible because it stops them from being tempted to change their mind. But of course, many of life's choices, including who to be, are reversible in the modern era of extensive freedom.

Social comparison arises from and then perpetuates uncertainty. What is the best today could be suboptimal tomorrow. A chooser could learn that someone else found a better choice at any time, and maximizers' reliance on social comparison to assure themselves they have the best means that their identities are inherently invested in the relative standing of their choice. *Relative standing* is, fundamentally, an unstable position for the self, given that new information and new people will be commonly encountered, requiring updating of self-knowledge. Thus, lacking internal standards to evaluate their choices (and themselves), maximizers are left with the malleability inherent to comparisons (Festinger, 1957). Indeed, research shows that frequent social comparisons and self-uncertainty and instability are positively associated (Butzer & Kuiper, 2006; Lee, 2014; Vartanian & Dey, 2013).

How widespread is this problem? Previous individual difference approaches to maximizing typically theorized that people are dispositionally inclined to engage in satisficing or maximizing, and thus choice overload, neurotic social comparisons, and uncertainty were predominantly outcomes for individuals who routinely sought the best. While we agree that there are important individual differences in maximizing, we also propose that extensive freedom and abundant choice may be *creating* maximizers, moving choosers towards a need for the best and away from satisfaction with good enough. We think the role of the self in choice is the key factor here—when having more choice makes choices more self-expressive (Cheek et al., 2023), it then becomes more important to make the best choice. When a pair of socks is just a pair of socks, it is enough to find a pair that gets the job done. But when the choice of a pair of socks becomes a statement about the self and carries with it the potential to influence how oneself and others understand the self, then it becomes much more important to choose the best pair of socks. Or, indeed, to choose the best self.

In the consumer domain, we have found evidence to support this line of theorizing (Cheek et al., in progress). In one study, we surveyed customers in a shopping mall and found that those who reported having chosen from larger assortments also reported maximizing more, an effect mediated by the perceived self-expressiveness of choices. Looking experimentally, we have found that participants randomly assigned to choose from a larger assortment report maximizing more, an effect again mediated by self-expression. Participants who chose from larger choice sets also reported greater overload, and this was predicted by their reported increases in maximizing. Simply encountering more options makes choices feel more expressive, which increases maximizing, which then spurs overload. Accordingly, the problems of abundant choice may not be restricted to individuals already high in maximizing, because the abundance itself may cause people to adopt a maximizing goal. (Said more technically, maximizing may not only be a moderator of overload but, in fact, a mediator).

Converging evidence for our claim that proliferating choice is creating more maximizing could be found in research on age differences and regional differences in maximizing. Research has shown that younger generations, who are growing up in a world of increasingly abundant choice, maximize more than older generations (Bruine de Bruin et al., 2016b), though this cross-sectional research cannot rule out developmental rather than generational effects. Recent research also suggests that urbanization and the adoption of neoliberal values are associated with greater maximizing (Srivastava et al., 2023). As cultural change causes societies to place greater value on independence and other neoliberal ideals (e.g., unlimited freedom in markets), there may be a resulting shift in consumer goals. Free markets are about competition and unchecked growth, and becoming the best is both a goal more common in capitalist, urbanizing environments and the standard that people adopt to evaluate their progress (Curran & Hill, 2019; Davies, 2014; Verhaeghe, 2014). As many societies around the world continue to trend toward urbanization and the further adoption of neoliberal market values, it may be that maximizing is also increasing around the world.

Suffering from Freedom

What is the evidence that modern consumers, particularly Westerners, are suffering from freedom? First, mental health, especially among younger people, is getting worse. There has been a significant rise in the incidence of clinical depression and suicide, both of which are befalling people at younger and younger ages (e.g., Keyes et al., 2019; Mojtabai et al., 2016), and an accompanying substantial increase in the rate at which college students are flocking to counseling centers (e.g., Lipson et al., 2019). Young college graduates report a palpable unease about their futures, seeming to lack a clear idea of what they are meant to do in their lives (Robbins & Wilner, 2001).

Other lines of research converge to illuminate the costs of unrestricted choice. Finkel (2017), discussing the decline over time in marriage satisfaction, suggests increases in perceived self-expression may be to blame. Over time, the freedom to marry whomever one wanted increased as marriages shifted from being about practical arrangements (e.g., land, property, and financial agreements) to being about true love, and then to being about identity expression and self-actualization. He argues that unconstrained choices of whom to marry precipitated a change in what people seek in their marriages—it's not just about love anymore, but about maximizing the self. While this might make the very best marriages more satisfying, it renders the typical marriage, filled with a natural balance of love and frustrations, more unsatisfying and unfulfilling.

In this volume, McGregor and Marigold (Chapter 13) outline how the uncertainty that freedom may cause can drive people to extreme behavior, including hate and violence. Freedom's value may also be eroded by the stress it causes—for instance, Sweeney and Howell (Chapter 19) discuss how people may avoid information even when it is available to them and might be useful. Increased freedom might make more information and more resources available, but it might also yield enough anxiety and stress that people cannot take advantage of those benefits.

Hook and Markus (2020) review evidence that the U.S.'s obsession with free choice is undermining Americans' physical health while also creating a culture where people are blamed for their own health problems, even when blame would be more accurately located in insufficient public health policies that place the burden of healthcare decisions on struggling individuals. Relatedly, Cheek et al. (2022) review research showing that a commitment to unlimited freedom can undermine safety and security, both in everyday life and especially when disasters and crises strike.

More generally, when free choice is the most salient value in people's minds, people are more self-focused, less empathetic, and more likely to blame others for their circumstances, ultimately creating a more divided and less caring world (for a review, see Madan et al., 2020).

Finally, research also specifically links high levels of freedom to lower well-being. Gelfand's (2018) research has shown that people suffer both from extremely tight, constricted, low-freedom cultures and from extremely loose, unconstrained, high-freedom cultures. For instance, data from 32 nations showed that both of these extremes were associated with worse physical health (e.g., greater mortality from cardiovascular disease, lower life expectancy) and mental health (e.g., lower happiness, higher suicide rates) compared to nations with a more balanced tradeoff between freedom and constraint (Harrington et al., 2015). Relatedly, there is evidence to suggest that low-income *and* high-income individuals, perhaps especially adolescents, are at a greater risk for depression, anxiety disorders, drug addiction, and other clinical conditions compared to middle-income individuals (Korous et al., 2023; Luthar et al., 2020). When laws are too relaxed, norms are too weak, and high income creates boundless possibilities, freedom may be a catalyst for uncertainty.

Conclusion: Balancing Freedom and Constraints

We opened this chapter with the idea that freedom, autonomy, and choice are essential to human well-being. We then proceeded to spend the remainder of the chapter arguing there can be too much of a good thing. Whereas there is no denying that "choice is good," it isn't always and only good. A point may be reached where the negative effects of choice so overwhelm the positive effects that the resulting psychological state is worse than neutral, meaning that the effects of choice overall follow an inverted-U shape (Grant & Schwartz, 2011; Reutskaja & Hogarth, 2009).

Here, we conclude by suggesting that the best route to eliminating some of the negative effects of choice overload without also eliminating the liberating effects of freedom might be through a change in awareness, sensibility, and aspiration on the part of individuals and of collectives (see Alpert, 2022). If people can come to see that, sometimes, unfettered choice is paralyzing while constrained choice may be liberating, they may seek and embrace constraints in their own lives instead of avoiding them (for suggestive evidence that this intuition may be accessible to people, see Haesevoets et al., 2022). Indeed, chapters in this volume review how romantic relationships (Murray, Chapter 16) and group membership (Hogg, Chapter 22) offer solutions to self-uncertainty (though see also Paredes et al., Chapter 5, on identity fusion and uncertainty). And a vast literature on the fundamental role connections with others play in well-being complements these perspectives (e.g., Araki, 2024; Diener et al., 1999; Diener & Suh, 2001; Myers, 2000). But in the context of the value people place on freedom, there is an interesting feature of interpersonal relationships and group memberships: they typically come with new constraints that seemingly *reduce* freedom.

Schwartz (2000) suggested that perhaps the best model we have for the importance of constraints for freedom comes from our understanding of human language abilities. The capacity to use language is perhaps the single most liberating characteristic of human beings. It frees people up in significant ways from the temporal and material limitations that afflict other organisms. People can say anything about any thing, any time, or any place—even things, times, and places that have never existed. They can produce new combinations of words no one has ever spoken or heard before. And they can be understood. So, language is probably as vivid an embodiment of human freedom and autonomy as anything. But what decades of research on language ability have made clear is that the thing that makes the liberating features of language possible is that language is heavily constrained by rules. The reason people can say anything and be understood is that they can't say *everything*. It is linguistic constraint, in the form of these rules, that makes linguistic freedom possible.

What we have suggested in this chapter is that exactly the same thing may be true in connection with the determination of the self. Unconstrained freedom leads to paralysis and becomes a kind of self-defeating tyranny. It is freedom of choice within significant constraints—within "rules" of some sort—that leads to well-being, to optimal functioning. Relationships and group membership can be one way of introducing constraints without necessarily eliminating freedom. For instance, research on group norms (Kouchaki et al., 2018; Mooijman et al., 2018) shows that norms constrain choice and behavior, sometimes to such an extent that potential actions are not even considered to be real choices (e.g., moral norms against meat consumption that forbid certain food choices).

Norms don't have to be laws. They can help people cope with uncertainty without compromising freedom. They can maintain the *freedom to* live the life they want while preventing the *freedom from* constraints from paralyzing people with uncertainty (Berlin, 1958). Cross-cultural research offers an illustration of the benefits of balancing constraints and freedoms—societies that have norms that are neither too loose nor too tight tend to be the happiest and healthiest (Harrington et al., 2015; Gelfand, 2018). And our own recent work suggests that consumers in cultural contexts that are less singularly focused on prioritizing individual self-expression through choice experience less choice overload when they encounter assortments larger than they want (Reutskaja et al., 2022). Western, individualistic, loose cultural contexts epitomized by the U.S. may not offer the optimal balance between individualism and relational bonds, or between freedom and constraint. A significant future task for psychology is to identify which constraints on self-determination are the crucial ones—the ones that will help people as they navigate the dark side of freedom.

References

Alpert, A. (2022). *The good-enough life.* Princeton University Press.

Araki, S. (2024). The societal determinants of happiness and unhappiness: Evidence from 152 countries over 15 years. *Social Psychological and Personality Science, 15*, 603–615.

Barkley-Levenson, E. E., & Fox, C. R. (2016). The surprising relationship between indecisiveness and impulsivity. *Personality and Individual Differences, 90,* 1–6.

Baumeister, R. F. (1986). *Identity: Cultural change and the struggle for self.* Oxford University Press.

Belk, R. W. (1988). Possessions and the extended self. *Journal of Consumer Research, 15,* 139–168.

Bellah, R. N., Madsen, R., Sullivan, W. M., Swidler, A., & Tipton, S. M. (1985). *Habits of the heart: Individualism and collectivism in American life*. Harper & Row.

Belli, A., Carrillat, F. A., Zlatevska, N., & Cowley, E. (2022). The wellbeing implications of maximizing: A conceptual framework and meta-analysis. *Journal of Consumer Psychology, 32,* 573–596.

Bem, D. J. (1972). Self-perception theory. In L. Berkowitz (Ed.), *Advances in experimental social psychology* (Vol. 6, pp. 1–62). Academic Press.

Berlin, I. (1958). Two concepts of liberty. In I. Berlin (Ed.), *Four essays on liberty* (pp. 6–67). Oxford University Press.

Bhargava, S., Loewenstein, G., & Sydnor, J. (2017). Choose to lose: Health plan choice from a menu with dominated options. *Quarterly Journal of Economics, 132,* 1319–1372.

Bone, S. A., Christensen, G. L., & Williams, J. D. (2014). Rejected, shackled, alone: The impact of systemic restricted choice on minority consumers' construction of self. *Journal of Consumer Research, 41,* 451–474.

Botti, S., & Iyengar, S. S. (2004). The psychological pleasure and pain of choosing: When people prefer choosing at the cost of subsequent outcome satisfaction. *Journal of Personality and Social Psychology, 87,* 312–326.

Bruine de Bruin, W., Dombrovski, A. Y., Parker, A. M., & Szanto, K. (2016a). Late-life depression, suicidal ideation, and attempted suicide: The role of individual differences in maximizing, regret, and negative decision outcomes. *Journal of Behavioral Decision Making, 29,* 363–371.

Bruine de Bruin, W., Parker, A. M., & Strough, J. (2016b). Choosing to be happy? Age differences in "maximizing" decision strategies and experienced emotional well-being. *Psychology and Aging, 31,* 295–300.

Bruner, J. (1990). *Acts of meaning*. Harvard University Press.

Butzer, B., & Kuiper, N. A. (2006). Relationships between the frequency of social comparisons and self-concept clarity, intolerance of uncertainty, anxiety, and depression. *Personality and Individual Differences, 41,* 167–176.

Cheek, N. N., & Cheek, J. M. (2018). Aspects of identity: From the inner-outer metaphor to a tetrapartite model of the self. *Self and Identity, 17,* 467–482.

Cheek, N. N., & Goebel, J. (2020). What does it mean to maximize? "Decision difficulty," indecisiveness, and the jingle-jangle fallacies in the measurement of maximizing. *Judgment and Decision Making, 15,* 7–24.

Cheek, N. N., Reutskaja, E., & Schwartz, B. (2022). Balancing the freedom-security tradeoff during crises and disasters. *Perspectives on Psychological Science, 17,* 1024–1049.

Cheek, N. N., & Schwartz, B. (2016). On the meaning and measurement of maximization. *Judgment and Decision Making, 11,* 126–146.

Cheek, N. N., & Schwartz, B., & Shafir, E. (2023). Choice set size shapes self-expression. *Personality and Social Psychology Bulletin, 49,* 267–281.

Cheek, N. N., Schwartz, B., & Shafir, E. (in progress). *A self-expression-based account of choice overload.* Unpublished manuscript.

Cheek, N. N., & Ward, A. (2019). When choice is a double-edged sword: Understanding maximizers' paradoxical experiences with choice. *Personality and Individual Differences, 143,* 55–61.

Chernev, A., Böckenholt, U., & Goodman, J. (2015). Choice overload: A conceptual review and meta-analysis. *Journal of Consumer Psychology, 25,* 333–358.

Curran, T., & Hill, A. P. (2019). Perfectionism is increasing over time: A meta-analysis of birth cohort differences from 1989 to 2016. *Psychological Bulletin, 145,* 410–429.

Dalal, D. K., Diab, D. L., Zhu, X. S., & Hwang, T. (2015). Understanding the construct of maximizing tendency: A theoretical and empirical evaluation. *Journal of Behavioral Decision Making, 5,* 437–450.

D'Angelo, J. D., & Toma, C. L. (2017). There are plenty of fish in the sea: The effects of choice overload and reversibility on online daters' satisfaction with selected partners. *Media Psychology, 20,* 1–27.Dar-Nimrod, I., Rawn, C. D., Lehman, D. R., & Schwartz, B. (2009). The maximization paradox: The costs of seeking alternatives. *Personality and Individual Differences, 46,* 631–635.

Davies, W. (2014). *The limits of neoliberalism: Authority, sovereignty, and the logic of competition.* Sage.

Deci, E. L., & Ryan, R. M. (Eds.) (2002). *Handbook of self-determination research.* University of Rochester Press.

Diab, D. L., Gillespie, M. A., & Highhouse, S. (2008). Are maximizers really unhappy? The measurement of maximizing tendency. *Judgment and Decision Making, 3,* 364–370.

Diener, E., Suh, E. M., Lucas, R. E., & Smith, H. L. (1999). Subjective well-being: Three decades of progress. *Psychological Bulletin, 125,* 276–302.

Diener, E., & Suh, E. M. (Eds.) (2001). *Subjective well-being across cultures.* MIT Press.

Elembilassery, V., Jain, N. K., & Aggarwal, D. (2024). What influences individuals' tolerance for ambiguity? Exploring the roles of social comparison orientation, tendency to maximize and feel regret. *Personality and Individual Differences, 217,* 112436.

Escalas, J. E., & Bettman, J. R. (2003). You are what they eat: The influence of reference groups on consumers' connections to brands. *Journal of Consumer Psychology, 13,* 339–348.

Finkel, E. J. (2017). *The all-or-nothing marriage: How the best marriages work.* Dutton.

Festinger, L. (1957). *A theory of cognitive dissonance*. Stanford University Press.

French, J. E., & Meltzer, A. L. (2019). Maximizing tendencies in marriage: Accentuating the implications of readily observer partner characteristics for intimates' satisfaction. *Personality and Social Psychology Bulletin, 45,* 1468–1481.

Gelfand, M. (2018). *Rule makers, rule breakers: How tight and loose cultures wire our world.* Scribner.

Goffman, E. (1959). *The presentation of self in everyday life.* Doubleday.

Grant, A. M., & Schwartz, B. (2011). Too much of a good thing: The challenge and opportunity of the inverted U. *Perspectives on Psychological Science, 6,* 61–76.

Haesevoets, T., Dierckx, K., & Van Hiel, A. (2022). Do people believe that you can have too much money? The relationship between hypothetical lottery wins and expected happiness. *Judgment and Decision Making, 17,* 1229–1254.

Harrington, J. R., Boski, P., & Gelfand, M. J. (2015). Culture and national well-being: Should societies emphasize freedom or constraint? *PLoS ONE, 10,* e0127173.

Hill, R. P., & Cunningham, D., & The Gramercy Gentlemen. (2016). Dehumanization and restriction inside a maximum security prison: Novel insights about consumer acquisition and ownership. *Journal of the Association for Consumer Research, 1,* 295–313.

Hook, C. J., & Markus, H. R. (2020). Health in the United States: Are appeals to choice and personal responsibility making Americans sick? *Perspectives on Psychological Science, 15,* 643–664.

Ishiguro, I. (2022). Maximizing tendency predicts delayed marriage among Japanese adults. *Japanese Psychological Research, 64,* 53–63.

Iyengar, S. S., Jiang, W., & Huberman, G. (2004). How much choice is too much: Determinants of individual contributions to 401K retirement plans. In O. S. Mitchell & S. Utkus (Eds.), *Pension design and structure: New lessons from behavioral finance* (pp. 83–95). Oxford University Press.

Iyengar, S. S., & Lepper, M. (2000). When choice is demotivating: Can one desire too much of a good thing? *Journal of Personality and Social Psychology, 79,* 995–1006.

Iyengar, S. S., Wells, R. E., & Schwartz, B. (2006). Doing better but feeling worse: Looking for the "best" job undermines satisfaction. *Psychological Science, 17,* 143–150.

Jackson, J. C., Gelfand, M., De, S., & Fox, A. (2019). The loosening of American culture over 200 years is associated with a creativity-order trade-off. *Nature Human Behaviour, 3,* 244–250.

Kelley, H. H. (1973). The processes of causal attribution. *American Psychologist, 28,* 107–128.

Keyes, K. M., Gary, D., O'Malley, P. M., Hamilton, A., & Schulenberg, J. (2019). Recent increases in depressive symptoms among US adolescents: Trends from 1991 to 2018. *Social Psychiatry and Psychiatric Epidemiology, 54,* 987–996.

Khan, U, Dhar, R., & Wertenbroch, K. (2005). A behavioral decision theory perspective on hedonic and utilitarian choice. In S. Ratneshwar & D. G. Mick (Eds.), *Inside consumption: Frontiers of research on consumer motives, goals, and desires* (pp. 144–165). Routledge.

Kim, K. (2022). Who reads customer reviews after product choice? Maximizing, satisficing, and postchoice information search. *Personality and Individual Differences, 184,* 111192.

Kim, H., & Markus, H. R. (1999). Deviance or uniqueness, harmony or conformity? A cultural analysis. *Journal of Personality and Social Psychology, 77,* 785–800.

Kokkoris, M. D. (2019). New insights into the association of maximizing and facets of perfectionism. *Personality and Individual Differences, 142,* 100–102.

Kokkoris, M. D. (2020). Choice as a meaning-making device for maximizers: Evidence from reactance to restrictions of choice freedom during lockdown. *Frontiers in Psychology, 11,* 571462.

Korous, K. M., Causadias, J. M., Bradley, R H., Levy, R., Cahill, K. M., Li, L., & Luthar, S. S. (2023). "More is better" or "better near the middle"? A U.S.-based individual participant data meta-analysis of socioeconomic status and depressive symptoms. *American Psychologist, 78,* 305–320.

Kim, H., & Markus, H. R. (1999). Deviance or uniqueness, harmony or conformity? A cultural analysis. *Journal of Personality and Social Psychology, 77,* 785–800.

Kouchaki, M., Smith, I. H., & Savani, K. (2018). Does deciding among morally relevant options feel like making a choice? How morality constrains people's sense of choice. *Journal of Personality and Social Psychology, 115,* 788–804.

Labroo, A. A., & Pocheptsova, A. (2016). Metacognition and consumer judgment: Fluency is pleasant but disfluency ignites interest. *Current Opinion in Psychology, 10,* 154–159.

Lai, L. (2010). Maximizing without difficulty: A modified maximizing scale and its correlates. *Judgment and Decision Making, 5,* 164–175.

Lee, S. Y. (2014). How do people compare themselves with others on social network sites? The case of Facebook. *Computers in Human Behavior, 32,* 253–260.

Levy, S. J. (1959). Symbols for sale. *Harvard Business Review, 37,* 117–124.

Lipson, S. K., Lattie, E. G., & Eisenberg, D. (2019). Increased rates of mental health service utilization by U.S. college students: 10-year population-level trends (2007–2017). *Psychiatric Services, 70,* 60–63.

Luthar, S. S., Kumar, N. L., & Zillmer, N. (2020). High-achieving schools connote risks for adolescents: Problems documented, processes implicated, and directions for interventions. *American Psychologist, 75,* 983–995.

Ma, J., & Roese, N. J. (2014). The maximizing mind-set. *Journal of Consumer Research, 41,* 71–92.

Madan, S., Nanakdewa, K., Savani, K., & Markus, H. R. (2020). The paradoxical consequences of choice: Often good for the individual, perhaps less so for society? *Current Directions in Psychological Science, 29,* 80–85.

Malhotra, N. K. (1982). Information load and consumer decision making. *Journal of Consumer Research, 8,* 419–430.

Markus, H. R., & Kitayama, S. (1991). Culture and the self: Implications for cognition, emotion, and motivation. *Psychological Review, 98,* 224–253.

Markus, H. R., & Nurius, P. (1986). Possible selves. *American Psychologist, 41,* 954–969.

Markus, H. R., & Schwartz, B. (2010). Does choice mean freedom and well-being? *Journal of Consumer Psychology, 37,* 344–355.

McCracken, G. (1989). Who is the celebrity endorser? Cultural foundations of the endorsement process. *Journal of Consumer Research, 16,* 310–321.

Misuraca, R., Reutskaja, E., Fasolo, B., & Iyengar, S. (2020). How much choice is "good enough"? Moderators of information and choice overload. In R. Viale (Ed.), *Routledge handbook of bounded rationality* (pp. 637–649). Routledge.

Mojtabai, R., Olfson, M., & Han, B. (2016). National trends in the prevalence and treatment of depression in adolescents and young adults. *Pediatrics, 138,* e20161878.

Mooijman, M., Meindl, P., & Graham, J. (2018). Resisting temptatión for the good of the group: Binding moral values and the moralization of self-control. *Journal of Personality and Social Psychology, 115,* 585–599.

Moyano-Díaz, E., Martínez-Molina, A., & Ponce, F. P. (2014). The price of gaining: Maximization in decision-making, regret, and life satisfaction. *Judgment and Decision Making, 9,* 500–509.

Mull, A. (2019, February 12). How fancy water bottles became a 21**st**-century status symbol. *The Atlantic.* https://www.theatlantic.com/health/archive/2019/02/luxury-water-bottles/582595/

Myers, D. (2000). *The American paradox.* Yale University Press.

Polman, E. (2010). Why are maximizers less happy than satisficers? Because they maximize positive and negative outcomes. *Journal of Behavioral Decision Making, 23,* 179–190.

Reibstein, D., Youngblood, S., & Fromkin, H. (1975). Number of choices as a factor in consumer satisfaction: An empirical study. *Journal of Applied Psychology, 60,* 434–437.

Reutskaja, E., Cheek, N. N., Iyengar, S., & Schwartz, B. (2022). Choice deprivation, choice overload, and satisfaction with choices across six nations. *Journal of International Marketing, 30,* 18–34.

Reutskaja, E., & Hogarth, R. M. (2009). Satisfaction in choice as a function of the number of alternatives: When "goods satiate." *Psychology & Marketing, 26,* 197–203.

Reutskaja, E., Linder, A., Nagel, R., Andersen, R. A., & Camerer, C. F. (2018). Choice overload reduces neural signatures of choice set value in dorsal striatum and anterior cingulate cortex. *Nature Human Behaviour, 2,* 925–935.

Rios Morrison, K., & Johnson, C. S. (2011). When what you have is who you are: Self- uncertainty leads individualists to see themselves in their possessions. *Personality and Social Psychology Bulletin, 37,* 639–651.

Robbins, A., & Wilner, A. (2001). *Quarterlife crisis: The unique challenges of life in your twenties.* Putnam.

Rozenkrants, B., Wheeler, S. C., & Shiv, B. (2017). Self-expression cues in product rating distributions: When people prefer polarizing products. *Journal of Consumer Research, 44,* 759–777.

Ryan, R. M., & Deci, E. L. (2000). Self-determination theory and the facilitation of intrinsic motivation, social development, and well-being. *American Psychologist, 55,* 68–78.

Savani, K., Markus, H. R., & Conner, A. L. (2008). Let your preference be your guide? Preferences and choices are more tightly linked for North Americans than for Indians. *Journal of Personality and Social Psychology, 95,* 861–876.

Savary, J., & Dhar, R. (2020). The uncertain self: How self-concept structure affects subscription choice. *Journal of Consumer Research, 46,* 887–903.

Scheibehenne, B., Greifeneder, R., & Todd, P. M. (2010). Can there ever be too many options? A meta-analytic review of choice overload. *Journal of Consumer Research, 37,* 409–425.

Schepman, S., Weyandt, L., Schlect, S. D., & Swentosky, A. (2012). The relationship between ADHD symptomology and decision making. *Journal of Attention Disorders, 16,* 3–12.

Schwartz, B. (2000). Self-determination: The tyranny of freedom. *American Psychologist, 55,* 79–88.

Schwartz, B. (2016). *The paradox of choice: Why more is less* (2nd ed.). Ecco Press.

Schwartz, B., & Cheek, N. N. (2017). Choice, freedom, and well-being: Considerations for public policy. *Behavioural Public Policy, 1,* 106–121.

Schwartz, B., Ward, A., Monterosso, J., Lyubomirsky, S., White, K., & Lehman, D. R. (2002). Maximizing versus satisficing: Happiness is a matter of choice. *Journal of Personality and Social Psychology, 83,* 1178–1197.

Sela, A., Berger, J., & Kim, J. (2017). How self-control shapes the meaning of choice. *Journal of Consumer Research, 44*, 724–737.

Seligman, M. E. P. (1975). *Helplessness: On depression, development, and death*. W. H. Freeman.

Shah, A. M., & Wolford, G. (2007). Buying behavior as a function of parametric variation of number of choices. *Psychological Science, 18*, 369–370.

Shiner, R. L. (2015). Maximizers, satisficers, and their satisfaction with and preferences for reversible versus irreversible decisions. *Social Psychological and Personality Science, 6*, 896–903.

Shrestha, S. (2016). Dollars to dimes: Disparity, uncertainty, and marketing to the poor at US dollar stores. *International Journal of Cultural Studies, 19*, 373–390.

Shrum, L. J., Chaplin, L. N., & Lowrey, T. M. (2022). Psychological causes, correlates, and consequences of materialism. *Consumer Psychology Review, 5*, 69–86.

Simon, H. A. (1955). A behavioral model of rational choice. *Quarterly Journal of Economics, 59*, 99–118.

Simon, H. A. (1956). Rational choice and the structures of the environment. *Psychological Review, 63*, 129–138.

Simon, H. A. (1957). *Models of man, social and rational: Mathematical essays on rational behavior*. Wiley.

Sirgy, M. J. (1982). Self-concept in consumer behavior: A critical review. *Journal of Consumer Research, 9*, 287–300.

Sirgy, M. J., Johar, J. S., & Wood, M. (1986). Determinants of product value-expressiveness: Another look at conspicuousness, differentiation, and common usage. In N. K. Malhotra (Ed.), *Developments in marketing science* (Vol. 9, pp. 229–241). Academy of Marketing Science.

Snibbe, A. C., & Markus, H. R. (2005). You can't always get what you want: Social class, agency, and choice. *Journal of Personality and Social Psychology, 88*, 703–720.

Socks n' Socks (2018, May 22). *Use your socks as a form of self-expression*. Retrieved from: https://www.socksnsocks.com/blogs/news/use-your-socks-as-of-form-of-self-expression

Sparks, E. A., Ehrlinger, J., & Eibach, R. P. (2012). Failing to commit: Maximizers avoid commitment in a way that contributes to reduced satisfaction. *Personality and Individual Differences, 52*, 72–77.

Srivastava, A., Kühnen, U., Simunovic, D., & Boehnke, K. (2023). "More" or "enough"? Rural- urban differences in maximizing: The case of India. *Current Research in Ecological and Social Psychology, 5*, 100140.

Stephens, N. M., Markus, H. R., & Townsend, S. S. M. (2007). Choice as an act of meaning: The case of social class. *Journal of Personality and Social Psychology, 93*, 814–830.

Tamir, D. I., & Mitchell, J. P. (2012). Disclosing information about the self is intrinsically rewarding. *Proceedings of the National Academy of Sciences, 109*, 8038–8043.

Taylor, C. (1989). *Sources of the self*. Harvard University Press.

Taylor, C. (1992). *The ethics of authenticity*. Harvard University Press.

Thai, N. T., & Yuksel, U. (2017). Too many destinations to visit: Tourists' dilemma? *Annals of Tourism Research, 62*, 38–53.

Trilling, L. (1972). *Sincerity and authenticity*. Harvard University Press.

Turner, R. H. (1976). The real self: From institution to impulse. *American Journal of Sociology, 81*, 989–1016.

Tversky, A., & Shafir, E. (1992). Choice under conflict: The dynamics of deferred decisions. *Psychological Science, 3*, 358–361.

Vartanian, L. R., & Dey, S. (2013). Self-concept clarity, thin-ideal internalization, and appearance-related social comparison as predictors of body dissatisfaction. *Body Image, 10*, 495–500.

Veblen, T. (1899/2009). *The theory of the leisure class*. Oxford University Press.

Verhaeghe, P. (2014). *What about me? The struggle for identity in a market-based society*. Scribe.

von Neumann, J., & Morgenstern, O. (1944). *Theory of games and economic behavior*. Princeton University Press.

Weaver, K., Daniloski, K., Schwarz, N., & Cottone, K. (2015). The role of social comparison for maximizers and satisficers: Wanting the best or wanting to be the best? *Journal of Consumer Psychology, 25*, 372–388.

5

CONFIDENCE VS. DOUBT

A Metacognitive Model on the Antecedents and Consequences of Identity

Borja Paredes, Pablo Briñol and Richard E. Petty

This chapter explores the topic of identity, its antecedents and consequences under the conceptual umbrella of Self-Validation Theory (SVT, Briñol & Petty, 2022). The particular mental content subject to validation (and invalidation) processes that are the main focus of this chapter concerns a person's identity. Identity is typically viewed as the part of a person's self-concept that stems from psychological affiliation with groups that are important to the person (Brewer, 2001). It is one of the most universal, longstanding, and important concepts in social psychology. From classic authors (Tajfel & Turner, 1979) to more contemporary theorists (Fiske, 2018), identity has played a central role in explaining human behavior. Identity in its various forms (i.e., belonging, inclusion, and acceptance in a particular social group or category) fulfills essential functions for people, including the need to make sense (Fiske, 2018), to keep positive self-esteem (Levine & Kerr, 2007) and healthy well-being (Williams, 2007). Given its relevance, this chapter examines the antecedents and consequences of identity from a new perspective that emphasizes metacognitive processes of validation and invalidation.

The key notion of SVT is that thoughts become more consequential (i.e., will be relied upon more for making judgments and engaging in behavior) as the perceived validity of those thoughts increases. Perceived validity often stems from having confidence rather than doubt in one's thoughts. Perceiving validity in one's thoughts involves thinking about thinking, and according to SVT, these metacognitive assessments can emerge from factors that are completely incidental to the thoughts, such as merely recalling past episodes of confidence or chronic levels of self-confidence. Thus, two people might have the very same thought become salient (i.e., the same mental content), but one person might believe that this thought is more valid or appropriate to use than the other person does for some reason (e.g., the person is feeling confident at the time) and would thus be more likely to form a judgment based on that thought and act upon it.

The accumulated SVT research conducted so far suggests that perceived validity can be applied to whatever the salient mental elements are in a person's mind at the time of a judgment or behavior, regardless of their specific content, valence, and nature. For example, SVT research shows that validation processes are applicable to many different types of thoughts including goals (DeMarree et al., 2012), attitudes (Rucker et al., 2014), emotional thoughts (Avnet et al., 2012), and traits (Paredes et al., 2021). Also, the thoughts subjected to validation processes have involved a diversity of topics including the self (Briñol et al., 2010), stigmatized others (Requero et al., 2020),

DOI: 10.4324/9781003363385-6

health campaigns (Requero, Santos et al., 2020), consumer products (Briñol et al., 2004), job candidates (Briñol et al., 2012), and organizations (Stavraki et al., 2017), to name just a few. Thus, perceived validity can be applied to all kinds of thoughts and mental contents.

The chapter is divided into five sections. The first section focuses on the ability of group attitudes to guide group identity as a function of attitude confidence versus doubt. The second section focuses on the consequences of identity revealing that the predictive validity of identity can be improved by taking confidence versus doubt about that identity into account. A third block of research focuses on SVT research specifying when confidence and doubt assessments are more likely to be taken into consideration in the domain of identity (i.e., under high elaboration conditions, when people have high motivation and ability to think about the validity of their attitudes or identities). A fourth section compares the impact of direct versus compensatory confidence in identity. That is, we discuss instances in which doubt can not only reduce but also *enhance* the impact of thoughts on identity relative to control. The fifth and final section provides a summary of the chapter as well as a brief discussion of potential avenues for future research relevant to this domain.

Throughout the chapter, we will use the term confidence/certainty (used as synonyms) as one end of a continuum that ranges from being doubtful to being confident. We focus on these constructs because they are core determinants of the perceived validity of one's mental contents. Because of this continuum, saying that one becomes more confident in one's mental content is comparable to saying that one grows *less* doubtful in one's mental content.

Attitudes Predicting Identity Is Moderated by Confidence/Doubt

Attitudes, one's global evaluations of people, objects, and issues (Petty & Cacioppo, 1996), are related to a number of constructs ranging from behavior (Fazio & Zanna, 1978; Moreno et al., 2022) to values (Maio & Olson, 1995). In this section, we focus on a relatively understudied associate of attitudes; the extent to which attitudes can predict identity, and especially those attitudes that are held with confidence (see left side of Figure 5.1).

Prior research has clearly linked attitudes with the concept of identity. For example, in reviewing the functions of attitudes, Maio and Olson (2000) noted that attitudes are important not only because they can guide behavior but also because they serve to define and express who we are (i.e., give us individual identity). As Hogg and Smith (2007) claimed, "*Attitudes can be windows on identity. When someone expresses an attitude, we feel we have learned something about who that person is, and when we express attitudes ourselves, we feel we are communicating something about who we are.*" (p. 89). Of course, attitudes can vary in the extent to which they are self-defining, with some more connected to people's identities than others (Zunick et al., 2017; Turner-Zwinkels & Brandt, 2023; Vaughan-Johnston et al., 2023). One particularly important source of a person's own identity is the groups with which the person affiliates. Indeed, group identification is an important source of self-esteem that helps people feel that they belong (Tajfel, 1982).

Empirical research has provided some evidence showing that attitudes toward groups are relevant predictors of group identity. For example, Robnett et al. (2012) showed that feminist identity was negatively correlated with gender-traditional attitudes. On a different topic, Van der Werff et al. (2013) showed that attitudes toward the biosphere were significantly related to having an environmental identity. In the context of education and critical thinking, Celuch et al. (2009) found a correlation between attitudes and identity such that attitudes towards critical thinking predicted the extent to which students identified as critical thinkers themselves. Therefore, the literature on attitudes is clear about the contribution attitudes make to identity. That is, the more a person

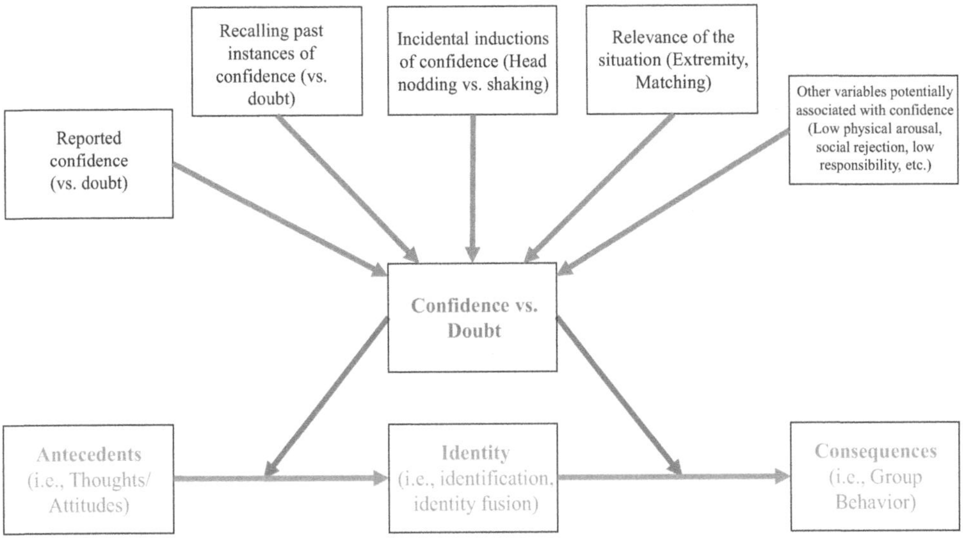

Figure 5.1 Selection of variables described in the current chapter that affect the perceived validity of thoughts/attitudes and identity.

likes or favors a domain, the more a person identifies with it. Although mostly correlational, this research supports the attitude-identity linkage.

Despite this evidence, not all researchers agree that attitudes are important predictors of identity. For example, although some theoretical models of identity formation explicitly include certain aspects of group evaluations (e.g., attitudes toward group norms) as precursors of group identity (e.g., Baudson & Ziemes, 2016), other models do not refer to any kind of attitudinal involvement when describing identity formation processes (Faye & Sharpe, 2008). Furthermore, still other researchers (Greenwald et al., 2002) have argued that attitudes toward the self are associated with group identity, but only at the automatic level (see also, Nosek et al., 2007).

To address this potential gap, the research described in this first section addresses the link between attitudes and identity by arguing that group attitudes can predict identity with a group, but that some attitudes are less impactful than others. Specifically, we propose that attitudes are more likely to predict one's identity when those attitudes are held with certainty rather than when they are held with doubt. This prediction is consistent with previous research on attitude strength (Petty & Krosnick, 1995) and also with SVT. As noted, the core tenet of SVT is that mental content in general becomes more consequential for judgment and action as the perceived validity of the thoughts is increased. In general, the less certain people are in their attitudes, the less they should predict relevant outcomes, including identity.

Paredes, Grande, and colleagues (2024) explored the extent to which this SVT notion could be applied to understanding the association between group attitudes and group identity. In their first study, participants reported attitudes towards a particular policy (i.e., recycling) and also rated the confidence with which those attitudes were held. Those two variables were used to predict their identity fusion with the issue (i.e., the overlap of the self with the issue; Swann et al., 2009, 2012), which served as the dependent measure. Identity fusion (IF) is defined as a remarkably strong form of alignment with a group and/or a construct (Gómez et al., 2020). Consistent with prior literature in this domain, identity was measured using a seven-item verbal scale (Gómez et al., 2011). Example items include: "I am one with recycling" and "I am strong because of recycling" This IF measure has been shown to be a reliable and valid instrument capable of predicting endorsement of pro-group behavior (Gómez & Vázquez, 2015). Results of this study revealed that attitudes were a significant predictor of identity. More importantly, it was found that the correlation of attitudes with IF was moderated by attitude confidence. As expected, as confidence in participants′ attitudes increased (or doubt decreased), attitudes' ability to predict identity increased.

A second study of this series was conducted with two main goals. First, this study was designed to replicate and generalize findings to a more classic identity object (i.e., people's own country). Second, this study used a full experimental design by manipulating both attitudes as well as confidence in those attitudes within the same study. In this experiment, participants were first asked to generate either positive or negative thoughts about their own country. Consistent with prior literature in persuasion (Briñol et al., 2012), manipulating the direction of thoughts served to vary the favorability of attitudes. After this induction, confidence was manipulated to be relatively high or low. Participants were randomly assigned to either recall past episodes of confidence or past episodes of doubt. The idea behind this induction is based on SVT according to which variables completely incidental to mental contents can have an impact on their perceived validity (Petty et al., 2002). Specifically, the logic is that recalling past episodes of confidence gives people a momentary feeling of confidence that can be then misattributed to whatever is in mind at the time (in this case, people′s attitudes). Following these two inductions (thought direction and confidence), participants were asked to complete a scale about identification with their country (Mael & Ashforth, 1992). This scale served as the dependent variable and consisted of six items assessing fusion with the country including: "When someone criticizes my country, it feels like a personal insult." and "When I talk about my country, I usually say 'we' rather than 'they.'"

Despite all of these variations, we found the same interaction between attitudes and confidence in predicting identity. Specifically, it was found that those who were assigned to the favorable attitudes condition were more highly identified with their country than those who were assigned to the unfavorable attitudes condition. More importantly, the induced attitudes of participants assigned to the high confidence condition had more impact on subsequent identity compared to the attitudes of those assigned to the doubt condition. In other words, this study showed that manipulated attitudes toward their country were more predictive of country identity when participants were randomly assigned to feel confident (vs. doubtful).

Taken together, the results of these two studies support the conclusion that attitudes can serve as antecedents of identity. We say this because manipulating certainty in attitudes affected how strongly those attitudes predicted identity. Consistent with SVT, the greater the confidence in one′s attitudes, the greater correspondence between attitudes and identity. Among other things, these findings are important because previous research has not always considered attitudes as an important determinant of identity (for exceptions, Celuch et al., 2009; Robnett et al., 2012). Of course, it is also possible that identity can be a determinant of attitudes such that manipulating certainty in identity could determine how strongly identity predicts attitudes (e.g., Horcajo et al., 2010; Paredes et al., 2024).

Consequences of Identity Are Moderated by Confidence/Doubt

Confidence and doubt have not only been shown to influence the relationship between attitudes and identity, but also to affect the association between identity and subsequent behavior (see right side of Figure 5.1). Recently, Paredes et al. (2020) examined the extent to which IF was more/less predictive of endorsement of extreme pro-group behavior as a function of confidence/doubt.

In the first study of this series, participants first completed the IF scale (Gómez et al., 2011) with their country. Then, they reported their confidence in their responses to the IF scale. These two variables served as predictors of the dependent measure that was completed at the end of the study. The dependent measure was responses to the willingness to fight and die scale (e.g. I would fight someone physically threatening another member of my country;" "I would sacrifice my life if it saved another group member's life"), taken from Swann et al. (2009). Results showed that IF was a significant predictor of willingness to fight and die, conceptually replicating the results of previous research in this domain (Swann et al., 2009; Gómez et al., 2011). Consistent with SVT, participants' IF was associated with their willingness to fight and die to a greater extent as confidence increased (or doubt decreased), introducing a new moderator in this context. These results were replicated by changing measures and materials in subsequent studies. Among other implications, these findings suggested that researchers interested in assessing IF can benefit by adding additional measures regarding certainty.

Further Evidence: Extremity of the Sacrifice

Recent research has also shown how situations that are indirectly related to confidence (high validity) or doubt (low validity) can also affect the association between identity and subsequent behavior (and/or behavioral intentions). For example, Paredes et al. (2021) examined the extent to which IF was more or less predictive of endorsement of extreme pro-group behavior as a function of the relevance of the situation. It was hypothesized that, given the strong link proposed between IF and extreme behavior (Swann et al., 2009; Swann et al., 2012), it might be that extreme (i.e., relevant) situations activate IF concerns whereas they are not as salient or as relevant for non-extreme situations. That is, thinking about extreme behaviors activates how much people are fused to the group whereas thinking about moderate situations does not activate any concerns about fusion because one does not need to concern oneself with how fused one is with a group to engage in moderate behaviors. The prediction was that high extremity situations would increase the perceived validity of thoughts about IF as a whole (regardless of whether people score high or low) and that low extremity would decrease the perceived validity of thoughts about IF as a whole.

Studies in this series by Paredes et al. (2021) tested whether people differed in the extent to which they are fused with a particular value, and the extent to which such fusion would predict sacrifice for that value, especially when the situation is of high extremity (i.e., high validity) relative to low extremity (i.e., low validity). As noted, this prediction is based on the previously established association between IF and extremity, and the possibility of extremity increasing the perceived validity associated with the concept of IF.

In the first study, participants reported their level of IF with a value, such as merit-based justice. That is, instead of using IF with a group, in this study IF was assessed with regard to a different psychological construct (i.e., a value). Participants were asked to answer the identity fusion verbal-scale items considering the following definition of merit-based justice: "*Merit based justice is a system in which positions are placed in a hierarchy based on a person's merit including one's talent, education, competence, and specific aptitude for a job.*" Indeed, previous research has shown that people can fuse with concepts other than their own groups, such as consumer brands (Hawkins, 2019), values and religious causes (Fredman et al., 2017), and also with particular individuals (Vázquez et al., 2015). Next, participants were assigned to either a high self-sacrifice or a low self-sacrifice version of a dilemma. The high sacrifice (extremity) required potentially giving away one's life for the value whereas the low sacrifice (extremity) implied the possibility of getting sick to preserve this value. After reading the dilemma, participants were given the option to betray the value they reported their identity with (i.e., cheating), thus avoiding the consequences described in the induction (dying vs. getting sick). Including their name on that list would be a form of not upholding the value of merit-based justice, given that they were warned that they did not meet the requirements to be on the list. As hypothesized, the effect of IF on self-sacrifice was moderated by the extremity of the situation. IF predicted simulated sacrifice for the value to a greater extent when participants were randomly assigned to a high (vs. low) extremity situation. Thus, for those participants who were assigned to the high extremity situation, the ability of this individual difference variable (IF) to predict endorsement of self-sacrifice was increased relative to those assigned to the low extremity situation.

A second study was designed to replicate and extend these results with more reliable measures, with refined inductions, and also with new materials. In this second study, participants first reported their IF with their country. Then, they received the critical manipulation of extremity. In the high extremity condition, participants were asked to list three reasons that would justify sacrificing their lives for a fellow countryman. In the low extremity condition, participants were asked to list three reasons to justify donating a non-vital organ to a fellow countryman. Finally, self-report sacrificial behavior was measured using a different dilemma (trolley dilemma) using both a continuous and a dichotomous measure. Specifically, participants were introduced to the "summoning the death train scenario" (Swann et al., 2014). In this paradigm, participants learn that a runaway train was about to crush and kill five citizens of his/her country unless they flipped a switch that diverted the train to their own railway track, killing them but leaving the five in-group members unharmed.

Despite all these changes, IF was associated with simulated self-sacrifice to a greater extent when a high (vs. low) extremity situation was activated. That is, the extent to which participants used their fusion levels when reporting self-sacrifice was higher in situations of higher (vs. lower) extremity. One possibility is that the extremity manipulations could have induced a sense of confidence or doubt that was misattributed to the responses to the IF scale. In turn, this higher certainty in IF scores (presumably produced by the relevant situation of high extremity) could have increased its predictive validity of simulated self-sacrifice (for another instance of indirect inductions of certainty increasing the predictive validity of IF, see Paredes, Martínez et al., 2021). Indeed, previous research on attitudes has shown that extremity is a consistent correlate of certainty (Krosnick et al., 1993; Petrocelli et al., 2007). We also argued that consideration of extreme sacrifices increases the relevance of fusion concerns. Thinking about extreme situations activates how fused people are with the group and that is why fusion scores were expected to guide willingness to self-sacrifice in those particular situations. Conversely, one must also consider the lack of relationship between identity fusion and self-sacrifice in non-extreme conditions. We argue that in non-extreme situations people are not likely to check on their level of identity fusion. For that reason, the extent of fusion does not make a difference in non-extreme situations because it is not considered as a relevant dimension to guide decisions.

Confidence versus Doubt in Other Forms of Identity

So far, the current chapter has focused on forms of identity that are directly linked to group belongingness or one's values. However, identity goes beyond groups and values. Identity is a reflective exercise of an object looking on to itself (Harré, 1998; Leary, 2004). As William James (1892/1953) suggested, a person can reflexively attribute an endless amount of qualities to the self (e.g., personality traits), but also characteristics of body and physiology, interpersonal relationships and social roles, and even aspects of the material world. From this approach to identity, a wide variety of dispositions and individual differences might be explored as aspects of identity too.

One instance of this broad definition of identity is provided by work on validation of primed identities. A primed identity occurs when a person's identity is changed by seemingly irrelevant group primes to the point where the person comes to act like a member of the primed group (DeMarree et al., 2005; Wheeler et al., 2001) and/or expects to be treated as a member of the activated social group (Briñol et al., 2015). Consistent with SVT, Briñol and colleagues (2015) argued that primes should especially influence perceptions of the self to the extent that they are seen as valid. In this study, Briñol and colleagues experimentally manipulated conditions that foster perceptions of prime validity using a head movement induction. Previous research had linked head nodding to higher levels of confidence than head shaking (Briñol & Petty, 2003). Consistent with SVT, participants primed with the African American stereotype (versus control) expected more future discrimination, but only if they were nodding their heads.

Another instance of this broad definition of identity is provided by work on the validation of personality traits. For example, Santos et al. (2019) examined whether a person's confidence in their responses on an aggressive identity scale (measured with The Aggression Questionnaire by Buss & Perry, 1992) could enhance the scale's ability to predict relevant aggression outcomes. Their first study examined to what extent confidence vs. doubt about one´s aggressive identity can help to predict aggressive behavioral intentions. Specifically, aggressive behavioral intentions were measured by having participants assess the likelihood of engaging in aggressive behavior in the future. As hypothesized, they found that aggressive identity predicted aggressive behavioral intentions to a greater extent as participants were more confident (less doubtful) in their reported aggressive identities.

Study 2 by Santos et al. (2019) used the same design and procedure but included behavioral measures of aggression. A common method of studying aggressive behavior is the hot sauce paradigm (Lieberman et al., 1999). In this method, participants are provided with an opportunity to aggress against a target by choosing the amount of extremely spicy hot sauce to give to a fellow participant. As in Study 1, the authors found that participants' self-reported aggressive identity predicted their aggressive behavioral intentions to a greater extent as confidence increased. In addition to replicating Study 1's findings, they also found that confidence moderated the relationship between aggressive identity and aggressive behavior.

In another research instance in which contextual variables might have indirectly induced confidence (vs. doubt) in participants´ identity, Santos et al. (2022) examined to what extent aggressive identity (measured with the 12-item Brief Aggression Questionnaire, BAQ; Webster et al., 2014) was more likely to predict aggressive outcomes (i.e., hot sauce paradigm; Lieberman et al., 1999) when the person is put in situations (playing a violent videogame) and in roles (being the agent of aggression) that are of high confidence (a valid basis) rather than when the situation and/or the role are of low confidence (a less valid basis). Across two studies, they examined to what extent a situation that fits a participant's aggressive identity can help increase the predictive validity of aggressive identity on aggressive behavior, and whether that effect is more likely to emerge in the agent as compared to the victim role.

The results of these studies showed that the effect of aggressive identity on aggressive behavior was moderated by the situation participants were put in and by the role they were assigned to adopt. When an agent role was made salient, the results indicated that aggressive identity predicted aggressive behavior to a greater extent when participants played a high-violence (vs. low-violence) videogame. Thus, the ability of this identity measure to predict actual aggression was more likely to emerge when the situation fit the participants' dispositional tendency—when participants were cast in the agent role. In other words, randomly assigning participants to an agent role might have increased confidence in their aggressive identity, making it more predictive of subsequent aggressive behavior. On the other hand, randomly assigning participants to a victim role might have increased doubt in their aggressive identity. Beyond aggressive identity, other recent research has shown that measuring confidence in a trait can also improve the predictive validity of other forms of identity including work in the domain of political ideology (Shoots-Reinhard et al., 2015), self-efficacy (Horcajo et al., 2022), addiction predisposition (Paredes et al., 2021), vaccine hesitancy (Paredes et al., 2022), holistic styles of thinking (Santos et al., in press), feelings of power, (Toader et al., in press), and even clinically relevant styles of thinking (Díaz et al., in press).

Elaboration Moderates the Use of Confidence/Doubt

Recent research on SVT has started to explore the conditions under which confidence/doubt in one's mental content is more likely to be taken into consideration. This work is based on SVT and predicts that reliance on certainty and doubt (metacognitive assessments) is more likely to occur as the extent of thinking is increased (Briñol & Petty, 2009, 2022). Specifically, SVT postulates that metacognitive processes (both experiences and usage of metacognition) are more likely to occur when thinking is increased at the time of decision-making or action. Because considering one's confidence/doubt is a metacognitive process, it takes more thought to generate such metacognition and then use that metacognition than it does to generate and use primary cognition. The implication of this SVT postulate for the current work is that, for identity confidence to be consequential, not only must people consider their identity, but they also need some motivation and ability to engage in additional thought about the validity of that mental content.

Moreno and colleagues (2024) conducted a number of studies to put this moderation prediction to the test in the context of identity. The main goal of this research was to examine whether scientific identity would be associated with performance in STEMM-relevant tasks, and to what extent confidence/doubt would moderate that relationship. Most relevant, the second and most important goal of this research was testing for the first time the circumstances under which people are more likely to use (rely on) their identity confidence to impact their behavior (i.e., engage in metacognitive usage).

In two correlational studies, students were first asked to complete a validated measure of scientific identity. Specifically, students' scientific identity was assessed with a 5-item visual scale previously validated by McDonald et al. (2019). To assess scientific identity, participants were asked questions such as *"Select the picture that best describes: the extent to which your capacity to use STEMM skills in a public setting matches that of a scientist."* There were 5 questions in all and for every item participants had to select among a set of seven overlapping circles varying in the degree of overlap from 1 (*no overlap*) to 7 (*near complete overlap*). Then, participants were asked to answer two questions about their confidence in their responses to the identity measures. Next, participants completed a self-report measure of elaboration in which they had to rate how much they thought or they completed a measure of their need for cognition (Cacioppo & Petty, 1982), depending on study. Finally, participants were asked to complete a STEMM-relevant task consisting of completing the Vandenberg Mental Rotation Test (VMRT, Vandenberg & Kuse, 1978). The VMRT consists of 20 questions with each question contained one target image and four alternative images. Of the four alternative images, only two were identical to the target. Participants must mentally rotate each item and choose the two images that were identical to the target. One point was given for each correct response for a maximum of 40 points (Casey et al., 1992). This measure was selected because spatial abilities are crucial cognitive skills that influence academic success in STEMM domains (Wai et al., 2009).

Results showed that STEMM identity was a better predictor of performance when it was held with higher rather than lower confidence. Even more important, the results showed for the first time that confidence moderated the correspondence between scientific identity and performance to a greater extent when participants reported having engaged in relatively higher degrees of thinking. Thus, among participants who reported being more thoughtful, the ability of identity to predict performance was stronger for those who indicated a relatively high versus low degree of confidence. This was not the case for those reported being less thoughtful. This study introduced a new finding by specifying for whom identity confidence or doubt is more or less likely to be taken into consideration.

In a third study, the main goal was to replicate and extend the findings of the previous studies by manipulating the two moderating variables: confidence/doubt and elaboration. First, participants in this study were asked to report their scientific identity combining both visual and verbal scales. Then, confidence was manipulated (rather than measured as in previous studies) to be relatively high or low. Specifically, participants were randomly assigned to either recall past episodes of confidence or past episodes of doubt (Moreno et al., 2022; Petty et al., 2002; Requero et al., 2020). Therefore, both scientific identity and confidence/doubt were introduced in this study before varying elaboration. This order of variables is a critical aspect of this study designed to distinguish between having and using metacognition. Thus, only after creating different levels of confidence/doubt was elaboration was manipulated. The manipulation of elaboration included both ability and motivation factors. Finally, participants were asked to solve a math test consisting of 20 multiple-choice questions from the Graduate Record Examination (Moreno et al., 2022).

Despite these variations, we expected and found scientific identity to predict math performance. Second, the predicted identity-performance effect was especially likely to emerge when confidence was manipulated to be high rather than low. Even more relevant, we also found that manipulated elaboration moderated the two-way interaction between identity and confidence/doubt on math performance. Specifically, it was found that the effect of induced confidence/doubt on identity-performance correspondence was more likely to emerge for participants assigned to the high rather than low elaboration condition. Thus, we obtained the predicted three-way interaction between scientific identity, manipulated confidence/doubt, and manipulated elaboration on math performance. Among other things, these results are important because they provided evidence of the conditions proposed by SVT that can enhance the likelihood of engaging in greater usage of metacognitions. Results supported the SVT prediction that the use of confidence/doubt to moderate scientific identity-behavior correspondence would be most apparent among those relatively high in their thinking at the time of the behavioral choice or action.

Direct vs. Compensatory Confidence in Identity

As shown in the research described so far, confidence can come from many different sources. For example, confidence versus doubt was induced in many of the studies described up to this point by asking participants to recall past episodes of confidence (vs. doubt), and by putting them in situations that matched (vs. mismatched) with their identity. In contrast to these direct inductions of confidence and doubt, there are other cases in which low confidence does not just feel doubtful but also feels threatening. As described by Briñol and Petty (this volume), threatening doubt can actually *enhance* thought use relative to a control. When experiencing a threatening uncertainty, individuals can be motivated to behave in ways that restore their sense of confidence (to mitigate the threat) such as by adopting more extreme attitudes (*compensatory conviction*; McGregor et al., 2001) or behaviors (Siev et al., 2023) or using one's thoughts more (Horcajo et al., 2022) or relying more on their identities (Paredes et al., 2023). When a threat is present, inductions of doubt can result in an increased (rather than decreased) impact on current thoughts (Hart, 2014).

In recent research, Moreno et al. (2023) examined the extent to which perceived threat from COVID-19 could lead people to defend themselves psychologically via thought validation. All participants in these studies were placed in high thinking conditions and were first asked to generate some thoughts to then be validated. The thoughts validated in these studies were thoughts about themselves (Studies 1 and 2) or about other people (Study 3). Different thoughts were used for generalization purposes and to ensure that the content of the thoughts was unrelated to the threat from COVID-19. Participants' initial thoughts were coded for favorability (Study 1) or directly manipulated to be positive versus negative (Study 2, and 3). After measuring or manipulating the valence of thoughts, the second independent variable was introduced, a measure of the perceived threat from COVID-19. In each of the studies, it was expected that the perceived threat from COVID-19 would moderate the effect of previously generated thoughts on subsequent evaluations. Specifically, we hypothesized that individuals perceiving COVID-19 as more threatening would show a greater effect of thought valence on evaluation.

Results showed that increased feelings of threat from COVID-19 (vs. getting cold) were associated with a greater use of thoughts about the self in forming self-esteem regardless of whether the accessible thoughts were measured or manipulated. The main notion is that whereas getting cold might induce a sense of doubt, the possibility of catching COVID-19 poses a *threatening* doubt (similar to mortality salience; Greenberg et al., 1990; Horcajo et al., 2022), one that participants wanted to compensate for by seeking confidence. Importantly, perceptions of COVID-19 threat, affected thought usage even though the initial thoughts were not directly related to the threat.

Although it is generally accepted and supported by research that individuals tend to act more on beliefs and attitudes about which they have greater certainty, some recent research showed that being more *uncertain* in a threatening context (e.g., when having concerns about COVID-19) can be associated with a greater willingness to support extreme mitigation-related behaviors (Siev et al., 2023). Thus, this research introduced *behavioral extremity* as a novel moderator of the relationship between uncertainty and the tendency to act on one's mental content. Additionally, the positive associations between uncertainty and extreme behaviors were strongest when the topic was highly threatening, consistent with the notion that the relationship reflects defensive motivation producing efforts among those with doubts to bolster their position.

Summary and Future Research

The research described in this chapter has revealed that the metacognitions of confidence and doubt can moderate the relationship between identity and its antecedents (attitudes) and consequences (behavior). Also, this SVT-inspired work revealed that confidence and doubt can be measured and manipulated, and that it applies to whatever measures of identity were available in the study. Furthermore, as shown in Figure 5.1, confidence and doubt inductions can come from many different sources, including recalling past episodes of these states or having people engage in situations and roles that match their identity.

We close this chapter by first suggesting that new forms of identity can be subject to the impact of confidence and doubt. We then explore new forms of inducing confidence or doubt in people′s identity. Next, we review potentially new consequences of identity that could be moderated by metacognition. Finally, we conclude by reinterpreting previous research in which relative confidence or doubt about one´s identity might have been induced unintentionally.

As noted, perceived validity can be applied to whatever mental elements are salient at a given point in time, regardless of the specific content, valence, and nature of the thoughts. In the studies reviewed in this chapter, self-validation processes operated for group belongingness, values, scientific identity, and dispositional traits. Future research should explore other identity objects (e.g., brand identity, organizational identity) and other forms of identity (e.g., identities that are stigmatized, multiple, secret, fragile, and/or ambivalent) that could be moderated by metacognition. Furthermore, different forms of identity can not only serve as the mental content to be validated but also serve as the validating variable. Consistent with this possibility, early SVT research revealed that people rely on their thoughts more when they are perceived to be similar to the thoughts of other in-group members (Petty et al., 2002; see Santos et al., 2024, for a recent replication). Furthermore, SVT research on validation by expectancy confirmation has illustrated how identity threat can influence important outcomes (e.g., intellectual performance) through validation processes. The key notion behind stereotype validation (as opposed to stereotype threat; Steele et al., 2002) is that members of (stigmatized) groups may feel more certain of their own (poor) performance when their identity (associated with negative stereotypes) is made accessible after finishing a task (Clark et al., 2009, 2015).

Similarly, research on SVT has demonstrated that a wide range of variables can affect people´s metacognition about their mental content. Future studies could also examine how variables associated with the person and the situation can not only be examined in isolation but also interact with each other to influence validation processes. According to SVT, when the situation matches or fits one's nature, thought use is increased (Briñol & Petty, 2005; Evans & Clark, 2012) because people likely feel confident when these matches occur. Although some matches have already been investigated empirically and discussed in the current chapter (e.g., a violent videogame and an agent role; Santos et al., 2022), there are many unexplored person-situation combinations that can be examined as determinants of validation processes such as matching personal identity and occupation (Schmader & Sedikides, 2018), and matching virtually any dispositions and situations more generally (see, Briñol & Petty, in press; Teeny et al., 2021; for more on validation by matching).

Another potential future avenue worth exploring is that what we call antecedents and consequences of identity could have a bidirectional relationship with identity itself. That is, just as thoughts and attitudes impact identity as a function of confidence or doubt in those mental contents (Paredes et al., 2023), identity held with doubt versus confidence could also impact subsequent identity-related attitudes (e.g., Paredes et al., 2024). Likewise, identity-related behavior could in turn impact identity as a function of the doubt versus confidence associated with such behavior (for recent research on the impact of behavior on identity, see Randers & Thøgersen, 2023). Lastly, given the wide range of constructs that have been shown to impact participants' metacognitions about their mental content, the research described in the present chapter can also be useful in reinterpreting past results. For example, although speculative, Swann et al. (2010) may have unintentionally moderated the relationship between IF and pro-group behavior by manipulating confidence versus doubt through induction of physical arousal (with high arousal being associated with more confidence). In another instance, Gómez et al. (2011) may have induced threatening doubt and triggered compensatory confidence by inducing feelings of social rejection, which in turn increased the association between IF and pro-group behavior in a manner similar to the compensatory effects described in this chapter for Moreno and colleagues (2023: see also Siev et al., 2023).

Beyond physical arousal and social rejection, other variables such as an induced low (vs. high) sense of morality and responsibility decreased the association between identity fusion with one's country and pro-group behavior for the country (Chinchilla et al., 2022). Specifically, after reporting their levels of identity fusion, participants learned that "most ingroup members do not feel viscerally responsible towards the ingroup, and that the feelings that they experience do not compel them to do things to protect and defend the ingroup." Notably, the induction in this research took place after participants reported their levels of identity fusion, suggesting that the induction of lack of morality and responsibility within the country might have increased participants´ doubts about their identity fusion, subsequently weakening its link with pro-group behavior. Although these interpretations are speculative at this point, future research should examine the potential link between confidence/doubt and variables like arousal, social rejection, and lack of responsibility.

References

Avnet, T., Pham, M. T., & Stephen, A. T. (2012). Consumers' trust in feelings as information. *Journal of Consumer Research, 39*(4), 720–735.

Baudson, T. G., & Ziemes, J. F. (2016). The importance of being gifted: Stages of gifted identity development, their correlates and predictors. *Gifted and Talented International, 31*(1), 19–32.

Brewer, M. B. (2001). The many faces of social identity: Implications for political psychology. *Political Psychology, 22*(1), 115–125.

Briñol, P., DeMarree, K. G., & Petty, R. E. (2010). Processes by which confidence (vs. doubt) influences the self. In R. Arkin, K. Oleson, & P. Carroll (Eds.), *Handbook of the uncertain self* (pp. 13–35). Psychology Press.

Briñol, P., DeMarree, K. G., & Petty, R. E. (2015). Validating a primed identity leads to expectations of group-relevant outcomes. *International Journal of Social Psychology, 30*, 614–630.

Briñol, P., & Petty, R. E (2003). Overt head movements and persuasion: A self-validation analysis. *Journal of Personality and Social Psychology, 84*, 1123–1139.

Briñol, P., Petty, R. E., & Tormala, Z. L. (2004). The self-validation of cognitive responses to advertisements. *Journal of Consumer Research, 30,* 559–573.

Briñol, P., & Petty, R. E. (2005). Individual differences in attitude change. In D. Albarracín, B. T. Johnson, & M. P. Zanna (Eds.), *The handbook of attitudes and attitude change* (pp. 575–616). Erlbaum.

Briñol, P., & Petty, R. E. (2009). Persuasion: Insights from the self-validation hypothesis. *Advances in Experimental Social Psychology, 41,* 69–118.

Briñol, P., Petty, R. E., & Stavraki, M. (2012). Power increases the reliance on first-impression thoughts. *Revista de Psicología Social, 27,* 293–303.

Briñol, P., & Petty, R. E. (in press). Mechanisms of personalized persuasion: Multiple processes, meanings, and outcomes. In R. E. Petty, A. Luttrell & J. D. Teeny (Eds.), *The handbook of personalized persuasion: Theory and application.* Taylor and Francis.

Briñol, P., & Petty, R. E. (2022). Self-validation theory: An integrative framework for understanding when thoughts become consequential. *Psychological Review, 129*(2), 340.

Buss, A. H., & Perry, M. (1992). The aggression questionnaire. *Journal of Personality and Social Psychology, 63*, 452–459.

Cacioppo, J. T., & Petty, R. E. (1982). The need for cognition. *Journal of Personality and Social Psychology, 42*(1), 116–131.

Casey, M. B., Colón, D., & Goris, Y. (1992). Family handedness as a predictor of mental rotation ability among minority girls in a math-science training program. *Brain and Cognition, 18*(1), 88–96.

Celuch, K., Black, G., & Warthan, B. (2009). Student self-identity as a critical thinker: The influence of attitudes, attitude strength, and normative beliefs. *Journal of Marketing Education, 31*(1), 31–39.

Chinchilla, J., Vazquez, A., & Gómez, Á. (2022). Identity fusion predicts violent pro-group behavior when it is morally justifiable. *The Journal of Social Psychology, 162*(6), 701–715.

Clark, J. K., Thiem, K. C., Barden, J., Stuart, J. O., & Evans, A. T. (2015). Stereotype validation: The effects of activating negative stereotypes after intellectual performance. *Journal of Personality and Social Psychology, 108*(4), 531–552.

Clark, J. K., Wegener, D. T., Brinol, P., & Petty, R. E. (2009). Discovering that the shoe fits: The self-validating role of stereotypes. *Psychological Science, 20*(7), 846–852.

DeMarree, K. G., Loersch, C. A., Briñol, P., Petty, R. E., Payne, B. K., & Rucker, D. D. (2012). From primed construct to motivated behavior: Validation processes in goal pursuit. *Personality and Social Psychology Bulletin, 38,* 1659–1670.

DeMarree, K. G., Wheeler, S. C., & Petty, R. E. (2005). Priming a new identity: Self-monitoring moderates the effects of non-self primes on self-judgments and behavior. *Journal of Personality and Social Psychology, 89,* 657–671.

Díaz, D., Briñol, P., Bajo, M., Stavraki, M., Beato-Fernández, L., & Petty, R. E. (2024). The association of the Persecutory Ideation Questionnaire with clinically-relevant and other outcomes: The moderating role of confidence. *Scientific Reports.*

Evans, A. T., & Clark, J. K. (2012). Source characteristics and persuasion: The role of self-monitoring in self-validation. *Journal of Experimental Social Psychology, 48*(1), 383–386.

Faye, C., & Sharpe, D. (2008). Academic motivation in university: The role of basic psychological needs and identity formation. *Canadian Journal of Behavioural Science, 40*(4), 189–199.

Fazio, R. H., & Zanna, M. P. (1978). On the predictive validity of attitudes: The roles of direct experience and confidence. *Journal of Personality, 46*(2), 228–243.

Fiske, S. T. (2018). Social beings: *Core motives in social psychology.* John Wiley & Sons.

Fredman, L. A., Bastian, B., & Swann Jr, W. B. (2017). God or country? Fusion with Judaism predicts desire for retaliation following Palestinian stabbing Intifada. *Social Psychological and Personality Science, 8*(8), 882–887.

Gómez, A., Brooks, M. L., Buhrmester, M. D., Vázquez, A., Jetten, J., & Swann Jr, W. B. (2011). On the nature of identity fusion: insights into the construct and a new measure. *Journal of Personality and Social Psychology, 100,* 918–933.

Gómez, A., Chinchilla, J., Vázquez, A., López-Rodríguez, L., Paredes, B., & Martínez, M. (2020). Recent advances, misconceptions, untested assumptions, and future research agenda for identity fusion theory. *Social and Personality Psychology Compass, 14*(6), e12531.

Gómez, Á., & Vázquez, A. (2015). The power of 'feeling one'with a group: Identity fusion and extreme pro-group behaviors. *Revista de Psicología Social, 30*(3), 481–511.

Greenberg, J., Pyszczynski, T., Solomon, S., Rosenblatt, A., Veeder, M., Kirkland, S., & Lyon, D. (1990). Evidence for terror management theory II: The effects of mortality salience on reactions to those who threaten or bolster the cultural worldview. *Journal of Personality and Social Psychology, 58*(2), 308–318.

Greenwald, A. G., Banaji, M. R., Rudman, L. A., Farnham, S. D., Nosek, B. A., & Mellott, D. S. (2002). A unified theory of implicit attitudes, stereotypes, self-esteem, and self-concept. *Psychological Review, 109*(1), 3–25.

Harré, R. (1998). *The singular self: An introduction to the psychology of personhood.* Sage Publications.

Hart, J. (2014). Toward an integrative theory of psychological defense. *Perspectives on Psychological Science, 9*(1), 19–39.

Hawkins, M. A. (2019). The effect of activity identity fusion on negative consumer behavior. *Psychology & Marketing, 36*(4), 395–409.

Hogg, M. A., & Smith, J. R. (2007). Attitudes in social context: A social identity perspective. *European Review of Social Psychology, 18*(1), 89–131.

Horcajo, J., Briñol, P., & Petty, R. E. (2010). Consumer persuasion: Indirect change and implicit balance. *Psychology & Marketing, 27,* 938–963.

Horcajo, J., Briñol, P., Paredes, B., Petty, R. E., DeMarree, K. G., & See, Y. H. M. (2022). Polarization of attitudes as a function of mortality salience: A meta-cognitive analysis. *Psicothema, 34*(2), 226–232.

Horcajo, J., Santos, D., & Higuero, G. (2022). The effects of self-efficacy on physical and cognitive performance: An analysis of meta-certainty. *Psychology of Sport and Exercise, 58,* 102063.

James, W. (1892/1953). *Psychology: A briefer course.* Fawcett.

Krosnick, J. A., Boninger, D. S., Chuang, Y. C., Berent, M. K., & Carnot, C. G. (1993). Attitude strength: One construct or many related constructs? *Journal of Personality and Social Psychology, 65*(6), 1132–1151.

Leary, M. R. (2004). What is the self? A plea for clarity. *Self and Identity, 3*(1), 1–3.

Levine, J. M., & Kerr, N. L. (2007). Inclusion and exclusion: Implications for group processes. In A. W. Kruglanski & E. T. Higgins (Eds.), *Social psychology: Handbook of basic principles* (pp. 759–784). The Guilford Press.

Lieberman, J. D., Solomon, S., Greenberg, J., & McGregor, H. A. (1999). A hot new way to measure aggression: Hot sauce allocation. *Aggressive Behavior, 25,* 331–348.

Mael, F., & Ashforth, B. E. (1992). Alumni and their alma mater: A partial test of the reformulated model of organizational identification. *Journal of Organizational Behavior*, *13*(2), 103–123.

Maio, G. R., & Olson, J. M. (1995). Relations between values, attitudes, and behavioral intentions: The moderating role of attitude function. *Journal of Experimental Social Psychology*, *31*(3), 266–285.

Maio, G. R., & Olson, J. M. (2000). Emergent themes and potential approaches to attitude function: The function-structure model of attitudes. In G. R. Maio & J. M. Olson (Eds.), *Why we evaluate: Functions of attitudes* (pp. 417–442). Psychology Press.

McDonald, M. M., Zeigler-Hill, V., Vrabel, J. K., & Escobar, M. (2019). A single-item measure for assessing STEM Identity. *Frontiers in Education, 4,* 78.

McGregor, I., Zanna, M. P., Holmes, J. G., & Spencer, S. J. (2001). Compensatory conviction in the face of personal uncertainty: Going to extremes and being oneself. *Journal of Personality and Social Psychology, 80*(3), 472–488.

Moreno, L., Briñol, P., & Petty, R. E. (2022). Metacognitive confidence can increase but also decrease performance in academic settings. *Metacognition and Learning, 17*, 139–165.

Moreno, L., Briñol, P., Paredes, B., & Petty, R. E. (2024). Scientific identity and STEMM-relevant outcomes: Elaboration moderates use of identity-certainty. *Journal of Experimental Social Psychology, 115*, 1–16. https://doi.org/10.1016/j.jesp.2024.104663

Moreno, L., Paredes, B., Horcajo, J., Briñol, P., See, M., DeMarree, K. G., & Petty, R. E. (2023). The effects of perceived COVID-19 threat on compensatory conviction, thought reliance, and attitudes. *European Journal of Social Psychology*, *53*(6), 1309–1325.

Nosek, B. A., Smyth, F. L., Hansen, J. J., Devos, T., Lindner, N. M., Ranganath, K. A., … & Banaji, M. R. (2007). Pervasiveness and correlates of implicit attitudes and stereotypes. *European Review of Social Psychology*, *18*(1), 36–88.

Paredes, B., Briñol, P., Petty, R. E., & Gómez, Á. (2021). Increasing the predictive validity of identity fusion in leading to sacrifice by considering the extremity of the situation. *European Journal of Social Psychology*, *51*(2), 239–250.

Paredes, B., Briñol, P., Bustos, D., Moreno, L., & Petty, R. E. (2024, February). *The impact of elaboration on spreading of attitude change: A new approach to assessing attitude strength. To be presented at the Attitudes Preconference of the Society of Personality and Social Psychology.* San Diego, CA.

Paredes, B., Cárdaba, M. A. M., Moreno, L., Cano, N., Briñol, P., Cuesta, U., & Petty, R. E. (2022). Strengthening the link between vaccine predispositions and vaccine advocacy through certainty. *Vaccines*, *10*(11), 1970.

Paredes, B., Grande, A., Moreno, L., Briñol, P., & Petty, R. E. (2024). Confidence moderates the impact of attitudes on related group identities. *Manuscript under Review*.

Paredes, B., Martínez, L., Cuesta, U., Briñol, P., Petty, R., & Moreno, L. (2021). The role of meta-cognitive certainty on pornography consumption. *Psicothema, 33*(3), 442–448.

Paredes, B., Santos, D., Briñol, P., Gómez, Á., & Petty, R. E. (2020). The role of meta-cognitive certainty on the relationship between identity fusion and endorsement of extreme pro-group behavior. *Self and Identity*, *19*(7), 804–824.

Petrocelli, J. V., Tormala, Z. L., & Rucker, D. D. (2007). Unpacking attitude certainty: Attitude clarity and attitude correctness. *Journal of Personality and Social Psychology, 92*(1), 30–41.

Petty, R. E., Briñol, P., & Tormala, Z. L. (2002). Thought confidence as a determinant of persuasion: the self-validation hypothesis. *Journal of Personality and Social Psychology, 82*(5), 722–741.

Petty, R. E., & Cacioppo, J. T. (1996). *Attitudes and persuasion: Classic and contemporary approaches*. Westview Press.

Petty, R. E., & Krosnick, J. A. (1995). *Attitude strength: Antecedents and consequences*. Erlbaum Associates.

Randers, L., & Thøgersen, J. (2023). From attitude to identity? A field experiment on attitude activation, identity formation, and meat reduction. *Journal of Environmental Psychology*, *87*, 101996.

Requero, B., Paredes, B., Gandarillas, B., & Moreno, L. (2020). Promoting healthy eating by enhancing the correspondence between attitudes and behavioral intentions. *Psicothema*, *32*(1), 60–66.

Requero, B., Santos, D., Paredes, B., Briñol, P., & Petty, R. E. (2020). Attitudes toward hiring people with disabilities: A meta-cognitive approach to persuasion. *Journal of Applied Social Psychology, 50,* 276–288.

Robnett, R. D., Anderson, K. J., & Hunter, L. E. (2012) Predicting feminist identity: associations between gender-traditional attitudes, feminist stereotyping, and ethnicity. *Sex Roles, 67*, 143–157.

Rucker, D. D., Tormala, Z. L., Petty, R. E., & Briñol, P. (2014). Consumer conviction and commitment: An appraisal-based framework for attitude certainty. *Journal of Consumer Psychology*, *24*(1), 119–136.

Santos, D., Briñol, P., Petty, R. E., Gandarillas, B., & Mateos, R. (2019). Trait aggressiveness predicting aggressive behavior: The moderating role of meta-cognitive certainty. *Aggressive Behavior, 45*, 255–264.
Santos, D., Horcajo, J., Gil, R., & Guyer, J. J. (2024). Changing attitudes regarding a pro-environmental proposal about solar power: The self-validating role of ingroup versus outgroup sources. *Psicothema, 36*(1), 46–54.
Santos, D., Paredes, B., Briñol, P., & Petty, R. E. (2022). Trait aggressiveness and aggressive behavior: The simultaneous influence of contextual variables. *Psychology of Violence. 12*(6), 438–449.
Santos, D., Requero, B., Moreno, L., Briñol, P., & Petty, R. E., (2024). Certainty in holistic thinking and responses to contradiction: Dialectical proverbs, counter-attitudinal change, and ambivalence. *British Journal of Social Psychology*.
Schmader, T., & Sedikides, C. (2018). State authenticity as fit to environment: The implications of social identity for fit, authenticity, and self-segregation. *Personality and Social Psychology Review*, *22*(3), 228–259.
Siev, J. J., Petty, R. E., Paredes, B., & Briñol, P. (2023). Behavioral extremity moderates the association between certainty in attitudes about COVID and willingness to engage in mitigation-related behaviors. *Social and Personality Psychology Compass*, *17*(8), e12767.
Stavraki, M., Santos, D., Cancela, A., Requero, B., & Briñol, P. (2017). The evaluation of green companies changes after remembering tip of the tongue experiences. *Psicothema, 29*, 502–507.
Steele, C. M., Spencer, S. J., & Aronson, J. (2002). Contending with group image: The psychology of stereotype and social identity threat. *Advances in Experimental Social Psychology, 34,* 379–440.
Shoots-Reinhard, B., Petty, R. E., DeMarree, K. G., & Rucker, D. D. (2015). Personality certainty and politics: Increasing the predictive utility of individual difference inventories. *Political Psychology*, *36*, 415–430.
Swann Jr, W. B., Gómez, A., Seyle, D. C., Morales, J., & Huici, C. (2009). Identity fusion: the interplay of personal and social identities in extreme group behavior. *Journal of Personality and Social Psychology, 96*, 995–1011.
Swann Jr, W. B., Gómez, A., Huici, C., Morales, J., & Hixon, J. G. (2010). Identity fusion and self-sacrifice: arousal as a catalyst of pro-group fighting, dying, and helping behavior. *Journal of Personality and Social Psychology*, *99*(5), 824–841.
Swann Jr, W. B., Gómez, Á., Buhrmester, M. D., López-Rodríguez, L., Jiménez, J., & Vázquez, A. (2014). Contemplating the ultimate sacrifice: Identity fusion channels pro-group affect, cognition, and moral decision making. *Journal of Personality and Social Psychology, 106*, 713–727.
Swann, W. B., Jetten, J., Gómez, A., Whitehouse, H., & Bastian, B. (2012). When group membership gets personal: a theory of identity fusion. *Psychological Review*, *119*(3), 441–456.
Tajfel, H. (1982). *Social identity and intergroup relations*. Cambridge University Press.
Tajfel, H., & Turner, J. C. (1979). An integrative theory of intergroup conflict. *The Social Psychology of Intergroup Relations*, *33*, 33–47.
Teeny, J. D., Siev, J. J., Briñol, P., & Petty, R. E. (2021). A review and conceptual framework for understanding personalized matching effects in persuasion. *Journal of Consumer Psychology*, *31*(2), 382–414.
Toader, I., Moreno, L., Briñol, P., & Petty, R. E. (2024). Power corrupts and being sure of felt power corrupts even more: Implications for immoral decisions and cheating. *European Journal of Social Psychology.* https://doi.org/10.1002/ejsp.3099
Turner-Zwinkels, F. M., & Brandt, M. J. (2023). Ideology strength versus party identity strength: Ideology strength is the key predictor of attitude stability. *Personality and Social Psychology Bulletin*, 01461672231189015.
Vandenberg, S. G., & Kuse, A. R. (1978). Mental rotations, a group test of three-dimensional spatial visualization. *Perceptual and Motor Skills, 47*(2), 599–604.
Van der Werff, E., Steg, L., & Keizer, K. (2013). The value of environmental self-identity: The relationship between biospheric values, environmental self-identity and environmental preferences, intentions and behavior. *Journal of Environmental Psychology*, *34*, 55–63.
Vaughan-Johnston, T. I., Fowlie, D. I., & Jacobson, J. A. (2023). Connecting attitude position and function: The role of self-esteem. *Personality and Social Psychology Bulletin, 49*(9), 1344–1362.
Vázquez, A., Gómez, Á., Ordoñana, J. R., & Paredes, B. (2015). From interpersonal to extended fusion: relationships between fusion with siblings and fusion with the country. *Revista de Psicología Social*, *30*(3), 512–530.

Wai, J., Lubinski, D., & Benbow, C. P. (2009). Spatial ability for STEM domains: aligning over 50 years of cumulative psychological knowledge solidifies its importance. *Journal of Educational Psychology, 101*, 817–835.

Webster, G. D., DeWall, C. N., Pond, R. S., Deckman, T., Jonason, P. K., Le, B. M.,... Smith, C. V. (2014). The brief aggression questionnaire: Psychometric and behavioral evidence for an efficient measure of trait aggression. *Aggressive Behavior, 40*(2), 120–139.

Wheeler, S. C., Jarvis, W. B., & Petty, R. E. (2001). Think unto others…The self-destructive impact of negative stereotypes. *Journal of Experimental Social Psychology*, *37*, 173–180.

Williams, K. D. (2007). Ostracism: The kiss of social death. *Social and Personality Psychology Compass, 1*(1), 236–247.

Zunick, P. V., Teeny, J. D., & Fazio, R. H. (2017). Are some attitudes more self-defining than others? Assessing self-related attitude functions and their consequences. *Personality and Social Psychology Bulletin, 43*(8), 1136–1149.

6

SELF-UNCERTAINTY AS CAUSE & CONSEQUENCE OF POSSIBLE SELF-REVISION

Patrick J. Carroll, Radhika Kothari and Rease Haley

Introduction

One of the primary endeavors of the individual human mind is to create a lasting representation of the self. Of course, there is nothing inherently magical or special about the self that makes it a necessity. Rather, the construction and maintenance of self makes sense simply because it's the only thing in life that remains constant over time and circumstance (Carroll et al., 2011). That is, whereas one can break up with partners, quit jobs, or move away from cities, one cannot just break up with self, quit the self, or move away from the self for a fresh start. As such, it is in one's best adaptive interests to represent and "know thyself" because it is the only tool that one can depend on throughout life to advance self-regulatory ends.

Although the personal narrative is arguably the most sophisticated self-representation (McAdams, 1996) that integrates past ("me last year"), present ("me today"), and possible future ("me next year") selves within a continuous and coherent timeline, it is the last to emerge on the developmental timeline (Nelson & Fivush, 2004; Fivush & Nelson, 2006). Moreover, it does not arise out of thin air but, instead, develops from the foundation of a slightly less elaborated, yet critical, form of temporal self-representation–The Temporally Extended Self (Peetz & Wilson, 2008).

The Temporally Extended Self arises with the development of linguistic competencies early in life. By around age 4, the child learns to differentiate and connect their present self to their past and potential future selves. For example, in parent-child conversations, the child begins to refer to their past selves ("me as a baby" or "me in preschool") as distinct from, albeit connected to, their present self ("me in first grade") and, in turn, the future self they could become one day ("Me when I grow up") (Fivush & Nelson, 2006). Although it links the selves of the past, present, and future, the temporally extended self does not embody the thematic coherence and sophistication of a fully developed self-narrative.

From adolescence through adulthood, the transition from temporal self-extension to full self-narrative accelerates as the individual learns cultural rules of narrative construction and development (Nelson & Fivush, 2006). For example, in contrast to the simple connections formed earlier in life, the teenager learns to apply cultural rules of narrative coherence to the ongoing development and integration of different storylines within their own life narrative. Now, the selves of past, present, and future are not merely connected—they become seamlessly integrated within

DOI: 10.4324/9781003363385-7

a unified personal narrative that displays temporal, causal, and thematic coherence and direction over life (McAdams, 1996; Landau et al., 2009). Moreover, recent work shows that the elaboration of new story lines continues to increase during important transitions beyond adolescence. For example, students show an increasing application of culturally based *redemptive* and *contaminated* thematic storylines to their narrative (Dunlop et al., 2016). Over time, the self emerges as new possible selves are elaborated from core selves across life stages within an increasingly coherent, whole, personal narrative (Wilson et al., 2009).

However, just as self-representations emerge in life, so too can questions, or uncertainty, emerge over the validity of those self-representations. Moreover, when these questions arise and linger, we argue that they can even become a catalyst of changes in those self-representations (see also Chang-Schneider, 2010). This chapter reviews prior work on self-uncertainty as both a cause and consequence of self-revisions. Rather than adding or removing self-representations, self-revision involves the ongoing adjustment of current self-representations to enhance their correspondence with feedback from the environment (Carroll et al., 2015). For example, the downward revision of a possible self occurs when a student forsakes commitment to her goal to become a doctor in response to threatening feedback from a faculty advisor that she simply lacks the ability or qualifications to succeed in medicine. By contrast, the upward revision of a possible self occurs when a student embraces the commitment to her goal of becoming a doctor in response to validating feedback from an advisor that she has what it takes to succeed in medicine. Of course, the student may also revise a core self. For example, although she may hold the initial core belief that she has scientific competencies, she may subsequently revise that belief to conclude that she is not as competent as she thought after several later failures.

Having articulated the definition of self-revision, we now turn to review prior work that outlines how changes in self-uncertainty initiate revisions in possible selves or personal goals. Next, we review prior work that outlines how those revisions, or changes, in personal goals, can influence more chronic experiences of self-uncertainty (E.g., chronic self-doubt, self-concept clarity). In the process, we consider how self-uncertainty ties together processes of identity revision (or stability) over time.

Conceptualizing Self-Uncertainty

Before proceeding, we first define the key construct of this chapter and the volume—self-uncertainty. Whether momentary or chronic, self-uncertainty can be defined as the experience of uncertainty in one's representation of the self, the world, and the interrelation between the two (see Carroll et al., 2010). Thus, it is distinct from informational uncertainty which simply refers to uncertainty over whether one has enough information to render a judgment (e.g., being unsure of whether one knows the correct answer to a *Trivial Pursuit* question) (Van den bos & Lind, 2010). Unlike informational uncertainty, self-uncertainty is always about the self and is often experienced as threatening (see Van den bos & Lind, 2010).

Consistent with prior work, moreover, self-uncertainty is not a monolithic construct. Rather, it consists of two dimensions of clarity and correctness (both low in the case of self-uncertainty) (Petrocelli et al., 2007). Whereas clarity is typically defined as the degree to which one truly has access to and awareness of the "true" representation in question, correctness is typically defined by the degree of social consensus or consensual validation of the representation in question (Petrocelli et al., 2007). The important point, however, is that self-uncertainty is defined by the dual experiences of low self-clarity and correctness. Although both are important to recognize from a conceptual standpoint and for attitudes more generally, our chapter will focus primarily on the clarity (rather than correctness) dimension given that is where most of the empirical work on self-uncertainty has been done. Thus, later in this chapter, we will discuss work showing changes in self-clarity, which can be viewed as part of the experience of self-uncertainty.

Two final points are worth making regarding the nature of self-uncertainty. First, it is important to clarify our view of the nature of the relationship between self-uncertainty and self-certainty. We propose that the relationship is bipolar, with uncertainty and certainty representing opposite poles of the same construct of self-certainty rather than two independent constructs that can vary from low. In the context of the present discussion, this *means* that high uncertainty can be considered low certainty whereas low uncertainty can be considered high certainty. Throughout this chapter, we will also use the terminology of high doubt to also mean low confidence and vice-versa.

Second, it is important to clarify that, as a meta-cognitive experience, self-uncertainty (or lack thereof) can apply to *any* aspect of cognition. It can apply to general or specific contents of cognition. That is, you can have doubt (or confidence) in your quality as a parent just as easily as you can have doubt (or confidence) in your quality as a good person overall. It can also apply to itself when someone comes to doubt their own doubt, a possibility to which we will return later. Having addressed these preliminary points, we now turn to the primary substance of this chapter on the relationship between self-uncertainty and self-change. We begin by focusing on the role of self-uncertainty in initiating the process of revisions in possible selves or personal goals.

Possible Self-Change from Self-Uncertainty

In this section, we draw from theory and evidence to suggest that self-uncertainty is a crucial part of self-change and, in particular, changes in possible selves or personal goals. We will argue that just as high or rising levels of self-certainty seal and lock in self-views, high or rising levels of self-uncertainty loosen and undermine stability in self-views. Consistent with this point, prior work suggests that doubt may help facilitate revisions or changes in identity. For example, in addition to undermining overly positive self-views, this work suggests that doubt can prompt those with overly negative self-views to yield to and internalize positive feedback that they would normally eschew (Chang-Schneider & Swann, 2010). Similarly, Julie Exline and colleagues persuasively argue in this volume that religious doubt, while painful and distressing at times, can be an important engine for personal change, transformation, and even growth (see this volume).

Our own approach to the study of possible self-stability and revision borrows much from this work and the Self-Validation Theory (SVT) framework discussed in this volume. Generally speaking, any mental contents (possible selves included) held with doubt will be less stable and enduring whereas mental contents (including possible selves) held with confidence will be more stable and enduring. Applied to the present context, it would suggest that stability and increased commitment to a possible identity goal would result when feelings of confidence are used as a meta-cognitive cue to infer that those identity representations are valid; by contrast, identity instability and lower commitment would result when feelings of doubt are used as a meta-cognitive cue to infer that those identity representations are invalid. Within this framework, self-uncertainty mediates the process of stability and change in self.

Of course, the important role of self-uncertainty in driving both stability and change in possible selves is something that is nicely supported by theory and evidence. Within this volume, it is clearly consistent with SVT but, beyond this volume, it is clearly consistent with other work on possible self-representations. In this regard, prior work by Landau and colleagues (2014) has shown how the application of a life journey metaphor can enhance readiness to engage with and motivation to achieve possible selves. Important for our purposes, however, it was shown that confidence mediated the link between metaphor use and possible self-engagement.

Consistent with these perspectives, our own work suggests that stability or change in the representation of possible self (or identity) goals is determined by the degree to which those representations are held with confidence or doubt. For example, in multiple independent studies, participants were exposed to a novel Masters in Business Psychology program that would train them in one year to become top-paying consultants (Carroll et al., 2009). Participants were then encouraged to imagine and form some initial commitment to the idea of becoming a business psychologist. Next, they were exposed to threatening or validating feedback that varied in the extent to which it specified the meaning or implications of the feedback for the likelihood of the desired relative to the undesired self of failure.

Beyond showing that more specified social threats and validations were more likely to trigger the revision of commitment to possible selves, these studies showed that changes in self-uncertainty initiate both the downward and upward revision of commitment to possible selves. The difference lies in direction, and downstream processes govern both. Whereas rising certainty represents the sole mediator of upward revisions in commitment to possible selves (Carroll, 2014), falling certainty initiates rising anxiety which, in turn, drives the effect of falling certainty into the collapse of expectations supporting commitment to the possible self (Carroll et al., 2009). Again, though, changes in initial certainty are the only constant in both forms of change.

It is worth noting that the concept of action crisis, characterized by *doubts* about whether to hold onto or let go of an important personal goal, also seems relevant to the current discussion on the important role of self-uncertainty in possible self-revisions. The reason is that the action crisis squarely focuses on the experience of uncertainty in goal pursuits (Ghassemi et al., 2020). While people mostly experience confidence in pursuing important personal goals, setbacks, and adversities may arise that shake one's confidence. Given a large enough setback, one may experience an action crisis state. Importantly, like the work on downward self-revision, this work suggests that goal adjustment and revision are more likely to take place when people experience the doubt associated with an action crisis. Consistent with this point, prior scholars have suggested that an action crisis "prepares the ground for goal disengagement" (Brandstätter & Schüler, 2013).

Moreover, this point of view is supported by evidence. For example, one study measured levels of action crisis along with a commitment to academic and non-academic personal goals over a year and a half (18 month) period (Herrmann & Brandstätter, 2015). In this work, action crisis is assessed using the 6-item action crisis scale developed by Brandstätter and colleagues. Consistent with its intimate relationship to doubt, the first example item is "I doubt whether I should continue striving for my goal or disengage from it." Participants rate their level of agreement with each item using a 5-point scale, ranging from 1 (no agreement) to 5 (very much agreement). The findings showed that those with higher levels of action crisis were faster to abandon commitment to their personal goals (Herrmann & Brandstätter, 2015). Our work would only add that the experience of doubt associated with an action crisis would indirectly rather than directly prompt goal disengagement via rising anxiety and falling expectations. By the same token, the action crisis work adds greater clarity on the initial role of self-uncertainty in triggering goal revision than our work.

Of course, if an action crisis prepares the ground for goal disengagement, it raises the question of what, if anything, prepares the ground for initial or sustained goal engagement. In our view, just as the action crisis prepares the ground for goal disengagement and downward revision of possible identity goals, one can experience action conviction that prepares the ground for identity goal engagement. Unlike an action crisis, we suggest that an action conviction is characterized by the confidence that one should pursue a given personal goal (Carroll, 2023). In many ways, this shift away from goal doubts to confidence would characterize the process of upward revision in possible selves. And, just as an action crisis seems to mimic many of the processes (e.g., cost-benefit thinking; deliberation between pros and cons) involved with a deliberative mindset, the action conviction experience would parallel the experience of adopting an implemental mindset, whereby rising optimism and confidence shifts attention away from deliberative concerns to focus squarely on issues related to goal achievement (see Brandstätter & Schüler, 2013; Gollwitzer, 2012). In both cases, however, self-uncertainty is a key defining feature of action crisis (high uncertainty) or action conviction (low uncertainty).

In our view, moreover, self-uncertainty may ironically provide a mechanism through which to transform an action crisis into action conviction (double-doubt induction). As alluded to earlier, within the SVT perspective, certainty or doubt can characterize *any* contents of mental experience—including certainty or doubt itself. That is, just as it can be a meta-cognitive or secondary experience, self-doubt can sometimes be the primary cognition when one considers their own doubt in their ability to succeed. Consistent with this SVT logic, people can then vary in the extent to which they have certainty or doubt in that doubt (see Briñol & Petty, 2022 and this volume), with significant and sometimes ironic consequences. Importantly, empirical evidence from the SVT tradition supports this line of reasoning. This work shows that inducing doubts in one's doubts can provide a formula for confidence (Wichman et al., 2010). Participants in one of the first studies on this topic were (1) primed with doubt or certainty and, then, exposed to (2) an overt head movement manipulation designed as a meta-cognitive validation induction (Briñol & Petty, 2003). Whereas those who nod their heads experience confidence because they use their own head nodding (as if to say "yes") as a cue that their thoughts must be valid, those who shake their heads (as if to say "no") experience doubt because they use their own head shaking as a cue that their thoughts are invalid.

Following the meta-cognitive validation induction, participants read a brief description of another person and rated the person on how certain he was. As expected, participants reported higher target certainty ratings when primed with certainty (vs. doubt) and when nodding (vs. shaking) their own heads. In contrast, participants rated the target as less certain when they were primed with certainty rather than doubt and were shaking rather than nodding their heads (invalidation induction). Importantly, moreover, this work showed that participants rated the target as more certain when they were primed with doubt rather than certainty *but* were shaking rather than nodding their heads. That is, when induced to doubt their own doubt, the effect of that doubt on target judgments was actually reversed. This line of research was *the first* to demonstrate that a secondary manipulation of certainty or uncertainty can interact with an initial induction of the same construct in the non-additive manner (doubt+doubt=*less* doubt) specified by SVT rather than in the additive way (doubt+doubt=more doubt) that might have been expected from prior work on sequential inductions of constructs (Kidder et al., 2018).

Drawing from this work specifically and self-validation theory more generally, recent work from our own lab suggests how to turn an action crisis into action conviction by taking into account the distinction between cognitive and meta-cognitive levels of awareness (Carroll, 2023). We reasoned that, if an action crisis involves thinking about goal doubts, then the induction of meta-cognitive doubt while or just after reflecting upon an action crisis should reverse its typical effect on goal commitment. Across two studies, we first measured the level of action crisis using the standard action crisis scale either before or during induction of self-uncertainty. For example, in one study, participants completed the action crisis scale measuring goal doubts while simultaneously undergoing the induction of meta-cognitive doubt by writing with their dominant (confidence) or non-dominant (doubt) hand. Whereas those who write with the dominant hand experience confidence because they use their steady handwriting as a cue that their thoughts are valid, those who write with their non-dominant hand experience *doubt* because they use their *shaky* handwriting as a cue that their thoughts must be invalid. Next, they were asked to report their level of confidence in the responses on the action crisis scale and, finally, to indicate their level of commitment to achieving the personal goal.

As expected, our findings showed that inducing meta-cognitive doubt in the goal doubts (associated with an action crisis) actually inspired greater goal conviction and commitment. Whereas participants higher (vs. lower) on action crisis reported lower commitment when induced to experience meta-cognitive confidence, participants higher (vs. lower) on action crisis—or higher goal doubts—actually reported *greater* goal commitment when exposed to an induction of meta-cognitive doubt. Moreover, consistent with the proposed mediation hypothesis, secondary analyses showed that self-uncertainty in participants' responses on the action crisis (goal doubts) scale mediated the effect of the action crises by doubt induction interaction on commitment.

Action Crisis Severity as Predictor of Permanence of Revisions in Possible Identity Goals

In addition to determining whether downward revisions in goal commitment (goal disengagement) occur in the first place, we propose that the severity of an action crisis or goal doubts may determine *the permanence* of these changes in commitment. This is something that our work has never explored but would be worthwhile to investigate. That is, in our past work, it has been assumed that the downward revision of commitment to a personal goal initiated by uncertainty represents a permanent change. However, some work has distinguished between abandoned or disengaged goals, on the one hand, and *frozen* or shelved goals, on the other, in terms of the permanence of change (Davydenko et al., 2019). In both cases, people appear to have ceased the active pursuit of the goal. However, there are important differences.

Abandoned goals are ones that the individual no longer considers important and has abandoned effort and commitment to achieve. Such a type of goal would seem likely to follow from a severe action crisis or goal doubts. Whereas abandoned goals are one's in which the person withdraws both effort and commitment, Davydenko and colleagues define frozen goals as personally important goals that individuals remain committed to (and so are not abandoned), yet no steps are actively taken towards attaining the goal (commitment without effort) (Davydenko et al., 2019).

An example may help to illustrate this. Suppose that Erica wants to learn to play guitar. She buys a guitar and even begins to take lessons. However, after being laid off, she may have to put that goal "on hold" until she can find another job. During that time, she keeps her guitar next to her bed but stops practicing and taking lessons. Yet, she vows to resume that pursuit as soon as the "job situation gets worked out." That is, even though she does not take active steps toward the goal, she still values it and fully intends to resume its pursuit at a later time. Put simply, frozen goals like Erica's are personally important goals that the person withdraws behavioral effort from while maintaining psychological commitment to. Unlike abandoned goals, the frozen goal is one to which the person is fully committed and intends to resume effort in the future.

Consistent with this point, the work of Daveydenko and colleagues not only showed that the majority of people had frozen goals (92% of the sample) but, in addition, that they regarded those frozen goals as important ones that they remained committed to achieve. For instance, participants rated their frozen goals as significantly higher than the scale midpoint of importance and commitment, thereby further suggesting some level of psychological investment despite the ceasing of behavioral efforts due to obstacles. In our view, such a type of goal would seem likely to follow from a mild or moderate action crisis or, put otherwise, mild to moderate goal doubt. Moreover, whereas the abandoned goal represents the type of goal that would remain permanently lost, frozen goals seem like the perfect candidate for the type of goal that may appear lost but yet is only temporarily suspended and recovered ultimately over time once the proper opportunities arise. There would likely be many factors that might expedite the "unfreezing" process. In this regard, one can draw from our earlier work (Carroll, 2023) to suggest that an incidental induction of meta-cognitive doubt may be sufficient to melt the uncertainty surrounding the frozen goal (double-doubt induction).

Before proceeding, it is important to note that we are not the first to suggest a link between the concepts of action crisis and frozen goals. In their work, Hubley and Scholer (2022) go so far as to suggest a time-dependent relationship between action crisis and frozen goals. Specifically, they suggest that an action crisis may precede or accompany the freezing of goals. We concur and would only add that the severity of the action crisis, or goal doubts, may dictate whether frozen goals are "unfrozen" in a renewal of effort and commitment or, alternatively, permanently abandoned with a complete disengagement of effort and commitment. We anticipate that less severe action crises, or goal doubts, would maintain goal freezing for full reengagement at a later point whereas more severe action crises would discontinue goal freezing and initiate complete disengagement of both commitment and effort. The important point for our purposes is the connection between the level of self-uncertainty in the form of an action crisis and, in turn, goal freezing or complete disengagement. Of course, this is admittedly speculative but still an intriguing possibility worth exploring in future work. We shall revisit this point later.

Summary of Section 1

In this first portion, we have focused on the role of self-uncertainty as a precipitate of revisions in possible identity goals. In the process, we have connected the work on uncertainty-driven revisions in possible selves to work on action crises and other important goal concepts (frozen goals). In the second half of this chapter, we now turn to consider self-uncertainty as an outcome of self-change. This portion of the chapter will consider self-uncertainty as defined by chronic self-doubt or self-concept unclarity.

(Core) Self-Uncertainty Changes from Changes in Possible Selves

Whereas the first portion focused on the role of self-uncertainty as a precipitate of possible self-change, we now turn in this second half of the review to consider changes in self-uncertainty as an outcome of possible self-change. Importantly, in this section, we treat self-concept clarity as one of the primary markers of self-uncertainty along with measured chronic self-doubt. As noted earlier, though, this is justified by the fact that prior work considers clarity an important element of overall self-certainty along with perceived correctness (Petrocelli et al., 2007). With that preliminary point in mind, we return to our proposal that self-uncertainty can arise from as well as initiate revisions in possible selves.

Consistent with this proposal, Slotter et al. (2010) have argued and demonstrated that break-ups may reduce well-being via changes in the content and clarity of one's self-concept. Important for our purposes, though, they claim that break-ups may involve discarding shared possible self-goals (e.g., building a family together) as well as shared values, activities, and social circles. These changes in the size of the self-concept content (due to having to discard shared identities and adopt new ones) can create reductions in self-clarity given that one must re-negotiate their sense of self without the former self-aspects associated with the relationship.

Lewandowski and colleagues (Lewandowski et al., 2006) have also shown that participants who merely imagined a possible future relationship loss, even if they had not yet experienced one, reported losses in their sense of self. As Emery and Gardner (2020) have pointed out, although not exactly self-concept clarity, the measure of loss of self has substantial overlap, including items like "I don't know who I am" (Lewandowski et al., 2006). There are, of course, several moderators of this effect. For example, those who change more of their specific self-concepts after the end of the relationship show higher losses in self-clarity (Emery & Gardner, 2020), *especially* when the change is appraised negatively but not positively (Slotter & Walsh, 2017). Despite these moderating factors, the bulk of the evidence suggests that the discarding of shared possible identity goals in relational changes can create changes in self-concept clarity.

Outside of the domain of interpersonal relationships, recent work suggests that one may experience a self-expanding relationship between their current self and a possible-self career pursuit in the same way that one may experience self-expanding relationships between the self and others (McIntyre et al., 2014). Specifically, the active pursuit of a rewarding career promotes the expansion of core selves into new possible job roles and commitments (e.g., law students pursuing a legal career). Thus, the loss of a self-expanding career would diminish self-clarity partly because one loses the sense of direction afforded by possible self-opportunities promised by the ongoing pursuit of that career.

As predicted, the results showed that the loss of a self-expanding career possibly self produces declines in self-clarity. Moreover, unlike the prior studies that examined the effects of relational loss, these findings directly examine the effect of losing a possible career self on changes in clarity. In addition to the effect of single job losses, researchers have examined the effect of repeated job losses (exits) on self-concept clarity. In a nationally representative sample of adults, they asked participants to report the number of both job role exits as well as job role entries and complete a measure of self-concept clarity. The evidence shows that repeated job losses or role exits further predicted self-clarity declines over a year, controlling for other factors (e.g., role entries) (Light & Visser, 2013).

Beyond the impact of losses in relational or career possible selves, some research has demonstrated that imagining the loss of a possible group identity can influence self-clarity (Slotter et al., 2015). In this work, students first reported the importance of their university (group) identity. Next, researchers randomly assigned participants to a group identity threat or control condition. Whereas participants in the control condition imagined realizing their possible group identity as valued university alums, those in the threat condition imagined losing their possible group identity after graduation. After writing about the anticipated identity realization or loss, all participants completed measures of anticipated self-change upon graduation. Finally, all participants completed the post-self-clarity measures. Consistent with expectations, when highly identified with their group, participants showed diminished self-clarity after exposure to the possible group identity threat (loss) condition. Moreover, the final study demonstrated that anticipated self-change (or possible self-change) mediated the interactive effect of identity importance and threat (loss) on self-concept clarity.

An important point is worth making about these findings and the type of identity presumed to drive these effects. Although interpreted as evidence for the effect of actual group identity loss, the studies actually measured and, thus, demonstrated the unique effect of possible identity loss (valued alumni possible self) on self-clarity. To their credit, the authors acknowledge this under limitations, though they suggest that the effects would only be stronger for actual identity loss. Although we agree that actual identity loss should produce bigger effects, that in no way diminishes the empirical fact that possible identity loss *did* produce changes in self-clarity in this study.

Similarly, Slotter and Gardner (2014) provided further support for the reciprocal pathway from possible self-revision to revisions in core self-clarity in a series of studies focusing on the benefits of social support for helping an individual to reconfirm a threatened aspect of self and recover any losses in self-concept clarity. Of note, this also reveals an important point of the present chapter—that momentary and chronic levels of self-uncertainty overlap in the process of self-change. Compared to pre-med students who received emotional support (reassurance with acceptance after threat), pre-med students who received evidentiary support (direct support for threatened self-knowledge) reported significantly greater confidence in their threatened self-aspect of "becoming a doctor" and, in turn, significantly lower declines in self-clarity. That is, just as drops in possible self-confidence are proposed to be associated with core self-clarity revisions via possible self-revision, so too is the restoration of core selves (in terms of clarity) associated with the restoration of possible self-confidence. Even though it does not refer to possible selves, it is clear that these studies all threatened pre-med (vs. control) students' *possible self* of "becoming a doctor." As such, this work provides further direct evidence for the unique reciprocal effect of changes in possible selves on broader changes in self-clarity.

Given this focus on the responses to possible self-validation (or invalidation), this work has relevance to the work on identity control and verification processes evoked by possible self-disruptions as well as core self-disruptions (Kerpelman & Lamke, 1997; Kerpelman & Pittman, 2001). Although that work suggested that possible and actual identity disruptions evoke the same identity control processes independently, this work is more consistent with the present claim that possible self disruptions evoke distress primarily because they undermine the certainty of the core selves that they derive from (Slotter & Gardner, 2014).

In particular, two findings support the latter claim. First, the failure to resolve threats to important possible selves diminished both specific possible self-confidence and self-concept clarity. Moreover, increases in possible self-confidence mediated the effect of successful threat resolution into increased self-concept clarity. It is worth noting that, like self-confidence, self-concept clarity is a meta-cognitive experience of having a certain and clear sense of self. Moreover, because it is a meta-cognitive experience like self-confidence, one can experience momentary fluctuations in self-concept clarity in response to possible self-changes. Taken together, the work on confidence changes in possible-self revision and this recent work suggests that declines in self-concept clarity may be the first aspect of core identity to change following possible-self revision initiated by the meta-cognitive experience of falling confidence.

Before closing, although several of the foregoing studies demonstrate changes in measures of chronic self-certainty with one experience of possible self-revision, we argue that *repeated* experiences of downward possible-self revisions will evoke stronger patterns of revision in core self-certainty measures. Consistent with this point, recent work from our own lab has shown that greater (numbers of) experiences of downward possible-self revision (or failure) uniquely predicted greater subsequent elevations in self-doubt (Carroll et al., 2011, 2015; see also Carroll, 2018), even after controlling for other transitional experiences (e.g., move).

Summary of Section 2

Whereas the first section focused on how uncertainty initiates revisions in commitment to possible selves, the second section examined how those revisions might contribute to changes or revisions in more chronic forms of self-uncertainty. Whether changes in career, relational, or even group possible identities, the work reviewed here seems to suggest that those changes induced by momentary self-uncertainty can ultimately influence more chronic self-uncertainty in core aspects of identity. Taken together, both sections underscore the importance of self-uncertainty as a consequence and cause of identity change.

Future Work

The present work raises important questions that should be explored in future work. Although not exhaustive, we offer an example of future directions for both the first and second sections, respectively. With respect to the first section, future work should examine the proposed relationship between the severity of action crisis or goal doubts and the likelihood of goal freezing versus abandonment. As noted earlier, the prediction would be that more severe action crisis or goal doubts should be more likely to lead to goal abandonment whereas less severe action crisis or goal doubts should be more likely to lead to goal freezing.

Connecting the first to the second section, future work could compare the effects of frozen versus abandoned goals on chronic self-uncertainty. Given that people do not completely abandon commitment to frozen goals, some work suggests that frozen goals may cause more distress (see Wrosch & colleagues, 2003). Indeed, the recent work by Hubley and Scholer (2022) mentioned earlier showed a negative association between frozen goal rumination and life satisfaction. However, they found no deleterious effect of thought frequency or commitment to frozen goals on measures like life satisfaction. Moreover, this past work did not examine the effect on measures of chronic self-uncertainty, like self-doubt and self-concept unclarity. Given that frozen goals remain an important part of personal identity, it could also be that the long-term effect is that frozen goals will not enhance chronic self-uncertainty as much as abandoned goals from which one has completely withdrawn.

Conclusion

Over the course of this chapter, we discussed how experiences of and changes in self-uncertainty might precipitate downward or upward revisions in commitment to possible selves or personal goals. In the process, we connected the topic of uncertainty-driven revisions in possible selves to several important concepts within the goal literature, including action crises and frozen goals. Second, we turned to explore the reverse pattern, whereby revisions in possible selves might ultimately precipitate revisions or changes in chronic measures of self-uncertainty, including chronic self-doubt and self-clarity. One thing that should be certain as we close this chapter is the importance of self-uncertainty for identity stability as well as change.

References

Brandstätter, V., & Schüler, J. (2013). Action crisis and cost–benefit thinking: A cognitive analysis of a goal-disengagement phase. *Journal of Experimental Social Psychology, 49*(3), 543–553.Briñol, P., & Petty, R. E. (2022). Self-validation theory: An integrative framework for understanding when thoughts become consequential. *Psychological Review, 129*(2), 340–367.

Briñol, P., & Petty, R. E. (2003). Overt head movements and persuasion: A self-validation analysis. *Journal of Personality and Social Psychology, 84*, 1123–1139.

Carroll, P. J. (2014). Upward self-revision: Constructing possible selves. *Basic and Applied Social Psychology, 36*, 377–385.

Carroll, P. J. (2018). The reciprocal path from possible self to core self-revision. *The Review of General Psychology, 22*(3), 264–277.

Carroll, P. J. (2023). *Examining the pathway from goal crisis to conviction*. Unpublished Manuscript, The Ohio State University-Lima.

Carroll, P. J., Agler, R., & Newhart, D. (2015). From cause to consequence: The road from possible self to core self-revision. *Self & Identity, 14*(4), 482–498.

Carroll, P. J., Arkin, R. M., & Oleson, K. C. (2010). Introduction. In R. M. Arkin, K.C. Oleson, & P. J. Carroll (Eds.) *Handbook of the Uncertain Self.* New York: Taylor and Francis.

Carroll, P. J., McCaslin, M., & Norman, G. (2011). The revision and expansion of self-theory through preparedness. *Social and Personality Psychology Compass, 10*, 1–15.

Carroll, P. J., Shepperd, J. A., & Arkin, R. M. (2009). Downward self-revision: Erasing possible selves. *Social Cognition, 27*, 550–578.

Chang-Schneider, C., & Swann, W. B., Jr. (2010). The role of uncertainty in self-evaluative processes: Another look at the cognitive-affective crossfire. In R. M. Arkin, K. C. Oleson, & P. J. Carroll (Eds.), *Handbook of the uncertain self* (pp. 216–231). Psychology Press. Davydenko, M., Werner, K. M., & Milyavskaya, M. (2019). Frozen goals: Identifying and defining a new type of goal. *Collabra Psychology, 5*(1), 17.

Dunlop, W. L., Guo, J., & McAdams, D. (2016). The autobiographical author through time examining the degree of stability and change in redemptive and contaminated personal narratives. *Journal of Social Psychological and Personality Science, 7*(5), 428–436.

Emery, L. F., & Gardner, W. L. (2020). Who in the world am I? Self-concept clarity and self-change in relationships. In B. Mattingly, K. McIntyre, & G. Lewandowski, Jr. (Eds.), *Interpersonal relationships and the self-concept* (pp. 89–104). Springer.

Fivush, R., & Nelson, C. (2006). Parent–child reminiscing locates the self in the past. *British Journal of Developmental Psychology, 24*, 235–251.

Ghassemi, M., Wolf, B. M., Bettschart, M., Kreibich, A., Herrmann, M., & Brandstätter, V. (2020). The dynamics of doubt: Short-term fluctuations and predictors of doubts in personal goal pursuit. *Motivation Science, 7*(2), 153–164.

Gollwitzer, P. M. (2012). Mindset theory of action phases. In P. A. M. Van Lange, A. W. Kruglanski, & E. T. Higgins (Eds.), *Handbook of theories of social psychology* (pp. 526–545). London: Sage Publications Ltd.

Herrmann, M., & Brandstätter, V. (2015). Action crises and goal disengagement: Longitudinal evidence on the predictive validity of a motivational phase in goal striving. *Motivation Science, 1*(2), 121–136.

Hubley, C., & Scholer, A. A. (2022). Melting COVID-frozen goals: How goal disengagement supports well-being during the COVID-19 pandemic. *Motivation and Emotion, 46*(6), 752–768.

Kerpelman, J. L., & Lamke, L. K. (1997). Anticipation of future identities: A control theory approach to identity development within the context of serious dating relationships. *Personal Relationships, 4*, 47–62.

Kerpelman, J. L., & Pittman, J. F. (2001). The instability of possible selves: Identity processes within late adolescents' close peer relationships. *Journal of Adolescence, 24*, 491–512.

Kidder, C. K., White, K. R., Hinojos, M. R., Sandoval, M., & Crites, S. L. (2018). Sequential stereotype priming: A meta-analysis. *Personality and Social Psychology Review, 22*, 199–227. DOI: 10.1177/1088868317723532

Lewandowski, G., Aron, A., Bassis, S., & Kunak, J. (2006). Losing a self-expanding relationship: Implications for the self-concept. *Personal Relationships, 13*(3), 317–331.

Landau, M. J., Greenberg, J., & Sullivan, D. (2009). Defending a coherent autobiography: When past events appear incoherent, mortality salience prompts compensatory bolstering of the past's significance and the future's orderliness. *Personality and Social Psychology Bulletin, 35*, 1012–1020.

Landau, M. J., Oyserman, D., Keefer, L. A., & Smith, G. C. (2014). The college journey and academic engagement: how metaphor use enhances identity-based motivation. *Journal of Personality and Social Psychology, 106*(5), 679–698.

Light, A. E., & Visser, P. S. (2013). The ins and outs of the self: Contrasting role exits and role entries as predictors of self-concept clarity. *Self and Identity, 12*(3), 291–306.

McAdams, D. P. (1996). Narrating the self in adulthood. In J. Birren, G. Kenyon, J. E. Ruth, J. J. F. Shroots, & J. Svendson (Eds.), *Aging and biography: Explorations in adult development* (pp. 131–148). New York: Springer.

McIntyre, K. P., Mattingly, B. A., Lewandowski, G. W., & Simpson, A. (2014). Workplace self-expansion: Implications for job satisfaction, commitment, self-concept clarity, and self-esteem among the employed and unemployed. *Basic and Applied Social Psychology, 36*, 59–69.

Nelson, C., & Fivush, R. (2004). The emergence of autobiographical memory: A social cultural developmental theory. *Psychological Review, 111*(2), 486–511.

Peetz, J., & Wilson, A. E. (2008). The temporally extended self: The relation of past and future selves to current identity, motivation, and goal pursuit. *Social and Personality Psychology Compass, 2*, 2090–2106.
Petrocelli, J. V., Tormala, Z. L., & Rucker, D. D. (2007). Unpacking attitude certainty: Attitude clarity and attitude correctness. *Journal of Personality and Social Psychology, 92*(1), 30–41.
Slotter, E. B., Gardner, W. L., & Finkel, E. J. (2010). Who am I without you? The influence of romantic breakup on the self-concept. *Personality and Social Psychology Bulletin, 36*, 147–160.
Slotter, E., & Gardner, W. (2014). Remind me of Who I am: Social interaction strategies for maintaining the threatened self-concept. *Personality and Social Psychology Bulletin, 40*(9), 1148–1161.
Slotter, E. B., & Walsh, C. M. (2017). All role transitions are not experienced equally: Associations among self-change, emotional reactions, and self-concept clarity. *Self and Identity, 16*(5), 531–556.
Slotter, E. B., Winger, L., & Soto, N. (2015). Lost without each other: The influence of group identity loss on the self-concept. *Group Dynamics: Theory, Research, & Practice, 19*(1), 15–30.
Lind, E. A., & Van den Bos, K. (2010). The social psychology of fairness and the regulation of personal uncertainty. In R. M. Arkin, K. C. Oleson, & P. J. Carroll (Eds.), *Handbook of the Uncertain Self* (pp. 122–141). New York: Psychology Press.
Wichman, A. L., Briñol, P., Petty, R. E., Rucker, D. D., Tormala, Z. L., & Weary, G. (2010). Doubting one's doubt: A formula for confidence. *Journal of Experimental Social Psychology, 46*, 350–355.
Wilson, A. O., Gunn, G. R., & Ross, M. (2009). The role of subjective time in identity regulation. *Applied Cognitive Psychology, 23*(8), 1164–1178.
Wrosch, C., Scheier, M. F., Miller, G. E., Schulz, R., & Carver, C. S. (2003). Adaptive self-regulation of unattainable goals: Goal disengagement, goal reengagement, and subjective well-being. *Personality and Social Psychology Bulletin, 29*, 1494–1508.

7

THE SOCIAL PSYCHOLOGY OF FAIRNESS AND THE REGULATION OF PERSONAL UNCERTAINTY

Implications for Understanding the Role of Trust in Society

Kees van den Bos and E. Allan Lind

The Social Psychology of Fairness and the Regulation of Personal Uncertainty

Implications for Understanding the Role of Trust in Society

This chapter focuses on the relationship between the uncertain self and how people respond to fair and unfair events. In this chapter, we argue for two general messages.

First, we propose that experienced fairness may have some special qualities that cause fairness judgments to have an especially strong impact on people's reactions when they are uncertain about themselves or even when they have only been reminded briefly about their personal uncertainties. We will base our review of these issues on our 2009 treatment of these issues (Van den Bos & Lind, 2009), which appeared in the first edition of the current *Handbook on the Uncertain Self* (Arkin et al., 2009). Our review will suggest that fairness judgments function as a crucial tool with which people manage uncertainty about themselves, the world around them, and the interrelation between the two. The importance of fairness judgments arises, we think, because fair and unfair events are experiences that occur at the social interface where the individual meets the collective. For example, how fairly or unfairly an individual is treated often communicates important information about how groups regard the individual (Lind & Tyler, 1988). This quintessentially social quality of fairness judgments makes the experience of fair treatment especially well-suited for people to rely upon as they seek to manage personal uncertainty.

Second, in this revised version of our 2009 chapter, we will zoom into insights into the important role of trust in society. This part of our review will focus on the relationship between uncertainty and trust. This part of our chapter will rely on recent treatments on these issues, related to radicalization into violent extremism (Van den Bos, 2018), distrust in social institutions (Van den Bos, 2023), and polarization in society (Van den Bos, 2024). The reader is directed to those publications for more insights and more details about these societally important and scientifically

 DOI: 10.4324/9781003363385-8

intriguing issues that entail many different components interesting for both psychologists and other scientists and practitioners.

From Informational Uncertainty to Personal Uncertainty

There are many different types of uncertainties that people can encounter (Van den Bos & Lind, 2002). We would like to focus on two important varieties here. One noteworthy type of uncertainty that people often face when forming social judgments is informational uncertainty, which involves having less information available than one ideally would like to have to confidently form a given social judgment. For example, the work by Nobel laureates Kahneman and Phelps notes that human judgments are often formed under conditions of incomplete information and that these conditions can lead to predictable effects on human decision and social judgment processes (e.g., Kahneman et al., 1982; Phelps, 1970). Thus, when studying how people make social judgments, including how they make fairness judgments, a pivotal issue is what information people have available.

In the social psychological study of how people form fairness judgments, we also have found that information uncertainty can have a substantial impact on the formation of fairness judgments and that this finding provides important social psychological insights into such issues as affect and cognition (e.g., Van den Bos, 2003), social and organizational theories pertaining to authority's trustworthiness (e.g., Van den Bos et al., 1998), fairness theories such as equity theory (e.g., Van den Bos et al., 1997; Van den Bos et al., 1998), and fairness phenomena such as how people react to the absence of opportunities to voice their opinions (e.g., Van den Bos, 1999). Informational uncertainty plays a pivotal role in the fairness judgment process and involves many issues, including interesting consequences of incomplete information about *both* outcome justice (e.g., Van den Bos et al., 1997; Van den Bos, 2003) *and* procedural justice issues (e.g., Van den Bos, 1999, 2003). Thus, our uncertainty management model is not a model that focuses on either outcome or procedural justice issues, but rather is a model that focuses on both aspects simultaneously.

While investigating the importance of informational uncertainty we have come across another type of uncertainty, personal uncertainty, that we now think is even more important to the social psychology of fairness. There are different versions of personal uncertainty and related concepts in the literature (see, e.g., Marigold et al., 2009; McGregor et al., 2001; Sedikides, De Cremer et al., 2009), but we define personal or self-uncertainty as a subjective sense of doubt or instability in self-views, world-views, or the interrelation between the two. Furthermore, personal uncertainty, as we conceive of it, involves the implicit and explicit feelings and other subjective reactions people experience as a result of being uncertain about themselves (Van den Bos, 2001, 2007; Van den Bos et al., 2005). It entails both stable individual differences, such as differences in emotional uncertainty (Greco & Roger, 2001; Sedikides et al., 2009), and situational fluctuations, such as conditions in which people's personal uncertainties have (versus have not) been made salient (Van den Bos, 2001). Furthermore, we assume that experiencing personal uncertainty is a hot-cognitive social psychological process (Abelson, 1963), involving a combination of both cognitive and affective reactions (Van den Bos, 2007). We also think that personal uncertainty more often than not involves visceral and intuitive (instead of more reasoned and rationalistic) reactions. Experiencing personal uncertainty about one's attitudes, beliefs, feelings, and perceptions, as well as about one's relationship to other people, is generally aversive (e.g., Hogg, 2007; Marigold et al., 2009; Sedikides et al., 2009; Sorrentino & Roney, 1986), and personal uncertainty therefore often motivates behavior that seeks to reduce it. Although experiencing personal uncertainty may sometimes be sought out and occasionally may instigate contemplation or introspection (e.g., McGregor & Marigold, 2003; Sorrentino et al., 1988; Weary & Jacobson, 1997), we argue that it is more common for people to find experiencing personal uncertainty an alarming event that does not allow for contemplation and introspection, but requires people to respond rather quickly to what is going on (Van den Bos et al., 2008).

The study of personal uncertainty is of special relevance to social psychologists interested in processes related to uncertainty management and self-regulation. In the current chapter, we will focus, therefore, on the psychological effects of personal uncertainty and the relevance this may have for the social psychology of both the uncertain self and fairness judgments. The next two sections of this chapter will include a discussion of the prevailing methodology and strategy of our research program.

Salience of Personal Uncertainty and Reactions toward Fair and Unfair Events

A substantial and growing body of research shows that people react more vigilantly to their being treated in fair or unfair ways when they are coping with personal uncertainty. In our opinion, this line of research may well be related to vigilance being the result of activation of the behavioral inhibition system. Marigold et al. (2009) argue that activation of the behavioral inhibition system (Gray & McNaughton, 2000) is essentially a state of aroused uncertainty; a state in which people and other animals remain in an inhibited approach orientation, with aroused attention vigilantly focused for awareness of threat cues or "tenable alternative goals."

One of the first studies on uncertainty and fairness was a series of experiments one of us published in 2001. In these experiments (Van den Bos, 2001), half of the participants were asked to think about, and write a description of, the emotional experiences they feel when they encounter uncertainty in their personal lives. The other half of the participants thought about and wrote about the emotional experiences involved in their watching television, an issue which does not salientize personal uncertainty among the population of university students where we conducted our studies. In a later, ostensibly unrelated study, the same participants were exposed to standard procedural fairness manipulations: In some of the experiments this involved participants, after completing a task in which they worked with another person, either being or not being allowed to voice their views about how much they should be paid relative to the other participant. In another experiment, participants were informed that in a selection process in which they took part either all (accurate procedure) or only some (inaccurate procedure) of their test items would be taken into account. These voice and accuracy manipulations are common procedural fairness manipulations, reliably leading those who do not receive voice or who experience inaccurate procedures to feel they have been unfairly treated and those who receive voice or are accurately treated to feel they have been fairly treated.

The principal dependent variable in the Van den Bos (2001) experiments was the participants' ratings of positive or negative affect toward the way they were treated. The results support our uncertainty salience hypothesis: When personal uncertainty had been made salient, the fair procedures resulted in more positive and less negative affects whereas the unfair procedures yielded more negative and less positive affect than was the case when uncertainty had not been made salient. In other words, when personal uncertainty was salient, the fair process effect (Van den Bos, 2005) on participants' affective treatment ratings was magnified. Subsequent research revealed that similar moderating effects of salience of personal uncertainty can also be found in other reactions to events that violate or bolster people's cultural norms and values, including behavioral reactions (Van den Bos et al., 2007), reactions to religious issues (Van den Bos et al., 2006), and other world-view defense reactions (Van den Bos et al., 2005). We believe that this suggests that reactions to fair and unfair treatment are part of general world-view defense reactions (Van den Bos, 2004; Van den Bos & Miedema, 2000; Van den Bos et al., 2005) and that these effects indicate the robustness of the influence of personal uncertainty concerns on human reactions.

To the best of our knowledge, no prior uncertainty studies had shown such sensitive effects: in the studies described here using only two short questions to salientize people's personal uncertainty concerns yielded strong and reliable effects on how people react to fair and unfair treatment (Van den Bos, 2001) or on how they respond to other experiences that violate or bolster their cultural norms and values (Van den Bos et al., 2005). That people show such strong sensitivity to even modest uncertainty salience manipulations seems to us to indicate the social psychological significance of personal uncertainty in general and our manipulation of personal uncertainty salience in particular.

These are also noteworthy findings for the fairness literature. While there are other factors that seem to enhance or diminish the impact of procedural fairness manipulations, the greater part of the existing fairness literature has tended to focus on factors concerned with the workings of the voice or accuracy processes themselves or on factors relating more generally to the psychological dynamics of fairness judgments. For example, research has shown that the voiced information has to be perceived to be considered by those in positions of authority in order to be effective or appropriate (Van den Bos & Spruijt, 2002). Other studies have shown that procedural fairness effects are stronger in the presence of negative outcomes (Brockner & Wiesenfeld, 1996). But few fairness researchers would have expected that merely asking people to complete two simple questions that in a rather subtle way make personal uncertainty a salient concern would reliably amplify the effects of fairness manipulations. Other fairness studies have found similar effects not just for the salience of personal uncertainty, but also for real experienced personal uncertainty (Maas & Van den Bos, 2011) and for stable differences in uncertainty orientation (Hofstede, 2001) in the context of important real-world situations or in organizational contexts (see, e.g., Elovainio et al., 2005; Kausto et al., 2005; Patterson et al., 2006; See, 2009; Thau et al., 2007). The implication seems to be that there is something about personal uncertainty that makes people to react more strongly and more vigorously toward fair and unfair events.

An interesting implication of the role of uncertainty in the social psychology of fairness judgments is that, upon re-examination, many of the factors that had been found, over the course of three decades of research, to moderate fairness effects are things that appear to be linked to uncertainty. Consider, for example, the moderating effects of positive or negative outcomes on procedural fairness judgments, described by Brockner and Wiesenfeld (1996). The pattern observed by Brockner and Wiesenfeld is that fairness effects are stronger in the presence of negative outcomes. Because under most circumstances negative outcomes are more likely than positive outcomes to induce feelings of self-related uncertainty, the outcome-based moderation may in fact be a special case of the more general moderation of fairness effects by uncertainty. That is, it may be that it is especially when negative outcomes salientize feelings of personal uncertainty that the procedure x outcome interaction reported by Brockner and Wiesenfeld (1996) is found. If this is the case, it would explain why some studies have not observed significant procedure x outcome interaction effects (Thibaut & Walker, 1975): When negative outcomes or procedures do not trigger greater feelings of personal uncertainty, no or only weak procedure x outcome interactions are to be expected.

Uncertainty and Trust

We propose that many of the issues regarding uncertainty and perceived fairness have to do with the issue of whether you can trust others, especially those with power, not to exclude us from important relationships or exploit us (Lind, 1995; Van den Bos, 2023). Trust is a complex issue. It has been defined in many ways, building on various conceptual perspectives. In this chapter, we rely on earlier treatments of this issue (see Van den Bos, 2011, 2023) and define trust as the conviction that others are well-intentioned towards us, will consider our interests if possible, and will not harm us intentionally if they can avoid doing so (Sztompka, 1999; see also Colquitt et al., 2007).

Contrary to what is assumed in the literature on trust and trustworthiness (Brewer, 2008; Damasio, 2005; Giffin, 1967; Güth et al., 1997; Kramer, 2001), people often lack the information they need to decide whether others (including those who hold powerful positions in our environments) can be trusted and regarded as reliable interaction partners (Van den Bos & Miedema, 2000; Van den Bos et al., 1998). It is indeed often difficult to determine whether you really can trust another party. You need for example a lot of experience with the other party before you can reach such a decision with certainty, and in general, we do not have such information. Under such circumstances, when you have less information than you would like to have about the other party's trustworthiness, you will have to make do with the information you do have at your disposition. This often concerns fairness: people can often form a good impression of how fairly they are being treated based on relatively little information (Lind, 1995). The impressions gained from some encounters are often enough to allow people to decide whether they are being treated fairly and in a just manner by the other person.

People thus often use information about how fairly or unfairly they are treated by another person as a proxy for the lack of information on the level of trust they can have in that person (Van den Bos, 2023; Van den Bos et al., 1998). If the person behaves fairly, this is viewed as an important indication that the person can be trusted. And if the person acts in clearly unfair ways, then important doubts about the legitimacy and trustworthiness of the person arise. Perceived fairness is thus important because it gives people information about the extent to which they can trust other persons, including representatives of government, law, science, and other social institutions (Van den Bos, 2023; Van den Bos et al., 2002).

As mentioned earlier, besides informational uncertainty, personal uncertainty is one of the other main reasons why fairness is important to people (Van den Bos & Lind, 2002, 2009, 2011). People often feel uncertain and insecure in their dealings with other persons, for example, because these persons can exert power or influence over them (Tyler & Huo, 2002) and may even exploit them or cut off social links that are important to them, excluding them from society as a whole or important groups within society (Tyler & DeGoey, 1996). Furthermore, people in modern society often have experiences that make them feel unsure of themselves. This feeling of personal uncertainty is experienced by people as unpleasant (Hogg, 2007), often as very unpleasant (Van den Bos & Lind, 2002, 2009). In fact, personal uncertainty is often seen as an alarm signal ("What's going on here?", "I'll have to watch out in this situation: it doesn't feel good," Van den Bos, Ham, Lind, Simonis, Van Essen & Rijpkema, 2008). In short, most people regard personal uncertainty as unpleasant and try to cope with it in some way. A possible coping mechanism is to explore the extent to which one forms part of one's social environment and the society in which one lives, in other words, to explore the extent of one's social integration (Hogg & Gaffney, 2023; Hogg et al., 2007). This makes it important for people to feel that they are accepted and respected by important people or groupings in their environment or in wider society. A key indicator of this acceptance and respect is being fairly and decently treated by important people in society or important individuals in the group to which one belongs (Lind & Tyler, 1988; Lind & Van den Bos, 2002; see also See, 2009; Thau et al., 2007; Thau et al., 2009). In this way, perceived fairness can help people to cope with personal uncertainty. It may even turn uncertainty from a threat into an agreeable challenge

(Van den Bos & Lind, 2009), perhaps because people associate fair treatment with positive affect (Van den Bos, 2007, 2009, 2011).

Managing Personal Uncertainty by Means of Fairness Judgments

When discussing uncertainty management by means of fairness judgments, two things are important to note here. The first is that although the findings discussed thus far are intriguing and corroborate to a large extent our earlier uncertainty management predictions (Lind & Van den Bos, 2002; Van den Bos & Lind, 2002), we do not now believe that these findings imply that fairness *in general* matters more to people when they are uncertain about themselves or have been reminded about their personal uncertainties. That is, an issue that, in retrospect, we should have emphasized more in our earlier writing is that most of the empirical findings that have been reported thus far suggest that people who are busy with personal uncertainty concerns respond with stronger reactions toward how fairly they themselves have been treated. But these stronger responses to fair or unfair events do not really show that "fairness matters more" in a general way; rather they show that "one's own personal fairness matters more." Specifically, these findings indicate that under conditions of personal uncertainty people react more positively toward *their own* fair treatment and more negatively toward *their own* unfair treatment. This suggests that under conditions of personal uncertainty, *personal* treatment, and *personal* fairness matter more when trying to explain people's reactions. Thus there is nothing in these findings that necessarily implies that the fairness of how other people are treated becomes a more important issue for people when they are confronted with personal uncertainty (see also Loseman et al., 2009). Research is needed to determine when or whether reactions to the fair treatment of others are stronger under uncertain conditions. Furthermore, in exploring this issue, it will be important to examine the potential for different psychological effects for different types of uncertainties (such as personal uncertainty, e.g., Van den Bos, 2001; group-related uncertainty, e.g., Hogg, 2007; and global uncertainty, e.g., Giroux, 2006) on how people react to different types of injustices (such as personal injustice, e.g., Van den Bos, 2001; group-related injustice, e.g., Runciman, 1966; and global injustice, e.g., Hertz, 2001).

The second thing that we think is important to note here pertains to the influence of fair events on the management of uncertainty concerns. The findings reviewed here may have important implications for the issue of why personal fairness matters to people: It may be the case that fair situations are sought out because the experience of fair treatment or fair events provide protection against things that people are uncertain about or because it makes uncertainty more tolerable. In other words, fairness may be important for people because they use fairness judgments in processes of regulating uncertainty. There is indeed some evidence that suggests that experiencing fair events positively influences perceived uncertainty.

Van den Bos et al. (2006) examined how employees cope with job-related uncertainty caused by reorganizations and whether perceptions of outcome fairness play a helpful role in these uncertainty management processes. The authors present findings of a survey study in which the respondents were employees at a chemical business company in the Netherlands who had survived a substantial reorganization process in which the majority of the company's employees had been laid off. As expected on the basis of uncertainty management hypotheses, the experience that the outcomes of the reorganization process were fair made people feel less uncertain about their current jobs. This suggests that after reorganizations outcome fairness can have ameliorative effects on job uncertainty, and these findings in turn provide some evidence for the uncertainty management model's claim that people may use fairness judgments to cope with the uncertainty resulting from reorganizations.

That said, it should be noted that not a lot of research findings have been reported on the actual *management* of uncertainty concerns. This may have to do with issues such as the difficulty of measuring state uncertainty, with people not having very good insight into whether they are indeed experiencing personal uncertainty, with people being reluctant to confess that they are uncertain about themselves, or people not wanting to think deeply about personal things that make them feel uncertain about important aspects of themselves. Whatever factors have constrained research to date, though, future research on these issues clearly is warranted.

Even if the direct measurement of uncertainty is difficult, however, the management of personal uncertainty concerns may be reflected in other dependent variables, such as measures of how well respondents in uncertain situations sleep. In fact, recently there have been some interesting papers published that show that experiencing fair treatment during uncertain times (such as times of organizational turmoil or reorganizations) can lead people to sleep better (Greenberg, 2006). Future studies on the management and regulation of uncertainty concerns might do well to incorporate these kinds of dependent measures in order to assess uncertainty management processes more reliably.

On the Social Psychology of Uncertainty Management

As mentioned above, we think that a particularly fruitful avenue for future research would be to focus on the social psychological antecedents and processes that drive the effects of personal uncertainty reported in the research literature. We will briefly discuss here two recent attempts to do this.

Affective-Experiential Processes

Marjolein Maas developed one very interesting line of work that was inspired by the uncertainty findings we have reported here. A core assumption that drove a series of studies by Maas and Van den Bos (2009) was the idea that personal uncertainty often leads people to react more strongly toward fair and unfair events because being uncertain or being reminded about things one is uncertain about often instigates strong affective-experiential processes. Thus, in terms of cognitive-experiential self-theory (Epstein & Pacini, 1999), the idea was that experiencing feelings of uncertainty would lead people to start processing the information they subsequently receive in experiential-intuitive ways.

Cognitive-experiential self-theory distinguishes between two conceptual systems that people use to process information, namely the experiential-intuitive and the rational-cognitive systems (Epstein & Pacini, 1999). The experiential way of processing information is intuitive, preconsciously encoding information into concrete images or metaphors, and making associative connections. In experiential modes, events are experienced passively, and people can be seized by their emotions. The rationalistic way of processing information, on the other hand, is analytic, encoding information in abstract ways, based on making logical cause-and-effect connections and requiring intentional, effortful processing. In rationalistic modes of information processing, people experience events actively and consciously while thinking things over and making justifications for what happened in these events, and in these modes, people are in control of their thoughts.

Cognitive-experiential self-theory also assumes that the operation of experiential mindsets is intimately associated with affect-related experiences (see, e.g., Epstein & Pacini, 1999). If experiential mindsets do indeed make people's fairness reactions more susceptible to affect-related processes, then the intensity with which people react affectively to daily life events (Larsen et al., 1987) should interact with people's mindsets. Earlier fairness studies had shown that individual differences in affect intensity can moderate people's fairness reactions (Van den Bos et al., 2003). Integrating this line of work with cognitive-experiential self-theory, Maas and Van den Bos (2009) predicted that under conditions of uncertainty, individual differences in affect intensity (Larsen et al., 1987) would moderate people's fairness reactions, especially when they have been primed with experiential (as opposed to rationalistic) modes of information processing.

Introducing a new manipulation of experiential versus rationalistic mindsets to the research literature, the findings of the Maas and Van den Bos (2009) studies indeed showed that, in uncertain conditions, people who had been primed with experiential mindsets and who score high on the affect intensity scale react more strongly to fair and unfair events (compared to those who have been brought in rationalistic mindsets and/or who score low on affect intensity). These findings suggest that focusing on the combination of affective and experiential processes is important for the social psychology of uncertainty effects reported in the literature.

The Human Alarm System

Another line of research that was inspired by the uncertainty effects reported in the literature, and that may well be related to the affective-experiential work of Maas and Van den Bos (2009), argues that the uncertainty effects described here occur because experiencing feelings of personal uncertainty constitutes an alarming experience (Van den Bos, Ham et al., 2008). Specifically, in this line of research we examined a possible connection between, on the one hand, the augmentation of fairness effects in the presence of personal uncertainty (e.g., Van den Bos, 2001; Van den Bos et al., 2005) and other self-threatening conditions (Miedema et al., 2006) and, on the other hand, related phenomena in social cognition and social neuroscience showing the possible existence of a "human alarm system" (Eisenberger et al., 2003).

As noted earlier, it is now well-established in the fairness literature that personal uncertainty (Van den Bos, 2001; Van den Bos et al., 2005) and other self-threats (Miedema et al., 2006) lead to more extreme reactions to fair and unfair events. Interestingly, in the literatures on close relationships and on social neuroscience, it has been suggested that personal uncertainty and self-threats lead to the activation of the "human alarm system," a psychological system that people use to detect and handle alarming situations and that prompts people to process more alertly what is going on in the situations in which they find themselves. For example, Murray et al. (2005) suggested that personal uncertainty and felt insecurity in close relationships activate the human alarm system with the result that people process more alertly what is happening in their relationships.

Along similar lines, Eisenberger et al. (2003) have argued that being ostracized or experiencing other self-threatening events activates parts of the human brain which Eisenberger et al. have labeled the "human alarm system." The alarm system is responsible for detecting cues that might be harmful to survival and, after activation, for recruiting attention and coping responses to minimize threats. Eisenberger et al. (2003) have argued that experiencing social exclusion or other self-threatening events may be an experience of social pain. Like physical pain, the experience of social pain may trigger the human alarm system, "alerting us when we have sustained injury to our social connections" (Eisenberger et al., 2003, p. 292). From an evolutionary perspective, the working of such an alarm system would be adaptive: An activated alarm system prompts the human organism to act and respond more quickly or otherwise more alertly to what is going on in the organism's environment; this in turn makes the survival of the organism more likely.

One way to triangulate the relationships linking personal uncertainty, the human alarm system, and the fairness literature is to conceptualize an overlap between the alarm system and the fairness judgment process. An intriguing, indeed we think potentially a very exciting, hypothesis that can be derived from such a postulated overlap is that factors that people associate with alarming conditions would be expected to enhance the sensitivity of the alarm system and thus, given the postulated overlap, potentiate sensitivity to the fairness-related events people subsequently experience. So, just as Eisenberger and Lieberman (2004) postulated that the brain bases of social pain are similar to those of physical pain and hypothesized that "factors that enhance the sensitivity to one type of pain should enhance the sensitivity of this alarm system and thus potentiate sensitivity to the other type of pain as well" (p. 297). We postulated that presenting alarm-related symbols to people would activate the human alarm system and hence potentiate sensitivity to other types of processes associated with it as well, including enhanced sensitivity to the fairness judgment process. This would be expected to make people react more sensitively to subsequently experienced fair or unfair events.

More specifically, the literature reviewed in this section suggests two conclusions in line with this analysis: (1) personal uncertainty and other self-threatening conditions activate the human alarm system (Eisenberger et al., 2003; Murray et al., 2005); (2) personal uncertainty and self-threatening conditions lead to more extreme judgments about procedural and outcome justice (Miedema et al., 2006; Van den Bos 2001; Van den Bos et al., 2005). Thus, we now know that the same conditions that are thought to activate the human alarm system, might also lead to more extreme fairness and justice judgments. Given this observation, we proposed that activating the human alarm system directly, by presenting alarm-related stimuli to people, would lead to more extreme reactions toward fair and unfair events.

Thus, an intriguing hypothesis that follows from the alarm-system perspective is that the presentation of cues that are closely, even subtly, related to alarming conditions might lead people to form more extreme judgments about subsequently presented fair and unfair events. Findings of various experiments (scenario studies, an experiential experiment, and fMRI testing) in fact provided evidence for this line of reasoning. Specifically, we found that viewing large exclamation points prior to making evaluations of the justice of accurate or inaccurate procedures, good or bad outcomes, and voice or no-voice procedures indeed made people react more extremely to the procedures or outcomes. Another experimental study replicated and extended these findings by showing that a flashing warning light produced similar effects on outcome justice judgments among participants with varied educational backgrounds and from different age groups who were walking in a shopping center in a typical Dutch city (Van den Bos, Ham et al., 2008). In accord with the alarm-system view of the justice judgment process, the findings reveal that the mere presence of an illuminated flashing light leads people to show more extreme justice judgments in response to variations in good and bad outcomes.

The studies reported in the Van den Bos, Ham, et al. (2008) paper were in part inspired by the conjecture that the uncertainty management findings reported in the fairness literature (see, e.g., Van den Bos, 2001; Van den Bos & Lind, 2002; Van den Bos et al., 2005) might be explained by the notion that experiences of personal uncertainty often constitute alarming events to people and that it is this alarm-related component of uncertainty manipulations that is driving some or perhaps all of the uncertainty effects reported in the social psychological literature. Especially interesting in this respect are some findings from functional magnetic resonance imaging (fMRI) testing (Van den Bos & Rijpkema, 2007). This study showed that watching an exclamation point leads to a brain activation pattern that shares areas (medial frontal gyrus, Brodmann area [BA] 9) with the brain regions that have been found to be active in personal moral judgment tasks. These brain areas are known to be sensitive to tapping the combined effects of cognitive and emotional responses (Greene et al., 2001). This might indicate that a combination of cognition and emotion best explains how people will form fairness and justice judgments (cf. Van den Bos et al., 2008) and make personal moral decisions (cf. Greene et al., 2001). In other words, the social psychology of personal uncertainty and fairness judgments may well involve hot cognitive, not cold cognitive, processes (Van den Bos, 2007).

Future research might do well to pursue and test the implications of this line of thinking. One thing we proposed is a close connection between personal uncertainty, relational insecurity, fairness, and the human alarm system. Clearly more conceptual development and future research are needed to sort out how these different concepts are related to each other. For example, we see the concepts of personal uncertainty and relational insecurity as potentially sharing many important elements with each other, and we would encourage more research on how the personal uncertainty of partners involved in close relationships affect the partners' interpretations and appraisals of those relationships, especially with respect to fairness. As we see it, elements of the risk regulation system by Murray et al. (2006) are in many ways similar to those of the human alarm system, but empirical findings are needed to sort out whether the risk regulation model (Murray et al., 2006) and uncertainty management models (e.g., Hogg, 2007; Marigold et al., 2009; Sedikides et al., 2009; Van den Bos & Lind, 2002) are wholly consistent with the human alarm system perspective.

Conclusions

In closing, we want to make some final remarks about the issues we discussed in this chapter. One of the things that we tried to show here is that, because of its social quality (Lind & Tyler, 1988), the study of fairness has much to contribute to core issues in social psychology, because the focus in fairness works on the self-collective interface may help to keep social psychology really *social* psychology. In particular, the social psychology of fairness judgments may well provide some new insights with respect to more mainstream social psychological theories and processes (e.g., Van den Bos et al., 2005). In addition, we proposed that fairness research should focus more on process-oriented research, broadening its attention to other relevant social psychological processes. In this chapter, we have highlighted several social psychological processes that we think may help to advance theory and research on the social psychology of fairness judgments. These include processes studied in research on worldview defense, self-regulation, experiential mindsets, the human alarm system, groups and group entativity, processes pertaining to affect intensity, and the relationship between affect and social cognition. We encourage future research to study these processes in greater depth and detail. There are other potentially relevant processes that we have not mentioned, but that certainly might bear on how people form and use fairness judgments: processes such as those studied in the literatures on system justification (e.g., Jost & Hunyady, 2002) and cognitive fluency (e.g., Winkielman et al., 2003). Work along these lines would help develop a better social *psychology* of fairness judgments.

We should note here that there often seems to be confusion in the fairness literature between fairness models that focus on self-regulatory psychological processes in order to understand the fairness judgment process and more egoistic, "instrumental" accounts of why fairness matters to people. One of the reasons for the confusion, we believe, is that there are variations in how broadly or narrowly one defines the term "instrumentality." If one defines instrumental accounts narrowly, as being oriented toward attaining better material or economic outcomes, there is a substantial problem in applying the label "instrumental," because—with the exception of some radical descriptions such as the version of equity theory as formulated by Walster et al. (1978), which states that people care primarily about maximizing their material outcomes—most justice theories would eschew such a narrow conception.

If one adopts a broader version of instrumentality, with the term "instrumental" referring to something (e.g., justice) being not regarded as an end in itself, but rather as a means towards the achievement of another end, independent of what that end is, and independent of whether the end is of material or symbolic nature (Mikula, 2005), then the problem becomes that the term is so broad that it runs the big risk of becoming meaningless and nonfalsifiable. That is, adopting such a broad definition of instrumentality makes it almost impossible (if not indeed impossible) to state that people care about fairness and justice (and related concepts such as morality) simply for the sake of fairness or justice. We work from the assumption that fairness and justice often are important motivators of people's judgments and their reactions, but typically it is very hard to falsify that no other reasons are important in explaining why people care about fairness and justice. This is the case especially when one defines broadly such concepts "instrumentality" and "self-interest." Rather than continuing the endless debate on instrumental and noninstrumental justice concerns, we think it is more fruitful to start investigating justice from the following notions: (1) people care a lot about justice, (2) other concerns are important as well, (3) research should focus on the conditions that lead justice versus the other concerns to gain or lose importance, and (4) modern social psychological theories should be developed that specify in greater detail the social psychological processes involved in the fairness judgment process (Van den Bos et al., 2006). The uncertainty management framework, the self-regulatory alarm-system model that may well follow from this framework, and the research reviewed here have all been inspired by these views, and all focus especially on the last notion.

Modern social psychological theories note correctly that self-regulatory processes play an important role in how humans perceive and react to their environments, and the uncertainty management, affective-experiential, and alarm-system models discussed here accord with this trend by paying substantial attention to processes of self-regulation. In this, our perspective is a truly psychological one, adopting the view that fairness and justice really are in the eye of the beholder. Building on that view, we therefore focus on how the beholder forms fairness judgments and reacts to events he or she perceives to be fair or unfair. This does not imply that our conception of the justice judgment process adopts an "instrumental" perspective, but rather that we think fairness judgments should be studied from a truly social psychological point of view, with the goal of revealing the conditions and processes that affect fairness judgments and fairness responses. We believe that it is appropriate to give a good deal of attention to the self-regulatory affective-experiential processes that may be going on when people form fairness judgments and try to manage their uncertain selves. It is our hope that this will be conducive to the social psychology of fairness and to the psychology of the regulation of personal uncertainty.

References

Abelson, R. P. (1963). Computer simulation of "hot cognitions." In S. S. Tomkins & S. Messick (Eds.), *Computer simulation and personality: Frontier of psychological theory* (pp. 277–298). Wiley.

Arkin, R. M., Oleson, K. C., & Carroll, P. J. (Eds.) (2009). *Handbook of the uncertain self*. Psychology Press.

Brewer, M. B. (2008). Depersonalized trust and intergroup cooperation. In J. I. Krueger (Ed.), *Rationality and social responsibility* (pp. 215–232). Psychology Press.

Brockner, J., & Wiesenfeld, B. M. (1996). An integrative framework for explaining reactions to decisions: Interactive effects of outcomes and procedures. *Psychological Bulletin, 120*, 189–208.

Colquitt, J. A., Scott, B. A., & LePine, J. A. (2007). Trust, trustworthiness, and trust propensity: A meta-analytic test of their unique relationships with risk taking and job performance. *Journal of Applied Psychology, 92*, 909–927.

Damasio, A. (2005). Brain trust. *Nature, 435*, 571–572.

Eisenberger, N. I., Lieberman, M. D., & Williams, K. D. (2003). Does rejection hurt? An fMRI study of social exclusion. *Science*, *302*, 290–292.

Eisenberger, N. I., & Lieberman, M. D. (2004). Why rejection hurts: A common neural alarm system for physical and social pain. *Trends in Cognitive Sciences*, *8*, 294–300.Elovainio, M., Van den Bos, K., Linna, A., Kivimäki, M., Ala-Mursula, L., Pentti, J., & Vahtera, J. (2005). Combined effects of uncertainty and organizational justice on employee health: Testing the uncertainty management model of fairness judgments among Finnish public sector employees. *Social Science & Medicine*, *61*, 2501–2512.

Epstein, S., & Pacini, R. (1999). Some basic issues regarding dual-process theories from the perspective of cognitive-experiential self-theory. In S. Chaiken & Y. Trope (Eds.), *Dual-process theories in social psychology* (pp. 462–482). Guilford.

Giffin, K. (1967). The contribution of studies of source credibility to a theory of interpersonal trust in the communication process. *Psychological Bulletin*, *68*, 104–120.

Giroux, H. A. (2006). *Beyond the spectacle of terrorism: Global uncertainty and the challenge of the new media*. Paradigm.

Gray, J. A., & McNaughton, N. (2000). *The neuropsychology of anxiety: An enquiry into the functions of the septo-hippocampal system*. Oxford University Press.

Greco, V., & Roger, D. (2001). Coping with uncertainty: The construction and validation of a new measure. *Personality and Individual Differences*, *31*, 519–534.

Greenberg, J. (2006). Losing sleep over organizational injustice: Attenuating insomiac reactions to underpayment inequity with supervisory training in interactional justice. *Journal of Applied Psychology*, *91*, 58–69.

Greene, J. D., Sommerville, B., Nystrom, L. E., Darley, J. M., & Cohen, J. D. (2001). An fMRI investigation of emotional engagement in moral judgment. *Science*, *293*, 2105–2108.

Güth, W., Ockenfels, P., & Wendel, M. (1997). Cooperation based on trust: An experimental investigation. *Journal of Economic Psychology*, *18*, 15–43.

Hertz, N. (2001). *The silent takeover: Global capitalism and the death of democracy*. Heinemann.

Hofstede, G. (2001). *Culture's consequences: Comparing values, behaviors, institutions, and organizations across nations* (2nd ed.). Sage.

Hogg, M. A. (2007). Uncertainty-identity theory. In M. P. Zanna (Ed.), *Advances in experimental social psychology* (Vol. 39, pp. 70–126). Academic Press.

Hogg, M. A., & Gaffney, A. M. (2023). Social identity dynamics in the face of overwhelming uncertainty. In J. P. Forgas, W. D. Crano, & K. Fiedler (Eds.), *The psychology of insecurity: Seeking certainty where none can be found* (pp. 244–264). Routledge.Hogg, M. A., Sherman, D. K., Dierselhuis, J., Maitner, A. T., & Moffitt, G. (2007). Uncertainty, entitativity, and group identification. *Journal of Experimental Social Psychology*, *43*, 135–142.

Jost, J. T., & Hunyady, O., (2002). The psychology of system justification and the palliative function of ideology. In W. Stroebe & M. Hewstone (Eds.), *European review of social psychology* (Vol. 13, pp. 111–153). Psychology Press.

Kahneman, D., Slovic, P., & Tversky, A. (Eds.) (1982). *Judgment under uncertainty: Heuristics and biases*. Cambridge University Press.

Kausto, J., Elo, A. L., Lipponen, J., & Elovainio, M. (2005). Moderating effects of job insecurity in the relationships between procedural justice and employee well-being: Gender differences. *European Journal of Work and Organizational Psychology*, *14*, 431–452.

Kramer, R. M. (2001). Identity and trust in organizations: One anatomy of a productive but problematic relationship. In M. A. Hogg & D. J. Terry (Eds.), *Social identity processes in organizational contexts* (pp. 167–180). Psychology Press.

Larsen, R. J., Diener, E., & Cropanzano, R. S. (1987). Cognitive operations associated with individual differences in affect intensity. *Journal of Personality and Social Psychology*, *53*, 767–774.

Lind, E. A. (1995). *Social conflict and social justice: Lessons from the social psychology of justice judgments*. Inaugural address, Leiden University.

Lind, E. A., & Tyler, T. R. (1988). *The social psychology of procedural justice*. Plenum.

Lind, E. A., & Van den Bos, K. (2002). When fairness works: Toward a general theory of uncertainty management. In B. M. Staw & R. M. Kramer (Eds.), *Research in organizational behavior* (Vol. 24, pp. 181–223). JAI Press.

Loseman, A., Miedema, J., Van den Bos, K., & Vermunt, R. (2009). Exploring how people respond to conflicts between self-interest and fairness: The influence of threats to the self on affective reactions to advantageous inequity. *Australian Journal of Psychology*, *61*, 13–21.

Maas, M., & Van den Bos, K. (2009). An affective-experiential perspective on reactions to fair and unfair events: Individual differences in affect intensity moderated by experiential mindsets. *Journal of Experimental Social Psychology*, *45*, 667–675.

Maas, M., & Van den Bos, K. (2011). Real personal uncertainty induced by means of task-related feedback: Effects on reactions to voice and no-voice procedures. *Social Justice Research*, *24*, 107–125.

Marigold, D. C., McGregor, I., & Zanna, M. P. (2009). Defensive conviction as emotion regulation: Goal mechanisms and interpersonal implications. In R. M. Arkin, K. C. Oleson, & P. J. Carroll (Eds.), *Handbook of the uncertain self* (pp. 232–248). Psychology Press.

McGregor, I., & Marigold, D. C. (2003). Defensive zeal and the uncertain self: What makes you so sure? *Journal of Personality and Social Psychology*, *85*, 838–852.

McGregor, I., Zanna, M. P., Holmes, J. G., & Spencer, S. J. (2001). Compensatory conviction in the face of personal uncertainty: Going to extremes and being oneself. *Journal of Personality and Social Psychology*, *80*, 472–488.

Miedema, J., Van den Bos, K., & Vermunt, R. (2006). The influence of self-threats on fairness judgments and affective measures. *Social Justice Research*, *19*, 228–253.

Mikula (2005). Some observations and critical thoughts about the present state of justice theory and research. In S. Gilliland, D. Steiner, D. Skarlicki, & K. van den Bos (Eds.), *What motivates fairness in organizations* (pp. 197–210). Information Age Publishing.

Murray, S. L., Holmes, J. G., & Collins, N. L. (2005). *The relational signature of felt security*. Paper presented at the 2005 Conference of the Society of Experimental Social Psychology, San Diego, CA.

Murray, S. L., Holmes, J. G., & Collins, N. L. (2006). Optimizing assurance: The risk regulation system in relationships. *Psychological Bulletin*, *132*, 641–666.

Patterson, P. G., Cowley, E., & Prasongsukarn, K. (2006). Service failure recovery: The moderating impact of individual-level cultural value orientation on perceptions of justice. *International Journal of Research in Marketing*, *23*, 263–277.

Phelps, E. S. (1970). *Microeconomic foundations of employment and inflation theory*. Norton.

Runciman, W. G. (1966). *Relative deprivation and social justice: A study of attitudes to social inequality in twentieth-century England*. Routledge & Kegan Paul.

Sedikides, C., De Cremer, D., Hart, C. M., & Brebels, L. (2009). Procedural fairness responses in the context of self-uncertainty. In R. M. Arkin, K. C. Oleson, & P. J. Carroll (Eds.), *Handbook of the uncertain self* (pp. 142–159). Psychology Press.

See, K. E. (2009). Reactions to decisions with uncertain consequences: Reliance on perceived fairness versus predicted outcomes depends on knowledge. *Journal of Personality and Social Psychology*, *96*, 104–117.

Sorrentino, R. M., Bobocel, D. R., Gitta, M. Z., Olson, J. M., & Hewitt, E. C. (1988). Uncertainty orientation and persuasion: Individual differences in the effects of personal relevance on social judgments. *Journal of Personality and Social Psychology*, *55*, 357–337.

Sorrentino, R. M., & Roney, C. J. R. (1986). Uncertainty orientation, achievement–related motivation and task diagnosticity as determinants of task performance. *Social Cognition*, *4*, 420–436.

Sztompka, P. (1999). *Trust: A sociological theory*. Cambridge: Cambridge University Press.

Thau, S., Aquino, K., & Wittek, R. (2007). An extension of uncertainty management theory to the self: The relationship between justice, social comparison orientation, and antisocial work behaviors. *Journal of Applied Psychology*, *92*, 286–295.

Thau, S., Bennett, R. J., Mitchell, M. S., & Marrs, M. B. (2009). How management style moderates the relationship between abusive supervision and workplace deviance: An uncertainty management theory perspective. *Organizational Behavior and Human Decision Processes*, *108*, 79–92.

Thibaut, J., & Walker, L. (1975). *Procedural justice: A psychological analysis*. Erlbaum.

Tyler, T. R., & DeGoey, P. (1996). Trust in organizational authorities: The influence of motive attributions on willingness to accept decisions. In R. Kramer & T. R. Tyler (Eds.), *Trust in organizations: Frontiers of theory and research* (pp. 331–356). Sage.

Tyler, T. R., & Huo, Y. J. (2002). *Trust in the law: Encouraging public cooperation with the police and courts*. Russell Sage Foundation.

Van den Bos, K. (1999). What are we talking about when we talk about no-voice procedures? On the psychology of the fair outcome effect. *Journal of Experimental Social Psychology*, *35*, 560–577.

Van den Bos, K. (2001). Uncertainty management: The influence of uncertainty salience on reactions to perceived procedural fairness. *Journal of Personality and Social Psychology*, *80*, 931–941.

Van den Bos, K. (2003). On the subjective quality of social justice: The role of affect as information in the psychology of justice judgments. *Journal of Personality and Social Psychology*, *85*, 482–498.

Van den Bos, K. (2004). An existentialist approach to the social psychology of fairness: The influence of mortality and uncertainty salience on reactions to fair and unfair events. In J. Greenberg, S. L. Koole, & T. Pyszczynski (Eds.), *Handbook of experimental existential psychology* (pp. 167–181). Guilford Press.

Van den Bos, K. (2005). What is responsible for the fair process effect? In J. Greenberg & J. A. Colquitt (Eds.), *Handbook of organizational justice: Fundamental questions about fairness in the workplace* (pp. 273–300). Erlbaum.

Van den Bos, K. (2007). Hot cognition and social justice judgments: The combined influence of cognitive and affective factors on the justice judgment process. In D. de Cremer (Ed.), *Advances in the psychology of justice and affect* (pp. 59–82). Information Age Publishing.

Van den Bos, K. (2009). Making sense of life: The existential self trying to deal with personal uncertainty. *Psychological Inquiry*, *20*, 197–217.

Van den Bos, K. (2011). *Vertrouwen in de overheid: Wanneer hebben burgers het, wanneer hebben ze het niet, en wanneer weten ze niet of de overheid te vertrouwen is?* [*Trust in government: When do people have it, when don't they, and when don't they know whether they trust the government or not?*]. Netherlands Ministry of the Interior and Kingdom Relations.

Van den Bos, K. (2018). *Why people radicalize: How unfairness judgments are used to fuel radical beliefs, extremist behaviors, and terrorism*. Oxford University Press.

Van den Bos, K. (2023). Trust in social institutions: The role of informational and personal uncertainty. In J. P. Forgas, W. D. Crano, & K. Fiedler (Eds.), *The psychology of insecurity: Seeking certainty where none can be found* (pp. 287–306). Routledge.

Van den Bos, K. (2024). *The fair process effect: Overcoming distrust, polarization, and conspiracy thinking*. Cambridge University Press.

Van den Bos, K., Euwema, M. C., Poortvliet, P. M., & Maas, M. (2007). Uncertainty management and social issues: Uncertainty as important determinant of reactions to socially deviating people. *Journal of Applied Social Psychology*, *37*, 1726–1756.

Van den Bos, K., Ham, J., Lind, E. A., Simonis, M., Van Essen, W. J., & Rijpkema, M. (2008). Justice and the human alarm system: The impact of exclamation points and flashing lights on the justice judgment process. *Journal of Experimental Social Psychology*, *44*, 201–219.

Van den Bos, K., Heuven, E., Burger, E., & Fernández Van Veldhuizen, M. (2006). Uncertainty management after reorganizations: The ameliorative effect of outcome fairness on job uncertainty. *International Review of Social Psychology*, *19*, 75–86.

Van den Bos, K., Lind, E. A., Vermunt, R., & Wilke, H. A. M. (1997). How do I judge my outcome when I do not know the outcome of others? The psychology of the fair process effect. *Journal of Personality and Social Psychology*, *72*, 1034–1046.

Van den Bos, K., & Lind, E. A. (2002). Uncertainty management by means of fairness judgments. In M. P. Zanna (Ed.), *Advances in experimental social psychology* (Vol. 34, pp. 1–60). Academic Press.

Van den Bos, K., & Lind, E. A. (2009). The social psychology of fairness and the regulation of personal uncertainty. In R. M. Arkin, K. C. Oleson, & P. J. Carroll (Eds.), *Handbook of the uncertain self* (pp. 122–141). Psychology Press.Van den Bos, K., Maas, M., Waldring, I. E., & Semin, G. R. (2003). Toward understanding the psychology of reactions to perceived fairness: The role of affect intensity. *Social Justice Research*, *16*, 151–168.

Van den Bos, K., & Miedema, J. (2000). Toward understanding why fairness matters: The influence of mortality salience on reactions to procedural fairness. *Journal of Personality and Social Psychology*, *79*, 355–366.Van den Bos, K., Peters, S. L., Bobocel, D. R., & Ybema, J. F. (2006). On preferences and doing the right thing: Satisfaction with advantageous inequity when cognitive processing is limited. *Journal of Experimental Social Psychology*, *42*, 273–289.

Van den Bos, K., Poortvliet, P. M., Maas, M., Miedema, J., & Van den Ham, E.-J. (2005). An enquiry concerning the principles of cultural norms and values: The impact of uncertainty and mortality salience on reactions to violations and bolstering of cultural worldviews. *Journal of Experimental Social Psychology*, *41*, 91–113.

Van den Bos, K., & Rijpkema, M. (2007). *Studying effects of exclamation point primes using functional neuroimaging*. Unpublished manuscript.

Van den Bos, K., & Spruijt, N. (2002). Appropriateness of decisions as a moderator of the psychology of voice. *European Journal of Social Psychology*, *32*, 57–72.

Van den Bos, K., Van Ameijde, J., & Van Gorp, H. (2006). On the psychology of religion: The role of personal uncertainty in religious worldview defense. *Basic and Applied Social Psychology*, *28*, 333–341.

Van den Bos, K., Van Schie, E. C. M., & Colenberg, S. E. (2002). Parents' reactions to child day care organizations: The influence of perceptions of procedures and the role of organizations' trustworthiness. *Social Justice Research*, *15*, 53–62.

Van den Bos, K., Wilke, H. A. M., & Lind, E. A. (1998). When do we need procedural fairness? The role of trust in authority. *Journal of Personality and Social Psychology*, *75*, 1449–1458.

Van den Bos, K., Wilke, H. A. M., Lind, E. A., & Vermunt, R. (1998). Evaluating outcomes by means of the fair process effect: Evidence for different processes in fairness and satisfaction judgments. *Journal of Personality and Social Psychology*, *74*, 1493–1503.

Walster, E., Walster, G. W., & Berscheid, E. (1978). *Equity: Theory and research*. Allyn & Bacon.

Weary, G., & Jacobson, J. A. (1997). Causal uncertainty beliefs and diagnostic information seeking. *Journal of Personality and Social Psychology*, *73*, 839–848.

Winkielman, P., Schwarz, N., Fazendeiro, T., & Reber, R. (2003). The hedonic marking of processing fluency: Implications for evaluative judgment. In J. Musch & K. C. Klauer (Eds.), *The psychology of evaluation: Affective processes in cognition and emotion* (pp. 189–217). Erlbaum.

8

AN ANTIDOTE TO SELF-UNCERTAINTY

Nostalgia Prevents Self-Uncertainty from Lowering Self-Continuity

Constantine Sedikides, Marios Biskas, Jacob Juhl and Tim Wildschut

We are concerned with self-uncertainty, nostalgia, and self-continuity. We begin by defining these constructs. Then, we discuss the relations among them. Subsequently, we argue that nostalgia buffers against a negative consequence of self-uncertainty, namely, self-discontinuity. We proceed to present relevant evidence and draw broader implications.

Definitions

Self-Uncertainty

We conceptualize self-uncertainty as ambiguity, doubt, or confusion about major aspects of one's life such as career, close relationships, or financial stability (Yang et al., 2017). Self-uncertainty is generally aversive (Hogg, 2014; Landau et al., in press). It is also highly disruptive to the self-concept. For example, self-uncertainty increases the subjective distance between one's present and past selves (Yang et al., 2020). It is also linked to a lack of direction due to blocking one's ability for decisions and actions (Marigold et al., 2010; McGregor & Marigold, in press), is associated with lower self-esteem (Baumgardner, 1990; Story, 2004), and it conduces to higher pessimism and self-handicapping (Martin et al., 2003).

Self-Continuity

We conceptualize self-continuity as a sense of connection between one's past and present selves (Sedikides, Wildschut, Gaertner, et al, 2008). Self-continuity entails psychological benefits. For example, it facilitates the formation of attitudes and judgments, strengthens motivation and decision-making, and conduces to gains in psychological and physical health (Sedikides et al., 2023). Conversely, we conceptualize self-discontinuity as a sense of disconnect between one's past and future selves (Sedikides et al., 2008). Self-discontinuity is a psychological liability. For example, it is associated with depression, anxiety, stress, and suicidal ideation (Sokol & Eisenheim, 2016).

DOI: 10.4324/9781003363385-9

Nostalgia

We conceptualize nostalgia as sentimental longing for important aspects of one's past (Sedikides, Wildschut, Arndt, & Routledge, 2008). The emotion is self-relevant, social, and mostly positive (Hepper et al., 2012; Van Tilburg et al., 2018). Nostalgic recollections typically involve personally meaningful events (e.g., graduation ceremony, the birth of a child, wedding) that focus on the self within social contexts (e.g., friends, family, romantic partners; Abeyta et al., 2015; Wildschut et al., 2006). Nostalgic recollections comprise a mixture of positive affect and negative affect, with the former outweighing the latter (Leunissen et al., 2021; Sedikides & Wildschut, 2016).

Relations Among Self-Uncertainty, Self-Continuity, and Nostalgia

Self-Uncertainty and Self-Continuity

As mentioned above, self-uncertainty has several negative consequences. In particular, it magnifies the felt distance between one's present self and past self, which may lower self-continuity (Yang et al., 2020). Also, self-uncertainty undermines the ability for decision-making and relevant action (Marigold et al., 2010; McGregor & Marigold, this volume), which can disrupt self-continuity. In addition, self-uncertainty contributes to an unclear and inconsistent self-view (Kusec et al., 2016), and a fragmented self-view will likely obstruct self-continuity. Similarly, individuals high on self-uncertainty lack a firm sense of who they have been and who they are now (Butzer & Kuiper, 2006; Kusec et al., 2016), thus hindering self-continuity. In all, self-uncertainty is likely to engender lower self-continuity.

Self-Uncertainty and Nostalgia

No research has directly examined the relationship between self-uncertainty and nostalgia. Yet, as stated previously, self-uncertainty is an aversive state (Hogg, 2014; Proulx & Inzlicht, 2012; Van den Bos & Lind, 2002; but see Sweeny & Howell, in press). Aversive states present a psychological threat, which nostalgia is known to counteract. We will review literature indicating that nostalgia can buffer aversive states. If so, nostalgia is likely to buffer self-uncertainty as well.

Let us consider trait nostalgia first. Pondering threatening thoughts about death increases anxiety about death, but only for participants who are low on trait nostalgia, not for those high on it (Juhl et al., 2010). Similarly, thinking about death decreases meaning in life for those low on trait nostalgia, but not for those high on it (Routledge et al., 2008).

Induced nostalgia is also known to buffer psychological threat. In an experiment by Vess et al. (2012), participants completed an analytical reasoning test and received bogus feedback indicating that they had either performed well on the test or failed it. Next, participants reflected for a few minutes on a nostalgic or ordinary event from their lives (i.e., Event Reflection Task; Sedikides, Wildschut, Routledge, Arndt et al., 2015; Wildschut et al., 2006) and described this event in writing; this constituted the nostalgia manipulation. Lastly, they indicated the extent to which their test performance was caused by their ability. People typically respond defensively to failure by eschewing internal (i.e., ability-related) attributions for it (Campbell & Sedikides, 1999). Indeed, in the ordinary event condition, those who learned that they had failed the test attributed their performance to their own ability to a lesser extent than those who learned that they had performed well. However, this defensive response was attenuated in the nostalgic event condition. In all, nostalgia thwarted defensive responses to self-threatening information.

In a related line of research, Routledge et al. (2011) examined whether nostalgia curtails defensive responses to meaning threat. They induced nostalgia by having participants think and write about a nostalgic or ordinary event from their lives (i.e., Event Reflection Task). Then, they experimentally threatened meaning by having participants read an essay on the meaninglessness of life (meaning-threat condition) or an essay on the limitations of computers (no-threat condition). Lastly, they assessed participants' views about the essay that they had read and its author. People typically respond defensively to such threatening information by derogating its source (Greenberg et al., 1990). Indeed, Routledge et al. reported that, among participants who recalled an ordinary event, those in the meaning-threat condition derogated the essay and its author to a greater extent than those in the no-threat condition. However, this pattern was not evident among participants who recalled a nostalgic event: they refrained from source derogation. In short, nostalgia warded off defensive responses to meaningful threats. A similar investigation (Routledge et al., 2012) further examined whether induced nostalgia offsets an established effect, namely, drops in meaning caused by viewing absurd art (Proulx et al., 2010). Participants viewed either an absurd painting or a representational painting, were subject to a nostalgia induction (vs. control), and completed a meaning in life scale (i.e., the Presence of Meaning in Life subscale of the Meaning in Life Questionnaire; Steger et al., 2006). Viewing an absurd (vs. representational) painting reduced meaning among participants who recalled an ordinary autobiographical event, but not among those who recalled a nostalgic event.

Conceptually similar results have been reported with other types of threats. Examples are loneliness (i.e., perceived lack of social support due to fewer and less satisfying relationships than desired; Abeyta & Juhl, 2023; Zhou et al., 2008, 2022), disillusionment (i.e., experience of loss, confusion, and hopelessness following the realization that deeply held beliefs have been discredited; Maher et al., 2021), and procedural injustice in the workplace (i.e., perceived unfairness of the decision making or outcome allocation process in the organization; Van Dijke et al., 2015). Nostalgia alleviated the discomfort that accompanied these threats.

Nostalgia and Self-Continuity

Nostalgia fosters self-continuity. Sedikides et al. (2016, Experiment 3) induced nostalgia with the Event Reflection Task. Subsequently, participants indicated their level of self-continuity by responding to such items as "I feel connected with my past" and "I feel there is continuity in my life." Nostalgic participants reported higher self-continuity than control participants. This finding has been replicated in several experiments and across Western, Chinese, and Syrian participants (Jiang et al., 2021; Ju et al., 2016; Sedikides et al., 2016, Experiment 2; Wildschut et al., 2018, 2019).

Further, Sedikides, Wildschut, Routledge, and Arndt (2015, Experiment 3) compared the influence of thinking and writing about a nostalgic event in one's life to thinking and writing about a positive event in one's life (i.e., a time when participants were lucky) on self-continuity. Again, nostalgia (vs. control) increased self-continuity. In replication experiments, nostalgia was induced with features that were prototypical of the construct (e.g., keepsakes, rose-tinted memories) or non-prototypical of it (e.g., daydreaming, wishing; Abakoumkin et al., 2019, Experiment 2), as well as with nostalgic or non-nostalgic song lyrics (Sedikides et al., 2016, Experiment 1), music (Van Tilburg et al., 2019, Experiments 3–4), and scents (Reid et al., 2014).

Nostalgia as a Buffer against Self-Uncertainty

People cope with self-uncertainty in various ways. They may compare themselves (e.g., their attitudes, accomplishments, or possessions) to similar others (Gerber et al., 2018). They may engage in revision of identity goals (Carroll et al., in press). They may respond positively to events that uphold their cultural worldview (e.g., values, norms) and negatively to events that challenge it (Van den Bos, 2009; Van den Bos & Lind, in press). They may identify strongly with their social group (Choi & Hogg, 2020), especially if they are peripheral group members (Hohman & Kuljian, in press). They may trust, or even support, autocratic leaders (Rast et al., 2013, 2016) while distrusting the public (Pfattheicher & Böhm, 2018). They may become more vocal when in a minority status (Rios et al., 2012). And they may become more materialistic (Martin et al., 2019; Morrison Rios & Johnson, 2011).

We propose that people also cope with self-uncertainty through nostalgia—whether at the trait or state (e.g., experimentally induced) level. Not only does the emotion serve as a psychological refuge in times of crisis, but it also motivates processes that contribute to the re-establishment of intrapersonal equilibrium. The foundational process here is approach motivation. Nostalgia is positively associated with, and activates, approach motivation. For example, in a cross-sectional investigation, Stephan et al. (2014, Study 1) assessed trait nostalgia both with the Southampton Nostalgia Scale (Barrett et al., 2010; Routledge et al., 2008; see also Wildschut & Sedikides, 2022a) and the Nostalgia Inventory (Batcho, 1995). The former scale comprises seven items pertaining to the personal relevance of nostalgia (e.g., "How valuable is nostalgia for you?"), proneness to nostalgia (e.g., "How prone are you to feeling nostalgic?"), and frequency of nostalgizing (e.g., "Generally speaking, how often do you bring to mind nostalgic experiences?"). The latter scale measures nostalgia for 20 objects, persons, or situations from one's past (e.g., "toys," "my family," "the way people were"). Stephan et al. assessed approach motivation with the 13-item Behavioral Activation System (BAS) subscale of the BIS/BAS Scales (Carver & White, 1994); sample items are "I will often do things for no other reason than that they might be fun" (Fun Seeking subscale), "I go out of my way to get things I want" (Drive subscale), and "It would excite me to win a contest" (Reward Responsiveness subscale). The two nostalgia scales were positively associated with BAS. In a follow-up experimental investigation, Stephan et al. (Study 3) induced nostalgia with the Event Reflection Task and assessed state approach motivation with the BAS. Nostalgic participants experienced higher approach motivation (as indicated by their scores on the Fun Seeking and Drive subscales, but not on the Reward Responsiveness subscale) than control participants. We propose that approach motivation underlies nostalgia's capacity to evoke self-continuity.

The dynamic relations among self-uncertainty, self-continuity, and nostalgia are captured by the restorative property of nostalgia (Wildschut & Sedikides, 2023). Self-uncertainty is likely to cause a discomforting state, self-discontinuity (or, to be more precise, drops in self-continuity). Nostalgia, however, at the trait or state (i.e., induced) level, will alleviate the said discomfort by minimizing reductions in self-continuity. More formally, nostalgia—assessed as a trait or experimentally manipulated—buffers aversiveness by weakening its negative consequences. As such, nostalgia will protect against reductions in self-continuity that are caused by self-uncertainty, maintaining homeostasis.

We examined the restorative property of nostalgia in an experiment that we describe below. As an overview, we induced self-uncertainty (vs. self-certainty) and then induced nostalgia (vs. control). Next, we assessed self-continuity. Lastly, following the collection of demographic information, we assessed trait nostalgia. We formulated two hypotheses. First, if nostalgia buffers the adverse impact of self-uncertainty on self-continuity, then self-uncertainty (vs. self-certainty) will reduce self-continuity, but only for participants low (not high) on nostalgia. This hypothesis is tested by the statistical interaction between self-uncertainty and trait nostalgia. Second, self-uncertainty (vs. self-certainty) will reduce self-continuity, but only for participants in the control (not in the nostalgia) condition. This hypothesis is tested by the statistical interaction between self-uncertainty and induced nostalgia. We also explored the three-way interaction among self-uncertainty, induced nostalgia, and trait nostalgia.

Description of Methodology

We began by estimating our sample size. Previous experiments on the buffering role of nostalgia reported medium to large effect sizes, ranging from $f = .23$ ($\eta^2 = .05$) to $f = .54$ ($\eta^2 = .21$). However, these experiments were conducted in controlled laboratory environments. Given that we intended for our experiment to be online, and hence in a less controlled environment, we estimated our sample size based on a small to medium effect size ($f = .18$; $\eta^2 = .03$), the typical effect size range in social psychology (Richard et al., 2003). Specifically, we used G*Power (Faul et al., 2009) to conduct an a-priori power analysis with a power of.80, significance level of $\alpha = .05$, and effect size of $f = .18$. This analysis recommended a target sample size of 245. We rounded this to 250 to hedge against attrition. We recruited MTurk workers for $1.00. We excluded eight of them because they failed to complete the experimental manipulations, yielding a final sample of 242 participants (151 women, 88 men, 1 other, 2 unknown; $M_{age} = 32.26$, $SD_{age} = 9.77$, $Range_{age} = 18–70$; one participant did not provide age-related information).

We experimentally manipulated self-uncertainty by randomly assigning participants to either the self-uncertainty ($n = 113$) or self-certainty ($n = 129$) condition. In the *self-uncertainty condition*, we initially provided participants with a few examples such as: "People face a lot of uncertainties in life. For instance, they are typically uncertain about their job or career, relationships, and financial stability." Following this, we instructed them to "make a detailed list of the specific uncertainties you face in your life." Finally, we asked them to "explain in detail your thoughts on these uncertainties and how they make you feel." In the *self-certainty condition*, we initially gave participants examples such as: "People face a lot of certainties in life. For instance, they are typically certain about the hobbies they have, the types of food they generally eat, and the friends they tend to see." Next, we instructed them to "make a detailed list of the specific certainties you have in your life." Lastly, we asked them to "explain in detail your thoughts on these certainties and how they make you feel."

We proceeded to induce nostalgia with the Event Reflection Task (Sedikides, Wildschut, Routledge, Arndt et al., 2015; Wildschut et al., 2006). In particular, we randomly assigned participants to the nostalgia or control condition. In the *nostalgia condition*, we provided them with a dictionary definition of the emotion (i.e., "a sentimental longing for the past;" The New Oxford Dictionary of English, 1998, p. 1266). Then, we instructed them to

> Think of a nostalgic event in your life. Specifically, try to think of a past event that makes you feel most nostalgic. Bring this nostalgic experience to mind. Immerse yourself in the nostalgic experience and spend a couple minutes thinking about how it makes you feel.

Afterward, we asked participants to "type four keywords relevant to this nostalgic event (i.e., words that describe the experience)." In the *control condition*, we instructed participants to "bring to mind the activities of your day yesterday. Specifically, try to think of the series of events that took place throughout your day. Bring these to mind and spend a couple of minutes thinking about them." Subsequently, we instructed them to "type four keywords relevant to yesterday's activities (i.e., words that describe what you did yesterday)." We asked these participants to reflect upon yesterday's activities in order to prevent them from bringing to mind a nostalgic event.

Afterward, we measured self-continuity (Sedikides et al., 2016; Sedikides, Wildschut, Routledge, & Arndt, 2015). We asked participants to indicate the extent to which they agreed (1 = *strongly disagree,* 6 = *strongly agree*) with four statements (e.g., "I feel there is continuity in my life," "I feel important aspects of my personality remain the same across time"). We averaged responses to compute self-continuity scores (α = .76, M = 4.36, SD = 0.96).

Finally, after collecting responses to demographic questions, we requested that participants complete the Southampton Nostalgia Scale; 1 = *not at all*, 7 = *very much*). We averaged responses to compute relevant scores (α = .94, M = 4.45, SD = 1.44). We administered this scale at the end (rather than the beginning) of the experiment to prevent it from activating the construct "nostalgia" among participants in the control condition.

Findings

Preliminary Analyses

To ascertain that trait nostalgia was not influenced by the experimental manipulation, we submitted trait nostalgia scores to a 2 (self-uncertainty vs. self-certainty) × 2 (induced nostalgia vs. control) Analysis of Variance. Neither the main effects of self-uncertainty, $F(1, 238) = 2.41$, $p = .122$, $\eta^2 = .01$, nor that of induced nostalgia, $F(1, 238) = 1.65$, $p = .201$, $\eta^2 = .01$, was significant. The interaction between self-uncertainty and induced nostalgia was not significant either, $F(1, 238) = 0.53$, $p = .469$, $\eta^2 = .002$. Trait nostalgia was not impacted by the manipulations.

Self-Uncertainty and Trait Nostalgia

Next, we tested the hypothesis that self-uncertainty reduces self-continuity, but only for participants low (not high) on trait nostalgia. We conducted a moderation analysis using model 1 of PROCESS (Hayes, 2017). We entered self-uncertainty (self-certainty = 0, self-uncertainty = 1) as the independent variable, self-continuity as the dependent variable, and trait nostalgia proneness as the moderator. The analysis revealed a significant interaction between self-uncertainty and trait nostalgia, $b = 0.17$, $SE = 0.08$, $t(238) = 2.03$, $p = .043$ (Figure 8.1). The analysis also yielded simple effects of self-uncertainty on self-continuity for participants with low (−1 SD) and high (+1 SD) levels of trait nostalgia. At low levels of trait nostalgia, self-uncertainty decreased self-continuity, $b = -0.42$, $SE = 0.17$, $t(238) = -2.46$, $p = .015$. However, at high levels of trait nostalgia, self-uncertainty did not influence self-continuity, $b = 0.07$, $SE = 0.17$, $t(238) = 0.41$, $p = .684$. Taken together, self-uncertainty decreased self-continuity, but highly nostalgic individuals were buffered from this negative outcome. Trait nostalgia protects against self-uncertainty.

Self-Uncertainty and Induced Nostalgia

In the next step, we tested the hypothesis that self-uncertainty (vs. self-certainty) reduces self-continuity, but only for participants in the control (not in the nostalgia) condition. We submitted the self-continuity scores to a 2 (self-uncertainty vs. self-certainty) × 2 (induced nostalgia vs. control) Analysis of Variance. There was no main effect of self-uncertainty, $F(1, 238) = 0.68$, $p = .409$, $\eta^2 = .003$. There was a trending main effect of induced nostalgia $F(1, 238) = 3.23$, $p = .073$, $\eta^2 = .01$, such that participants in the nostalgia condition (M = 4.46, SD = 0.93) reported higher levels of self-continuity than those in the control condition (M = 4.24, SD = 0.99).

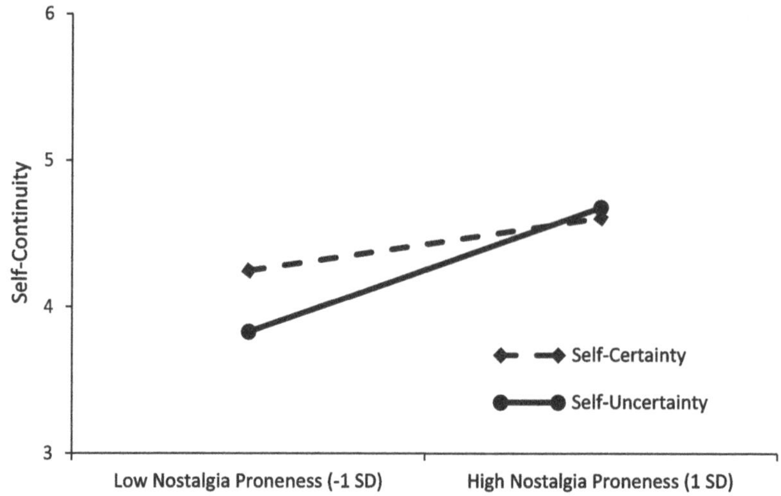

Figure 8.1 Self-uncertainty, self-continuity, and trait nostalgia.

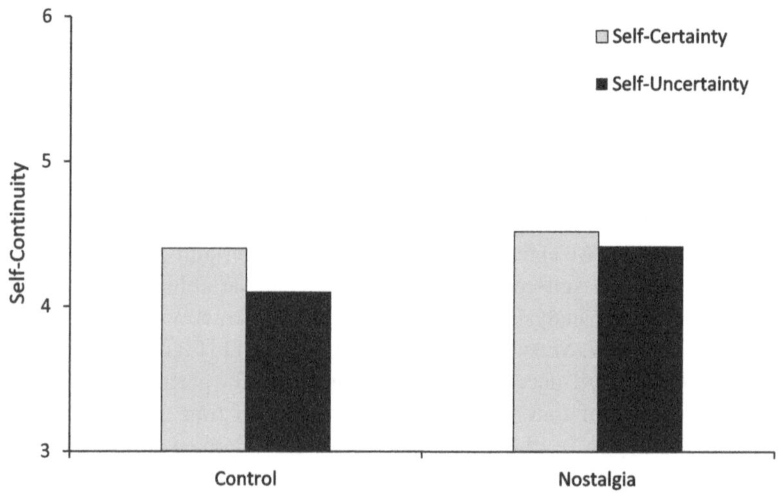

Figure 8.2 Self-uncertainty, self-continuity, and induced nostalgia.

The interaction between self-uncertainty and induced nostalgia was not significant, $F(1, 238) = 2.64$, $p = .106$, $\eta^2 = .01$ (Figure 8.2). Nevertheless, we proceeded to examine whether the pattern of this interaction is consistent with the hypothesis. To do so, we carried out simple effect tests. First, we tested the simple effects of self-uncertainty (vs. self-certainty) for participants in the control and nostalgia conditions. Within the control condition, participants in the self-uncertainty condition tended to exhibit lower levels of self-continuity than those in the self-certainty condition, $F(1, 238) = 2.90$, $p = .090$, $\eta^2 = .01$. However, within the nostalgia condition, there was no difference between participants in the self-uncertainty and self-certainty conditions, $F(1, 238) = 0.33$, $p = .567$, $\eta^2 = .001$. This pattern of results is suggestive. It shows that self-uncertainty likely reduces self-continuity and that induced nostalgia buffers this outcome of self-uncertainty.

Self-Uncertainty, Induced Nostalgia, and Trait Nostalgia

In order to explore the three-way interaction, we conducted a moderation analysis using model 3 of PROCESS macro (Hayes, 2017). We entered self-uncertainty as the independent variable, self-continuity as the dependent variable, induced nostalgia as the first moderator, and trait nostalgia as the second moderator. The three-way interaction was not significant, $b = 0.07$, $SE = 0.17$, $t(234) = 0.39$, $p = .697$.

Summary

The evidence we obtained in this experiment generally aligns with the idea that nostalgia buffers the adverse influence of self-uncertainty on self-continuity. In particular, the results provided strong support for the first hypothesis: self-uncertainty reduced self-continuity, but only for those low on trait nostalgia, not for those high on trait nostalgia. Stated otherwise, individuals chronically high on nostalgia were buffered from the negative impact of self-uncertainty on self-continuity. The results provided weak support for the second hypothesis: self-uncertainty tended to reduce self-continuity, but only for participants who recalled a recent (i.e., yesterday) autobiographical event, not for those who recalled a nostalgic event. The findings have theoretical and practical implications.

Theoretical Implications

Nostalgia appeared to act as a buffer against the negative (i.e., declines in self-continuity) consequences of self-uncertainty. But how so? What is the mechanism of nostalgia that neutralizes the impact of self-uncertainty on self-continuity? There are two likely mechanisms that can act independently of each other. One is the *self-oriented function* of nostalgia (Sedikides, Wildschut, Arndt, Routledge et al., 2015; Wildschut & Sedikides, 2022b). Nostalgic accounts revolve around the self (Brown & Humphreys, 2002; Wildschut et al., 2006). Also, experimentally induced nostalgia increases self-esteem (Hepper et al., 2012; Wildschut et al., 2006), optimism (Cheung et al., 2013, 2016), and inspiration (Evans et al., 2021; Stephan et al., 2015). It is possible, then, that, in the experiment we described, nostalgia bolstered the self, which in turn warded off the impact of self-uncertainty. Another mechanism is the *social function* of nostalgia (Sedikides & Wildschut, 2019; Sedikides, Wildschut, Arndt, Routledge et al., 2015; see also Murray, in press). Nostalgic accounts refer to important people from one's life (Abeyta et al., 2015; Madoglou et al., 2017). Also, in nostalgizing, the person is imbued with social connectedness (i.e., feeling loved, protected, and accepted; Hepper et al., 2012; Wildschut et al., 2006), empathy (Juhl et al., 2020; Zhou et al., 2012), and attachment security (Wildschut et al., 2006, 2010). It is possible, then, that, in the described experiment, nostalgia affirmed the self (cf. Crocker et al., 2008; Kumashiro & Sedikides, 2005), thus withstanding the negative repercussions of self-uncertainty.

Given that nostalgia buffers the adverse influence of self-uncertainty on self-continuity, nostalgia may directly render self-uncertainty (and the downstream consequence of self-discontinuity) more tolerable. As a result of this, nostalgia may increase the likelihood that people will choose to place themselves in uncertain or risky situations. For example, nostalgia may strengthen people's willingness to pursue a further educational degree, despite uncertainty about their capacity to fund it or complete it. Similarly, nostalgia may fortify people's resolve to initiate midlife career changes despite some uncertainty about monetary consequences for their family. Further, nostalgia may provide the spark needed to end a dissatisfying relationship, notwithstanding the uncertainty of a single life or the availability of desirable partners. Generally speaking, nostalgia may, in some circumstances, provide the impetus needed to take risks.

Consistent with the above assertion, research indicates that nostalgia increases financial risk-taking (Zou et al., 2019). In a cross-sectional study, trait nostalgia was positively related to the proclivity for risk-taking (e.g., "What is your preferred way of running your business?") among business owners. Further, in experimental studies, nostalgia increased risk-taking. In one experiment, risk-taking was assessed with the Automatic Balloon Analogue Risk Task (Pleskac et al., 2008), in which risk is operationalized as the number of pumps that participants choose for each of the 30 virtual balloons. Participants do not know when each balloon will pop. They receive a small monetary reward for each pump but lose all their earnings if the balloon pops. The more pumps participants choose, the riskier they are considered. In the said experiment, nostalgic participants chose a higher number of pumps than control participants. Nostalgic participants took more financial risks than controls. These findings were replicated in two additional experiments with a different operationalization of risk-taking (i.e., a stock market investment task; but see Lilleholt & Zettler, 2023).

Nostalgia buffered the adverse influence of *self-uncertainty*, that is, uncertainty about major aspects of life such as one's career, relationships, and financial stability. This raises the question of whether nostalgia could also protect against uncertainty more generally, not just self-uncertainty. There are several domains about which people can be uncertain, and not all of these uncertainties concern major aspects of life. For example, people can be uncertain about the meaning of an ambiguously worded sentence, whether to bring snacks instead of drinks to a party, or whether it is best to purchase a gas weed trimmer or an electric one. Does nostalgia also buffer the effects of these relatively minor uncertainties? The literature does not offer a definitive answer. On the one hand, empirical efforts have focused on nostalgia's capacity to buffer the impact of existential threats (e.g., meaning in life, mortality awareness). Given that nostalgia largely refers to meaningful life events and time periods (Abeyta & Pillarisetty, 2023; Sedikides & Wildschut, 2018), and that nostalgia affords the opportunity to reflect more broadly on one's life (providing, for example, self-continuity; Sedikides et al., 2023; Zou et al., 2018), there are solid grounds to expect that nostalgia buffers the effects of more serious psychological threats. However, there is less reason to advocate that nostalgia will buffer more minor uncertainties. They do not pose serious threats to self-continuity. They can, however, arouse negative affect (Bar-Anan et al., 2009) and, because nostalgia can foster positive affect (Leunissen et al., 2021; Wildschut et al., 2006), the emotion may help circumvent this negative affect (Sedikides, Wildschut, Routledge, Arndt et al., 2015; Wildschut & Sedikides, 2023). Future research may address whether nostalgia buffers the effects of more minor uncertainties.

Practical Implications

The work we reported is relevant to the developmental periods of late adolescence and early adulthood. These periods are marked by changes and self-uncertainty in several life domains, including relationships, education, and career. Being nostalgic may contribute to the maintenance of self-continuity during this transformative time. For example, nostalgia may facilitate coping with career-related uncertainty.

Career uncertainty can plague some individuals, necessitating the need for career counselors. High levels of career uncertainty, characterized by greater indecision about one's self and future, can be harmful to well-being (Meldahl & Muchinsky, 1997). Individuals facing career uncertainty often express fears of failing, making the wrong choices, or displeasing close others (Serling &

Betz, 1990). These individuals are also more likely to be pessimistic about their career opportunities as well as their control over the employment and career in which they eventually find themselves (Saka et al., 2008). To overcome these discomforting states, people often accept the first available career opportunity, rather than tolerating a period of uncertainty that could lead to more valuable career opportunities (Trevor-Roberts, 2006). The findings of the experiment we reported suggest that nostalgia may increase tolerance for this uncertainty and thus enable individuals to pursue optimal professional prospects.

This possibility seems likely in light of evidence that people who struggle to maintain a stable self-concept are more vulnerable to career uncertainty. Specifically, those with lower self-esteem (Lin et al., 2015), and ill-defined self-concepts (Saka et al., 2008) or vocational self-concepts (Garrison et al., 2017) are more likely to manifest career indecision. Unsurprisingly, one of the main goals of career counseling programs is to help people who struggle with career uncertainty to reconnect with their life values, interests, and goals, and subsequently to script their own personal and career stories, thus strengthening self-continuity (Bright & Pryor, 2011; Mitchell et al., 1999). Given that nostalgia prevents self-uncertainty from disrupting self-continuity, career counselors could utilize nostalgia to assist with this process.

The findings of our experiment have clinical relevance as well. Maintaining self-continuity contributes to well-being. Specifically, self-continuity is related to greater self-esteem (Sheldon et al., 1997; Usborne & Taylor, 2010), more self-concept clarity (Jiang et al., 2020), enhanced self-acceptance (Diehl & Hay, 2011), and increased self-efficacy (Mattingly & Lewandowski, 2013). Moreover, self-continuity is associated with increased positive affect (Diehl & Hay, 2011), greater meaning in life (Shin et al., 2016), lower stress, anxiety, and depression (Anderzén & Arnetz, 1999; Sheldon et al., 1997) as well as augmented satisfaction with life (Ritchie et al., 2011; Zou et al., 2018). In addition, reducing uncertainty contributes to well-being. Specifically, uncertainty can be detrimental to well-being, as it is associated with decreased self-esteem (Baumgardner, 1990; Story, 2004) and greater pessimism (Martin et al., 2003). Furthermore, people who struggle with uncertainty report more negative affects (Carleton et al., 2010), worry (Dugas et al., 2004), anxiety (Wright et al., 2016), and rumination (de Jong-Meyer et al., 2009). Lastly, uncertainty is related to several mental disorders, such as generalized anxiety disorder (Sexton et al., 2003), social anxiety (Carleton et al., 2010), panic disorder (Carleton et al., 2014), obsessive-compulsive disorder (Gentes & Ruscio, 2011), and depression (Boswell et al., 2013). Given the undesirable consequences of uncertainty, clinicians have developed treatments to reduce uncertainty or increase tolerance for it (Dugas & Ladouceur, 2000; Ladouceur et al., 2000).

Nostalgia's capacity to maintain self-continuity in the face of self-uncertainty suggests that nostalgia could complement and enhance therapeutic approaches. For instance, Layous et al. (2022; see also Layous & Kurtz, 2023) carried out an intervention to assess the psychological well-being benefits of nostalgia. These researchers induced nostalgia (vs. control) weekly, for six weeks. They assessed well-being at baseline, mid-intervention (after three weeks), post-intervention, and one-month post-intervention. At mid-intervention, nostalgic (vs. control) participants reported more positive affect, satisfaction with life, and eudaimonic well-being, but less negative affect. These well-being benefits, however, did not persist at the two post-intervention points. Additional research has shown that nostalgia can evoke behavioral changes (i.e., increased physical activity) when it is induced repeatedly (Kersten et al., 2016; see also Kersten & Cox, 2023), raising the possibility that the effects of nostalgia in the Layous et al. study would be stronger had the nostalgia induction been repeated throughout. Taken together, the implementation of nostalgia in clinical environments, perhaps in the face of self-uncertainty, appears promising.

Concluding Remarks

We set to understand the relations among self-uncertainty, self-continuity, and nostalgia. We hypothesized that the emotion buffers the negative consequences (i.e., declines in self-continuity) of self-uncertainty. We provided initial support for this hypothesis in an experiment and considered broader theoretical and practical implications. In all, preliminary evidence indicates that nostalgia serves as an antidote to the perils of self-uncertainty.

References

Abakoumkin, G., Hepper, E. G., Wildschut, T., & Sedikides, C. (2019). From nostalgia through social connectedness to self-continuity: Replication and extension. *Hellenic Journal of Psychology, 16*(2), 127–144. https://doi.org/10.26262/hjp.v16i2.7893

Abeyta, A. A., & Juhl, J. (2023). Nostalgia restores meaning in life for lonely people. *Emotion, 23*(6), 1791–1795. https://doi.org/10.1037/emo0001190

Abeyta, A. A., & Pillarisetty, S. (2023). Nostalgia supports a meaningful life. *Current Opinion in Psychology, 49,* Article 101520. https://doi.org/10.1016/j.copsyc.2022.101520

Abeyta, A., Routledge, C., Roylance, C., Wildschut, R. T., & Sedikides, C. (2015). Attachment-related avoidance and the social and agentic content of nostalgic memories. *Journal of Social and Personal Relationships, 32*(3), 406–413. https://doi.org/10.1177/0265407514533770

Anderzén, I., & Arnetz, B. B. (1999). Psychophysiological reactions to international adjustment. *Psychotherapy and Psychosomatics, 68*(2), 67–75. https://doi.org/10.1159/000012316

Bar-Anan, Y., Wilson, T. D., & Gilbert, D. T. (2009). The feeling of uncertainty intensifies affective reactions. *Emotion, 9*(1), 123–127. https://doi.org/10.1037/a0014607

Barrett, F. S., Grimm, K. J., Robins, R. W., Wildschut, T., Sedikides, C., & Janata, P. (2010). Music-evoked nostalgia: Affect, memory, and personality. *Emotion, 10*(3), 390–403. https://doi.org/10.1037/a0019006

Batcho, K. I. (1995). Nostalgia: A psychological perspective. *Perceptual and Motor Skills, 80*(1), 131–143. https://doi.org/10.2466/pms.1995.80.1.131

Baumgardner, A. H. (1990). To know oneself is to like oneself: Self-certainty and self-affect. *Journal of Personality and Social Psychology, 58*(6), 1062–1072. https://doi.org/10.1037/0022-3514.58.6.1062

Boswell, J. F., Thompson-Hollands, J., Farchione, T. J., & Barlow, D. H. (2013). Intolerance of uncertainty: A common factor in the treatment of emotional disorders. *Journal of Clinical Psychology, 69*(6), 630–645. https://doi.org/10.1002/jclp.21965

Bright, J. E., & Pryor, R. G. (2011). The chaos theory of careers. *Journal of Employment Counseling, 48*(4), 163–166. https://doi.org/10.1177/103841620301200304

Brown, A. D., & Humphreys, M. (2002). Nostalgia and the narrativization of identity: A Turkish case study. *British Journal of Management, 13*(2), 141–159. https://doi.org/10.1111/1467-8551.00228

Butzer, B., & Kuiper, N. A. (2006). Relationships between the frequency of social comparisons and self-concept clarity, intolerance of uncertainty, anxiety, and depression. *Personality and Individual Differences, 41*(1), 167–176. https://doi.org/10.1016/j.paid.2005.12.017

Campbell, K. W., & Sedikides, C. (1999). Self-threat magnifies the self-serving bias: A meta-analytic integration. *Review of General Psychology, 3*(1), 23–43. https://doi.org/10.1037/1089-2680.3.1.23

Carleton, R. N., Collimore, K. C., & Asmundson, G. J. (2010). "It's not just the judgements—It's that I don't know": Intolerance of uncertainty as a predictor of social anxiety. *Journal of Anxiety Disorders, 24*(2), 189–195. https://doi.org/10.1016/j.janxdis.2009.10.007

Carleton, R. N., Duranceau, S., Freeston, M. H., Boelen, P. A., McCabe, R. E., & Antony, M. M. (2014). "But it might be a heart attack": Intolerance of uncertainty and panic disorder symptoms. *Journal of Anxiety Disorders, 28*(5), 463–470. https://doi.org/10.1016/j.janxdis.2014.04.006

Carver, C. S., & White, T. L. (1994). Behavioral inhibition, behavioral activation and affective responses to impending reward and punishment: The BIS/BAS scales. *Journal of Personality and Social Psychology, 67*(2), 319–333. https://doi.org/10.1037/0022-3514.67.2.319

Cheung, W. Y., Sedikides, C., & Wildschut, T. (2016). Induced nostalgia increases optimism (via social connectedness and self-esteem) among individuals high, but not low, in trait nostalgia. *Personality and Individual Differences, 90*, 283–288. https://doi.org/10.1016/j.paid.2015.11.028

Cheung, W. Y., Wildschut, T., Sedikides, C., Hepper, E. G., Arndt, J., & Vingerhoets, A. J. J. M. (2013). Back to the future: Nostalgia increases optimism. *Personality and Social Psychology Bulletin, 39*(11), 1484–1496. https://doi.org/10.1177/0146167213499187

Choi, E. U., & Hogg, M. A. (2020). Self-uncertainty and group identification: A meta-analysis. *Group Processes & Intergroup Relations, 23*(4), 483–501. https://doi.org/10.1177/1368430219846990

Crocker, J., Niiya, Y., & Mischkowski, D. (2008). Why does writing about important values reduce defensiveness? Self-affirmation and the role of positive other-directed feelings. *Psychological Science, 19*(7), 740–747. https://doi.org/10.1111/j.1467-9280.2008.02150.x

de Jong-Meyer, R., Beck, B., & Riede, K. (2009). Relationships between rumination, worry, intolerance of uncertainty and metacognitive beliefs. *Personality and Individual Differences, 46*(4), 547–551. https://doi.org/10.1016/j.paid.2008.12.010

Diehl, M., & Hay, E. L. (2011). Self-concept differentiation and self-concept clarity across adulthood: Associations with age and psychological well-being. *The International Journal of Aging and Human Development, 73*(2), 125–152. https://doi.org/10.2190/AG.73.2.b

Dugas, M. J., & Ladouceur, R. (2000). Treatment of GAD: Targeting intolerance of uncertainty in two types of worry. *Behavior Modification, 24*(5), 635–657. https://doi.org/10.1177/0145445500245002

Dugas, M. J., Schwartz, A., & Francis, K. (2004). Intolerance of uncertainty, worry, and depression. *Cognitive Therapy and Research, 28*(6), 835–842. https://doi.org/10.1007/s10608-004-0669-0

Evans, N. D., Reyes, J., Wildschut, T., Sedikides, C., & Fetterman, A. K. (2021). Mental transportation mediates nostalgia's psychological benefits. *Cognition and Emotion, 35*(1), 84–95. https://doi.org/10.1080/02699931.2020.1806788

Faul, F., Erdfelder, E., Buchner, A., & Lang, A. G. (2009). Statistical power analyses using G* Power 3.1: Tests for correlation and regression analyses. *Behavior Research M*ethods, *41*(4), 1149–1160. https://doi.org/10.3758/BRM.41.4.1149

Garrison, Y. L., Lee, K. H., & Ali, S. R. (2017). Career identity and life satisfaction: The mediating role of tolerance for uncertainty and positive/negative affect. *Journal of Career Development, 44*(6), 516–529. https://doi.org/10.1177/0894845316668410

Gentes, E. L., & Ruscio, A. M. (2011). A meta-analysis of the relation of intolerance of uncertainty to symptoms of generalized anxiety disorder, major depressive disorder, and obsessive–compulsive disorder. *Clinical Psychology Review, 31*(6), 923–933. https://doi.org/10.1016/j.cpr.2011.05.001

Gerber, J. P., Wheeler, L., & Suls, J. (2018). A social comparison theory meta-analysis 60+ years on. *Psychological Bulletin, 144*(2), 177–197. https://doi.org/10.1037/bul0000127

Greenberg, J., Pyszczynski, T., Solomon, S., Rosenblatt, A., Veeder, M., Kirkland, S., & Lyon, D. (1990). Evidence for terror management II: The effects of mortality salience on reactions to those who threaten or bolster the cultural worldview. *Journal of Personality and Social Psychology, 58*(2), 308–318. https://doi.org/10.1037/0022-3514.58.2.308

Hayes, A. F. (2017). *Introduction to mediation, moderation, and conditional process analysis: A regression-based approach.* Guilford Press.

Hepper, E. G., Ritchie, T. D., Sedikides, C., & Wildschut, T. (2012). Odyssey's end: Lay conceptions of nostalgia reflect its original Homeric meaning. *Emotion, 12*(1), 102–119. https://doi.org/10.1037/a0025167

Hogg, M. A. (2014). From uncertainty to extremism: Social categorization and identity processes. *Current Directions in Psychological Science, 23*(5), 338–342. https://doi.org/10.1177/0963721414540168

Hohman, Z., & Kuljian, O. (in press). Prototypicality threat and self-uncertainty motivate ingroup behavior. In P. J. Carroll, K. Rios, & K. C. Oleson (Eds.), *Handbook of the uncertain self* (2nd ed.). Routledge Press.

Jiang, T., Chen, Z., & Sedikides, C. (2020). Self-concept clarity lays the foundation for self-continuity: The restorative function of autobiographical memory. *Journal of Personality and Social Psychology, 119*(4), 945–959. https://doi.org/10.1037/pspp0000259

Jiang, T., Chen, Z., Wang, S., & Hou, Y. (2021). Ostracism disrupts self-continuity. *Personality and Social Psychology Bulletin, 47*(9), 1390–1400. https://doi.org/10.1177/0146167220974496

Ju, I., Kim, J., Chang, M. J., & Bluck, S. (2016). Nostalgic marketing, perceived self-continuity, and consumer decisions. *Management Decision, 54*(8), 2063–2083. https://doi.org/10.1108/MD-11-2015-0501

Juhl, J., Routledge, C., Arndt, J., Sedikides, C., & Wildschut, T. (2010). Fighting the future with the past: Nostalgia buffers existential threat. *Journal of Research in Personality, 44*(3), 309–314. https://doi.org/10.1016/j.jrp.2010.02.006

Juhl, J., Wildschut, T., Sedikides, C., Diebel, T., Cheung, W. Y., & Vingerhoets, A. J. (2020). Nostalgia proneness and empathy: Generality, underlying mechanism, and implications for prosocial behavior. *Journal of Personality, 88*(3), 485–500. https://doi.org/10.1111/jopy.12505

Kersten, M., Cox, C. R., & Van Enkevort, E. A. (2016). An exercise in nostalgia: Nostalgia promotes health optimism and physical activity. *Psychology & Health, 31*(10), 1166–1181. https://doi.org/10.1080/08870446.2016.1185524

Kersten, M., & Cox, C. R. (2023). The past promotes the picture of health: Nostalgia as a resource for physical well-being. *Current Opinion in Psychology, 49*, Article 101522. https://doi.org/10.1016/j.copsyc.2022.101522

Kumashiro, M., & Sedikides, C. (2005). Taking on board liability-focused feedback: Close positive relationships as a self-bolstering resource. *Psychological Science, 16*(9), 732–739. https://doi.org/10.1111/j.1467-9280.2005.01603.x

Kusec, A., Tallon, K., & Koerner, N. (2016). Intolerance of uncertainty, causal uncertainty, causal importance, self-concept clarity and their relations to generalized anxiety disorder. *Cognitive Behaviour Therapy, 45*(4), 307–323. https://doi.org/10.1080/16506073.2016.1171391

Ladouceur, R., Dugas, M. J., Freeston, M. H., Léger, E., Gagnon, F., & Thibodeau, N. (2000). Efficacy of a cognitive–behavioral treatment for generalized anxiety disorder: Evaluation in a controlled clinical trial. *Journal of Consulting and Clinical Psychology, 68*(6), 957–964. https://doi.org/10.1037/0022-006X.68.6.957

Landau, M. J., Ryu, Y. J., Greenberg, J., Chur, M., & Pyszczynski, T., (2025). A terror management perspective on life's "big" uncertainties. In P. J. Carroll, K. Rios, & K. C. Oleson (Eds.), *Handbook of the Uncertain Self*, Second Edition. Routledge.

Layous, K., Kurtz, J. L., Wildschut, T., & Sedikides, C. (2022). The effect of a multi-week nostalgia intervention on well-being: Mechanisms and moderation. *Emotion, 22*(8), 1952–1968. https://doi.org/10.1037/emo0000817

Layous, K., & Kurtz, J. L. (2023). Nostalgia: A potential pathway to greater well-being. *Current Opinion in Psychology, 49*, Article 101548. https://doi.org/10.1016/j.copsyc.2022.101548

Leunissen, J. M., Wildschut, T., Sedikides, C., & Routledge, C. (2021). The hedonic character of nostalgia: An integrative data analysis. *Emotion Review, 13*(2), 139–156. https://doi.org/10.1177/1754073920950455

Lilleholt, L., & Zettler, I. (2023). A closer Look on the relation between nostalgia and risk-taking. *Personality and Social Psychology Bulletin, 49*(4), 600–611. https://doi.org/10.1177/01461672221074113

Lin, S. H., Wu, C. H., & Chen, L. H. (2015). Unpacking the role of self-esteem in career uncertainty: A self-determination perspective. *The Journal of Positive Psychology, 10*(3), 231–239. https://doi.org/10.1080/17439760.2014.950178

Madoglou, A., Gkinopoulos, T., Xanthopoulos, P., & Kalamaras, D. (2017). Representations of autobiographical nostalgic memories: Generational effect, gender, nostalgia proneness and communication of nostalgic experiences. *Journal of Integrated Social Sciences, 7*(1), 60–88.

Maher, P. J., Igou, E. R., & Van Tilburg, W. A. P. (2021). Nostalgia relieves the disillusioned mind. *Journal of Experimental Social Psychology, 92*, Article 104061. https://doi.org/10.1016/j.jesp.2020.104061

Marigold, D. C., McGregor, I., & Zanna, M. P. (2010). Defensive conviction as emotion regulation: Goal mechanisms and interpersonal implications. In R. M. Arkin, K. C. Oleson, & P. J. Carroll (Eds.), *The uncertain self: A handbook of perspectives from social and personality psychology* (pp. 232–248). Psychology Press.

Martin, A. J., Marsh, H. W., & Debus, R. L. (2003). Self-handicapping and defensive pessimism: A model of self-protection from a longitudinal perspective. *Contemporary Educational Psychology, 28*(1), 1–36. https://doi.org/10.1016/S0361-476X(02)00008-5

Martin, C., Czellar, S., & Pandelaere, M. (2019). Age-related changes in materialism in adults – A self-uncertainty perspective. *Journal of Research in Personality, 78*, 16–24. https://doi.org/10.1016/j.jrp.2018.09.007

Mattingly, B. A., & Lewandowski Jr, G. W. (2013). An expanded self is a more capable self: The association between self-concept size and self-efficacy. *Self and Identity, 12*(6), 621–634. https://doi.org/10.1080/15298868.2012.718863

McGregor, I., & Marigold, D. (in press). Reactive approach motivation: From personal uncertainty to love or hate, and meaning in life. In P. J. Carroll, K. Rios, & K. C. Oleson (Eds.), *Handbook of the uncertain self* (2nd ed.). Routledge Press.

Meldahl, J. M., & Muchinsky, P. M. (1997). The neurotic dimension of vocational indecision: Gender comparability? *Journal of Career Assessment, 5*(3), 317–331. https://doi.org/10.1177/106907279700500305

Mitchell, K. E., Al Levin, S., & Krumboltz, J. D. (1999). Planned happenstance: Constructing unexpected career opportunities. *Journal of Counseling & Development*, *77*(2), 115–124. https://doi.org/10.1002/j.1556-6676.1999.tb02431.x
Morrison Rios, K., & Johnson, C. S. (2011). When what you have is who you are: Self-uncertainty leads individualists to see themselves in their possessions. *Personality and Social Psychology Bulletin, 37*(5) 639–651. https://doi.org/10.1177/0146167211403158
Murray, S. L. (in press). Certainty through social connection? Protecting the self in an uncertain social world. In P. J. Carroll, K. Rios, & K. C. Oleson (Eds.), *Handbook of the uncertain self* (2nd ed.). Routledge Press.
Pfattheicher, S., & Böhm, R. (2018). Honesty-humility under threat: Self-uncertainty destroys trust among the nice guys. *Journal of Personality and Social Psychology, 114*(1), 179–194. https://doi.org/10.1037/pspp0000144
Pleskac, T. J., Wallsten, T. S., Wang, P., & Lejuez, C. W. (2008). Development of an automatic response mode to improve the clinical utility of sequential risk-taking tasks. *Experimental and Clinical Psychopharmacology, 16*(6), 555–564. https://doi.org/10.1037/a0014245
Proulx, T., Heine, S. J., & Vohs, K. D. (2010). When is the unfamiliar the uncanny? Meaning affirmative after exposure to absurdist literature, humor, and art. *Personality and Social Psychology Bulletin, 36*(6), 817–829. https://doi.org/10.1177/0146167210369896
Proulx, T., & Inzlicht, M. (2012). The five "A"s of meaning maintenance: Finding meaning in the theories of sense-making. *Psychological Inquiry, 23*(4), 317–335. https://doi.org/10.1080/1047840X.2012.702372
Rast III, D. E., Hogg, M. A., & Giessner, S. R. (2013). Self-uncertainty and support for autocratic leadership. *Self and Identity*, *12*(6), 635–649. https://doi.org/10.1080/15298868.2012.718864
Rast, D. E. III, Hogg, M. A., & Giessner, S. R. (2016). Who trusts charismatic leaders who champion change? The role of group identification, membership centrality, and self-uncertainty. *Group Dynamics: Theory, Research, and Practice, 20*(4), 259–275. https://doi.org/10.1037/gdn0000053
Reid, C. A., Green, J. D., Wildschut, T., & Sedikides, C. (2014). Scent-evoked nostalgia. *Memory, 23*(2), 157–166. https://doi.org/10.1080/09658211.2013.876048
Richard, F. D., Bond, C. F., Jr., & Stokes-Zoota, J. J. (2003). One hundred years of social psychology quantitatively described. *Review of General Psychology, 7*(4), 331–363. https://doi.org/10.1037/1089-2680.7.4.331
Rios, K., Wheeler, S. C., & Miller, D. T. (2012). Compensatory nonconformity: Self-uncertainty and low implicit self-esteem increase adoption and expression of minority opinions. *Journal of Experimental Social Psychology, 48*(6), 1300–1309. https://doi.org/10.1016/j.jesp.2012.07.005
Ritchie, T. D., Sedikides, C., Wildschut, T., Arndt, J., & Gidron, Y. (2011). Self-concept clarity mediates the relation between stress and subjective well-being. *Self and Identity*, *10*(4), 493–508. https://doi.org/10.1080/15298868.2010.493066
Routledge, C., Arndt, J., Sedikides, C., & Wildschut, T. (2008). A blast from the past: The terror management function of nostalgia. *Journal of Experimental Social Psychology, 44*(1), 132–140. https://doi.org/10.1016/j.jesp.2006.11.001
Routledge, C., Arndt, J., Wildschut, T., Sedikides, C., Hart, C., Juhl, J., Vingerhoets, A. J., & Scholtz, W. (2011). The past makes the present meaningful: Nostalgia as an existential resource. *Journal of Personality and Social Psychology, 101*(3), 638–652. https://doi.org/10.1037/a0024292
Routledge, C., Wildschut, T., Sedikides, C., Juhl, J., & Arndt, J. (2012). The power of the past: Nostalgia as a meaning-making resource. *Memory, 20*(5), 452–460. https://doi.org/10.1080/09658211.2012.677452
Saka, N., Gati, I., & Kelly, K. R. (2008). Emotional and personality-related aspects of career-decision-making difficulties. *Journal of Career Assessment*, *16*(4), 403–424. https://doi.org/10.1177/1069072708318900
Sedikides, C., Hong, E., & Wildschut, T. (2023). Self-continuity. *Annual Review of Psychology, 74*, 333–361. https://doi.org/10.1146/annurev-psych-032420-032236
Sedikides, C., & Wildschut, T. (2016). Nostalgia: A bittersweet emotion that confers psychological health benefits. In A. M. Wood, J. Johnson, A. M. Wood, & J. Johnson (Eds.), *The Wiley handbook of positive clinical psychology* (pp. 125–136). Wiley-Blackwell. https://doi.org/10.1002/9781118468197.ch9
Sedikides, C., & Wildschut, T. (2018). Finding meaning in nostalgia. *Review of General Psychology, 22*(1), 48–61. https://doi.org/10.1037/gpr0000109
Sedikides, C., & Wildschut, T. (2019). The sociality of personal and collective nostalgia. *European Review of Social Psychology, 30*(1), 123–173. https://doi.org/10.1080/10463283.2019.1630098
Sedikides, C., Wildschut, T., Arndt, J., & Routledge, C. (2008). Nostalgia: past, present, and future. *Current Directions in Psychological Science, 17*(5), 304–307. https://doi.org/10.1111/j.1467-8721.2008.00595.x

Sedikides, C., Wildschut, T., Cheung, W.-Y., Routledge, C., Hepper, E. G., Arndt, J., Vail, K., Zhou, X., Brackstone, K., & Vingerhoets, A. J. J. M. (2016). Nostalgia fosters self-continuity: Uncovering the mechanism (social connectedness) and the consequence (eudaimonic well-being). *Emotion, 16*(4), 524–539. https://doi.org/10.1037/emo0000136

Sedikides, C., Wildschut, T., Gaertner, L., Routledge, C., & Arndt, J. (2008). Nostalgia as enabler of self-continuity. In F. Sani (Ed.), *Self-continuity: Individual and collective perspectives* (pp. 227–239). Psychology Press.

Sedikides, C., Wildschut, T., Routledge, C., & Arndt, J. (2015). Nostalgia counteracts self-discontinuity and restores self-continuity. *European Journal of Social Psychology, 45*(1), 52–61. https://doi.org/10.1002/ejsp.2073

Sedikides, C., Wildschut, T., Routledge, C., Arndt, J., Hepper, E. G., & Zhou, X. (2015). To nostalgize: Mixing memory with affect and desire. *Advances in Experimental Social Psychology, 51,* 189–273. https://doi.org/10.1016/bs.aesp.2014.10.001

Serling, D. A., & Betz, N. E. (1990). Development and evaluation of a measure of fear of commitment. *Journal of Counseling Psychology*, *37*(1), 91–97. https://doi.org/10.1037/0022-0167.37.1.91

Sexton, K. A., Norton, P. J., Walker, J. R., & Norton, G. R. (2003). Hierarchical model of generalized and specific vulnerabilities in anxiety. *Cognitive Behaviour Therapy*, *32*(2), 82–94. https://doi.org/10.1080/16506070302321

Sheldon, K. M., Ryan, R. M., Rawsthorne, L. J., & Ilardi, B. (1997). Trait self and true self: Cross-role variation in the Big-Five personality traits and its relations with psychological authenticity and subjective well-being. *Journal of Personality and Social Psychology*, *73*(6), 1380–1393. https://doi.org/10.1037/0022-3514.73.6.1380

Shin, J. Y., Steger, M. F., & Henry, K. L. (2016). Self-concept clarity's role in meaning in life among American college students: A latent growth approach. *Self and Identity*, *15*(2), 206–223. https://doi.org/10.1080/15298868.2015.1111844

Sokol, Y., & Eisenheim, E. (2016). The relationship between continuous identity disturbances, negative mood, and suicidal ideation. *Primary Care Companion for CNS Disorders, 18*(1). https://doi.org/10.4088/PCC.15m01824

Steger, M. F., Frazier, P., Oishi, S., & Kaler, M. (2006). The meaning in life questionnaire: Assessing the presence of and search for meaning in life. *Journal of Counseling Psychology, 53*(1), 80–93. https://doi.org/10.1037/0022-0167.53.1.80

Stephan, E., Sedikides, C., Wildschut, T., Cheung, W. Y., Routledge, C., & Arndt, J. (2015). Nostalgia-evoked inspiration: Mediating mechanisms and motivational implications. *Personality and Social Psychology Bulletin, 41*(10), 1395–1410. https://doi.org/10.1177/0146167215596985

Stephan, E., Wildschut, T., Sedikides, C., Zhou, X., He, W., Routledge, C., Cheung, W. Y., & Vingerhoets, A. J. J. M. (2014). The mnemonic mover: Nostalgia regulates avoidance and approach motivation. *Emotion, 14*(3), 545–561. https://doi.org/10.1037/a0035673

Story, A. L. (2004). Self-esteem and self-certainty: A mediational analysis. *European Journal of Personality, 18*(2), 115–125. https://doi.org/10.1002/per.502

Sweeny, K., & Howell, J. L. (in press). Managing acute uncertainty about the future. In P. J. Carroll, K. Rios, & K. C. Oleson (Eds.), *Handbook of the uncertain self* (2nd ed.). Routledge Press.

The New Oxford Dictionary of English. (1998) (J. Pearsall, Ed.). Oxford University Press.

Trevor-Roberts, E. (2006). Are you sure? the role of uncertainty in career. *Journal of Employment Counseling, 43*(3), 98–116. https://doi.org/10.1002/j.2161-1920.2006.tb00010.x

Usborne, E., & Taylor, D. M. (2010). The role of cultural identity clarity for self-concept clarity, self-esteem, and subjective well-being. *Personality and Social Psychology Bulletin*, *36*(7), 883–897. https://doi.org/10.1177/0146167210372215

Van den Bos, K. (2009). Making sense of life: The existential self trying to deal with personal uncertainty. *Psychological Inquiry, 20*(4), 197–217. https://doi.org/10.1080/10478400903333411

Van den Bos, K., & Lind, E. A. (2002). Uncertainty management by means of fairness judgments. *Advances in Experimental Social Psychology, 34*, 1–60. https://doi.org/10.1016/S0065-2601(02)80003-X

Van den Bos, K., & Lind, E. A. (in press). The social psychology of fairness and the regulation of personal uncertainty: Implications for understanding unrest and discontent in society. In P. J. Carroll, K. Rios, & K. C. Oleson (Eds.), *Handbook of the uncertain self* (2nd ed.). Routledge Press.

Van Dijke, M., Wildschut, T., Leunissen, J., & Sedikides, C. (2015). Nostalgia buffers the negative impact of low procedural justice on cooperation. *Organizational Behavior and Human Decision Processes, 127*, 15–29. https://doi.org/10.1016/j.obhdp.2014.11.005

Van Tilburg, W. A. P., Sedikides, C., Wildschut, T., & Vingerhoets, A. J. J. M. (2019). How nostalgia infuses life with meaning: from social connectedness to self-continuity. *European Journal of Social Psychology, 49*(3), 521–532. https://doi.org/10.1002/ejsp.2519

Van Tilburg, W. A., Wildschut, T., & Sedikides, C. (2018). Nostalgia's place among self-relevant emotions. *Cognition and Emotion, 32*(4), 742–759. https://doi.org/10.1080/02699931.2017.1351331

Vess, M., Arndt, J., Routledge, C., Sedikides, C., & Wildschut, T. (2012). Nostalgia as a resource for the self. *Self and Identity, 11*(3), 273–284. https://doi.org/10.1080/15298868.2010.521452

Wildschut, T., Sedikides, C., Arndt, J., & Routledge, C. (2006). Nostalgia: Content, triggers, functions. *Journal of Personality and Social Psychology, 91*(5), 975–993. https://doi.org/10.1037/0022-3514.91.5.975

Wildschut, T., Sedikides, C., Routledge, C., Arndt, J., & Cordaro, F. (2010). Nostalgia as a repository of social-connectedness: The role of attachment-related avoidance. *Journal of Personality and Social Psychology, 98*(4), 573–586. https://doi.org/10.1037/a0017597

Wildschut, T., Sedikides, C., & Robertson, S. (2018). Sociality and intergenerational transfer of older adults' nostalgia. *Memory, 26*(8), 1030–1041. https://doi.org/10.1080/09658211.2018.1470645

Wildschut, T., Sedikides, C., & Alowidy, D. (2019). *Hanin*: Nostalgia among Syrian refugees. *European Journal of Social Psychology, 49*(7), 1368–1384. https://doi.org/10.1002/ejsp.2590

Wildschut, T., & Sedikides, C. (2022a). The measurement of nostalgia. In W. Ruch, A. B. Bakker, L. Tay, & F. Gander (Eds.), *Handbook of positive psychology assessment* (pp. 438–451). Hogrefe.

Wildschut, T., & Sedikides, C. (2022b). Psychology and nostalgia: Towards a functional approach. In M. H. Jacobsen (Ed.), *Intimations of nostalgia: Multidisciplinary explorations of an enduring emotion* (pp. 110–128). Bristol University Press.

Wildschut, T., & Sedikides, C. (2023). Benefits of nostalgia in vulnerable populations. *European Review of Social Psychology, 34*(1), 44–91. https://doi.org/10.1080/10463283.2022.2036005

Wright, K. D., Lebell, M. A. A., & Carleton, R. N. (2016). Intolerance of uncertainty, anxiety sensitivity, health anxiety, and anxiety disorder symptoms in youth. *Journal of Anxiety Disorders, 41*, 35–42. https://doi.org/10.1016/j.janxdis.2016.04.011

Yang, Q., Bi, C. Z., Li, L., & Huang, X. T. (2017). Self-uncertainty: Concepts, structures, and theories. *Advances in Psychological Science, 25*(6), 1012–1024. https://doi.org/10.3724/SP.J.1042.2017.01012

Yang, Q., Ybarra, O., Zhao, Y., & Huang, X. (2020). Restoring meaning: Self-uncertainty increases subjective distance between the past and present self. *Social Behavior and Personality: An International Journal, 48*(7), e8823. https://doi.org/10.2224/sbp.8823

Zhou, X., Sedikides, C., Wildschut, C., & Gao, D.-G. (2008). Counteracting loneliness: On the restorative function of nostalgia. *Psychological Science, 19*(10), 1023–1029. https://doi.org/10.1111/j.1467-9280.2008.02194.x

Zhou, X., Sedikides, C., Mo . T., Li, W., Hong, E. K., & Wildschut, T. (2022). The restorative power of nostalgia: Thwarting loneliness by raising happiness during the COVID-19 pandemic. *Social Psychological and Personality Science, 13*(4), 803–815. https://doi.org/10.17605/OSF.IO/U5RJB

Zhou, X., Wildschut, T., Sedikides, C., Shi, K., & Feng, C. (2012). Nostalgia: The gift that keeps on giving. *Journal of Consumer Research, 39*(1), 39–50. https://doi.org/10.1086/662199

Zou, X., Lee, M., Wildschut, T., & Sedikides, C. (2019). Nostalgia increases financial risk-taking. *Personality and Social Psychology Bulletin, 45*(5), 907–919. https://doi.org/10.1177/0146167218799717

Zou, X., Wildschut, T., Cable, D., & Sedikides, C. (2018). Nostalgia for host culture facilitates repatriation success: The role of self-continuity. *Self and Identity, 17*(3), 327–342. https://doi.org/10.1080/15298868.2017.1378123

9

JUMPING TO CONCLUSIONS

Carmen Sanchez, Steffen Moritz and David Dunning

Reaching decisions may be especially difficult in uncertain environments because they require people to compile, weigh, and sort information before reaching a conclusion. Given the difficulty of these tasks, it is not surprising ample social psychological research suggests people commit a host of systematic errors when making judgments under uncertainty, with people often expressing undue confidence in their abilities in these complex tasks (Dunning et al., 1990; Griffin & Tversky, 1992; Lichtenstein et al., 1982). Dealing with uncertainty is one of the most common problems people face and requires people to choose the amount of information to gather before reaching a decision. When does one stop and reach a conclusion? Some people agonize and take far too long before making decisions. Other people jump to a conclusion far more quickly than most people would consider wise.

Interestingly, the topic of who gathers too little information has received extensive study but much of the research is done with a specialized group where the tendency to jump to conclusions carries significant implications, schizophrenia patients (Dudley et al., 2015; Dudley et al., 2016; Garety & Freeman, 1999; Huq et al., 1988; Moritz & Woodward, 2005; Ross et al., 2015; So et al., 2016). In this chapter, we integrate findings from that literature in clinical psychology with research from social psychology to explore who might be the most vulnerable to the types of errors, illusions, impairments, and overconfidence that characterize everyday judgment and decision-making. In doing so, we discuss implications for learning, with an emphasis on probabilistic learning, and how jumping to conclusions impacts perceptions of abilities.

We begin our chapter with a discussion of findings related to cognitive biases. Cognitive biases encompass a broad range of systematic errors people face when they are interpretating and explaining the world around them (Ehrlinger et al., 2016). Our focus on cognitive biases is specifically related to information gathering. After that, we then ask which biases may be exacerbated when people collect too little information. That is, when do people fail to act rationally when they reach conclusions based on minimal information gathering?

Cognitive Biases in Social Psychology

From a social psychological perspective, people in general are vulnerable to reaching a conclusion based on too little information. They are inattentive to small sample sizes and exaggerate the

DOI: 10.4324/9781003363385-10

degree to which these small samples represent the truth (Benjamin et al., 2016; Griffin & Tversky, 1992; Tversky & Kahneman, 1971; Williams et al., 2013), In doing so, they make conclusions from too little information and infer meaningful patterns from random or chaotic data (Camerer, 1987; Chapman & Chapman, 1969; Guthrie et al., 1993; Ono, 1987; Rabin, 2002). Further, people tend to be disproportionately influenced by the very first piece of information they encounter (Asch, 1946; Jones et al., 1968; Kelley, 1950), and thus again reach conclusions that vary from the truth (Kamin, 1968; Yarritu et al., 2015). They also tend not to question what they do not know before reaching conclusions, and reach decisions solely on the information presented to them (Kardes et al., 2022; Walters et al., 2017).

Thus, extensive research in social and cognitive psychology has shown just how comfortable people are taking a small amount of information, generalizing it to large populations, and forming highly confident conclusions from it (Heider & Simmel, 1944; Risen et al., 2007; Sanchez & Dunning, 2018). When people make decisions or form beliefs, they use the first piece of information or the first few pieces of evidence they initially encounter, and they fail to temper their beliefs given how little information they have (Griffin & Tversky, 1992; Wang et al., 2022).

Cognitive Biases in Schizophrenia Patients

From a clinical perspective, an exaggeration of cognitive biases is believed to lead to the development of schizophrenia, especially positive symptoms such as delusions (Bell et al., 2006; Bentall, 1992; Garety & Freeman, 2013; Savulich et al., 2012; Van Der Gaag, 2006). Schizophrenia is a chronic and severe mental condition, affecting roughly 1% of the population (Cooper et al., 2007). People with schizophrenia experience disabling symptoms that affect how they think, feel, and behave.

Amongst these symptoms are delusions and hallucinations (American Psychiatric Association, 2013). Delusions are firmly held beliefs with little to no evidence to substantiate them (Balzan, 2016; Moritz et al., 2014). These delusions have themes of grandiosity (e.g. "I am immortal") and paranoia (e.g. "My spouse is trying to poison me") and are often distressing for the patient and those around them (Freeman, 2007; Turner et al., 2014), although ambivalence towards positive symptoms is frequent (Schneider et al., 2023). They are believed to occur because of deficits in probabilistic learning: When two unrelated events happen together, people form a pattern based on them, and reach incorrect conclusions about their relationship (Moritz et al., 2014). For example, if the phone rings and a car drives by, people may believe they are being surveilled. Unfortunately, schizophrenia patients usually attach strong certainty to their delusional beliefs (Balzan, 2016; Köther et al., 2012; Moritz & Woodward, 2006a), reaching firmly held conclusions when alternative conclusions are still possible (Moritz & Woodward, 2006c).

Consequently, schizophrenia patients tend to be overconfident in the judgments they formulate (Balzan, 2016; Köther et al., 2012; Moritz & Woodward, 2006a). Overconfidence, which may result in "knowledge corruption" in schizophrenia, is broadly defined as errors and biases in decisions and judgments people fail to anticipate in themselves. Knowledge corruption occurs if the proportion of errors on all high-confidently held cognitions is high. Schizophrenia patients tend to be less calibrated than non-clinical samples about their abilities and weaknesses (Gawęda et al., 2015; Moritz & Woodward, 2002; Peters et al., 1999). When they engage in recall tasks, they display less confidence in their correct memories and have greater overconfidence in their erroneous recollections (Moritz & Woodward, 2002; Moritz & Woodward, 2006a; Moritz & Woodward, 2006c). Yet, not all studies were able to replicate this finding, and studies at times also report underconfidence in patients with schizophrenia for correct responses. Antipsychotic medication, which is routinely given in this population, likely moderates findings as antipsychotic medication may induce doubt (Moritz et al., 2016). Confidence scores in clinical samples with psychosis-related disorders also predict the therapy length needed for hospital discharge. In fact, thoughts and attitudes become less consequential for judgments as the perceived validity of the thoughts is decreased (for a further discussion see Chapter by Briñol and Petty in this volume).

The confidence gap in schizophrenia patients results in greater difficulty in distinguishing between correct and incorrect subjective facts, which may further promote delusional thoughts (Moritz, Andreou et al., 2014; Moritz, Ramdini et al., 2014; Moritz & Woodward, 2006b). Given that people are more likely to act on their behaviors when they are overconfident (Barber & Odean, 2001; Moritz & Van Quaquebeke, 2014), understanding the development of overconfidence is of interest to schizophrenia researchers (Hoven et al., 2019).

What Is Jumping to Conclusions in Clinical Psychology?

The propensity for schizophrenia patients to display cognitive biases led schizophrenia researchers to explore whether there might be individual differences in their occurrence and whether individual variations in cognitive biases were linked to greater delusion and impaired decision-making. Specifically, researchers became interested in individual differences among schizophrenia patients in information gathering, or the propensity to jump to conclusions (JTC), in which individuals collect only a few pieces of evidence before reaching a conclusion in a decision-making task, often doing so when alternative conclusions are still possible (Dudley et al., 2015; Garety & Freeman, 1999; Huq et al., 1988; Moritz & Woodward, 2005).

Typically, decision-making tasks that have some degree of uncertainty are used to measure JTC. The tasks can be quite simple and sparse, and thus focus on material far-afield from schizophrenia. In one common task, participants are shown two urns and told that each contains a different proportion of beads. For example, one urn has 80 red beads and 20 white beads and the second contains red and white beads in the opposite proportion. Beads are then drawn, one at a time, from one of the urns, until players stop the process because they believe they know which urn the beads are being drawn from. Some players require seeing many beads before reaching a decision. Others, stop more quickly, even after seeing only one or two beads (Dudley et al., 2015; Moritz & Woodward, 2005). These are the players who show the "jumping to conclusions" style (Dudley et al., 2015; Moritz & Woodward, 2005).

Roughly half of all schizophrenia patients exhibit the jumping to conclusions bias measured in this way (Fine et al., 2007; Freeman, 2007; Freeman et al., 2008). Those who demonstrate the JTC bias are more likely to exhibit psychosis (Dudley et al., 2015), a conviction in delusional ideas, and cognitive inflexibility (i.e., no possibility that one could be wrong). They show no differences in terms of anxiety and depression (Garety et al., 2005). Thus, JTC does appear to be primarily a cognitive bias instead of an affective one.

To be sure, the key JTC finding among schizophrenia patients is those who jump to conclusions are more likely to believe and act on their delusions (Garety et al., 2005; Ross et al., 2015; Moritz & Woodward, 2004; Warman et al., 2007; Zawadski, 2012), and the JTC bias is taken to represent liability to delusions (Dudley et al., 2015). JTC also appears to be a trait difference, rather than momentary carelessness, with high test-retest reliability of.88 after three months and.84 after 12 months (So et al., 2012).

Jumping to Conclusions in Non-Clinical Samples

There is nothing inherent about the JTC bias that constrains it to schizophrenia patients. Indeed, measures of JTC contain no schizophrenia-relevant material. Thus, it is not a surprise that the JTC bias has been found in studies of the general population as well, with about 10–20% of respondents exhibiting it using the same measures applied to schizophrenia patients (Fine et al., 2007; Freeman, 2007; Freeman et al., 2008).

This has led some researchers to explore whether findings from schizophrenia research replicate in nonclinical samples. Indeed, many of the findings using nonclinical samples that examine the relationship between JTC and unrealistic beliefs are reminiscent of those in schizophrenia research. Using nonclinical samples, those higher in JTC are more likely to endorse conspiracy theories, express paranoia, harbor delusional ideation, and endorse the occurrence of perceptual anomalies (Freeman et al., 2008; Pytlik et al., 2020; Ross et al., 2015; Warman et al., 2007; Zawadski, 2012; Ziegler et al., 2008, although see Ross et al., 2016).,

Those higher in JTC endorse more oddball beliefs, such as medical myths (e.g. *Health officials know that cell phones cause cancer but are doing nothing to stop it because large corporations won't let them)*, conspiracy theories (e.g. *Princess Diana's death was not an accident but rather an organized assassination by members of the British royal family who disliked her*), and paranormal beliefs (e.g. *During altered states, such as sleep or trances, the spirit can leave the body*) (Sanchez & Dunning, 2021). JTC is also associated with higher levels of conviction in delusional thoughts. That is, those higher in JTC are more convinced that harm is occurring or about to occur to them, and that the person causing the harm has the express intention to do so. Much like in clinical samples, JTC in the general population is unrelated to symptoms involving mood and emotion, such as depression, anxiety, or worry (Freeman et al., 2008; Garety et al., 2005).

In terms of the relationship in the general population between JTC and "knowledge corruption" there is much less work on this topic. However, in the judgment and decision-making literature, much of the work referred to as knowledge corruption in the schizophrenia literature would be referred to as overconfidence or miscalibration (Dunning et al., 1990; Lichtenstein et al., 1982). Here, the topic of JTC and overconfidence in a nonclinical sample has been explored. Much like in schizophrenia research, JTC behavior is related to exacerbated overconfidence and greater miscalibration about which specific answers are right versus wrong (Sanchez & Dunning, 2021).

Jumping to conclusions is also related to common reasoning errors among the general population. For example, high JTC individuals score lower on the Cognitive Reflection Test, in which people confront questions that tempt test-takers with intuitive answers that are wrong (Frederick, 2005). For example, when asked, *If John can drink one barrel of water in 6 days, and Mary can drink one barrel of water in 12 days, how long would it take them to drink one barrel of water together?* The intuitive but incorrect answer that quickly comes to mind is 9 days, but the actual answer is 4.

High JTC individuals also show similar "belief bias" errors in solving logical problems, endorsing wrong conclusions that fit common knowledge about the world but which are invalid under the laws of formal logic (Evans et al., 1983). For example, if presented with the logical syllogism *Flowers need water. Roses need water. Therefore, roses are flowers,* high JTC individuals are more likely to claim the syllogism is logically valid even though its conclusion cannot be reached from the logical structure of the syllogism.

High JTC individuals also make gambling decisions that are not wise, in a phenomenon known as denominator neglect (Reyna & Brainerd, 2008). For example, choose to gamble that a red ball will be drawn from an urn that has nine red balls out of 100 rather than drawing from the alternative urn that contains one red ball out of ten. The number 9 may seem more impressive than the number 1, but the odds of winning are better on that second urn, 10% versus 9% (Sanchez & Dunning, 2021).

Proposed Mechanisms

Why do people show the JTC bias? Among schizophrenia researchers, several cognitive processes that might underlie the relationship between JTC and judgmental errors and biases have been proposed. The two most popular proposed mechanisms are hyper-salience of evidence and liberal acceptance of conclusions, both of which are supported by empirical research. These two mechanisms proposed are reminiscent of system 1 versus system 2 thinking in judgment and decision-making research, or automatic versus controlled thought (Kahneman, 2011; Sloman, 1996). That is, cognitive processes can either be automatic, intuitive, with little thought (i.e., system 1), or conscious and logical (system 2). Failures of either may lead to the jumping-to-conclusions bias.

Under the hyper-salience of evidence account, individuals who exhibit JTC imbue current stimuli with "hyper-salience." That is, they over-adjust their conclusions based on the most recent piece of evidence they encounter. In the urn task, when asked to report the confidence of judgments after each draw, schizophrenia patients are more confident from the onset (Speechley et al., 2010) and they make more drastic changes in their confidence ratings after each additional piece of evidence is seen (Garety, 1991; Huq et al., 1988; Langdon et al., 2008) or reward gained (Joyce et al., 2013).

The hyper-salience of the evidence mechanism is suggestive of an error in the automatic processing of misdirected thought in schizophrenia, delusion, and misguided belief. Whatever evidence toward a conclusion that is currently available in the environment is overweighted when making a decision. It looms larger than other information that is less perceptually salient or to information acquired in the past. For example, if it was sunny yesterday but raining today a person might be more likely to forecast rain for tomorrow because they would relatively overvalue weather conditions that are present and perceptually available. This is consistent with the notion that schizophrenia patients have more difficulty inhibiting sensory information perceived in the immediate environment (Ventura et al., 2013).

As an alternative, under the liberal acceptance account, people have lax decision thresholds when they make decisions. That is, schizophrenia patients require less evidence to accept an option (Moritz & Woodward, 2004). In two-choice tasks, like the beads task, when choices are mutually exclusive conclusions are reached more hastily. Similarly, under the liberal acceptance account, if one choice stands out among many others, JTC behaviors are expected (Moritz et al., 2006). However, when there are more alternatives with more ambiguity a delay in decision making may occur (Moritz & Woodward, 2004). Schizophrenia patients are also less inclined to change their behavior even when receiving contrary feedback, and this error is not due to lower cognitive ability (Everett et al., 2001: Pantelis et al., 1999).

In judgment and decision-making research, the liberal acceptance mechanism suggests that JTC is absent in controlled processing. Specifically, JTC is a willingness to reach a conclusion based on a small amount of evidence lightly considered. As such, those higher in JTC may not have heightened automatic experiences, but instead, they fail to exert cognitive effort over their deliberate thoughts. In support of this mechanism in the general population, Sanchez and Dunning (2021) examined performance in logical puzzles and gambling situations, decomposing participants' responses to system 1 and system 2 components and found that high JTC participants showed less system 2 reasoning than their low JTC peers, whereas both groups showed equivalent levels of system 1 thought.

Hyper-salience of evidence and liberal acceptance are the most popular psychological mechanisms that explain the jumping-to-conclusions bias. However, others have suggested that the two mechanisms are not mutually exclusive and may interact to form the bias (Evans et al., 2015).

Unfortunately, this relationship is not fully understood because it takes considerable resources to establish a causal link in the biological, psychological, and social mechanisms at play.

Other plausible explanations for JTC have been ruled out by data. For example, JTC does not appear to be a deficit in motivation. If a task is more difficult, both those high and low in JTC behavior increase the amount of evidence they obtain before reaching a decision, inconsistent with the notion those high in JTC are simply unmotivated to do well (Dudley et al., 1997; Garety et al., 2005). When the experimenter shows everyone the same amount of information, those who are high in JTC do just as well as others (Dudley et al., 1997), and take a similar amount of time to reach decisions (Moritz & Woodward, 2005). JTC is also not a result of the need for closure, or due to misunderstandings of probabilistic inference (Dudley et al., 2015). That said, there is some empirical evidence suggesting JTC may be linked to impairments in working memory, but not general deficits in cognitive ability (Broome et al., 2007; Garety et al., 2013b). However, the evidence is inconsistent, and memory aids and impulsivity do not eliminate the JTC effects (Dudley et al., 1997; Gabbert, 2020; Moritz & Woodward, 2005).

Given that the JTC bias is highly prevalent in the schizophrenia population and yet can be studied as an individual difference in a nonclinical population, greater insights for clinical psychologists might be gained by social and personality psychologists studying JTC. Clinical psychologists may be able to use findings gained from these experiments to assist in the treatment of schizophrenia patients and to better understand the underpinnings of the psychological mechanisms that lead to delusion formation. To be sure, this was the catalyst that has led some to study how those high versus low in JTC learn probabilistically in a nonclinical sample (Sanchez & Dunning, 2021).

JTC and Learning in Clinical and Social Psychology

In clinical settings, deficits in probabilistic learning have been proposed as a precursor to delusion formation (Moritz et al., 2014). Beliefs formed early, with too little evidence, may also exacerbate downstream biases like confirmation bias, illusory correlation, and ultimately overconfidence. Others should conduct further research examining the development of cognitive biases and their relationship to belief formation. Those who fail to adequately learn correlations between events in the environment, or the lack thereof, will tend to arrive at erroneous theories about how the world works.

Given that JTC is associated both with delusions and overconfidence in the face of uncertain environments, probabilistic learning is another area of study in clinical psychology. To be sure, schizophrenia patient performance is worse than non-clinical participants on probabilistic tasks (Averbeck et al., 2011; Dowd et al., 2016; Weiler et al., 2009). However, the rates of learning among schizophrenia patients and control participants are similar, ruling out that these are caused solely by a lack of attention (Kéri et al., 2001; Weickert et al., 2002; Weiler et al., 2009).

Others have sought to explore the role of JTC in probabilistic learning in nonclinical samples. In these studies, JTC was measured then participants engaged in a completely novel probabilistic learning task (Sanchez & Dunning, 2021). They were asked to imagine they were medical residents in a post-apocalyptic world that has been overrun by zombies, a task they were certain participants had no actual experience with. Participants were required to learn by trial and error how to diagnose patients based on imperfect symptom clues over 60 repeated trials. Along with each diagnosis, participants reported their confidence.

Across all the trials, changes in learning, confidence, and overconfidence were assessed. Both high and low jumpers learned the task. However, high jumpers had lower levels of performance and higher levels of confidence as they were learning. Thus, those higher in JTC were more overconfident because of their higher confidence in their poor performance. Among high JTC participants, the elevated rise in overconfidence they expressed arose because they were more likely to generate theories, with no or little information, about how to approach the task early on (Sanchez & Dunning, 2021). In fact, even before they began the task and saw their first "patient"—that is, even before they had any experience whatsoever on the task—high JTC participants were much more likely to generate a theory about how to diagnose zombie disease than did low JTC peers.

In a subsequent study, Sanchez and Dunning (2021) sought to explore whether overconfidence as people learned could be dampened using interventions from schizophrenia research. In recent schizophrenia research, Metacognitive Training (MCT) interventions have been developed to correct cognitive biases that are associated with hallucinations and delusions in psychosis (Aghotor et al., 2010; Balzan et al., 2014; Favrod et al., 2014; for a review see: Moritz, Andreou et al., 2014; Moritz, Kerstan et al., 2011; Moritz, Veckenstedt et al., 2011; Moritz, Veckenstedt et al., 2014; Moritz et al., 2011). MCT has been shown to reduce delusional thinking and severity, and psychotic symptoms among schizophrenia patients (Gawęda et al., 2015; So et al., 2015). Specially, MCT has been shown to reduce positive symptoms (e.g. delusions, hallucinations, disorganized behavior) in the short and mid-term and it also exerts a significant effect on negative symptoms (e.g. lack of interest in the world, social withdrawal, lack of motivation) and function (Liu et al., 2018; Penney et al., 2022; Philipp et al., 2020).

Borrowing from MCT research among schizophrenia patients, intervention materials used in schizophrenia treatment were adapted to train participants to avoid jumping to conclusions. The intervention dampened overconfidence in the probabilistic learning task in a nonclinical population (Sanchez & Dunning, 2021). It is important to note that the MCT training impacted all participants, lowering their confidence, not just those who were high in JTC. This research suggests that fruitful crosstalk may exist between clinical psychology and work on social cognition in the general population. Other studies have shown that interventions derived from MCT may result in less hostility toward political opponents (Reininger et al., 2020) and reduce religious prejudice (Moritz et al., 2021).

Areas for Future Research

When do people jump to conclusions? Are there situations where some people might be vulnerable to falling prey to the JTC bias? Even though JTC is thought of as a relatively stable trait difference (So et al., 2012), there may be situations that make people especially vulnerable to JTC. The question of whether JTC is situational in the general population is an intriguing research question. Consider this: a car survey showed that 41% of Americans visit only one dealership before buying a car—a rather consequential decision (Cox Automotive, 2019). Does that behavior bear any relation to behavior on the JTC task, or to the types of decisions confronting the person matter as well?

Much of the research on JTC focuses on uncertain environments when imperfect cues are used to forecast probabilistic events. Under these conditions, JTC appears to occur when there is one alternative that stands out among others (Moritz et al., 2006). In tasks that require a decision with two mutually exclusive choices, like the urn task, schizophrenia patients are more likely to jump to conclusions (Moritz et al., 2007).

In contrast, in situations where there is a high level of ambiguity and uncertainty, schizophrenia patients show a different pattern. When a situation has greater ambiguity, with more alternatives with lower probabilities attached to each event, schizophrenia patients display a delay in decision making, the opposite of JTC. This occurs because multiple options are deemed as appropriate, and one does not stand out. More alternatives seem plausible, they surpass the threshold of acceptance. For example, schizophrenia patients judged more interpretations as plausible in the traditional thematic apperception test than did control participants. Thus, control participants were more likely to reach a plausible conclusion more quickly in these types of tasks than schizophrenia patients (Moritz & Woodward, 2004).

Can Clinical and Social Psychology Profit from a Crosstalk? A potential crosstalk between clinical and social/personality psychologists may be mutually beneficial. Work on schizophrenia is hampered because the condition is rare (Cooper et al., 2007). Conducting research with such a small population is effortful, costly, and time-consuming. Moreover, mechanisms are often revealed only after experimental work, essential for establishing causality. Generating the statistical power needed to establish such causal pathways may require greater numbers of participants than possible when only schizophrenia patients are studied. However, clinical psychology reveals psychological phenomena, such as jumping to conclusions, that might contain great importance and general applicability in populations beyond where they are discovered, and so should be of interest beyond the clinic.

Thus, as an alternative, once research questions are specified by clinical researchers, empirical studies using the general population could provide faster and more precise answers about processes and mechanisms associated with JTC. Clinical psychologists could suggest psychological phenomena that could be more easily explored in the general population, which could later be applied to understanding phenomena with schizophrenia patients.

Several areas are ripe for research on JTC in clinical psychology. For example, JTC may be a mechanism to cope with the complexity of the world. People may jump to conclusions, especially when cognition fails. Specifically, those higher in JTC who experience doubt might be more prone to harden their beliefs to avoid the cognitive discomfort of ambiguity. Those higher in JTC may collect less information because ambiguity or uncertainty feels uncomfortable. To resolve this discomfort as quickly as possible they collect little information and simultaneously form excessive confidence around this information because both of these cognitive habits in combination reduce the most uncertainty in the fastest possible manner. They compensate in uncertain environments by demonstrating excessive confidence.

To be sure, this has been tested in an unaffected population. Participants who score higher in positive symptoms for schizophrenia were more likely to jump to conclusions, show greater confidence, and make greater errors. However, the experimental condition to induce doubt did not result in significant differences compared to the control condition (Moritz et al., 2019). However, the tasks used may not have involved enough personal relevance, and the sample size is limited. Thus, the question of whether those high in JTC are more likely to harden their beliefs to compensate for discomfort from ambiguity remains.

There may also be beneficial personality characteristics associated with JTC. For example, people who make quick decisive decisions may be admired. Overconfident people are more likely to be esteemed by their peers (Anderson et al., 2012). Quick decision-making may be rewarded in daily life as people tend to admire people who make decisive actions. There may be unexplored circumstances and situations that exacerbate JTC behaviors. Even though there is evidence that JTC is a trait difference, are there environmental factors that improve or worsen decision-making among these individuals? What is the impact of anxiety, stress, or medications on decision-making? Finally, what type of information are jumpers using to make decisions? JTC may be especially dangerous when the quality of information is poor.

Conclusion: On Overthinking

In this chapter, we have gathered evidence from two fields, clinical and social psychology, on jumping to conclusions. We explored whether those who jump to conclusions might be the most vulnerable to the types of errors, illusions, impairments, and overconfidence that characterize everyday judgment and decision-making. Such a relationship has long been studied among schizophrenia patients.

It is important to note that much of the research on JTC focuses on its relationships with maladaptive behaviors. The focus of the review was on people who are prone to collect too little information before deciding. There also may be situations and circumstances in which jumping to conclusions is favorable. Collecting too much information can also be an error in decision-making (Wang et al., 2022). Overthinking can also be negative. For example, overthinking leads people to make decisions that diverge from expert opinions (Wilson & Schooler, 1991), and reduces preference consistency, especially in complex decisions (Nordgren & Dijksterhuis, 2009). Many would even rather administer electric shocks to themselves than be left alone with their own thoughts (Wilson et al., 2014).

In clinical psychology, people with obsessive-compulsive disorders are overly cautious and collect too much information, they are low jumpers (Fear & Healy, 1997). Those with obsessive-compulsive disorders fail to perceive risk correctly, spending more time deliberating on low-risk decisions and yet they do not spend more time than others on high-risk decisions (Foa et al., 2003). Sometimes a decision hastily made can be better than no decision at all. Others should explore the consequences and situations when low jumping is more likely to impact decision-making negatively.

Thus, one should not necessarily jump to conclusions when it comes to jumping to conclusions, and there is a long list of interesting questions and complications for future research to address. A frequent and important question is whether people should think things through or go with their gut. When it comes to gathering evidence, it may be important to ask whether one could use just a little bit more information, before jumping to any conclusions. It is this decision, rather than the final one, that may be the most consequential one of all.

References

Aghotor, J., Pfueller, U., Moritz, S., Weisbrod, M., & Roesch-Ely, D. (2010). Metacognitive training for patients with schizophrenia (MCT): Feasibility and preliminary evidence for its efficacy. *Journal of Behavior Therapy and Experimental Psychiatry, 41*, 207–211.

American Psychiatric Association. (2013). *Diagnostic and statistical manual of mental disorders* (5th ed.). Washington, DC: Author.

Anderson, C., Brion, S., Moore, D. A., & Kennedy, J. A. (2012). A status-enhancement account of overconfidence. *Journal of Personality and Social Psychology, 103*, 718–735.

Asch, S. E. (1946). Forming impressions of personality. *The Journal of Abnormal and Social Psychology, 41,* 258–290.

Averbeck, B. B., Evans, S., Chouhan, V., Bristow, E., & Shergill, S. S. (2011). Probabilistic learning and inference in schizophrenia. *Schizophrenia Research, 127*, 115–122.

Balzan, R. P. (2016). Overconfidence in psychosis: The foundation of delusional conviction?. *Cogent Psychology, 3*, 1–11.

Balzan, R. P., Delfabbro, P. H., Galletly, C. A., & Woodward, T. S. (2014). Metacognitive training for patients with schizophrenia: Preliminary evidence for a targeted, single-module programme. *Australian & New Zealand Journal of Psychiatry, 48*, 1126–1136.

Barber, B. M., & Odean, T. (2001). Boys will be boys: Gender, overconfidence, and common stock investment. *The Quarterly Journal of Economics, 116*, 261–292.

Bell, V., Halligan, P. W., & Ellis, H. D. (2006). Explaining delusions: A cognitive perspective. *Trends in Cognitive Sciences, 10*, 219–226.

Benjamin, D. J., Rabin, M., & Raymond, C. (2016). A model of nonbelief in the law of large numbers. *Journal of the European Economic Association, 14,* 515–544.

Bentall, R. P. (1992). A proposal to classify happiness as a psychiatric disorder. *Journal of Medical Ethics, 18*, 94–98.

Broome, M. R., Johns, L. C., Valli, I., Woolley, J. B., Tabraham, P., Brett, C., Valmaggia, L., Peters, E., Garety, P. A., & Mcguire, P. K. (2007). Delusion formation and reasoning biases in those at clinical high risk for psychosis. *The British Journal of Psychiatry, 191*, s38–s42.

Camerer, C. F. (1987). Do biases in probability judgment matter in markets? Experimental evidence. *The American Economic Review*, *77*, 981–997.

Chapman, L. J., & Chapman, J. P. (1969). Illusory correlation as an obstacle to the use of valid psychodiagnostic signs. *Journal of Abnormal Psychology, 74,* 271–280.

Cooper, S. A., Smiley, E., Morrison, J., Allan, L., Williamson, A., Finlayson, J., Jackson, A., & Mantry, D. (2007). Psychosis and adults with intellectual disabilities. *Social Psychiatry and Psychiatric Epidemiology*, *42*, 530–536.

Cox Automotive (2019). *Car buyer journey 2019.* Cox Automotive.

Dowd, E. C., Frank, M. J., Collins, A., Gold, J. M., & Barch, D. M. (2016). Probabilistic reinforcement learning in patients with schizophrenia: Relationships to anhedonia and avolition. *Biological Psychiatry: Cognitive Neuroscience and Neuroimaging, 1*, 460–473.

Dudley, R. E., John, C. H., Young, A. W., & Over, D. E. (1997). Normal and abnormal reasoning in people with delusions. *British Journal of Clinical Psychology, 36*, 243–258.

Dudley, R., Taylor, P., Wickham, S., & Hutton, P. (2015). Psychosis, delusions and the "jumping to conclusions" reasoning bias: A systematic review and meta-analysis. *Schizophrenia Bulletin, 42*, 652–665.

Dudley, R., Taylor, P., Wickham, S., & Hutton, P. (2016). Psychosis, delusions and the "jumping to conclusions" reasoning bias: a systematic review and meta-analysis. *Schizophrenia Bulletin, 42*, 652–665. Dunning, D., Griffin, D. W., Milojkovic, J. H., & Ross, L. (1990). The overconfidence effect in social prediction. *Journal of Personality and Social Psychology, 58*, 568–592.

Ehrlinger, J., Readinger, W. O., & Kim, B. (2016). Decision-making and cognitive biases. *Encyclopedia of Mental Health, 12*, 83–87.

Evans, S., Averbeck, B., & Furl, N. (2015). Jumping to conclusions in schizophrenia. *Neuropsychiatric Disease and Treatment, 11,* 1615–1624.

Evans, J. S. B., Barston, J. L., & Pollard, P. (1983). On the conflict between logic and belief in syllogistic reasoning. *Memory & Cognition, 11,* 295–306.

Everett, J., Lavoie, K., Gagnon, J. F., & Gosselin, N. (2001). Performance of patients with schizophrenia on the Wisconsin Card Sorting Test (WCST). *Journal of Psychiatry and Neuroscience, 26*, 123–130.

Foa, E. B., Mathews, A., Abramowitz, J. S., Amir, N., Przeworski, A., Riggs, D. S., ... & Alley, A. (2003). Do patients with obsessive–compulsive disorder have deficits in decision-making?. *Cognitive Therapy and Research, 27*, 431–445.

Favrod, J., Rexhaj, S., Bardy, S., Ferrari, P., Hayoz, C., Moritz, S., Conus, P., & Bonsack, C. (2014). Sustained antipsychotic effect of metacognitive training in psychosis: A randomized-controlled study. *European Psychiatry*, *29*, 275–281.

Fear, C. F., & Healy, D. (1997). Probabilistic reasoning in obsessive–compulsive and delusional disorders. *Psychological Medicine*, *27*, 199–208.

Fine, C., Gardner, M., Craigie, J., & Gold, I. (2007). Hopping, skipping or jumping to conclusions? Clarifying the role of JTC behavior in delusions. *Cognitive Neuropsychiatry, 12*, 46–77.

Frederick, S. (2005). Cognitive reflection and decision making. *Journal of Economic Perspectives, 19,* 25–42.

Freeman, D. (2007). Suspicious minds: The psychology of persecutory delusions. *Clinical Psychology Review, 27*, 425–457.

Freeman, D., Pugh, K., & Garety, P. (2008). Jumping to conclusions and paranoid ideation in the general population. *Schizophrenia Research, 102*, 254–260.

Gabbert, T. (2020). *Decision-making and risk taking propensity in individuals with high schizotypy.* Unpublished manuscript.University of Bremen.

Garety, P. (1991). Reasoning and delusions. *The British Journal of Psychiatry*, *159*, 14–18.

Garety, P. A., & Freeman, D. (1999). Cognitive approaches to delusions: A critical review of the evidence. *British Journal of Clinical Psychology, 38,* 113–154.

Garety, P. A., Freeman, D., Jolley, S., Dunn, G., Bebbington, P. E., Fowler, D. G., … & Dudley, R. (2005). Reasoning, emotions, and delusional conviction in psychosis. *Journal of Abnormal Psychology, 114*, 373–384.
Garety, P. A., & Freeman, D. (2013). The past and future of delusions research: From the inexplicable to the treatable. *The British Journal of Psychiatry, 203*, 327–333.Garety, P., Joyce, E., Jolley, S., Emsley, R., Waller, H., Kuipers, E., … Freeman, D. (2013b). Neuropsychological functioning and jumping to conclusions in delusions. *Schizophrenia Research, 150*, 570–574.
Gawęda, Ł., Krężołek, Gawęda, M., Olbryś, J., Turska, A., & Kokoszka, A. (2015). Decreasing self-reported cognitive biases and increasing clinical insight through meta-cognitive training in patients with chronic schizophrenia. *Journal of Behavior Therapy and Experimental Psychiatry, 48*, 98–104.
Griffin, D., & Tversky, A. (1992). The weighing of evidence and the determinants of confidence. *Cognitive Psychology, 24,* 411–435.
Guthrie, J. T., Weber, S., & Kimmerly, N. (1993). Searching documents: Cognitive processes and deficits in understanding graphs, tables, and illustrations. *Contemporary Educational Psychology, 18,* 186–221.
Heider, F., & Simmel, M. (1944). An experimental study of apparent behavior. *The American Journal of Psychology, 57*, 243–259.
Hoven, M., Lebreton, M., Engelmann, J. B., Denys, D., Luigjes, J., & van Holst, R. J. (2019). Abnormalities of confidence in psychiatry: An overview and future perspectives. *Translational Psychiatry, 9*, 268.
Huq, S. F., Garety, P. A., & Hemsley, D. R. (1988). Probabilistic judgments in deluded and non-deluded subjects. *Quarterly Journal of Experimental Psychology, 40*, 801–812.
Jones, E. E., Rock, L., Shaver, K. G., Goethals, G. R., & Ward, L. M. (1968). Pattern of performance and ability attribution: An unexpected primacy effect. *Journal of Personality and Social Psychology, 10,* 317–340.
Joyce, D. W., Averbeck, B. B., Frith, C. D., & Shergill, S. S. (2013). Examining belief and confidence in schizophrenia. *Psychological Medicine, 43*, 2327–2338.
Kahneman, D. (2011). *Thinking, fast and slow*. Farrar, Straus and Giroux.
Kamin, L. J. (1968). "Attention-like" processes in classical conditioning. In M. R. Jones (Ed.), *Miami symposium on the prediction of behavior, 1967: Aversive stimulation* (pp. 9–31). University of Miami Press.
Kardes, F. R., Posavac, S. S., & Gaffney, D. R. (2022). Omission neglect and consumer judgment and inference based on limited evidence. In L. R. Kahle, T. M. Lowrey, & J. Huber (Eds.), *APA handbook of consumer psychology* (pp. 529–549). Washington, DC: American Psychological Association.
Kelley, H. H. (1950). The warm-cold variable in first impressions of persons. *Journal of Personality, 18,* 431–439.
Kéri, S., Kelemen, O., Benedek, G., & Janka, Z. (2001). Intact prototype learning in schizophrenia. *Schizophrenia Research, 52*, 261–264.
Köther, U., Veckenstedt, R., Vitzthum, F., Roesch-Ely, D., Pfueller, U., Scheu, F., & Moritz, S. (2012). "Don't give me that look"—Overconfidence in false mental state perception in schizophrenia. *Psychiatry Research, 196*, 1–8.
Langdon, R., Ward, P. B., & Coltheart, M. (2008). Reasoning anomalies associated with delusions in schizophrenia. *Schizophrenia Bulletin, 36*, 321–330.
Lichtenstein, S., Fischhoff, B., & Phillips, L. D. (1982). Calibration of probabilities: The state of the art to 1980. In D. Kahneman, P. Slovic, & A. Tversky (Eds.), *Judgment under uncertainty: Heuristics and biases* (pp. 306–334). New York: Cambridge University Press.
Liu, Y. C., Tang, C. C., Hung, T. T., Tsai, P. C., & Lin, M. F. (2018). The efficacy of metacognitive training for delusions in patients with schizophrenia: A meta-analysis of randomized controlled trials informs evidence-based practice. *Worldviews on Evidence-Based Nursing, 15*, 130–139.
Moritz, S., Ahmed, K., Krott, N. R., Ohls, I., & Reininger, K. M. (2021). How education and metacognitive training may ameliorate religious prejudices: A randomized controlled trial. *The International Journal for the Psychology of Religion, 31*, 121–137.
Moritz, S., Andreou, C., Schneider, B. C., Wittekind, C. E., Menon, M., Balzan, R. P., & Woodward, T. S. (2014). Sowing the seeds of doubt: A narrative review on metacognitive training in schizophrenia. *Clinical Psychology Review, 34*, 358–366.
Moritz, S., Kerstan, A., Veckenstedt, R., Randjbar, S., Vitzthum, F., Schmidt, C., Heise, M., & Woodward, T. S. (2011). Further evidence for the efficacy of a metacognitive group training in schizophrenia. *Behaviour Research and Therapy, 49*, 151–157.
Moritz, S., Kolbeck, K., & Andreou, C. (2016). Antipsychotics decrease response confidence. *Journal of Psychopharmacology, 30*, 831–833.

Moritz, S., Ramdani, N., Klass, H., Andreou, C., Jungclaussen, D., Eifler, S., … & Zink, M. (2014). Overconfidence in incorrect perceptual judgments in patients with schizophrenia. *Schizophrenia Research: Cognition, 1*, 165–170.

Moritz, S., Stojisavlevic, M., Göritz, A. S., Riehle, M., & Scheunemann, J. (2019). Does uncertainty breed conviction? On the possible role of compensatory conviction in jumping to conclusions and overconfidence in psychosis. *Cognitive Neuropsychiatry, 24*, 284–299.

Moritz, S., & Van Quaquebeke, N. (2014). Are you sure? Delusion conviction moderates the behavioural and emotional consequences of paranoid ideas. *Cognitive Neuropsychiatry, 19*, 164–180.

Moritz, S., Veckenstedt, R., Randjbar, S., Vitzthum, F., & Woodward, T. S. (2011). Antipsychotic treatment beyond antipsychotics: Metacognitive intervention for schizophrenia patients improves delusional symptoms. *Psychological Medicine, 41*, 1823–1832.

Moritz, S., Veckenstedt, R., Andreou, C., Bohn, F., Hottenrott, B., Leighton, L., Köther, U., Woodward, T.S., Treszl, A., Menon, M., & Schneider, B. C. (2014). Sustained and "sleeper" effects of group metacognitive training for schizophrenia: A randomized clinical trial. *JAMA Psychiatry, 71*, 1103–1111.Moritz, S., & Woodward, T. S. (2002). Memory confidence and false memories in schizophrenia. *The Journal of Nervous and Mental Disease, 190*, 641–643.

Moritz, S., & Woodward, T. S. (2004). Plausibility judgment in schizophrenic patients: Evidence for a liberal acceptance bias. *German Journal of Psychiatry, 7*, 66–74.

Moritz, S., & Woodward T. S. (2005). Jumping to conclusions in delusional and non-delusional schizophrenic patients. *British Journal of Clinical Psychology, 44*, 193–207.

Moritz, S., & Woodward, T. S. (2006a). The contribution of metamemory deficits to schizophrenia. *Journal of Abnormal Psychology, 115*, 15–25.

Moritz, S., & Woodward, T. S. (2006b). Metacognitive control over false memories: A key determinant of delusional thinking. *Current Psychiatry Reports, 8*, 184–190.

Moritz, S., & Woodward, T. S. (2006c). A generalized bias against disconfirmatory evidence in schizophrenia. *Psychiatry Research, 142*, 157–165.

Moritz, S., Woodward, T. S., & Hausmann, D. (2006). Incautious reasoning as a pathogenetic factor for the development of psychotic symptoms in schizophrenia. *Schizophrenia Bulletin, 32*, 327–331.

Moritz, S., Woodward, T. S., & Lambert, M. (2007). Under what circumstances do patients with schizophrenia jump to conclusions? A liberal acceptance account. *British Journal of Clinical Psychology, 46*, 127–137.

Nordgren, L. F., & Dijksterhuis, A. P. (2009). The devil is in the deliberation: Thinking too much reduces preference consistency. *Journal of Consumer Research, 36*, 39–46.

Ono, K. (1987). Superstitious behavior in humans. *Journal of the Experimental Analysis of Behavior, 47*, 261–271.

Pantelis, C., Barber, F. Z., Barnes, T. R., Nelson, H. E., Owen, A. M., & Robbins, T. W. (1999). Comparison of set-shifting ability in patients with chronic schizophrenia and frontal lobe damage. *Schizophrenia Research, 37*, 251–270.

Penney, D., Sauve, G., Mendelson, D., Thibaudeau, E., Moritz, S., & Lepage, M. (2022). Immediate and sustained outcomes and moderators associated with metacognitive training for psychosis: a systematic review and meta-analysis. *JAMA Psychiatry, 79*, 417–429.

Peters, E. R., Joseph, S. A., & Garety, P. A. (1999). The measurement of delusional ideation in the normal population: Introducing the PDI (Peters et al. Delusions Inventory). *Schizophrenia Bulletin, 25*, 553–576.

Philipp, R., Kriston, L., Kühne, F., Härter, M., & Meister, R. (2020). Concepts of metacognition in the treatment of patients with mental disorders. *Journal of Rational-Emotive & Cognitive-Behavior Therapy, 38*, 173–183.

Pytlik, N., Soll, D., & Mehl, S. (2020). Thinking preferences and conspiracy belief: Intuitive thinking and the jumping to conclusions-bias as a basis for the belief in conspiracy theories. *Frontiers in Psychiatry, 11*, 568942.

Rabin, M. (2002). A perspective on psychology and economics. *European Economic Review*, 46, 657–685.

Reininger, K. M., Krott, N. R., Hoenisch, M., Scheunemann, J., & Moritz, S. (2020). Targeting our blind spot: A metacognitive intervention ameliorates negative feelings, evaluations, and stereotypes towards conservatives in a liberal sample. *Journal of Social and Political Psychology, 8*, 453–472.

Reyna, V. F., & Brainerd, C. J. (2008). Numeracy, ratio bias, and denominator neglect in judgments of risk and probability. *Learning and Individual Differences, 18*, 89–107.

Risen, J. L., Gilovich, T., & Dunning, D. (2007). One-shot illusory correlations and stereotype formation. *Personality and Social Psychology Bulletin, 33*, 1492–1502.

Ross, R. M., Mckay, R., Coltheart, M., & Langdon, R. (2015). Jumping to conclusions about the beads task? A meta-analysis of delusional ideation and data-gathering. *Schizophrenia Bulletin, 41*, 1183–1191.

Ross, R. M., Pennycook, G., McKay, R., Gervais, W. M., Langdon, R., & Coltheart, M. (2016). Analytic cognitive style, not delusional ideation, predicts data gathering in a large beads task study. *Cognitive Neuropsychiatry, 21*, 300–314.

Sanchez, C., & Dunning, D. (2018). Overconfidence among beginners: Is a little learning a dangerous thing? *Journal of Personality and Social Psychology, 114*, 10–28.

Sanchez, C., & Dunning, D. (2021). Jumping to conclusions: Implications for reasoning errors, false belief, knowledge corruption, and impeded learning. *Journal of Personality and Social Psychology, 120*, 789–815.

Savulich, G., Shergill, S., & Yiend, J. (2012). Biased cognition in psychosis. *Journal of Experimental Psychopathology, 3,* 514–536.

Schneider, B. C., Rahmede, M., Pillny, M., Karow, A., Moritz, S., & Veckenstedt, R. (2023). In the eyes of the beholders: Subjective experiences of positive symptoms among patients with symptoms of psychosis seeking psychotherapy. *Schizophrenia Research, 254*, 14–21.

Sloman, S. A. (1996). The empirical case for two systems of reasoning. *Psychological Bulletin, 119*, 3.

So, S. H., Chan, A. P., Chong, C. S., Wong, M. H., Lo, W. T., Chung, D. W., & Chan, S. S. (2015). Metacognitive training for delusions (MCTd): Effectiveness on data-gathering and belief flexibility in a Chinese sample. *Frontiers in Psychology, 6*, 730.

So, S. H., Freeman, D., Dunn, G., Kapur, S., Kuipers, E., Bebbington, P., … & Garety, P. A. (2012). Jumping to conclusions, a lack of belief flexibility and delusional conviction in psychosis: A longitudinal investigation of the structure, frequency, and relatedness of reasoning biases. *Journal of Abnormal Psychology, 121*, 129–139.

So, S. H. W., Siu, N. Y. F., Wong, H. L., Chan, W., & Garety, P. A. (2016). 'Jumping to conclusions' data-gathering bias in psychosis and other psychiatric disorders—Two meta-analyses of comparisons between patients and healthy individuals. *Clinical Psychology Review, 46*, 151–167.

Speechley, W. J., Whitman, J. C., & Woodward, T. S. (2010). The contribution of hypersalience to the "jumping to conclusions" bias associated with delusions in schizophrenia. *Journal of Psychiatry & Neuroscience: JPN, 35*, 7.

Turner, D. T., van der Gaag, M., Karyotaki, E., & Cuijpers, P. (2014). Psychological interventions for psychosis: a meta-analysis of comparative outcome studies. *American Journal of Psychiatry, 171*, 523–538.

Tversky, A., & Kahneman, D. (1971). Belief in the law of small numbers. *Psychological Bulletin, 76,* 105–110.

Van Der Gaag, M. (2006). A neuropsychiatric model of biological and psychological processes in the remission of delusions and auditory hallucinations. *Schizophrenia Bulletin, 32*, S113–S122.

Ventura, J., Wood, R. C., Jimenez, A. M., & Hellemann, G. S. (2013). Neurocognition and symptoms identify links between facial recognition and emotion processing in schizophrenia: Meta-analytic findings. *Schizophrenia Research, 151*, 78–84.

Walters, D. J., Fernbach, P. M., Fox, C. R., & Sloman, S. A. (2017). Known unknowns: A critical determinant of confidence and calibration. *Management Science, 63*(12), 4298–4307.

Warman, D. M., Lysaker, P. H., Martin, J. M., Davis, L., & Haudenschield, S. L. (2007). Jumping to conclusions and the continuum of delusional beliefs. *Behaviour Research and Therapy, 45*, 1255–1269.

Weickert, T. W., Terrazas, A., Bigelow, L. B., Malley, J. D., Hyde, T., Egan, M. F., … & Goldberg, T. E. (2002). Habit and skill learning in schizophrenia: Evidence of normal striatal processing with abnormal cortical input. *Learning & Memory, 9*, 430–442.

Weiler, J. A., Bellebaum, C., Brüne, M., Juckel, G., & Daum, I. (2009). Impairment of probabilistic reward-based learning in schizophrenia. *Neuropsychology, 23*, 571–580.

Williams, J. J., Lombrozo, T., & Rehder, B. (2013). The hazards of explanation: Overgeneralization in the face of exceptions. *Journal of Experimental Psychology: General, 142,* 1006–1014.

Wilson, T. D., Reinhard, D. A., Westgate, E. C., Gilbert, D. T., Ellerbeck, N., Hahn, C., … & Shaked, A. (2014). Just think: The challenges of the disengaged mind. *Science, 345*, 75–77.

Wilson, T. D., & Schooler, J. W. (1991). Thinking too much: Introspection can reduce the quality of preferences and decisions. *Journal of Personality and Social Psychology, 60*, 181–192.Wang, Y., Luan, S., & Gigerenzer, G. (2022). Modeling fast-and-frugal heuristics. *PsyCh Journal, 11*, 600–611.

Yarritu, I., Matute, H., & Luque, D. (2015). The dark side of cognitive illusions: When an illusory belief interferes with the acquisition of evidence-based knowledge. *British Journal of Psychology, 106,* 597– 608.
Zawadzki, J. A. (2012). Cognitive factors associated with subclinical delusional ideation in the general population. *Psychiatry Research, 197*, 345–349.
Ziegler, M., Rief, W., Werner, S. M., Mehl, S., & Lincoln, T. M. (2008). Hasty decision-making in a variety of tasks: Does it contribute to the development of delusions? *Psychology and Psychotherapy: Theory, Research and Practice, 81*, 237–245.

10

INAUTHENTIC OR MERELY UNCERTAIN

When Do People Tolerate Situations of Identity Misfit?

Yingchi Guo and Toni Schmader

Inauthentic or Merely Uncertain: When Do People Tolerate Situations of Identity Misfit?

People gravitate to situations where they can feel authentic. State authenticity, or the sense of being aligned with one's real self, can be cued by environments that fit one's sense of self, afford one's goals, or otherwise socially validate key aspects of one's identity. And yet, people often find themselves in situations that feel like a poor fit for who they are. In this chapter, we explore conceptual similarities and distinctions between states of self-uncertainty and inauthenticity. Extending the SAFE model (State Authenticity as Fit to Environment, Schmader & Sedikides, 2018), we seek to understand why people sometimes seek out and sometimes avoid situations of identity misfit. We suggest that situational appraisals of the self as malleable, predicted by certain individual differences and cultural variables, will determine whether situations of person-environment misfit are experienced as a temporary state of self-uncertainty or as state inauthenticity. We apply this modified SAFE model to better understand experiences of self-uncertainty at the individual, intergroup, and cultural levels of analysis.

State Authenticity as Fit to Environment (SAFE) Model

Humanists put self-actualization atop other internal drives, maintaining that all individuals have a deep-seated drive to become their 'real self' (Maslow, 1964; Rogers, 1980). Contemporary psychologists have adopted and advanced this view, studying authenticity as a stable personality trait. For example, Wood and colleagues (2008) articulated and validated individual difference measures of three components of authenticity: authentic living, refusing external influence, and self-alienation (see also Kernis & Goldman, 2006). In support of the trait perspective, experiencing authenticity across different contexts is associated with better psychological well-being (as summarized in Sheldon et al., 1997; Sheldon & Kasser, 2001). Despite the evidence for the benefits of trait authenticity, conceptualizations of the authentic personality cannot explain situational variation in authentic feelings (Lenton et al., 2013a, 2013b). As such, state authenticity, defined as *the sense that one is currently in alignment with one's true or real self* (Sedikides

DOI: 10.4324/9781003363385-11

et al., 2017), is now studied as a unique phenomenon that differs from trait authenticity (e.g., Lenton et al., 2016).

Recently, Schmader and Sedikides (2018) proposed the State Authenticity as Fit to Environment (SAFE) model, to emphasize how environmental features elicit state authenticity. The SAFE model posits that state authenticity can be experienced as a function of three distinct types of self-environment fit: self-concept fit (a cognitive component), goal fit (a motivational component), and social fit (a social component). Self-concept fit occurs when cues in the environment activate the most chronically accessible or default aspects of the self (facilitating cognitive fluency and a sense of the self as true). Goal fit occurs when institutional structures or norms in the environment afford one's internalized goals (facilitating motivational fluency or fluid progress toward one's goals). Finally, social fit occurs when other people in the environment accept and validate a person's sense of self (facilitating social fluency and a sense of being at ease with others). Although environments can elicit more than one type of fit, these three types of fit need not always co-occur. For example, a person might join a soccer team because the sport is a key aspect of their self-concept (high self-concept fit), but find that the coaching style is mismatched to their training goals (low goal fit) or that other players do not appreciate their talents (low social fit).

Research has empirically validated this tripartite model of fit in a series of cross-sectional and experience-sampling studies of undergraduate students' experience of fit at their university or in classes related to their major (Aday et al., 2023; Guo, 2023). In these studies, not only did each type of fit explain unique variance in students' experiences of state authenticity, but these three types of fit were also cued from distinct contextual cues. For instance, students experienced greater self-concept fit in environments they had chosen to be in, greater goal fit in environments where they were actively engaging in purposeful activities, and greater social fit in environments with close (but not with non-close) others (Aday et al., 2023).

This research also points to the negative consequences of feeling inauthentic in a given situation. When environmental features triggered one or more types of misfit, students experienced lower working memory capacity (in the case of low self-concept fit), lower grades (for lower self-concept and goal fit), and lower social well-being (for social fit). These experiences of fit and state authenticity also predicted students' willingness to return to that specific situation on campus as well as their broader feelings of attachment and thoughts of leaving their university or major. These possible negative implications of person-environment misfit motivate a desire to better understand variability in people's experiences of inauthenticity. In this chapter, we propose that self-uncertainty might play a key role in understanding when people tolerate the experience of environmental misfit.

Incorporating Self-Uncertainty into the SAFE Model

Fundamental to the sense of feeling authentic is the prerequisite that individuals know themselves or have a default sense of self that feels true. However, people do not always have a clear or certain view of themselves or their goals. Some research examines self-uncertainty as a stable trait (e.g., individual differences in self-concept clarity, Campbell, 1990) that has implications for both individuals and groups. For example, in this volume, Schwartz and Cheek focus on self-uncertainty at the individual level, identifying predictors and consequences of self-uncertainty in modern society. Other chapters discuss how self-uncertainty contributes to identity formation (see Landau et al. this volume), self-continuity (see Sedikides et al. this volume), and belonging uncertainty (see Brady et al. this volume). Self-uncertainty is also discussed at the intergroup level; uncertainty-identity

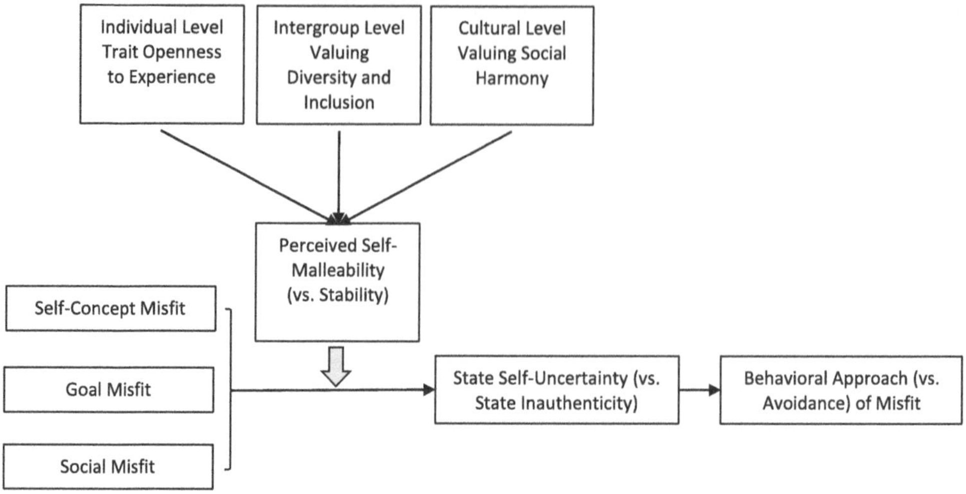

Figure 10.1 Theoretical representation of incorporating self-uncertainty into the SAFE model.

theory proposes that people identify with groups as a means to reduce self-uncertainty (Hogg, 2009) and with implications for prosocial behavior (see Paredes, Briñol, Petty this volume).

In contrast to work examining self-uncertainty as a relatively stable individual difference, we are interested in how states of self-uncertainty are elicited by situations of person-environment mismatch. We conceive of state inauthenticity and perceived state self-uncertainty as being related but distinct constructs. As shown in Figure 10.1, we propose that both can reflect having one's sense of self called into question by experiencing a misfit with the surrounding environment. One's appraisal of person-environment misfit is key to understanding whether one experiences state inauthenticity (a sense of currently being out of alignment with one's real self, Sedikides et al., 2017) or self-uncertainty (a sense of being unsure of what the real self is). Below, we elucidate how the perceived malleability or stability of the self shifts one's interpretation of misfit and might subsequently influence an individual's approach or avoidance of an environment. Briefly, we argue that when one believes the self is malleable (rather than stable), person-environment misfit will elicit a temporary state of self-uncertainty that merely signals that one is currently redefining or adapting themselves in that context. As such, people will be less motivated to avoid or leave situations that cue state self-uncertainty. In contrast, when one believes the self is stable (rather than malleable), person-environment misfit will be experienced as inauthenticity and people will be motivated to exit or avoid that setting.

Appraising the Self as Malleable

Although people have a sense of the self as being stable over time at the gestalt level, more specific self-aspects can vary and change (Chen, 2019; Markus & Kunda, 1986). For example, empirical research has revealed that personality traits, often characterized as being stable across situations and time, actually shift and change over the course of development (Bleidorn et al., 2022; Roberts & Mroczek, 2008, 2017) and alongside environmental changes such as transitioning into university or embarking on a career path (Parker et al., 2012; Lüdtke et al., 2011).

Distinct from this evidence that the self can truly change, people vary in their beliefs about the malleability of the self either due to individual differences in lay beliefs or situationally-induced appraisals (Dweck & Leggett, 1988; Dweck, 2006). These malleability beliefs have implications for how people appraise self-relevant information. For example, people who endorse an entity theory of personality uphold the notion that one's traits and abilities are intrinsic and impervious to change, while incremental theorists embrace a developmental perspective, believing that one's traits and abilities can be modified or enhanced through deliberate practice. As such, people with incremental theories of intelligence are inclined to attribute failure to themselves and linger in such situations for self-improvement (Hong et al., 1999; see neurological evidence in Mangels et al., 2006). Recent theorizing also suggests that people's needs propel them to enter and experience situations in ways that can guide their personality development (Dweck, 2017).

Extending this past work, we assert that when people appraise the self as malleable, they will be more willing to tolerate experiences of person-environment misfit. In a given situation, self-identities relevant to the current situation are activated, but as we will discuss below, people's appraisal of their context-cued self as malleable or stable will be informed by various individual and cultural variables (as well as other situational cues). Perceiving the potential for self-malleability and change in the current environment, individuals may construe situations of misfit as serving other goals including opportunities for self-growth, self-expansion, or adaptability. In such cases, the experience of dissonance stemming from a sense of misfit would be assessed as a transient state of self-uncertainty, reflecting the process of identity development or accommodation that might occur as one adapts, learns, and harmonizes within the surrounding context. As a consequence, self-change may take place in tandem with uncertainty reduction, ultimately leading to a state where the evolved self becomes aligned with the environment. On the other hand, in situations where the self is perceived as stable and unchangeable, misfit would instead cue a sense of inauthenticity, signifying an immutable mismatch between the self and the environment.

We can find examples of people tolerating situations of person-environment misfit in the literature. For example, according to uncertainty identity theory, heightened identification with the dominant group is expected to occur to the degree that one assimilates with the norms, beliefs, and culture of that group (Hogg, 2009). Similar identity transformation can happen when one takes on new roles. For instance, in alignment with the leadership identity development model (Komives et al., 2006), receiving a promotion to a leadership position may initially evoke a sense of misfit between the current self and the new environment; however, if that misfit is appraised in terms of personal growth, individuals will feel self-uncertainty, but perhaps not inauthenticity, if they believe in their capacity to adapt and align themselves with the environment. Although this proposition has not been explicitly tested, studies have investigated discomfort as an indicator of self-growth, suggesting that individuals may prefer to seek out discomfort as a means to motivate their personal growth (Woolley & Fishbach, 2022).

Interpreting person-environment misfit in ways that elicit either self-uncertainty or inauthenticity should engender distinct behavioral inclinations towards either staying in or leaving the current situation. If individuals perceive the self as malleable, they might be inclined to endure short-term self-environment misfit and self-uncertainty in pursuit of personal growth or harmony. Conversely, if the self is perceived as stable and individuals experience a sense of being inauthentic in this environment, they will be more inclined to leave. In line with this perspective, individuals who adhere to entity theory, believing that intelligence is fixed, tend to exhibit lower resilience and a greater propensity toward helplessness when confronted with academic challenges (Blackwell et al., 2007; Yeager & Dweck, 2012). Similarly, when individuals experience belonging uncertainty, due to incongruence between cues in the environment and a valued social identity (i.e., their race or gender), they tend to avoid such environments even while explicitly acknowledging the value or utility of those domains (Cheryan et al., 2009; Murphy et al., 2007; Walton & Cohen,

2007, 2011). However, an intervention that encourages marginalized students to reframe their experience of misfit as a normal part of transition or development (or belongingness uncertainty) can be effective at mitigating these effects (Walton et al., 2023).

When Do People Embrace Person-Environment Misfit?

We have thus far argued that people might be more likely to tolerate or even embrace experiences of person-environment misfit if they appraise themselves as likely to change or adapt to the situation. When self-change is perceived to be possible or likely, people will experience situations of misfit more in terms of self-uncertainty than state inauthenticity. We next turn to a consideration of three distinct individual differences or cultural factors that should predict these malleability appraisals. This is not meant to be an exhaustive list of predictors but rather represents examples occurring at the individual, intergroup, and cultural levels of analysis.

At the individual level, we propose that variation in trait levels of openness to experience should predict people's willingness to approach situations of self-concept misfit with an appraisal of such situations as providing the potential for personal growth. At the intergroup level, we propose that individual variation in diversity and inclusion values should predict people's willingness to approach situations of group-based social misfit with an appraisal of the potential for self-expansion. Finally, at the cultural level, we propose that cultural variation in harmony values will predict people's willingness to approach situations of goal misfit with an appraisal of self-improvement or one's ability to adapt oneself to the expectations of the environment.

Individual Level: Openness to Experience and Self-Concept Misfit

At the individual level, personality traits guide how people approach and appraise situations (Dweck, 2017; Mischel & Shoda, 1995). In contemporary models of personality (e.g., the Big Five, McCrae & Costa, 1987; HEXICO, Lee & Ashton, 2004), openness to experience is the dimension that should influence how people appraise situations of person-environment misfit. Openness to experience has been linked to a preference for engaging with complex, novel, and nontraditional ideas and experiences (Connelly et al., 2014), as evidenced by the link between openness and risk-taking (Nicholson et al., 2005). As such, individuals high in openness to experience are regarded as better at adapting to changing situations (LePine et al., 2000). For example, students high on openness adapted better to online learning during COVID to achieve better performance (Audet et al., 2021); while employees high on openness were more satisfied with jobs that required a diverse array of skills (de Jong et al., 2001).

The adaptability enjoyed by highly open people might be partially attributed to having more of a growth mindset (Connelly et al., 2014; Zarrinabadi et al., 2022). Moreover, openness is linked with cognitive flexibility to switch between different mental sets and adjust cognitive strategies (e.g., Tseng et al., 2020) as well as a tolerance of ambiguity (Jach & Smillie, 2019). Given this evidence of cognitive flexibility in novel environments, individuals high in openness might view the discomfort or dissonance experienced in ambiguous situations of self-environment misfit not in terms of having an inauthentic self but in terms of temporary self-uncertainty. Some work even suggests that for highly open people, engaging in openness activities (e.g., introspective and curious thoughts) actually feels more authentic (van Allen & Zelenski, 2018).

Because openness to experience is specifically linked to viewing novel situations as opportunities for self-growth and desire for self-expansion (Hughes et al., 2020), openness might moderate the specific link between self-concept (rather than goal or social) misfit and approach behaviors.

According to the SAFE model, self-concept misfit induces cognitive disfluencies when the environment does not activate default aspects of one's self-concept. When environments instead activate the default self-concept, people experience cognitive fluency (Aday et al., 2024). Relatedly, neuroimaging research has discovered that people high in openness to experience exhibit greater efficiency in the activation of their default network, a functional system of brain regions involved in introspective and creative thought (Beaty et al., 2016). Thus, the neural efficiency that underlies openness to experience might allow highly open individuals the ability to enter into and tolerate situations of identity misfit without experiencing cognitive disfluency.

If we are correct that openness to experience allows one to approach and tolerate the self-uncertainty experienced in situations of person-environment misfit, then we should see that this trait predicts people's willingness to self-select into and persist in situations of identity misfit. Indeed, people high in openness to experience are more likely to take jobs outside their country of birth and adjust better to their cross-cultural environment when they do (Albrecht et al., 2014). Similarly, although women tend to avoid going into gender-atypical occupations if the masculine defaults in those environments cue self-concept misfit and state inauthenticity (Schmader, 2023), women high in openness to experience might exhibit more tolerance for self-concept misfit. For example, in one unique study, George and colleagues (2011) analyzed 50 years of longitudinal data from a cohort of women to assess how their personality as young adults predicted their entry and progression in the workforce. Openness to experience measured in their early 20s predicted women's tendency to have and sustain a career, to get an advanced degree, and to have unconventional, entrepreneurial, and/or high-status jobs (all outcomes considered unusual for these women in the 1960s when the study began).

In summary, as individuals high in openness are more motivated by a growth mindset, they are more likely to appraise the self as malleable. As a result, experiences of self-environment misfit should elicit a state of self-uncertainty rather than inauthenticity, resulting in less avoidance motivation and more exploration of ways to adapt themselves to the situation. Conversely, individuals low in openness are more likely to appraise the self as stable, and thus feel inauthentic in situations of self-environment misfit, leading them to avoid rather than tolerate those contexts.

Intergroup Level: Diversity and Inclusion Values and Social Misfit

A second context where individuals routinely approach or avoid situations of person-environment misfit involves intergroup interactions. A challenge in modern society is to foster greater inclusion among diverse people by encouraging a willingness to seek out and learn from those who are different from oneself. Indeed, seeking out situations where one might experience intergroup misfit can have several benefits. Developing relationships with people of different backgrounds can lead to self-expansion as people tend to 'include the other in the self' (Turner et al., 2008; Wright et al., 1997). In addition, positive cross-group experiences can help reduce inequities by motivating members of advantaged groups to engage in allyship (Brannon, 2018) and fostering greater fit and belonging for those who are disadvantaged (Carey et al., 2022; Mendoza-Denton & Page-Gould, 2008). In this section, we propose that those who value diversity and inclusion might be more motivated to approach intergroup interactions with a mindset of personal growth that allows them to avoid feeling inauthentic, and instead merely uncertain, in such encounters.

According to social identity theory (Tajfel & Turner, 1979), any interaction across salient group boundaries has the potential to be framed in terms of different social identities (e.g., based on race, ethnicity, cultural background, gender identity, sexual orientation, disability status, socioeconomic status, etc.). Moreover, even in the absence of outgroup prejudice, individuals often exhibit homophilic tendencies to prefer the ingroup over outgroups (McPherson et al., 2001; Melamed et al., 2020). This preference to seek out relationships with other ingroup members is particularly strong among those most identified with that group identity (Leszczensky & Pink, 2019) and distinct from the mere opportunity to meet people different than oneself given base rates of people in the surrounding context (Currarini et al., 2010). Such evidence of homophily suggests that people are inclined to seek out the sense of fit they feel with similar others.

There is also evidence, however, that many people specifically experience cross-group interactions as situations of social misfit to be avoided. For example, the tendency to avoid interracial interactions can be fueled by intergroup anxiety and a fear of being rejected (Amodio & Hamilton, 2012; Shelton & Richeson, 2005; Stephan & Stephan, 1985). These anxieties can take different forms for members of advantaged and disadvantaged groups. For example, when anticipating an interracial interaction, White participants worry about being perceived as racist whereas Black and Latino participants are more likely to worry about seeming incompetent (Bergsieker et al., 2010). Given that impression management concerns are central to why intergroup situations can feel like a mismatch to one's identity, such situations seem to be specifically characterized by an experience of low social fit, in terms of the SAFE model.

There is some direct evidence that this experience of low social fit might lead people to feel inauthentic during interracial interactions. Members of the advantaged racial groups tend to avoid interactions with racial outgroup members because they expect to feel anxiety and stress (Trawalter et al., 2009), and that they do not have a clear script to follow, decreasing their executive function (Trawalter & Richeson, 2006). During interracial interactions, White Americans with stronger implicit racial associations exhibit more speech hesitations (Dovidio et al., 2002; McConnell & Leibold, 2001), indicative of impaired social fluency in situations of social misfit. Members of disadvantaged groups often have more experience trying to integrate with those who are relatively advantaged. They find themselves aiding in efforts to find common ground with an advantaged partner in order to get along with someone who might harbor prejudices against them (Schmader et al., 2013). However, in the process, a tendency to avoid sharing unique aspects of their lived experience as a member of a marginalized group can also leave them feeling misunderstood and inauthentic in these interactions (Holoien et al., 2015; Shelton et al., 2005).

The evidence above suggests that interracial interactions are experienced as episodes of low social fit. We suggest that such encounters elicit a sense of either uncertainty or inauthenticity, depending on how these situations are appraised. If the focus is on oneself (and perhaps also the other person) as stable and unchangeable, then one might predominantly feel inauthentic in such encounters and avoid them in the future. But if the focus is on these situations as providing an opportunity for growth, inclusion, and understanding, then perhaps the sense of misfit elicits only a temporary state of uncertainty while those changes take place.

Although these ideas have not been directly tested, there is evidence that people's appraisal of intergroup interactions can alter their willingness to engage in outgroup contact (Murphy et al., 2011). For example, when Black adults adopt a goal to learn from an outgroup member's different experience (as opposed to a focus on one's own performance), they expect to be perceived more positively (Green et al., 2021) and are less worried about the impression they are making (Trawalter & Richeson, 2006), suggesting they feel greater social fit. Such framing manipulations often encourage people to see intergroup encounters in terms of self-growth, that is, as a means of expanding their view of the self and the world. Interestingly, manipulations of the malleability of the outgroup's views can also be an effective way to encourage people's willingness to approach and cooperate in these intergroup situations of social misfit (Goldenberg et al., 2018; Halperin et al., 2012).

Those who intrinsically value diversity and inclusion, we suggest, should be more inclined to approach intergroup encounters with this more approach-oriented mindset of the malleability of self and others. Although research has not directly tested this idea, some evidence points to individual differences that moderate people's interest in approaching outgroup contact. For example, individuals with egalitarian motivations are willing to interact with individuals from diverse cultural backgrounds despite the discomfort, with the hope that positive interactions will contribute to establishing an inclusive environment (Allport, 1954; Pettigrew, 1998). In a large longitudinal study of German, Dutch, Swedish, and English adolescents, teens who developed more positive attitudes toward outgroups, and decreased identification with their ingroup, were less likely to exhibit a more general shift toward homophily in their friendship networks (Wölfer & Hewstone, 2018). In more focused research, the experience of having close cross-group friendships (which we surmise might change one's value for diversity and inclusion) can mitigate the anxiety often elicited in subsequent intergroup encounters, making those experiences less aversive (Page-Gould et al., 2008).

Interestingly, some research has recently examined how personality differences predict racial diversity in one's friendship networks. Connected to our discussion above, openness to experience is the big five personality trait that best predicted having a less homophilic friendship network, an effect that is held among both members of minority and majority groups (Antonoplis & John, 2022). That said, because the typical measure of openness was only a weak predictor, Antonoplis and John developed a new measure they called Openness to Other that showed a consistently positive relationship with the odds of having different race friends. This openness-to-other construct, defined as "people's appreciation, embrace of, and preference for others who are different" is conceptually similar to what we mean by valuing diversity and inclusion. We suggest that such beliefs might allow one to also appraise the self as more malleable to intergroup self-expansion and thus motivated to seek out diversity in one's social relationships. We see potential for future research to examine how diversity and inclusion values do not just mitigate feelings of inauthenticity that lead to intergroup avoidance but actually foster a willingness to embrace the self-uncertainty that one experiences among diverse others.

Culture Level: Harmony Values and Goal Misfit

Finally, as a third example, we consider a cultural variable that might also predict people's willingness to tolerate situations of person-environment misfit. Specifically, cultural variations in harmony values associated with an interdependent view of the self can shape how people appraise and approach situations (Markus & Kitayama, 1991; Schwartz, 2012). For example, whereas individualistic cultures tend to view the self as independent of others and having personal agency, collectivistic cultures tend to view the self as being fundamentally interdependent with other people (Markus & Kitayama, 1991). As a result, people from interdependent cultures are more comfortable than those from independent cultures in having a sense of self that is inherently uncertain because it shifts from one context to the next in order to facilitate social harmony (English & Chen, 2007; Heine et al., 1999; Kashima et al., 2004; Spencer-Rodgers et al., 2010; Suh, 2002). For example, Japanese (a typical non-independent culture) adolescents develop an identity that allows for more instability and uncertainty compared to their Western peers (Sugimura, 2020).

Cultural variation in having an independent vs. interdependent self-construal has implications for the relationships among people's attitudes, personal preferences, and behavioral tendencies. Western psychologists have long assumed a person-centered view of how personal attitudes guide individual preference and behavioral choices (Ajzen & Fishbein, 1980; Katz, 1960; Petty & Krosnick,

2014; Zanna & Rempel, 1988). However, Riemer et al. (2014) proposed the normative-contextual model arguing that, in non-Western sociocultural contexts, an individual's attitudes need not be consistent either with each other or one's behavior. Rather, non-Westerners enter into situations with the readiness to incorporate others' attitudes into their own, such that adapting to situations does not require a pronounced internal conflict between maintaining one's true self and conforming to external forces (Riemer et al., 2014). From this perspective, in non-Western cultures that endorse a more interdependent sense of self, the contextual characteristics (e.g., others' attitudes) that induce feelings of misfit and inauthenticity for those in the West, might only be interpreted as a transient and uncertain stage of adaptation.

Such evidence leads us to expect cultural variation in the norm to act authentically, or in line with one's own attitudes. Indeed, individuals from Eastern (as compared with Western) cultures tend to place less value on authentic living and its presumed relationship with life satisfaction (Xia & Xu, 2023). Moreover, self-consistency is less important in predicting psychological well-being for Easterners with highly relational self-construal (Cross et al., 2003). In addition, although role consistency is reported to universally predict adjustment across cultures, a lower level of cross-role consistency is observed for those in collectivistic cultures (Church et al., 2008), especially those from East Asian cultures (e.g., Japanese culture) that embrace Confucian dialecticalism.

We postulate that harmony values, together with an interdependent self-construal, might guide how individuals appraise situations of person-environment misfit, especially goal misfit, to predict either self-uncertainty or state-inauthenticity. Given that those with an interdependent view of the self value acting in harmony with others, they appraise the self in malleable ways (Heine, et al., 2001) and become adept at attending to and adapting oneself to other people's expectations and goals. Those from independent cultures, on the other hand, view the self as a stable entity and are more motivated to make choices that align with their own goals and preferences (Hoshino-Browne et al., 2005). As such, for those with strong harmony values (e.g., in China, Korea, and Japan; Zhang et al., 2005), situations in which one's own goals do not align with the goals of others should not feel intensely inauthentic or as something to be avoided. Rather, goal misfit might be appraised as a temporary state of self-uncertainty as one discerns how to adapt oneself to the expectations of others.

Although research has not examined a direct link between fit and authenticity as a function of cultural variation in harmony values, our assertion is consistent with some prior evidence. For instance, the Japanese, compared to North Americans, are adept at fostering goal fit on tasks that have interpersonal benefits (Nguyen et al., 2022). In addition, for the sake of interpersonal harmony, individuals from interdependent vs. independent cultures may put different weights towards goal fit vs. relational harmony. In business settings, self-organizational misfit (similar to goal misfit) is less predictive of job dissatisfaction and intent to quit in collectivistic compared with individualistic cultures (Astakhova, 2016; meta-analysis in Oh et al., 2014). Likewise in social relationships, relational harmony motives trump goal misfit in guiding interpersonal behaviors for collectivists (Hook et al., 2009; Karremans et al., 2011). As such, interdependent individuals are less likely to use goal misfit as a criterion to guide avoidance; rather, experiences of goal misfit merely signal a need for adaptation for the sake of interpersonal harmony.

In summary, interdependent self-construal, in combination with the emphasis on harmony values, leads to a more malleable self-appraisal that enables the preference of tolerating some degree of goal misfit. We suggest that such situations of goal misfit might only elicit self-uncertainty but not inauthenticity for those with an interdependent self-construal that is malleable to the expectations of others in that environment. In contrast, for those with an independent self-construal, similar situations of goal misfit feel inauthentic with their more stable sense of self, thus inducing higher avoidance. Future research is needed to better understand these processes directly.

Summary

Through the lens of the SAFE model, we have discussed the conceptual similarities and distinctions between state authenticity and self-uncertainty, with a focus on the appraisal of self-malleability. Self-environmental misfit may be experienced as a transient state of uncertainty when individuals feel that the self is malleable and can flexibly change, adapt, or grow in an unfamiliar environment. On the contrary, if the self is considered fixed, situations of misfit or more likely to feel inauthentic compelling people to leave or avoid those situations. We illustrate this appraisal divergence at individual, intergroup, and cultural levels by conceptually analyzing one possible moderator at each level that could elicit more malleable appraisals of the self. Specifically, we posit that, at the individual level, those embracing high openness tend to tolerate self-concept misfit for personal growth. At the intergroup level, valuing diversity and inclusion might motivate appraisals of self-expansion that allow people to seek out and embrace situations of social difference. At the cultural level, individuals with an interdependent self-concept are motivated to adapt who they are to maintain harmony, thus remaining in goal-misfit situations to meet the expectations and goals of others. Feelings of self-environment misfit in these situations are interpreted as short-term uncertainty in the self-situation adaptation process. Through these processes, individuals are able to tolerate and even seek out novel situations for exploration, expansion, and adaptation.

We have focused our analysis on the appraisal of self-malleability as a means of better understanding the relationships between self-uncertainty and inauthenticity. However, it is worth noting that appraisals of environmental malleability could also moderate one's experience of person-environment misfit. In intergroup contexts, for example, the belief that others' biases can change motivates greater tolerance for intergroup encounters (Halperin et al., 2012). Individuals may further respond to a malleable environment by directly manipulating physical or social aspects of the environment as a co-adaptation strategy, which in the long run, may shape one's own personality characteristics (Mischel & Shoda, 1995). Although the topic is outside the scope of the current chapter, future theory and research should explore when people tolerate situations of misfit because they believe in their own ability to shape and change the situation itself. Such an analysis would broaden our understanding of when and why people embrace uncertainty and seek out or remain in situations that are mismatched with their sense of self.

References

Aday, A. E., Guo, Y.C., Mehta, S., Chen, S., Goetz, F., Hall, W., Sedikides, C., & Schmader, T. (2024). The SAFE model: State authenticity as a function of three types of fit. *Personality and Social Psychology Bulletin.* Advance online publication. DOI: 10.1177/01461672231223597

Ajzen, I. (1980). *Understanding attitudes and predictiing social behavior*. Englewood Cliffs.

Albrecht, A-G., Dilchert, S., Deller, J., & Paulus, F. M. (2014). Openness in cross-cultural work settings: A multicountry study of expatriates. *Journal of Personality Assessment, 96*(1), 64–75. https://doi.org/10.1080/00223891.2013.821074

Allport, G. W. (1954). *The nature of prejudice*. Addison-Wesley.

Amodio, D. M., & Hamilton, H. K. (2012). Intergroup anxiety effects on implicit racial evaluation and stereotyping. *Emotion, 12*(6), 1273.

Antonoplis, S., & John, O. P. (2022). Who has different-race friends, and does it depend on context? Openness (to other), but not agreeableness, predicts lower racial homophily in friendship networks. *Journal of Personality and Social Psychology, 122*(5), 894.

Audet, É. C., Levine, S. L., Metin, E., Koestner, S., & Barcan, S. (2021). Zooming their way through university: Which Big 5 traits facilitated students' adjustment to online courses during the COVID-19 pandemic. *Personality and Individual Differences, 180*, 110969.

Beaty, R. E., Kaufman, S. B., Benedek, M., Jung, R. E., Kenett, Y. N., Jauk, E., Neubauer, A. C., & Silvia, P. J. (2016). Personality and complex brain networks: The role of openness to experience in default network efficiency. *Human Brain Mapping, 37*(2), 773–779. https://doi.org/10.1002/hbm.23065

Bergsieker, H. B., Shelton, J. N., & Richeson, J. A. (2010). To be liked versus respected: Divergent goals in interracial interactions. *Journal of Personality and Social Psychology, 99*(2), 248.

Blackwell, L. S., Trzesniewski, K. H., & Dweck, C. S. (2007). Implicit theories of intelligence predict achievement across an adolescent transition: A longitudinal study and an intervention. *Child Development, 78*(1), 246–263.

Bleidorn, W., Schwaba, T., Zheng, A., Hopwood, C. J., Sosa, S. S., Roberts, B. W., & Briley, D. A. (2022). Personality stability and change: A meta-analysis of longitudinal studies. *Psychological Bulletin, 148* (7–8), 588.

Brannon, T. N. (2018). Reaffirming King's vision: The power of participation in inclusive diversity efforts to benefit intergroup outcomes. *Journal of Social Issues, 74*(2), 355–376.

Campbell, J. D. (1990). Self-esteem and clarity of the self-concept. *Journal of Personality and Social Psychology, 59*(3), 538. https://doi.org/10.1037/0022-3514.59.3.538

Carey, R. M., Stephens, N. M., Townsend, S. S., & Hamedani, M. G. (2022). Is diversity enough? Cross-race and cross-class interactions in college occur less often than expected, but benefit members of lower status groups when they occur. *Journal of Personality and Social Psychology, 123*(5), 889.

Chen, S. (2019). Authenticity in context: Being true to working selves. *Review of General Psychology, 23*(1), 60–72.

Cheryan, S., Plaut, V. C., Davies, P. G., & Steele, C. M. (2009). Ambient belonging: how stereotypical cues impact gender participation in computer science. *Journal of Personality and Social Psychology, 97*(6), 1045.

Church, A. T., Anderson-Harumi, C. A., del Prado, A. M., Curtis, G. J., Tanaka-Matsumi, J., Valdez Medina, J. L., Mastor, K. A., White, F. A., Miramontes, L. A., & Katigbak, M. S. (2008). Culture, cross-role consistency, and adjustment: Testing trait and cultural psychology perspectives. *Journal of Personality and Social Psychology, 95*(3), 739–755. https://doi.org/10.1037/0022-3514.95.3.739

Connelly, B. S., Ones, D. S., & Chernyshenko, O. S. (2014). Introducing the special section on openness to experience: Review of openness taxonomies, measurement, and nomological net. *Journal of Personality Assessment, 96*(1), 1–16.

Cross, S. E., Gore, J. S., & Morris, M. L. (2003). The relational-interdependent self-construal, self-concept consistency, and well-being. *Journal of Personality and Social Psychology, 85*(5), 933.

Currarini, S., Jackson, M. O., & Pin, P. (2010). Identifying the roles of race-based choice and chance in high school friendship network formation. *Proceedings of the National Academy of Sciences, 107*(11), 4857–4861.

De Jong, R. D., Van Der Velde, M. E., & Jansen, P. G. (2001). Openness to experience and growth need strength as moderators between job characteristics and satisfaction. *International Journal of Selection and Assessment, 9*(4), 350–356.

Dovidio, J. F., Kawakami, K., & Gaertner, S. L. (2002). Implicit and explicit prejudice and interracial interaction. *Journal of Personality and Social Psychology, 82*(1), 62.

Dweck, C. S. (2006). *Mindset: The new psychology of success*. Random house.

Dweck, C. S. (2017). From needs to goals and representations: Foundations for a unified theory of motivation, personality, and development. *Psychological Review, 124*(6), 689.

Dweck, C. S., & Leggett, E. L. (1988). A social-cognitive approach to motivation and personality. *Psychological Review, 95*(2), 256.

English, T., & Chen, S. (2007). Culture and self-concept stability: Consistency across and within contexts among Asian Americans and European Americans. *Journal of Personality and Social Psychology, 93*(3), 478.

George, L. G., Helson, R., & John, O. P. (2011). The "CEO" of women's work lives: How Big Five Conscientiousness, Extraversion, and Openness predict 50 years of work experiences in a changing sociocultural context. *Journal of Personality and Social Psychology, 101*(4), 812–830. https://doi.org/10.1037/a0024290

Goldenberg, A., Cohen-Chen, S., Goyer, J. P., Dweck, C. S., Gross, J. J., & Halperin, E. (2018). Testing the impact and durability of a group malleability intervention in the context of the Israeli–Palestinian conflict. *Proceedings of the National Academy of Sciences, 115*(4), 696–701.

Green, P. A., Briffa, M., & Cant, M. A. (2021). Assessment during intergroup contests. *Trends in Ecology & Evolution, 36*(2), 139–150.

Guo, Y. (2023). *Finding your place at school: Momentary fit, state authenticity and academic experiences* (Master dissertation, University of British Columbia).

Halperin, E., Crisp, R. J., Husnu, S., Trzesniewski, K. H., Dweck, C. S., & Gross, J. J. (2012). Promoting intergroup contact by changing beliefs: Group malleability, intergroup anxiety, and contact motivation. *Emotion, 12*(6), 1192.

Heine, S. J., Kitayama, S., Lehman, D. R., Takata, T., Ide, E., Leung, C., & Matsumoto, H. (2001). Divergent consequences of success and failure in Japan and North America: An investigation of self-improving motivations and malleable selves. *Journal of Personality and Social Psychology, 81*(4), 599.

Heine, S. J., Lehman, D. R., Markus, H. R., & Kitayama, S. (1999). Is there a universal need for positive self-regard? *Psychological Review, 106*(4), 766–794. https://doi.org/10.1037/0033-295x.106.4.766

Hogg, M. A. (2009). Managing self-uncertainty through group identification. *Psychological Inquiry, 20*(4), 221–224. https://doi.org/10.1080/10478400903333452

Holoien, D. S., Bergsieker, H. B., Shelton, J. N., & Alegre, J. M. (2015). Do you really understand? Achieving accuracy in interracial relationships. *Journal of Personality and Social psychology, 108*(1), 76.

Hong, Y. Y., Chiu, C. Y., Dweck, C. S., Lin, D. M. S., & Wan, W. (1999). Implicit theories, attributions, and coping: a meaning system approach. *Journal of Personality and Social Psychology, 77*(3), 588.

Hook, J. N., Worthington Jr, E. L., & Utsey, S. O. (2009). Collectivism, forgiveness, and social harmony. *The Counseling Psychologist, 37*(6), 821–847.

Hoshino-Browne, E., Zanna, A. S., Spencer, S. J., Zanna, M. P., Kitayama, S., & Lackenbauer, S. (2005). On the cultural guises of cognitive dissonance: The case of easterners and westerners. *Journal of Personality and Social Psychology, 89*(3), 294.

Hughes, E. K., Slotter, E. B., & Lewandowski, G. W., Jr. (2020). Expanding who I am: Validating the self-expansion preference scale. *Journal of Personality Assessment, 102*(6), 792–803. https://doi.org/10.1080/00223891.2019.1641109

Jach, H. K., & Smillie, L. D. (2019). To fear or fly to the unknown: Tolerance for ambiguity and Big Five personality traits. *Journal of Research in Personality, 79*, 67–78.

Karremans, J. C., Regalia, C., Paleari, F. G., Fincham, F. D., Cui, M., Takada, N., ... & Uskul, A. K. (2011). Maintaining harmony across the globe: The cross-cultural association between closeness and interpersonal forgiveness. *Social Psychological and Personality Science, 2*(5), 443–451.

Kashima, Y., Kashima, E., Farsides, T., Kim, U., Strack, F., Werth, L., & Yuki, M. (2004). Culture and context-sensitive self: The amount and meaning of context-sensitivity of phenomenal self differ across cultures. *Self and Identity, 3*(2), 125–141.

Katz, D. (1960). The functional approach to the study of attitudes. *Public Opinion Quarterly, 24*(2), 163–204.

Kernis, M. H., & Goldman, B. M. (2006). A multicomponent conceptualization of authenticity: Theory and research. *Advances in Experimental Social Psychology, 38*, 283–357.

Komives, S. R., Longerbeam, S. D., Owen, J. E., Mainella, F. C., & Osteen, L. (2006). A leadership identity development model: Applications from a grounded theory. *Journal of College Student Development, 47*(4), 401–418.

Lee, K., & Ashton, M. C. (2004). Psychometric properties of the HEXACO personality inventory. *Multivariate Behavioral Research, 39*(2), 329–358.

Lenton, A. P., Bruder, M., Slabu, L., & Sedikides, C. (2013a). How does "being real" feel? The experience of state authenticity. *Journal of Personality, 81*(3), 276–289.

Lenton, A. P., Slabu, L., Sedikides, C., & Power, K. (2013b). I feel good, therefore I am real: Testing the causal influence of mood on state authenticity. *Cognition & Emotion, 27*(7), 1202–1224.

Lenton, A. P., Slabu, L., & Sedikides, C. (2016). State authenticity in everyday life. *European Journal of Personality, 30*(1), 64–82.

LePine, J. A., Colquitt, J. A., & Erez, A. (2000). Adaptability to changing task contexts: Effects of general cognitive ability, conscientiousness, and openness to experience. *Personnel Psychology, 53*(3), 563–593.

Leszczensky, L., & Pink, S. (2019). What drives ethnic homophily? A relational approach on how ethnic identification moderates preferences for same-ethnic friends. *American Sociological Review, 84*(3), 394–419.

Lüdtke, O., Roberts, B. W., Trautwein, U., & Nagy, G. (2011). A random walk down University Avenue: Life paths, life events, and personality trait change at the transition to university life. *Journal of Personality and Social Psychology, 101*(3), 620.

Mangels, J. A., Butterfield, B., Lamb, J., Good, C., & Dweck, C. S. (2006). Why do beliefs about intelligence influence learning success? A social cognitive neuroscience model. *Social Cognitive and Affective Neuroscience, 1*(2), 75–86.
Markus, H. R., & Kitayama, S. (1991). Culture and the self: Implications for cognition, emotion, and motivation. *Psychological Review, 98*(2), 224.
Markus, H., & Kunda, Z. (1986). Stability and malleability of the self-concept. *Journal of Personality and Social Psychology, 51*(4), 858.
Maslow, A. H. (1964). A theory of human motivation. In H. J. Leavitt & L. R. Pondy (Eds.), *Readings in managerial psychology* (pp. 6–24). University of Chicago Press.
McConnell, A. R., & Leibold, J. M. (2001). Relations among the Implicit Association Test, discriminatory behavior, and explicit measures of racial attitudes. *Journal of Experimental Social Psychology, 37*(5), 435–442.
McCrae, R. R., & Costa, P. T. (1987). Validation of the five-factor model of personality across instruments and observers. *Journal of Personality and Social Psychology, 52*(1), 81.
McPherson, M., Smith-Lovin, L., & Cook, J. M. (2001). Birds of a feather: Homophily in social networks. *Annual Review of Sociology, 27*(1), 415–444.
Melamed, D., Sweitzer, M., Simpson, B., Abernathy, J. Z., Harrell, A., & Munn, C. W. (2020). Homophily and segregation in cooperative networks. *American Journal of Sociology, 125*(4), 1084–1127.
Mendoza-Denton, R., & Page-Gould, E. (2008). Can cross-group friendships influence minority students' well-being at historically white universities? *Psychological Science, 19*(9), 933–939.
Mischel, W., & Shoda, Y. (1995). A cognitive-affective system theory of personality: Reconceptualizing situations, dispositions, dynamics, and invariance in personality structure. *Psychological Review, 102*(2), 246.
Murphy, M. C., Richeson, J. A., & Molden, D. C. (2011). Leveraging motivational mindsets to foster positive interracial interactions. *Social and Personality Psychology Compass, 5*(2), 118–131.
Murphy, M. C., Steele, C. M., & Gross, J. J. (2007). Signaling threat: How situational cues affect women in math, science, and engineering settings. *Psychological Science, 18*(10), 879–885.
Nguyen, T., Togawa, T., Scholer, A. A., Miele, D. B., & Fujita, K. (2022). A cross-cultural investigation of metamotivational beliefs about regulatory focus task-motivation fit. *Personality and Social Psychology Bulletin, 48*(5), 807–820. https://doi.org/10.1177/01461672211025423
Nicholson, N., Soane, E., Fenton-O'Creevy, M., & Willman, P. (2005). Personality and domain-specific risk taking. *Journal of Risk Research, 8*(2), 157–176. https://doi.org/10.1080/1366987032000123856
Oh, I. S., Guay, R. P., Kim, K., Harold, C. M., Lee, J. H., Heo, C. G., & Shin, K. H. (2014). Fit happens globally: A meta-analytic comparison of the relationships of person–environment fit dimensions with work attitudes and performance across East Asia, Europe, and North America. *Personnel Psychology*, 67(1), 99–152.
Page-Gould, E., Mendoza-Denton, R., & Tropp, L. R. (2008). With a little help from my cross-group friend: Reducing anxiety in intergroup contexts through cross-group friendship. *Journal of Personality and Social Psychology, 95*(5), 1080.
Parker, P. D., Lüdtke, O., Trautwein, U., & Roberts, B. W. (2012). Personality and relationship quality during the transition from high school to early adulthood. *Journal of Personality, 80*(4), 1061–1089. https://doi.org/10.1111/j.1467-6494.2012.00766.x
Pettigrew, T. F. (1998). Intergroup contact theory. *Annual Review of Psychology, 49*(1), 65–85.
Petty, R. E., & Krosnick, J. A. (2014). *Attitude strength: Antecedents and consequences.* Psychology Press.
Riemer, H., Shavitt, S., Koo, M., & Markus, H. R. (2014). Preferences don't have to be personal: Expanding attitude theorizing with a cross-cultural perspective. *Psychological Review, 121*(4), 619–648.
Roberts, B. W., Luo, J., Briley, D. A., Chow, P. I., Su, R., Rong Su, Su, R., & Hill, P. L. (2017). A systematic review of personality trait change through intervention. *Psychological Bulletin, 143*(2), 117–141. https://doi.org/10.1037/bul0000088
Roberts, B. W., & Mroczek, D. (2008). Personality trait change in adulthood. *Current Directions in Psychological Science, 17*(1), 31–35.
Roberts, B. W., Walton, K. E., & Viechtbauer, W. (2006). Patterns of mean-level change in personality traits across the life course: A meta-analysis of longitudinal studies. *Psychological Bulletin, 132*(1), 1.
Rogers, Carl. (1980). *A way of being.* Boston: Houghton Mifflin.
Schmader, T. (2023). Gender inclusion and fit in STEM. *Annual Review of Psychology, 74*, 219–243.

Schmader, T., Croft, A., Whitehead, J., & Stone, J. (2013). A peek inside the targets' toolbox: How stigmatized targets deflect discrimination by invoking a common identity. *Basic and Applied Social Psychology, 35*(1), 141–149. https://doi.org/10.1080/01973533.2012.746615

Schmader, T., & Sedikides, C. (2018). State authenticity as fit to environment: The implications of social identity for fit, authenticity, and self-segregation. *Personality and Social Psychology Review, 22*(3), 228–259.

Schwartz, S. H. (2012). An overview of the Schwartz theory of basic values. *Online Readings in Psychology and Culture, 2*(1), 11.

Sedikides, C., Slabu, L., Lenton, A., & Thomaes, S. (2017). State authenticity. *Current Directions in Psychological Science, 26*(6), 521–525.

Sheldon, K. M., & Kasser, T. (2001). Goals, congruence, and positive well-being: New empirical support for humanistic theories. *Journal of Humanistic Psychology, 41*(1), 30–50.

Sheldon, K. M., Ryan, R. M., Rawsthorne, L. J., & Ilardi, B. (1997). Trait self and true self: Cross-role variation in the Big-Five personality traits and its relations with psychological authenticity and subjective well-being. *Journal of Personality and Social Psychology, 73*(6), 1380.

Shelton, J. N., & Richeson, J. A. (2005). Intergroup contact and pluralistic ignorance. *Journal of Personality and Social Psychology, 88*(1), 91.

Shelton, J. N., Richeson, J. A., & Salvatore, J. (2005). Expecting to be the target of prejudice: Implications for interethnic interactions. *Personality and Social Psychology Bulletin, 31*(9), 1189–1202.

Spencer-Rodgers, J., Williams, M. J., & Peng, K. (2010). Cultural differences in expectations of change and tolerance for contradiction: A decade of empirical research. *Personality and Social Psychology Review, 14*(3), 296–312.

Stephan, W. G., & Stephan, C. W. (1985). Intergroup anxiety. *Journal of Social Issues, 41*(3), 157–175.

Sugimura, K. (2020). Adolescent identity development in Japan. *Child Development Perspectives, 14*(2), 71–77. https://doi.org/10.1111/cdep.12359

Suh, E. M. (2002). Culture, identity consistency, and subjective well-being. *Journal of Personality and Social Psychology, 83*(6), 1378–1391. https://doi.org/10.1037/0022-3514.83.6.1378

Tajfel, H., & Turner, J. C. (1979). An integrative theory of intergroup conflict. In W. G. Austin & S.Worchel (Eds.), *The social psychology of intergroup relations* (pp. 33–48). Monterey, CA: Brooks/Cole.

Trawalter, S., & Richeson, J. A. (2006). Regulatory focus and executive function after interracial interactions. *Journal of Experimental Social Psychology, 42*(3), 406–412.

Trawalter, S., Richeson, J. A., & Shelton, J. N. (2009). Predicting behavior during interracial interactions: A stress and coping approach. *Personality and Social Psychology Review, 13*(4), 243–268.

Tseng, H., Kuo, Y. C., & Walsh, E. J. (2020). Exploring first-time online undergraduate and graduate students' growth mindsets and flexible thinking and their relations to online learning engagement. *Educational Technology Research and Development, 68*, 2285–2303.

Turner, R. N., Hewstone, M., Voci, A., & Vonofakou, C. (2008). A test of the extended intergroup contact hypothesis: The mediating role of intergroup anxiety, perceived ingroup and outgroup norms, and inclusion of the outgroup in the self. *Journal of Personality and Social Psychology, 95*(4), 843.

van Allen, Z. M., & Zelenski, J. M. (2018). Testing trait-state isomorphism in a new domain: An exploratory manipulation of openness to experience. *Frontiers in Psychology, 9*, 1964. https://doi.org/10.3389/fpsyg.2018.01964

Walton, G. M., & Cohen, G. L. (2007). A question of belonging: Race, social fit, and achievement. *Journal of Personality and Social Psychology, 92*(1), 82.

Walton, G. M., & Cohen, G. L. (2011). A brief social-belonging intervention improves academic and health outcomes of minority students. *Science, 331*(6023), 1447–1451.

Walton, G. M., Murphy, M. C., Logel, C., Yeager, D. S., Goyer, J. P., Brady, S. T., ... & Krol, N. (2023). Where and with whom does a brief social-belonging intervention promote progress in college? *Science, 380*(6644), 499–505.

Wölfer, R., & Hewstone, M. (2018). What buffers ethnic homophily? Explaining the development of outgroup contact in adolescence. *Developmental Psychology, 54*(8), 1507.

Wood, A. M., Linley, P. A., Maltby, J., Baliousis, M., & Joseph, S. (2008). The authentic personality: A theoretical and empirical conceptualization and the development of the Authenticity Scale. *Journal of Counseling Psychology, 55*(3), 385–399.

Woolley, K., & Fishbach, A. (2022). Motivating personal growth by seeking discomfort. *Psychological Science, 33*(4), 510–523.

Wright, S. C., Aron, A., McLaughlin-Volpe, T., & Ropp, S. A. (1997). The extended contact effect: Knowledge of cross-group friendships and prejudice. *Journal of Personality and Social Psychology, 73*(1), 73.

Xia, M., & Xu, X. (2023). Does authenticity always breed mental health? A cross-cultural comparison between the United States and China. *Asian Journal of Social Psychology, 26*(1), 132–145. https://doi.org/10.1111/ajsp.12549

Yeager, D. S., & Dweck, C. S. (2012). Mindsets that promote resilience: When students believe that personal characteristics can be developed. *Educational Psychologist, 47*(4), 302–314.

Zanna, M. P., & Rempel, J. K. (1988). Attitudes: A new look at an old concept. In D. Bar-Tal & A. W. Kruglanski (Eds.), *The social psychology of knowledge* (pp. 315–334). Cambridge University Press.

Zarrinabadi, N., Rezazadeh, M., Karimi, M., & Lou, N. M. (2022). Why do growth mindsets make you feel better about learning and your selves? The mediating role of adaptability. *Innovation in Language Learning and Teaching, 16*(3), 249–264.

Zhang, Y. B., Lin, M. C., Nonaka, A., & Beom, K. (2005). Harmony, hierarchy and conservatism: A cross-cultural comparison of Confucian values in China, Korea, Japan, and Taiwan. *Communication Research Reports, 22*(2), 107–115.

PART II

Motivation & Uncertainty in Self

11

WHY IS EXISTENTIAL UNCERTAINTY DISTRESSING AND PERSISTENT? A TERROR MANAGEMENT PERSPECTIVE

Mark Landau, Young Ju Ryu, Jeff Greenberg, Marcus Chur and Tom Pyszczynski

People's knowledge about the world and themselves encompasses various elements, such as beliefs, values, and episodic memories. Each element can be assigned a (figurative) certainty coefficient representing one's subjective confidence in its alignment with reality. For instance, the current author holds the belief "My name is Mark" with a certainty coefficient of 0.99 (sure it's true) and his opinion "Honda makes the most reliable cars" with a coefficient of.61 (not sure it's true).

Psychologists generally agree that people are motivated to maintain high certainty coefficients (e.g., Kruglanski & Orehek, 2012). Supporting evidence shows that when people encounter circumstances or entertain thoughts that undermine their confidence in their knowledge, they employ compensatory strategies to restore that confidence to its baseline levels (Briñol & Petty, this volume). The literature on attitude certainty suggests that there may be two components of uncertainty: clarity and correctness (Petrocelli et al., 2007). Our focus in this chapter is on people's desire to maintain certainty about the *correctness* of their beliefs, attitudes, and other elements of knowledge.

Why do people crave certainty? The conventional answer, proposed by pragmatist philosophers (Dewey, 1925; James, 1890), is that certainty facilitates goal pursuit. To accomplish nearly anything, individuals need to confidently categorize things, predict future events, and generally interpret their social and physical environments as structured in such a way that performing a given action reliably produces expected outcomes or achieves desired ends. Conversely, perceiving one's environment incorrectly or lacking confidence in the correctness of one's knowledge interferes with effective goal-directed actions.

But if certainty is for doing, what are people trying to do? At a practical level, they want to accomplish day-to-day tasks like commuting to work and planning birthday parties. Consequently, they wrestle with uncertainty about mundane issues such as the attributes of common stimuli ("Is the grocery store open?"), expectations of others' behaviors ("Will mom be upset if I skip Mother's Day?"), and solutions to everyday problems ("How do I tune up this lawnmower?").

On top of their practical goals, people are also trying to view themselves as significant members of a meaningful world. As a result, they grapple with not only mundane uncertainty but also

 DOI: 10.4324/9781003363385-13

existential uncertainty, which we define as a lack of certainty that one's life is making a positive, enduring impact on the world. Existential uncertainty can be caused by uncertainties regarding a number of more specific beliefs that form the basis for the individual's sense of their enduring personal value. The following questions illustrate some of the more common of these uncertainties:

- Am I merely an animal, no different from that squirrel over there, or am I something special?
- Am I on my own or do I belong to something bigger than myself?
- Do the groups I belong to possess accurate knowledge about how the world works and the correct way to live?
- Am I a "good" person? Do I have valuable qualities? Am I accomplished or at least on the right path?
- Do we inhabit a world where virtuous individuals succeed while wicked ones suffer?

To clarify, we don't believe there is (or perhaps even can be) a single adequate self-report measure of one's existential certainty coefficient. We treat the term existential (un)certainty as a theoretical construct that refers to a person's global conception of themselves as a person of enduring value. This global conception rests on a network of beliefs that can vary in certainty, such as "humans are special," "cultural ideals are worth pursuing," and "my experiences fit into a coherent whole." This theoretical approach has the advantage of widening the scope of relevant evidence to include studies examining perceptions of distinct dimensions (e.g., purpose, continuity, fairness) that contribute to one's global sense of existential certainty or uncertainty.

To better understand existential uncertainty and its significance for social behavior, we analyze it through the lens of terror management theory, or TMT (Solomon et al., 2015). We hope to show that TMT offers a unique and empirically corroborated perspective on two questions:

Why Is Existential Uncertainty Distressing at Its Core?

Although people actually very often seek out and enjoy experiences involving mundane uncertainty (e.g., visiting exotic locales, gambling at casinos and online, playing and watching sports, going to new restaurants), and while they occasionally derive intellectual satisfaction from contemplating the mysteries of existence, they generally dislike being uncertain about whether their life amounts to anything. In numerous studies spanning various phenomena like loneliness (Cacioppo & Patrick, 2008), well-being (Ryff et al., 2004), and political ideology (Jost et al., 2013), even temporary uncertainty about sources of meaning in life and personal worth elicits negative emotions, while chronic uncertainty about them undermines mental and physical health. It may seem obvious that existential uncertainty is distressing, but what exactly makes it so bad?

Why Does Existential Uncertainty Persist Stubbornly?

When it comes to knowledge about mundane matters, people rarely go to great lengths to bolster their certainty (e.g., they don't wear t-shirts proclaiming, "The grocery store opens at 7:30am!!"). Also, once they've addressed their uncertainty (e.g., by looking up store hours online), they typically move on and put the matter to rest. In stark contrast, people fiercely promote their knowledge of life's meaning and their personal significance, and they react defensively to even relatively minor events that threaten to invalidate that knowledge. Why is it that people can't seem to settle on a picture of their existential significance and relax their vigilance?

Theory

To understand people's struggles with existential uncertainty, we begin by recognizing their unparalleled aptitude for overcoming mundane uncertainty. Humans' ability to think using symbols—to conceive and communicate about things beyond the immediate present—allows them to detect patterns in their physical and social environments, envision hypothetical future outcomes and counterfactual past scenarios, and respond flexibly to a given situation in a much wider range of ways than is possible for any other form of life.

Unfortunately, this cognitive adaptation to uncertainty comes with a price tag: People are aware of the most indisputable truth about life: *it ends*. Despite the practical advantages of symbolic intelligence, it also makes individuals acutely aware that their death is always a potential and ultimately an inevitable occurrence. While people may be uncertain about the circumstances of their death—when and how it will happen—they hold the knowledge that it will happen with a 1.0 certainty coefficient.

According to TMT, this awareness conflicts with people's biological and psychological predispositions to avoid threats to continued existence, thereby creating a constant potential for anxiety. To minimize the conscious experience of death-related anxiety, people invest in two knowledge structures that work together to deny that death marks the self's annihilation. The first structure is a *cultural worldview*—a network of beliefs created and shared by a group that imbues the world with meaning, prescribes actions to accrue personal value, and promises culturally valued individuals a means of transcending death, such as gaining admittance to a literal afterlife or leaving a personal legacy through creative and generative endeavors. The second structure is *self-esteem*—an evaluation of oneself as meeting or exceeding internalized standards of value associated with one's social roles within the broader culture. For example, American soldiers engaged in their country's "crusade" against evil, members of Thailand's Mien tribe performing rituals to invite benevolent spirits, and social psychologists spending their days engrossed in computer screens can all perceive their actions as conforming to culturally sanctioned paths towards enduring personal significance, thus alleviating potential death anxiety.

With this summary of TMT in mind, let's return to the two questions about existential uncertainty that we posed earlier. The first question was why existential uncertainty is so distressing. Here, TMT builds on the aforementioned pragmatist notion that certainty facilitates goal pursuit, but it expands our understanding of the goals people strive for. In addition to navigating the practical aspects of their daily lives, people also seek to maintain psychological equanimity despite their certain knowledge of death's inevitability. In this view, the distal (or ultimate) psychological goal is keeping anxiety-provoking thoughts about death at bay. People pursue this goal by maintaining existential certainty—a theoretical construct referring to a global conception of the self as leading a life of death-transcending significance. Existential certainty is sustained by maintaining confidence in the correctness of one's cultural worldview and in the correctness of one's perceived satisfaction of the worldview's standards of personal value (i.e., self-esteem). Maintaining confidence in one's worldview and self-esteem requires maintaining confidence in many specific elements of one's knowledge (e.g., that cultural institutions are trustworthy; that rituals are effective; that accomplishments will be remembered; that one doesn't have a piece of spinach stuck in one's teeth). When this knowledge is held with confidence, existential certainty is high, and the individual is protected against anxiety-inducing thoughts of death.

When, however, the individual encounters stimuli (e.g., information, social situations, performances) that decrease certainty about the correctness of any of the knowledge constituting one's cultural worldview or self-esteem, they suffer a drop in existential certainty (*aka* a spike in existential uncertainty). To illustrate, if your current author starts to doubt that publishing manuscripts represents a legitimate path towards enduring personal significance, or if he sanctions that path but perceives himself as failing to cut the proverbial mustard, then he starts to wonder (most likely at an implicit level of consciousness) whether any part of his life or self will continue to exist in a significant way after his body dies. Such thoughts are distressing because they conflict with his desire to continue living.

That brings us to the second question: Why is existential uncertainty so difficult to put to rest? Why can't people simply endorse their worldview's explanation of how the world works and how to transcend death? The answer lies in the nature of worldviews—they are essentially stories, symbolic accounts of reality and existence that can never be definitively validated. They consist of ideas (e.g., supernatural realms, science will solve all our problems) that cannot be proven through personal experience.

Confidence in the worldview instead relies on social consensus: The more people who subscribe to a particular worldview, the more it appears to be correct (Berger & Luckmann, 1967; Festinger, 1954). This consensus is established and maintained through various mechanisms present in all cultures. Even before individuals are born (e.g., at baby showers), they are the target of an immersive socialization process that reinforces prevailing norms, values, and ideals through lifelong participation in collective ceremonies, rituals, and rites of passage, and through constant engagement with cultural products embodying local ideologies. This immersion provides individuals with a comprehensive understanding of which lifestyles are considered significant contributions to the culture and which are not.

The problem is that social consensus is tenuous. It must compete with common social experiences and environmental conditions that lead individuals to question the correctness of their worldview, even if only implicitly. One of the most apparent threats is encountering (or merely learning of the existence of) individuals or groups who hold competing or alternative worldviews. For instance, imagine a Christian who believes in an afterlife meeting a Hindu who believes in reincarnation. This encounter undermines the social consensus that typically reinforces the validity of their respective death-denying worldviews. Though it's unlikely they consciously experience this challenge, such encounters imply that if an objective reality exists, then one of us must be right and the other wrong.

Self-esteem, too, relies on a fragile social consensus. It is sustained by perceiving one's qualities and actions as adhering to a culturally prescribed formula for literal or symbolic continuance beyond death, which includes principles to live by and standards for appropriate behavior. However, this formula is not provably "true." No empirical observations definitively establish that any human activities, such as engaging in military crusades or writing book chapters, guarantee death transcendence.

People's confidence in the validity of this formula, as well as their embodiment of it, can be undermined by various threats encountered in everyday life. Consider the example of a student working towards her PhD in social psychology. She will encounter individuals gaining acclaim for pursuing alternative paths to value. Even within her academic community, standards of value appear ambiguous: Her advisor says that success requires making bold, novel discoveries, but her classes prioritize incremental replication attempts and conservative statistical analyses. Moreover, because she lives in a culture where there is a considerable time gap between one's pursuit of value and the feedback one receives, she is uncertain whether the broader culture will continue to value social psychology and thus her personal achievements in the long run.

In summary, TMT posits that the knowledge structures of cultural worldview and self-esteem that give people hope of transcending death are social constructs that cannot be conclusively proven.

They buffer death-related anxiety only as long as individuals can maintain subjective confidence in their correctness, thereby bolstering a global sense of death-denying value. This confidence is constantly challenged by common sources of existential uncertainty—stimuli that cast doubt on any of the knowledge constituting one's worldview or self-esteem. This is why people appear to be perpetually striving to reinforce the correctness of their worldviews and their positive self-views.

Speaking of confidence, how can we be confident that this theoretical analysis of the sting and persistence of existential uncertainty holds water? By turning to a substantial body of empirical research inspired by TMT.

Research: The Dynamic Relation between Existential Uncertainty and Death-Related Cognitions

Because TMT is broad in scope, it can be used to formulate several testable hypotheses. For the purposes of this chapter, we focus on two hypotheses that correspond to our guiding questions about existential uncertainty.

Hypothesis 1: Sources of existential uncertainty → death-related cognitions. If, as TMT claims, subjective confidence in the correctness of one's worldview and self-esteem function to keep death-related thoughts at bay, then we would expect that encounters with sources of existential uncertainty—stimuli that undermine confidence in aspects of one's worldview or bases of self-esteem—will increase the extent to which death-related cognitions (but not just any negative cognitions) are mentally accessible outside consciousness.

Hypothesis 2: Death-related cognitions → compensating for sources of existential uncertainty. If confidence in one's worldview and bases of self-esteem serves to alleviate mortality concerns, then activating people's awareness of their mortality (but not other negative cognitions) should increase their need for the psychological protection provided by these knowledge structures, and therefore, should lead people to more vehemently bolster and defend sources of culturally derived meaning and to more vigorously do (or at least believe that they are doing) whatever provides them a sense of personal value. Also, threatening or affirming sources of meaning and self-esteem should moderate the effects of activating death-related cognitions on other compensatory processes.

These hypotheses have been supported in hundreds of studies conducted by independent researchers in more than 30 countries and using demographically diverse samples and wide-ranging methods (for comprehensive reviews, see Burke et al., 2010; Greenberg et al., 2008; Hayes et al., 2010). Research testing the first broad hypothesis mentioned—also known as the death-thought accessibility hypothesis—uses various paradigms to measure the accessibility of death-related cognitions. In one paradigm, researchers ask participants to complete ambiguous word fragments and measure the number of death-related (vs. non-death-related) completions (e.g., completing GRA_ _ as *grave* vs. *grape*). Other studies measure the speed of lexical decisions for death-related versus neutral words.

In the typical paradigm used for testing variations of the mortality salience (or "MS") hypothesis, participants answer open-ended items about their death (e.g., "Describe the emotions that the thought of death arouses in you") and are subsequently assessed on attitudinal and behavioral efforts to bolster and defend aspects of their worldview and self-esteem. Other operationalizations of MS include proximity to funeral homes and subliminal primes of death-related stimuli (e.g., the word *death*).

The next few sections offer a selective review of this large research literature. We organize findings around four sources of existential uncertainty that have preoccupied humans across cultural contexts and historical epochs.

Animality vs. Specialness: "Am I Merely My Finite Body?"

One source of existential uncertainty people routinely confront is the awareness that they are flesh-and-blood creatures who are subject to deterioration and vulnerable to sudden destruction. In the words of Ernest Becker, the intellectual predecessor of TMT, people face "an existential contradiction between a symbolic self, that seems to give [them] infinite worth in a timeless scheme of things, and a body that is worth about 98 cents" (1973, p. 34). People strive to shore up confidence in their life's enduring significance, but their bodies frustrate this goal by making apparent their animal nature and vulnerability to death.

Empirical support for TMT's perspective on existential uncertainty's core threat comes from evidence that reminders of animality increase the accessibility of death-related cognitions (Goldenberg et al., 2002). In one study, participants were asked to read an essay that discussed either the similarities between humans and other animals or the special position that humans occupy among living things. Participants were then primed with either the physical aspects of sex (e.g., "Feeling my partner's sweat on my body") or the romantic, culturally valued aspects of sex (e.g., "The romantic feelings surrounding sex"). When participants were reminded of their similarity to other animals, priming physical, but not romantic, sex increased death-thought accessibility. In contrast, when confidence in human specialness was fortified, priming physical sex did not make death thoughts more accessible.

Supporting TMT's perspective on people's vehement compensation for sources of existential uncertainty, studies show that MS instigates attitudinal and behavioral efforts to distance from stimuli that blur the human-animal boundary (Goldenberg et al., 2001). In one study, participants were asked to write about their death or their experience with intense pain (as a comparison condition) as part of a purported study of personality. They were then asked to evaluate an essay describing either humans' similarity or dissimilarity to other animals. Mortality salient participants preferred the essay emphasizing human specialness over the essay emphasizing humans' animality. MS also increased self-reported disgust sensitivity in response to bodily products (e.g., "You see a bowel movement left unflushed on a public toilet") and animals (e.g., "You see maggots on a piece of meat in an outdoor garbage pail").

Isolation vs. Belonging: "Am I Part of Something Real and Enduring?"

To supply their lives with confident meaning and death-transcending significance, individuals often envision a role or function within a social entity that is more significant and enduring than themselves (Becker, 1973). Belonging to a group, relationship, or cause offers people the social consensus necessary to maintain confidence in their worldview and its paths to enduring significance. Others also provide acknowledgement of one's existence and validation for one's claims to culturally prescribed identities and achievements. Without this sense of belonging, individuals would struggle to sustain confidence in the enduring value of their lives and would therefore be susceptible to death anxiety.

Accordingly, research shows that death-related cognitions interact with tendencies to merge with and support others who represent power, safety, and continuity.

Groups. According to uncertainty-identity theory (Hogg, 2007), individuals are motivated to alleviate unpleasant feelings of uncertainty about themselves by identifying with groups that provide a sense of certainty through defined roles and norms. Similarly, TMT suggests that group identification helps individuals alleviate aversive self-relevant uncertainty, emphasizing the psychological benefit of feeling connected to something greater and more enduring than own's own existence. While death is inevitable, people find solace in belonging to ancestral lines, national or religious groups, political movements, scientific or artistic fields, or other enduring groups that symbolically carry a part of their identity forward. Whereas uncertainty-identity theory views a confident sense of group belonging as a goal in its own right, TMT views it as serving the superordinate goal of alleviating death anxiety.

Supporting TMT is evidence that MS heightens group identification across cultural contexts. Following an MS induction, Italians expressed a heightened sense of identification with Italy and considered Italian identity as a concrete entity rather than a mere collection of individuals (Castano et al., 2002); Dutch students were more favorable to and more optimistic about the performance of their local soccer team and university (Dechesne et al., 2000); Spanish participants became more likely to view fellow Spaniards as constituting a real and enduring group (Sani et al., 2009); Chinese participants showed an increased bias in resource allocation to people from their native city and country (Tam et al., 2007); and Israelis showed greater motivation to serve in the national military and endure hardships for the sake of their country (Taubman-Ben-Ari & Findler, 2006).

TMT gives rise to more nuanced hypotheses regarding group identification. It posits that people seek more than just identification; they ultimately rely on groups for self-esteem. This suggests that mortality-primed individuals will strongly identify with groups that are framed positively, but will distance themselves from groups framed negatively. Indeed, when Hispanics or women were reminded of their mortality and primed with negative aspects of their group membership (e.g., the stereotype of Latinos being drug dealers; the stereotype of women being bad at math), they distanced themselves from their ethnic or gender identity (Arndt et al., 2002).

Leaders. In addition to identifying with groups, individuals seek a confident sense of belonging by aligning themselves with leaders—individuals with extra power, status, and responsibility. In their effort to secure death-transcending significance, people are especially drawn to leaders with a charismatic style—those who, with great self-confidence, offer followers a central role in a grand, heroic mission to triumph over evil and bring about a better future (Becker, 1975).

Supporting the terror management function of leader identification, Landau, Solomon et al. (2004) showed that, just prior to the 2004 Presidential Election, reminders of death or the September 11, 2001, terrorist attacks (which increased death-thought accessibility) heightened participants' support for then-President George W. Bush, who portrayed himself as spearheading a divinely sponsored crusade against evil. More recent studies show that experimental and naturalistic inductions of mortality increase support for then-presidential candidate Donald J. Trump, who, like Bush, presented himself as a larger-than-life figure leading a heroic mission (Cohen et al., 2017).

Romantic relationships. Theorist Otto Rank (1936) proposed that romantic relationships have, in modern times, largely taken the place of religion as a primary source of existential meaning and self-esteem. A romantic partner becomes someone who knows and cares about one's life story and personal aspirations, thereby witnessing and validating one's existence and its significance. Backing up Rank's claim is evidence that people are increasingly expecting their committed romantic relationships to fulfill their psychological needs for self-esteem and self-actualization (Finkel et al., 2014).

Going a step further, TMT suggests that the meaning and value derived from romantic relationships function to alleviate mortality concerns, even if individuals are not consciously aware of this function. Mikulincer et al. (2003) proposed that romantic relationships are particularly crucial for managing death anxiety because they provide the same kind of physical and emotional closeness individuals relied on as children when feeling scared. Their studies show that threats to committed relationships or thoughts of separation from romantic partners increased the accessibility of death-related cognitions, implying that the confidence in the meaning and value attributed to romantic relationships helps suppress such cognitions. Moreover, MS intensified people's desire for closeness in their romantic relationships, and it led individuals not in a romantic relationship to report an increased desire to have one.

Descendants. TMT's analysis of belonging also helps us understand the culturally widespread desire for and love of one's children. Although having children likely satisfies a variety of psychological and biological needs, it can bolster confidence that a part of the self will live on beyond death. Studies show that, among young married adults without children, thinking about becoming parents reduced the accessibility of death-related cognitions (Yaakobi et al., 2014). Also, MS increased positive thoughts of parenthood and desire for offspring among Dutch, German, and Chinese individuals (Fritsche et al., 2007; Wisman & Goldenberg, 2005; Zhou et al., 2008). MS also increased interest in naming future children after oneself (Vicary, 2011). Among German participants, bringing offspring to mind eliminated outgroup derogation typically induced by MS (Fritsche et al., 2007). Particularly in cultures where the continuation of the lineage symbolizes transcending death by passing on the ancestral heritage, the significance of descendent continuity acts as a buffer against death-related anxiety for both parents and non-parents (Qi, 2023).

Shared Reality vs. Relativism: "Does My Group Know How the World *Really* Works?"

During the process of socialization into a worldview that gives life meaning, individuals acquire a host of beliefs about reality—about how things work, what's good and bad, and what goals to strive for. From a TMT perspective, individuals must maintain confidence in these beliefs to be assured that their worldview offers dependable routes to literal or symbolic immortality. When confidence in these beliefs is shaken, it frustrates one's goal of leading a life of enduring significance and thereby creates the potential to experience death-related anxiety.

Supporting this perspective, studies show that when people encounter people, messages, or other stimuli that threaten the validity of their cultural beliefs, thoughts of death become more accessible. For instance, Canadians exposed to insults to the Canadian way of life (but not just any negative stimulus) exhibited increased death-thought accessibility (Schimel et al., 2007). In a related study, when the belief in fundamentalism was challenged through the presentation of contradictions and inconsistencies in the Bible's account of the resurrection, Christian fundamentalists exhibited increased death-thought accessibility, whereas non-fundamentalists did not (Friedman & Rholes, 2007).

Related research shows that MS heightens efforts to reinforce confidence in one's cultural beliefs. For example, proximity to a cemetery or funeral home led people to overestimate social consensus for their attitudes (Pyszczynski et al., 1996). MS also leads people to react more favorably to others who validate aspects of their worldview and react more negatively to others who violate or dispute those aspects of their worldview. In one study (Greenberg et al., 1990), American participants were asked to evaluate two essays purportedly written by foreign exchange students. One essay criticized the United States and its way of life, while the other praised the country's virtues. MS increased positive reactions toward the pro-US author and negative reactions toward the anti-US author. Mortality-induced worldview defense emerges in response to implicit as well as explicit worldview threats. For example, mortality salient Christian participants were especially attracted to someone who appeared to be Christian and were especially averse to someone who appeared to be Jewish (Greenberg et al., 1990). MS even led participants to physically aggress against targets who opposed their political ideologies (McGregor et al., 1998).

MS also motivates people to seek new information as a means of reinforcing confidence in their beliefs (Jonas et al., 2003). German participants were asked to read about a controversy regarding German health insurance policies. After making a preliminary decision on which of two policies should be implemented by the German parliament, participants were provided with a list of additional resources, such as newspaper articles with headlines biased in favor of different policies. Mortality salient participants were eager to view additional information so long as it was consistent with their initial viewpoint.

The Vagaries of Self-Esteem: "Am I a Valuable Person?"

Recall that, according to TMT, sustaining confidence in the validity of one's worldview is not sufficient for the distal goal of assuaging mortality concerns. The person also needs self-esteem—to feel as though they are personally living up to their worldview's standards of value and therefore qualify for continuation beyond physical death. However, people remain existentially uncertain to varying degrees in part because their self-esteem can never be verified with absolute certainty. Indeed, because self-esteem hinges on fickle social validation for one's claims to culturally prescribed identities and achievements, refers to intangible constructs (e.g., personality traits), and is often gained through achievements largely outside of individual control, it is almost guaranteed that people experience persistent uncertainty regarding their value.

Does this uncertainty really weaken the psychological shield that keeps thoughts of death from entering consciousness, as TMT claims? Yes. Study participants who experienced a threat to their self-esteem showed increased death-thought accessibility (Hayes et al., 2008). The pattern emerged when individuals were faced with threats that are highly relevant to their personal sense of self-worth, such as receiving false feedback indicating poor performance on an intelligence test for those who value intelligence or being informed that their personality is not suitable for their desired career. Related studies show a similar effect in response to more general threats, such as the anticipation of delivering an inadequately prepared speech to peers or reflecting on past instances of failing to uphold one's most significant values (Routledge, 2012). Lifshin and colleagues (2021) provided more direct evidence supporting TMT's claim that the effect of self-esteem threat on death-thought accessibility is attributable to reduced certainty in symbolic immortality, or the belief that one's personal significance will endure beyond physical death.

Other studies show that MS increases self-serving biases, leading Dutch students to report stronger belief in the validity of positive information about themselves (e.g., from a horoscope or a personality test; Dechesne et al., 2003) and Israeli students to make self-serving attributions on an achievement-related task (e.g., attributing poor performance following failure to external causes; Mikulincer & Florian, 2002).

Moreover, MS leads people to engage in (or perceive themselves as engaging in) activities from which they derive personal value. Mortality salient participants were more likely to conform to cultural values and norms (e.g., by increasing generosity toward valued charities; Jonas et al., 2002) and conversely were more reluctant to violate cultural standards for appropriate conduct (Greenberg et al., 1995). Related studies show that MS increases people's efforts to perform well in domains on which they stake their self-esteem (Peters et al., 2005; Zestcott et al., 2016).

MS can even lead people to engage in dangerous activities if it makes them feel valuable. Israeli soldiers who valued their driving ability as a source of self-esteem drove more recklessly if they were first reminded of their mortality (Ben-Ari et al., 1999). MS also led women, but not men, to strive to attain cultural standards of bodily appearance with greater intentions to tan their skin and restrict their calorie consumption (Goldenberg & Arndt, 2008). Although it may seem counterintuitive that thinking about death can lead people to do things that pose lethal health risks, it is consistent with TMT's claim that self-esteem striving is a distal defense that is not logically or directly related to the problem of death (Solomon et al., 2015).

Dispositional Factors in Response to Existential Uncertainty

TMT research has examined individual differences in the degree of reactivity to sources of existential uncertainty—that is, threats to aspects of one's worldview or self-esteem. Researchers have hypothesized that individuals predisposed to experience death anxiety will respond to such threats with particularly high death-thought accessibility. We would also expect them to respond to MS with exaggerated defenses. To test these hypotheses, researchers have assessed the moderating role of individual-difference variables associated with susceptibility to negative affect and anxiety, such as trait self-esteem, neuroticism, depression, attachment style, religiosity, and nostalgia.

Let's consider neuroticism as an example. Individuals with high levels of neuroticism report higher levels of death anxiety (Loo, 1984) and are more likely to ruminate about mortality (Abdel-Khalek, 1998). In line with TMT, studies conducted by Goldenberg and her colleagues show that neuroticism predicts particularly strong negative reactions to aspects of the human body that imply animal nature (e.g., excrement, reproduction) because these stimuli remind people that they are mortal animals. Individuals with high neuroticism were more likely to exhibit death-thought accessibility in response to priming the physical aspects of sex and exhibit decreased interest in physical sex following MS (Goldenberg et al., 1999). High levels of neuroticism even predicted reduced compliance with body-focused health recommendations (e.g., to undergo a mammogram) under mortality salience (Goldenberg et al., 2009), suggesting that dispositional sensitivity to the threatening mortal implications of the physical body can ironically increase the risk of lethal health conditions.

On the flip side of the same coin, other dispositional factors predict lower susceptibility to death anxiety, which predicts relaxed defensiveness in response to worldview and self-esteem threats. Consider trait mindfulness, which refers to the ability to attentively perceive stimuli as they arise in the present moment without the intrusion of higher-order appraisals and distractions. Niemiec et al. (2010) proposed that individuals with high levels of mindfulness would be better equipped to directly confront death-related cognitions. In this way, they would avoid the defensive suppression of death-related cognitions shown to mediate MS effects on worldview defense (Hayes et al., 2010). Accordingly, individuals with high trait mindfulness did not respond to MS with increased defense of their cultural beliefs, and this effect was partially mediated by more deliberate processing of death-related thoughts during MS inductions.

Besides the degree of defense, what about variations in people's "style" of defense? According to TMT, the dominant worldview typically offers a broad set of possibilities for what to believe and what to personally strive for, and individuals select from this buffet the sources of meaning and self-esteem that they prefer to use as a protective buffer against mortality concerns. This analysis leads us to expect that individuals within the same cultural milieu will share many aspects of the dominant worldview but also will allay mortality concerns by adhering to diverging subsystems of beliefs, preferences, standards of personal value, and behaviors.

Supporting this analysis is the aforementioned evidence that MS-induced self-esteem striving is moderated by individual differences in domain investment (e.g., Goldenberg & Arndt, 2008; Peters et al., 2005). Other studies examine dispositional variability in people's desire for clear, coherent knowledge and their corresponding aversion to ambiguity and disorder. This variability is measured using instruments like the Personal Need for Structure (PNS) Scale, which assesses agreement with statements such as "It upsets me to go into a situation without knowing what I can expect from it" (Thompson et al., 2001).

From a TMT perspective, to manage mortality concerns, all people need to sustain the perception that they live in an ordered world in which people and nature can be engaged with confidence, and in which they reliably can establish a sense of lasting personal significance. Nevertheless, TMT acknowledges that individual worldviews can be personalized, allowing for the possibility that individuals with a stronger dispositional preference for structured knowledge may be especially likely to invest in well-structured (i.e., clearly defined, consistent, stable) conceptions of their environment and experiences as a characteristic means of managing mortality concerns, whereas low-structure-seeking individuals may be more tolerant of ambiguity and novelty in cognizing the world and themselves.

Accordingly, many studies show that MS increases high-PNS participants' tendencies to seek out and defend well-structured interpretations of other people, interpersonal relations, and social events, whereas MS does not prompt these structuring tendencies among low-PNS individuals. For example, MS increased high-PNS participants' desire to believe in a just world (where people get what they deserve and do not suffer randomly or arbitrarily; Hirschberger, 2006; Landau, Johns et al., 2004), to view others in line with simplifying stereotypes (Schimel et al., 1999), and to integrate memories of past events with their current self-concept (Landau et al., 2009). Are high-PNS individuals simply more defensive overall than their low-PNS counterparts? No. Low-PNS individuals are no less defensive; rather, they derive protective meaning from exploratory engagement with novel information rather than from epistemic structure (Vess et al., 2009).

Outlook: Existential Uncertainty and Terror Management in Modern Times

Sources of existential uncertainty have persisted throughout history, likely stemming from the complexity of the human brain. In the oldest recorded story, the 5,000-year-old Epic of Gilgamesh, the protagonist's awareness of death sets him off on a quest for immortality. Ancient Greek and East Asian philosophers contemplated death and the purpose of existence, as did Medieval and Renaissance writers like Omar Khayyam and Shakespeare.

However, the Industrial Revolution, Darwin's theories, and the rise of psychoanalysis turned up the volume on existential uncertainty. Marx highlighted the challenge of maintaining self-worth in mass-production societies. Schopenhauer argued that life lacks inherent meaning. Durkheim observed a growing alienation from mainstream cultural values. Nietzsche proclaimed the demise of an all-powerful deity working on our behalf.

As the 20th century dawned, writers like Thomas Mann, Freud, and Otto Rank emphasized the void in meaning and purpose as religion waned in its role as a widely shared foundation for identity, social connection, and transcending death (Greif, 2015). World wars and genocides took millions of lives with cruel indifference, and an expanding mass media exposed people to horrors and tragedies not only within their own geographical and social sphere but around the world. Advancements in fields like astronomy further reinforced the notion that humans were being demoted from "Masters of the Universe" to inconsequential specks in the grand cosmic scheme.

As humanity progresses into the third decade of the 21st century, the din of challenges to existential certainty has grown even louder. One factor is the looming threat of species extinction caused by climate change and related environmental disasters. Terrorism and ongoing wars continue to contribute to a sense of imminent global disaster. The pervasive influence of social media has fostered mass doubt regarding what or whom to believe, leading to political polarization and the proliferation of conspiracy theories. The global COVID-19 pandemic and intensified social justice issues have further amplified these trends, as have rapid social and technological changes that challenge long-standing beliefs, such as the equivalence of biological sex and gender.

In short, a perfect storm of cultural-historical factors has resulted in an unprecedented level of awareness of a multitude of often conflicting beliefs, norms, values, and lifestyles. Consequently, existential uncertainty is likely at an all-time high. Considering TMT and related research, we can draw some implications regarding the likely consequences of this development. One is the heightened prevalence of death anxiety. Growing evidence points to death anxiety as a common underlying factor contributing to a wide range of mental health issues, including anxiety disorders, depression, obsessive-compulsive disorder, substance abuse disorders, PTSD, and potentially even schizophrenia (Menzies & Menzies, 2023). Therefore, it is plausible that mounting existential uncertainty is fueling profound death anxiety, which, in turn, contributes to the documented rise in chronic mental health problems (Twenge et al., 2019).

A second likely consequence of growing existential uncertainty is the tendency to seek relief in extremist worldviews. In their analysis of the causes and consequences of the September 11th terrorist attacks on the World Trade Center and Pentagon, Pyszczynski, Solomon, and Greenberg (2003) posited that humankind is caught between two basic types of worldviews: "rocks" and "hard places." Rock-type worldviews are characterized by absolutism, moral judgment, and a strict belief in right and wrong. They uphold rigid power hierarchies and promote anger as the default response to those perceived as wrong or evil. Fundamentalist and extremist worldviews fall into this category, offering a single, defined path toward heroism by combating perceived evils.

In contrast, hard place-type worldviews are more relativistic and less certain about matters of right and wrong. They emphasize tolerance, uncertainty, and humility, and are associated with feelings of anxiety rather than anger. Leading a significant life, within this general scope, involves attempting to make the world a better place but with much less certainty about the best approach to achieving that goal.

Terror management theory and research suggest that conditions that increase the accessibility of death-related thoughts, as sources of existential uncertainty demonstrably do, heighten the appeal of rock-type worldviews and those who promote them. Consequently, TMT provides a framework for understanding the proliferation of extremist views observed in the United States and elsewhere, as well as the resulting polarization and hostility within and between subcultures. (Of course, TMT is not the only theoretical perspective positing that uncertainty and extremism often go hand in hand).

Future research on the existential uncertainty-extremism link could focus on specific, practically important expressions of extremism. For example, despite their differences, extremist worldviews often share a similar solution to rising existential uncertainty in the present: reconnecting with a largely mythical, sanitized bygone era when, it is believed, the world made sense and there was one consensually agreed-upon way to live.

This is a common strategy used by charismatic leaders, epitomized by former President Trump's motto, "Make America Great Again." It's also a popular strategy among neo-masculinity groups, such as the cultish following of Andrew Tate, which promise followers circumscribed gender roles (e.g., "Men protect; women nurture"), strict power hierarchies, and an attainable code of conduct. The argument for the correctness of this chauvinist worldview rests on a nostalgic caricature of men and women's "natures" for most of recorded history and even further back in the distant hominid past.

Extremist white supremacy groups similarly fetishize the past, basing their ideology on a romanticized image of an ancestral homeland for White Europeans—where, it is imagined, people were homogenously white and ruled the world. For example, in 2017, white supremacists descended on Charlottesville, Virginia for the "Unite the Right" rally. As they chanted anti-Semitic, Nazi-associated slogans, they carried shields bearing iconography appropriated from medieval Europe and ancient Germanic and Norse mythology.

This analysis leads us to expect that when mortality is salient, especially when combined with the salience of ambiguous or shifting value standards in the mainstream culture, people will be drawn to, and identify more zealously with, extremist worldviews that reach back into history for a seemingly "pure," irrefutable basis of existential significance. The aforementioned research on MS and the appeal of charismatic leaders supports this idea, but more focused investigations are warranted.

We'll conclude by discussing another facet of contemporary life, which we might call "folk postmodernism." Postmodernist philosophy tends to downplay and sometimes reject concepts of objectivity, rationality, and universal truth, while instead emphasizing diversity of perspectives and the role of ideology and culture in all human thought and experience. There seems to be a recent epistemological shift in some realms of contemporary society in which the criteria for confident beliefs resemble the precepts of postmodernist philosophy. Truth has come to depend less on the correspondence between an idea and a mutually agreed upon reality—based on shared observations and prior knowledge—and more on consistency with one's preferred ideology. Hence the embrace by some political figures of "alternative facts" and the denial of seemingly strong evidence, such as widespread scientific consensus, audio and video recordings of behavior, and eyewitness testimony from multiple observers.

These more relativistic bases of truth have allowed ideological factions to feel strong collective certainty in worldviews that look very different from each other. Those to the right of the political spectrum champion a mythical, perfect past and condemn those outsiders perceived to be threatening their view of traditional American values, while those on the left strive for a mythical counterfactual reality in which history can somehow be undone ("decolonizing"), and they condemn the current system as uniquely guilty of societal ills that are arguably present in every society, past and present.

Truth may be shifting toward relativism from a bird's eye perspective, but that is probably not how most people view it. According to Pyszczynski and Greenberg's (1987) biased hypothesis-testing model of social inference, people need to maintain an *illusion of objectivity*—to believe that their beliefs follow logically from available information. At first blush, one might suspect that this need to be able to convince oneself and others of the rationality and objectivity of one's beliefs has diminished in recent years—and this may indeed be the case for some people. But we suspect that the need for an illusion of objectivity still governs the thinking of most people. The informational landscape that most people inhabit provides what appears to individuals as compelling evidence for whatever interpretation of world events best fits their worldviews and maintains effective anxiety-buffering protection. When major news events occur, reporting from conservative and liberal media outlets spin them in ways that confirm the network's (and their viewers') ideological agendas and often don't even mention aspects that don't fit.

Ironically, the fact that people are aware of this bias in the media and in the statements of politicians and opinion leaders helps them maintain an illusion of objectivity about their own biased worldviews (Lavine et al., 2005). In a world where all sources of information are suspect, it feels rational to discount information that supports ideological agendas different from one's own. *Of course* nothing *they* say can be trusted, and *of course* people on *our* own side care only about truth, fairness, and objectivity!

As noted earlier, Petrocelli et al. (2007) have noted that uncertainty may have two separable components: correctness and clarity. In current times, both one's clarity regarding what one believes and how correct one is may be more in doubt than ever before. However, we believe that uncertainty about correctness is the primary existential threat that calls into question one's bases of meaning and value, and therefore sense of death transcendence. From a TMT perspective, being correct is what provides certainty. And, as research has shown, lack of social consensus, so salient in the contemporary world, affects correctness more than it does clarity (Cheatham & Tormala, 2014). In addition, studies investigating these two components have found that correctness predicts advocacy of one's views, whereas clarity does not, and that level of correctness rather than clarity predict anger and assertiveness toward those with different views (Niedbala et al., 2018).

After MS, negative reactions are intensified toward an essay by someone who holds very different beliefs (e.g., Greenberg et al., 2990). Such essays are more likely to call into question one's correctness rather than one's clarity. That said, the clarity versus correctness distinction does point to a missing piece of evidence in the TMT literature. Uncertainty regarding one's worldview or self-worth has only rarely been assessed directly. Still, it may be difficult to do so because any direct measure may inadvertently provide participants with a means of reasserting their confidence in the correctness and worthiness of their worldview and self-concept.

Indeed, that is why the many threats to certainty are leading to such extreme and polarizing worldviews, creating a post-modern landscape in which rationality and objectivity are less important determinants of beliefs and behavior than subjective preferences. Ironically, despite the changes brought on by the enlightenment of past centuries and the wealth of knowledge produced by the scientific method, blind faith in one's preferred worldview and ideology may be a more potent determinant of beliefs and attitudes in today's world than objective information and rational analysis. The irony is that this blind faith leads to a lot more professed certainty about life than is warranted as a way to cope with the uncertainties posed by the conflicted state of today's world and the rumble of death anxiety generated by those uncertainties.

References

Abdel-Khalek, A. M. (1998). The structure and measurement of death obsession. *Personality and Individual Differences, 24*, 159–165.

Arndt, J., Greenberg, J., Schimel, J., Pyszczynski, T., & Solomon, S. (2002). To belong or not to belong, that is the question: Terror management and identification with gender and ethnicity. *Journal of Personality and Social Psychology, 83*, 26–43.

Becker, E. (1973). *The denial of death.* Free Press.

Becker, E. (1975). *Escape from evil.* Free Press.

Ben-Ari, O., Florian, V., & Mikulincer, M. (1999). The impact of mortality salience on reckless driving: A test of terror management mechanisms. *Journal of Personality and Social Psychology, 76*, 35–45.

Berger, P., & Luckmann, T. (1967). *The social construction of reality: A treatise in the sociology of knowledge*. Doubleday Anchor.

Burke, B., Martens, A., & Faucher, E. (2010). Two decades of terror management theory: A meta-analysis of mortality salience research. *Personality and Social Psychology Review, 14*, 155–195.

Cacioppo, J., & Patrick, W. (2008). *Loneliness: Human nature and the need for social connection.* Norton.

Castano, E., Yzerbyt, V., Paladino, M. & Sacchi, S. (2002). I belong, therefore, I exist: Ingroup identification, ingroup entitativity, and ingroup bias. *Personality and Social Psychology Bulletin, 28*, 135–143.

Cheatham, L., & Tormala, Z. (2014). Fostering advocacy: How the underlying constructs of attitude certainty affect persuasion intentions. *ACR North American Advances*, 42, 428–429.

Cohen, F., Solomon, S., & Kaplin, D. (2017). You're hired! Mortality salience increases Americans' support for Donald Trump. *Analyses of Social Issues and Public Policy, 17*, 339–357.

Dechesne, M., Greenberg, J., Arndt, J., & Schimel, J. (2000). Terror management and the vicissitudes of sports fan affiliation: The effects of mortality salience on optimism and fan identification. *European Journal of Social Psychology, 30*, 813–835.

Dechesne, M., Pyszczynski, T., Arndt, J., Ransom, S., Sheldon, K. M., van Knippenberg, A., & Janssen, J. (2003). Literal and symbolic immortality: The effect of evidence of literal immortality on self-esteem striving in response to mortality salience. *Journal of Personality and Social Psychology*, *84*, 722–737.

Dewey, J. (1925). *Experience and nature*. Open Court.

Festinger, L. (1954). A theory of social comparison processes. *Human Relations*, *7*, 117–140.

Finkel, E., Hui, C., Carswell, K., & Larson, G. (2014). The suffocation of marriage: Climbing Mount Maslow without enough oxygen. *Psychological Inquiry*, *25*, 1–41.

Friedman, M., & Rholes, W. S. (2007). Successfully challenging fundamentalist beliefs results in increased death awareness. *Journal of Experimental Social Psychology*, *43*, 794–801.

Fritsche, I., Jonas, E., Fischer, P., Koranyi, N., Berger, N., & Fleischmann, B. (2007). Mortality salience and the desire for offspring. *Journal of Experimental Social Psychology*, *43*, 753–762.

Goldenberg, J., & Arndt, J. (2008). The implications of death for health: A terror management health model for behavioral health promotion. *Psychological Review*, *115*, 1032–105.

Goldenberg, J., Cox, C. R., Pyszczynski, T., Greenberg, J., Solomon, S. (2002). Understanding human ambivalence about sex: The effects of stripping sex of meaning. *Journal of Sex Research*, *39*, 310–320.

Goldenberg, J., Pyszczynski, T., McCoy, S. K., Greenberg, J., & Solomon, S. (1999). Death, sex, love, and neuroticism: Why is sex such a problem? *Journal of Personality and Social Psychology*, *77*, 1173–1187.

Goldenberg, J., Pyszczynski, T., Greenberg, J., Solomon, S., Kluck, B., & Cornwell, R. (2001). I am not an animal: Mortality salience, disgust, and the denial of human creatureliness. *Journal of Experimental Psychology*, *130*, 427–435.Goldenberg, J., Routledge, C., & Arndt, J. (2009). Mammograms and the management of existential discomfort: Threats associated with the physicality of the body and neuroticism. *Psychology and Health*, *24*, 563–581.Greenberg, J., Porteus, J., Simon, L., Pyszczynski, T., & Solomon, S. (1995). Evidence of a terror management function of cultural icons: The effects of mortality salience on the inappropriate use of cherished cultural symbols. *Personality and Social Psychology Bulletin*, *21*, 1221–1228.

Greenberg, J., Pyszczynski, T., Solomon, S., Rosenblatt, A., Veeder, M., Kirkland, S., & Lyon, D. (1990). Evidence for terror management II: The effects of mortality salience on reactions to those who threaten or bolster the cultural worldview. *Journal of Personality and Social Psychology*, *58*, 308–318.

Greenberg, J., Solomon, S., & Arndt, J. (2008). A basic but uniquely human motivation: Terror management. In J. Shah & W. Gardner (Eds.), *Handbook of motivation science* (pp. 113–134). The Guilford Press.

Greif, M. (2015). *The age of the crisis of man: Thought and fiction in America, 1933–1973*. Princeton University Press.

Hayes, J., Schimel, J., Faucher, E. H., & Williams, T. J. (2008). Evidence for the DTA hypothesis II: Threatening self-esteem increases death-thought accessibility. *Journal of Experimental Social Psychology, 44*, 600–613.

Hayes, J., Schimel, J., Arndt, J., & Faucher, E. H. (2010). A theoretical and empirical review of the death-thought accessibility concept in terror management research. *Psychological Bulletin, 136*, 699–739. Hirschberger, G. (2006). Terror management and attributions of blame to innocent victims: Reconciling compassionate and defensive responses. *Journal of Personality and Social Psychology, 91*, 832–844.

Hogg, M. A. (2007). Uncertainty-identity theory. In M. Zanna (Ed.), *Advances in experimental social psychology* (Vol. 39, pp. 69–126). Academic Press.

James, W. (1890). *The principles of psychology* (Vol. 1). Harvard University Press.

Jonas, E., Greenberg, J., & Frey, D. (2003). Connecting terror management and dissonance theories: Evidence that mortality salience increases the preference for supportive information after decisions. *Personality and Social Psychology Bulletin, 29*, 1181–1189.

Jonas, E., Schimel, J., Greenberg, J., & Pyszczynski, T. (2002). The Scrooge effect: Evidence that mortality salience increases prosocial attitudes and behavior. *Personality and Social Psychology Bulletin, 28*, 1342–1353.

Jost, J. T., Hennes, E., & Lavine, H. (2013). "Hot" political cognition: Its self-, group-, and system-serving purposes. In D. Carlston (Ed.), *The Oxford handbook of social cognition* (pp. 851–875). Oxford University Press.

Kruglanski, A. W., & Orehek, E. (2012). The need for certainty as a psychological nexus for individuals and society. In M. Hogg & D. Blaylock (Eds.), *Extremism and the psychology of uncertainty* (pp. 3–18). Wiley-Blackwell.

Landau, M. J., Greenberg, J., Sullivan, D., Routledge, C., & Arndt, J. (2009). The protective identity: Evidence that mortality salience heightens the clarity and coherence of the self-concept. *Journal of Experimental Social Psychology, 45*, 796–807.

Landau, M.J., Johns, M., Greenberg, J., Pyszczynski, T., Martens, A., Goldenberg, J. L., & Solomon, S. (2004). A function of form: Terror management and structuring the social world. *Journal of Personality and Social Psychology, 87*, 190–210.

Landau, M.J., Solomon, S., et al. (2004). Deliver us from evil: The effects of mortality salience and reminders of 9/11 on support for President George W. Bush. *Personality and Social Psychology Bulletin, 30*, 1136–1150.

Lavine, H., Lodge, M., & Freitas, K. (2005). Threat, authoritarianism, and selective exposure to information. *Political Psychology, 26*, 219–244.

Lifshin, U., Horner, D., Helm, P., Solomon, S., & Greenberg, J. (2021). Self-esteem and immortality: Evidence regarding the terror management hypothesis that high self-esteem is associated with a stronger sense of symbolic immortality. *Personality and Individual Differences, 175*, 110712.

Loo, R. (1984). Personality correlates of the fear of death and dying scale. *Journal of Clinical Psychology, 40*, 120–122.

McGregor, H., Lieberman, J. D., Greenberg, J., Solomon, S., Arndt, J., Simon, L., & Pyszczynski, T. (1998). Terror management and aggression: Evidence that mortality salience motivates aggression against worldview threatening others. *Journal of Personality and Social Psychology, 74*, 590–605.

Menzies, R. E., & Menzies, R. G. (2023). Death anxiety and mental health: Requiem for a dreamer. *Journal of Behavior Therapy and Experimental Psychiatry, 78*, 101807.

Mikulincer, M., & Florian, V. (2002). The effects of mortality salience on self-serving attributions: Evidence for the function of self-esteem as a terror management mechanism. *Basic and Applied Social Psychology, 24*, 261–271.

Mikulincer, M., Florian, V., & Hirschberger, G. (2003). The existential function of close relationships: Introducing death into the science of love. *Personality and Social Psychology Review, 7*, 20–40.

Niedbala, E. M., Hohman, Z. P., & Elleby, J. S. (2018). When I'm right you're wrong: attitude correctness facilitates anger and approach motivation toward opposing individuals, *Social Influence, 13*, 150–162.

Niemiec, C. P., Brown, K. W., Kashdan, T. B., Cozzolino, P. J., Breen, W. E., Levesque-Bristol, C., & Ryan, R. M. (2010). Being present in the face of existential threat: The role of trait mindfulness in reducing defensive response to mortality salience. *Journal of Personality and Social Psychology, 99*, 344–365.

Peters, H., Greenberg, J., Williams, J., & Schneider, N. (2005). Applying terror management theory to performance: Can reminding individuals of their mortality increase strength output? *Journal of Sport and Exercise Psychology, 27*, 111–116.

Petrocelli, J. V., Tormala, Z. L., & Rucker, D. D. (2007). Unpacking attitude certainty: Attitude clarity and attitude correctness. *Journal of Personality and Social Psychology, 92*, 30.

Pyszczynski, T., & Greenberg, J. (1987). Toward an integration of cognitive and motivational perspectives on social inference: A biased hypothesis-testing model. *Advances in Experimental Social Psychology, 20*, 297–340.

Pyszczynski, T., Solomon, S., & Greenberg, J. (2003). *In the wake of 9/11: The psychology of terror*. American Psychological Association.

Pyszczynski, T., Wicklund, R. A., Floresku, S., Koch, H., Gauch, G., Solomon, S., & Greenberg, J. (1996). Whistling in the dark: Exaggerated estimates of social consensus in response to incidental reminders of mortality. *Psychological Science, 7*, 332–336.

Qi, J. (2023). The terror management function of descendent continuity: Evidence that descendent continuity acts as a distal and proximal defense. *Personality and Social Psychology Bulletin, 49*, 125–137.

Rank, O. (1936). *Truth and reality: A life history of the human will*. Knopf.

Routledge, C. (2012). Failure causes fear: The effect of self-esteem threat on death-anxiety. *The Journal of Social Psychology, 152*, 665–669.

Ryff, C. D., Singer, B., & Dienberg Love, G. (2004) Positive health: connecting well-being with biology. *Philosophical Transactions of the Royal Society B: Biological Sciences, 359*, 1383–1394.

Sani, F., Herrera, M., & Bowe, M. (2009). Perceived collective continuity and ingroup identification as defence against death awareness. *Journal of Experimental Social Psychology, 45*, 242–245.

Schimel, J., Hayes, J., Williams, T., & Jahrig, J. (2007). Is death really the worm at the core? Converging Evidence that worldview threat increases death-thought accessibility. *Journal of Personality and Social Psychology, 92*, 789–803.

Schimel, J., et al. (1999). Stereotypes and terror management: Evidence that mortality salience enhances stereotypic thinking and preferences. *Journal of Personality and Social Psychology, 77*, 905–926.

Solomon, S., Greenberg, J., & Pyszczynski, T. (2015). *The worm at the core: On the role of death in life*. Random House.

Tam, K., Chiu, C., & Lau, I. (2007). Terror management among Chinese: Worldview defense and intergroup bias in resource allocation. *Asian Journal of Social Psychology, 10*, 93–102.

Taubman-Ben-Ari, O., & Findler, L. (2006). Motivation for military service: A terror management perspective. *Military Psychology, 18*, 149–159.

Thompson, M., Naccarato, M., Parker, K., & Moskowitz, G. (2001). The personal need for structure and personal fear of invalidity measures. In G. Moskowitz (Ed.), *Cognitive social psychology* (pp. 19–39). Lawrence Erlbaum Associates.

Twenge, J., Cooper, A., Joiner, T., Duffy, M., & Binau, S. (2019). Age, period, and cohort trends in mood disorder indicators and suicide-related outcomes in a nationally representative dataset, 2005–2017. *Journal of Abnormal Psychology, 128*, 185–199.

Vess, M., Routledge, C., Landau, M. J., & Arndt, J. (2009). The dynamics of death and meaning: The effects of death-relevant cognitions and personal need for structure on perceptions of meaning in life. *Journal of Personality and Social Psychology, 97*, 728–744.

Vicary, A. M. (2011). Mortality salience and namesakeing: Does thinking about death make people want to name their children after themselves? *Journal of Research in Personality, 45*, 138–141.

Wisman, A., & Goldenberg, J. (2005). From the grave to the cradle: Evidence that mortality salience engenders a desire for offspring. *Journal of Personality and Social Psychology, 89*, 46–61.

Yaakobi, E., Mikulincer, M., & Shaver, P. (2014). Parenthood as a terror management mechanism: The moderating role of attachment orientation. *Personality and Social Psychology Bulletin, 40*, 762–774.

Zestcott, C., Lifshin, U., Helm, P., & Greenberg, J. (2016). He dies he scores: The effects of reminders of death on athletic performance in basketball. *Journal of Sport and Exercise Psychology, 38*, 470–480.

Zhou, X., Liu, J., Chen, C., & Yu, Z. (2008). Do children transcend death? An examination of the terror management function of offspring. *Scandinavian Journal of Psychology, 49*, 413–418.

12
THE INTEGRATED CAUSAL UNCERTAINTY MODEL

Jae-Eun Namkoong, Marlone D. Henderson and Stephanie J. Tobin

Introduction

Causal uncertainty (CU) refers to the feeling of not knowing why something happens or happened (Weary & Edwards, 1996; Weary et al., 2010). The world is full of events that induce CU, ranging from mundane experiences (e.g., someone staring at you) to extraordinary events that fill our news feeds (e.g., mass shootings). Understanding causality appears to be a fundamental human need. From as early as three years old, people intuitively question why things happen, especially when events are unusual (Legare et al., 2010) or negative (Wong & Weiner, 1981).

The inability to resolve CU has been associated with a host of psychological issues, including anxiety, depression, rumination, and a perceived lack of control (Tobin et al., 2014; Tobin & Raymundo, 2010). This may explain why the desire to understand causality activates various cognitive processes, such as seeking out diagnostic information (Weary & Jacobson, 1997), carefully examining causal explanations (Tobin & Weary, 2008), and correcting for cognitive biases (Vaughn & Weary, 2003). These processes demonstrate how individuals effortfully and deliberately strive to accumulate greater knowledge in order to reduce CU (for a review, see Weary et al., 2010).

In recent research, significant progress has been made in understanding how CU can activate a more automatic cognitive process, specifically abstract thinking (see Namkoong & Henderson, 2019). Studies on abstract thinking and causal reasoning have revealed a strong link between more abstract (vs. concrete) thinking and a reduced sense of CU, even when individuals do not necessarily exert more cognitive effort or accumulate greater knowledge. While much is understood about the interplay between controlled cognitive processes and CU (Weary et al., 2010), the role of automatic processes in reducing CU remains less explored.

Moreover, there is limited understanding of how deliberate and automatic responses to CU interact, or which of the two is more likely to take precedence in reducing CU. Although past research has been informative, more work is needed to provide a comprehensive understanding of the antecedents and consequences of CU resolution efforts. This chapter aims to address these gaps by reviewing past research on CU and integrating it to develop a more complete model of the motivational-cognitive processes activated in response to CU.

DOI: 10.4324/9781003363385-14

Empirical Approaches in Causal Uncertainty Research

Here we present a summary of existing research on CU, organized by empirical approaches. The purpose is to offer more details and context before synthesizing the different bodies of work in this research area.

Causal Uncertainty as a Trait

Research on CU had initially focused on the construct as a dispositional variable. The notion that some individuals have a chronically stronger tendency to experience CU derived from studies showing patterns of information processing in those with depressive symptoms. Depressed individuals often experience a lack of control and feelings of uncertainty, leading to effortful and systematic processing of social information (Weary et al., 1993).

To facilitate further research on the topic, Weary and Edwards (1994) developed the Causal Uncertainty Scale (CUS) to capture individual differences in the chronic sense of not understanding why things happen. Since then, research has tested the scale's validity and explored its underlying factor structure (Edwards et al., 1998).

As researchers gained the ability to reliably capture CU as a chronic trait, the relationship between CU and other socio-psychological variables has been widely studied. For instance, the connection between CU and depressive symptoms has been further examined (Chang, 2000; Rounding et al., 2016; Weary & Edwards, 1994). The relationship between CU and effortful information processing has also received continued attention, showing that those with high (vs. low) CU were more likely to correct their biases in judgment tasks when warned about unwanted influences (Vaughn & Weary, 2003, Study 2) and were less likely to rely on stereotypes in social judgment (Tobin et al., 2009). In other notable studies, higher CU scores were associated with more self-handicapping (Thompson & Hepburn, 2003) and negative social interactions (Boucher & Jacobson, 2012).

CU as a trait has also been examined as a moderator. For instance, to better understand the accuracy motivation associated with causal understanding, several studies have documented how individuals with high (vs. low) chronic CU respond differently to potential sources of biases or cues to correct for biases (Tobin et al., 2009; Vaughn & Weary, 2003; Weary et al., 2006).

Longitudinal Studies of Causal Uncertainty

A number of longitudinal studies have utilized the CUS, as the temporal order in which changes in variables occur can shed light on causal directions. This design has also allowed researchers to test the role of chronic CU in different parts of the model, not only as an antecedent but also as the outcome variable or mediator.

Confirming the link between a perceived lack of control and CU, negative life events often associated with low control (e.g., illness) predicted higher CU levels two weeks later (McConnell et al., 2005) and one year later (Stahl & Jacobson, 2007). More directly, studies have shown that a perceived lack of control predicted higher CU six weeks later (Edwards & Weary, 1998; Jacobson et al., 1999). The findings also revealed a reciprocal relationship, suggesting that CU may further reinforce one's sense of low control. Another longitudinal study found that, among those with a lower sense of secondary control (e.g., sense of acceptance), higher CU regarding the self was associated with greater negative affect 4–12 weeks later (Tobin & Raymundo, 2010, Study 2).

Research indicates that CU may explain how certain relationship dynamics result in dysphoria. In a study spanning four to eight weeks, CU was confirmed as a mediator between reassurance-seeking and depressive symptoms (Jacobson, 2007). The finding highlights how excessive attempts to validate one's own value in relationships may elicit confusing reactions from close others and lead to dysphoria. A similar CU-inducing social dynamic was observed in the research by Rounding and Jacobson (2013), who examined how parents' depressive symptoms can be associated with CU among their children, predicting the onset of depressive symptoms in children.

Causal Uncertainty as an Accessible Construct

Due to the prevalence of the CU experience, the notion of the self as someone who does not understand causal relationships is a belief that can be temporarily activated. In doing so, uncertainty tied to the self will activate strong motivational processes (see Carroll et al., in this Handbook). The accessibility of CU as a construct has been directly tested by measuring response latency to words and phrases associated with CU, confirming that both chronic and situationally activated CU results in shorter reaction times (Edwards et al., 2009).

CU primes have been widely used to study the influence of situationally induced CU on various cognitive states and activities, such as stereotype usage (Weary et al., 2001), information processing (Jacobson et al., 2008), construal level (Helzer & Edwards, 2012; Namkoong & Henderson, 2016; Namkoong et al., 2019), and judgment confidence (Wichman et al., 2010). This section provides a summary of the different CU priming methods developed and employed in these studies. The findings of these studies, particularly those concerning the conceptual models of CU, will be explained later when discussing the self-regulatory processes activated by CU.

The CU priming methods can be categorized into several groups. The first set of priming methods utilizes items from the CUS. For instance, Weary et al. (2001, Study 3) and Jacobson et al. (2008; Study 3) asked participants to memorize statements from the CUS (prime) versus neutral statements (control). In a later study, Edwards et al. (2009, Study 2) used modified items from the CUS versus neutral statements and asked participants to indicate whether each statement was true or false.

Another type of CU prime relies on sentence unscrambling tasks adapted from Srull and Wyer (1979); see Wichman et al. (2008, Study 1), Wichman et al. (2010, Study 1), and Helzer and Edwards (2012, Studies 1–3). Participants in these studies received 20 scrambled sentences with five words each and were instructed to remove one word to construct a grammatically correct sentence. The control group was only given neutral sentences (e.g., "He took the container"), whereas the treatment group received a mix of sentences, half of which were CU-related (e.g., "Their behavior puzzles me"). Tobin et al. (2012) used a similar method to prime CU and causal importance. While this method does not involve the memorization or rating of the CUS items, it relies on the same underpinning mechanism of semantic CU activation.

A third type of CU manipulation directs participants to focus on their internal states. Wichman et al. (2008, Study 2) and Wichman (2010) asked participants in the CU prime condition to describe their thoughts, emotions, and physical states that arise when they feel uncertain about why something happened. The control group described these internal states in relation to watching TV. This method was an adaptation of the uncertainty induction method used by Van den Bos (2001), which itself was a modified version of a manipulation commonly employed in Terror Management Theory research (see Hayes et al., 2010).

A fourth group of CU induction methods instructs participants to elaborate on aspects of negative events for which they had either a good or poor causal understanding. Namkoong and

Henderson (2014, Study 1) had participants reflect on a recent product failure and write about aspects they still did not understand well regarding why it happened (high CU) or understood well regarding why it happened (low CU). The same instructions were applied to various negative events, such as relationship conflicts (Namkoong & Henderson, 2016) or salient events at the time (e.g., a recent train derailment; Namkoong et al., 2019, Study 2).

Finally, researchers have conducted CU studies around naturally occurring events. In Namkoong and Henderson (2014, Studies 2, 3A, and 3B), for instance, the Sandy Hook mass shooting (a recent event at the time) was used as a high CU event. Importantly, natural experiments have been conducted to compare the impact of high versus low CU events or to compare what happened before versus after a high CU event (Namkoong et al., 2019). While these approaches deviate from the CU priming methods used in previous studies, they provide unique opportunities to study the influence of spontaneously occurring CU in natural environments (also see Landau et al., in this Handbook).

Previous Models of Causal Uncertainty

CU research has been guided by a theoretical model introduced by Weary and Edwards (1996) and revised by Weary et al. (2010). Namkoong and Henderson (2019) presented an independent model based on their work on CU and automatic abstraction. We review these models before presenting the Integrated CU Model.

The Original and Revised Causal Uncertainty Model

The original CU model (Weary & Edwards, 1996) specified how various factors could activate beliefs that one does not fully understand the causes of social events and the accompanying feelings of confusion, leading to a motive to resolve the uncertainty. Factors contributing to CU include low perceived control, task instructions (e.g., to explain an outcome), priming, and causally relevant information. The motive structure involves a negative feedback loop: negative affect signals a discrepancy between one's current and desired level of understanding, leading to action plans aimed at reducing the discrepancy. Amplification of negative affect can occur with high levels of error sensitivity (e.g., when the cost of not understanding is high). Action plans were thought to involve searching for and using causally relevant information, with an assessment of their likely success determining whether people engage with them. Efforts continue until either goal attainment or disengagement occurs.

A large body of work supports the CU model. For example, longitudinal studies have identified a lack of perceived control as an important antecedent and consequence of chronic CU (Edwards & Weary, 1998; Jacobson et al., 1999). The close relationship between CU and a perceived lack of control may explain why CU is positively associated with depression, anxiety, and discomfort with ambiguity (Edwards & Weary, 1998; Jacobson et al., 1999; Weary & Edwards, 1994). CU and the associated need to improve one's sense of control can lead to increased cognitive efforts to achieve a more accurate causal understanding. For instance, in a high CU context, those with a greater need for cognitive closure exerted more effort into causal learning, which helped restore their sense of control (Sankaran et al., 2023). Studies have also found that higher CU is associated with less reliance on stereotypes (Weary et al., 2001), greater correction for strong situation constraints when forming attributions for events (Weary et al., 2006), greater adjustment for possible bias (Vaughn & Weary, 2003), and more diagnostic information seeking (Weary & Jacobson, 1997). These cognitive efforts are reactive in nature, motivated by the urgency to mitigate aversive negative affect generated by CU, rather than to satisfy intrinsic cognitive pleasures, such as curiosity or intellectual mastery (Edwards & Weary, 1998; Jacobson et al., 1999; Weary & Edwards, 1994). Indeed, studies have shown that chronic CU is negatively associated with one's need for cognition (Edwards et al., 1998; Weary & Edwards, 1994).

Weary et al. (2010) revised the CU model by expanding upon goal importance, referred to as causal importance, and action plans. They added causal importance to the model to capture the value that people place on causal understanding. Causal importance can vary across individuals and situations. It can increase attempts to reduce CU by (a) increasing the window of action to include both large and small discrepancies that might otherwise be dismissed as too difficult or inconsequential and (b) amplifying the negative affect generated by discrepancies between current and desired levels of understanding. In terms of action plans, Weary et al. noted that although much of the early research had focused on effortful information processing strategies, relatively automatic processes such as recategorization could also be used to reduce CU (Tobin et al., 2009).

Supporting the role of causal importance, studies have found that chronic causal importance moderates the effects of CU on judgments. Weary et al. (2001) found that high levels of either CU or causal importance reduced reliance on stereotypes when judging an ambiguous scenario. Tobin and Weary (2008) found greater persuasion by strong (vs. weak) counter-attitudinal causal arguments among those high in both CU and causal importance. Tobin et al. (2012) later replicated this finding with primed CU and causal importance. These studies highlight the relevance of causal importance as a moderator and suggest the amount of uncertainty in the stimulus materials may affect the nature of moderation.

The original and revised CU models raised the possibility of disengaging from attempts to reduce CU (Weary & Edwards, 1996; Weary et al., 2010). However, they noted that due to the importance of the goal and the fact that attainment often takes time and multiple attempts, expectancies for success would need to be very low for disengagement to occur. Weary and Edwards (1996) noted that options for disengaging could include withdrawing from the situation, focusing on a different goal, or attempting to reduce goal importance or error sensitivity. Disengaging could help to protect people from negative affect produced by CU. Indeed, Tobin and Weary (2008) found that at high levels of CU, lower levels of causal importance were associated with lower levels of depression. Further, Tobin and Raymundo (2010) found that higher levels of harmony control or flexible goal adjustment buffered causally uncertain individuals from increases in negative affect over time. Other research points toward potentially maladaptive responses to CU, such as disengaged coping in an academic context (Chang, 2000), self-handicapping (Thompson & Hepburn, 2003), and using alcohol to manage depression (Tobin et al., 2014).

Recent Work on Causal Uncertainty and Abstraction

Recent studies have examined the relationship between CU and abstract thinking (see Namkoong & Henderson, 2019). The premise of this body of work is that being in an abstract mindset likely makes causal inference-making easier, improving one's perceived causal understanding. This is because the process of investigating and comprehending cause-and-effect relationships necessitates some level of controlled or automatic abstraction, which may involve considering someone's behavioral intentions (e.g., personal goals), relying on generalizable traits, or activating stereotypes (Fiske, 1998; Winter & Uleman, 1984). It may also involve taking a step back and examining the bigger picture, such as extracting meaningful patterns observed across different behaviors or events (Kelley, 1973).

Namkoong and Henderson (2014) found that thinking more abstractly, whether through an unrelated mindset prime or considering the uncertainty-inducing event at a higher level, reduced participants' levels of CU. Furthermore, they showed that this reduction was due to a spontaneous simplification process. Abstraction involves a process of decontextualization, which means that an abstract representation of causal relationships will contain fewer details, nuances, and complexities. The resulting, simpler explanation provides a sense of clarity and reduces CU.

Given this finding, individuals are expected to develop a propensity for abstract thinking when faced with CU due to the repeated experience of benefiting from such thinking in resolving CU. In other words, the goal to understand causal relationships would activate a subgoal to think more abstractly. Namkoong and Henderson (2016) tested this idea using the task interruption and resumption protocol (Bargh et al., 2001; Förster et al., 2007; also see Namkoong & Henderson, 2017). They found that participants who were manipulated to experience high (vs. low) CU were more likely to resume an interrupted task if the task was expected to involve more abstract (vs. concrete) thinking. Another study showed that participants who were manipulated to experience high CU preferred an abstract stimulus after finishing a task that involved concrete thinking (goal unsatisfied), but no longer preferred an abstract stimulus after finishing a task that involved abstract thinking (goal satisfied).

Importantly, research shows that individuals are generally effective at automatically fulfilling the abstract thinking goal activated by CU. Helzer and Edwards (2012) found that priming CU, especially among those with low chronic CU, resulted in an overall more abstract mindset. This is consistent with the effortless and efficient nature of automatic goal pursuits (Bargh, 1994). Without an alternative cognitive goal or directive (see Namkoong & Henderson, 2016; Experiments 1A and 1B), motivated abstraction would efficiently fulfill its course.

An extension of this body of work involved natural and lab experiments centered around prominent socio-political events associated with high CU (Namkoong et al., 2019), revealing that abstract (vs. concrete) messages on social media generated more positive engagement when CU was high, especially when the message source was socially prominent. CU and the resulting motivated abstraction seem to not only influence individuals' thinking styles but also their interaction with the social world.

The Integrated Causal Uncertainty Model

The Integrated CU Model (see Figure 12.1) retains key elements and processes depicted in the two existing models. The Integrated CU Model builds upon the negative feedback loop of the previous models, while integrating the two distinct response systems activated by CU, demonstrating how these systems coexist and interact. We now turn to these discussions.

Antecedents of Causal Uncertainty

CU is a subjective experience, likely influenced by various factors. CU may increase due to forces that dampen one's perceived causal understanding, increase one's desired understanding, or both. The factors that will likely contribute to the level of perceived and/or desired causal understanding are listed in the Integrated CU Model. This allows us to elaborate on the model and offer guidance for future research.

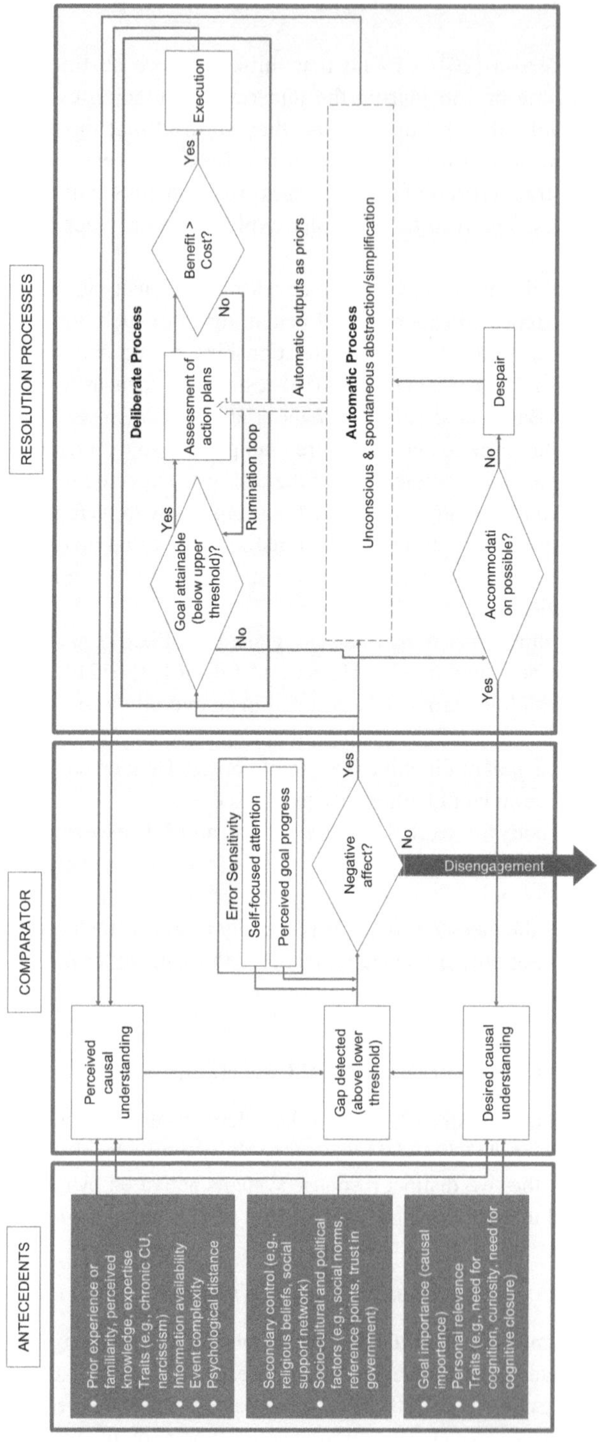

Figure 12.1 The integrated causal uncertainty model.

Determinants of Perceived Causal Understanding

Perceived causal understanding is likely influenced not only by actual expertise but also by familiarity and perceived knowledge. Personality traits such as chronic CU or narcissism would impact one's confidence in their causal understanding. Additionally, characteristics of the CU-inducing event may alter individuals' sense of understanding. The lack of available information surrounding the event or information overload would both negatively impact perceived understanding. Events that are complex and multifaceted, or those that are too psychologically close, can also reduce one's sense of causal understanding, while simpler and more abstract representations enhance perceived understanding (see Namkoong & Henderson, 2014). Similarly, broad-stroked inferences made in the absence of contradicting information can increase perceived causal understanding (Edwards, 1998).

Determinants of Desired Causal Understanding

Stronger goal importance (i.e., causal importance), predicts a higher level of desired causal understanding. Causal importance may vary individually but can be heightened if there is greater personal relevance, such as when the causal understanding is tied to one's identity or future risks (see Carroll et al. and Rios & Morales, in this Handbook). Temporal or physical proximity (e.g., an accident that happened recently or in one's own community) would likely increase personal relevance, and hence, causal importance and desired causal understanding. Causal importance may explain why desired causal understanding is higher for unexpected negative events than it is for unexpected positive events (Wong & Weiner, 1981), as the former is more likely to threaten one's sense of control. Those with higher curiosity or need for cognition may be predisposed to desire greater causal understanding.

Determinants of Perceived and Desired Causal Understanding.

To cope with CU, some individuals may draw upon secondary sources of control, such as their social network or belief in a higher power. This reliance can enhance their perceived causal understanding by accessing shared community knowledge or attributing events to a higher power. It may also reduce their desire for causal understanding by restoring a sense of control in CU-inducing situations. Socio-political factors can set reference points and establish norms for causal understanding. A society that promotes open access to information and transparent public discourse would likely lead its members to both develop a higher perceived causal understanding and hold a higher standard for desired causal understanding.

Comparator

The Integrated CU Model illustrates that the negative feedback loop continues until an individual's perceived causal understanding matches their desired level, ultimately ceasing the generation of negative affect and resolving CU (Weary & Edwards, 1996; Weary et al., 2010). Negative affect is generated when the discrepancy between one's perceived and desired causal understanding is sufficiently large (i.e., above the lower threshold for detecting CU). This disrupts psychological equilibrium and serves as a cue that a problem needs resolving, thereby activating a self-regulatory process in which conscious and/or unconscious resolution attempts are made until negative affect is sufficiently reduced. Individuals may need repeated attempts to resolve CU. The presence of negative affect when repeating the feedback loop would indicate that the discrepancy is still significant, necessitating continued efforts to close the gap. Conversely, a lack of negative affect would signal successful achievement of the CU resolution goal, leading to goal disengagement.

We noted earlier the concept of error sensitivity, which incorporates factors that amplify the intensity of negative affect. Self-focused attention may increase error sensitivity, especially when involving ruminative self-focus (Mor & Winquist, 2002). Ruminative tendencies are likely to direct more attention to the unsatisfied CU resolution goal, resulting in greater negative affect. Distraction from self-awareness (e.g., through intoxication) may have the opposite effect by decreasing sensitivity to the discrepancy in causal understanding (see Tobin et al., 2014).

We added goal progress as an error sensitivity factor in the integrated model. Negative affect should be a function of both one's current standing in goal pursuit and whether the goal pursuit is on the right path, i.e., getting closer to (vs. farther away from) the goal at an optimal rate (Carver & Scheier, 2001). Negative affect may lessen during goal pursuit if speedy progress is registered, signaling that current attempts are effective and should be continued. In contrast, negative affect may intensify if progress is slowing down or regressing, cueing the need for changes in self-regulatory strategies.

It is worth noting the depiction of causal importance in the integrated model. As described earlier, causal importance was considered a factor that influences both desired causal understanding and error sensitivity in the previous version of the model (Weary et al., 2010). The underlying idea is that a stronger value placed on causal understanding will make the gap between perceived and desired causal understanding less tolerable, generating stronger negative affect. The current model describes the role of causal importance in a way that is more concise while retaining the meaning of its role as an amplifier. Specifically, we describe causal importance only as an antecedent that directly impacts desired causal understanding. As causal importance raises the level of desired causal understanding, the gap between perceived and desired causal understanding widens, leading to a stronger negative affect generated by the gap.

Resolution Processes

As reviewed earlier, previous literature has explored two distinct CU resolution processes. The earlier CU model primarily focused on systematic and deliberate attempts to reduce CU, whereas the latter work examined the simplifying cognitive process (i.e., abstraction) spontaneously activated in response to CU. The current model's main contribution lies in describing the relationship between these two systems. This understanding is critical for gaining insights into how people respond to CU because the process of reducing CU is unlikely to be entirely effortful or automatic. Rather, it is likely to be a combination of both modes, depending on one's motivation, ability, and opportunity at a given moment. The CU resolution goal itself may be conscious (e.g., deliberately activated to reduce uncertainty about a particular cause-effect relationship) or unconscious (e.g., primed). Even when the goal to reduce CU is conscious, the resolution process would likely involve a combination of effortful and automatic processes. Drawing on Bargh's analogy (1994), an individual may have a deliberate motive to drive a car to a destination, but the actual process of driving would include numerous automatic behaviors, guided by subconsciously activated subgoals, such as driving safely or swiftly.

The Integrated CU Model thus presents a dynamic CU resolution process where both automatic and deliberate modes may be simultaneously active, and one mode may serve as a fallback when the other is deemed unproductive or unfeasible. We elaborate on these points below.

Primary/Automatic vs. Secondary/Deliberate Responses

We posit that the automatic mode of reducing CU begins and continues to operate in the background once a CU resolution goal is active. The automatic mode of resolving CU is instantaneous, unconscious, and effortless (commonly known as "System 1" processing; Kahneman, 2003). This automatic process has been described as one of the "unintended consequences" activated by the CU resolution goal (p. 157; Weary & Edwards, 1996). For instance, the goal to reduce CU in social judgment (e.g., to understand someone's behavioral motive) may begin with an instantaneous broad-stroked categorization process, such as trait-based attributions or the use of stereotypes (Fiske, 1998; Winter & Uleman, 1984). Attribution bias and stereotyping are forms of oversimplification, and thus abstraction because they discount individuating contextual information.

Simpler or more abstract explanations contribute to one's sense of understanding (FeldmanHall & Shenhav, 2019; Namkoong & Henderson, 2014). Thus, if the gap between perceived and desired causal understanding is relatively small, to begin with, the initial automatic abstraction process may suffice in satisfying the CU resolution goal. For instance, while the world is full of events that activate CU, many of them could be of low relevance and thus be accompanied by a relatively low level of desired causal understanding. Perhaps these events are occurrences involving distant others (e.g., the sudden death of a stranger in a different state) or experiences directly encountered but without significant ramifications (e.g., receiving rude service at a restaurant one seldom visits). When the level of desired understanding is low, the automatic simplification process may be sufficient for resolving CU. This aligns with findings indicating that people tend to quickly form judgments when evaluating others and decline opportunities for further learning (Klein & O'Brien, 2018; also see Sanchez, Dunning, & Moritz, in this Handbook).

Due to the antecedents of perceived causal understanding mentioned earlier, some individuals may already be close to reaching their desired level of understanding. Those with low chronic CU, for instance, may be able to quickly resolve CU through automatic abstraction. This may explain why individuals with low (vs. high) chronic CU are more likely to judge others based on traits and stereotypes (Tobin et al., 2009; Weary et al., 2001; Weary et al., 2006). Similarly, narcissistic individuals are overly confident (Campbell et al., 2004) and thus may reach CU resolution through automatic abstraction without engaging in effortful processing. Indeed, research shows that hubristic pride, a component of narcissism, leads to a more abstract mindset by activating a positive trait-based self-attribution process (Yang & Zhang, 2018).

However, if the automatic process alone is insufficient in resolving CU, a controlled secondary response will be pursued, involving a more systematic approach. Here, individuals will deliberately consider whether, and which, cognitive efforts should be made to improve causal understanding. The initial consideration is to assess the attainability of CU resolution through conscious efforts. Deliberate attempts to reduce CU are pursued only if sufficient CU reduction seems achievable, that is, if the size of the gap between one's perceived and desired causal understanding falls below the upper threshold, beyond which CU resolution is deemed unattainable through conscious efforts.

Given that CU resolution seems attainable, available action plans will be evaluated, and those with the highest expectancy of success will be selected. These action plans prioritize accuracy, favoring rational and effortful thinking over intuitive responses (Edwards, 2003; Weary et al., 2010). For instance, individuals with higher CU are more likely to seek diagnostic information when trying to understand outgroup members (Weary & Jacobson, 1997). They are also more sensitive to argument strength (Weary et al., 2006) and cues that signal potential influence of biases (Vaughn & Weary, 2003).

Expanding on the previous model (Weary et al., 2010), we have incorporated a cost-benefit analysis into the consideration of action plans. The choice of any action plan will involve considering not just the benefits of the plan's outcome (i.e., better causal understanding) but also the potential costs associated with the plan. For instance, to understand the sudden death of a neighbor, approaching the neighbor's immediate family may provide the clearest answer, yet this action plan has the potential to inflict pain on others. For an individual struggling with depression, therapy may be the most effective at understanding the source of the depression, but this action plan may seem expensive, time-consuming, or, depending on the culture, potentially damaging to one's self-esteem. The benefits must outweigh the costs for an action plan to be chosen and implemented. Of course, a very strong CU resolution goal will make the potential cost of any action plan seem comparatively small and thus justified.

Further, the Integrated CU Model deviates from the earlier CU model by temporally separating when the lower and upper thresholds are applied. Previously, the thresholds were considered together: the goal to resolve CU would become active if the discrepancy between perceived and desired causal understanding is large enough to generate a negative affect (above the lower threshold), but small enough that the goal seems attainable (below the upper threshold). While this version accurately describes the activation of a conscious CU resolution process, it does not account for the automatic abstraction process initiated by a sufficiently high CU, irrespective of the perceived attainability of resolving CU.

For this reason, the current model introduces the thresholds in stages. The lower threshold acts as an affect generator, triggering the CU resolution goal and automatic abstraction when surpassed. Subsequently, the upper threshold, because it is the point up to which a goal is seen as attainable through deliberate efforts, determines whether conscious attempts will be made to resolve CU. This separation is a crucial aspect of the integrated model, as it allows for a motivational process that continues even when the goal may not seem consciously attainable. We now discuss the said self-regulatory response activated by perceived goal unattainability.

Response to Perceived Goal Unattainability

What happens when the CU resolution goal is active but deemed unattainable through deliberate efforts? In the earlier CU model, it was suggested that perceived goal unattainability will result in goal disengagement, albeit only when the discrepancy is extremely large. However, based on new research, we put forth the idea that the motivational process does not come to a halt; instead, it shifts to a different mode. We propose there are two simultaneous processes that sustain the motivational process.

First, even if conscious attempts to reduce CU are abandoned, the automatic process of abstraction and simplification is likely to persist due to the effortless nature of unconscious goal pursuits (Bargh, 1994). We propose this continued unconscious motivational process because of the fundamental importance of the need for causal understanding (Weary et al., 2010). Consider the experience of hunger. If food is unavailable, we might be able to distract ourselves from hunger and stop consciously thinking about food, but our brain's automatic functions that could help satisfy the fundamental need (e.g., heightened sensitivity to food smells) will continue to operate in the background. Similarly, disengagement from an active CU resolution goal may only happen at the conscious level while individuals continue to make sense of the world through unconscious processes. Although this automatic and effortless process may not provide explicit answers through systematic information seeking and processing, it can facilitate generalization and simplification, ultimately improving one's subjective sense of causal understanding

(Namkoong & Henderson, 2014). We further elaborate on this point in the section "Falling Back to Automatic Mode."

Second, if a CU resolution goal seems unattainable, individuals may consider accommodation, i.e., whether CU can be resolved by lowering the level of desired causal understanding. This may involve utilizing the aforementioned factors that influence desired causal understanding, such as relying on secondary sources of control (Tobin & Raymundo, 2010). For instance, spiritual individuals may find a sense of control by surrendering to a higher power and accepting a lack of precise understanding as a way of life. A lack of causal understanding may also be acceptable among those who have a strong social network to support them in troubling times. If accommodation proves difficult (e.g., due to a lack of strong spiritual belief or social network), individuals would rely on the automatic CU resolution mode.

The underlying assumption for these ideas is that one cannot truly disengage from an active CU resolution goal—that the only way to conclude the motivational process is through goal resolution, indicated by a lack of associated negative affect. If the goal is deemed unattainable, then the negative feedback loop will persist and repeat outside of conscious awareness until enough changes occur that the goal becomes seemingly attainable. For example, perceived causal understanding might increase due to the automatic abstraction/simplification process described earlier or because new information becomes available over time. Desired causal understanding may be adjusted downward through accommodation or simply diminish over time as personal relevance decreases. Once the CU resolution goal seems attainable, a deliberate assessment of action plans will be attempted to engage in systematic causal reasoning.

Interaction between Automatic and Deliberate Processes

The Integrated CU Model describes how the automatic and deliberate modes of CU resolution intertwine. The integrated model incorporates a deliberate correction of automatic causal inferences, as discovered in previous research. Importantly, it explores the conditions that lead individuals to forego conscious processing for automatic CU resolution and accounts for the role of automatic abstract inferences as priors in the conscious CU resolution process.

DELIBERATE CORRECTION OF AUTO-GENERATED CAUSAL OUTPUTS

The automatic versus deliberate modes of CU resolution are often at odds with each other. The former mode, automatic abstraction, relies on cognitive shortcuts, making quick judgements based on intuitions and automatic associations, while the latter mode involves systematic and effortful analyses and perhaps even piecemeal processing. Indeed, research has shown that more abstract processing facilitates a more simultaneous rather than piecemeal consideration of information (Henderson & Trope, 2009; also see Henderson et al., 2006). Thus, conscious efforts to improve causal understanding often involve correcting abstract, overgeneralized judgments formed automatically. For instance, individuals with high CU are more likely to correct their dispositional inferences based on new situational information (Weary et al., 2006). Similarly, high CU motivates individuals to see beyond initial stereotypes and consider stereotype-inconsistent information (Tobin et al., 2009; Weary et al., 2001). This is not to say that conscious CU resolution efforts rely solely on concrete, piecemeal processing. Certain forms of abstraction, such as identifying similarities or overarching themes across events, are often used as deliberate strategies in causal reasoning (Kelley, 1973). In other words, inferential outputs from automatic abstraction, rather than intentional abstraction, are likely the target of deliberate corrections.

FALLING BACK TO AUTOMATIC MODE

The deliberate mode of CU resolution is rooted in accuracy motives and requires effortful and systematic thinking. However, when individuals encounter limitations in their ability or opportunity to engage in this demanding process, they are likely to switch to the effortless and automatic mode of CU resolution. For instance, mental bandwidth may be consumed by stress, distractions, or time pressure, leaving little cognitive capacity for systematic causal reasoning, allowing automatic inferences to take over. Indeed, spontaneous dispositional attributions are more readily made under cognitive load (Gilbert, Krull et al., 1988; Gilbert, Pelham et al., 1988).

Moreover, repeated failures to identify an effective action plan can lower one's confidence in achieving the goal, leading to a shift towards the automatic CU resolution mode until perceived attainability is restored. Additionally, those with high chronic CU may discard the outputs of their systematic processing—that is, the lack of self-confidence in their ability to understand cause-effect relations may lead them to discount the diagnosticity of the information they produced through conscious efforts and revert to causal inferences that had been automatically generated (Edwards, 1998).

PRIORS SET BY AUTOMATIC MODE

Due to the efficient and effortless nature of the automatic abstraction process, it becomes activated from the beginning when CU is experienced and continues to operate beneath conscious attempts to resolve CU. Similar to other dual processing models (Chaiken & Trope, 1999; Fiske & Neuberg, 1990), the conscious and unconscious CU resolution processes coexist and interact with each other. As mentioned earlier, automatic causal inferences can be corrected through more conscious and effortful approaches (Tobin et al., 2009; Weary et al., 2001; Weary et al., 2006). However, we have not yet discussed how conscious causal reasoning may be influenced by unconscious automatic processes.

Automatically generated causal inferences would serve as "priors" in the Bayesian sense of understanding causal relationships, shaping how subsequent information is sought out and processed (FeldmanHall & Shenhav, 2019). Furthermore, the automatic abstraction process may render some action plans more readily available than others. This raises the question: how much are the controlled responses to CU influenced by the unconscious processes that preceded them? The answer likely depends on various personal, situational, and motivational factors, including the relative strength of the priors (i.e., outputs from automatic abstraction) in relation to (1) access to diagnostic information, (2) the quality of readily available action plans, and (3) behavioral commitments made based on the initial automatic abstraction process. We elaborate on this next.

First, the more access one has to diagnostic information about the CU-inducing situation, the less the impact of automatic abstraction. Social, physical, or temporal distance is likely to influence such access. For instance, individuals are more likely to have access to diagnostic information when understanding the motive of a close other, as they can obtain clarifications directly from the person or through a shared social network, facilitating more accurate causal reasoning. In contrast, understanding a distant other lacks this benefit, leading initial abstract judgments to have an outsized impact during conscious causal reasoning. Similarly, it would be easier to gather diagnostic information about an event that occurred recently or in a proximal location, as opposed to a long time ago or in a distant location.

Second, being equipped with potentially effective action plans to enhance causal understanding can help reduce the influence of automatic abstraction outputs. Systematic causal reasoning is a skill that can improve with practice. Thus, individuals with previous experience in successful causal reasoning or familiarity with common inferential biases would possess strong action plans to resolve CU. Even if the initially available set of action plans is shaped by automatic abstraction, such individuals may be able to widen their set of plans or consciously look for specific biases such as overgeneralization. In contrast, for those lacking experience (e.g., being too young or unfamiliar with the topic) or ability (e.g., having poor systematic reasoning skills or intelligence), the automatically generated priors will have a strong influence on how the subsequent conscious inference-making unfolds.

Third, automatic priors may exert a significant influence when individuals have made behavioral commitments based on those priors. In the aftermath of intense negative events (e.g., the 9/11 attack or the death of a child), CU may persist for an extended period. Although various systematic ways to reduce CU will likely be considered, the magnitude of the event may render many of these insufficient, leading to ruminative thinking. In the background, the automatic abstraction process would continue to operate and influence behavior, nudging individuals to gravitate toward certain individuals, ideologies, or social groups that offer generalizable and simplified explanations. This could result in engagement with leaders who communicate at a higher level of abstraction (Namkoong et al., 2019), adopting religious beliefs or conspiracy theories that provide all-encompassing explanations for events (Rounding et al., 2016; Wichman, 2010; also see Markman et al., in this Handbook), or affiliating with groups that hold simplistic and perhaps even extreme political ideologies (Hogg, 2014). Over time, some of these behavioral commitments may become firmly established and hard to reverse, leading cognitive dissonance and confirmation bias to constrain conscious reasoning. In such cases, systematic and effortful attempts for accurate causal understanding would be made, but within a limit set by a-priori stereotypes, ideologies, or other generalizing frameworks.

Concluding Remark

The reality is that many events that induce CU are complex and multifaceted. Take, for instance, the goal to comprehend the underlying causes behind the high occurrence of mass shootings in the United States. This problem likely arises from a combination of factors, including the abundance of guns, weak gun regulations, lax policy enforcement, ideological polarization influencing legislation, breakdown of social communities, and mental health challenges. Furthermore, these factors likely influence each other or form hierarchical causal chains. As such, the process of causal inference often involves multiple lower-order causal reasonings. Some of these reasonings will undergo deliberate and systematic processing. But for the ones that overwhelm our cognitive or emotional capacity for systematic processing, relying primarily on automatic abstraction and simplification is likely. The combined output of both conscious and unconscious CU resolution efforts will feed back into our current perceived causal understanding.

Through the synthesis of the two existing streams of research on CU, we aspire for the Integrated CU Model to offer a more comprehensive depiction of the CU resolution process and ignite further research in this area. The novel components of the model especially warrant further attention. The ruminative state of CU, i.e., being trapped in a set of seemingly ineffective action plans, and the consequences of being in such a state should be examined. We need a better understanding of how cultural factors influence both the levels of perceived and desired causal understanding, as well as their impact on the cost-benefit analysis of action plans considered for CU resolution. Furthermore, the paths by which unchecked automatic abstraction leads to extreme tendencies, and how such tendencies shape conscious causal reasoning, should be empirically examined. We also urge future research to explore the practical implications of the Integrated CU model in socio-political domains and in business. This includes identifying better ways to communicate with constituents or consumers in times of high CU, such as during global conflicts or economic recessions.

References

Bargh, J. A. (1994). The four horsemen of automaticity: Intention, awareness, efficiency, and control in social cognition. In R. S. Wyer, Jr. & T. K. Srull (Eds.), *The handbook of social cognition* (2nd ed., Vol. 1, pp. 1–40). Lawrence Erlbaum Associates.

Bargh, J. A., Gollwitzer, P. M., Lee-Chai, A., Barndollar, K., & Trötschel, R. (2001). The automated will: Nonconscious activation and pursuit of behavioral goals. *Journal of Personality and Social Psychology*, *81*(6), 1014–1027. https://doi.org/10.1037/0022-3514.81.6.1014

Boucher, E. M., & Jacobson, J. A. (2012). Causal uncertainty during initial interactions. *European Journal of Social Psychology*, *42*(5), 652–663. https://doi.org/10.1002/ejsp.1876

Campbell, W. K., Goodie, A. S., & Foster, J. D. (2004). Narcissism, confidence, and risk attitude. *Journal of Behavioral Decision Making*, *17*(4), 297–311. https://doi.org/10.1002/bdm.475

Carver, C. S., & Scheier, M. F. (2001). *On the self-regulation of behavior*. Cambridge University Press.

Chaiken, S., & Trope, Y. (1999). *Dual-process theories in social psychology*. Guilford Press.

Chang, E. C. (2000). Causal uncertainty and depressive symptoms: Appraisals and coping as mediating variables. *Journal of Social and Clinical Psychology, 19*(3), 420–436. https://doi.org/10.1521/jscp.2000.19.3.420

Edwards, J. A. (1998). Effects of causal uncertainty on the dispositional attribution process. *Journal of Experimental Social Psychology*, *34*(2), 109–135. https://doi.org/10.1006/jesp.1997.1345

Edwards, J. A. (2003). The interactive effects of processing preference and motivation on information processing: Causal uncertainty and the MBTI in a persuasion context. *Journal of Research in Personality*, *37*(2), 89–99. https://doi.org/10.1016/s0092-6566(02)00537-8

Edwards, J. A., & Weary, G. (1998). Antecedents of causal uncertainty and perceived control: A prospective study. *European Journal of Personality*, *12*(2), 135–148. https://doi.org/10.1002/(SICI)1099-0984(199803/04)12:2<135::AID-PER301>3.0.CO;2-Y

Edwards, J. A., Weary, G., & Reich, D. A. (1998). Causal uncertainty: Factor structure and relation to the big five personality factors. *Personality and Social Psychology Bulletin*, *24*(5), 451–462. https://doi.org/10.1177/0146167298245001

Edwards, J. A., Wichman, A. L., & Weary, G. (2009). Causal uncertainty as a chronically accessible construct. *European Journal of Social Psychology*, *39*(5), 694–706. https://doi.org/10.1002/ejsp.567

FeldmanHall, O., & Shenhav, A. (2019). Resolving uncertainty in a social world. *Nature: Human Behaviour*, *3*(5), 426–435. https://doi.org/10.1038/s41562-019-0590-x

Fiske, S. T. (1998). Stereotyping, prejudice, and discrimination. In *The handbook of social psychology* (pp. 357–411). McGraw-Hill.

Fiske, S. T., & Neuberg, S. L. (1990). A continuum of impression formation, from category-based to individuating processes: Influences of information and motivation on attention and interpretation. In M. P. Zanna (Ed.), *Advances in experimental social psychology* (Vol. 23, pp. 1–74). Elsevier.

Förster, J., Liberman, N., & Friedman, R. S. (2007). Seven principles of goal activation: A systematic approach to distinguishing goal priming from priming of non-goal constructs. *Personality and Social Psychology Review*, *11*(3), 211–233. https://doi.org/10.1177/1088868307303029

Gilbert, D. T., Krull, D. S., & Pelham, B. W. (1988). Of thoughts unspoken: Social inference and the self-regulation of behavior. *Journal of Personality and Social Psychology*, *55*(5), 685–694. https://doi.org/10.1037/0022-3514.55.5.685

Gilbert, D. T., Pelham, B. W., & Krull, D. S. (1988). On cognitive busyness: When person perceivers meet persons perceived. *Journal of Personality and Social Psychology*, *54*(5), 733–740. https://doi.org/10.1037/0022-3514.54.5.733

Hayes, J., Schimel, J., Arndt, J., & Faucher, E. H. (2010). A theoretical and empirical review of the death-thought accessibility concept in terror management research. *Psychological Bulletin*, *136*(5), 699–739. https://doi.org/10.1037/a0020524

Helzer, E. G., & Edwards, J. A. (2012). Causal uncertainty prompts abstract construal of behavior. *Social Cognition*, *30*(5), 519–536. https://doi.org/10.1521/soco.2012.30.5.519

Henderson, M. D., Trope, Y., & Carnevale, P. J. (2006). Negotiation from a near and distant time perspective. *Journal of Personality and Social Psychology*, *91*(4), 712–729. https://doi.org/10.1037/0022-3514.91.4.712

Henderson, M. D., & Trope, Y. (2009). The effects of abstraction on integrative agreements: When seeing the forest helps avoid getting tangled in the trees. *Social Cognition*, *27*(3), 402–417. https://doi.org/10.1521/soco.2009.27.3.402

Hogg, M. A. (2014). From uncertainty to extremism: Social categorization and identity processes. *Current Directions in Psychological Science*, *23*(5), 338–342. https://doi.org/10.1177/0963721414540168

Jacobson, J. A. (2007). The relationship among causal uncertainty, reassurance seeking, and dysphoria. *Journal of Social and Clinical Psychology*, *26*(8), 922–939. https://doi.org/10.1521/jscp.2007.26.8.922

Jacobson, J. A., Weary, G., & Edwards, J. A. (1999). Certainty-related beliefs and depressive symptomatology: Concurrent and longitudinal relationships. *Social Cognition*, *17*(1), 19–45. https://doi.org/10.1521/soco.1999.17.1.19

Jacobson, J. A., Weary, G., & Lin, Y. S. (2008). Causal uncertainty and metacognitive inferences about goal attainment. *Cognition & Emotion*, *22*(7), 1276–1305. https://doi.org/10.1080/02699930701739849

Kahneman, D. (2003). Maps of bounded rationality: Psychology for behavioral economics. *American Economic Review*, *93*(5), 1449–1475. https://doi.org/10.1257/000282803322655392

Kelley, H. H. (1973). The processes of causal attribution. *American Psychologist*, *28*(2), 107–128. https://doi.org/10.1037/h0034225

Klein, N., & O'Brien, E. (2018). People use less information than they think to make up their minds. *Proceedings of the National Academy of Sciences*, *115*(52), 13222–13227. https://doi.org/10.1073/pnas.1805327115

Legare, C. H., Gelman, S. A., & Wellman, H. M. (2010). Inconsistency with prior knowledge triggers children's causal explanatory reasoning. *Child Development*, *81*(3), 929–944. https://doi.org/10.1111/j.1467-8624.2010.01443.x

McConnell, A. R., Renaud, J. M., Dean, K. K., Green, S. P., Lamoreaux, M. J., Hall, C. E., & Rydell, R. J. (2005). Whose self is it anyway? Self-aspect control moderates the relation between self-complexity and well-being. *Journal of Experimental Social Psychology*, *41*(1), 1–18. https://doi.org/10.1016/j.jesp.2004.02.004

Mor, N., & Winquist, J. (2002). Self-focused attention and negative affect: a meta-analysis. *Psychological Bulletin*, *128*(4), 638–662. https://doi.org/10.1037/0033-2909.128.4.638

Namkoong, J.-E., & Henderson, M. D. (2014). It's simple and I know it! Abstract construals reduce causal uncertainty. *Social Psychological and Personality Science*, *5*(3), 352–359. https://doi.org/10.1177/1948550613499240

Namkoong, J.-E., & Henderson, M. D. (2016). Wanting a bird's eye to understand why: Motivated abstraction and causal uncertainty. *Journal of Experimental Social Psychology*, *64*, 57–71. https://doi.org/10.1016/j.jesp.2016.01.014

Namkoong, J.-E., & Henderson, M. D. (2017). Task interruption and resumption paradigm for testing the activation and pursuit of an abstract thinking goal. *Journal of Visualized Experiments*, *122*, e55650. https://doi.org/10.3791/55650

Namkoong, J.-E., & Henderson, M. D. (2019). Responding to causal uncertainty through abstract thinking. *Current Directions in Psychological Science*, *28*(6), 547–551. https://doi.org/10.1177/0963721419859346

Namkoong, J.-E., Ro, J. H., & Henderson, M. D. (2019). Responding to causal uncertainty in the Twitterverse: When abstract language and social prominence increase message engagement. *Journal of Interactive Marketing*, *45*, 81–98. https://doi.org/10.1016/j.intmar.2018.11.002

Rounding, K., & Jacobson, J. A. (2013). The role of causal uncertainty in the relationship between perceived parental dysphoria and offspring's own dysphoria. *Cognitive Therapy and Research*, *37*(5), 1058–1069. https://doi.org/10.1007/s10608-013-9539-y

Rounding, K., Jacobson, J. A., & Hart, K. E. (2016). Religiosity as a moderator of causal uncertainty's mediational role in the parental–offspring dysphoria relationship. *Psychology of Religion and Spirituality*, *8*(1), 1–12. https://doi.org/10.1037/a0039690

Sankaran, S., Kossowska, M., & Von Hecker, U. (2023). When do they push the right buttons? Need for closure and the role of perceived control in situations of uncertainty. *Personality and Individual Differences*, *213*, 112316.

Srull, T. K., & Wyer, R. S. (1979). The role of category accessibility in the interpretation of information about persons: Some determinants and implications. *Journal of Personality and Social Psychology*, *37*(10), 1660–1672. https://doi.org/10.1037/0022-3514.37.10.1660

Stahl, J., & Jacobson, J. (2007). Effects of negative and positive life events on levels of causal uncertainty. Poster accepted for presentation at the annual meeting of the Society for Personality and Social Psychology, Memphis, TN,

Thompson, T., & Hepburn, J. (2003). Causal uncertainty, claimed and behavioural self-handicapping. *British Journal of Educational Psychology*, *73*(2), 247–266. https://doi.org/10.1348/00070990360626967

Tobin, S. J., Capuozzo, K. I., & Raymundo, M. M. (2012). The effects of primed causal uncertainty and causal importance on persuasion. *Social Influence*, *7*(4), 269–284. https://doi.org/10.1080/15534510.2012.66772

Tobin, S. J., Loxton, N. J., & Neighbors, C. (2014). Coping with causal uncertainty through alcohol use. *Addictive Behaviors*, *39*(3), 580–585. https://doi.org/10.1016/j.addbeh.2013.11.009

Tobin, S. J., & Raymundo, M. M. (2010). Causal uncertainty and psychological well-being: The moderating role of accommodation (secondary control). *Personality and Social Psychology Bulletin*, *36*(3), 371–383. https://doi.org/10.1177/0146167209359701

Tobin, S. J., & Weary, G. (2008). The effects of causal uncertainty, causal importance, and initial attitude on attention to causal persuasive arguments. *Social Cognition*, *26*(1), 44–65. https://doi.org/10.1521/soco.2008.26.1.44

Tobin, S. J., Weary, G., Brunner, R. P., Gonzalez, J., & Han, H. A. (2009). Causal uncertainty and stereotype avoidance: The role of perceived category fit. *Social Cognition*, *27*(6), 917–928. https://doi.org/10.1521/soco.2009.27.6.917

Van den Bos, K. (2001). Uncertainty management: The influence of uncertainty salience on reactions to perceived procedural fairness. *Journal of Personality and Social Psychology*, *80*(6), 931–941. https://doi.org/10.1037/0022-3514.80.6.931

Vaughn, L. A., & Weary, G. (2003). Causal uncertainty and correction of judgments. *Journal of Experimental Social Psychology*, *39*(5), 516–524. https://doi.org/10.1016/S0022-1031(03)00028-3

Weary, G., & Edwards, J. A. (1994). Individual differences in causal uncertainty. *Journal of Personality and Social Psychology*, *67*(2), 308–318. https://doi.org/10.1037/0022-3514.67.2.308

Weary, G., & Edwards, J. A. (1996). Causal-uncertainty beliefs and related goal structures. In M. Sorrentino & E. T. Higgins (Eds.), *The handbook of motivation and cognition* (Vol. 3, pp. 148–181). Guilford Press.

Weary, G., & Jacobson, J. A. (1997). Causal uncertainty beliefs and diagnostic information seeking. *Journal of Personality and Social Psychology*, *73*(4), 839–848. https://doi.org/10.1037/0022-3514.73.4.839

Weary, G., Jacobson, J. A., Edwards, J. A., & Tobin, S. J. (2001). Chronic and temporarily activated causal uncertainty beliefs and stereotype usage. *Journal of Personality and Social Psychology*, *81*(2), 206–219. https://doi.org/10.1037//0022-3514.81.2.206

Weary, G., Marsh, K. L., Gleicher, F., & Edwards, J. A. (1993). Depression, control motivation, and the processing of information about others. In G. Weary, F. Gleicher, & K. L. Marsh (Eds.), *Control motivation and social cognition* (pp. 255–287). Springer. https://doi.org/10.1007/978-1-4613-8309-3_10

Weary, G., Tobin, S. J., & Edwards, J. A. (2010). The causal uncertainty model revisited. In R. M. Arkin, K. C. Oleson, & P. J. Carroll (Eds.), *Handbook of the uncertain self* (pp. 78–100). Psychology Press.

Weary, G., Vaughn, L. A., Stewart, B. D., & Edwards, J. A. (2006). Adjusting for the correspondence bias: Effects of causal uncertainty, cognitive busyness, and causal strength of situational information. *Journal of Experimental Social Psychology*, *42*(1), 87–94. https://doi.org/10.1016/j.jesp.2005.01.003

Wichman, A. L. (2010). Uncertainty and religious reactivity: Uncertainty compensation, repair, and inoculation. *European Journal of Social Psychology*, *40*(1), 35–42. https://doi.org/10.1002/ejsp.712

Wichman, A. L., Briñol, P., Petty, R. E., Rucker, D. D., Tormala, Z. L., & Weary, G. (2010). Doubting one's doubt: A formula for confidence? *Journal of Experimental Social Psychology*, *46*(2), 350–355. https://doi.org/10.1016/j.jesp.2009.10.012

Wichman, A. L., Brunner, R. P., & Weary, G. (2008). Immediate and delayed effects of causal uncertainty inductions on uncertainty accessibility. *Journal of Experimental Social Psychology*, *44*(4), 1106–1113. https://doi.org/10.1016/j.jesp.2007.12.002

Winter, L., & Uleman, J. S. (1984). When are social judgments made? Evidence for the spontaneousness of trait inferences. *Journal of Personality and Social Psychology*, *47*(2), 237–252. https://doi.org/10.1037/0022-3514.47.2.237

Wong, P. T., & Weiner, B. (1981). When people ask "why" questions, and the heuristics of attributional search. *Journal of Personality and Social Psychology*, *40*(4), 650–663. https://doi.org/10.1037/0022-3514.40.4.650

Yang, P., & Zhang, Q. (2018). How pride influences product evaluation through construal level. *European Journal of Marketing*, *52*(7/8), 1750–1775. https://doi.org/10.1108/EJM-12-2016-0777

13

TOWARD LOVE OR HATE AND MEANING EITHER WAY

From Anxious Uncertainty to Proactive or Reactive Approach Motivation

Ian McGregor and Denise Marigold

Early Ideas about Uncertainty as a Cause of Fascist Hostility

In the early 20th century Freud, Pavlov, and Lewin noticed their patients, dogs, and toddlers reacting with weird extremes to uncertainty-related predicaments. The psychodynamic perspective of the day framed the extremes as defensive reactions to intrapsychic conflicts. For example, Pavlov conditioned dogs to associate electric shocks at specific leg-locations with a gravy reward. The shocks were then migrated to increasingly distant locations, and once they got far enough away to arouse uncertainty about reward expectations a "most violent reaction occurred...the animals became restless and excited in an extreme degree, which they had never been before." Frenzies of barking and biting ensued that Pavlov labeled with the psychodynamic terms "neurosis" and "hysteria," but interpreted more simply as serving to supplant motivational conflict with a singular focus: "clashing of excitation with inhibition led to … pathological disturbances...and finally gave way to an undisputed predominance of one of them" (Pavlov, 1927, Lecture 17).[1] This chapter traces the evolution of related ideas through experimental social psychology and the humanities to arrive at a contemporary understanding of how uncertainty can animate love or hate.

The use of psychodynamic terms by a Nobel Prize winner like Pavlov attests to their currency at the time. Indeed, a few years later when shapes of WWII were forming on the horizon, Einstein wrote an open letter to Freud asking, "Why War?" (Einstein, 1932). Meanwhile, the Frankfurt School was integrating psychodynamic ideas with sociological and existential ones, converging on the conclusion that bewildered uncertainties about how to live are "the worst of all pains" (Fromm, 1941, p. 35; cf. Carroll et al., this volume) that can cause fascist extremes, leaps of faith, sadistic compulsions, and rigid identity claims (Barnes, 1973; Oaklander, 1996).

Frankfurt School affiliates fled Nazi Germany in the early 1930s and disseminated the idea that uncertainty was a potent cause of personal and social convulsions. For instance, Fromm interpreted rigid submission to authority as an "escape from freedom" way to shirk uncertainty about life choices.

> Man, lacking instinctive determination and having a brain that permits him to think of many directions in which he could go, needs an object of total devotion … to be the focal point of all his strivings … The need for devotion itself is a primary existentlal need.
>
> (Fromm, 1973, pp. 260–261)

 DOI: 10.4324/9781003363385-15

Citing Fromm, Adorno similarly saw authoritarian hostility as arising from uncertainty about what to value. Authoritarianism is rewarding because it eliminates choices about how to live. Adorno et al. (1950, p. 975) accordingly concluded that the solution to fascism was "an increase in people's capacity to see themselves and to be themselves."

Before and after WWII similar ideas were shaping clinical, developmental, and experimental psychology, led by other European scholars who had been forced to flee the very phenomena around which their theories revolved (e.g., Adler, Erickson, Lewin). Academic psychology embraced the neoanalytic idea that while some people try to repress psychological conflicts and uncertainties with reactive ideology and hostile extremes, others prevail over them with authentic commitment to self-transcendent values. For example, mature and non-defensive character development requires commitment to social interest according to Adler, and generative identity according to Erikson. Related ideas and evidence supporting the psychological power of authentic values to supplant defenses re-appeared in the 1980s as self-affirmation theory (Steele, 1988).

On the early experimental side, Lewin (an occasional affiliate of the Frankfurt School) began his graduate training immersed in Gestalt ideas related to cognitive conflict and harmony. His "field theory" depicted conflicts among goals and environmental factors as incompatible force-fields in "life space" that acted on each other like same-charged poles of magnets to cause uncomfortable "tension" and violent deflections (Lewin, 1939). His demonstrations and experiments in the 1930s showed children becoming aggressive and dysregulated when faced with conflicts or uncertainties about how to act (Lewin, 1933; Lewin, 1935; Lewin et al., 1939). The psychodynamically inspired frustration-aggression hypothesis forwarded a similar idea that aggression and scapegoating are defensively oblique ways to release the pressure build-up from drives blocked by conflict or uncertainty (Dollard et al., 1939; all authors had psychoanalytic backgrounds). Several decades and hundreds of frustration-aggression experiments later, the psychodynamic emphasis on visceral motivation for aggression after frustration gave way to cooler cognitive models of how negative affect can sometimes lead to aggressive decisions and habits, for some people, in some circumstances (Anderson & Bushman, 2002; see also Berkowitz, 1989).

While frustration-aggression ideas were cooling, the academic lineage from Lewin's Research Center for Group Dynamics (RCGD) at MIT stayed with a hot conception of conflict-induced motivation for aggression. Lewin's RCGD's mandate in 1945 was to understand the psychological factors that had motivated people to perpetrate and cooperate with the atrocities of WWII (Patnoe, 1988). The RCGD's most seminal product was Festinger's theory of cognitive dissonance, and its demonstrations that confronting people with "non fitting cognitions" (1957, p. 3) caused defensive extremes and exaggerated consensus about opinions. Festinger and colleagues famously used this model to interpret the tenacious extremes cult-members used to cope with uncertainty about their beliefs (Festinger et al., 1956). Like Pavlov, both Lewin and Festinger viewed defensive extremes as serving to restore motivational singularity because "only the really extreme exclusion of the majority of all the simultaneously present psychical tensions ... and the practically exclusive connection of the motor sphere with one special region of inner tensions make an ordered action possible" (Lewin, 1935, p. 56). MIT's RCGD seeded the field of experimental social psychology with generations of researchers raised on this core idea that psychological conflicts and the uncertainties they imply can cause irrationally extreme, defensive reactions. By the 1980s, however, it was becoming apparent that diverse psychological threats beyond goal conflict, and uncertainty could cause the same kinds of extreme reactions.

Emergence of Competing Ideas

Various theories emerged, with hundreds of experiments supporting each, to explain rigid and hostile tendencies in terms of a critical psychological currency that various threats (i.e., aversive thoughts or experiences) could presumably undermine and that non-consciously mediated defenses could presumably restore (reviewed in Jonas et al., 2014). Dissonance researchers assumed that cognitive consistency (i.e., freedom from conflict and uncertainty) was the critical currency people were defending. Self-affirmation and related theories came next with their demonstrations that focus on values or worth could relieve the need for cognitive consistency. As self-affirmation theory evolved it then came to see the maintenance of a positive self-image, not freedom from conflict/uncertainty, as the critical currency people are motivated to defend. Terror management theory (TMT) focuses on anxiety about death and the culturally embedded ways people defend against it. From the TMT perspective, a positive and cognitively consistent self-image justified by consensual cultural values confers a worldview-defense buffer against death anxiety. People cling to their worldviews with hostile tenacity because they make people feel symbolically immortal. Confident worldviews are self-transcendent life-vests inflated with cognitive-consistency and worth. Threats to cognitive consistency and worth puncture the vest, and make people cling all the more tightly in fear of the abyss below (cf. Landau et al., this volume).

Ego depletion theory proposed an even more general motivational account of threats that make people lose self-control and go to lazy, self-serving, and aggressive extremes (Baumeister & Vohs, 2016). Initial exercises of self-control cause lapses in subsequent self-control because they sap a limited resource of ego-energy. This depleted state leaves people vulnerable to impulsive and extreme indulgence in whatever habits or temptations are salient e.g., in "overeating, overspending, prejudice, aggression, and passivity" (Baumeister & Vohs, 2018). Ego-depletion researchers found that mortality salience can cause such depletion effects (Gailliot et al., 2006) and that self-affirmations can eliminate them (Schmeichel & Vohs, 2009), and concluded (p. 772) "it may be that efforts to cope with threats to the self deplete the resource for self-control." A key consideration for our interpretation of ego-depletion effects is that the depleting manipulations always confront participants with motivational conflicts that imply uncertainty about whether or not to continue—typically instructing participants to do something that goes against the grain of what they want to do (as in Lewin's early studies with children, and cognitive dissonance experiments). Cognitive dissonance manipulations that induce people to act in ways that conflict with their beliefs can similarly cause irrational extreme and hostile reactions (Randles et al., 2015).

Theoretical Integration

To integrate these and other competing ideas about why people go to defensive extremes after diverse threats, and why values relieve defenses, McGregor (2006) and Jonas et al. (2014) focused on basic motivational processes, beneath the presenting phenomena, that evolved to respond to uncertainty-arousing experiences. They started with the postulate that vertebrate goals are regulated by two motivational subsystems that interact with each other and the environment (Carver & White, 1994). The first, the BAS (behavioral approach system) is a 'lock in' system that mediates eager engagement and focus on goals one is committed to (Corr, 2004; Gray & McNaughton, 2000). When BAS is highly activated, attention zeroes in on stimuli relevant to the focal goal and becomes relatively impervious to distractions and peripheral worries or conflicts (Harmon-Jones & Gable, 2009; Harmon-Jones et al., 2009). State activation of the BAS confers energy, vitality, and flow (Van der Linden, 2021). The second, the BIS (behavioral inhibition system) is a 'look out!' system that readies organisms for disengagement from goals rendered uncertain by novelty, impedance, or conflict (Gray & McNaughton, 2000; cf. Hirsh et al., 2012; Proulx et al., 2012). With BIS activation, attention becomes biased toward aversive information, arousal is heightened, and commitments become fragil—state activation of the BIS feels bored, agitated, and distracted and culminates in anxiety if not resolved (Gray & McNaughton, 2000; Mercer-Lynn et al., 2014; cf. Inzlicht et al., 2015;). Such unstable states are conducive to goal disengagement and to noticing and impulsively seizing on alternative goals or commitments that might be better bets for the restoration of focused and more sanguine BAS states.

State activity of each subsystem emits a generalized pattern of affect and attention that either fortifies or destabilizes focal goal pursuit. The arousal of each subsystem also mutes the activity of the other (Corr, 2004). The resulting BIS-BAS disengagement-re-engagement toggling is a primitive goal regulation loop for vertebrates immersed in concrete goals. We lock in with BAS until uncertainty cues the BIS to "look out!" thereby temporarily stalling BAS long enough to notice and switch to more viable goals to restore BAS (and mute BIS). Adaptive cycles of this loop allow the BIS and BAS to automatically manage goal regulation for rats and humans alike, without the need for conscious oversight.

The human capacity for abstraction and existential uncertainty adds intrigue, however. BIS-activating uncertainty can loom over and destabilize any concrete goal subjected to the many abstracts "why" questions/answers that our promiscuous imaginations can conjure. Capacity for chronic uncertainty about 'why?' accordingly makes humans uniquely vulnerable to BIS-activated demotivation and instability even when concrete goals are going well (cf. Exline et al., this volume; Schwartz & Cheek, this volume). Without some way to manage this vulnerability, chronic BIS activation can cascade into paralyzing anxiety (recall that the BIS is the system that mediates anxious distress, goal hesitation, loss of interest, and disengagement; Gray & McNaughton, 2000).

The key idea in this chapter is that eager engagement with abstract values can fortify BAS activation and thereby mute the BIS (cf. Namkoong et al., this volume) for a solution to this vexing human conundrum. The "higher power" capacity of values to activate BAS with little behavioral investment or risk makes them alluring to lock in on as antidotes to the drag of personal uncertainty endemic to the human condition (McGregor, Tran et al., 2022). Indeed, mere contemplation and identification with abstract values can be enough to activate BAS and mute BIS to sustain a sanguine sense of meaning in life (see "Values → BAS → Meaning" section below). The highest values are usually prosocial and self-transcendent, but they can also be self-enhancing, jingoistic, and hateful (Sagiv et al., 2017; Schumann et al., 2014; Sibley & Duckitt, 2008). Indeed, self-righteous and aggressive values may be especially alluring because power and anger are potent BAS-activators even on their own (reviewed in Jonas et al., 2014; e.g., see the section below on collective hate). Reactively cleaving to values animated by either love or hate can accordingly be rewarding in BIS-activating circumstances. Either way, the resulting reactive approach motivation (RAM) they spur can mute BIS-linked distress and negatively reinforce the reaction.

According to Jonas et al. (2014) the motivational crux of diverse threats people experience in their everyday lives is BIS-activation. Conflicts, failures, frustrations, reminders of death, insults, depleting experiences, rejection/exclusion, dilemmas, unfairness, weird experiences, and loss of control, all confront people with varieties of goal impedance and uncertainty that arouse BIS-activation. The eliciting threat can fade from awareness, but the generalized BIS activation can linger leaving people in a motivationally volatile state—less absorbed, more distressed, and more vigilant for problems and inclined to leap impulsively toward any alternative goal or idea that can reactivate BAS to mute BIS. The palliative allure of BAS for BIS relief is why people lock into their values and worldviews with extreme conviction under diverse conditions of uncertainty

(Jonas et al., 2014). Uncertainty-related threats spur the urge to surge more eagerly toward whatever BAS-activating affordances are salient or habitual. The surge can be toward mundane and concrete rewards like chocolate or phone-scrolling, but values and worldviews are especially potent as BAS-activating levers for BIS-relief. They can be wielded effortlessly and reliably by mere identification, without the need for immediate action or risk of friction in the outside world because they are abstract goals—self-guides that can be approached conceptually, at the pinnacle of human goal systems (cf. Carver & Scheier, 2001; Sagiv & Schwartz, 2022; Van Hook & Higgins, 1988).[3]

What is the evidence for this higher power of abstraction to mute anxious distress? Dozens of experiments guided by self-affirmation theory (reviewed in McGregor et al., 2012) reveal that focusing on personally important values mutes anxious arousal as indicated by cortisol evidence, decreased rumination, decreased subjective salience of unrelated worries, and decreased tendency toward extreme and hostile reactions after threats. Value-focus makes people more reasonable, poised, resilient, and magnanimous (Cohen & Sherman, 2014). As illustrated in Figures 13.1 and 13.2 (adapted from McGregor, Tran et al., 2022) we accordingly propose that BAS activation via proactive value-focus (which is usually prosocial; Schwartz & Bardi, 2001) supplants the need to engage reactive approach motivation (RAM) via antisocial defenses for BIS-relief. Figure 13.1 depicts the use of RAM via extremes for relief from the discomfort of uncertainty-instigated BIS-activation. Figure 13.2 illustrates how proactive focus on self-transcendent values can supplant the need to use of RAM to activate BAS for BIS-relief. This is why proactively engaging with loving values can supplant reactively hateful ones. They pre-emptively serve the same motivational function (BIS-relief).

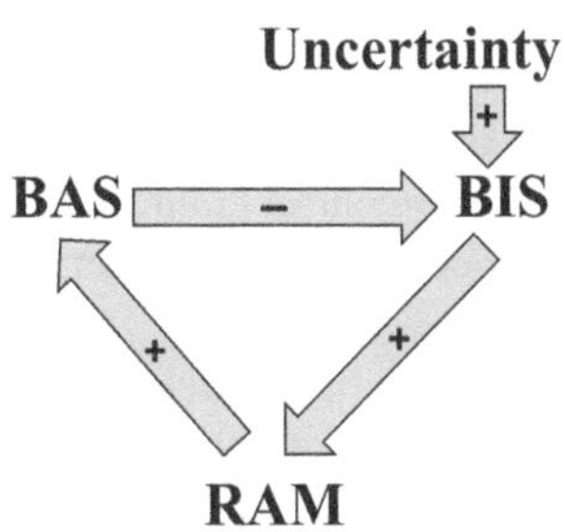

Figure 13.1 RAM for BAS relief from BIS.

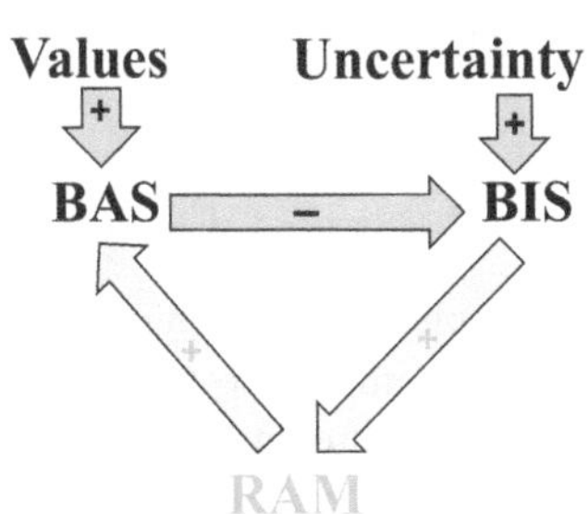

Figure 13.2 Proactive values supplant RAM.

Some New, Higher-N, and Pre-Registered Evidence for a BIS-BAS Integration

The motivational explanation and model in the previous section has potential to integrate 70+ years of social psychological theory and research on how people react to threats, and on how loving and hateful values and worldviews can quell those threats and make lives feel meaningful. However, the thousands of between-subject laboratory experiments that this integration is based on, and that had been considered best practice when conducted, have recently been critiqued as having fatal flaws related to sample size (too small) and experimenter degrees of freedom (too many) (e.g., Simmons et al., 2011). The next section reviews empirical work from the past few years with larger samples and fewer experimenter degrees of freedom that has begun to corroborate and extend the evidence base that the Figure 13.1 model and the Jonas et al. (2014) integration came from.

Mortality Salience and Personal Uncertainty → BIS → Loss of Self Control

Evidence for the role of BIS-activation in the threat-defense research integrated by Jonas et al. (2014) came from mostly low-N experiments showing that the various threats (e.g., mortality salience, cognitive dissonance, low control, social exclusion, dilemmas) that cause reactive defenses also initially heighten self-reports and neural indices of uncertainty and BIS-activation. Two new, preregistered studies (N = 819) now corroborate this older work with the finding that experimentally manipulated mortality salience causes self-reported affect linked to uncertainty and BIS activation (Britton, 2023). Moreover, that affect predicted feelings of boredom (also closely linked with BIS activation; Mercer-Lynn et al., 2016) which mediated effects on reduced self-control for personal projects and for a behavioral task (data entry) at the end of the study, even among participants who had reported intentions to work on the task diligently. These findings are consistent with the idea that mortality salience, one of the most prominently researched threats in experimental social psychology, effects subsequent self-control failure via BIS-activation (See also Hayes et al., 2016 for evidence that mortality salience manipulations can make people give up on goals and life as a way to relieve BIS activation).

In another pre-registered experiment with a different threat (N = 337; Alquist et al., 2018) participants randomly assigned to write about personal uncertainties in their lives performed more poorly on a subsequent anagram task that required self-control and persistence than participants who had written about their highest values. Importantly, as in the previously described mortality salience study, self-reported BIS-affect mediated the self-control deficit. We propose that this kind of uncertainty/BIS-induced low self-control on subsequent tasks is similar to typical findings in ego depletion experiments (that confront participants with motivational conflicts). BIS activation dulls commitment and makes people less determined to do the right thing and more attracted to impulsive extremes.

Ego-Depletion → BIS → Loss of Self-Control

Since the 1990s, hundreds of ego-depletion experiments have demonstrated that initial tasks requiring self-control can make people impulsive and less persistent on subsequent tasks in unrelated domains. A recent replication attempt supports a BIS-activation interpretation of such ego-depletion effects. In a large, pre-registered, multi-site project (Vohs et al., 2021) 3531 participants were randomly assigned to standard ego-depletion conditions in which participants completed initial tasks in non-intuitive ways that repeatedly conflicted with their natural tendencies. Control condition participants instead followed their natural tendencies (no conflict). The pre-registered main-effect results were equivocal but exploratory analyses revealed a large effect of the depletion manipulations on feelings of fatigue that we see as closely linked to BIS activation (Hockey, 2013; because one of the main outputs of BIS activation is the muting of enthusiasm and energy for all ongoing goals, Gray & McNaughton, 2000). Most relevant to this chapter, there was also a significant condition x fatigue interaction effect. The depletion/conflict manipulations caused fatigue and it was specifically this conflict-induced fatigue that moderated poor performance in the depletion/conflict conditions. Additional exploratory analyses indicated that fatigue also mediated poor performance in the depletion condition. The depleted participants retained their (self-reported) intention to perform well but just lost the motivational tenacity to actually do so.[2]

Reactive Approach Motivation (RAM): BIS → Risk-Taking/Worldview Defense/ Hate → BAS

In our view, loss of self-control in the aforementioned new experiments could have resulted either directly from the bored fatigue of BIS activation or from impulsive, BAS-activating RAM reactions. Evidence for RAM involvement in the impulsive loss of self-control after BIS-activating threats comes from a new, pre-registered experiment (n = 432) on how uncertainty affects impulsive risk-taking. A BIS-activating academic-uncertainty manipulation, unrelated to the rest of the study materials, caused participants to over-pump and burst balloons, thereby losing money (money was earned by fully pumping but not bursting the balloons; Leota et al., 2023). This balloon task has face-validity as one that prioritizes the approach of what one wants (pumping to win money) over caution about bursting and losing. The academic uncertainty manipulation was the same one used in the original RAM research (McGregor et al., 2010). Importantly the reactive riskiness occurred only among participants with high scores on a BAS-related trait. Presumably, people high on BAS traits have easier access to BAS-states to use for muting BIS.

Trait BAS similarly moderated results in three other studies (N =1163) more directly linked to hate. Uncertainty-related threats that have caused BIS-linked affect in past research caused reactive religious zeal, intergroup hostility, and authoritarian belligerence only among participants with high BAS traits (McGregor, Britton et al., 2022). Similarly, across three other studies (N = 1078) uncertainty and mortality salience manipulations most extremely heightened ethnocentric disdain for outgroup members among high-BAS participants (Klackl et al., 2024). Consistent with Figure 13.2 these findings indirectly implicate involvement of BAS activation in rigid and hostile reactions to threats.

More direct evidence for the BAS-activating function of defenses after threats comes from three studies (Stollberg et al., 2024; N = 683) showing that threats (mortality salience, loss of control, and relationship conflict) aroused BIS-linked affect. Importantly, participants in the threat (but not in the neutral control) conditions reported significantly more BAS-affect after being presented with an opportunity to focus on BAS-linked phenomena (personal goals and desires) than after more neutral phenomena (morning routine). When BIS had been activated by threat, they threw themselves more eagerly into BAS activating phenomena. Finally, two pre-registered experiments (Elnakouri et al., 2022; N = 762) focusing on collective, outgroup-related hate significantly elevated BAS-linked affect (determined, eager, enthusiastic). Together, these findings support the idea that after threats, people use defensive and hateful worldview convictions to shift motivational orientation from BIS to BAS.

Values → BAS → Meaning

In the Elnakouri et al. (2022) hate condition almost all participants spontaneously wrote about value-and-morality related reasons for hating outgroup members. This kind of collective, value-linked hate may be especially potent because anger, groups, and values can all independently activate BAS (Carver & Harmon-Jones, 2009; Fritsche, 2022; McGregor et al., 2022). Importantly, in both studies, the collective hate effect on BAS-activation mediated an increase in self-reported feelings of meaning in life. Past theory and research have linked engagement with values to meaning in life (e.g., McGregor & Little, 1998; Sagiv & Schwartz, 2022) but these new findings indicate that even hateful values can fortify feelings of meaning in life. For the first time, they also reveal the motivational basis for how they do so, while also helping make sense of why intentional focus on values can be so remarkably effective at relieving anxious distress and defensiveness. As illustrated in Figure 13.2, value-focus heightens state-BAS, which mutes BIS-linked feelings of boredom and uncertainty. The motivational shift toward BAS and away from BIS feels vigorous, hopeful, and meaningful (McGregor et al., 2012).

Elnakouri et al. (2022) showed that people can find dark inspiration and meaning in value-ideological hate if focused on that. Importantly, however, when explicitly asked to nominate their highest values, religious identifications, or meanings in life, most people in every culture intentionally focus on loving-value themes related to generativity, helping, and connecting with other people (e.g., Schumann et al., 2014; Schwartz & Bardi, 2001; King & Napa, 1998). In research guided by self-affirmation theory, focus on such loving values (vs. on self-enhancing values) has been especially good at supplanting anxiety and defensiveness (Burson et al., 2012; Crocker et al., 2008; Shnabel et al., 2013), and recent evidence indicates BAS activation is the mechanism here as well. Focus on prosocial values increases blood flow to dopaminergically specialized parts of the brain that mediate approach-motivated states (reviewed in McGregor, Tran et al., 2022). Moreover, this effect of prosocial value on approach-motivation-related blood-flow is highest among participants who report the highest commitment to living meaningful lives (Kang et al., 2018). In sum, new evidence supports the Jonas et al. (2014) claim that values bolster meaning and mute defenses by proactively arousing BAS-states (as depicted in Figure 13.2).

Converging evidence that loving values can supplant hate-related defenses via BAS-activation, as per Figure 13.2, comes from two studies (N = 677) showing that proactive focus on self-transcendent values (related to love, compassion, and spirituality) activates BAS (measured with EEG and self-report; McGregor, Tran et al., 2022), which in turn mediates a decrease in hostile worldview defenses. In both studies, the BAS activated by self-transcendence mediated less punitive and less dismissive reactions toward others who offended participants' moral and religious beliefs. Importantly, in both studies, this effect of self-transcendence on approach motivation and magnanimity occurred only among meaning-seeking participants. This moderation by meaning-seeking indicates it is not the mere priming of love-related topics (linked to the values) that boosts magnanimity. Meaningful identification with the self-transcendent foci is the consequential thing. Self-transcendent value commitments confer a kind of meaningful higher power—the BAS activation they arouse is personally energizing and conducive to self-control, freedom from malice, and meaning in life.

To further probe the BIS-BAS motivational bases of meaning a series of pre-registered studies found that writing about high-value-related experiences elevated BAS and muted BIS, and that these changes jointly mediated feelings of meaning in life and meaning in experiences (McGregor et al., 2024). Importantly, in the same series of experiments, another experimentally manipulated condition focused participants on what they most intensely desired. The intense-desire condition similarly elevated feelings of meaning in life, jointly mediated by the same BAS/BIS motivational shifts that occurred after values-focus. This indicates that at least in the short term, passionate desire can operate on the same motivational platform as abstract values, with similar effects on meaning in life. Feelings of meaning in life are thus not necessarily diagnostic of noble intentions. They can also arise, at least temporarily, from hate, passionate desire, or presumably anything that can arouse BAS vitality and mute BIS malaise.

The shared (approach) motivational substrate of loving, hateful, and other kinds of passionate aspirations that can mediate feelings of meaning in life fits with recent scholarship calling for the need to demote meaning from its virtuous pedestal (Heintzelman & King, 2014; King & Hicks, 2021). It also helps explain why so many of the world's wisdom stories feature choices protagonists face between loving, hateful, and self-enhancing priorities. Identification with love, power, desire, or hate may lead to different outcomes in the long run, but the motivational tone and feelings of meaning they can support in the short term are similar (cf. Womick et al., 2019). This may be why hypocritical and morally dubious choices and convictions can be so seductive and easy to rationalize. Their motivational bases can feel right even when they are morally wrong.

Connecting with Big-Picture Perspectives on Human Nature

Redemption Stories in Myth and Religion

Themes around the redemptive power of self-transcendent values as an antidote to anxious distress and evil are ubiquitous across the world's wisdom traditions. For example, in humanity's first wisdom story on record (Mitchell, 2004), King Gilgamesh has a "restless heart" (BIS activation) beneath his hostile and exploitive habits (BAS-activating RAM). When his best friend dies (mortality salience) he becomes especially anxious. At first, he doubles down on desperate heroics in a quest for relief (RAM). Doing so leaves him exhausted and bewildered over time, however. Finally, after a grueling overnight race against death through a dark tunnel, it is the experience of a host's graceful compassion that moves Gilgamesh to adopt self-transcendent values as the solution to his angst. His moral conversion to a new identity focused on being a benevolent king finally brings serenity and effectiveness. As in Figure 13.2, proactive commitment to self-transcendence supplanted his BIS activation and RAM. We can now understand the basic motivational dynamics that make such primordial conversion stories so intuitive.

A similar redemptive theme characterized popular religious practices in ancient Greece. They all began with ritual re-enactments of a mythical protagonist's anguish, torture or abduction, and death and/or descent into darkness (metaphors for uncertainty) due to conflicts arising from hate or jealous desire. After simmering in vicarious and actual despair for a few days in a dark cave or crypt, augmented by exposure to an array of bewildering and terrifying trials, participants' anxious distress was finally relieved via contact with deities personifying compassionate virtue (e.g., Isis, Demeter). At this point, in solidarity with the protagonist's compassion-mediated resurrection or rebirth, participants' despair flipped to collective joy. These rituals experientially purveyed salvation from BIS-activating distress via self-transcendent virtue. Variations of this theme repeated across Osirian, Dionysian, and Eleusinian mystery cult rituals (Bowden, 2010). Pythagoras and Plato, founders of idealistic Greek philosophy, participated in these rituals and spoke highly of them. The 1st-century BCE statesman and philosopher, Cicero, claimed that these initiation rituals conferred power to live happily (Bowden, 2010). Plato's famous cave allegory tells the same story—of redemption from chains of ignorance in a shadowy cave by turning toward the light of virtuous ideals.

In Buddhism, the Four Noble truths preach relief from the anxious dukkha (frustration-related suffering) of aimlessness and angry wandering and ignorance via the enlightened Eightfold Path of disciplined commitment to moral virtue (Bodhi, 2010). Metaphorical and psychological interpretations of Christianity similarly view redemption and salvation stories as symbolizing a psychological shift from the ultimately dull preoccupation with personal pleasure/advantage/status/evil to rebirth in a new identity focused on self-transcendent generosity that confers persistent and surprisingly buoyant joy (Borg, 2009). Across stories in these and other myths and religious traditions, BIS-activating uncertainty is poetically depicted as akin to friction, darkness, blindness, ignorance, wilderness, being lost, shackled, exiled, flooded, or pulled into the murky underworld. Such metaphors depict people as uncertain about what to do in bewildering and frustrating circumstances. Wisdom stories discourage angry and self-enhancing reactions, which are often framed as being what caused the story predicaments in the first place. The stories advise paths to salvation via self-transcendent value commitments, instead. As such, they serve to bolster faith that commitment to self-transcendent values can confer power and resilience even in the face of human uncertainty. They point out that whereas self-enhancing values glimmer in the sun but go cold in the dark, self-transcendent values can shine either way because they do not require worldly success.

The BAS-BIS dynamics illustrated in Figure 13.2 may help explain why self-transcendent story themes are so enduring across cultures and millennia, and why they are so regularly used to scaffold the redemptive "stories we live by" (McAdams, 1993, 2013). There really is a mysterious power—BAS-activation—that can be accessed via commitment to the approach of adaptive, self-transcendent values but that can also be aroused, at least temporarily, by more selfish or antisocial extremes that ultimately degrade lives and groups (Elnakouri et al., 2022; McGregor, Tran et al., 2022; Cho & Keltner, 2020; Pearce & Huta, 2023). The joy and energy that can come from commitment to selfless abstractions is so surprising and paradoxical that it feels like an infusion of other-worldly inspiration.

Evolution of Abstraction, Uncertainty, Values, and Culture

The neo-cortex accounts for most of humans' bigger brains (than other primates; Kaas, 2013). Evolution of neocortical capacity for abstract thought liberated capacity to simulate and deliberate about alternatives for action and thriving in diverse habitats. We became less constrained by instinct as the lost capacity to smell was replaced by the found capacity to think (Gilad et al., 2003). Capacity for creative exploitation of environmental affordances, guided by abstract priorities, allowed groups of humans to migrate, cooperate, and thrive across diverse niches (Ash & Gallup, 2007; Bailey & Geary, 2009).

Abstract priorities and values lack objective arbiters for truth, however, and so groups rely on consensus with others for answers to abstract questions such as, "what is worth doing?" and "what is good?" We negotiate and validate consensus about values in relationships and communities of shared reality (Durkheim, 1897/1951; Festinger, 1954; Hardin & Higgins, 1996; Sagiv et al., 2017; cf. Hohman & Kuljian, this volume; cf. Murray, this volume; cf. Schmader & Guo, this volume). To be readily endorsable by others, however, values must hold some collective value. Values related to "I love you" or "I love us" can usually garner buy-in from others better than those that revolve around "I love me." Across all cultures and eras notions of virtue accordingly revolve around norms and values that focus on care for and contribution to others, even if those others are a relatively small circle of ingroup members (Graham et al., 2009; Sagiv et al., 2017; Twenge & King, 2005; Waytz et al., 2019). Across 63 countries from all continents, people rate self-transcendent values as most important and self-enhancing values as least important as guiding priorities in their lives (Schwartz & Bardi, 2001). Self-transcendent values also correlate positively, and self-enhancement values correlate negatively, with self-reported meaning in life (Bojanowska & Piotrowski, 2021). Without allegiance to self-transcendent values, humans are accordingly more likely to find themselves in the relatively uncertain predicament of having to navigate the welter of possibilities they can imagine without a clear guidance system.

Self-transcendent value-priorities (vs. self-enhancing ones) are endorsed especially strongly by religious people as compared to non-religious (Saroglou et al., 2004). Beyond how groups help people have confidence and commit to values by providing consensual validation, values also help people commit to groups. Indeed, the propagation of cooperative and generous values (even if only parochial) has been proposed as a reason for the cultural evolution and persistence of religions (Norenzayan et al., 2014). Groups use self-transcendent "sacred values" as binding agents to draw and keep members connected and cooperating without conflict (Durkheim, 1912/2008; Elnakouri et al., 2023; Graham & Haidt, 2010). We propose that the unique human vulnerability to BIS-activating uncertainty (from the capacity to think abstractly), together with our capacity to lock in on BAS-activating values to mute BIS, created conditions that rewarded self-transcendent convictions. Such convictions are palliative, but also adaptive because they fostered group cohesion, communal cooperation, and the invigorating experience of collectively fortified meaning in life (what Durkheim referred to as "collective effervescence;" Rimé & Páez, 2023).

Existential and Psychodynamic Ideas

Approaching self-transcendent moral virtue may have benefits for reliable BAS activation and group functioning, but desires for temporal pleasure, success, power, or fun can sometimes make for easier and more immediate rewards, and can also activate the BAS and support feelings of meaning in life, at least when going well (Heintzelman & King, 2014; King & Hicks, 2021). For much of recorded human history, however, identification with such "lower" motivations was discouraged as selfish ignorance or evil by wisdom traditions that encouraged self-transcendent virtue, instead, by decree. Virtuous, God-given, inner-essence was seen as preceding human existence and defining its being, and humans accordingly self-actualized (Aristotle's term) and approached virtue by striving to live in accordance with this inner essence. As the renaissance and enlightenment shifted attention to the here-and-now empirical world of science and aesthetic experiences, however, religious moral hegemony receded and the (BAS-activating) power of worldly incentives regained legitimacy. Fruits of the industrial revolution and romanticism popularized creaturely pleasures, and Darwin's ideas positioned sexual success, not virtuous values, as the most potent essence of human nature. Power and pleasure regained status as legitimate preoccupations. An uncertainty storm ensued.

Weakened consensus about essential virtue tilted people into an uncertain world where "existence precedes essence" without objective or consensual bases for being (Sartre, 1946/2007 p. vii). Value-consolidating identities accordingly became personal responsibilities to build either via desperately uncertain leaps of faith toward arbitrary worldview options or by Nietzschean feats of personal agency (Oaklander, 1996; Wicks, 2022). Either way took courage to face the radical uncertainty of trying to sustain meaning in an absurd world. Sartre (1943/1992) claimed people mask existential nausea arising from this bewildering existential freedom by turning to authoritarian rigidity about inauthentic identity-claims ("bad faith," p. 496) and by indulging in sadistic and hateful orientations toward others. The impulsive, grandiose, and hostile ways of coping with uncertainty described by Kierkegaard, Nietzsche, and Sartre (Oaklander, 1996) map onto the kinds of zealous, self-serving, hostile, risky, and extreme RAM reactions reviewed above that result from uncertainty-related threats in the lab (Jonas et al., 2014; Leota et al., 2023; McGregor et al., 2013).

Freud was born in the decade between when Marx and Engel published their manifesto and Darwin published his ideas about natural selection. Echoing their emphasis on worldly power and sexual selection, Freud demoted identification with idealistic values to the status of a defense mechanism—moral obsessions people use to repress their darker id-essences and uncertainties. To explain how people accomplish repression via moral extremes, Freud compared the extremes to bouncers who eject unruly patrons (the unwanted thoughts and feelings) and then guard the door; to barking dogs that keep the unwanted thoughts cowering at bay; or to mental dams that block the flow of unwanted thoughts. RAM and BIS-BAS dynamics provide a parsimonious account of how this kind of repression could occur. Idealistic (and-or hostile) extremes are rewarding and effective defense mechanisms because they activate BAS, which terminates BIS-linked rumination and distress over uncertainties and conflicts. This simple explanation fits with how Freud thought repression worked: "The reactive thought keeps the objectionable one under repression by means of a certain surplus of intensity" (Freud, 1905, in Strachey et al., 1953).

Most neoanalytic theorists who started out close to Freud eventually distanced themselves from the sexual focus of his ideas, but retained the belief that narcissistic, aggressive, and rigid extremes are defense mechanisms people non-consciously use to repress distressing thoughts and feelings about their uncertain selves. Most also promoted the hopeful theme that reactive extremes could be supplanted by proactive commitment to ideals. Adler, for example, believed people would react to vulnerabilities with rigid and hostile compensation efforts (superiority complex) unless they could find a way to reorient to other-focused, self-transcendent values and commitments (Ansbacher & Ansbacher, 1956). Fromm (1941) argued that aggression, hate, conformity, and greed are what people are left with if they are not able to commit to "love and productive work" (p. 30). Horney (1937) saw hostility and defensive pride as defenses against the basic anxiety of disconnection from others. Maslow (1987, pp. 156–157, 87–88) held that self-actualization required a common-humanity capacity to love others for their own sake, a "being" love that supplants the urge to use and exploit others. Erikson (1959, p. 134) viewed successful adult development as involving identity achievement, intimacy, and generativity as a way to escape from cycles of narcissistic hostility. Moreover, Erikson (like Kierkegaard) viewed an anxious crisis as a catalyst for proactive identity commitment. Together, neoanalytic theories converge on the idea that human thriving depends on authentic commitment to prosocial values that can quell anxious distress and supplant reactive extremes. The BIS-BAS dynamics depicted in Figure 13.2 provide a simple way to understand the basic motivational forces beneath neo-analytic claims.

Discussion

> Religious rapture, moral enthusiasm… are…unifying states of mind, in which the sand and grit of the selfhood incline to disappear.
>
> (James, 1902/1958, p. 240)

This chapter has attempted to integrate theory and research on how anxious uncertainties and BAS-activating abstractions can interact to account for dynamics of loving and hating. Figure 13.2 depicts the basic template for how these dynamic processes work. We maintain that this parsimonious template can make integrative sense of most threat and defense findings in experimental social psychology (cf. Brinol & Petty, this volume; Landau et al., this volume;

Murray, this volume; Van den Bos & Lind, this volume) and also account for core themes in the humanities and classic psychological theories. In their own ways and with discipline-specific jargon and bases for persuasion, each tradition converges on the problem of anxious uncertainties and frustrations in life, on the reflex for hostile and self-serving reactions to them, and on the power of self-transcendent-value commitment to help people overcome their anxious-uncertainties and maladaptive reactions.

Over the course of human history, related ideas have been repeatedly invoked as wisdom, only to be forgotten or suppressed as misguided or ill-informed when epistemological limitations of the truth criteria came into view. Narrative myths and rituals that used metaphor to allude to the processes gave way to monotheistic religions that appealed to absolute truth. Religions were then discarded as superstitious ignorance when God died with Nietzsche in the age of reason, to be replaced by existential philosophy and psychodynamic theory, which was in turn discarded by many as a cult of wooly and unfalsifiable ideas. Neoanalytic ideas about non-conscious defenses and the power of identity and prosocial values, together with ideas from existential philosophy about the agony of personal uncertainty, then formed the foundation for most of the psychological theories of human motivation that prevailed after WWII and that still persist in introductory psychology textbooks today. These grand theories are in-turn routinely dismissed as too vague and grandiose by hard-nosed, experimental researchers, but even such researchers' theories are often tacitly rooted in psychodynamic assumptions. Most recently, the methods of experimental researchers have been found wanting, and their conclusions are now viewed with suspicion by many on the cutting edge of the current methods revolution. Despite its storied history, confidence in the map has once again been undermined by fear that the previous generation of explorers who drew it up may have been akin to empirical pirates collecting their evidence by illicit or dubious means.

Our hope is that the convergence of theory, research, and interdisciplinary relevance outlined in this chapter will help people see beyond methodological imperfections to appreciate the utility of the template depicted in Figure 13.2. We hope it helps destigmatize and re-legitimize the higher-power of self-transcendent values, for people and societies to use as antidotes to the languishing and reactive malevolence that blight our world and distract people from making it better. In the 20th century, idealistic values were pummeled by Freud's promotion of pleasure as an alternative to defensively rigid idealism. Still today, disgust over how regularly hypocrisy and hate infiltrate religious, political, ingroup, and personal values make it seem reasonable to jettison earnest ideals to focus more on rational pragmatics of self-care and hedonic expedience. A massive marketing complex armed with addictive technologies and pernicious algorithms further bolsters the idea that living for pleasure and self-enhancement (spiced with resentment) is reasonable common sense. Further, even for those who might yearn to strive for self-transcendence, there is scant cultural support or consensus about what values are worthy of commitment. Idealistic values have accordingly fallen out of fashion. Over the last 50 years, young people's engagement with major life goals related to the pursuit of self-transcendent values has dropped from 80% to 40%, with a reciprocal increase in self-enhancing goals (Twenge et al., 2012), narcissism, and anxiety-related disturbances (Collishaw et al., 2004; Duffy et al., 2019; Twenge & Foster, 2010). Angry ideological polarization and the global appeal of fascism seem also to be filling the void. Based on the theoretical, empirical, and interdisciplinary convergence reviewed above, we hold that self-transcendent, idealistic values may be more vital for human well-being than is commonly understood. Without them, people are at risk of over-exposure to the radical uncertainty of being human, and either simmering in its anxiety or using hostile maneuvers to mask it.

Notes

1 Pavlov seems to have regarded bewildered-Russia's political extremes as having the same (uncertainty-linked) cause as his uncertain dogs' outbursts. The year he published his experiments on uncertainty causing dog-tantrums he wrote an open letter rebuking Stalin's fascism (Cavendish, 2011).
2 These fatigue findings need a pre-registered replication but are consistent with the pre-registered findings in the previous section.
3 Given links between nostalgia, approach motivation, and authentic communal values (Sedikides & Wildschut, 2023), part of the palliative and invigorating power of nostalgia may arise from this same BAS-muting-BIS power of values (cf. Sedikides et al., this volume), helping to account for the appeal of traditional-worldview defenses after mortality salience and other uncertainty-related threats (e.g., (Jonas et al., 2014).

References

Adorno, T. W., Frenkel-Brunswik, E., Levinson, D. J., & Sanford, R. N. (1950). *The authoritarian personality.* Harpers.
Alquist, J. L., Baumeister, R. F., McGregor, I., Core, T. J., Benjamin, I., & Tice, D. M. (2018). Personal conflict impairs performance on an unrelated self-control task: Lingering costs of uncertainty and conflict. *Journal of Experimental Social Psychology, 74,* 157–160. https://doi.org/10.1016/j.jesp.2017.09.010
Anderson, C. A., & Bushman, B. J. (2002). Human aggression. *Annual Review of Psychology, 53*(1), 27–51. https://doi.org/10.1146/annurev.psych.53.100901.135231
Ansbacher, H. L., & Ansbacher, R. R. (Eds.) (1956). *The individual psychology of Alfred Adler.* Basic Books.
Ash, J., & Gallup, G. G., Jr. (2007). Paleoclimatic variation and brain expansion during human evolution. *Human Nature, 18*(2), 109–124. https://doi.org/10.1007/s12110-007-9015-z
Bailey, D. H., & Geary, D. C. (2009). Hominid brain evolution: Testing climatic, ecological, and social competition models. *Human Nature, 20*(1), 67–79. https://doi.org/10.1007/s12110-008-9054-0
Barnes, H. E. (1973). *Sartre*. J. B. Lippincott and Co.
Baumeister, R. F., & Vohs, K. D. (2016). Strength model of self-regulation as limited resource: Assessment, controversies, update. In J. M. Olson & M. P. Zanna (Eds.), *Advances in experimental social psychology* (pp. 67–127). Elsevier Academic Press. https://doi.org/10.1016/bs.aesp.2016.04.001
Baumeister, R. F., & Vohs, K. D. (2018). Strength model of self-regulation as limited resource: Assessment, controversies, update. In *Self-regulation and self-control* (pp. 78–128). Routledge.
Berkowitz, L. (1989). Frustration-aggression hypothesis: Examination and reformulation. *Psychological Bulletin, 106*(1), 59–73. https://doi.org/10.1037/0033-2909.106.1.59
Bodhi, B. (2010). *The noble eightfold path: The way to the end of suffering*. Buddhist Publication Society.
Bojanowska, A., & Piotrowski, K. (2021). Two levels of personality: Temperament and values and their effects on hedonic and eudaimonic well-being. *Current Psychology: A Journal for Diverse Perspectives on Diverse Psychological Issues, 40*(3), 1185–1193. https://doi.org/10.1007/s12144-018-0043-0
Borg, M. J. (2009). *The heart of Christianity: Rediscovering a life of faith*. Harper Collins.
Bowden, H. (2010). *Mystery cults of the ancient world.* Princeton University Press.
Britton. (2023). *The uncertainty model of boredom and self-control failure: How ambient uncertainty influences affect and behaviour during unrelated goal pursuit* (Unpublished doctoral dissertation). University of Waterloo.
Burson, A., Crocker, J., & Mischkowski, D. (2012). Two types of value-affirmation: Implications for self-control following social exclusion. *Social Psychological and Personality Science, 3*(4), 510–516. https://doi.org/10.1177/1948550611427773
Carver, C. S., & Harmon-Jones, E. (2009). Anger is an approach-related affect: Evidence and implications. *Psychological Bulletin, 135*(2), 183–204. https://doi.org/10.1037/a0013965
Carver, C. S., & Scheier, M. F. (2001). *On the self-regulation of behavior.* Cambridge University Press. https://doi.org/10.1017/CBO9781139174794
Carver, C. S., & White, T. L. (1994). Behavioral inhibition, behavioral activation, and affective responses to impending reward and punishment: The BIS/BAS Scales. *Journal of Personality and Social Psychology, 67*(2), 319–333. https://doi.org/10.1037/0022-3514.67.2.319
Cavendish, R. (2011, February). Death of Ivan Pavlov: February 27th 1936. *History Today, 61*(2), 9.

Cho, M., & Keltner, D. (2020). Power, approach, and inhibition: Empirical advances of a theory. *Current Opinion in Psychology, 33,* 196–200. https://doi.org/10.1016/j.copsyc.2019.08.013

Cohen, G. L., & Sherman, D. K. (2014). The psychology of change: Self-affirmation and social psychological intervention. *Annual Review of Psychology*, *65*, 333–371.

Collishaw, S., Maughan, B., Goodman, R., & Pickles, A. (2004). Time trends in adolescent mental health. *Journal of Child Psychology and Psychiatry, 45*(8), 1350–1362. https://doi.org/10.1111/j.1469-7610.2004.00335.x

Corr, P. J. (2004). Reinforcement sensitivity theory and personality. *Neuroscience and Biobehavioral Reviews, 28*(3), 317–332. https://doi.org/10.1016/j.neubiorev.2004.01.005

Crocker, J., Niiya, Y., & Mischkowski, D. (2008). Why does writing about important values reduce defensiveness? Self-affirmation and the role of positive other-directed feelings. *Psychological Science, 19*(7), 740–747. https://doi.org/10.1111/j.1467-9280.2008.02150.x

Dollard, J., Doob, L. W., Miller, N. E., Mowrer, O. H., & Sears, R. R. (1939). *Frustration and Aggression.* Yale University Press.

Duffy, M. E., Twenge, J. M., & Joiner, T. E. (2019). Trends in mood and anxiety symptoms and suicide-related outcomes among U.S. undergraduates, 2007–2018: Evidence from two national surveys. *Journal of Adolescent Health, 65*(5), 590–598. https://doi.org/10.1016/j.jadohealth.2019.04.033

Durkheim, E. (1951). *Suicide: A study in sociology* (J. A. Spaulding & G. Simpson, Trans). Free Press. (Original work published 1897).

Durkheim, E. (2008). *The elementary forms of the religious life* (J. W. Swain, Trans). Courier Corporation. (Original work published 1912).Einstein, A. (1932, July 30). *Letter from Albert Einstein to Sigmund Freud*, 1932. Retrieved from https://en.unesco.org/courier/may-1985/why-war-letter-albert-einstein-sigmund-freud

Elnakouri, A., Hubley, C., & McGregor, I. (2022). Hate and meaning in life: How collective, but not personal, hate quells threat and spurs meaning in life. *Journal of Experimental Social Psychology, 98,* Article 104227. https://doi.org/10.1016/j.jesp.2021.104227

Elnakouri, A., Rossignac-Milon, M., Krueger, K. L., Forest, A. L., Higgins, E. T., & Scholer, A. A. (2023). In it together: Shared reality with instrumental others is linked to goal success. *Journal of Personality and Social Psychology.* Advance online publication. https://doi.org/10.1037/pspi0000427

Erikson, E. H. (1959). *Identity and the life cycle: Selected papers*. International Universities Press.

Festinger, L. (1954). A theory of social comparison processes. *Human Relations, 7,* 117–140. https://doi.org/10.1177/001872675400700202

Festinger, L. (1957). *A theory of cognitive dissonance.* Stanford University Press.

Festinger, L., Riecken, H. W., & Schachter, S. (1956). *When prophecy fails.* University of Minnesota Press. https://doi.org/10.1037/10030-000

Fritsche, I. (2022). Agency through the we: Group-based control theory. *Current Directions in Psychological Science, 31*(2), 194–201. https://doi.org/10.1177/09637214211068838

Fromm, E. (1941). *Escape from freedom.* Farrar & Rinehart.

Fromm, E. (1973). *The anatomy of human destructiveness*. Fawcett Publications.

Gailliot, M. T., Schmeichel, B. J., & Baumeister, R. F. (2006). Self-regulatory processes defend against the threat of death: Effects of self-control depletion and trait self-control on thoughts and fears of dying. *Journal of Personality and Social Psychology, 91*(1), 49–62. https://doi.org/10.1037/0022-3514.91.1.49

Gilad, Y., Man, O., Pääbo, S., & Lancet, D. (2003). Human specific loss of olfactory receptor genes. *Proceedings of the National Academy of Sciences, 100*(6), 3324–3327. https://doi.org/10.1073/pnas.0535697100

Graham, J., Haidt, J., & Nosek, B. A. (2009). Liberals and conservatives rely on different sets of moral foundations. *Journal of Personality and Social Psychology, 96*(5), 1029–1046. https://doi.org/10.1037/a0015141

Graham, J., & Haidt, J. (2010). Beyond beliefs: Religions bind individuals into moral communities. *Personality and Social Psychology Review, 14*(1), 140–150. https://doi.org/10.1177/1088868309353415

Gray, J. A., & McNaughton, N. (2000) *The neuropsychology of anxiety: An inquiry into the functions of the septo-hippocampal system* (2nd ed.). Oxford University Press.

Hardin, C. D., & Higgins, E. T. (1996). Shared reality: How social verification makes the subjective objective. In R. M. Sorrentino & E. T. Higgins (Eds.), *Handbook of motivation and cognition, Vol. 3. The interpersonal context* (pp. 28–84). The Guilford Press.

Harmon-Jones, E., Amodio, D. M., & Harmon-Jones, C. (2009). Action-based model of dissonance: A review, integration, and expansion of conceptions of cognitive conflict. In M. P. Zanna (Ed.), *Advances in experimental social psychology* (Vol. 41, pp. 119–166). Elsevier.

Harmon-Jones, E., & Gable, P. A. (2009). Neural activity underlying the effect of approach-motivated positive affect on narrowed attention. *Psychological Science, 20*(4), 406–409. https://doi.org/10.1111/j.1467-9280.2009.02302.x

Hayes, J., Ward, C. L., & McGregor, I. (2016). Why bother? Death, failure, and fatalistic withdrawal from life. *Journal of Personality and Social Psychology, 110*(1), 96.

Heintzelman, S. J., & King, L. A. (2014). Life is pretty meaningful. *American Psychologist, 69*(6), 561–574. https://doi.org/10.1037/a0035049

Hirsh, J. B., Mar, R. A., & Peterson, J. B. (2012). Psychological entropy: A framework for understanding uncertainty-related anxiety. *Psychological Review, 119*(2), 304–320. https://doi.org/10.1037/a0026767

Hockey, R. (2013). *The psychology of fatigue: Work, effort and control.* Cambridge University Press. https://doi.org/10.1017/CBO9781139015394

Horney, K. (1937). *The neurotic personality of our time.* W W Norton & Co.

Inzlicht, M., Bartholow, B. D., & Hirsh, J. B. (2015). Emotional foundations of cognitive control. *Trends in Cognitive Sciences, 19*(3), 126–132. https://doi.org/10.1016/j.tics.2015.01.004

James, W. (1958). *The varieties of religious experience.* The New American Library, Inc. (Original work published in 1902).

Jonas, E., McGregor, I., Klackl, J., Agroskin, D., Fritsche, I., Holbrook, C., Nash, K., Proulx, T., & Quirin, M. (2014). Threat and defense: From anxiety to approach. In J. M. Olson & M. P. Zanna (Eds.), *Advances in experimental social psychology* (Vol. 49, (pp. 219–286). Elsevier Academic Press.

Kaas, J. H. (2013). The evolution of brains from early mammals to humans. *WIREs Cognitive Science, 4*(1), 33–45. https://doi.org/10.1002/wcs.1206

Kang, Y., Cooper, N., Pandey, P., Scholz, C., O'Donnell, M. B., Lieberman, M. D., Taylor, S.E., Strecher, V.J., Dal Cin, S., Konrath, S., Polk T.A., Resnicow, K., An, L., & Falk, E. B. (2018). Effects of self-transcendence on neural responses to persuasive messages and health behavior change. *Proceedings of the National Academy of Sciences, 115*(40), 9974–9979. https://doi.org/10.1073/pnas.1805573115

King, L. A., & Hicks, J. A. (2021). The science of meaning in life. *Annual Review of Psychology, 72*, 561–584.

King, L. A., & Napa, C. K. (1998). What makes a life good? *Journal of Personality and Social Psychology, 75*(1), 156–165. https://doi.org/10.1037/0022-3514.75.1.156

Klackl, J., Lüders, A., & Jonas, E. (2024). Q: What is the recipe for defense? A: Threat, anxiety, and approach motivation. *Motivation Science, 10*, 63–77.

Leota, J., Nash, K., & McGregor, I. (2023). Reactive risk-taking: Anxiety regulation via approach motivation increases risk-taking behavior. *Personality and Social Psychology Bulletin, 49*(1), 81–96. https://doi.org/10.1177/01461672211059689

Lewin, K. (1933). Environmental forces. In C. Murchison (Ed.), *A handbook of child psychology* (2nd ed., pp. 590–625). Clark University Press.

Lewin, K. (1935). *A dynamic theory of personality* (D. K. Adams & K. E. Zaner, Trans.). McGraw-Hill (Original work published 1935).

Lewin, K. (1939). Field theory and experiment in social psychology: Concepts and methods. *American Journal of Sociology, 44*(6), 868–896. https://doi.org/10.1086/218177

Lewin, K., Lippitt, R., & White, R. K. (1939). Patterns of aggressive behavior in experimentally created "social climates." *The Journal of Social Psychology, 10*, 271–299. https://doi.org/10.1080/00224545.1939.9713366

Maslow, A. H. (1987). *Motivation and Personality* (3rd ed.). Addison-Wesley. (Original work published 1954).

McAdams, D. P. (1993). *The stories we live by: Personal myths and the making of the self.* William Morrow & Co.

McAdams, D. P. (2013). *The redemptive self: Stories Americans live by* (Revised and expanded edition). Oxford University Press.

McGregor, I. (2006). Offensive defensiveness: Toward an integrative neuroscience of compensatory zeal after mortality salience, personal uncertainty, and other poignant self-threats. *Psychological Inquiry, 17*(4), 299–308. https://doi.org/10.1080/10478400701366977

McGregor, I., Britton, E., Elnakouri, A., & Sharpinskyi, K. (2022). Weak personal ideals incline proud people towards religious radicalization in anxious circumstances (Research Brief). *Canadian Network for Research on Terrorism, Security, and Society.* https://www.tsas.ca/publications/weak-personal-ideals-incline-proud-people-towards-religious-radicalization-in-anxious-circumstances/

McGregor, I., Britton, E., Auger, E., & Elnakouri, A. (2024). *Unpublished raw data on the effect of value-focus on felt-meaning in life*. University of Waterloo.

McGregor, I., & Little, B. R. (1998). Personal projects, happiness, and meaning: On doing well and being yourself. *Journal of Personality and Social Psychology, 74*(2), 494–512. https://doi.org/10.1037/0022-3514.74.2.494

McGregor, I., Nash, K., Mann, N., & Phills, C. E. (2010). Anxious uncertainty and reactive approach motivation (RAM). *Journal of Personality and Social Psychology, 99*(1), 133–147. https://doi.org/10.1037/a0019701

McGregor, I., Prentice, M., & Nash, K. (2012). Approaching relief: Compensatory ideals relieve threat-induced anxiety by promoting approach-motivated states. *Social Cognition, 30*(6), 689–714. https://doi.org/10.1521/soco.2012.30.6.689

McGregor, I., Prentice, M., & Nash, K. (2013). Anxious uncertainty and Reactive Approach Motivation (RAM) for religious, idealistic, and lifestyle extremes. *Journal of Social Issues, 69*(3), 537–563. https://doi.org/10.1111/josi.12028

McGregor, I., Tran, A., Auger, E., Britton, E., Hayes, J., Elnakouri, A., Eftekhari, E., Sharpinskyi, K., Arbiv, O. A., & Nash, K. (2022). Higher power dynamics: How meaning search and self-transcendence inspire approach motivation and magnanimity. *Journal of Experimental Social Psychology, 102,* 1–17. https://doi.org/10.1016/j.jesp.2022.104350

Mercer-Lynn, K. B., Bar, R. J., & Eastwood, J. D. (2016). Causes of boredom: The person, the situation, or both? *Personality and Individual Differences, 56,* 122–126. https://doi.org/10.1016/j.paid.2013.08.034

Mitchell, S. (2004). *Gilgamesh: A new English version*. Simon and Schuster.

Norenzayan, A., Shariff, A. F., Gervais, W. M., Willard, A. K., McNamara, R. A., Slingerland, E., & Henrich, J. (2014). The cultural evolution of prosocial religions. *Behavioral and Brain Sciences, 39,* Article e1. https://doi.org/10.1017/S0140525X14001356

Oaklander, L. N. (1996). *Existentialist philosophy: An introduction*. Prentice Hall.

Patnoe, S. (1988). *A narrative history of experimental social psychology: The Lewin tradition.* New York: Springer-Verlag.

Pavlov, I. (1927). Lecture 17: *The different types of nervous, system. -- Pathological disturbances of the cortex, result of functional interferences* [Transcript]. https://psychclassics.yorku.ca/Pavlov/lecture17.htm

Pearce, K., & Huta, V. (2023). When are people willing to help others? Links with eudaimonic versus hedonic motives. *Motivation and Emotion*, 524–537. https://doi.org/10.1007/s11031-022-10004-z

Proulx, T., Inzlicht, M., & Harmon-Jones, E. (2012). Understanding all inconsistency compensation as a palliative response to violated expectations. *Trends in Cognitive Sciences, 16*(5), 285–291. https://doi.org/10.1016/j.tics.2012.04.002

Randles, D., Inzlicht, M., Proulx, T., Tullett, A. M., & Heine, S. J. (2015). Is dissonance reduction a special case of fluid compensation? Evidence that dissonant cognitions cause compensatory affirmation and abstraction. *Journal of personality and social psychology*, *108*(5), 697.

Rimé, B., & Páez, D. (2023). Why we gather: A new look, empirically documented, at Émile Durkheim's theory of collective assemblies and collective effervescence. *Perspectives on Psychological Science.*

Sagiv, L., Roccas, S., Cieciuch, J., & Schwartz, S. H. (2017). Personal values in human life. *Nature Human Behaviour*, *1*(9), 630–639.

Sagiv, L., & Schwartz, S. H. (2022). Personal values across cultures. *Annual Review of Psychology, 73,* 517–546. https://doi.org/10.1146/annurev-psych-020821-125100

Saroglou, V., Delpierre, V., & Dernelle, R. (2004). Values and religiosity: A meta-analysis of studies using Schwartz's model. *Personality and Individual Differences, 37*(4), 721–734. https://doi.org/10.1016/j.paid.2003.10.005

Sartre, J-P. (1992). *Being and nothingness* (H. E. Barnes, Trans.). Washington Square Press. (Original work published 1943)

Sartre, J-P. (2007). *Existentialism is a humanism.* (C. Macomber, Trans.). New Haven: Yale University Press. (Original work published 1946)

Schmeichel, B. J., & Vohs, K. (2009). Self-affirmation and self-control: Affirming core values counteracts ego depletion. *Journal of Personality and Social Psychology, 96*(4), 770–782. https://doi.org/10.1037/a0014635

Schumann, K., McGregor, I., Nash, K. A., & Ross, M. (2014). Religious magnanimity: Reminding people of their religious belief system reduces hostility after threat. *Journal of Personality and Social Psychology, 107*(3), 432–453. https://doi.org/10.1037/a0036739

Schwartz, S. H., & Bardi, A. (2001). Value hierarchies across cultures: Taking a similarities perspective. *Journal of Cross-Cultural Psychology, 32*(3), 268–290. https://doi.org/10.1177/0022022101032003002

Sedikides, C., & Wildschut, T. (2023). Nostalgia as motivation. *Current Opinion in Psychology, 49,* Article 101537. https://doi.org/10.1016/j.copsyc.2022.101537

Shnabel, N., Purdie-Vaughns, V., Cook, J. E., Garcia, J., & Cohen, G. L. (2013). Demystifying values-affirmation interventions: Writing about social belonging is a key to buffering against identity threat. *Personality and Social Psychology Bulletin, 39*(5), 663–676. https://doi.org/10.1177/0146167213480816

Sibley, C. G., & Duckitt, J. (2008). Personality and prejudice: A meta-analysis and theoretical review. *Personality and Social Psychology Review, 12*(3), 248–279. https://doi.org/10.1177/1088868308319226

Simmons, J. P., Nelson, L. D., & Simonsohn, U. (2011). False-positive psychology: Undisclosed flexibility in data collection and analysis allows presenting anything as significant. *Psychological Science, 22*(11), 1359–1366. https://doi.org/10.1177/0956797611417632

Steele, C. M. (1988). The psychology of self-affirmation: Sustaining the integrity of the self. In L. Berkowitz (Ed.), *Advances in experimental social psychology, Vol. 21. Social psychological studies of the self: Perspectives and programs* (pp. 261–302). Academic Press.

Stollberg, J., Klackl, J., & Jonas, E. (2024). Empirical test of a general process model of threat and defense: A systematic examination of the affective-motivational processes underlying proximal and distal reactions to threat. *Journal of Experimental Social Psychology, 110,* 1-14.

Strachey, J., Freud, A., Strachey, A., & Tyson, A. (1953). *The standard edition of the complete psychological works of Sigmund Freud, Volume VII (1901–1905): A case of hysteria, three essays on sexuality and other works.* Hogarth Press and the Institute of Psychoanalysis.

Twenge, J. M., Campbell, W. K., & Freeman, E. C. (2012). Generational differences in young adults' life goals, concern for others, and civic orientation, 1966–2009. *Journal of Personality and Social Psychology, 102*(5), 1045–1062. https://doi.org/10.1037/a0027408

Twenge, J. M., & Foster, J. D. (2010). Birth cohort increases in narcissistic personality traits among American college students, 1982–2009. *Social Psychological and Personality Science, 1*(1), 99–106. https://doi.org/10.1177/1948550609355719

Twenge, J. M., & King, L. A. (2005). A good life is a personal life: Relationship fulfillment and work fulfillment in judgments of life quality. *Journal of Research in Personality, 39*(3), 336–353. https://doi.org/10.1016/j.jrp.2004.01.004

Van Der Linden, D., Tops, M., & Bakker, A. B. (2021). Go with the flow: A neuroscientific view on being fully engaged. *European Journal of Neuroscience, 53,* 947-963.

Van Hook, E., & Higgins, E. T. (1988). Self-related problems beyond the self-concept: Motivational consequences of discrepant self-guides. *Journal of Personality and Social Psychology, 55*(4), 625–633. https://doi.org/10.1037/0022-3514.55.4.625

Vohs, K. D., Schmeichel, B. J., Lohmann, S., Gronau, Q. F., Finley, A. J., Ainsworth, S. E., Alquist, J. L., Baker, M. D., Brizi, A., Bunyi, A., Butschek, G. J., Campbell, C., Capaldi, J., Cau, C., Chambers, H., Chatzisarantis, N. L. D., Christensen, W. J., Clay, S. L., Curtis, J., … Albarracín, D. (2021). A multisite preregistered paradigmatic test of the ego-depletion effect. *Psychological Science, 32*(10), 1566–1581. https://doi.org/10.1177/0956797621989733

Waytz, A., Iyer, R., Young, L., Haidt, J., & Graham, J. (2019). Ideological differences in the expanse of the moral circle. *Nature Communications, 10*(1), 1–12. https://doi.org/10.1038/s41467-019-12227-0

Wicks, R. (2022). Nietzsche's life and works. In Edward N. Zalta (Ed.), *The Stanford encyclopedia of philosophy.* https://plato.stanford.edu/archives/spr2022/entries/nietzsche-life-works

Womick, J., Ward, S. J., Heintzelman, S. J., Woody, B., & King, L. A. (2019). The existential function of right-wing authoritarianism. *Journal of Personality, 87*(5), 1056–1073. https://doi.org/10.1111/jopy.12457

14
PROTOTYPICALITY THREAT AND SELF-UNCERTAINTY MOTIVATE GROUP BEHAVIOR

Olivia R. Kuljian and Zachary P. Hohman

Prototypicality Threat and Self-uncertainty Motivate Group Behavior

Our social world is composed of group memberships, categorical boundaries between groups, and drawn contrasts between ingroups and outgroups. Given the identity-defining power that groups provide, people aim to feel secure in their group memberships. Knowing oneself as part of a collective allows people to place themselves within the world and gain some degree of control and prediction over the environment. On the contrary, feeling as if one is on the periphery of an important ingroup is threatening because it inhibits the construction of a group-referenced self-identity. When people are unable to access a clear understanding of who they are within their social world, they tend to experience uncertainty (Hogg, 2007). Feeling uncertain about domains relevant to the self (e.g., one's standing as a member of a valued ingroup) is aversive and motivates efforts to alleviate feeling uncertain (Hogg, 2007; Hogg, 2021). Within a social context, efforts may take many forms, such as behaviors directed at enhancing how one appears to others within the group (Hogg, 2007; Smith et al., 2007), engaging in prosocial behaviors that raise the status of the ingroup (e.g., Grieve & Hogg, 1999; Hohman et al., 2017; Mullin & Hogg, 1998), or endorsing extreme intergroup behaviors (e.g., Goldman & Hogg, 2016; Hogg & Adelman, 2013; Kuljian, 2023; Niedbala & Hohman, 2019). This chapter details the impact of peripheral group membership on identity construction and feeling certain about the self, as well as the motivating role of self-uncertainty in spurring group behavior. The research covered within this chapter highlights contributions and current directions of the field, identifies measures and manipulations of uncertainty, and outlines opportunities for future contributions to the field.

Social Identities

Social identity theory broadly describes that people source and understand their identities from their memberships with important groups (Tajfel, 1972). Groups provide members with prescriptive guidelines for how to think, act, and behave in a complex social world (Hogg, 2004, 2005, 2007). In addition, identities crafted through group membership provide structure for the way in which people view and understand reality, the world, others, and themselves (Hogg & Rinella, 2018).

DOI: 10.4324/9781003363385-16

When individuals identify and self-categorize as members of an ingroup, they understand and define their self-identity on the core values, mannerisms, and characteristics that compose the ingroup identity. Ingroup identities do not exist in a vacuum—ingroups are also defined by how they differ from outgroups (Hogg, 2004). The central attributes, values, and typical behaviors that define the ingroup also mark the categorical boundaries that differentiate the ingroup from relevant outgroups. Attributes that are deemed to be essential to the categorization of groups are emphasized, highlighting the similarities within groups and the differences between groups (Tajfel, 1959; Tajfel & Wilkes, 1963). As a result, people understand themselves and others in perceptually separate categories according to group membership. This shift in cognition to view one's social world in terms of group membership is termed depersonalization (Abrams & Hogg, 1990, 2010; Tajfel & Turner, 1986; Turner et al., 1987). When people depersonalize, they view themselves and others in reference to the central, essential qualities of their group (group prototypes; Abrams & Hogg, 1990, 2010; Turner et al., 1987). Group prototypes provide an exemplary definition of categorical group membership within a social context and offer a basis for the evaluation of group members.

Group Prototypes

The essential values and properties that define group identity and distinguish the group from other groups are termed prototypes. Prototypes are fuzzy constellations of norms and attributes that are essential to a given ingroup identity (Turner et al., 1987). Prototypes simultaneously promote ingroup similarities and emphasize differences that differentiate the ingroup from relevant outgroups (maximizing the meta-contrast ratio, Hogg et al., 1990; Turner, 1991; Turner et al., 1987; Turner & Oakes, 1989). Prototypes serve to distance the ingroup from relative outgroups, and thus often represent the qualities of an idyllic, rather than average, group member (Abrams & Hogg, 2010). Due to the identify-defining properties that group prototypes provide, people often strive to conform to the group prototype (Abrams & Hogg, 1990; Hogg & Turner, 1987), especially when they feel they are distant from the prototype.

Prototypical Group Membership

Group members vary in their distance to the ingroup prototype, and proximity to the group prototype has implications for representation, self-definition, and identification processes (Hogg, 2005). Members who align closely with the ingroup prototype tend to be endowed with higher status, influential power (McGarty et al., 1992), positive evaluations (Hogg & Hardie, 1991), charisma (Platow et al., 2006), and trust (Giessner & van Knippenberg, 2008). Moreover, those who have higher prototypicality in conjunction with enhanced social identification tend to report more positive psychological health and well-being (Hoffman et al., 2020). Due to their proximity to the ingroup prototype, prototypical members are afforded clear access to a group-referenced self-identity. In contrast, peripheral members' distance from the ingroup prototype limits the use of the prototype as a reference to define the social self.

Under the umbrella of peripheral status, members may fall on the periphery of the ingroup that is distant from relevant outgroups (far-peripheral), or on the periphery of the ingroup that is closer to relevant outgroups (near-peripheral). The ingroup prototype is often composed of idealized qualities aimed at distancing the ingroup from relevant outgroups, thus far-peripheral members' embodiment of extreme ingroup qualities may validate their status as ideal ingroup members (Gaffney et al., 2014; McGarty et al., 1992). Falling on the far-periphery of a valued ingroup may not threaten one's group-referenced self-identity. Rather, far-peripheral group members may be viewed in a positive light because their membership aids in maximizing the contrast between the ingroup and relevant outgroups. In contrast, near-peripheral membership status is threatening due to the distance from ideal ingroup attributes and the proximity to undesirable outgroup qualities. Given the relevance of near-peripheral (compared to far-peripheral) membership for discussions surrounding group status, self-definition, and resulting action, this chapter references near-peripheral group status with the term *non-prototypical.*

Feeling as if one is different from the strived-for qualities of the ingroup prototype and approaching the prototypical qualities of relevant outgroups is uncomfortable and threatening (Pickett & Brewer, 2001). Moreover, non-prototypical members' separation from other ingroup members and increased approximation to outgroup members violate the metacontrast ratio (Turner et al., 1987) by threatening perceptions of similarity among ingroup members and the ingroup's collective distinctiveness from close outgroups. Non-prototypical members' distance from the ingroup prototype inhibits understanding and self-categorizing oneself as a group member. To gain a better understanding of the self in a social context, non-prototypical group members tend to be driven to redefine self-identity by enhancing their membership with valued ingroups through a variety of methods.

Consequences of Feeling Peripheral

Feeling as if one is on the margins of a valued ingroup is uncomfortable because it signifies that one is different from other group members and distant from the idealistic attributes of a prototypical member. Non-prototypical group members are thus often subject to feelings of insecurity (Jetten et al., 2002), negative affect (Sassenberg et al., 2011), and uncertainty about their identity as group members (Hohman et al., 2017). Research contends that when people feel that they are distant from an identity-defining ingroup prototype, they work to align themselves more closely with the ingroup prototype membership (e.g., Goldman & Hogg, 2016; Noel et al., 1995; Schmitt & Branscombe, 2001; Steinel et al., 2010; Van Kleef et al., 2013; Van Kleef et al., 2011). To lessen the discrepancy between the group identity and their peripheral, and thus questionable identity, non-prototypical group members tend to act in ways that justify their group membership and reaffirm their status as prototypical members. For example, non-prototypical group members self-stereotype and endorse ingroup qualities (Burris & Jackson, 2010), follow ingroup norms (Noel et al., 1995; Steinel et al., 2010), and engage in pro-ingroup behavior (Jetten et al., 2002; Hohman et al., 2017) more than prototypical members (see also, Gómez et al., 2014). Moreover, non-prototypical group members display increased motivations to derogate relevant outgroups (Goldman & Hogg, 2016), and even other non-prototypical group members whose status threatens the cohesivity of the ingroup identity (Schmitt & Branscombe, 2001).

Non-prototypical members may be especially driven to perform pro-ingroup action when they feel that their efforts may be witnessed by other group members. Noel et al. (1995) found that, compared to their prototypical counterparts, peripheral participants indicated more support for the use of coercive strategies against the outgroup and negative trait ratings of outgroup targets as a function of the visibility of their actions. Non-prototypical members who perceived their ratings to be public, as opposed to private, demonstrated increased outgroup derogation and ingroup bias. Additional research by Van Kleef and colleagues (2011, 2013) demonstrated that non-prototypical participants who felt that their actions were visible to fellow ingroup members tended to work harder on behalf of the ingroup in an intergroup negotiation (e.g., sent more competitive messages to the opposing group representative, made higher demands during negotiation; bought and recalled more information to benefit the ingroup) than prototypical and/or nonvisible non-prototypical group members. Feeling non-prototypical and as if one's actions are visible to peers increases peoples' efforts and willingness to engage in behaviors that advance a valued ingroup.

Previous research also suggests that belief in prospective acceptance is a moderator of non-prototypical members' pro-ingroup behavior (Goldman & Hogg, 2016; Jetten et al., 2003). Goldman and Hogg (2016) found that non-prototypical members who felt that their future acceptance into the group was likely, demonstrated stronger intent and support for extreme intergroup behaviors. Additional work contends that when non-prototypical group members believe that it is possible and easy to gain ingroup acceptance, they tend to demonstrate more loyalty, enhanced motivation to work harder for the ingroup, and increased willingness to engage in extreme and aggressive intergroup behaviors to benefit the ingroup (Jetten et al., 2003).

Collectively, previous work on peripheral group status suggests that feeling non-prototypical is aversive and motivates actions to reestablish oneself as a prototypical group member. Prototypical status is desirable because it offers a satisfactory definition of self-identity. Members who recognize themselves as central members within the ingroup are granted with a greater understanding of who they are, as prescribed by the ingroup prototype. In contrast, non-prototypical group status inhibits a clear group-based definition of self-identity, thus increasing uncertainty surrounding the self. Previous work has theorized that uncertainty surrounding one's group-based self-identity (self-uncertainty) may serve as the underlying motivational reasoning as to why non-prototypical members perform group behaviors to attain prototypical status (Hohman et al., 2017).

Prototypicality Threat and Uncertainty

Unlike those who closely approximate the ingroup prototype, non-prototypical group members are not afforded a clear definition of who they are as group members. Vagueness surrounding self-identity within a group context manufactured by non-prototypical status elicits self-uncertainty and motivates behaviors to redefine self-identity (e.g., ingroup identification, ingroup bias). This line of reasoning was theorized and investigated by Hohman et al. (2017), exploring self-uncertainty as a motivational process explaining the relationship between peripheral status and group behavior across three experiments. Experiment 1 randomly assigned participants to feel prototypical or non-prototypical of their group (a.k.a. prototypicality threat) and then measured self-uncertainty. Results demonstrated that participants who were made to feel non-prototypical indicated greater endorsement for items of a self-uncertainty measure than participants in the prototypical condition. Experiment 2 manipulated both prototypicality threat and self-uncertainty, and measured ingroup identification. There was a marginal difference in ingroup identification between those in the prototypical and non-prototypical conditions—evidence suggested that non-prototypical participants demonstrated slightly more ingroup identification than prototypical participants. This effect was qualified by self-uncertainty. Non-prototypical participants who were made to feel uncertain demonstrated more ingroup identification than those who were assigned to the low uncertainty condition. Self-uncertainty did not impact prototypical participants' identification with the ingroup. Moreover, Experiment 3 demonstrated that peripheral group status and high self-uncertainty led to increased ingroup bias (and this effect was mediated by ingroup identification). Overall, this work demonstrates that feeling peripheral in a group leads to increased self-uncertainty, ingroup identification, and ingroup bias.

The results of Hohman et al.'s (2017) research illuminate the consequences of feeling non-prototypical for self-definition. This work provides a crucial linking of the prototypicality threat and self-uncertainty literatures, illustrating that the motivations for group behavior stemming from prototypicality threat can be explained by self-uncertainty. The mediating role of self-uncertainty has been conceptually replicated in subsequent work (Kuljian, 2023; Kuljian et al., 2023), and demonstrates that those who are distant from the identity-defining prototype of an important ingroup tend to experience self-uncertainty and are motivated to resolve such uncertainty.

Self-Uncertainty

Uncertainty is a prevalent part of life and people encounter uncertainty within a range of domains (e.g., moving across the country, entering a new job, concern for a global future). Some forms of uncertainty can be exciting and even positively valanced, provided one feels that they are equipped with the necessary tools to tackle the source of uncertainty (Hogg, 2015). With "positive" forms of uncertainty, people may view obstacles instead as challenges—opportunities to rise to the occasion and to gain mastery (Anderson et al., 2019; Hogg & Adelman, 2013; Hogg, 2015). However, forms of uncertainty that draw into question one's own capabilities, social standing, and identity may instead produce stress and anxiety (Brown et al. 2021). People view uncertainty as threatening when they feel that they do not have sufficient tools or resources for which to resolve such uncertainty (Hogg, 2007). Existential forms of uncertainty, as detailed within the terror management perspective in Chapter 12 (Landau et al., this volume), are deeply uncomfortable and motivate efforts for resolution through a variety of means, such as bolstering one's cultural worldview. The research covered in Chapter 7 describes that experiencing disruption in one's self-concept and possible self-goals, for example, through a break-up or loss of group identity, elicits uncertainty (Carroll et al., this volume). Moreover, Chapter 19 demonstrates that experiencing conflicts in one's personal identities and beliefs can cast doubts on one's "true identity" (Rios & Morales, this volume).

Of all forms of uncertainty, uncertainty surrounding the self is particularly aversive (Hogg, 2007, 2021). People are motivated to reduce self-uncertainty to define self-identity, improve predictions about others and their environment, and understand their place within the world (Hogg, 2007, 2021). Uncertainty identity theory posits that identification with a valued social group serves as a powerful way to reduce uncertainty about the self (Hogg, 2000, 2007, 2012, 2015, 2021). Through the identification process, people cognitively represent their social world in terms of categorical group memberships composed of group boundaries and idealistic prototypes (Turner et al., 1987). Group prototypes offer prescriptive definitions of group membership that provide members with a clear structure for their thoughts, actions, and behaviors. Having a prescribed definition of how to operate and understand oneself effectively reduces self-referential uncertainty (Hogg, 2021). Knowing oneself as part of a collective not only reduces uncertainty about the self but also uncertainty about others. Understanding others in terms of their group memberships allows people to make predictions about how others will likely behave (Hogg, 2007). Moreover, identification with a group offers a sense of inclusion, acceptance, shared reality, mutual understanding, and validation of worldviews that serve to further reduce uncertainty (Hogg, 2015; Hogg & Rinella, 2018). Considering the benefits of ingroup membership for understanding the self, people strive to maintain a clear and positive social identity through their ingroup. As such, previous research has primarily constructed operationalizations, measures, and manipulations of self-uncertainty on the basis of group membership and one's place within the social world.

Self-uncertainty Measures and Manipulations

Measured Self-Uncertainty

Established measures of self-uncertainty primarily reference uncertainty about one's collective identity, as uncertainty surrounding one's group is projected to have the strongest relationship with group identification and group behaviors (Hogg & Mahajan, 2018). While the number of items and content within items vary slightly, the measures demonstrate moderate to high internal consistency and ask participants to report on their certainty or uncertainty regarding aspects of themselves, their relationships, their future, or their beliefs. For example, the items present within Grant and Hogg's (2012) 8-item measure (α =.87,.95), Hogg et al.'s (2007) 9-item measure (α =.93; adapted from social identity work; Hains et al., 1997; Hogg & Hains, 1996; Hogg et al., 1998), and Hohman and Hogg's (2015) 12-item measure (α =.68; adapted from a self-concept clarity scale; Campbell, 1990; Campbell et al., 1996), involve themes of what kind of person one is, how one's understanding of the self may fluctuate, and uncertainty for future conceptions of the self. However, as with many forms of written response assessments, these measures are vulnerable to self-presentational concerns, the ability to accurately report one's feelings and motivations, and other self-report errors and biases.

Recent work has investigated physiological markers of self-uncertainty, which may serve to alleviate concerns surrounding self-report and offer continuous monitoring of self-uncertainty-linked processes (Brown et al., 2021). As detailed in Chapter 14 (McGregor & Marigold, this volume), threats that induce uncertainty can activate behavioral systems designed to increase physiological arousal and direct attention to resources to reduce uncertainty (see also, Jonas et al., 2014). A variety of studies offer additional support and demonstrate that increased physiological arousal, such as elevated skin conductance and heart rate, accompanies increased self-uncertainty (e.g., Brown et al., 2021; Eisenbarth et al., 2016; Niedbala et al., 2018). Measuring physiological stress and arousal responses such as skin conductance and heart rate may allow future research to continuously evaluate self-uncertainty correlates across a multitude of group contexts and threats. As well, future work may evaluate other possible biological markers of uncertainty, such as cortisol or alpha-amylase (both biological markers of stress, e.g., see Niedbala et al., 2018).

Manipulated Self-Uncertainty

Self-uncertainty has largely been manipulated in past and present research using a writing prime (e.g., Grant & Hogg, 2012; Hogg et al., 2007; Hohman & Hogg, 2015; Hohman et al., 2017; Hogg & Mahajan, 2018). The writing prime instructs participants to, "take a few minutes to think about the aspects in your life that make you feel the most uncertain about yourself, your future, or your place in the world. Then please list/write three of those below" (Hohman et al., 2017). The writing prime may also be presented to participants in a measurement format to assess self-uncertainty regarding specific personal domains (Choi & Hogg, 2020).

Grant and Hogg's (2012) work demonstrated supporting evidence for an additional manipulation of self-uncertainty, adapted from previous work (Hogg et al., 2007; Hogg et al., 2010). The manipulation involves asking participants to read a news article and underline words or sentences that make them experience uncertainty in reference to themselves, their place in the world, or their future (also see, Hohman et al., 2010).

Additional manipulations, such as Schuit and Hogg's (1999) manipulation of subjective uncertainty, present participants with a difficult task designed to threaten performance in a self-relevant domain (e.g., performance on the given task) (see also Reid & Hogg, 2005; Grieve & Hogg, 1999). Such manipulations appear to be less commonly used in present literature, as uncertainty manipulations that speak directly to uncertainty about the self in one's social world (e.g., the written uncertainty prime) may be more relevant for investigating collective self-uncertainty.

The development of uncertainty manipulations has allowed researchers to experimentally investigate the motivations and outcomes of those who experience self-uncertainty. People who feel self-uncertain tend to be driven to pursue certainty surrounding their ingroup identity (Hogg, 2007) and may do so through a variety of group behaviors that clarify and bolster their status as an ingroup member.

Consequences of Self-Uncertainty

Experiencing uncertainty about who one is within a complex social world motivates actions to resolve self-referential uncertainty (Hogg, 2007). Feeling as if one is on the fringes of an important group and unable to define identity by referencing the ingroup prototype is an especially intense form of uncertainty that motivates group behavior (Hogg, 2021; Hohman et al., 2017; Wagoner & Hogg, 2016). A myriad of previous research, including both measured and manipulated self-uncertainty, illustrates that increased self-uncertainty relates to increased ingroup identification (for a meta-analysis, see Choi & Hogg, 2020). Understanding oneself through ingroup identification offers an avenue for enhanced self-definition and uncertainty reduction. However, research also suggests that feeling uncertain about the self may motivate additional behaviors to promote oneself as an established group member and enhance group membership. Behaviors, such as working harder on behalf of the ingroup, may be especially helpful to those who feel uncertain in response to prototypicality threat, as pro-ingroup actions provide an avenue to establish oneself as a legitimate and central group member. Such behaviors may occur within the group (intragroup behaviors) as well as directed towards relevant outgroups (intergroup behaviors).

Motivated Intragroup Behavior

INGROUP IDENTIFICATION

Previous research offers extensive detail for the relationship between self-uncertainty and ingroup identification (Choi & Hogg, 2020). When people feel uncertain about their personal identity and where they stand as ingroup members, they tend to bolster their ingroup identification and alignment with group norms, as the ingroup serves as a source of reference to construct and enhance self-definition (Hogg, 2007; Smith et al., 2007). Uncertainty moderates the self-categorization process, such that those who self-categorize as part of the ingroup under uncertainty demonstrate more ingroup identification and ingroup bias (Grieve & Hogg, 1999). Moreover, those high in uncertainty tend to be especially willing to strengthen identification with highly prominent identities (e.g., national identities; Grant & Hogg, 2012), demonstrating that uncertainty drives identification with groups that are central to the self and distinctive from other personal identities. Group identities that have high personal relevance, are focalized, and maintain distinctiveness from other personal identities provide a clear sense of identity to those experiencing self-uncertainty (Grant & Hogg, 2012).

IDENTIFICATION WITH ENTITATIVE GROUPS

The conception that distinctive and focal identities should moderate the relationship between uncertainty and group identification was formed out of group entitativity literature. Entitativity describes the qualities of groups that maintain a high degree of distinctiveness from other groups and member cohesiveness. Groups that are highly entitative have clear conditions for membership as well as common attributes, goals, and outcomes among members (Campbell, 1958; Hamilton & Sherman, 1996). Highly entitative groups provide members with clear guidelines for constructing social identity, thus identification with a highly entitative group is a particularly effective path for uncertainty reduction (Hogg, 2004). Hogg et al. (2007) found support for this rationale through two studies, demonstrating that participants who were primed to feel highly uncertain reported increased identification as a function of increased ingroup entitativity. Additional research consistently demonstrates the positive relationship between uncertainty and group entitativity on group identification, suggesting that people experiencing high self-uncertainty are motivated to identify with highly entitative groups to construct their group-referenced self-identity (e.g., Jetten et al., 2000; Yzerbyt et al., 2000).

Research conducted by Brown and colleagues (2021) suggests that identifying with a highly entitative group is indeed fruitful for uncertainty reduction. Brown et al. (2021) used markers of physiological arousal throughout their study to indirectly measure uncertainty. Following a written uncertainty manipulation, participants in the high uncertainty condition demonstrated elevated arousal and stress responses that were indicative of a physiological response to uncertainty. Next, participants read a vignette that either painted their ingroup as high or low in entitativity. Participants who identified with a highly entitative group experienced sharper decreases in the physiological responses to uncertainty than participants who identified with a group that was described to be lower in entitativity. Overall, this work demonstrates that identification with a highly entitative group reduces uncertainty.

Additional support for the link between self-uncertainty and ingroup entitativity can be found in research on extremist groups. Radical and extremist groups often contain a strong sense of unity, strict requirements for membership, a clear internal structure, and strong leaders who embody and dictate the ideal attributes of the group prototype (Hogg et al., 2010). These groups offer clear guidelines for who one is and how one should act—desirable directions for those experiencing self-uncertainty. Moreover, radical and extremist groups possess strong potential for action and often go to great lengths to achieve group-based goals (Hogg et al., 2010). Identification with a group that is capable of combating threats and raising the status of its members may be especially attractive for highly uncertain individuals. Indeed, Hogg et al. (2010) found that participants who were primed to feel highly uncertain demonstrated more identification with groups that possessed radical motives than for groups that offered more moderate positions. However, to date, the impact of prototypicality threat on the relationship between uncertainty and identification with radical groups remains underinvestigated. Future research should investigate the interactive role between prototypicality threat and self-uncertainty on support for radical groups, as such groups often offer a strong and highly entitative basis for constructing social identity.

If highly uncertain individuals perceive that a valued ingroup is low in entitativity, they tend to engage in behaviors aimed at bolstering the entitativity of the ingroup (Sherman et al., 2009). For example, Schmitt and Branscombe (2001) demonstrated that prototypicality threat motivates members' efforts to derogate other non-prototypical members. Non-prototypical group members threaten the entitativity of a group, as their membership threatens ingroup homogeneity and obfuscates the boundaries between the ingroup and relevant outgroups. Non-prototypical members may combat their marginal group status and clarify their group identity by derogating other non-prototypical members, thus strengthening the entitativity of a valued ingroup. Because self-identities are inextricably linked with group identities (Hogg & Reid, 2006), behaviors that bring clarity to the ingroup identity also serve to reduce uncertainty about the self (Hogg, 2007; see also Kuljian, 2023). Moreover, performing behaviors that advance ingroup entitativity can signal one's value as a qualified group member and reduce uncertainty surrounding membership status. Future research should continue to explore the role of prototypicality threat in conjunction with self-uncertainty for entitativity-bolstering behaviors. Those who feel non-prototypical and self-uncertain may be motivated to enhance ingroup entitativity as a way to clarify the ingroup prototype and justify their membership as central group members who uphold the important norms and qualities of the ingroup.

In sum, highly uncertain group members display motivations to clarify their social identity by identifying with highly entitative groups, or by strengthening the entitativity of their ingroup. Identification with a highly entitative ingroup offers members a prescriptive recipe for defining social identity and reducing self-uncertainty. Those under uncertainty may also perform behaviors that clarify and strengthen ingroup identity through additional avenues, such as promoting leaders that define and advance the ingroup.

LEADERSHIP SUPPORT

Leaders are central figureheads of a group—they embody and represent the ideal qualities of ingroup membership (Hogg, 2001; Reicher & Hopkins, 1996). Group members under uncertainty strive to support leadership styles that clearly define ingroup attributes and thus strengthen self-identity (Hogg, 2001). Previous work illustrates that those experiencing high uncertainty demonstrate increased support for extremist leadership, particularly autocratic leaders who dictate unambiguous norms for group behavior and qualities of the ingroup prototype (Rast et al., 2013). Of note, uncertainty also appears to drive general support for group leadership, as even leaders who are low in prototypicality receive support from group members when members experience high uncertainty (Rast et al., 2012; see also Gaffney et al., 2018). This tendency to support even non-prototypical leaders when uncertain may reflect a desire to strengthen the ingroup identity by any means necessary (e.g., an atypical new leader may offer innovative solutions to advance the ingroup; Hogg, 2021). However, additional research is needed to understand why uncertain individuals support non-prototypical leaders.

As well, future work may examine the relationship between self-uncertainty and preferential leadership support among non-prototypical *members*. Non-prototypical, uncertain group members may be more inclined to support prototypical leaders who represent and dictate the ingroup prototype than non-prototypical leaders. Prototypical leaders offer non-prototypical members a clear reference point for which to align with the ingroup prototype, attain prototypical status, and reduce self-uncertainty. Moreover, non-prototypical members who experience self-uncertainty may be expressly concerned with enhancing their ingroup identity by backing highly efficacious, even extremist leaders who are capable of advancing the ingroup identity above that of relevant outgroups (Rast et al., 2013).

Whereas leaders can reduce members' self-uncertainty by bringing definition to group membership, leadership processes can also increase uncertainty ingroup members. Kuljian et al. (2023) explored the consequences of losing a prototype-defining leader for group members' conceptions of self-prototypicality and self-uncertainty. When leaders fall from their position of power and influence, for example, due to the course of a national election, their exit is accompanied by the loss of an accessible portrayal of the current ingroup prototype. As a consequence, followers may experience lowered self-prototypicality and increased self-uncertainty as they question their representativeness and identity in reference to an unclear prototype. Across two studies that used longitudinal data and separate measures to assess pre- and post-election perceptions, Kuljian et al. (2023) found that Republicans, whose leader (Donald Trump) lost the 2020 election, viewed Trump as a less prototypical Republican post-election. This effect was not present for Democrat participants, whose leader, Joe Biden, won the election. Results demonstrated that lowered perceptions of one's leader's prototypicality related to lowered perceptions of self-prototypicality, which in turn related to increased self-uncertainty. Future work may investigate downstream consequences of self-uncertainty resulting from the loss of a political leader. Heightened uncertainty accompanying the loss of defining leadership may motivate members to define and strengthen ingroup and self-identity through other outlets, such as extreme intra and inter-group behavior.

Groups and the leaders that head them offer powerful prescriptive definitions for self-identity (Hogg, 2001). Thus, contexts that threaten the ingroup identity such as deviant ingroup members (Schmitt & Branscombe, 2001) or the loss of the ingroup leader (Kuljian et al., 2023) create uncertainty and inspire action to enhance the ingroup identity. Highly uncertain individuals are motivated to strengthen their identification with groups that are best served at reducing uncertainty, as well as bolstering aspects of groups that enhance the clarity of group membership (e.g., Kuljian, 2023; Sherman et al., 2009; Schmitt & Branscombe, 2001). Whereas such behaviors may be performed within the ingroup (e.g., selecting an autocratic leader), people may also perform intergroup-directed behaviors that advance the ingroup over relevant outgroups.

Motivated Intergroup Behavior

Within the social world, group-referenced identities do not exist within a social vacuum—identities are composed not only of shared ingroup qualities but also of the categorical boundaries between the ingroup and relevant outgroups and the attributes that distance *us* from *them* (Hogg, 2004). The processes involved in the construction of a socially referenced self-identity and resulting consequences for behavior thus vary as a function of the intergroup context. Those who feel self-uncertain may be especially motivated to strengthen and uplift the ingroup identity in an intergroup context to clarify and construct a positive image of the self. In the presence of close outgroups, uncertain individuals can generate a positive and distinct self-identity by aligning closely with the ingroup prototype and distancing themselves from the prototypes of relevant outgroups.

POLARIZATION

Group prototypes that define the self and social identities in an intergroup context are structured to emphasize within-group similarities and between-group differences (the metacontrast principle; Oakes, 1987; Turner, 1985). As a result, ingroup prototypes are often polarized to distance the ingroup from the content and positions of relevant outgroup prototypes (Abrams et al., 1990). Research conducted by Hogg et al. (1990) demonstrates the dynamic nature of ingroup prototypes. When confronted with an outgroup that promoted risk, participants polarized their opinions away from the outgroup and converged on a contrasting ingroup prototype that promoted caution. When participants were presented with an outgroup that endorsed caution, the resulting ingroup prototype was polarized toward risk. Given the power that social identities, prototypes, and norms hold for reducing uncertainty (Hogg, 2007, 2021) coupled with uncertain individuals' motivations to align with ingroup norms (Smith et al., 2007), those who feel highly self-uncertain may further contribute to intergroup polarization (Sherman et al., 2009). To investigate this line of reasoning, Gaffney et al. (2014) examined the impact of self-uncertainty on support for political positions that polarized a partisan ingroup identity away from relevant political outgroups. Republicans who were primed with self-uncertainty and exposed to an intergroup context exhibited the most support for an extremist far-right message, as compared to Republicans who were exposed to a self-certainty prime and/or an intragroup context. For uncertain group members, supporting a polarizing, pro-norm message is alluring—it maximizes the differences between the positions of the ingroup and the outgroup and clarifies social identity. The clarification of group-referenced self-identity offered by polarization may be especially attractive to non-prototypical group members. Those who feel highly uncertain by way of prototypicality threat may demonstrate increased motivations to polarize their thoughts and opinions away from relevant outgroups as a strategy to increase proximity to the ingroup prototype. Members' prototypicality often varies within groups, thus future work needs to investigate the consequences of non-prototypical membership status for self-uncertainty and polarization.

PRO-INGROUP BEHAVIOR

Additional work contends that feeling self-uncertain motivates behaviors to clarify, benefit, and differentiate one's ingroup within an intergroup context. For example, when people categorize and identify as group members under uncertainty, they tend to demonstrate enhanced preference and bias for their ingroup over relevant outgroups. Previous work has evaluated the positive relationship between self-uncertainty and ingroup bias, with bias taking form as the preference for positive over negative descriptions of the ingroup (Hohman et al., 2017) or the preferential allocation of points or resources to the ingroup (Grieve & Hogg, 1999; Mullin & Hogg, 1998).

In addition to ingroup bias, uncertainty may also inspire extreme forms of intergroup behavior. Recent data collected by Kuljian (2023) offer initial evidence for the relationship between self-uncertainty and extreme pro-ingroup behavioral intentions. Results of a path analysis demonstrated that concerns surrounding the clarity of group-level qualities contributed to lowered perceptions of self-prototypicality, which related to increased self-uncertainty. In turn, increased self-uncertainty related to increased motivations to fight or die for the ingroup. The fight-or-die intentions assessment consists of items that represent an extreme form of motivated group behavior: participants are asked to indicate their willingness to fight, gain revenge, and hurt outgroup members in defense of the ingroup, as well as their willingness to sacrifice their own life for the benefit of the ingroup (Swann et al., 2009). The results parallel research covered within Chapter 13 (Paredes et al., this volume), which demonstrates that individuals who feel an intense alignment with their ingroup (identity fusion) tend to display a greater willingness to fight or die for their ingroup. Relevant to Kuljian (2023), threats to one's ingroup identity and resulting concerns for self-prototypicality may increase self-uncertainty and motivate intentions to defend the ingroup identity at nearly any cost.

Results echo additional work that investigates the role of uncertainty in intergroup relations; for example, research conducted by Hogg and Adelman (2013) investigated measured and manipulated uncertainty within the context of the Israeli-Palestinian conflict. For surveyed Palestinian Muslims and Israeli Jews, national identification and self-uncertainty moderated support for violent war tactics, such that participants who strongly identified with their national identity and felt highly self-uncertain demonstrated the strongest support for extreme military practices. Further work regarding perceptions of immigrants and refugees offers evidence that uncertainty promoted by media sources may contribute to the dehumanization of such targets (Esses et al., 2013). As well, Niedbala and Hohman (2019), demonstrated that outgroup threats produce uncertainty and enhance group members' willingness to retaliate against the threatening outgroup as a strategy to strengthen the ingroup identity and reduce uncertainty.

The influence of self-uncertainty on extreme intergroup behavior and perceptions, coupled with uncertainty-spurred motivations to identify with the extremist groups and leaders that are capable of acting on such views and intentions, elicits concern. World events that threaten people's cultural identities, health, and safety may spark self-relevant uncertainty and inspire extreme action. As detailed in Chapter 8, uncertainty tends to elicit more extreme reactions to unfair circumstances and perceived injustice (van den Bos & Lind, this volume), which may contribute to intensified intergroup relations and collective action tendencies. In addition to group-level threats, threats to individuals' prototypical status within the group may also intensify the consequences of uncertainty. Non-prototypical members who experience self-uncertainty and strive to be accepted by their group may be more willing to engage in extreme behavior on behalf of their ingroup (e.g., Kuljian, 2023). Building off of work conducted by Kuljian (2023) and Niedbala and Hohman (2019), future work should examine how threats to individuals' group membership coupled with threats to the group as a whole contribute to group behavior. Those who feel self-uncertainty due to prototypicality and outgroup-based threats may be more likely to act in ways that retaliate against the outgroup (e.g., Niedbala & Hohman, 2019), derogate and dehumanize outgroup members (e.g., Esses et al., 2013), or act in self-sacrifice for the ingroup (e.g., Kuljian, 2023).

Conclusion

Across the world, the tides of uncertainty appear to be rising. The development of global conflicts, extremist social agendas, and exclusive social practices incite speculation about where one stands within a valued social group and impacts conceptions of self-identity. A diverse set of experimental and longitudinal research demonstrates the impact of non-prototypical membership status on self-definition and uncertainty, as well as the consequences for intra- and intergroup behaviors. The studies covered within this chapter involve a wide variety of methodologies, manipulations, and measures that illustrate the consequences of feeling non-prototypical on identity conception and resulting motivations. In an attempt to rectify feeling uncertain about one's ingroup and oneself, people may engage in a host of group behaviors—ranging from favoring positive perceptions of the ingroup to the justification of extreme acts of violence committed against outgroup members. Such actions can serve to satiate prototypicality and uncertainty concerns by enhancing one's status with the ingroup and providing increased clarity to one's social identity, but come at the cost of harshened outgroup perceptions, intensified intergroup relations, and personal self-sacrifices.

References

Abrams, D., & Hogg, M. A. (1990). Social identification, self-categorization, and social influence. *European Review of Social Psychology*, *1*(1), 195–228. https://doi.org/10.1080/14792779108401862

Abrams, D., & Hogg, M. A. (2010). Social identity and self-categorization. In J. F. Dovidio, M. Hewstone, P. Glick, & V. M. Esses (Eds.), *The SAGE handbook of prejudice, stereotyping, and discrimination* (pp. 179–193). SAGE. https://doi.org/10.4135/9781446200919.n11

Anderson, E. C., Carleton, R. N., Diefenbach, M., & Han, P. K. J. (2019). The relationship between uncertainty and affect. *Frontiers in Psychology*, *10*, Article e2504. https://doi.org/10.3389/fpsyg.2019.02504

Brown, J. K., Hohman, Z. P., Niedbala, E. M., & Stinnett, A. J. (2021). Sweating the big stuff: Arousal and stress as functions of self-uncertainty and identification. *Psychophysiology*, *58*(8). Article e13836. https://doi.org/10.1111/psyp.13836

Burris, C. T., & Jackson, L. M. (2010). Social identity and the true believer: Responses to threatened self-stereotypes among the intrinsically religious. *British Journal of Social Psychology*, *39*(2), 257–278. https://doi.org/10.1348/014466600164462

Campbell, D. T. (1958). Common fate, similarity, and other indices of the status of aggregates of persons as social entities. *Behavioral Science*, *3*(1), 14–25. https://doi.org/10.1002/bs.3830030103

Campbell, J. D. (1990). Self-esteem and clarity of the self-concept. *Journal of Abnormal and Social Psychology*, *59*(3), 538–549. https://psycnet.apa.org/doi/10.1037/0022-3514.59.3.538

Campbell, J. D., Trapnell, P. D., Heine, S. J., Katz, I. M., Lavallee, L. F., & Lehman, D. R. (1996). Self-concept clarity: Measurement, personality correlates, and cultural boundaries. *Journal of Personality and Social Psychology*, *70*(1), 141–156. https://psycnet.apa.org/doi/10.1037/0022-3514.70.1.141

Choi, E. U., & Hogg, M. A. (2020): Self-uncertainty and group identification: A meta-analysis. *Group Processes and Intergroup Relations*, *23*(4), 483–501. https://doi.org/10.1177/1368430219846990

Eisenbarth, H., Chang, L. J., & Wager, T. D. (2016). Multivariate brain prediction of heart rate and skin conductance responses to social threat. *Journal of Neuroscience*, *36*(47), 11987–11998. https://doi.org/10.1523/JNEUROSCI.3672-15.2016

Esses, V. M., Medianu, S., Lawson, A. S. (2013). Uncertainty, threat, and the role of the media in promoting the dehumanization of immigrants and refugees. *Journal of Social Issues*, *69*(23), 518–536. https://doi.org/10.1111/josi.12027

Gaffney, A. M., Rast, D. E. III., Hackett, J. D., & Hogg, M. A. (2014). Further to the right: Uncertainty, political polarization and the American "Tea Party" movement. *Social Influence*, *9*(4), 272–288. https://doi.org/10.1080/15534510.2013.842495

Gaffney, A. M., Rast, D. E., III., & Hogg, M. A. (2018). Uncertainty and influence: The advantages (and disadvantages) of being atypical. *Journal of Social Issues*, *74*(1), 20–35. https://doi.org/10.1111/josi.12254

Giessner, S. R., & van Knippenberg, D. (2008). "License to fail": Goal definition, leader group proto- typicality, and perceptions of leadership effectiveness after leader failure. *Organizational Behavior and Human Decision Processes, 105,* 14–35. https://doi.org/10.1016/j.obhdp.2007.04.002

Goldman, L., & Hogg, M. A. (2016). Going to extremes for one's group: The role of prototypicality and group acceptance. *Journal of Applied Social Psychology*, *46*(9), 544–553. https://doi.org/10.1111/jasp.12382

Gómez, Á., Jetten, J., & Swann, W. B., Jr. (2014). The more prototypical the better? The allure of being seen as one sees oneself. *Group Processes and Intergroup Relations*, *17*(2), 221–239. https://doi.org/10.1177/1368430213510570

Grant, F., & Hogg, M. A. (2012). Self-uncertainty, social identity prominence, and group identification. *Journal of Experimental Social Psychology*, *48*(2), 538–542. https://doi.org/10.1016/j.jesp.2011.11.006

Grieve, P. G., & Hogg, M. A. (1999). Subjective uncertainty and intergroup discrimination in the minimal group situation. *Personality and Social Psychology Bulletin*, *25*(8), 926–940. https://doi.org/10.1177/01461672992511002

Hamilton, D. L., & Sherman, S. J. (1996). Perceiving persons and groups. *Psychological Review*, *103*(2), 336–355. https://psycnet.apa.org/doi/10.1037/0033-295X.103.2.336

Hains, S. C., Hogg, M. A., & Duck, J. M. (1997). Self-categorization and leadership: Effects of group prototypicality and leader stereotypicality. *Personality and Social Psychology Bulletin, 23*(10), 1087–1100. https://psycnet.apa.org/doi/10.1177/01461672972310009

Hoffman, P., Platow, M. J., Read, E., Mansfield, T., Carron-Arthur, B., & Stanton, M. (2020). Perceived self-in-group prototypicality enhances the benefits of social identification for psychological well-being. *Group Dynamics: Theory, Research, and Practice*, *24*(4), 213–226. https://doi.org/10.1037/gdn0000119

Hogg, M. A. (2000). Subjective uncertainty reduction through self-categorization: A motivational theory of social identity processes. *European Review of Social Psychology*, *11*(1), 223–255. https://doi.org/10.1080/14792772043000040

Hogg, M. A. (2001). A social identity theory of leadership. *Personality and Social Psychology Review*, *5*(3), 184–200. https://doi.org/10.1207/S15327957PSPR0503_1

Hogg, M. A. (2004). Uncertainty and extremism: Identification with high entitativity groups under conditions of uncertainty. In V. Yzerbyt, C. M. Judd, & O. Corneille (Eds.), *The psychology of group perception: Perceived variability, entitativity, and essentialism* (pp. 401–418). Psychology Press.

Hogg, M. A. (2005). Uncertainty, social identity and ideology. In S. R. Thye & E. J. Lawler (Eds.), *Advances in group processes* (Vol. 22, pp. 203–230). Elsevier.

Hogg, M. A. (2007). Uncertainty-identity theory. In M. P. Zanna (Ed.), *Advances in experimental social psychology* (Vol. 39, pp. 69–126). Elsevier Academic Press. https://doi.org/10.1016/S0065-2601(06)39002-8

Hogg, M. A. (2012). Uncertainty-identity theory. In P. A. M. Van Lange, A. W. Kruglanski, & E. T. Higgins (Eds.), *Handbook of theories of social psychology* (Vol. 2, pp. 62–80). Thousand Oaks, CA: Sage.

Hogg, M. A. (2015). To belong or not to belong: Some self-conceptual and behavioural consequences of identity uncertainty. *Revista de Psicologia Social*, *30*(3), 586–613. https://doi.org/10.1080/02134748.2015.1065090

Hogg, M. A. (2021). Self-uncertainty and group identification: Consequences for social identity, group behavior, intergroup relations, and society. *Advances in Experimental Social Psychology*, *64*, 236–316. https://doi.org/10.1016/bs.aesp.2021.04.004

Hogg, M. A., & Adelman, J. (2013). Uncertainty-identity theory: Extreme groups, radical behavior, and authoritarian leadership. *Journal of Social Issues*, 69(3), 436–454. https://psycnet.apa.org/doi/10.1111/josi.12023

Hogg, M. A., & Hains, S. C. (1996). Intergroup relations and group solidarity: Effects of group identification and social beliefs on depersonalized attraction. *Journal of Personality and Social Psychology, 70*(2), 295– 309. https://psycnet.apa.org/doi/10.1037/0022-3514.70.2.295

Hogg, M. A., Hains, S. C., & Mason, I. (1998). Identification and leadership in small groups: Salience, frame of reference, and leader stereotypicality effects on leader evaluations. *Journal of Personality and Social Psychology, 75*(5), 1248–1263. https://psycnet.apa.org/doi/10.1037/0022-3514.75.5.1248

Hogg, M. A., & Hardie, E. A. (1991). Social attraction, personal attraction, and self-categorization: A field study. *Personality and Social Psychology Bulletin*, *17*(2), 175–180. https://psycnet.apa.org/doi/10.1177/0146167291017002009

Hogg, M. A., & Mahajan, N. (2018). Domains of self-uncertainty and their relationship to group identification. *Journal of Theoretical Social Psychology*, *2*(3), 67–75. https://doi.org/10.1002/jts5.20

Hogg, M. A., Meehan, C., & Farquharson, J. (2010). The solace of radicalism: Self-uncertainty and group identification in the face of threat. *Journal of Experimental Social Psychology*, *46*(6), 1061–1066. https://doi.org/10.1016/j.jesp.2010.05.005

Hogg, M. A., & Reid, S. A. (2006). Social identity, self-categorization, and the communication of group norms. *Communication Theory*, *16*(1), 7–30. https://doi.org/10.1111/j.1468-2885.2006.00003.x

Hogg, M. A., & Rinella, M. J. (2018). Social identities and shared realities. *Current Opinion in Psychology*, *23*(1), 6–10. https://doi.org/ 10.1016/j.copsyc.2017.10.003

Hogg, M. A., Sherman, D. K., Dierselhuis, J., Maitner, A. T., & Moffitt, G. (2007). Uncertainty, entitativity, and group identification. *Journal of Experimental Social Psychology*, *43*(1), 135–142. https://doi.org/10.1016/j.jesp.2005.12.008

Hogg, M. A., & Turner, J. C. (1987). Social identity and conformity: A theory of referent informational influence. In W. Doise & S. Moscovici (Eds.), *Current issues in European social psychology* (Vol. 2, pp. 139–182). Cambridge University Press.

Hogg, M. A., Turner, J. C., & Davidson, B. (1990). Polarized norms and social frames of reference: A test of the self-categorization theory of group polarization. *Basic and Applied Social Psychology*, *11*(1), 77–100. https://psycnet.apa.org/doi/10.1207/s15324834basp1101_6

Hohman, Z. P., Gaffney, A. M., & Hogg, M. A. (2017). Who am I if I am not like my group? Self-uncertainty and feeling peripheral in a group. *Journal of Experimental Social Psychology*, *72*(1), 125–132. https://doi.org/10.1016/j.jesp.2017.05.002

Hohman, Z. P., Hogg, M. A., & Bligh, M. C. (2010). Identity and intergroup leadership: Asymmetrical political and national identification in response to uncertainty. *Self and Identity*, *9*(2), 113–128. https://psycnet.apa.org/doi/10.1080/15298860802605937

Hohman, Z. P., & Hogg, M. A. (2015). Fearing the uncertain: Self-uncertainty plays a role in mortality salience. *Journal of Experimental Social Psychology*, *57*, 31–42. https://psycnet.apa.org/doi/10.1016/j.jesp.2014.11.007

Jetten, J., Branscombe, N., & Spears, R. (2002). On being peripheral: Effects of identity insecurity on personal and collective self-esteem. *European Journal of Social Psychology*, *32*(1), 105–123. https://doi.org/10.1002/ejsp.64

Jetten, J., Hogg, M. A., & Mullin, B.-A. (2000). In-group variability and motivation to reduce subjective uncertainty. *Group Dynamics: Theory, Research, and Practice*, *4*(2), 184–198. https://psycnet.apa.org/doi/10.1037/1089-2699.4.2.184

Jetten, M. T., Branscombe, N. R., Spears, R., & McKimmie, B. M. (2003). Predicting the paths of peripherals: The interaction of identification and future possibilities. *Personality and Social Psychology Bulletin*, *29*(1), 130–140. https://doi.org/10.1177/0146167202238378

Jonas, E., McGregor, I., Klackl, J., Agroskin, D., Fritsche, I., Holdbrook, C., Nash, K., Proulx, T., & Quirin, M. (2014). Chapter four – threat and defense: From anxiety to approach. *Advances in Experimental Social Psychology*, *49*, 219–286. https://doi.org/10.1016/B978-0-12-800052-6.00004-4

Kuljian, O. R. (2023). *Who are we? Who am I?! Ingroup prototype ambiguity and self-prototypicality, uncertainty, and ingroup identification* [Doctoral thesis, Texas Tech University]. Texas Tech University Libraries.

Kuljian, O. R., Hohman, Z. P., & Gaffney, A. M. (2023). Who am I if I do not know who my leader is? Perceptions of leaders' prototypicality affects followers' self-prototypicality and uncertainty. *Social Psychological and Personality Science*, *14*(5), 599–609. https://doi.org/10.1177/19485506221111237

McGarty, C., Turner, J. C., Hogg, M. A., David, B., & Wetherell, M. S. (1992). Group polarization as conformity to the prototypical group member. *British Journal of Social Psychology, 31,* 1–19. https://doi.org/10.1111/j.2044-8309.1992.tb00952.x

Mullin, B., & Hogg, M. A. (1998). Dimensions of subjective uncertainty in social identification and minimal intergroup discrimination. *British Journal of Social Psychology*, *37*(3), 345–365. https://doi.org/10.1111/j.2044-8309.1998.tb01176.x

Niedbala, E. M., Hohman, Z. P., Harris, B. N., & Abide, A. C. (2018). Taking one for the team: Physiological trajectories of painful intergroup retaliation. *Physiology and Behavior*, *194*(1), 277–284. https://doi.org/10.1016/j.physbeh.2018.06.011

Niedbala, E. M., & Hohman, Z. P. (2019). Retaliation again the outgroup: The role of self-uncertainty. *Group Processes and Intergroup Relations*, *22*(5), 708–723. https://doi.org/10.1177/1368430218767027

Noel, J. G., Wann, D. L., & Branscombe, N. R. (1995). Peripheral ingroup membership status and public negativity toward outgroups. *Journal of Personality and Social Psychology*, *68*(1), 127–137. https://psycnet.apa.org/doi/10.1037/0022-3514.68.1.127

Oakes, P. J. (1987). The salience of social categories. In J. C. Turner, M. A. Hogg, P. J. Oakes, S. D. Reicher, & M. S. Wetherell (Eds.), *Rediscovering the social group* (pp. 117–141). Blackwell.

Pickett, C. L., & Brewer, M. B. (2001) Assimilation and differentiation needs as motivational determinants of perceived in-group and out-group homogeneity. *Journal of Experimental Social Psychology*, *37*(4), 341–348. https://psycnet.apa.org/doi/10.1006/jesp.2000.1469

Platow, M. J., van Knippenberg, D., Haslam, S. A., van Knippenberg, B., & Spears, R. (2006). A special gift we bestow on you for being representative of us: Considering leader charisma from a self- categorization perspective. *British Journal of Social Psychology, 45,* 303–320. https://doi.org/10.1348/014466605X41986

Rast, D. E. III., Gaffney, A. M., Hogg, M. A., & Crisp, R. J. (2012). Leadership under uncertainty: When leaders who are non-prototypical group members can gain support. *Journal of Experimental Social Psychology*, *48*(3), 646–653. https://doi.org/10.1016/j.jesp.2011.12.013

Rast, D. E. III., Hogg, M. A., & Geissner, S. R. (2013). Self-uncertainty and support for autocratic leadership. *Self and Identity*, *12*(6), 635–649. https://doi.org/10.1080/15298868.2012.718864

Reicher, S. D., & Hopkins, N. (1996). Self-category constructions in political rhetoric: An analysis of Thatcher's and Kinnock's speeches concerning the British miners' strike (1984–5). *European Journal of Social Psychology*, *26*(3), 353–371. https://doi.org/10.1002/(SICI)1099-0992(199605)26:3%3C353::AID-EJSP757%3E3.0.CO;2-O

Sassenberg, K., Matschke, C., & Scholl, A. (2011). The impact of discrepancies from ingroup norms on group members' well-being and motivation. *European Journal of Social Psychology*, *41*(7), 886–897. https://doi.org/10.1002/ejsp.833

Schmitt, M. T., & Branscombe, N. R. (2001). The good, the bad, and the manly: Threats to one's prototypicality and evaluations of fellow in-group members. *Journal of Experimental Social Psychology*, *37*(6), 510–517. https://doi.org/10.1006/jesp.2001.1476

Schuit, R., & Hogg, M. A. (1999). *Subjective uncertainty reduction, social identification, and prototype construction*. Unpublished manuscript, University of Queensland, Queensland, Australia.

Sherman, D. K., Hogg, M. A., & Maitner, A. T. (2009). Perceived polarization: Reconciling ingroup and intergroup perceptions under uncertainty. *Group Processes and Intergroup Relations*, *12*(1), 95–109. https://doi.org/10.1177/1368430208098779

Smith, J. R., Hogg, M. A., Martin, R., & Terry, D. J. (2007). Uncertainty and the influence of group norms in the attitude-behavior relationship. *British Journal of Social Psychology*, *46*(4), 769–792. https://doi.org/10.1348/014466606X164439

Steinel, W., van Kleef, G. A., van Knippenberg, D., Hogg, M. A., Hohman, A. C. & Moffitt, G. (2010). How intragroup dynamics affect behavior in intergroup conflict: The role of group norms, prototypicality,

and need to belong. *Group Processes & Intergroup Relations*, *13*(6), 779–794. https://psycnet.apa.org/doi/10.1177/1368430210375702
Swann, W. B., Gómez, A., Seyle, D. C., Morales, J. F., & Huici, C. (2009). Identity fusion: The interplay of personal and social identities in extreme group behavior. *Journal of Personality and Social Psychology*, *96*(5), 995–1011. https://doi.org/10.1037/a0013668
Tajfel, H. (1959). Quantitative judgement in social perception. *British Journal of Psychology*, *50*, 16–29. https://psycnet.apa.org/doi/10.1111/j.2044-8295.1959.tb00677.x
Tajfel, H. (1972). Social categorization. English manuscript of 'La categorisation sociale.' In S. Moscovici (Ed.), introduction a la Psychologie Sociale (Vol. 1, pp. 272–302). Paris: Larousse.
Tajfel, H., & Turner, J. C. (1986). The social identity theory of intergroup behavior. In S. Worchel & W. G. Austin (Eds.), *Psychology of intergroup relations* (pp. 7–24). Nelson-Hall.
Tajfel, H., & Wilkes, A. L. (1963). Classification and quantitative judgement. *British Journal of Psychology*, *54*(2), 101–114. https://psycnet.apa.org/doi/10.1111/j.2044-8295.1963.tb00865.x
Turner, J. C. (1985). Social categorization and the self-concept: A social cognitive theory of group behaviour. In E. J. Lawler (Ed.), *Advances in group processes* (Vol. 2, pp. 77–122). JAI Press.
Turner, J. C. (1991). *Social influence*. Open University Press.
Turner, J. C., Hogg, M. A., Oakes, P. J., Reicher, S. D., & Wetherell, M. S. (1987). *Rediscovering the social group: A self-categorization theory*. Blackwell.
Turner, J. C., & Oakes, P. J. (1989). Self-categorization theory and social influence. In P. B. Paulus (Ed.), *The psychology of group influence* (2nd ed. pp. 233–275). Erlbaum.
Van Kleef, G. A., Steinel, W., Van Knippenberg, D., Hogg, M. A., & Svensson, A. (2011). Group member prototypicality and intergroup negotiation: How one's standing in the group affects negotiation behaviour. *British Journal of Social Psychology*, *46*(1), 129–152. https://doi.org/10.1348/014466605X89353
Van Kleef, G. A., Steinel, W., & Homan, A. C. (2013). On being peripheral and paying attention: Prototypicality and information processing in intergroup conflict. *Journal of Applied Psychology*, *98*(1), 63–79. https://doi.org/10.1037/a0030988
Wagoner, J. A., & Hogg, M. A. (2016). Uncertainty and group identification: Moderation by warmth and competence as cues to inclusion and identity validation. *Self and Identity*, *15*(5), 525–535. https://psycnet.apa.org/doi/10.1080/15298868.2016.1163284
Yzerbyt, V., Castano, E., Leyens, J., & Paladino, M. (2000). The primacy of the ingroup: The interplay of entitativity and identification. *European Review of Social Psychology*, *11*(1), 257–295. https://doi.org/10.1080/14792772043000059

15

THE UNCERTAINTY SURROUNDING OSTRACISM

A Systematic Review and Future Directions

Zhansheng Chen, Yunqian (Fiona) Tian, Andrew Hales and Kipling Williams

The Uncertainty Surrounding Ostracism: A Systematic Review and Future Directions

To be ostracized is to be ignored and excluded (Williams, 2007). It is often unaccompanied by an explicit pronouncement (Williams et al., 1998), as it was used in Athens to send individuals into temporary exile (Forsdyke, 2000). The target of ostracism notices it but is not sure that it is indeed happening. Perhaps, the target thinks, he/she is being paranoid. Maybe the others are preoccupied with concerns of their own and thus their apparent inattention was coincidental. Then, when it becomes clearer that the others are indeed ostracizing the individual, there is still ambiguity. Why are they engaging in ostracism? Maybe the ostracism is due to misunderstandings other than something internal to the target. Thus, ostracism and uncertainty are ecologically intertwined and the impact of ostracism and subsequent responses are partly attributable to the uncertainty that envelops it. In this chapter, we review the research on ostracism especially as it pertains to uncertainty.

The feeling of uncertainty is frequently associated with negative emotions, such as anxiety, worry, and fear (Carleton, 2016; Gordon, 2003; van den Bos, 2001; Sweeny, 2018; Wilson et al., 2005). Such typical aversive experiences motivate people to think and act in ways to reduce uncertainty and its associated negative feelings (FeldmanHall & Shenhav, 2019). Empirical evidence suggests that these negative feelings can be reduced or eliminated when the level of uncertainty is reduced. For example, Pennebaker (1997) asked people who suffered a traumatic experience to write about their experiences on several consecutive days. It turned out that participants whose writing had increased in organization and detail over time benefited more from this writing exercise. It was argued that the increased organization in people's writing helped to resolve the uncertainty surrounding the event, and the reduced uncertainty helped to reduce negative emotions.

In light of the positive benefits gained in resolving uncertainty, there are times at which uncertainty could be appealing, particularly when certainty threatens one's self-image. Clarifying whether or not one is being ostracized may be such a situation[1]. Ostracized individuals face damaging implications and consequences. For many social animals, ostracism means death (Gruter & Masters, 1986), but for humans, it is more likely to mean immediate pain (Eisenberger et al., 2003) as well as threats to basic needs, including belonging, self-esteem, control, and meaningful existence (Williams et al., 2000; Zadro et al., 2004; Williams, 2009).

 DOI: 10.4324/9781003363385-17

And, given the powerful effect of ostracism on uncertainty, and the importance of certainty in general, recent ostracism theory has postulated *uncertainty* itself as a fifth need that is threatened by ostracism (Hales & Williams, 2021). Experiments have found that ostracism reliably induces feelings of uncertainty both about the event (based on endorsement of items like "I did not know what I should be doing") and also about *oneself* (based on endorsements of items like "I was unsure of what makes me who I am"; Hales & Williams, 2018, and see Williams et al., 2019 for an overview).

Ostracism and related constructs are examined with an exceptional variety of methods and manipulations. The methods used include scenario/hypotheticals, face-to-face and electronically communicated (via Inter-, Intranet, cell phones, and virtual reality) laboratory manipulations, role-play, surveys, diaries, and in-depth interviews. In experiments, ostracism/rejection/exclusion has been operationally defined by excluding individuals in an emergent face-to-face ball toss game, through an Internet game called Cyberball, conversations, through the use of bogus feedback about others not wanting to work with the individual, and through a personality-based prognosis of living a life alone (for a review of these methods, see Williams, 2007, 2009; Wirth, 2016). Although this may decrease certainty for researchers when differences emerge between experiments, the variety certainly strengthens researchers' confidence that the replicable effects are not the result of any specific method. In this chapter, we review the various roles uncertainty plays in ostracism. Specifically, we examine the two-edged sword of uncertainty: it threatens the individual's desire to understand what is going on, and to control the social situation on the one hand, but allows self-protection on the other. The underlying mechanism of these different roles is also discussed. Further, we propose directions regarding uncertainty surrounding ostracism for future research. To properly approach this, we will start by outlining ostracism and how uncertainty fits in.

Uncertainty in Ostracism

According to Williams's Model of Ostracism (Williams, 1997; Williams & Zadro, 2005), there are several dimensions on which ostracism can vary, many of which are centrally related to uncertainty or ambiguity. These include motives (why is the source ostracizing the target, or what is the objective or goal?), causal clarity (to what extent does the source reveal the reason for ostracism or the explicit intent to the target), quantity (is the ostracism all-encompassing, or does it occur some times and not others), and mode (is the channel through which ostracism happens). As Williams (1997) emphasized "all these dimensions allude to, directly or indirectly, a particular feature of ostracism: it is inherently ambiguous" (p. 142). Each of the four dimensions could be arranged on a scale with uncertainty on one end and certainty on the other end, and would likely affect the extent to which the specific need for certainty would be threatened overall. Perceived motives and causal clarity are tied with the certainty, or lack of it, behind the reason why one is being ostracized. The dimensions of modality and quantity are related to the uncertainty in determining whether or not one is being ostracized.

Motives

Williams (1997) proposed five perceived motives that the target surmises as the likely explanations for the ostracism they are receiving. Although little research has been done to distinguish these motives, we will present them in what we believe to be from least to most hurtful to the targets. The first is labeled *not ostracism*; a conclusion that the source did not intend to ignore and exclude them. Perhaps the source was preoccupied and did not hear the "hello!" offered by the target.

If the act in question passes through this gate, the target can consider another seemingly innocuous motive—*normative ostracism*. Empirical evidence suggests that, when exclusion is perceived as aligning with social norms, it can buffer the threats to basic needs following ostracism (Rudert & Greifeneder, 2016). Consider, for example, the change in group dynamics when you transition from being a colleague to becoming the new boss. In such a scenario, expectations of social exclusion are in harmony with established workplace norms that govern authority and rank, which in turn can mitigate the perceived threat to one's need for inclusion. As such, when normative ostracism is concluded, we (perhaps) can discount the inattention as nothing more than a shared cultural response that indicts neither one's behavior nor character. If, however, this conclusion is easily ruled out, then more hurtful motives become more plausible.

Perhaps the next motive on the hurtful continuum is *defensive ostracism*, in which the target perceives that the ostracism results from the source's attempt to avoid social pain. When direct aggression or confrontation is discouraged within a particular setting—be it a workplace, social circle, or community — options for conflict resolution are often constrained, and defensive ostracism emerges as a passive alternative for dealing with conflicts and managing relationships with troublesome or deviant others (Robinson et al., 2013). This motive is not about direct harm but rather about the source's self-protection, maintaining social order, and upholding group norms. It can be seen as less aggressive and perhaps more socially acceptable, reflecting the source's need to navigate complex social relationships while minimizing personal and collective discomfort.

A *punitive* motive is one in which targets perceive the source's motive as a form of punishment for the target's undesirable behavior or character. The perceived intent is to inflict pain, signaling the source's disapproval, dislike, disdain, or disgust toward the target. Perceiving ostracism to be punitive would undoubtedly be self-threatening for the target. However, the effects of punitive ostracism are not one-dimensional. While being deeply hurtful to the target, empirical evidence suggests that for ostracizers, punitive ostracism can be psychologically rewarding. Nezlek et al. (2012) found that individuals who engage in punitive ostracism may experience heightened feelings of control, an increase in self-esteem, and a stronger sense of meaningful existence, and they may feel less apologetic and even angrier. Within the punitive domain, there still remains ambiguity. Does the intended hurt mean to correct and reform the target for future inclusion, or does it signal a desire to permanently banish the target from the source?

Finally, targets may surmise that they are being *obliviously ostracized*. Here, the target perceives that the ostracizer(s) do not notice him or her, or that they (the target) do not warrant attention by others. It is the belief that one does not register on others' social radar. Whereas it could be argued that there is no harm intended, this type of ostracism strikes at the very core of one's being, or one's existence. To not merit recognition, or others' acknowledgment as an existing equal, is to not be regarded as a human. A related phenomenon is that of being *objectified*, often sexually. When people are sexually objectified, they sense that attention is not being paid to their personhood, but rather peripheral aspects of the self, and thus, feelings of ostracism and related negative outcomes follow (Dvir et al., 2021). While theories of objectification and dehumanization point to characterological dimensions of beast-ness and automaton-ness as the essence of not being human (Bastian & Haslam, 2010), we would argue that not being recognized as existing would trump either of these dimensions for potential hurt, anger, or self-loathing.

Causal Clarity

As the name suggests, the dimension of *causal clarity* is closely linked with uncertainty. When ostracism is low in causal clarity, the targets find themselves in the dark about why they are being ostracized. Such episodes are characterized by a lack of announcement or clear explanation, leaving the ostracized individual to grapple with an ambiguous situation. On the other hand, ostracism high in causal clarity is marked by an overt declaration, offering the target a specific reason for their exclusion. "We're not talking to you," is a common taunt of children. As mean-spirited as it is, it provides the target with certainty.

Recent research by Chen et al. (2023) revealed that the specific reason for rejection—whether it be a perceived lack of warmth or competence—elicits distinct social-cognitive and behavioral responses due to the differential threat to underlying psychological needs. Targets who are informed that their rejection is based on a perceived lack of warmth tend to react in more affiliative ways, as an attempt to fortify the threatened need of belonging. On the other hand, competence-rejected individuals tend to turn inwards, becoming more self-focused as responding to threatened control and belongingness. Thus, the degree of causal clarity not only influences the immediate emotional response of the target but can also shape the strategies to cope with rejection.

Quantity

The dimension of quantity in ostracism refers to the extent to which a person is excluded, and this variance plays a crucial role in the uncertainty and perceived meaning of the behavior. Some have argued that ostracism can range from coolness in tone of voice and denial of eye contact to the total absence of verbal address, eye contact, and attention to verbalizations of the target (Boehm, 1986). The certainty that one is being ostracized corresponds to the magnitude. If one receives only occasional subtle forms of ostracism, one is not certain that it is occurring at all, or if it is, what it means: Perhaps it is simply a characteristic of the source, something they do from time to time to everyone. If full-blown ostracism is experienced, it leaves little room for doubt about its occurrence, and likely narrows down the range of possible motives.

Recent studies have improved our understanding of ostracism's quantity and its effects. The quantity of ostracism and the manner in which it is executed can influence the target's causal attribution and coping response. Pancani et al. (2022) suggest that *ghosting* (i.e., ending a relationship without explanation or further communication), may be worse than direct rejection through social media; whereas *orbiting,* or maintaining some peripheral presence (e.g., viewing someone's social media stories without direct interaction), might be somewhere between. However, orbiting's ambiguous nature was found to fuel false hope of reconciliation, which could paradoxically hinder the healing process and inhibit the pursuit of new relationships (Pancani et al., 2022). Adding to the complexity, Büttner and Rudert (2022) found that being passively excluded from social interactions, such as not being tagged in a photo post, is less psychologically painful than active exclusion, such as being removed from a tag in a photo post. The former allows for self-serving attributions to buffer the threat, while the latter is a clear and deliberate action that eliminates ambiguity.

Mode

Finally, ostracism can be expressed through various modalities. Individuals can be ostracized from electronic communications, from social acknowledgment while in the presence of others, or by being placed in solitary confinement. Each modality delivers its own set of uncertainties. Electronically, one might consider the possibility that the server, phone lines, or satellite connections are down (Smith & Williams, 2004). Socially, one wonders whether others are merely preoccupied with other concerns. Physically, one wonders whether others are thinking of them or desiring reconnections. Still, it seems plausible to assume that physical ostracism is associated with less uncertainty, and electronic modes offer the most uncertainty.

Recent research by Lutz and Schneider (2021) investigated the effects of ostracism on social media, where being ignored or receiving rejections are common manifestations. When individuals are ignored on social media, they might grapple with uncertainty, questioning if their ostracism is intentional or merely an oversight due to social media feeds. Rejection, which is more explicit and can manifest as receiving dislikes, creates less ambiguity but inflicts greater harm on one's need for belonging and self-esteem. However, both forms were found to equally threaten one's sense of meaningful existence and control. In terms of coping responses, ignored individuals exhibit more prosocial behaviors, whereas rejected ones rather withdraw from social interactions. These findings suggest that while electronic modes may present the most uncertainty due to technological ambiguities, they also induce distinct psychological and behavioral responses.

In sum, the interplay of motive, causal clarity, quantity, and mode forms the uncertainty that characterizes an ostracism episode. The ambiguity of motive fuels uncertainty about the reasons behind being excluded. Causal clarity, or the lack thereof, further intensifies this uncertainty, as individuals struggle to comprehend why they are being ostracized. The quantity of ostracism, reflecting its frequency and intensity, influences the degree of doubt a person has about their current status and future social interactions. Lastly, the mode of ostracism can either induce or mitigate uncertainty, depending on the transparency of the channel employed. Each factor contributes to the overall uncertainty inherent in ostracism, pointing out the challenges people face when they are ostracized and the extent to which it threatens one's need for certainty.

When Uncertainty Matters Less: Immediate Response to Ostracism

Ostracism is often a method of punishment used to express displeasure and in extreme cases, a precursor to death. From an evolutionary standpoint, there is an importance for the existence of an alarming system to allow individuals to quickly detect and react to any potential signs of ostracism. Through time, this system was probably developed when codependency became important to an individual's survival and when ostracism was used to punish social deviants. MacDonald and Leary (2005) suggested a social pain system that (a) punishes individuals who do not avoid social exclusion and (b) motivates quick responses to signs of exclusion. Since pain is already a strong signal of danger in the environment that draws people's attention and focus; it is already equipped to serve as an alarm for detecting ostracism. This idea is consistent with various mechanisms suggested by other researchers on how people react to ostracism and/or social exclusion. Eisenberger and Lieberman (2004) suggest that social pain functions as an alarming system to detect cues that might be harmful to survival, such as physical danger or social separation, and to recruit attention and coping resources to minimize the threat.

Studies using a variety of different paradigms consistently find that ostracized individuals report a threat to their social needs of belonging, self-esteem, control, and meaningful existence as well as an increase in hurt feelings and negative emotions (Williams & Zadro, 2005; Williams, 2007). An fMRI study (Eisenberger et al., 2003) shows that being ostracized during a game of Cyberball activates the dorsal anterior cingulate cortex (dACC). The dACC is also activated when people are experiencing physical pain and the amount of activation is highly correlated ($r = .88$) with self-reported stress. This provides physiological evidence that being ostracized in a minimal situation like Cyberball is enough to trigger pain. Law and Williams (2007) created Minimal World by removing the social cues inherent in Cyberball. Player icons were replaced by squares and a circle replaced the ball that mimicked the actions of a game of Cyberball. When participants were asked to mentally visualize what was occurring, their social needs were threatened as in the Cyberball paradigm. This study suggests that the action of objects that share features of social interactions can trigger the detection system. In addition, after relieving a past socially painful experience, relative to a past physically painful experience, people experience a higher level of current pain (Chen et al., 2008). The most common socially painful experience reported was an instance of ostracism. It was also found that people reported higher levels of pain after imagining a future social rejection compared with imagining a future physical injury (Chen & Williams, 2012). This implies that the ostracism detection system is highly sensitive since remembering a past or imagining a future, social rejection situation will trigger pain.

The failure to detect ostracism occurring is much more detrimental than misperceiving a normal event such as ostracism. As a result, this detection system favors false alarms over misses and is therefore highly sensitive to detect any possibility of ostracism (Williams, 2007). It is less likely for uncertainty to moderate the immediate reactions of ostracism because of the quick and dirty nature of the alarming system. Indeed, it has been shown that people do not differentiate various situational factors that ought to diminish the immediate impact of ostracism (Williams & Zadro, 2005). People react negatively even when they are ostracized by a despised outgroup, the Ku Klux Klan (Gonsalkorale & Williams, 2007; Fayant et al., 2014), when they are ostracized by computers (Zadro et al., 2004; Jauch et al., 2022), and when ostracism wins money while inclusion loses it (van Beest & Williams, 2006). Furthermore, various individual difference variables, such as self-esteem (Williams et al., 2000), individualism/collectivism (Smith & Williams, 2004), and social anxiety (Zadro et al., 2006) did not moderate the immediate impact of ostracism.

Recent findings by Jauch et al. (2023) reinforce this perspective, demonstrating that the anticipation of exclusion does not meaningfully buffer against the psychological pains when exclusion is realized, as expected exclusion is as painful as unexpected exclusion. This absence of a moderating effect aligns with Williams' (2009) theoretical proposition that the immediate painful and negative response to social exclusion is reflexive. Therefore, uncertainty regarding the likelihood of occurrence may become irrelevant as the default reaction of the need threat dominates the experience of social exclusion. These insights collectively underscore that the immediate reactions to ostracism are painful and negative no matter what the goal of ostracism is, whether the ostracism is happening all the time or once in a while, to what extent the source reveals the reasons for ostracism, or through what medium it is delivered to the target.

Following the reflexive responses, ostracized individuals begin to cope with the pain and stress. During this reflective stage, individual differences (Zadro et al., 2006) and social factors (Williams, 2007) have been reported to moderate the recovery from ostracism. The various roles uncertainty plays in ostracism during this stage will be reviewed in detail later in this chapter.

Chronically ostracized targets progress to the last stage of ostracism: acceptance. Targets of chronic ostracism suffer from depression, alienation, and/or suicidal thoughts (Williams & Zadro, 2005). Interviews with 28 long-term targets of ostracism conducted by Zadro (2004) found targets learned to accept the detrimental effects of ostracism rather than fight to regain their basic needs. Uncertainty plays no major role here since it is apparent that ostracism has been and still occurring regardless of the reasons.

When Uncertainty Matters More: Reflection, Attributions, and Coping

As mentioned earlier, ostracized individuals begin to reflect upon the ostracism episode, make sense of it, determine its importance to self, and then, if necessary, cope with it. Uncertainty can play two opposing roles during this process. The absence of an explicit pronouncement of displeasure that often occurs with group ostracism and dyadic silent treatment may allow the individual to pretend that it is not happening to deny the potential threat. On the other hand, uncertainty can be detrimental and augment the pain because the individual can, without precise information that might otherwise accompany an unpleasant interaction, engage in self-deprecating and paranoid cognitions that only serve to amplify the negative impact. In the following, we review these two roles of uncertainty, a threat protector as well as a threat amplifier, followed by individual differences.

Uncertainty as a Threat Protector

There appear to be two distinct points of ambiguity. The first is raised by the question, "Is ostracism happening or am I just imagining it?" To the extent that the individual can convince him- or herself that the episode is not ostracism, then the potential threat of ostracism should be relatively easy to slough off. Indeed, in diary studies, when individuals at first think they are being subjected to the silent treatment but upon reflection decide it was not ostracism, they suffer little in terms of threatened needs (Nezlek et al., 2012). Thus, at this stage, ambiguity might promote a protective shield of denial. When denial is not a viable strategy to reduce ambiguity, some individuals may embrace it. Reich and Wheeler (2016) found that when people face uncertain outcomes, they non-consciously create a state of ambivalence to protect themselves from potential rejection. Similarly, ostracism can make prospects of inclusion ambiguous, thus embracing ambivalence may foster a hope of potential success and buffer against possible failure.

There are other situations when being uncertain may be a more preferred option to the targets of ostracism and reduce its negative effects. The quantity of ostracism that a target endures fluctuates with the amount of uncertainty surrounding the ostracism. In a Cyberball study by Williams et al. (2000), partially ostracised participants (receiving 20% of the throws) had fewer negative consequences compared with fully ostracised participants. Perhaps being partially ostracized affords them the ability to embrace the uncertainty that they are not ostracized. This indicates that complete ostracism, which leaves no room for uncertainty, can result in unresponsiveness towards behaviors that might help the recovery of the need to belong.

The different modes through which ostracism can be expressed are another domain where uncertainty offers some protection to targets from the effects of ostracism. As mentioned earlier, physical ostracism is associated with less uncertainty regarding whether or not one is being ostracized compared with electronic ostracism. In face-to-face communication, targets of ostracism can use various social cues, such as the sources' facial expression and vocal tone, to understand the social situation. Ostracism through cyber communication is more uncertain because it lacks this channel that allows targets to directly judge the sources' feelings, emotions, and intentions. Williams and colleagues found that cyber ostracism had a different impact on the four social needs than face-to-face ostracism (Williams et al., 2000; Williams et al., 2002). When ostracized face-to-face, the target's sense of belongingness, self-esteem, control, and meaningful existence were threatened. In a chat room environment, the ostracized target's sense of belongingness and meaningful existence were equally threatened but a sense of control and self-esteem were less affected when compared to face-to-face ostracism. In cyber communication, there are a lot more uncertainties involved within the experience that may buffer the effect of ostracism. Not only are social cues associated with intentional ostracism missing but also other reasons for an accidental exclusion, such as computer or other technical issues, are present.

These dynamics are especially relevant in the modern age with greater technology-mediated communication, and greater opportunity to both receive, and engage in *ghosting* (Pancani et al., 2021; Freedman et al., 2022). The experience of being ghosted is fraught with uncertainty (LeFebvre & Fan, 2020). People who are especially averse to uncertainty (as measured by being higher in the need for closure) react especially negatively to the experience of being ghosted (Leckfor et al., 2023).

In conclusion, the protective nature of ambiguity within the context of ostracism is multifaceted. Starting with denial and ambivalence cultivation, we have seen that these psychological strategies provide individuals with a means to shield themselves from the immediate hurt of exclusion. Empirical evidence further supports the notion that uncertainty, particularly regarding the quantity of ostracism, can mitigate the pain experienced: those who are partially ostracized often feel better than those who are completely excluded. Moreover, the mode of ostracism plays a critical role, with physical ostracism offering less room for uncertainty and, consequently, less opportunity for protective denial, compared to online ostracism, where the greater uncertainty can be used to one's advantage. These findings highlight the complex interplay between the objective reality of ostracism and the subjective perception of it, where ambiguity can serve as a subtle but powerful protection.

Uncertainty as a Threat Amplifier

However, once the ostracism is undeniable, because of its clarity, consensus, or length of time imposed, then we think that the ambiguity exists around the question, "Why are they doing this to me?" The principle of interpretive control (Rothbaum et al., 1982) states that the ability to understand an aversive event is important to cope with the event. Thus to cope with the ostracism, it would be beneficial to understand that ostracism is indeed occurring and perhaps more importantly, why the ostracism is happening. In understanding these reasons, the target also clears up uncertainties surrounding the ostracism event. It is not unreasonable to suggest that the targets who cannot explain why they were ostracized would suffer more from ostracism than those who can.

In a study by Ezrakhovich et al. (1998), participants were either informed they were late for the experiment or not informed at all before a group task with two confederates who either ostracized or included them in the activity. Ostracized participants, especially females, who were not told anything, worked harder in subsequent tasks, possibly due to greater uncertainty about the reason for ostracism compared with those who were given a reason for potential ostracism (i.e., late for the experiment). This suggests that causal uncertainty led them to exert more effort, perhaps as a way to counteract the threat to their social needs. Sommer et al. (2001) further explored the effect of causal uncertainty by having participants write about ostracism experiences, finding that those unable to pinpoint a cause for their exclusion felt a greater impact on their sense of belonging and self-esteem. The lack of an identifiable reason for ostracism intensified its negative effects, indicating that the harm from ostracism is magnified by not understanding the reason behind it.

People differ in their level of confidence regarding their ability to understand casual relations in social situations (Weary & Edwards, 1994). A study by Passey and Jacobson (2007) found that people who are less confident in their ability to understand social causation (high in casual uncertainty) had more negative reactions to ostracism by Cyberball than people who were more confident in their ability to understand social causation (low in casual uncertainty). This finding further supports the claim that not being able to clearly understand why ostracism is occurring is more detrimental to the target.

It is also important to understand the goal that the source of ostracism is trying to achieve through ostracism. The targets may view ostracism as intentional or simply perceive it as being an oblivious act (Williams, 1997). Oblivious ostracism is more uncertain than intentional ostracism in that it lacks clear information on why someone is ostracized. Intentional ostracism implies the target has an understanding or a guess of why they are ostracized. When targets interpret ostracism as being oblivious, it is difficult to understand what the goal behind the ostracism is. The simplest reason they could guess is that they are unworthy of attention and that their existence has no bearing on the sources of ostracism. Sommer and colleagues (2001) indeed found that oblivious ostracism posed a greater threat to belongingness, self-esteem, and meaningful existence than intentional ostracism does.

The above findings reveal the dark side of ambiguity, particularly when it relates to the causes and motives behind ostracism. Yet, despite sparse evidence, the literature does suggest strategies to reduce this causal uncertainty. Research indicates that adopting a higher-level construal of negative events induces a more simplified understanding and reduces causal uncertainty (Namkoong & Henderson, 2014, see also Namkoong et al., Chapter 6). Specifically, engaging in abstract rather than concrete thinking has been shown to aid in the emotional recovery from social exclusion, as abstract thinking can bolster the basic need of belonging when excluded (Pfundmair et al., 2015). By interpreting exclusion through a broader lens, individuals can potentially alleviate its pain.

In business settings, particularly within digital customer interactions, the ambiguous nature of ostracism can yield negative consequences and have practical implications. In online customer service, retailers often resort to automated replies to manage large volumes of inquiries, aiming to reduce the uncertainty that may arise from unattended queries. However, Mattila et al. (2013) revealed that such generic automated responses are ineffective in alleviating customers' feelings of uncertainty, as they do not provide the personalized feedback that consumers seek. The study found that customers felt equally ostracized whether they received a generic auto-reply or no response at all. This perceived neglect resulted in heightened negative emotions, diminished satisfaction, and higher intention to engage in negative behaviors. While an absence of feedback online could plausibly be attributed to technical difficulties, ambiguity does not seem to reduce feelings of being ignored (Smith & Williams, 2004). Without personalized acknowledgment, customers attributed a lack of direct response to a lack of concern on the company's part (Mattila et al., 2013).

On the flip side, retailers experience a similar sense of uncertainty when potential buyers do not respond. Alba and Slongo (2020) found that a lack of replies from customers prompted retailers to make causal attributions about the customer's interest. Such uncertainty led to tangible business decisions, like offering higher price discounts, significantly $88 more on average, based on the presumption of disinterest.

This evidence illustrates that non-responses or impersonal communication can initiate a detrimental cycle of negative assumptions that influence both parties' attitudes and behaviors. It shows a mutual aversion to ostracism and the uncertainty it produces among both consumers and retailers. Personalized communication emerges as a more effective approach in alleviating the uncertainty pervasive in online retailer-consumer relationships, thus reducing the feelings of ostracism and encouraging more constructive exchanges.

Individual Differences

While the previous sections have explored the general protective and threatening nature of ambiguity in ostracism, it is important to note that not all individuals will perceive and react to uncertainty in the same way. The degree to which ambiguity is perceived as protective or threatening can be influenced by various individual differences. Below we reviewed five individual differences that are particularly prone to detect or interpret ambiguity in a threatening way.

Rejection Sensitivity

Rejection sensitivity entails that anxiety about rejection leads to a readiness to perceive others' ambiguous behavior as rejection (Downey & Feldman, 1996). As rejection sensitivity is strongly linked to an increased expectation of being rejected, highly rejection-sensitive individuals should avoid putting themselves in ambiguous situations where rejection is possible. Rejection-sensitive people were found to respond more negatively than others to both overt and highly ambiguous rejections (Zimmer-Gembeck & Nesdale, 2013).

High Need to Belong

The need to belong is a basic drive to form connections (Baumeister & Leary, 1995). Those with a high need to belong place more importance on gaining acceptance, unlike individuals with a low need for belonging (Leary et al., 2013). Not being tagged on social media has been found to be an ambiguous ostracism episode that threatens fundamental needs, with individuals with a higher need to belong suffering greater pain (Büttner & Rudert, 2022).

Hostile Attribution Bias

Individuals who struggle with social information processing may exhibit hostile attribution bias, whereby they assume the negative intent of others, even in situations that are neutral or ambiguous (Dodge & Coie, 1987). Social exclusion has been found to foster such a bias, in which socially excluded participants were more likely to rate aggressive and ambiguous words as similar and to rate the ambiguous actions of another person as hostile, contributing to aggressive responses (DeWall et al., 2009).

Motivated Paranoid Cognition

Motivation to Acquire Relationship-Threatening Information (MARTI) stands out as a specific type of motivation that drives individuals to seek out cues indicating that others have communicated negative information about oneself behind one's back (Marr et al., 2012). Those with high levels of MARTI are more likely to selectively perceive and interpret social cues in a way that aligns with this motivation, often leading to paranoid cognition, including the assumption of malevolent intent (sinister attribution error) and the belief that one is often the focus of others' harmful actions (self-as-target bias). Marr et al. (2012) demonstrated a positive correlation between MARTI and tendencies toward these paranoid cognitions and suspicious behavior.

Negative Interpretation Bias

Interpretation biases toward negatively evaluating ambiguous situations are central to depression, as shown by meta-analyses demonstrating a medium effect size relationship (Everaert et al., 2017). Experienced ostracism and depression also reciprocally predict each other over time, with ostracism leading to later depression and vice versa according to a three-year longitudinal analysis (Rudert et al., 2021). Notably, ostracism elicits a stronger negative interpretation bias, particularly for individuals with a higher level of depressive symptoms, evidenced by a faster selection of negative interpretations from ambiguous social scenarios (Bar-Sella et al., 2022). These evidences together suggest a cyclic process whereby ostracism fosters depressive symptoms through increased negative interpretation biases, resulting in individuals evaluating uncertain situations in an overly negative manner.

Self-Enhancing Responses Following Ostracism

When to maintain uncertainty surrounding ostracism and when to reduce it? The above review suggests that uncertainty moderates the impact of ostracism during the coping stage. According to the principle of interpretive control (Rothbaum et al., 1982), understanding the negative event helps people to cope with it better. Thus, to cope with ostracism, people should prefer certainty to uncertainty. This seems to be the case when dealing with why ostracism is happening and what the goals of the source are. On the other hand, certainty could be more threatening than uncertainty, when dealing with whether and to what extent ostracism is happening.

However, we think it is inappropriate to draw a simple conclusion that people avoid uncertainty when dealing with why ostracism occurs and that they seek uncertainty when dealing with if ostracism occurs. After having run many participants through the face-to-face ball-tossing paradigm, we have noticed what we think is an interesting and peculiar use of uncertainty. No participant in this paradigm has ever confronted his or her ostracizers. No one has said, "Hey, why aren't you throwing me the ball?" No one has tried to intercept the ball. Indeed, almost every participant in this particular paradigm ends up slumped and dejected. Why don't they clear up the uncertainty by confronting those who are ostracizing them? Is this response functional in any way?

The earlier analysis of casual uncertainty suggests that unwillingness to clarify the situation is not a general response to ostracism. Interestingly, this lack of confrontation appears to be rather specific to the face-to-face ball-tossing paradigm. In chat rooms, ostracized participants provoke attention and response (Williams et al., 2002). Ostracized participants would challenge others to respond by asking why they were not including them, calling their names, and filling up the computer screen with a monologue, which we call "virtual bravado" (Williams et al., 2002). So, too, on cell phones (Smith & Williams, 2004). Even in face-to-face conversation paradigms, participants try to interject themselves into the conversation or at least obstruct the ongoing conversation (Zadro et al., 2004). But why does this just seem to occur in the ball-tossing paradigm?

We think this has to do with the unique nature of the face-to-face ball-tossing paradigm, and this has to do with why people seek uncertainty at some times but avoid uncertainty at others. There might be an underlying fear that confronting the ostracizers could lead to confirmation of a negative evaluation, which could be more painful than the uncertainty itself. By not asking, participants can hold onto a sliver of hope that the exclusion isn't personal or is just a misunderstanding. Also, participants may choose not to confront to avoid potential conflict escalation. They may fear that asking could lead to outright rejection or hostility, which would be more distressing than silent treatment. Although not confronting may appear maladaptive, it could serve a protective function by allowing individuals to avoid potential conflict, maintain hope, and preserve self-esteem.

Having explored the dual nature of ambiguity in ostracism, the role of individual differences, and boundary conditions to maintain or reduce ambiguity, we now turn to discussing the coping strategy following ostracism. It has been widely noticed that people prefer to maintain a positive self-image and that when they face threatening social situations, they engage in various strategies to serve the purpose of self-enhancement. For example, when facing negative outcomes or threats, people tend to make external rather than internal attributions, they also tend to make downward comparisons, comparing themselves with someone less fortunate, to improve subjective well-being; also, they are more likely to engage in self-handicapping, and tend to make more collective identifications than individual identifications (for a review, see Banaji & Prentice, 1994). People could also create positive illusions in threatening situations, such as an illusion of control over the social situation (Taylor & Brown, 1988). These various strategies and distorted perceptions help to buffer the negative events or situations.

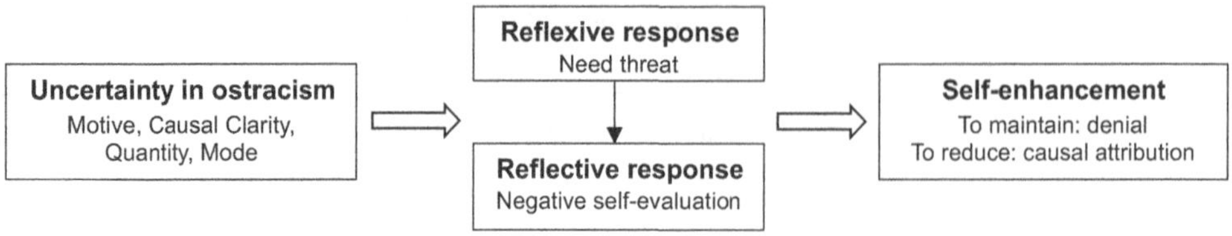

Figure 15.1 Self-enhancing responses following ostracism.

We believe that people will engage in similar strategies to serve the purpose of self-enhancement when they are ostracized. Figure 15.1 presents a conceptual model illustrating our assumptions. It has been shown repeatedly that ostracism threatens fundamental needs, such as belonging, self-esteem, meaningful existence, and control (for a review, see Williams, 2007). We believe that these threatened needs will lead to a change of self-evaluation. For example, when the target's self-esteem is threatened, he/she will have a more negative evaluation of himself/herself. We also believe that ostracized targets will then engage in self-enhancing responses to change their self-evaluations.

When the target can make external attributions (e.g., the others are friends) or certain internal attributions (e.g. I was late for the experiment, as in Ezrakhovich et al., 1998) then his/her self-evaluations can be adjusted and thus improved. However, when the target cannot make such attributions, he/she will begin to have self-doubt, which will lead to negative self-evaluation. One way to boost self-evaluation is to regain acceptance by others, which would explain why the female participants in Ezrakhovich et al. (1998) worked harder after they were ostracized but not provided any information. Another way is to confront the source on why he/she is ostracized. However, only those ostracized in virtual environments have the "virtual bravado" to do so.

When threatened by casual uncertainty in the face-to-face ball-tossing paradigm, the target has two options to deal with the situation. One option is not to do anything and to suffer from the threats of causal uncertainty, just as all the participants in our lab did. Another option is to confront the source and figure out why they are ostracized, which could help to buffer the threat caused by causal uncertainty. However, when the target chooses to do that, he/she will face another potential threat, that is, the fact that the others dislike him/her. When one is ostracized, the other people may be friends, but it is also possible that the others do not like him/her. In a lab setting, the latter seems more likely. This should be a general pattern for ostracism via different modules. Whether the target confronts the sources or not should be decided by the weight between the potential threat caused by causal uncertainty and the potential threat caused by the possible harsh reality. The major difference between face-to-face ostracism and chat-room ostracism is that it is much more threatening to learn that others do not like you in a face-to-face situation compared with a cyber situation.

When it's not clear whether the ostracism is happening, it is preferable to remain uncertain, because it helps to protect against the potential threat to self-evaluation caused by possible ostracism. We think participants use uncertainty as a protective device, forestalling or preventing a certain and devastating acknowledgment of being unwanted or disliked. This is consistent with the findings on whether ostracism is occurring and through which mode it is occurring (Williams et al., 2002).

When one is clear that the ostracism is happening, it is still better in some cases to seek uncertainty regarding why one is ostracized. Although most studies we have reviewed in this chapter demonstrate that causal uncertainty has a more negative impact on the target than causal certainty, we believe that people will seek causal uncertainty when the threat is caused by the possible reality that they are not liked or wanted by others weights over the threat caused by causal uncertainty. Uncertainty, in the form of perceiving the ostracism as not happening, and in the form of imagining several alternative reasons for not being included in the ball-tossing game provides some comfort, and in this instance, uncertainty might provide a cloak of ego-protection.

Future Directions

Uncertainty plays different roles in reacting to and coping with the impact of ostracism. Our analysis suggests having greater uncertainty in the quantity and mode can be somewhat beneficial because ostracized targets can believe that they are not ostracized due to the ambiguity surrounding the event rather than admitting that they are being ostracized. However, greater uncertainty in understanding the motives and casual clarity behind being ostracized is more detrimental to the targets. Ostracized targets may generate numerous causes, which can result in greater distress than the actual reason might bring (Williams, 2002). One caveat to this is that we may fear validating the worst-case scenario so much that we'd rather leave things ambiguous. In this case, uncertainty serves to protect our ego from facing a distressing reality.

Moving from this nuanced understanding of individual reactions to uncertainty in ostracism, it's important to consider the impacts on broader social contexts. Exclusion can provoke a sense of personal uncertainty (Güzel & Şahin, 2018), and such ostracism-induced uncertainty can have practical implications. For one, people may resort to undesirable or problematic means to restore certainty, particularly in the form of extremism (See also McGregor & Marigold, Chapter 14). According to uncertainty identity theory, an important motivation for identifying with groups is the need to manage and reduce uncertainty (Hogg, 2007). It has been theorized that groups that are particularly *extreme* are the best suited for this because they provide clear and rigid prescriptions of behavior and visions for change (Hogg, 2014). Indeed, research suggests that social exclusion is often a factor contribution to extremism and radicalization (Pfundmair et al., 2022; Williams et al., 2019).

Additionally, empirical evidence shows that the state of uncertainty about oneself can lead to a stronger belief in conspiracy theories (van Prooijen & Jostmann, 2013). Those who feel ostracized are more susceptible to feeling threatened, which can drive them to adopt conspiracy theories as a defense mechanism against the perceived dangers in their environment (Poon et al., 2020). Thus, the need to mitigate uncertainty and protect oneself can lead to the endorsement of such beliefs and affect attitudes and behaviors.

Looking forward, we propose five promising areas for further exploration into the uncertainty associated with ostracism. Firstly, there is a clear need for more research into the protective role of uncertainty in ostracism. While the current literature has predominantly examined the negative effects of uncertainty and ways to minimize it, only a limited number of studies have empirically explored its potential benefits, such as the cultivation of ambivalence (Reich & Wheeler, 2016). We advocate for more research into how uncertainty can be strategically used for self-enhancement, which could provide a deeper understanding of its dual nature and inform better-coping strategies for dealing with ostracism.

In terms of methodology, we recommend that future research incorporate uncertainty as a deliberate element of experimental manipulation. The traditional approach that manipulates partial versus complete ostracism indeed can generate varying levels of uncertainty based on quantity, but it has not systematically explored the effects of uncertainty in manipulation. We suggest that future studies embed manipulations of uncertainty directly into ostracism manipulations and include manipulation checks that assess participants' perceptions of uncertainty. This could help clarify the role of uncertainty in ostracism and its subsequent effects on attitudes and behaviors.

Additionally, existing studies are predominantly cross-sectional and offer only a snapshot of the immediate aftermath of ostracism, leaving a gap in our understanding of its long-term mental health impacts. Given the interplay between ostracism, cognitive biases, and depression (Bar-Sella et al., 2022; Rudert et al., 2021), future research should explore how these elements interact over time. Cognitive restructuring, which has shown promising therapeutic effects in meta-analyses ($d = 0.85$; Ezawa & Hollon, 2023), could be tested as a potential method to help those ostracized reinterpret ambiguous situations in a way that promotes self-enhancement and mental health resilience.

Also, further attention is needed to better understand the nature of certainty itself, viewed as a fundamental need. As the most recent need to be considered as part of the temporal need-threat model (Hales & Williams, 2021), it is less theoretically developed than the other four needs. Important questions surround the extent to which it is empirically related to the other needs, or perhaps even conceptually overlapping with some (e.g., when one feels a lack of meaning, how much of this is due to a lack of knowledge about their place in the social world). Further work is also needed to locate the need for certainty within the context of the more affiliation-based needs (belonging and self-esteem) versus the provocation-based needs (control and meaningful existence).

Lastly, the ubiquitous use of social media in daily life provides rich opportunities to examine how virtual interactions might alter the psychological processing of ostracism compared to traditional, face-to-face contexts. Social media is a dynamic environment where the manifestations and consequences of ostracism can be unique and profound. While we reviewed several recent studies examining the effects of ostracism on social media, this emerging field continues to grow rapidly, leaving ample gaps for future research. For example, acts such as being "blocked," "unfriended," "orbited," or "ghosted,"along with the visible counts of "comments," "likes," and "shares" as indicators of inclusionary status, and the permanence of digital records that serve as reminders to relive ostracism—these factors may uniquely contribute to the uncertainty experienced by ostracized individuals and influence their coping strategies.

Conclusion

For decades, research on ostracism has deepened our understanding of its antecedents, mechanisms, and consequences. Recently, the rising integration of information technology into everyday life has added complexity to these dynamics, especially through the mode of cyber-ostracism. However, despite these advancements, the role of uncertainty in reactions to ostracism remains underexplored. This chapter synthesized recent findings into the uncertainties surrounding ostracism, organizing them into categories of motive, mode, quantity, and causal clarity. We outlined the conditions under which uncertainty may play a prominent role in shaping people's responses to ostracism. We also differentiated the role of uncertainty as a threat protector versus a threat amplifier. In addition, we introduced a conceptual model of self-enhancement that reveals how individuals may cope with the uncertainties following ostracism. Nevertheless, there is still a lot of room for growth for research on this niche topic. We hope this review lays the groundwork for future empirical investigations into the uncertainty in ostracism, ultimately contributing to a more comprehensive understanding of this phenomenon.

Note

1 The empirical literature does not yet delineate the differences between ostracism, social exclusion and rejection. Ostracism is frequently defined in empirical literature as an individual or a group being ignored or excluded by other individuals or groups (Williams, 1997). Twenge et al. (2001) characterized social

exclusion as being isolated, rejected and/or excluded. A statement issued by a group or individual of not wanting another individual to be part of their company is termed as rejection (Leary, 2001). The terminology and definitions will be interchangeably used in reviewing the detrimental effects of ostracism.

References

Alba, G., & Slongo, L. A. (2020). Getting a no-reply is also a reply: An investigation of unreplied consumer attributions. *Journal of Retailing and Consumer Services*, *54*, 102054. https://doi.org/10.1016/j.jretconser.2020.102054

Banaji, M. R., & Prentice, D. A. (1994). The self in social contexts. *Annual Review of Psychology*, *45*, 297–332. https://doi.org/10.1146/annurev.ps.45.020194.001501

Bar-Sella, A., Richter, T., Zilcha-Mano, S., & Okon-Singer, H. (2022). How social experiences affect interpretation bias among individuals with non-clinical depression: The role of ostracism. *Frontiers in Psychiatry*, *13*, 819143. https://doi.org/10.3389/fpsyt.2022.819143

Bastian, B., & Haslam, N. (2010). Excluded from humanity: The dehumanizing effects of social ostracism. *Journal of Experimental Social Psychology*, *46*(1), 107–113. https://doi.org/10.1016/j.jesp.2009.06.022

Baumeister, R. F., & Leary, M. R. (1995). The need to belong: Desire for interpersonal attachments as a fundamental human motivation. *Psychological Bulletin*, *117*(3), 497–529. https://doi.org/10.1037/0033-2909.117.3.497

Boehm, C. (1986). Capital punishment in tribal Montenegro: Implications for law, biology, and theory of social control. *Ethology and Sociobiology*, *7*, 305–320. https://doi.org/10.1016/0162-3095(86)90056-7

Büttner, C. M., & Rudert, S. C. (2022). Why didn't you tag me?!: Social exclusion from Instagram posts hurts, especially those with a high need to belong. *Computers in Human Behavior*, *127*, 107062. https://doi.org/10.1016/j.chb.2021.107062

Carleton, R. N. (2016). Into the unknown: A review and synthesis of contemporary models involving uncertainty. *Journal of Anxiety Disorders*, *39*, 30–43. https://doi.org/10.1016/j.janxdis.2016.02.007

Chen, F., Guo, T., & Wang, J. (2023). Divergent effects of warmth and competence social rejection: An explanation based on the need-threat model. *Journal of Personality and Social Psychology*. Advance online publication. https://doi.org/10.1037/pspi0000440

Chen, Z., Williams, K. D., Fitness, J., & Newton, N. C. (2008).When hurt won't heal: Exploring the capacity to relive social pain. *Psychological Science*, *19*, 789–795. https://doi.org/10.1111/j.1467–9280.2008.02158.x

Chen, Z., & Williams, K. D (2012). Imagined future social pain hurts more now than imagined future physical pain. *European Journal of Social Psychology*, *42*, 314–317. https://doi.org/10.1002/ejsp.1861

DeWall, C. N., Twenge, J. M., Gitter, S. A., & Baumeister, R. F. (2009). It's the thought that counts: The role of hostile cognition in shaping aggressive responses to social exclusion. *Journal of Personality and Social Psychology*, *96*(1), 45–59. https://doi.org/10.1037/a0013196

Dodge, K. A., & Coie, J. D. (1987). Social-information-processing factors in reactive and proactive aggression in children's peer groups. *Journal of Personality and Social Psychology*, *53*(6), 1146–1158. https://doi.org/10.1037/0022-3514.53.6.1146

Downey, G., & Feldman, S. I. (1996). Implications of rejection sensitivity for intimate relationships. *Journal of Personality and Social Psychology*, *70*(6), 1327–1343. https://doi.org/10.1037/0022-3514.70.6.1327

Dvir, M., Kelly, J. R., Tyler, J. M., & Williams, K. D. (2021). I'm up here! Sexual objectification leads to feeling ostracized. *Journal of Personality and Social Psychology*, *121*(2), 332–353. https://doi.org/10.1037/pspi0000328

Eisenberger, N. I., Lieberman, M. D., & Williams, K. D. (2003). Does rejection hurt? An fMRI study of social exclusion. *Science*, *302*, 290–292. https://doi.org/10.1126/science.1089134

Eisenberger, N. I., & Lieberman, M. D. (2004). Why rejection hurts: The neurocognitive overlap between physical and social pain. *Trends in Cognitive Science*, *8*, 294–300. https://doi.org/10.1016/j.tics.2004.05.010

Everaert, J., Podina, I. R., & Koster, E. H. (2017). A comprehensive meta-analysis of interpretation biases in depression. *Clinical Psychology Review*, *58*, 33–48. https://doi.org/10.1016/j.cpr.2017.09.005

Ezawa, I. D., & Hollon, S. D. (2023). Cognitive restructuring and psychotherapy outcome: A meta-analytic review. *Psychotherapy*, *60*, 396–406. https://doi.org/10.1037/pst0000474

Ezrakhovich, A., Kerr, A., Cheung, S., Elliot, K., Jerrems, A., & Williams, K. D. (1998, April). *Effects of norm violation and ostracism on working with the group*. Paper presented at the meeting of the Society of Australasian Social Psychology, Christchurch, NZ.

Fayant, M-P., Muller, D., Hartgerink, C. H. J., & Lantian, A. (2014). Is ostracism by a despised outgroup really hurtful? A replication and extension of Gonsalkorale and Williams (2007). *Social Psychology, 45*(6), 489–494. https://doi.org/10.1027/1864-9335/a000209

FeldmanHall, O., & Shenhav, A. (2019). Resolving uncertainty in a social world. *Nature Human Behaviour, 3*(5), 426–435. https://doi.org/10.1038/s41562-019-0590-x

Forsdyke, S. (2000). Exile, ostracism and the Athenian democracy. *Classical Antiquity, 19,* 232–263. https://doi.org/10.2307/25011121

Freedman, G., Hales, A. H., Powell, D. N., Le, B., & Williams, K. D. (2022). The role of gender and safety concerns in romantic rejection decisions. *Journal of Experimental Social Psychology, 102*, 104368. https://doi.org/10.1016/j.jesp.2022.104368

Gonsalkorale, K., & Williams, K. D. (2007). The KKK won't let me play: Ostracism even by a despised outgroup hurts. *European Journal of Social Psychology, 37,* 1176–1185. https://doi.org/10.1002/ejsp.392

Gordon, K. (2003). The impermanence of being: Toward a psychology of uncertainty. *Journal of Humanistic Psychology, 43,* 96–117. https://doi.org/10.1177/0022167802250731

Gruter, M., & Masters, R. D. (1986). Ostracism as a social and biological phenomenon: An introduction. *Ethology & Sociobiology, 7*, 149–158. https://doi.org/10.1016/0162-3095(86)90043-9

Güzel, H. Y., & Şahin, D. N. (2018). The effect of ostracism on the accessibility of uncertainty-related thoughts. *Archives of Neuropsychiatry*, *55*(2), 183. https://doi.org/10.5152/npa.2017.19342

Hales, A. H., & Williams, K. D. (2018). Marginalized individuals and extremism: The role of ostracism in openness to extreme groups. *Journal of Social Issues*, *74*(1), 75–92. https://doi.org/10.1111/josi.12257

Hales, A. H., & Williams, K. D. (2021). Social ostracism: Theoretical foundations and basic principles. In P. A. M. Van Lange, E. T. Higgins, & A. W. Kruglanski (Eds.), *Social psychology: Handbook of basic principles* (3rd ed., pp. 337–349). Guilford.

Hogg, M. A. (2007). Uncertainty-identity theory. In M. P. Zanna (Ed.), Advances in experimental social psychology, Vol. 39, pp. 69–126). Elsevier Academic Press.

Hogg, M. A. (2014). From uncertainty to extremism: Social categorization and identity processes. *Current Directions in Psychological Science*, *23*(5), 338–342. https://doi.org/10.1177/0963721414540168

Jauch, M., Büttner, C. M., Rudert, S. C., & Greifeneder, R. (2023). Expecting exclusion: Does bracing for the worst buffer the pain of social exclusion? *European Journal of Social Psychology*, *53*(4), 746–765. https://doi.org/10.1002/ejsp.2934

Jauch, M., Rudert, S. C., & Greifeneder, R. (2022). Social pain by non-social agents: Exclusion hurts and provokes punishment even if the excluding source is a computer. *Acta Psychologica*, *230*, 103753. https://doi.org/10.1016/j.actpsy.2022.103753

Law, A. T., & Williams, K. D. (2007, January). *What does it take to feel ostracized? Effect of mental visualization and degraded presentation on ostracism's detection and impact.* Presented at the Society for Personality and Social Psychology, Memphis, TN.

Leary, M. R. (2001). Toward a conceptualization of interpersonal rejection. In M. R. Leary (Ed.), *Interpersonal rejection* (pp. 3–20). New York: Oxford University Press.

Leary, M. R., Kelly, K. M., Cottrell, C. A., & Schreindorfer, L. S. (2013). Construct validity of the need to belong scale: Mapping the nomological network. *Journal of Personality Assessment*, 95(6), 610–624. https://doi.org/10.1080/00223891.2013.819511

Leckfor, C. M., Wood, N. R., Slatcher, R. B., & Hales, A. H. (2023). From close to ghost: Examining the relationship between the need for closure, intentions to ghost, and reactions to being ghosted. *Journal of Social and Personal Relationships*, *40*(8), 2422–2444. https://doi.org/10.1177/02654075221149955

LeFebvre, L. E., & Fan, X. (2020). Ghosted?: Navigating strategies for reducing uncertainty and implications surrounding ambiguous loss. *Personal Relationships*, *27*(2), 433–459. https://doi.org/10.1111/pere.12322

Lutz, S., & Schneider, F. M. (2021). Is receiving dislikes in social media still better than being ignored? The effects of ostracism and rejection on need threat and coping responses online. *Media Psychology*, *24*(6), 741–765. https://doi.org/10.1080/15213269.2020.1799409

MacDonald, G., & Leary, M. (2005). Why does social exclusion hurt? The relationship between social and physical pain. *Psychological Bulletin, 131,* 202–233. https://doi.org/10.1037/0033-2909.131.2.202

Marr, J. C., Thau, S., Aquino, K., & Barclay, L. J. (2012). Do I want to know? How the motivation to acquire relationship-threatening information in groups contributes to paranoid thought, suspicion behavior, and social rejection. *Organizational Behavior and Human Decision Processes, 117* (2), 285–297. https://doi.org/10.1016/j.obhdp.2011.11.003

Mattila, A. S., Andreau, L., Hanks, L., & Kim, E. E. (2013). The impact of cyberostracism on online complaint handling: Is "automatic reply" any better than "no reply"? *International Journal of Retail & Distribution Management*, *41*(1), 45–60. https://doi.org/10.1108/09590551311288166

Namkoong, J. E., & Henderson, M. D. (2014). It's simple and I know it! Abstract construals reduce causal uncertainty. *Social Psychological and Personality Science*, *5*(3), 352–359. https://doi.org/10.1177/1948550613499240

Nezlek, J. B., Wesselmann, E. D., Wheeler, L., & Williams, K. D. (2012). Ostracism in everyday life. *Group Dynamics: Theory, Research, and Practice*, *16*(2), 91–104. https://doi.org/10.1037/a0028029

Pancani, L., Aureli, N., & Riva, P. (2022). Relationship dissolution strategies: Comparing the psychological consequences of ghosting, orbiting, and rejection. *Cyberpsychology: Journal of Psychosocial Research on Cyberspace*, *16*, 9. https://doi.org/ 10.5817/CP2022-2-9

Pancani, L., Mazzoni, D., Aureli, N., & Riva, P. (2021). Ghosting and orbiting: An analysis of victims' experiences. *Journal of Social and Personal Relationships*, *38*(7), 1987–2007. https://doi.org/10.1177/02654075211000417

Passey, J., & Jacobson, J. A. (2007, January). *Causal uncertainty and social rejection.* Presented at the Society for Personality and Social Psychology, Memphis, TN.

Pennebaker, J. W. (1997). Writing about emotional experience as a therapeutic process. *Psychological Science, 8,* 162–166. https://doi.org/10.1111/j.1467-9280.1997.tb00403.x

Pfundmair, M., Lermer, E., Frey, D., & Aydin, N. (2015). Construal level and social exclusion: Concrete thinking impedes recovery from social exclusion. *The Journal of Social Psychology*, *155*(4), 338–355. https://doi.org/10.1080/00224545.2015.1015475

Pfundmair, M., Wood, N. R., Hales, A. H., & Wesselmann, E. D. (2022). How social exclusion makes radicalism flourish. *Journal of Social Issues, 80,* 1–19. https://doi.org/10.1111/josi.12520

Poon, K. T., Chen, Z., & Wong, W. Y. (2020). Beliefs in conspiracy theories following ostracism. *Personality and Social Psychology Bulletin*, *46*(8), 1234–1246. https://doi.org/10.1177/0146167219898944

Reich, T., & Wheeler, S. C. (2016). The good and bad of ambivalence: Desiring ambivalence under outcome uncertainty. *Journal of Personality and Social Psychology*, *110*(4), 493. https://doi.org/10.1037/pspa0000047

Robinson, S. L., O'Reilly, J., & Wang, W. (2013). Invisible at work: An integrated model of workplace ostracism. *Journal of Management*, *39*(1), 203–231. https://doi.org/10.1177/0149206312466141

Rothbaum, F., Weisz, J. R., & Snyder, S. (1982). Changing the world and changing the self: A two process model of perceived control. *Journal of Personality and Social Psychology, 42,* 5–37. https://doi.org/10.1037/0022-3514.42.1.5

Rudert, S. C., & Greifeneder, R. (2016). When it's okay that I don't play: Social norms and the situated construal of social exclusion. *Personality and Social Psychology Bulletin*, *42*(7), 955–969. https://doi.org/10.1177/ 0146167216649606

Rudert, S. C., Janke, S., & Greifeneder, R. (2021). Ostracism breeds depression: Longitudinal associations between ostracism and depression over a three-year-period. *Journal of Affective Disorders Reports*, *4*, 100118. https://doi.org/10.1016/j.jadr.2021.100118

Smith, A., & Williams, K. D. (2004). R U There? Effects of ostracism by cell phone messages. *Group Dynamics: Theory, Research, and Practice, 8,* 291–301. https://doi.org/10.1037/1089-2699.8.4.291

Sommer, K. L., Williams, K. D., Ciarocco, N. J., & Baumeister, R. F. (2001). When silence speaks louder than words: Explorations into the interpersonal and intrapsychic consequences of social ostracism. *Basic and Applied Social Psychology, 83,* 606–615. https://doi.org/10.1207/S15324834BASP2304_1

Sweeny, K. (2018). On the experience of awaiting uncertain news. *Current Directions in Psychological Science*, *27*(4), 281–285. https://doi.org/10.1177/0963721417754197

Taylor, S. E., & Brown, J. D. (1988). Illusion and well-being: A social psychological perspective on mental health. *Psychological Bulletin, 103,* 193–210. https://doi.org/10.1037/0033-2909.103.2.193

Twenge, J. M., Baumeister, R. F., Tice, D. M., & Stucke, T. S. (2001). If you can't join them, beat them: Effects of social exclusion on aggressive behavior. *Journal of Personality and Social Psychology*, *81,* 1058–1069. https://doi.org/10.1037/0022-3514.81.6.1058

van Beest, I., & Williams, K. D. (2006). When inclusion costs and ostracism pays, ostracism still hurts. *Journal of Personality and Social Psychology, 91,* 218–228. https://doi.org/10.1037/0022-3514.91.5.918

van den Bos, K. (2001). Uncertainty management: The influence of uncertainty salience on reactions to perceived procedural fairness. *Journal of Personality and Social Psychology, 80,* 931–941. https://doi.org/10.1037/0022-3514.80.6.931

van Prooijen, J., & Jostmann, N. B. (2013). Belief in conspiracy theories: The influence of uncertainty and perceived morality. *European Journal of Social Psychology, 43*, 109–115. https:// doi.org/10.1002/ejsp.1922

Weary, G., & Edwards, J. A. (1994). Individual differences in causal uncertainty. *Journal of Personality and Social Psychology, 67,* 308–318. https://doi.org/10.1037/0022-3514.67.2.308

Williams, K. D. (1997). Social ostracism. In R. M. Kowalski (Ed.), *Aversive interpersonal behaviors* (pp. 133–170). Plenum Press.

Williams, K. D. (2007). Ostracism. *Annual Review of Psychology, 58*, 425–452. https://doi.org/10.1146/annurev.psych.58.110405.085641

Williams, K. D. (2009). Ostracism: A temporal need-threat model. In M. P. Zanna (Ed.), *Advances in experimental social psychology* (Vol. 41, pp. 275–314). Elsevier Academic Press. https://doi.org/10.1016/S0065-2601(08)00406-1

Williams, K. D., Cheung, C. K. T., & Choi, W. (2000). CyberOstracism: Effects of being ignored over the Internet. *Journal of Personality and Social Psychology, 79*, 748–762. https://doi.org/10.1037/0022-3514.79.5.748

Williams, K. D., Govan, C. L., Crocker, V., Tynan, D., Cruickshank, M. C., & Lam, A. (2002). Investigation into differences between social- and cyberostracism. *Group Dynamics: Theory, Research, and Practice. 6,* 65–77. https://doi.org/10.1037/1089-2699.6.1.65

Williams, K. D., Hales, A. H. & Michels, C. (2019). Social ostracism as a factor motivating interest in extreme groups. In S. C. Rudert, R. Greifeneder, & K. D. Williams (Eds.), *Current directions in ostracism, social exclusion and rejection research* (pp. 17–30). Routledge.

Williams, K. D., Shore, W. J., & Grahe, J. E. (1998). The silent treatment: Perceptions of its behaviors and associated feelings. *Group Processes and Intergroup Relations, 1,* 117–141. https://doi.org/10.1177/1368430298012002

Williams, K. D., & Zadro, L. (2005). Ostracism: The indiscriminate early detection system. In K. D. Williams, J. P. Forgas, & W. von Hippel (Eds.), *The social outcast: Ostracism, social exclusion, rejection, and bullying* (pp. 19–34). Psychology Press.

Wilson, T. D., Centerbar, D. B., Kermer, D. A., & Gilbert, D. T. (2005). The pleasure of uncertainty: Prolonging positive mood in ways people do not anticipate. *Journal of Personality and Social Psychology, 88,* 5–21. https://doi.org/10.1037/0022-3514.88.1.5

Wirth, J. H. (2016). Methods for investigating social exclusion. In P. Riva & J. Eck (Eds.), *Social exclusion: Psychological approaches to understanding and reducing its impact* (pp. 25–47). Springer International Publishing/Springer Nature. https://doi.org/10.1007/978-3-319-33033-4_2

Zadro, L. (2004). *Ostracism: Empirical studies inspired by real-world experiences of silence and exclusion.* Unpublished doctoral dissertation. University of New South Wales, Sydney, Australia.

Zadro, L., Boland, C, & Richardson, R. (2006). How long does it last? The persistence of the effects of ostracism in the socially anxious. *Journal of Experimental Social Psychology, 42*, 692–697. https://doi.org/10.1016/j.jesp.2005.10.007

Zadro, L., Williams, K. D., & Richardson, R. (2004). How low can you go? Ostracism by a computer lowers belonging, control, self-esteem, and meaningful existence. *Journal of Experimental Social Psychology, 40,* 560–567. https://doi.org/10.1016/j.jesp.2003.11.006

Zimmer-Gembeck, M. J., & Nesdale, D. (2013). Anxious and angry rejection sensitivity, social withdrawal, and retribution in high and low ambiguous situations. *Journal of Personality, 81*(1), 29–38. https://doi.org/10.1111/j.1467-6494.2012.00792.x

16

CERTAINTY THROUGH SOCIAL CONNECTION? PROTECTING THE SELF IN AN UNCERTAIN SOCIAL WORLD

Sandra L. Murray

A quick online search for dictionary definitions of the term "self" casts the self as a solitary figure—as standing "apart from others." However, we cannot escape our ties to others (Baumeister & Leary, 1995). Rather than standing apart, our sense of ourselves, and our sense of the world around us, is tied to the actions of those we hold dear, such as our spouses, children, and cherished friends (Murray et al., 2006). It is similarly tied to those we might never meet, such as a reclusive neighbor, a political pundit spreading conspiracy theories, a deadlocked Congress, or a divisive Prime Minister (Holt-Lunstad, 2018).

On the upside, these interdependent ties can strengthen or fortify the self. For instance, being able to count on the support of a romantic partner, the generosity of friends, or the love of a child can attenuate physical pain (Master et al., 2009), alleviate death anxiety (Cox & Arndt, 2012; Plusnin et al., 2018) and facilitate successful goal pursuit (Feeney & Collins, 2015; Fitzsimons et al., 2015). On the downside, these same interdependent ties can also threaten or undermine the self. For example, people can be left unsure of their identity after a romantic breakup (Slotter et al., 2010), nursing a wounded ego after soliciting advice from a friend (Leary et al., 1995), or stressed and distraught over a Presidential election (Blanton et al., 2012).

Because the myriad ties we share with others offer the possibility for benefit as well as harm, their very existence has the potential to increase uncertainty about our personal fate. Depending on the exigencies of the situation, a spouse could respond to a request for help with support or criticism, a friend could respond to good news with congratulations or jealousy, or a President could respond to a looming financial crisis with wisdom or obstruction (Murray, Lamarche et al., 2021). Recognizing this duality, Baumeister and Leary (1995) concluded that people are fundamentally motivated to belong—to be included in social connections where they are consistently cared for and protected, not hurt or exploited. In other words, people have a fundamental need for social connections that are *safe* (see Brady et al., this volume).

Reflecting the importance of this motivation for human survival, people seem to be equipped with regulatory systems for ensuring social connection is safe (Kenrick et al., 2010). For instance, the risk-regulation system motivates people to avoid intimates who might reject or ostracize them (Cameron & Granger, 2019; Murray et al., 2002), whereas the behavioral-immune system

 DOI: 10.4324/9781003363385-18

motivates people to avoid others when they are potentially infected with contagious diseases (Miller & Maner, 2011, 2012; Murray & Schaller, 2016).

However, in depending on others, people risk exposing themselves to more than emotional or physical harm. They also risk having their very understanding of themselves and the reality that surrounds them challenged by the actions of others (Heine et al., 2006; Jonas et al., 2014; Murray et al., 2017). The sources of such existential uncertainty are varied and plentiful. On any given day, Jamie might be taken aback by her left-leaning spouse's strident opposition to gender-affirming care, troubled by a conservative President's unexpectedly dovish position toward an adversary, puzzled by her teenage son's meltdown over a compliment, or questioning why her friends made such deep dives into conspiratorial thought.

This chapter reviews the pivotal role that romantic relationships play in creating and resolving uncertainty about the motivations of others, and thus, the consequent safety of social connection (see also Murray & Lamarche, 2023). Its first section explains why romantic relationships play a central world in shaping the operation of the social-safety system, which functions to protect people against everyday experiences of being perplexed or flummoxed by the behavior of others. Its second section reviews empirical research illustrating the operation of this system—documenting how romantic relationships create and alleviate uncertainty. Its concluding section provides intervention-based evidence that affirming the safety of social connection through romantic relationships provides an all-purpose antidote against uncertainty about one's safety in the social world, whether such uncertainty comes from the social or physical risks others pose to the self.

The Social-Safety System

Romantic relationships have long played an outsized role in affording physical and psychological protection against harm (Day, 2016). In evolutionary history, people relied on romantic partners for concrete protection from human foes, animal foes, and resource insecurity (e.g., food, shelter, Finkel et al., 2014). Romantic partners have even continued to confer physical protection today, as evidenced by the fact that people with supportive partners experience better physical health than people with less supportive partners (Robles et al., 2014). In recent decades, people have also come to rely almost exclusively on romantic partners to satisfy self-actualization needs (Finkel et al., 2014). Given the outsized role romantic partners play in protecting the self, experiences in this foundational relationship likely play a central role in shaping how safe people feel depending on others outside of this relationship as well.

People live immersed in multiple layers of social connection spanning the *personal* (Feeney & Collins, 2015) to the *sociopolitical* (Hudson, 2006). People share *personal* relationships with *close* others, such as siblings, parents, children, spouses, in-laws, friends, and teammates. Such personal relationships are typically chosen and voluntarily nurtured to a greater or lesser degree (Feeney & Collins, 2015). However, people also share community or societally-based *sociopolitical* relationships with *non-close* others, such as employers, teachers, neighbors, fellow citizens, governmental bodies (e.g., Congress), and Presidents or Prime Ministers. Such sociopolitical relationships are typically foisted on people as part of living as part of organized, often hierarchical, social collectives, such as schools, workplaces, and cities (Hudson, 2006).

Despite dissimilarities in familiarity and volition, the relationships that surround people nonetheless share a defining feature: One's outcomes ultimately depend on the behavior of others (Kelley, 1979). For instance, soliciting advice can result in a spouse's criticism or praise, cultivating a teen's excitement for a family trip can court excitement or indifference, and disclosing a secret to a friend can result in greater closeness or betrayed confidence. Similarly, depending on an employer for family leave can result in vacation days spent on a beach or taking one's children to doctors, trusting state or federal governments to enforce environmental safety regulations can result in safe or tainted water supplies, and relying on fellow community members to vote sensibly can elect experienced politicians or Q-Anon followers to Congress.

For people to feel relatively safe in the face of such dependence, they need to trust that others will behave in ways that are sensible, understandable, and foreseeable. Seeing others' behavior as sensible, understandable, and foreseeable is essential to the experience of safety because correctly anticipating others' actions allows people to adjust their own behavior accordingly (Kelley, 1979; Tooby & Cosmides, 1996). For instance, if Jamie can anticipate when Quinn is motivated to be supportive (vs. critical), her friends are motivated to be congratulatory (vs. jealous), or her President is motivated to be honest (vs. duplicitous), she can adjust her behavior to keep herself safer in her social ties to them. Namely, she can selectively seek advice when her spouse is motivated to be supportive, share good news when her friend is motivated to be congratulatory, and judiciously disbelieve a President she suspects of duplicity. Consequently, when Jamie correctly anticipates the behavior of others, it provides reassuring evidence that she understands the reality they inhabit well enough to know when she can and cannot safely depend on them to protect her (Higgins et al., 2021), keeping her relatively safe.

Inevitably, though, Jamie will err in her behavioral forecasts. Indeed, people often make mistakes in forecasting others' behavior because they naively assume that others perceive the same reality they perceive (Griffin & Ross 1991; Peetz et al., 2022). This results in individuals, entities, or institutions behaving in ways that violate personal (e.g., "My spouse is a feminist just like me"), historic (e.g., "I've never seen my son enjoy vegetables") and/or normative (e.g., "Presidents should be prudent") expectations. For instance, people overestimate how positively and negatively others are likely to feel (Pollmann & Finkenauer, 2009). Such a bias could leave people vulnerable to being confused or unsettled by a spouse's ennui after a promotion or an employer's nonchalance in the face of poor earnings. People also underestimate how much gratitude acts of kindness will elicit in others (Kumar & Epley, 2018). Such a bias could leave people unsettled or confused by friend's glee over what seemed like a small favor or a President's openness to dialogue with an adversary.

Finding Safety in the Face of the Unexpected

Unexpected behavior thus highlights the uncertainty inherent to interdependence: It is not always possible to predict what others will do, which makes it difficult to know when it is safe to depend on them. The social-safety system illustrated in Figure 16.1 gives people a reason to feel safe depending on others in the face of the threat that unexpected behavior poses to their understanding of others and the social world they share with them. In outlining the operation of this system, we first explain when unexpected behavior poses a greater threat to the safety of social connection. We then explain the role that romantic relationship bonds play in both creating and alleviating threats to the perception of safety in daily life (Murray, Lamarche et al., 2021).

Triggering a Safety Threat

Reflecting its roots in interdependence theory (Kelley, 1979), the model contends that people are especially motivated to feel safe in social connection when their personal outcomes are *more* (vs. less) dependent on others (Murray, Lamarche et al., 2021). Outcome dependence varies by *situation* because situations vary in their features (Kelley et al., 2003). For instance, Jamie's emotional

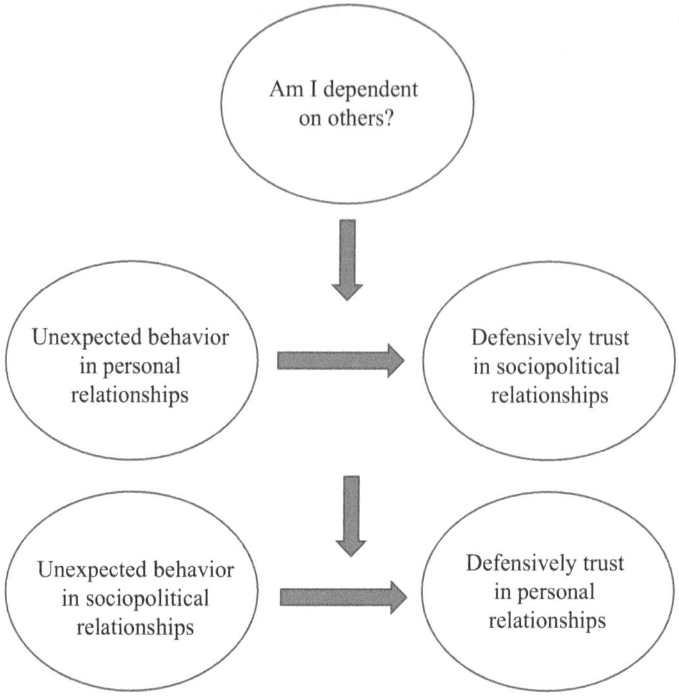

Figure 16.1 The social safety system.

well-being is more dependent on her spouse's willingness to provide comfort when she needs support than when she does not need support; her physical health is more dependent on her neighbors being vaccinated when COVID-19 cases are rising than falling in her community (Murray, Seery et al., 2021); and her personal finances are more dependent on her fellow citizens when votes are being cast in more (vs. less) pivotal elections (Blanton et al., 2012; Stanton et al., 2010; Trawalter et al., 2012).

Outcome dependence also varies by *person* because people differ in the extent to which they feel more (vs. less) vulnerable to being harmed by the actions of others. According to evolutionary theorists, people evolved to detect and seek out intimates they can reliably depend upon—intimates who see them as indispensable or special—because loyal alliances afford protection against harm (Tooby & Cosmides, 1996). In modern life, people rely heavily on romantic partners to provide such protection (Arriaga et al., 2018; Feeney & Collins, 2015; Finkel et al., 2014; Szepsenwol & Simpson, 2019). This reliance can leave people who are *less* certain they can trust their romantic partner *more* vulnerable to harm than people who are *more* certain they can trust their romantic partner. For instance, people who are *less* certain they can trust their romantic partners are *more* readily hurt by their partner's transgressions, as compared to people who are certain they can trust their partner (Murray et al., 2003). People who are less certain they can trust their romantic partner are also more readily agitated by the thought of physical pain or human mortality, suggesting they generally feel more vulnerable to the actions of others (Cox & Arndt, 2012; Plusnin et al., 2018).

The model further contends that outcome-dependence does not always generate worries about safety. Instead, whether outcome-dependence feels more or less safe depends on one's certainty about oneself and one's understanding of the world, which varies *situationally* (see van den Bos & Lind, this volume; Landau et al., this volume). According to the model, when a spouse, friend, community, government institution, or political leader behaves *expectedly*, it provides reassuring evidence that one shares their reality (Higgins et al., 2021). The resulting state of *certainty* validates the self and makes it acutely easier to believe one's power to keep oneself safe from harm in such situations (Heine et al., 2006; Jonas et al., 2014; Murray et al., 2017). Conversely, when a significant person behaves *unexpectedly*, it provides troubling evidence that reality is not consensually perceived, which puts one's own understanding of reality in question. The resulting state of *uncertainty* invalidates or undermines one's sense of self, and makes it acutely harder to believe in one's power to keep oneself safe from harm in such situations (Murray et al., 2018).

Being acutely uncertain of others' motivations and behavior heightens the vulnerability inherent to being dependent on them (see Namkoong et al., this volume). Therefore, when outcome dependence is high, experiencing *more* unexpected behavior makes it especially salient that one might not understand others or the reality they inhabit well enough to keep oneself safe. For instance, when Jamie is counting on Quinn for a specific sacrifice, Quinn's unexpected behavior could make Jamie question whether she really understands Quinn as well as she thought, making her feel acutely unsafe. Also, when *rising* COVID-19 cases make people more dependent on their neighbors to keep them safe from infection, a neighbor's unexpected support for a populist politician could make Jamie question whether she really understands her community, making her feel acutely unsafe. Similarly, when Jamie is less certain that she can trust Quinn, a President's unexpected change in tax policy should make Jamie question whether her financial future is secure in her government's hands, making her feel acutely unsafe.

The model further assumes that unexpected behavior poses *generalized* rather than localized threats to safety. That is, when Jamie's partner Quinn behaves unexpectedly, Jamie may do more than wonder whether she really understands Quinn. She might also wonder, however fleetingly, whether she actually understands anyone close to her. Why would uncertainty generalize in this way? Relationships within a given relationship world (personal versus societal/community/sociopolitical) are interconnected, both experientially and cognitively. Experiences depending on a spouse are bound up in experiences depending on children, in-laws, and family friends (Holt-Lunstad, 2018; Mikulincer & Shaver, 2003). Similarly, experiences depending on fellow community members to behave in socially or legally prescribed ways are bound up in experiences depending on local, state, and federal officials and institutions to behave responsibly (Hudson, 2006). Because the experiences people have with others share these past and present interconnections, unexpected behavior on the part of one inhabitant of a given relationship world can put the motivations of *other* inhabitants in that relationship world into question as well, threatening its safety *as a whole*.[1]

Defending against a Safety-Threat

To recap the "threat" side of Figure 16.1, ongoing experiences threaten feelings of safety in social connection when people are (1) *highly* outcome-dependent (i.e., highly dependent on others) and (2) *unable* to anticipate the behavior of the inhabitants of a specific relationship world (i.e., highly uncertain). The "defense" side of Figure 16.1 describes the reactive defenses that restore safety to social connection in the face of such acute vulnerability (see McGregor & Marigold, this volume for the effects of uncertainty on approach).

Much as pain motivates reflexively withdrawing from its source, we contend that being highly outcome-dependent on the unexpectedly-behaving inhabitants of one relationship world motivates people to psychologically escape this now riskier relationship world (Cavallo et al., 2009; Murray et al., 2006). People typically escape threatening experiences by adopting the beliefs that can most readily, and compellingly, restore feelings of equanimity (Heine et al., 2006). When unexpected behavior alerts people to the possibility that they might *not* understand one type of relationship world as well as they thought, the model contends that people can most readily convince themselves that they are still safe *nonetheless* by imposing caring and well-meaning intentions on the *alternate*, more perceptually *pliable*, relationship world (Kunda, 1990). Consistent with this logic, people can escape anxieties about being rejected by others by seeing greater acceptance in the tabula rasa afforded by *new* acquaintances (Maner et al., 2007; Richman & Leary, 2009; Williams et al., 2000). They also escape anxiety about death by turning to close relationship partners who best afford safety (Plusnin et al., 2018; Young et al., 2015).

In sum, operating in conjunction with daily life, the social-safety system's dual defenses link the threats to the safety of social connection in one relationship world to its associated *defense* for making social connections feel safer. Specifically, *personal-to-sociopolitical* threat-defense links anxiety about depending on the indecipherable or unforeseeable motivations of the inhabitants of one's *personal relationship* world to the defensive inclination to impose understandable, benevolent, and trustworthy motivations on the inhabitants of one's *sociopolitical relationship* world. Conversely, *sociopolitical-to-personal* threat-defense links anxiety about depending on the indecipherable or unforeseeable motivations of the inhabitants of one's *sociopolitical relationship* world to the defensive inclination to impose understandable, benevolent, and trustworthy motivations on the inhabitants of one's *personal relationship* world.

Personal-to-Sociopolitical Threat-Defense

Through this threat-defense, people counteract the uncertainty posed by having one's outcomes tied to *unexpectedly behaving close others* by defensively perceiving greater reason to trust in *sociopolitical* relationships. For instance, being surprised by a progressive spouse's agreement with a right-wing TV personality or a friend gushing over for a small favor might motivate people to defensively perceive their neighbors or legislators as being especially capable of looking out for their best interest.

Sociopolitical-to-Personal Threat-Defense

Through this threat-defense, people counteract the uncertainty posed by having one's outcomes tied to *unexpectedly behaving sociopolitical agents or entities* by defensively perceiving greater reason to trust in *personal relationships*. For instance, being surprised by a President reversing a longstanding position or an unexpected dip in the stock market despite good employment numbers might motivate people to defensively perceive their family members and friends as being *more* capable of taking care of them. Consistent with this logic, people acutely threatened by national economic uncertainty report more trust in people they know (Navarro-Carrillo et al., 2018). Similarly, people primed to think their country is doing poorly report more trust in their partner and in marriage (Day et al., 2011).

Empirical Examples of the Social-Safety System in Operation

In our research on the social-safety system, my collaborators and I have relied on naturalistic daily diary and longitudinal study designs so that we can capitalize on unexpected events as they happen in the real world. This section of the chapter summarizes findings drawn from two daily diary studies conducted during the initial years of the Trump administration (Murray, Lamarche et al., 2021), an 8-week longitudinal study of the 2018 U.S. Midterm election (Murray, Lamarche et al., 2021; Murray, Seery et al., 2021), and a three-week longitudinal study of the initial months of the COVID-19 pandemic in the United States (Murray, Seery et al., 2021). In all of these studies, we required participants to be involved in live-in romantic relationships. Given this constraint, most were married for more than a decade and had an average of two children still at home. In the daily diary studies, participants provided online daily reports each day for nine to ten consecutive days. In the midterm election study, participants provided once-weekly online reports for each of the six weeks preceding the 2018 U.S. midterm election, the day after the midterm election, and one week after the election. In the COVID-19 study, participants provided reports every other day for three weeks. We provide the evidence for *personal-to-sociopolitical* and *sociopolitical-to-personal* threat-defense in turn.

Personal-to-Sociopolitical Threat-Defense

When people exhibit this threat-defense, they counteract the uncertainty posed by depending on unexpectedly behaving intimates (i.e., the *threat*) by perceiving greater reason to trust in *sociopolitical* relationships (i.e., the defense). We examined these dynamics in one daily diary study and the 2018 midterm election study. In these studies, we expected people to defensively trust *more* in *sociopolitical relationships* when they were (1) *highly outcome-dependent* and (2) exposed to *unexpected* behavior on the part of close others.

The Daily-Diary Study

In this study, we operationalized *outcome-dependence* through differences between *people*—that is, through individual differences in expressions of romantic trust (i.e., "I can trust my romantic partner completely"; "I can always count on my romantic partner to be responsive to my needs and feelings"; "My romantic partner is always there for me"). As in prior research, we expected participants who were *less* certain they could trust their romantic partners to be more outcome-dependent or vulnerable to being harmed by others (Murray et al., 2006), sensitizing them to the threat posed by unexpected behavior. We operationalized intimates' *unexpected behavior* through daily "yes" responses to 6 items that asked participants to indicate whether their romantic partner or child(ren) had said or done anything "out-of-the-ordinary", "they did not expect", or anything that "did not make sense" that day. We operationalized *trust in sociopolitical relationships* through daily expressions of faith that the Trump administration was a trustworthy steward of the nation, which we captured through the daily value participants personally placed on political conservatism and their trust that the (Republican) federal government was doing a good job (Murray, Lamarche et al., 2021).

Because the data had a nested structure (i.e., day within-person), we used multilevel analyses to test our hypotheses. These analyses revealed that participants who were less certain they could trust their romantic partner (i.e., *high* outcome-dependence) reported *greater* faith that the Republican government's actions secured the country's welfare on the days after family members behaved *more* unexpectedly than usual (i.e., *high* uncertainty about the motivations of close others) as compared to days their family members behaved *less* unexpectedly (i.e., *low* uncertainty). However, people who were already certain they could trust their romantic partner evidenced no such compensatory effect (i.e., *low* outcome-dependence).

The 2018 Midterm Election Study

As we did in the daily diary study, we indexed *outcome-dependence* through individual differences in expressions of romantic trust. However, the midterm election study also allowed us to further index outcome-dependence *situationally.* With each passing week during the 2018 midterm election season, the public became increasingly aware of the eventual electoral result—Democrats gaining control of the House and Republicans retaining the Senate. Because neither party gained unilateral control of Congress on election day, we expected *not* knowing whether one's preferred party would ultimately wield enough power over the country's governance *in the future* to make the risks of having one's fate tied to the votes cast by fellow community members more salient to partisans of both stripes. Therefore, we expected participants to be more keenly aware of their dependence on the collective populace to cast the "right" votes *after* the election than before the election.

We operationalized the daily *unexpected behavior* of intimates through "yes" responses to eight items that asked participants to separately indicate whether their romantic partner or child had said or done anything "out-of-the-ordinary," anything "they did not expect," or anything that "did not make sense" and whether *they themselves* had any thoughts or feelings about their romantic partner or children "they did not expect to have" that day. We operationalized *trust in sociopolitical relationships* through sympathy for the brand of Republicanism President Trump routinely Tweeted. Namely, each week, we asked participants to report how much they personally (1) distrusted the media (e.g., "The mainstream media cannot be trusted"), (2) distrusted progressivism (e.g., "American society needs to be radically restructured," reversed, "The structure of American society needs to change," reversed), and (3) favored economic (e.g., "fiscal responsibility," "business") over social conservatism (e.g., "the family," "religion"). We targeted the relative priority of economic over social conservatism as a metric of sympathy for President Trump because perceiving such an economic bias in Trump's policies made him a more trustworthy and appealing candidate to swing voters in the 2016 federal election (Silver, 2019). So, in this study, we reasoned that perceiving such an economic bias in Trump's policies would also make it psychologically easier for participants to convince themselves they could trust in the Trump-led government on days when their family members behaved unexpectedly.

Multilevel analyses revealed the expected operation of the social-safety system. After the results of the election were known (i.e., *high* outcome-dependence), participants who were less certain they could trust their romantic partner (i.e., *high* outcome-dependence) reported significantly *greater* faith that the Republican government's actions secured the country's welfare on the days after family members behaved *more* unexpectedly than usual (i.e., high uncertainty about the motivations of close others) as compared to days their family members behaved *less* unexpectedly (i.e., low uncertainty). However, these compensatory effects were not evident well in advance of the election (i.e., *low* outcome dependence), nor were they evident when people were certain they could trust their romantic partner (i.e., *low* outcome dependence).

Of course, it is relatively easy for participants who are motivated to find safety in the *sociopolitical* relationships to profess greater trust in the Republican-led government. To provide a more difficult test of the social-safety system's power, we asked participants to report how they voted. Even though voting is strongly partisan in nature, these data nevertheless revealed a shift in voting preferences, but only when people needed to find *greater* safety in *sociopolitical relationships* to defend against unexpected behavior in their *personal* relationships. Specifically, participants who were *less* certain they could trust their romantic partner (i.e., *high* outcome-dependence) were *more* likely to cast votes for Republican candidates when their family members behaved *more* unexpectedly in the five weeks before the midterm (i.e., *high* uncertainty about the motivations of close others), as compared to less trusting participants whose family members behaved *less* unexpectedly (i.e., *low* uncertainty). In other words, when family members behaved especially unexpectedly, the hypothesized defensive need to trust and find safety in the Trump administration predicted being more likely to trust and support this administration by casting more votes in favor of Republican over Democratic candidates.

In sum, findings from both studies suggest that participants defensively professed *greater* trust in the safety of *sociopolitical* relationships when they were (1) *highly outcome-dependent* and (2) existentially confused by the unexpected behavior of their intimates.

Sociopolitical-to-Personal Threat-Defense

When people engage in this threat-defense, they counteract the uncertainty posed by *high* outcome-dependence on *unexpectedly behaving* sociopolitical agents and entities (i.e., the *threat*) by perceiving greater reason to trust in their intimates (i.e., the *defense*). We examined this threat-defense in the daily diary studies, the 2018 midterm election study, and our three-week study of the initial period of the COVID-19 pandemic in the United States. We expected people to defensively trust *more* in *personal relationships* when they were (1) *highly outcome-dependent*, and (2) exposed to the *unexpected* behavior of *sociopolitical* agents, entities, and institutions, whether the behavior of government leaders or fellow members of the U.S. community.

The Daily Diary Studies

As we did before, we operationalized *outcome-dependence* through differences between *people*—that is, through individual expressions of romantic trust. We then turned to two *real-world* indicators to operationalize *unexpected behavior* on the part of government leaders and institutions. Specifically, we categorized the *expectedness* of *government* behavior each day through (1) the Chicago Board Options Exchange Volatility Index, an economic marker of political instability[2] and (2) the Google searches of people living in the same zip code as the participant, assuming that Google searches that day would capture existential uncertainty about unexpected government behavior. For instance, the news cycle in the first study included Trump tweeting threats of nuclear war with North Korea and impugning the FBI director. So, we tracked how often people living in the same zip code as the participant searched for "uncertainty," "North Korea," "Trump lies," "Comey," and "terrorism," assuming that more frequent searches in the participant's community would capture greater collective uncertainty about these presumably unexpected behaviors. We operationalized *trust in personal relationships* through perceptions of love and acceptance from immediate family members (e.g., "my partner made me feel especially loved"; "my child expressed love and affection toward me") and the daily quality of these family relationships (from "terrible" to "terrific").

Multilevel analyses revealed that participants who were *less* certain they could trust their romantic partner (i.e., *high* outcome-dependence) reported greater trust or faith in the benevolent motivations of family members on days after the sociopolitical world behaved *more* unexpectedly, as captured by spikes in the VIX or Google-search activity (i.e., *high* uncertainty about the motivations of government leaders and institutions), as compared to days when sociopolitical powers behaved *less* unexpectedly (i.e., low uncertainty). However, people who were already certain they could trust their romantic partner evidenced no such compensatory effect (i.e., *low* outcome-dependence). In sum, participants defensively professed *greater* trust in the safety of their *personal* relationships when they were (1) *highly outcome-dependent* and (2) likely confused and uncertain in the face of *unexpected* government behavior.

The Midterm Election and Pandemic Studies

The midterm election and pandemic studies allowed us to operationalize both outcome-dependence and expectedness *situationally*. In the midterm study, we again operationalized *outcome-dependence* through knowledge of the election's results in the midterm study. As we explained earlier, we expected participants to feel *more* keenly dependent on fellow community members to vote the "right way" after the election resulted in a divided Congress (i.e., *high* outcome-dependence) than before (i.e., *low* outcome-dependence). In the pandemic study, we operationalized *outcome-dependence* through the total number of COVID-19 cases in the United States. We expected participants to feel *more* keenly dependent on their fellow community members to keep them safe from infection on days when the total number of U.S. cases increased *more* than usual (i.e., *high* outcome-dependence), as compared to *less* than usual (i.e., *low* outcome-dependence).

We operationalized expectedness through the *consistency* between one's personal view of President Trump's stewardship and popular consensus. We did this by tracking the percentage of social media posts mentioning the President that were *negative* on each assessment day. We then used political partisanship to define (1) days when U.S. citizens *more often* posted negative comments mentioning Donald Trump as *more* unexpected for conservatives, given the positive reality of his stewardship most conservatives perceived, and (2) days when U.S. citizens *less often* posted negative comments mentioning Donald Trump as *more* unexpected for liberals, given the *negative* reality of his stewardship most *liberals* perceived. We operationalized *trust in personal relationships* through participants reporting (1) the daily quality of their relationships with their romantic partners and children (from "terrible" to "terrific") and (2) daily doubt and conflict in these familial relationships, which we reversed, such that higher scores captured greater daily happiness, and thus safety, within these family relationship bonds.

Multilevel analyses revealed that on days when the election results were known (i.e., *high* outcome-dependence), *liberals* reported greater family relationship happiness on days when popular sentiment toward President Trump was *less negative* than usual (i.e., *high* uncertainty about the motivations of their fellow citizens for liberals) than *more negative* than usual (i.e., *low* uncertainty for liberals). However, *conservatives* reported greater family relationship happiness on days when popular sentiment toward President Trump was *more negative* than usual (i.e., *high* uncertainty about the motivations of their fellow citizens for conservatives) than *less negative* than usual (i.e., *low* uncertainty for conservatives). Similarly, on days when COVID-19 cases spread *more* rapidly (i.e., *high* outcome-dependence), *liberals* reported greater family relationship happiness on days when popular sentiment toward President Trump was *less negative* than usual (i.e., *high* uncertainty about the perceptions and motivations of their fellow citizens for liberals) than *more negative* than usual (i.e., *low* uncertainty about their fellow citizens for liberals). However, *conservatives* reported greater family relationship happiness on days when popular sentiment toward President Trump was *more negative* than usual (i.e., *high* uncertainty about the perceptions and motivations of their fellow citizens for conservatives) than *less negative* than usual (i.e., *low* uncertainty for conservatives). No such compensatory effects emerged for liberals or conservatives in either study on days when the election results were unknown or U.S. COVID-19 cases spread less rapidly (i.e., *low* outcome-dependence). Importantly, then, the predicted safety-affirming defenses emerged regardless of political orientation (which we examined only to index the consistency between participants' own likely views of President Trump (based on their partisanship) and popular sentiment on a given day).

In sum, we found evidence for *sociopolitical-to-personal* threat-defense in all four studies. Participants defensively professed *greater* trust in the safety of *personal* relationship worlds on days when they were highly *outcome-dependent* (i.e., vulnerable to others) and existentially confused by government leaders and community members behaving unexpectedly.

A Safety Intervention: Leveraging the Power of Romantic Relationships

The studies I have reviewed suggest that romantic relationships can create and resolve uncertainty about one's place, and one's safety, in the social world. However, these studies do not directly speak to the centrality of the role that romantic relationships play in affording a sense of safety in connection. If romantic relationships are indeed central to this experience, then actively intervening to make this specific relationship context feel safer should make the uncertainties of dependence less threatening. Specifically, such an intervention should help inoculate people who would otherwise feel uncomfortably vulnerable against the risks posed by depending on others. For instance, intervening to give a less trusting Jamie reason to feel safe depending on Quinn should make Quinn's unexpected behavior less threatening to Jamie – lessening Jamie's need to defensively affirm the trustworthiness of her community relationships. Indeed, such an intervention might also transform Jamie's general experience of the social world—broadly inoculating her against the social and physical risks inherent to depending on others.

The logic of a goal-system provides an apt metaphor for understanding how and why such a safety intervention could potentially work (Murray et al., 2023). Goal systems are typically conceptualized as hierarchically structured mental networks, ones that help people navigate their lives from one situation to the next. In such a network, a motivationally prioritized goal is thought to be linked to the means for its pursuit and embedded with other goals and their associated means. Importantly, these associated goals and means can complement or compete with the motivationally -prioritized goal pursuit (see Fishbach & Ferguson, 2007; Fitzsimons et al., 2015; Kruglanski et al., 2002; Kruglanski et al., 2015, for reviews). For instance, in the goal system of an aspiring dieter, the goal to lose weight is linked to the means for its pursuit—the complementary goals to eat healthy foods and exercise daily—which share links to the means supporting their pursuit (e.g., stocking the fridge with produce, cooking for oneself, committing to early morning hikes), furthering the pursuit of the motivationally-prioritized goal to lose weight. However, for this aspiring dieter, the goal to lose weight is also linked to the competing goal to self-indulge, such as (1) going out eating and drinking with friends or (2) sleeping in after a night spent playing video games, threatening the pursuit of the motivationally-prioritized goal.

When it comes to the risks posed by depending on others, people who normally feel *insufficiently* safe in social connections are like aspiring dieters. To meet their dieting goals, aspiring dieters need to prioritize eating healthy and exercise goals over alternative pursuits. Similarly, to meet the desired goals of feeling safer in social connections, people who feel *insufficiently* safe in social connections need to prioritize protecting themselves against being hurt by others. Indeed, as we have seen, people who feel *insufficiently* safe in social connection (either in the moment or in general) are more likely to defend against unexpected behavior. They are also highly motivated to defend themselves against other social risks—such as being rejected by a friend (Cameron & Granger, 2019) or infected by a stranger (Mortensen et al., 2010; Neuberg et al., 2011). In contrast, people who feel *sufficiently* safe in social connections (either in general or in the moment) are like accomplished dieters. Just like accomplished dieters can afford the occasional snack-infused Netflix binges with friends, *accomplished* safety-seekers can afford to pursue alternate, non-safety-related goals when it is riskier to depend on others.

With a romantic relationship-based intervention, my colleagues and I hoped to turn *aspiring safety-seekers* (i.e., people who feel *insufficiently* safe in social connections) into *accomplished safety-seekers* (i.e., people who feel *sufficiently* safe in social connections). In so doing, we hoped to reduce normally aspiring safety-seekers' need to defend against unexpected behavior—as well as other social (i.e., rejection) and physical (i.e., disease) risks that being connected to others imposes on individuals in day-to-day life.

What kind of romantic relationship intervention would be powerful enough to have such an effect? In ongoing relationships, spontaneous evaluative associations to romantic partners (e.g., good/bad, approach/avoid) capture actual experiences of being more or less valued and protected. A history of being treated *responsively* conditions more *positive* evaluative associations that signal the safety such responsive partners provide. In contrast, a history of being treated *unresponsively* conditions more *negative* evaluative associations that signal the vulnerability such unresponsive partners create (Hicks et al., 2016, 2018; Murray et al., 2010, 2013). This behavioral basis affords individuals with more positive automatic attitudes a resource for feeling safe, one that allows them to trust their romantic partner in situations where they might be hurt (Faure et al., 2018; McNulty et al., 2013, 2017; Murray et al., 2011, 2013).

Therefore, we decided to target evaluative associations to romantic partners with our intervention, with the hope of filling otherwise unfulfilled needs to feel safe in social connection in a sample of 555 U.S. adults in live-in romantic relationships (Murray et al., 2023). Building on an established evaluative-conditioning procedure for conditioning more positive automatic partner attitudes (McNulty et al., 2017), we designed our safety-intervention to *simulate* the experience of someone who spontaneously makes highly positive automatic associations to their romantic partner in daily interactions. Namely, every other day, over a three-week period, we repeatedly evaluatively conditioned *experimental* participants to associate their romantic partner with highly positive words and images—using an online protocol to nudge them to make safety-affording associations to them (above and beyond whatever associations they normally made, McNulty et al., 2017). In contrast, we repeatedly evaluatively conditioned *control* participants to associate their romantic partner with neutral words and images.

On each of the assessment/conditioning days, we also measured (1) daily unexpected behavior in *personal* relationships through self-reports that a romantic partner had behaved unexpectedly (e.g., "my romantic partner did/said something that made no sense to me") and (2) daily unexpected behavior in sociopolitical or community-based relationships through (a) self-reports that government officials had behaved unexpectedly and (b) objective evidence that government officials had behaved unexpectedly, indexed through increases in the VIX (aka fear) financial index, a marker of sociopolitical instability (Bloom, 2014). We also measured participants' self-reported trust in government officials, strangers, and personal relationship partners on each assessment day to examine if participants defensively restored safety.

The findings in the *control* condition replicated our previous research on the social safety system. Participants who felt *insufficiently* safe in social connection (i.e., participants who were less certain they could trust their romantic partner) protected themselves against unexpected behavior. That is, they defensively affirmed their trust in sociopolitical/community relationships on days when their romantic partner behaved *more* (vs. less) unexpectedly and they defensively affirmed their trust in those closest to them on days when the sociopolitical world behaved *more* (vs. less) unexpectedly. However, in the *experimental* condition, such defensive reaffirmations of safety disappeared. This suggests that intervening, and providing participants who are uncertain they can trust their partner with *advance* reason to feel safe in social connection, inoculated these vulnerable individuals against the threat that unexpected behavior posed to their sense of safety.

The risks of social connection are not limited to unexpected behavior, as noted earlier. Notably, people can be rejected or ostracized by others; they can also contract infectious illnesses from others (Miller & Maner, 2011, 2012; Murray & Schaller, 2016). Impressively, evaluatively conditioning participants to make positive, safety-affording associations to their romantic partner even inoculated people who are normally highly sensitive to the possibility of being rejected or hurt by others or the possibility of catching a contagious illness from others against these threatening experiences (Murray et al., 2023). For instance, in the *control* condition, people who were highly sensitive to interpersonal rejection (e.g., people low in self-esteem) self-protectively devalued their relationships with close others on days they were more (vs. less) hurt and rejected by them. And, in the *control* condition, people who felt highly vulnerable to infectious disease distanced themselves from strangers on days they were more (vs. less) worried about COVID-19. However, both of these self-protective responses to social risk were considerably attenuated and even disappeared in the *safety-intervention* condition.

Looking Forward

The findings that we have reviewed in this chapter suggest that romantic relationships play a central role in creating and resolving the uncertainties that are inherent to social connection. For instance, when Jamie questions Quinn's trustworthiness or fears a rapidly circulating virus, *not* being able to anticipate the behavior of her neighbors, fellow community members, or President threatens the collective safety of social connection, motivating her to perceive greater evidence of safety in her family relationships (i.e., *sociopolitical-to-personal* threat-defense). However, *not* being able to anticipate the behavior of her spouse or children motivates her to perceive greater evidence of safety in her relationship with her government or fellow community members (i.e., *personal-to-sociopolitical* threat-defense).

Of course, the evidence that people engage in these defenses in daily life does not address the question of whether the defense "works." While the initial evidence is not definitive, it does point to the effectiveness of the "safety-affirming" defenses. For instance, we took advantage of a longitudinal study of newlywed couples to examine whether newlyweds who were *more* likely to find a greater reason to be happy in their marriage on days when the VIX spiked fared better over time than newlyweds who were *less* likely to evidence this defense. For people who married *less* than completely certain they could trust their new spouse, being *more* likely to find happiness in their marriage on days when the VIX spiked was protective. Namely, being able to find greater safety in their marriage on days when the world behaved more unpredictably helped strengthen their trust in their partner and the security of their marriage over time (Murray, Lamarche et al., 2021).

Nevertheless, there is still more that we need to understand in delineating how people find a sense of safety in the relationships that surround them. For instance, future research might broaden the definition of sociopolitical relationships to include in-group or out-group members. On days when children or romantic partners behave acutely unexpectedly, perhaps people impose greater safety on the *sociopolitical* world by believing more in stereotypes that depict in-group members as warm and disbelieving stereotypes that depict out-group members as hostile. They might also profess greater than usual faith in the importance of religion in their lives. Future research should also examine the social-safety system's operation in different political contexts. The reviewed studies were conducted in the United States during the Trump administration, which confounds the motivation to believe in the prevailing sociopolitical powers with conservative (Republican) thinking. In this context, people had to believe in right-wing ideology and policy (no matter how personally foreign they normally found it) to impose safety on the sociopolitical world. In a Democratic-led administration, people might instead need to believe in more left-wing ideology and policy (no matter how personally foreign they find it) to impose safety on the sociopolitical world when close others they usually count on to meet their needs behave unexpectedly.

Future research could also examine whether *non-romantic* relationship bonds have similar power to desensitize people to the uncertainties that are inherent to living connected to others. The safety-intervention we deployed focused on romantic relationship bonds because one's bond to a romantic partner is arguably the most important social connection made in adult life (Day, 2016). Indeed, romantic partners are unique in the diversity of ways in which they can afford the experience of safety, both physical and psychological, including being a responsive sexual partner, listener, parent, conversationalist, goal-supporter, etc. However, romantic relationship bonds are not the only bonds that can make social connections feel safer, nor is evaluative conditioning the only way to increase feelings of relational safety. Therefore, future research might examine whether other interventions, such as focusing individuals on their longest-lasting friendships or reminding them of especially happy childhood memories of their parents, can also desensitize people to uncertainty and social risk.

Conclusion

The reviewed research sheds new light on how romantic relationships can be leveraged to protect the self in an uncertain social world. As this chapter has explored, the way people think about themselves, and their own vulnerability in the world, is inextricably tied to the bonds that share with those closest to them as well as the bonds that they share with people they will never meet and the collective institutions that surround them.

Notes

1 The model assumes that unexpected events can threaten perceptions of understandability and foreseeability, generating feelings of uncertainty, regardless of whether they are positive, negative or neutral (Murray et al., 2021). Consistent with this logic, prior research suggests that unexpected positive and unexpected negative events both generate uncertainty (e.g., Lee & Qiu, 2009; Quinn et al., 2021; van Dijk & Zeelenberg, 2006; Wilson et al., 2005).

2 Derived from the behavior of financial traders, the VIX is a daily economic indicator that tracks uncertainty in national and international events by forecasting greater volatility in the stock market over the next 30 days (Bloom, 2014).

References

Arriaga, X. B., Kumashiro, M., Simpson, J. A., & Overall, N. C. (2018). Revising working models across time: Relationship situations that enhance attachment security. *Personality and Social Psychology Review*, *22*, 71–96.

Baumeister, R. F., & Leary, M. R. (1995). The need to belong: Desire for interpersonal attachments as a fundamental human motivation. *Psychological Bulletin*, *117*, 497–529.

Blanton, H., Strauts, E., & Perez, M. (2012). Partisan identification as a predictor of cortisol response to election news. *Political Communication*, *29*, 447–460.

Bloom, N. (2014). Fluctuations in uncertainty. *Journal of Economic Perspectives*, *28*, 153–176.

Cameron, J. J., & Granger, S. (2019). Does self-esteem have an interpersonal imprint beyond self-reports? A meta-analysis of self-esteem and objective interpersonal indicators. *Personality and Social Psychology Review*, *23*, 73–102.

Cavallo, J., Fitzsimons, G. M., & Holmes, J. G. (2009). Taking chances in the face of threat: Romantic risk regulation and approach motivation. *Personality and Social Psychology Bulletin*, *35*, 737–751.

Cox, C. R., & Arndt, J. (2012). How sweet it is to be loved by you: The role of perceived regard in terror management in relationships. *Journal of Personality and Social Psychology*, *102*, 616–632.
Day, M. V. (2016). Why people defend relationship ideology. *Journal of Social and Personal Relationships*, *33*, 348–360.
Day, M. V., Kay, A. C., Holmes, J. G., & Napier, J. L. (2011). System justification and the defense of committed relationship ideology. *Journal of Personality and Social Psychology*, *101*, 291–306.
Faure, R., Righetti, F., Seibel, M., & Hofmann, W. (2018). Speech is silver, nonverbal behavior is gold: How implicit partner evaluations affect dyadic interactions in close relationships. *Psychological Science*, *29*, 1731–1741.
Feeney, B. C., & Collins, N. L. (2015). A new look at social support: A theoretical perspective on thriving through relationships. *Personality and Social Psychology Review*, *19*, 113–147.
Finkel, E. J., Hui, C. M., Carswell, K. L., & Larson, G. M. (2014). The suffocation of marriage: Climbing Mount Maslow without enough oxygen. *Psychological Inquiry*, *25*, 1–41.
Fishbach, A., & Ferguson, M. J. (2007). The goal construct in social psychology. In A. W. Kruglanski & E. T. Higgins (Eds.), *Social psychology: Handbook of basic principles* (pp. 490–515). The Guilford Press.
Fitzsimons, G. M., Finkel, E. J., & van Dellen, M. R. (2015). Transactive goal dynamics. *Psychological Review, 122*, 648–673.
Griffin, D. W., & Ross, L. (1991). Subjective construal, social inference and human misunderstanding. In M. P. Zanna (Ed.), *Advances in experimental social psychology* (Vol. 24, pp. 319–359). Academic Press.
Heine, S. J., Proulx, T., & Vohs, V. (2006). The meaning maintenance model: On the coherence of social motivations. *Personality and Social Psychology Review*, *10*, 88–110.
Hicks, L. L., McNulty, J. K., Meltzer, A. L., & Olson, M. A. (2016). Capturing the interpersonal implications of evolved preferences? Frequency of sex shapes implicit, but not explicit, partner evaluations. *Psychological Science*, *27*, 836–847.
Hicks, L. L., McNulty, J. K., Meltzer, A. L., & Olson, M. A. (2018). A dual-process perspective on how sexual experiences shape automatic versus explicit relationship satisfaction: Reply to Brody, Costa, Klapilova, and Weiss. *Psychological Science*, *29*, 670–672.
Higgins, E. T., Rossignac-Milon, M., & Echterhoff, G. (2021). Shared reality: From sharing-is-believing to merging minds. *Current Directions in Psychological Science*, *30*, 103–110.
Holt-Lunstad, J. (2018). Why social relationships are important for physical health: A systems approach to understanding and modifying risk and protection. *Annual Review of Psychology*, *69*, 437–458.
Hudson, J. (2006). Institutional trust and subjective well-being across the EU. *KYKLOS*, *59*, 43–62.
Jonas, E., McGregor, I., Klackl, J., Agroskin, D., Fritsche, I., Holbrook, C., Nash, K., Proulx, T., & Quirin, M. (2014). Threat and defense: From anxiety to approach. In J. M. Olson & M. P. Zanna (Eds.), *Advances in experimental social psychology* (pp. 219–286). Elsevier Inc.
Kelley, H. H. (1979). *Personal relationships: Their structures and processes*. Psychology Press.
Kelley, H. H., Holmes, J. G., Kerr, N. L., Reis, H. T., Rusbult, C. E., & Van Lange, P. A. M. (2003). *An atlas of interpersonal situations.* Cambridge University Press.
Kenrick, D. T., Griskevicius, V., Neuberg, S. L., & Schaller, M. (2010). Renovating the pyramid of needs: Contemporary extensions built upon ancient foundations. *Perspectives on Psychological Science, 5*(3), 292–314.
Kruglanski, A. W., Chernikova, M., Babush, M., Dugas, M., & Schumpe, B. M. (2015). The architecture of goal systems: Multi-finality, equi-finality, and counter-finality in means—end relations. In A. J. Elliot (Ed.), *Advances in motivation science* (Vol. 2, pp. 69–98). Elsevier.
Kruglanski, A. W., Shah, J. Y., Fishbach, A., Friedman, R., Chun, W. Y., & Sleeth-Keppler, D. (2002). A theory of goal systems. *Advances in Experimental Social Psychology*, *34*(2), 331–378.
Kumar, A., & Epley, N. (2018). Undervaluing gratitude: Expressers misunderstand the consequences of showing appreciation. *Psychological Science*, *29*, 1423–1435.
Kunda, Z. (1990). The case for motivated reasoning. *Psychological Bulletin, 108*(3), 480–498.
Leary, M. R., Tambor, E. S., Terdal, S. K., & Downs, D. L. (1995). Self-esteem as an interpersonal monitor: The sociometer hypothesis. *Journal of Personality and Social Psychology*, *68*, 518–530.
Lee, Y. H., & Qiu, C. (2009). When uncertainty brings pleasure: The role of prospect imageability and mental imagery. *Journal of Consumer Research*, *36*(4), 624–633.
Maner, J. K., DeWall, C. N., Baumeister, R. F., Schaller, M. (2007). Does social exclusion motivate interpersonal reconnection? Resolving the "porcupine problem." *Journal of Personality and Social Psychology*, *92*, 42–55.

Master, S. L., Eisenberger, N. I., Taylor, S. E., Naliboff, B. D., Shirinyan, D., & Lieberman, M. D. (2009). A picture's worth: Partner photographs reduce experimentally induced pain. *Psychological Science*, *20*, 1316–1318.
McNulty, J. K., Olson, M. A., Meltzer, A. L., & Shaffer, M. J. (2013). Though they may be unaware, newlyweds implicitly know whether their marriage will be satisfying. *Science*, *342*, 1119–1120.
McNulty, J. K., Olson, M. A., Jones, R. E., & Acosta, L. M. (2017). Automatic associations between one's partner and one's affect as the proximal mechanism of change in relationship satisfaction: Evidence from evaluative conditioning. *Psychological Science*, *28*, 1031–1040.
Mikulincer, M., & Shaver, P. R. (2003). The attachment behavioral system in adulthood: Activation, psychodynamics, and interpersonal processes. In M. Zanna (Ed.), *Advances in experimental social psychology* (Vol. 35, pp. 52–153). Academic Press.
Miller, S. L., & Maner, J. K. (2011). Sick body, vigilant mind: The biological immune system activates the behavioral immune system. *Psychological Science*, *22*, 1467–1471.
Miller, S. L., & Maner, J. K. (2012). Over-perceiving disease cues: The basic cognition of the behavioral immune system. *Journal of Personality and Social Psychology*, *102*, 1198–1213.
Mortensen, C. R., Becker, D. V., Ackerman, J. M., Neuberg, S. L., & Kenrick, D. T. (2010). Infection breeds reticence: The effects of disease salience on self-perceptions of personality and behavioral avoidance. *Psychological Science*, *21*, 440–447.
Murray, S. L., Bellavia, G., Rose, P., & Griffin, D. (2003). Once hurt, twice hurtful: How perceived regard regulates daily marital interaction. *Journal of Personality and Social Psychology*, *84*, 126–147.
Murray, S. L., Gomillion, S., Holmes, J. G., Harris, B., & Lamarche, V. (2013). The dynamics of relationship promotion: Controlling the automatic inclination to trust. *Journal of Personality and Social Psychology*, *104*, 305–334.
Murray, S. L., Holmes, J. G., & Collins, N. L. (2006). Optimizing assurance: The risk regulation system in relationships. *Psychological Bulletin*, *132*, 641–666.
Murray, S. L., Holmes, J. G., & Pinkus, R. T. (2010). A smart unconscious? Procedural origins of automatic partner attitudes in marriage. *Journal of Experimental Social Psychology*, *46*, 650–656.
Murray, S. L., Lamarche, V., Gomillion, S., Seery, M. D., & Kondrak, C. (2017). In defense of commitment: The curative power of violated expectations in relationships. *Journal of Personality and Social Psychology*, *13*, 627–729.
Murray, S. L., Lamarche, V., & Seery, M. D. (2018). Romantic relationships as shared reality defense. *Current Opinion in Psychology*, *23*, 34–37.
Murray, S. L., Lamarche, V., Seery, M. D., Jung, H. Y., Griffin, D. W., & Brinkman, C. (2021). The social-safety system: Fortifying relationships in the face of the unforeseeable. *Journal of Personality and Social Psychology*, *120*, 99–130.
Murray, S. L., & Lamarche, V. (2023). Beyond dyadic interdependence: Relationships in an uncertain social world. In J. Forgas, W. D. Crano, & K. Fiedler (Eds.), *The psychology of insecurity: Seeking certainty where none can be had* (pp. 205–223). Routledge.Murray, S. L., McNulty, J. K., Xia, J., Lamarche, V. M., Seery, M. D., Ward, D. E., Griffin, D. W., Hicks, L. L., & Jung, H. Y. (2023). Pursuing safety in social connection regulates the risk-regulation, social-safety, and behavioral-immune systems. *Journal of Personality and Social Psychology*. Advance online publication. https://doi.org/10.1037/pspi0000420
Murray, S. L., Pinkus, R. T., Holmes, J. G., Harris, B., Gomillion, S., Aloni, M., Derrick, J., & Leder, S. (2011). Signaling when (and when not) to be cautious and self-protective: Impulsive and reflective trust in close relationships. *Journal of Personality and Social Psychology*, *101*, 485–502.
Murray, S. L., Rose, P., Bellavia, G., Holmes, J., & Kusche, A. (2002). When rejection stings: How self-esteem constrains relationship-enhancement processes. *Journal of Personality and Social Psychology*, *83*, 556–573.
Murray, D. R., & Schaller, M. (2016). The behavioral immune system: Implications for social cognition, social interaction, and social influence. In *Advances in experimental social psychology* (Vol. 53, pp. 75–129). Elsevier Academic Press.
Murray, S. L., Seery, M. D., Lamarche, V., Jung, H. Y., Saltsman, T. L., Griffin, D. W., Dubois, D., Xia, J., Ward, D. E., & McNulty, J. (2021). Looking for safety in all the right places: When threatening political reality strengthens family relationship bonds. *Social Psychological and Personality Science*, *12*, 1193–1202.

Navarro-Carrillo, G., Valor-Segura, I., Lozano, L. M., & Moya, M. (2018). Do economic crises always undermine trust in others? The case of generalized, interpersonal, and in-group trust. *Frontiers in Psychology, 9*. https://doi.org/10.3389/fpsyg.2018.01955

Neuberg, S. L., Kenrick, D. T., & Schaller, M. (2011). Human threat management systems: Self-protection and disease avoidance. *Neuroscience and Biobehavioral Reviews, 35*, 1042–1051.

Peetz, J., Shimizu, J. P., & Royle, C. (2022). Projecting current feelings into the past and future: Better current relationship quality reduces negative retrospective bias and increases positive forecasting bias. *Journal of Social and Personal Relationships, 39*(8), 02654075221084280.

Plusnin, N., Pepping, C. A., & Kashima, E. S. (2018). The role of close relationships in terror management: A systematic review and research agenda. *Personality and Social Psychology Review, 22*, 307–346.

Pollmann, M. M. H., & Finkenauer, C. (2009). Empathic forecasting: How do we predict other people's feelings? *Cognition and Emotion, 23*, 978–1001.

Quinn, M. S., Campbell, K., Keane, M. T. (2021). Do we "fear for the worst" or "Hope for the best" in thinking about the unexpected? Factors affecting the valence of unexpected outcomes reported for everyday scenarios, *Cognition, 208*,104520. https://doi.org/10.1016/j.cognition.2020.104520.

Richman, L. S., & Leary, M. R. (2009). Reactions to discrimination, stigmatization, ostracism, and other forms of interpersonal rejection: A multi-motive model. *Psychological Review, 116*, 365–383.

Robles, T. F., Slatcher, R. B., Trombello, J. M., & McGinn, M. M. (2014). Marital quality and health: A meta-analytic review. *Psychological Bulletin, 140*, 140–187.

Silver, N. (2019). *Socially liberal, fiscally conservative voters preferred Trump in 2016*. Retrieved from: https://fivethirtyeight.com/features/socially-liberal-fiscally-conservative-voters-preferred-trump-in-2016/

Slotter, E. B., Gardner, W. L., & Finkel, E. J. (2010). Who am I without you? The influence of romantic breakup on the self-concept. *Personality and Social Psychology Bulletin, 36*, 147–160.

Stanton, S. J., LaBar, K. S., Saini, E. K., Kuhn, C. M., & Beehner, J. C. (2010). Stressful politics: Voters' cortisol responses to the outcome of the 2008 United States Presidential election. *Psychoneuroendocrinology, 35*, 768–774.

Szepsenwol, O., & Simpson, J. A. (2019). Attachment within life history theory: An evolutionary perspective on individual differences in attachment. *Current Opinion in Psychology, 25*, 65–70.

Tooby, J., & Cosmides, L. (1996). Friendship and the banker's paradox: Other pathways to the evolution of adaptations for altruism. In W. G. Runciman, J. M. Smith, & R. I. M. Dunbar (Eds.), *Evolution of social behaviour patterns in primates and man* (pp. 119–143). Oxford University Press.

Trawalter, S., Chung, V. S., DeSantis, A. S., Simon, C. D., & Adam, E. K. (2012). Physiological stress responses to the 2008 U. S. presidential election: The role of policy preferences and social dominance orientation. *Group Processes and Intergroup Relations, 15*, 333–345.

Van Dijk, E., & Zeelenberg, M. (2006). The dampening effect of uncertainty on positive and negative emotions. *Journal of Behavioral Decision Making, 19*(2), 171–176.

Williams, K. D., Cheung, C. K., & Choi, W. (2000). Cyberostracism: Effects of being ignored over the Internet. *Journal of Personality and Social Psychology, 79*(5), 748–762.

Wilson, T. D., Centerbar, D. B., Kermer, D. A., & Gilbert, D. T. (2005). The pleasures of uncertainty: Prolonging positive moods in ways people do not anticipate. *Journal of Personality and Social Psychology, 88*, 5.

Young, S. G., Slepian, M. L., & Sacco, D. F. (2015). Sensitivity to perceived facial trustworthiness is increased by activating self-protection motives. *Social Psychological and Personality Science, 6*, 607–613.

PART III

Clinical & Applied Implications of the Uncertain Self

17

COVID-19 THREAT AND UNCERTAINTY

How Outcome Anticipation Shapes Responses to the Unknown

Erica Molinario, Molly Ellenberg and Laura Prislei

In December 2019, the first case of SARS-CoV-2 [COVID-19] was reported in Wuhan, China, and began to spread across the world, to Iran, to Italy, to the United Kingdom, to the United States, and beyond. On March 12, 2020, the World Health Organization declared a global pandemic (Ciotti et al., 2020). Thus began an era of uncertainty. In the United States, what was expected by many politicians and laypeople to be a two-week lockdown to stop the spread of the virus turned into months of restrictions (Feuer & Higgins-Dunn, 2021). On one hand, people were afraid of the unpredictable and serious health consequences of the COVID-19 infection (Van Lissa et al., 2022). On the other hand, questions over when one would be able to return to work evolved into fears over one's ability to provide for oneself and one's family, meet their basic needs, and accomplish their goals (Blustein & Guarino, 2020; Ritchie et al., 2021), thus inducing uncertainty regarding the economic consequences of the pandemic. The lasting impacts of the COVID-19 era are still being uncovered, many related to the mental health toll of the pandemic. In Iceland, depression and poor well-being that increased at the start of the pandemic remained higher than pre-COVID levels even two years after the start of the pandemic (Thorisdottir et al., 2023). In Germany, adults' depression, loneliness, and life satisfaction worsened over the course of the first year of the pandemic (Benke et al., 2022).

While the pandemic's negative impacts have been widespread, there have been notable positive effects as well. Research during this period suggests that hope played a beneficial role in psychological well-being amidst the early stages of the COVID-19 outbreak (Yildirim & Arslan, 2020), serving as an adaptive mechanism for alleviating pandemic-related stress and enhancing overall well-being (Gallagher et al., 2021).

In a similar vein, in a study conducted by Cornell and colleagues (2022) involving 1,370 participants in Australia, it was found that 70% of respondents reported experiencing at least one positive effect during the COVID-19 pandemic. Among these positive effects, many participants highlighted the increased time spent with family, the ability to work from home or have more flexible work arrangements, and the enjoyment of a less busy lifestyle.

Therefore, while uncertainty surrounding the pandemic may be linked to negative emotions, it has also exhibited positive correlations with beneficial factors. Accordingly, although surprising for many, some studies have failed to establish a clear link between uncertainty and adverse

 DOI: 10.4324/9781003363385-20

mental health issues (Arroll et al., 2012). Instead, uncertainty has been associated with positive psychosocial factors like hope (Gill & Morgan, 2011), with some arguing that it fosters optimism in challenging circumstances (Brashers, 2001). Experimental evidence also suggests that uncertainty can yield positive effects or amplify existing ones (Kurtz et al., 2007; Bar-Anan et al., 2009). Moreover, interventions targeting uncertainty management in medical contexts have demonstrated positive impacts on mental health (Germino et al., 2013; Gil et al., 2006).

In this chapter, we propose that negative feelings associated with the uncertainty of the COVID-19 pandemic stem not from the uncertainty itself, but from expectations of negative outcomes, often shaped by individuals' past experiences. Through a review of experimental data and observations, we identify those factors that may influence individuals' sensitivity to negative outcome expectations. We also emphasize how individuals' anticipation of positive outcomes and their self-assurance in managing potential obstacles shape their responses to uncertainty.

Uncertainty and Negative Outcomes

Social psychology research has demonstrated how the perception of threats, whether physical or economic, renders society more vulnerable (Forgas & Crano, 2021). In this vein, when faced with threatening situations, individuals experience frustration in fulfilling their needs, prompting them to actively seek avenues to regain satisfaction. This parallels other motivational mechanisms where deprivation triggers the pursuit of need fulfillment (Kruglanski et al., 2022). Much interest related to needs triggered by threatening circumstances has revolved around the need for uncertainty avoidance as represented by constructs like the intolerance of uncertainty (e.g., Carleton, 2016) and the need for cognitive closure (Kruglanski & Webster, 1996), that is, the desire for certainty and the avoidance of unpredictability. According to the perspective that views the need for certainty as a fundamental human need (e.g., Van den Bos, 2009), individuals generally experience a need to eliminate uncertainty or, alternatively, to find ways to make it cognitively tolerable.

In the early days of the pandemic, people received conflicting and ever-changing information as experts' understanding of COVID-19 evolved (Nagler et al., 2020). This changing expert information was also muddied by the presence of misinformation, often spread over social media, leading to lower trust in the mainstream media and government authorities (Filkuková et al., 2021). Moreover, research shows that during stressful periods, individuals may avoid information to which they have ready access, even when acquiring the information may benefit them in various ways (see Sweeny & Howell, 2025, in this volume). For example, individuals might steer clear of health information to preserve valued beliefs about their identity (Hua & Howell, 2022). Studies on selective exposure reveal that people tend to actively pursue information that aligns with their existing beliefs and, conversely, tend to avoid information that contradicts their established convictions (Hart et al., 2009; Smith et al., 2008).

Research shows that in times of ecological threats, the need for cognitive closure becomes particularly salient as individuals seek ways to interpret and establish order in unknown circumstances. For this reason, during times of uncertainty and chaos, individuals high in need for cognitive closure may rely on authoritarian leaders to provide a sense of stability and order (Contu et al. 2023a). In the Italian context, Contu and colleagues (2023a) showed that concern about contingent ecological threats (i.e., COVID-19 and the Russia-Ukraine conflict) was positively related to the need for cognitive closure. Similarly, Molinario and colleagues (2024) found that the threat posed by the Ukrainian-Russian conflict and COVID-19 were positively related to the need for cognitive closure, which in turn led to a higher support for extreme ideologies such as populism.

The uncertainty triggered by the COVID-19 pandemic confronted individuals with challenges to their identities, shaking their confidence in safeguarding themselves and their families. The sense of uncertainty induced by the pandemic has manifested in observed self-affirming behavioral reactions, taking the form of increased aggression towards individuals from ethnic minority backgrounds, especially those from Asian communities, who were targeted due to their perceived association with the pandemic's origins (Aratani, 2020; Margolin, 2020). Moreover, there was a notable increase in prejudice towards foreign communities, particularly those most affected during the initial phase of the pandemic (e.g., Sorokowski et al., 2020; Yamagata et al., 2020). This increase in prejudice is likely attributable to a tendency to pathogen- avoidance tendency, leading individuals to steer clear of people from other communities believed to have higher infection rates. This inclination can extend to broader attitudes toward the group perceived as having infected members (Yamagata et al., 2020). Individuals with less resilient identities, whose confidence in coping was undermined, showed increased fear of COVID-19 and heightened distrust of science and scientists (Breakwell & Jaspal, 2021), fostering the dissemination of negationist and conspiratorial narratives (Sensales et al., 2024).

Uncertainty-Identity Theory (Hogg et al., 2007) explains these phenomena. According to the authors, when facing threats, individuals may experience a loss of self-certainty, compelling them to seek support and defense in social in-groups (Fritsche et al., 2011). In this vein, Hogg (2014) argues that individuals grappling with uncertainty tend to adhere to groups that furnish a distinct and clearly defined identity along with normative beliefs and behavioral guidelines. For this reason, more extreme groups and behaviors can be seen as more appealing for reducing uncertainty tied to identification. Controlled experiments have consistently supported these analyses. For example, in the context of Palestinian Muslims and Israeli Jews, Hogg and Adelman (2013) found that self-uncertainty was more strongly correlated to support for suicide bombing (Palestinians) or aggressive military action (Israelis) when national identity was central to self-definition. Similarly, threats to personal worth and significance (Kruglanski et al., 2021) prompt individuals to sacrifice for a cause (Jasko et al., 2019), adopt extreme religious views (Borum, 2014), and participate in radical behaviors (Jasko et al., 2017; Schumpe et al., 2020; Webber et al., 2018). In this regard, in field surveys with political extremists imprisoned in the Philippines and Sri Lanka and experiments conducted with American samples, Webber and colleagues (2018) found that threats to self-value and respect (i.e., loss of significance) instill a sense of uncertainty that motivates individuals to seek certainty and closure, thereby restoring personal significance through support for extremist ideologies (i.e., Islamic extremism, violent support for Liberation Tigers of Tamil Eelam movement, and conservative vs liberal ideology). Van den Bos and Lind (this volume) argue that perceptions of how fairly or unfairly an individual is treated may have a significant role in managing uncertainty and self-regulation, particularly when it comes to violent extremism.

The relationship between threats and the need to avoid uncertainty is also evident in studies related to the migratory context, with members of the host community frequently expressing apprehensions about potential cultural threats to their group privileges and cultural values. For instance, results of a study across several samples of both general populations and former violent extremists from different countries (i.e., Denmark, Afghanistan, Pakistan, France, Afghans, and former Mujahideen in Afghanistan) demonstrated that perceived cultural threats lead to violent extremism through an increase in people's need for cognitive closure (Obaidi et al., 2023). These findings align with Terror Management Theory (Greenberg et al., 1986), which posits that individuals are driven to alleviate the existential unease stemming from the inevitability of death by embracing significant cultural worldviews. These worldviews provide either concrete or symbolic persistence after death for those who adhere to predetermined standards value (see Landau et al., 2024, in this volume for a discussion).

Thus, the threat of COVID-19 led to increased epistemic uncertainty, leading individuals to turn to certainty- and closure-providing sources, even if those sources were conspiracy theorists or extremist ideologues promoting "wellness" alongside far-right authoritarianism (Van Bavel et al., 2020; Baker, 2022).

In an experimental study by Jutzi et al. (2020), priming COVID-19 salience through a poster highlighting the lack of existing treatment (inducing anxiety and uncertainty about the pandemic's course) resulted in greater activation of the behavioral inhibition system (BIS). The BIS, responsible for handling threatening situations, is associated with increased vigilance and anxiety. This heightened BIS activation, in turn, was associated with increased belief in conspiracy theories. These findings are also consistent with research showing that the risk of contagion and death from COVID-19 motivates antidemocratic beliefs, including conspiracy social representations, and practices, to regain a sense of control (e.g., Pizarro et al., 2023).

Much literature has tied these mental health challenges to the uncertainty induced by the pandemic, as well as to the lack of social connection engendered by prolonged lockdowns (Rettie & Daniels, 2021; Marroquín, Vine, & Morgan, 2020). These findings are well-supported by empirical results dating from long before the pandemic began. For instance, empirical data suggests that both humans and other mammals exhibit inherent acute stress responses when confronted with situations of uncertainty, such as greater skin conductance responses and greater pupil diameter (de Berker et al., 2016).

Building on this, research indicates a positive correlation between uncertainty and several negative mental health outcomes across various psychiatric conditions. In a recent scoping review by Massazza and colleagues (2023) exploring the link between uncertainty and mental health, findings revealed associations with anxiety disorders (Tarhani et al., 2020), depression (Sharkey et al., 2018), and post-traumatic stress disorder (PTSD; Moreland & Santacroce, 2018). Additionally, uncertainty has been associated with a deterioration in various psychosocial consequences, including challenges in psychosocial adjustment (Mauro, 2008), declines in quality of life (Niv et al., 2017), and heightened psychological distress (Hoff et al., 2002).

More recently, in the wake of the pandemic, the World Health Organization has highlighted that in the first year of COVID-19, the global prevalence of anxiety and depression surged by a massive 25% (WHO, 2020). Further underscoring this, the WHO's page on mental health and COVID-19 emphasized that "fear, worry, and stress are normal responses to perceived or real threats, at times when we are faced with uncertainty or the unknown" (WHO, 2020). In this regard, a study conducted by Han and colleagues (2021) with 54,845 participants from 112 countries highlighted that a higher perception of risk linked to COVID-19 was found to be significantly associated with emotional responses (especially negative emotions), which in turn were related to exacerbating self-rated mental health issues.

Thus, COVID-19 ushered in an era of uncertainty, both about the world and one's ability to thrive in it. Individuals differ in their ability to cope with uncertainty, however (Buhr & Dugas, 2002), and people who are less tolerant of uncertainty do seem to have suffered greater mental health challenges during the pandemic. In numerous studies, researchers have shown that around the world, people who were more intolerant of uncertainty were more negatively affected by the social isolation of the COVID-19 lockdowns (Smith et al., 2020; Parlapani et al., 2020), ruminated more on their fears and anxieties about COVID-19 (Satici et al., 2022), and were more anxious and depressed during the pandemic (del Valle et al., 2020). This evidence suggests that while the COVID-19 pandemic resulted in broad increases in personal and epistemic uncertainty (Baker et al., 2020; Freeston et al., 2020; Koffman et al., 2020), and while anxiety increased around the world (World Health Organization, 2022), people's affective responses to COVID-related uncertainty depended on individual differences in their abilities to tolerate and cope with uncertainty. Nonetheless, the idea that uncertainty is intrinsically harmful has faced criticism (Schiltz et al., 2019). In this vein, Mishel's theory of uncertainty in illness (Mishel, 1988) emphasizes that, depending on the context, uncertainty can be perceived not only as a threat but also as an opportunity. In the present chapter, we apply a novel theory of affective reactions to uncertainty (Kruglanski, 2023; Ellenberg, 2023) to the different levels of anxiety experienced by different people in response to the various uncertainties of the COVID-19 pandemic.

Uncertainty and Anticipated Outcomes

Despite the vast pool of literature on negative affective reactions to uncertainty, including as they relate to the COVID-19 pandemic, uncertainty may not be inherently threatening or frightening. Indeed, some individuals react positively to uncertainty (Sorrentino et al., 1988). Moreover, many research paradigms, though not conventionally associated with uncertainty, provide evidence of a proclivity to approach rather than avoid uncertain situations. For example, research suggests that individuals may sometimes embrace uncertainty stemming from a misfit between themselves and their environment when they believe that the self can flexibly adjust to the environment (see Schmader & Guo, this volume, for further discussion). Additionally, studies on sensation seeking (i.e., the pursuit of novel, thrilling, and intense experiences, Zuckerman, 2009) and risk-taking (Dekkers et al., 2017; Yates, 1992) indicate that there are at least some individuals who derive excitement and pleasure from the unknown and seek out novel and stimulating activities. Similarly, studies on creativity (Kaufman & Sternberg, 2010; Runco & Albert, 2010) and exploration and curiosity (Berlyne, 1960; Keller et al., 1994; Szumowska & Kruglanski, 2020) reveal the complex dimensions of how humans interact with uncertainty. For example, the deprivation/interest model of curiosity (Litman, 2005) proposes that curiosity may arise either from the positive feelings of interest and joy generated by the anticipation of learning new information or from the unpleasant experience of uncertainty due to the lack of knowledge. Moreover, studies on hope, surprise, and gift-giving have underscored individuals' positive responses to unexpected situations (Kagan, 2002; Noordewier et al., 2016; Snyder, 1995). In a broader context, research indicates that individuals with a strong sense of positivity (i.e., the inclination to assess life from a positive perspective; Caprara et al., 2012) are less likely to perceive uncertain situations as threats, thus avoiding negative effects on their emotional balance (Thartori et al., 2021). Moreover, research suggests that when facing uncertainty arising from both physical and social risks, affirming the safety of romantic relationships can also serve as a means of uncertainty resolution (see Murray, this volume). The positive effect of social connections can be related to positive emotional patterns derived from the sense of belonging (Baumeister & Leary, 2017) that a romantic relationship can elicit.

Positive emotions play a crucial role in promoting well-being and fortifying psychological resilience, especially in times of adversity. Indeed, resilient responses during a stressor are characterized, in part, by the use of positive emotions (Folkman & Moskowitz, 2000). Furthermore, coping strategies aimed at nurturing positive emotions have proven effective in addressing a range of everyday stressors (Ong et al., 2006) and major life stressors (Fredrickson, 2000).

One avenue through which individuals experience positive emotions is through anticipating positive events (Van Boven & Ashworth, 2007). Anticipation involves mentally simulating a potential future event and has been shown to elicit emotions comparable to those experienced during the actual event itself (Waugh et al., 2008), potentially to a greater degree as it remains novel and unanalyzed during the anticipation phase (Wilson & Gilbert, 2003). Previous studies on discrete stressors have demonstrated that anticipating positive events can lead to increases in positive emotion both before and after the stressor (Monfort et al., 2015). The authors propose that because these positive events are envisioned in the future, individuals can cultivate positive emotions associated with anticipation, even amidst stressful circumstances.

In this vein, Kruglanski and colleagues (2023) proposed that uncertainty is neither necessarily "bad," or experienced as aversive, nor "good," or experienced as pleasant or exciting. Rather, people's positive and negative affective reactions to uncertain situations may be determined by the expectations of positive and negative outcomes that the situation might bring, which manifest as optimism and positive affect and pessimism and negative affect, respectively.

Whether the uncertain situation elicits the expectation of positive or negative outcomes may be specifically conditioned by automatic activation of a schema characterized by thoughts about expected outcomes as a result of a given similar uncertain situation. These expectations are formed based on people's long-term and recent histories of outcomes (Kruglanski et al., 2023; Kruglanski, 2023). For instance, Ellenberg (2023) found that long-term positive and negative outcomes (including Adverse Childhood Experiences [ACEs]) predicted optimism and pessimism, respectively, which in turn predicted positive and negative reactions to a list of uncertain but not strongly emotionally charged situations (e.g., a pop quiz, the first day of a new job). Moreover, Contu and colleagues (2023b) found that short-term positive and negative outcomes caused people to react more positively or more negatively, respectively, to uncertain situations, but only when the uncertain situation was introduced immediately after the short-term outcome. When a time delay was introduced, people's affective reactions to uncertainty were instead driven by their long-term histories of positive and negative outcomes. This finding is consistent with prior findings regarding the accessibility of recent versus chronic primes, which similarly demonstrate that a recent prime is more accessible in its immediate aftermath but is overtaken by chronic primes as the time between the prime and the stimulus increases (Higgins, 1996). However, in some circumstances, when the uncertain situation is unprecedented to the individual's personal experience, such as with the COVID-19 pandemic, one's affective response might result from socially shared narratives (Higgins et al., 2021) about the given uncertain situations that highlight the valenced outcomes those situations may contain.

Application of the Novel Theory to the COVID-19 Pandemic

Based on a thorough review of past literature on reactions to uncertainty, Kruglanski and colleagues (2023) theorize that the valence of uncertain situations lies in the eye of the beholder; that is, people's expectations of what the outcome of an uncertain situation will be determine their reactions to those situations. In other words, if someone has long experienced positive outcomes when faced with an uncertain situation, they are likely to expect that it will end well for them, or at least not end poorly. Thus, they are more likely to react positively to that situation. In the context of the COVID-19 pandemic, someone who has generally experienced good outcomes throughout their lives may not expect the uncertainty of the pandemic to lead to overwhelmingly negative outcomes and may therefore react less negatively to the pandemic. They may even react positively, viewing it as an opportunity to spend more time with their children or work on a new hobby.

Of course, these individuals may also have the resources to foster positive outcomes; someone who is not worried about losing their job, because they are able to easily work from home, is unlikely to expect that the pandemic will bring about financial struggles. They may also be able to afford private tutoring for their children or higher-quality healthcare should they become sick. Resources may also be psychological, such as resilience, or the degree to which one believes that they will be able to effectively cope with any negative outcomes which may arise (Ellenberg, 2023). In contrast, someone who has experienced a lifetime of bad outcomes and who does not have the resources to succeed within the uncertain constraints of the pandemic is less likely to view COVID-19 as an opportunity, and rather as a situation which will lead to economic hardship, academic difficulties, and even death. These negative expectations thus drive their negative affective reactions to the COVID-related uncertainty in their lives.

The examples listed above are supported by extensive evidence from research produced during the COVID-19 pandemic. For instance, individuals who perceived themselves as more vulnerable to disease experienced more COVID-related anxiety (Mann et al., 2020), perhaps because they were more likely to expect that they would contract COVID-19. Similarly, older people, those with children, and those with chronic illnesses experienced higher COVID-related anxiety in a study of Polish participants at the beginning of the pandemic (Malesza & Kaczmarek, 2021). Additionally, COVID-related anxiety, depression, and other psychological symptoms were elevated among healthcare professionals, particularly nurses, who spend more time with patients and may have therefore been more vulnerable to contracting COVID (Pappa et al., 2020).

In contrast, COVID-related anxiety was lower in people who may have expected to fare better during the pandemic, such as people with a higher socioeconomic status (Zhou & Guo, 2021) and greater resilience (Paredes et al., 2021). Similarly, people who were more confident that their employment status would not be affected by the pandemic (e.g., those who could work remotely) experienced less COVID-related anxiety and depression (Wilson et al., 2020). It is also noteworthy that more optimistic people were less likely to engage in behavioral measures to prevent the spread of COVID-19, such as social distancing (Fragkaki et al., 2021), perhaps because they expected that they would not contract COVID, or that if they did, they would not become seriously ill.

Dealing with Uncertainty

The presently described theory of affective reactions to uncertainty as depending on past experiences and future expectations also suggests novel interventions for dealing with uncertainty (Kruglanski et al., 2023; Kruglanski, 2023; Ellenberg, 2023), particularly in non-clinical populations, as prior research on intolerance of uncertainty interventions tend to focus on those diagnosed with anxiety disorders (Robichaud & Dugas, 2006; Miller & McGuire, 2023). Considering the significant negative impacts of prolonged stress, it becomes imperative to explore adaptive strategies that effectively foster enduring positive emotions.

During periods of increased uncertainty, it is essential to maintain one's motivation to confront potential challenges that may arise. For instance, strategies focused on fostering positive emotions have proven effective in addressing various chronic conditions such as anxiety, depression, aggression, and stress-related health issues (Fredrickson, 2000). It has been proposed that cultivating positive anticipation contributes to successful stress recovery by replacing negative thoughts about the stressor with positive thoughts about upcoming events (Tanner et al., 2013; Monfort et al., 2015). Therefore, maintaining a positive and optimistic perspective toward stressors can facilitate effective resolution and pave the way for future endeavors (Nezu, 2004).

Correlational studies utilizing daily diaries support this notion. In a study conducted with an American sample, Leslie-Miller et al. (2021) found that optimism predicted positive emotions amid the relentless stress of uncontrollable events such as the COVID-19 pandemic. Additionally, they found that this relationship was partially mediated by a sense of positive anticipation throughout the day. This supports the concept that optimism serves as a trait-level predictor of positive anticipation. However, it also raises the possibility that optimism may influence positive emotions through alternative mechanisms not fully captured in their daily diaries.

Given the negative relationship between intolerance of uncertainty and optimism, and the role of optimism in predicting positive reactions to uncertainty, one might easily surmise that interventions aimed at increasing optimism (i.e., "learned optimism," Seligman, 2006) might be effective in reducing uncertainty-related anxiety. In a qualitative study conducted with Australian adults living in a senior community, participants reported that their optimism served to help them cope proactively and seek solutions during the stressful period of the pandemic (Craig et al., 2022).

Studies using psychological interventions further show that optimism can be increased through several methods which had other beneficial effects such as decreasing negative affect, depression, and pain, beyond merely increasing optimism. (Malouff & Schutte, 2017).

However, more studies testing the efficacy of optimism interventions in increasing positive and decreasing negative reactions to uncertainty are necessary, especially in light of more contemporary events including the pandemic.

Mindfulness-based methods have been proposed as especially beneficial in managing conditions marked by an inability to tolerate negative experiences (Bishop et al., 2004). In the context of anxiety, embracing mindfulness could aid in controlling adverse responses to uncertainty, as uncertainty may be perceived as less intolerable or in need of immediate resolution. Hence, Kruglanski and colleagues (2023) propose that mindfulness meditation might be effective in diminishing negative responses to uncertainty, albeit not by teaching participants to expect more positive outcomes. Rather, mindfulness meditation focuses on non-attachment to outcomes, allowing practitioners to observe what is happening in their environments without trying to control them (Whitehead et al., 2019). As such, people who are more mindful should be expected to simply worry less about the outcomes of uncertain situations, regardless of whether they expect those outcomes to be positive or negative. Indeed, Ellenberg (2023) found that participants who engaged in a mindfulness meditation exercise reacted more neutrally (i.e., closer to the midpoint of a scale from negative to positive) to a series of uncertain events. Similarly, Papenfuss et al. (2021) found that high levels of mindfulness predicted lower levels of intolerance for uncertainty.

During the COVID-19 pandemic, several factors were found to moderate the effects of COVID-related uncertainty on negative affect, each related to the perception of outcomes, consistent with Kruglanski and colleagues' theory (2023). For instance, American teachers who had a "creative growth mindset" and who viewed the COVID-19 pandemic as an opportunity to come up with new, creative ways of teaching were more buoyant and joyful in their teaching (Iheduru-Anderson & Foley, 2021). Among university employees in Thailand, having more support from supervisors reduced perceived uncertainty surrounding COVID-19, which subsequently predicted reduced emotional exhaustion, but only in workplaces with a climate of open-mindedness ("low intransigence") (Charoensukmongkol & Phungsoonthorn, 2021). Finally, among Russian participants, positive emotions related to COVID-19 were associated with "higher levels of harmony with life and subjective vitality, as well as tolerance for ambiguity and self-efficacy [...] and hardiness" (Leontiev et al., 2022, pp. 7–8).

Conclusion

The theory of affective reactions to uncertain situations as based on past experiences and expectations of positive and negative outcomes (Kruglanski et al., 2023; Kruglanski, 2023) clearly and succinctly explains why anxiety increased so dramatically during the COVID-19 pandemic (World

Health Organization, 2022) and why the effects of COVID-related uncertainty on anxiety were not universally experienced to the same degree. Whereas much prior research on uncertainty, including that on COVID-related uncertainty, assumes that uncertainty is inherently negative (e.g., Carleton, 2016), we posit that uncertainty as such is neutrally valenced. Rather, people ascribe their own valence to uncertain situations based on their expectations as to what the outcomes of those situations will be, which are in turn based on their past experiences of positive and negative outcomes. Therefore, general increases in anxiety and negative affect in response to COVID-related uncertainty may be attributed to the fact that negative outcomes to the uncertain situation—job loss, severe illness, death of loved ones—were so prevalent and thus so easy to imagine and expect. At the same time, people who were less vulnerable to these outcomes—younger, healthier, wealthier people—experienced less anxiety and negative affect because they did not expect negative outcomes or even expected positive outcomes to the COVID-19 uncertainty. These explanations clarify the ways that different people with diverse life experiences react to uncertainty and suggest novel paths for interventions to help people react less negatively to uncertain situations.

Acknowledgement

Erica Molinario's work on this manuscript was supported by the Polish National Science Center (SONATA 16, registration number 2020/39/D/HS6/02647).

References

Aratani, L. (2020, March 24). "Coughing while Asian": Living in fear as racism feeds off coronavirus panic. *The Guardian*. Retrieved from: https://www.theguardian.com/world/2020/mar/24/coronavirus-us-asian-americans-racism

Arroll, M., Dancey, C. P., Attree, E. A., Smith, S., & James, T. (2012). People with symptoms of Ménière's disease: The relationship between illness intrusiveness, illness uncertainty, dizziness handicap, and depression. *Otology & Neurotology: Official Publication of the American Otological Society, American Neurotology Society [AND] European Academy of Otology and Neurotology*, *33*(5), 816–823.

Baker, S. A. (2022). Alt. Health Influencers: How wellness culture and web culture have been weaponised to promote conspiracy theories and far-right extremism during the COVID-19 pandemic. *European Journal of Cultural Studies*, *25*(1), 3–24.

Baker, S. R., Bloom, N., Davis, S. J., & Terry, S. J. (2020). *Covid-induced economic uncertainty* (No. w26983). National Bureau of Economic Research. https://doi.org/10.3386/w26983

Bar-Anan, Y., Wilson, T. D., & Gilbert, D. T. (2009). The feeling of uncertainty intensifies affective reactions. *Emotion*, *9*(1), 123–127. https://doi.org/10.1037/a0014607

Baumeister, R. F., & Leary, M. R. (2017). The need to belong: Desire for interpersonal attachments as a fundamental human motivation. In R. Zukauskiene (Ed.), *Interpersonal Development* (pp. 57–89). Routledge.

Benke, C., Autenrieth, L. K., Asselmann, E., & Pané-Farré, C. A. (2022). Stay-at-home orders due to the COVID-19 pandemic are associated with elevated depression and anxiety in younger, but not older adults: Results from a nationwide community sample of adults from Germany. *Psychological Medicine*, *52*(15), 3739–3740. https://doi.org/10.1017/S0033291720003438

Berlyne, D. E. (1960). *Conflict, arousal, and curiosity*. McGraw-Hill Book Company.

Bishop, S. R., Lau, M., Shapiro, S., Carlson, L., Anderson, N. D., Carmody, J., Segal, Z. V., Abbey, S., Speca, M., Velting, D., & Devins, G. (2004). Mindfulness: A proposed operational definition. *Clinical Psychology: Science and Practice, 11*(3), 230–241. https://doi.org/10.1093/clipsy.bph077

Blustein, D. L., & Guarino, P. A. (2020). Work and unemployment in the time of COVID-19: The existential experience of loss and fear. *Journal of Humanistic Psychology*, *60*(5), 702–709. https://doi.org/10.1177/0022167820934229

Borum, R. (2014). Psychological vulnerabilities and propensities for involvement in violent extremism. *Behavioral Sciences & the Law*, *32*(3), 286–305. https://doi.org/10.1002/bsl.2110

Brashers, D. E. (2001). Communication and uncertainty management. *Journal of Communication, 51*(3), 477–497. https://doi.org/10.1111/j.1460-2466.2001.tb02892.x
Breakwell, G. M., & Jaspal, R. (2021). Identity change, uncertainty and mistrust in relation to fear and risk of COVID-19. *Journal of Risk Research, 24*(3–4), 335–351. https://doi.org/10.1080/13669877.2020.1864011
Buhr, K., & Dugas, M. J. (2002). The intolerance of uncertainty scale: Psychometric properties of the English version. *Behaviour Research and Therapy, 40*(8), 931–945. https://doi.org/10.1016/S0005-7967(01)00092-4
Caprara, G. V., Alessandri, G., Eisenberg, N., Kupfer, A., Steca, P., Caprara, M. G., Yamaguchi, S., Fukuzawa, A., & Abela, J. (2012). The Positivity Scale. *Psychological Assessment, 24*(3), 701–712. https://doi.org/10.1037/a0026681
Carleton, R. N. (2016). Fear of the unknown: One fear to rule them all? *Journal of Anxiety Disorders, 41*, 5–21. https://doi.org/10.1016/j.janxdis.2016.03.011
Charoensukmongkol, P., & Phungsoonthorn, T. (2021). The effectiveness of supervisor support in lessening perceived uncertainties and emotional exhaustion of university employees during the COVID-19 crisis: The constraining role of organizational intransigence. The *Journal of General Psychology, 148*(4), 431–450. https://doi.org/10.1080/00221309.2020.1795613
Ciotti, M., Ciccozzi, M., Terrinoni, A., Jiang, W. C., Wang, C. B., & Bernardini, S. (2020). The COVID-19 pandemic. *Critical Reviews in Clinical Laboratory Sciences, 57*(6), 365–388. https://doi.org/10.1080/10408363.2020.1783198
Contu, F., Ellenberg, M., Kruglanski, A. W., Pantaleo, G., & Pierro, A. (2023a). Need for cognitive closure and desire for cultural tightness mediate the effect of concern about ecological threats on the need for strong leadership. *Current Psychology, 43*(13), 11458–11469.https://doi.org/10.1007/s12144-023-05260-2
Cornell, S., Nickel, B., Cvejic, E., Bonner, C., McCaffery, K. J., Ayre, J., ... & Dodd, R. (2022). Positive outcomes associated with the COVID-19 pandemic in Australia. *Health Promotion Journal of Australia, 33*(2), 311–319. https://doi.org/10.1002/hpja.494
Craig, H., Gasevic, D., Ryan, J., Freak-Poli, R., & Talic, S. (2022). A qualitative study on how older adults perceive the meaning and shaping of optimism: Has the COVID-19 pandemic impacted their perceptions?. *Journal of Global Health Reports, 6*, e2022039.
de Berker, A. O., Rutledge, R. B., Mathys, C., Marshall, L., Cross, G. F., Dolan, R. J., & Bestmann, S. (2016). Computations of uncertainty mediate acute stress responses in humans. *Nature Communications, 7*(1), 10996.
Dekkers, L. M., Jansen, B. R., Salemink, E., & Huizenga, H. M. (2017). Intolerance of Uncertainty Scale: Measurement invariance among adolescent boys and girls and relationships with anxiety and risk taking. *Journal of Behavior Therapy and Experimental Psychiatry, 55*, 57–65. https://doi.org/10.1016/j.jbtep.2016.11.009
Del Valle, M. V., Andrés, M. L., Urquijo, S., Yerro-Avincetto, M., López-Morales, H., & Canet-Juric, L. (2020). Intolerance of uncertainty over COVID-19 pandemic and its effect on anxiety and depressive symptoms. *Revista Interamericana de Psicología/Interamerican Journal of Psychology, 54*(2), e1335–e1335. https://doi.org/10.30849/ripijp.v54i2.1335
Ellenberg, M. D. (2023). *Affective reactions to uncertainty as driven by past experiences, personality, and perceived valence* (Doctoral dissertation, University of Maryland, College Park).
Feuer, W., & Higgins-Dunn, N. (2021, March 13). A year later, Trump's '15 days to slow the spread' campaign shows how little we knew about Covid. *CNBN*. Retrieved from: https://www.cnbc.com/2021/03/16/covid-a-year-later-trumps-15-days-to-slow-the-spread-pledge-shows-how-little-we-knew.html#:~:text=Health%20and%20Science-,A%20year%20later%2C%20Trump%27s%20%2715%20days%20to%20slow%20the%20spread,little%20we%20knew%20about%20Covid&text=Former%20President%20Trump%20announced%20his,to%20combat%20the%20coronavirus%20pandemic
Filkuková, P., Ayton, P., Rand, K., & Langguth, J. (2021). What should I trust? Individual differences in attitudes to conflicting information and misinformation on COVID-19. *Frontiers in Psychology, 12*, 588478. https://doi.org/10.3389/fpsyg.2021.588478
Folkman, S., & Moskowitz, J. T. (2000). Positive affect and the other side of coping. *American Psychologist, 55*(6), 647–654. https://doi.org/10.1037/0003-066X.55.6.647
Forgas, J. P., & Crano, W. D. (2021). The psychology of populism: The tribal challenge to liberal democracy. In J. P. Forgas & W. D. Crano (Eds.), *The psychology of populism* (pp. 1–19). Routledge.
Fragkaki, I., Maciejewski, D. F., Weijman, E. L., Feltes, J., & Cima, M. (2021). Human responses to Covid-19: The role of optimism bias, perceived severity, and anxiety. *Personality and Individual Differences, 176*, 110781. https://doi.org/10.1016/j.paid.2021.110781

Freeston, M., Tiplady, A., Mawn, L., Bottesi, G., & Thwaites, S. (2020). Towards a model of uncertainty distress in the context of Coronavirus (COVID-19). *The Cognitive Behaviour Therapist, 13*, e31. https://doi.org/10.1017/S1754470X2000029X

Fredrickson, B. L. (2000). Cultivating positive emotions to optimize health and well-being. *Prevention & Treatment, 3*(1), A.1. https://doi.org/10.1037/1522-3736.3.1.31a

Fritsche, I., Jonas, E., & Kessler, T. (2011). Collective reactions to threat: Implications for intergroup conflict and for solving societal crises. *Social Issues and Policy Review, 5*(1), 101–136. https://doi.org/10.1111/j.1751-2409.2011.01027.x

Gallagher, M. W., Smith, L. J., Richardson, A. L., D'Souza, J. M., & Long, L. J. (2021). Examining the longitudinal effects and potential mechanisms of hope on COVID-19 stress, anxiety, and well-being. *Cognitive Behaviour Therapy, 50*(3), 234–245. https://doi.org/10.1080/16506073.2021.1877341

Germino, B. B., Mishel, M. H., Crandell, J., Porter, L., Blyler, D., Jenerette, C., & Gil, K. M. (2013). Outcomes of an uncertainty management intervention in younger African American and Caucasian breast cancer survivors. *Oncology Nursing Forum, 40*(1), 82–92.

Gil, K. M., Mishel, M. H., Belyea, M., Germino, B., Porter, L. S., & Clayton, M. (2006). Benefits of the uncertainty management intervention for African American and White older breast cancer survivors: 20-month outcomes. *International Journal of Behavioral Medicine, 13*(4), 286–294.

Gill, E. A., & Morgan, M. (2011). Home sweet home: Conceptualizing and coping with the challenges of aging and the move to a care facility. *Health Communication, 26*(4), 332–342. https://doi.org/10.1080/10410236.2010.551579

Greenberg, J., Pyszczynski, T., & Solomon, S. (1986). The causes and consequences of a need for self-esteem: A terror management theory. In R. F. Baumeister (Ed.), *Public self and private self* (pp. 189–212). Springer.

Han, Q., Zheng, B., Agostini, M., Bélanger, J. J., Gützkow, B., Kreienkamp, J., ... & PsyCorona Collaboration. (2021). Associations of risk perception of COVID-19 with emotion and mental health during the pandemic. *Journal of Affective Disorders, 284*, 247–255. https://doi.org/10.1016/j.jad.2021.01.049

Hart, W., Albarracín, D., Eagly, A. H., Brechan, I., Lindberg, M. J., & Merrill, L. (2009). Feeling validated versus being correct: A meta-analysis of selective exposure to information. *Psychological Bulletin, 135*(4), 555–588. https://doi.org/10.1037/a0015701

Hogg M. A. (2007). Uncertainty–identity theory. In Zanna M. P. (Ed.), *Advances in experimental social psychology* (Vol. 39, pp. 69–126). San Diego, CA: Elsevier Academic Press.

Higgins, E. T. (1996). Knowledge activation: Accessibility, applicability, and salience. In E. T. Higgins & A. W. Kruglanski (Eds.), *Social psychology: Handbook of basic principles* (pp. 133–168). The Giulford Press.

Higgins, E. T., Rossignac-Milon, M., & Echterhoff, G. (2021). Shared reality: From sharing-is-believing to merging minds. *Current Directions in Psychological Science, 30*(2), 103–110. https://doi.org/10.1177/0963721421992027

Hoff, A. L., Mullins, L. L., Chaney, J. M., Hartman, V. L., & Domek, D. (2002). Illness uncertainty, perceived control, and psychological distress among adolescents with type 1 diabetes. *Research and Theory for Nursing Practice, 16*(4), 223–236.

Hogg, M. A. (2014). From uncertainty to extremism: Social categorization and identity processes. *Current Directions in Psychological Science, 23*(5), 338–342. https://doi.org/10.1177/0963721414540168

Hogg, M. A., & Adelman, J. (2013). Uncertainty–identity theory: Extreme groups, radical behavior, and authoritarian leadership. *Journal of Social Issues, 69*(3), 436–454. https://doi.org/10.1111/josi.12023

Hua, J., & Howell, J. L. (2022). Coping self-efficacy influences health information avoidance. *Journal of Health Psychology, 27*(3), 713–725. https://doi.org/10.1177/1359105320965664

Iheduru-Anderson, K., & Foley, J. A. (2021). Transitioning to full online teaching during COVID-19 crisis: The associate degree nurse faculty experience. *Global Qualitative Nursing Research, 8*, 23333936211057545. https://doi.org/10.1177/23333936211057545

Jasko, K., LaFree, G., & Kruglanski, A. (2017). Quest for significance and violent extremism: The case of domestic radicalization. *Political Psychology, 38*(5), 815–831. https://doi.org/10.1111/pops.12376

Jasko, K., Szastok, M., Grzymala-Moszczynska, J., Maj, M., & Kruglanski, A. W. (2019). Rebel with a cause: Personal significance from political activism predicts willingness to self-sacrifice. *Journal of Social Issues, 75*(1), 314–349. https://doi.org/10.1111/josi.12307

Jutzi, C. A., Willardt, R., Schmid, P. C., & Jonas, E. (2020). Between conspiracy beliefs, ingroup bias, and system justification: How people use defense strategies to cope with the threat of COVID-19. *Frontiers in Psychology, 11*, 578586. https://doi.org/10.3389/fpsyg.2020.578586

Kagan, J. (2002). *Surprise, uncertainty, and mental structures.* Harvard University Press.
Kaufman, J. C., & Sternberg, R. J. (2010). *The Cambridge handbook of creativity.* Cambridge University Press.
Keller, H., Schneider, K., & Henderson, B. B. (1994). *Curiosity and exploration.* Springer-Verlag.
Koffman, J., Gross, J., Etkind, S. N., & Selman, L. (2020). Uncertainty and COVID-19: How are we to respond? *Journal of the Royal Society of Medicine, 113*(6), 211–216. https://doi.org/10.1177/0141076820930665
Kruglanski, A. (2023). *Uncertain: How to turn your biggest fear into your greatest power.* Random House.
Kruglanski, A. W., Ellenberg, M., Laurijssen, M., Szumowska, E., Molinario, E., Altungy, P. R., Jaume, L., Pierro, A., Contu, F., & Wang, M. (2023). Facing the unknown: On the affective reactions to uncertainty. [Under review].
Kruglanski, A. W., Molinario, E., Jasko, K., Webber, D., Leander, N. P., & Pierro, A. (2022). Significance-quest theory. *Perspectives on Psychological Science, 17*(4), 1050–1071. https://doi.org/10.1177/17456916211034825
Kruglanski, A. W., Szumowska, E., Kopetz, C. H., Vallerand, R. J., & Pierro, A. (2021). On the psychology of extremism: How motivational imbalance breeds intemperance. *Psychological Review, 128*(2), 264–282. https://doi.org/10.1037/rev0000260
Kruglanski, A. W., & Webster, D. M. (1996). Motivated closing of the mind: "Seizing" and "freezing". *Psychological Review, 103*, 263–283.Kurtz, J. L., Wilson, T. D., & Gilbert, D. T. (2007). Quantity versus uncertainty: When winning one prize is better than winning two. *Journal of Experimental Social Psychology, 43*(6), 979–985. https://doi.org/10.1016/j.jesp.2006.10.020
Landau, M. J., Ryu, Y. J., Greenberg, J., Chur, M., & Pyszczynski, T., (2025). A terror management perspective on life's "big" uncertainties. In P. J. Carroll, K. Rios, & K. C. Oleson (Eds.), *Handbook of the Uncertain Self*, Second Edition. Routledge.
Leontiev, D., Mospan, A., & Osin, E. (2022). Positive personality resources as buffers against psychological reactions to uncertainty. *Current Psychology, 43*(16), 14839–14850. https://doi.org/10.1007/s12144-022-03879-1
Leslie-Miller, C. J., Waugh, C. E., & Cole, V. T. (2021). Coping with COVID-19: The benefits of anticipating future positive events and maintaining optimism. *Frontiers in Psychology, 12*, 646047. https://doi.org/10.3389/fpsyg.2021.646047
Litman, J. (2005). Curiosity and the pleasures of learning: Wanting and liking new information. *Cognition & Emotion, 19*(6), 793–814. https://doi.org/10.1080/02699930541000101
Malouff, J. M., & Schutte, N. S. (2017). Can psychological interventions increase optimism? A meta-analysis. *The Journal of Positive Psychology, 12*(6), 594–604. https://doi.org/10.1080/17439760.2016.1221122
Malesza, M., & Kaczmarek, M. C. (2021). Predictors of anxiety during the COVID-19 pandemic in Poland. *Personality and Individual Differences, 170*, 110419. https://doi.org/10.1016/j.paid.2020.110419
Mann, F. D., Krueger, R. F., & Vohs, K. D. (2020). Personal economic anxiety in response to COVID-19. *Personality and Individual Differences, 167*, 110233. https://doi.org/10.1016/j.paid.2020.110233
Margolin, J. (2020, March 27). FBI warns of potential surge in hate crimes against Asian Americans amid coronavirus. *ABC News*. Retrieved from: https://abcnews.go.com/US/fbi-warns-potential-surge-hate-crimes-asian-americans/story?id=69831920
Marroquín, B., Vine, V., & Morgan, R. (2020). Mental health during the COVID-19 pandemic: Effects of stay-at-home policies, social distancing behavior, and social resources. *Psychiatry Research, 293*, 113419. https://doi.org/10.1016/j.psychres.2020.113419
Massazza, A., Kienzler, H., Al-Mitwalli, S., Tamimi, N., & Giacaman, R. (2023). The association between uncertainty and mental health: A scoping review of the quantitative literature. *Journal of Mental Health, 32*(2), 480–491. https://doi.org/10.1080/09638237.2021.2022620
Mauro, A. M. P. (2008). Exploring uncertainty and psychosocial adjustment after cardioverter defibrillator implantation. *Journal of Cardiovascular Nursing, 23*(6), 527–535. https://doi.org/10.1097/01.JCN.0000338932.73963.42
Miller, M. L., & McGuire, J. F. (2023). Targeting intolerance of uncertainty in treatment: A meta-analysis of therapeutic effects, treatment moderators, and underlying mechanisms. *Journal of Affective Disorders, 341*, 283–295. https://doi.org/10.1016/j.jad.2023.08.132
Mishel, M. H. (1988). Uncertainty in illness. *Image-The Journal of Nursing Scholarship, 20*(4), 225–232. https://doi.org/10.1111/j.1547-5069.1988.tb00082.x

Molinario, E., Di Cicco, G., Prislei, L., & Sensales, G. (2024). Navigating uncertainty: How war and COVID-19 threats shape populist sentiment through need for cognitive closure. *Psychology Hub*, *41*, 133–144. https://doi.org/10.13133/2724-2943/18443

Monfort, S. S., Stroup, H. E., & Waugh, C. E. (2015). The impact of anticipating positive events on responses to stress. *Journal of Experimental Social Psychology*, *58*, 11–22. https://doi.org/10.1016/j.jesp.2014.12.003

Moreland, P., & Santacroce, S. J. (2018). Illness uncertainty and posttraumatic stress in young adults with congenital heart disease. *The Journal of Cardiovascular Nursing*, *33*(4), 356–362. https://doi.org/10.1097/JCN.0000000000000471

Nagler, R. H., Vogel, R. I., Gollust, S. E., Rothman, A. J., Fowler, E. F., & Yzer, M. C. (2020). Public perceptions of conflicting information surrounding COVID-19: Results from a nationally representative survey of US adults. *PloS one*, *15*(10), e0240776. https://doi.org/10.1371/journal.pone.0240776

Nezu, A. M. (2004). Problem solving and behavior therapy revisited. *Behavior Therapy*, *35*, 1–33. https://doi.org/10.1016/S0005-7894(04)80002-9

Niv, G., Bar Josef, S., Ben Bassat, O., Avni, I., Niv, Y., & Barnoy, S. (2017). Quality of life and uncertainty in Crohn's disease. *Quality of Life Research*, *26*, 1609–1616. https://doi.org/10.1007/s11136-017-1509-5

Noordewier, M. K., Topolinski, S., & Van Dijk, E. (2016). The temporal dynamics of surprise. *Social and Personality Psychology Compass*, *10*(3), 136–149. https://doi.org/10.1111/spc3.12242

Obaidi, M., Anjum, G., Bierwiaczonek, K., Dovidio, J. F., Ozer, S., & Kunst, J. R. (2023). Cultural threat perceptions predict violent extremism via need for cognitive closure. *Proceedings of the National Academy of Sciences*, *120*(20), e2213874120. https://doi.org/10.1073/pnas.2213874120

Ong, A. D., Bergeman, C. S., Bisconti, T. L., & Wallace, K. A. (2006). Psychological resilience, positive emotions, and successful adaptation to stress in later life. *Journal of Personality and Social Psychology*, *91*(4), 730–749. https://doi.org/10.1037/0022-3514.91.4.730

Papenfuss, I., Lommen, M. J., Grillon, C., Balderston, N. L., & Ostafin, B. D. (2021). Responding to uncertain threat: A potential mediator for the effect of mindfulness on anxiety. *Journal of Anxiety Disorders*, *77*, 102332.

Pappa, S., Ntella, V., Giannakas, T., Giannakoulis, V. G., Papoutsi, E., & Katsaounou, P. (2020). Prevalence of depression, anxiety, and insomnia among healthcare workers during the COVID-19 pandemic: A systematic review and meta-analysis. *Brain, Behavior, and Immunity*, *88*, 901–907. https://doi.org/10.1016/j.bbi.2020.05.026

Paredes, M. R., Apaolaza, V., Fernandez-Robin, C., Hartmann, P., & Yañez-Martinez, D. (2021). The impact of the COVID-19 pandemic on subjective mental well-being: The interplay of perceived threat, future anxiety and resilience. *Personality and Individual Differences*, *170*, 110455. https://doi.org/10.1016/j.paid.2020.110455

Parlapani, E., Holeva, V., Nikopoulou, V. A., Sereslis, K., Athanasiadou, M., Godosidis, A., ... & Diakogiannis, I. (2020). Intolerance of uncertainty and loneliness in older adults during the COVID-19 pandemic. *Frontiers in Psychiatry*, *11*, 842. https://doi.org/10.3389/fpsyt.2020.00842

Pizarro, J. J., Cakal, H., Méndez, L., Zumeta, L. N., Gracia-Leiva, M., Basabe, N., ... & Páez, D. (2023). Sociopolitical consequences of COVID-19 in the Americas, Europe, and Asia: A multilevel, multicountry investigation of risk perceptions and support for antidemocratic practices. *Political Psychology*, *45*(2), 407–433. https://doi.org/10.1111/pops.12930

Rettie, H., & Daniels, J. (2021). Coping and tolerance of uncertainty: Predictors and mediators of mental health during the COVID-19 pandemic. *American Psychologist*, *76*(3), 427. https://doi.org/10.1037/amp0000710

Ritchie, L., Cervone, D., & Sharpe, B. T. (2021). Goals and self-efficacy beliefs during the initial COVID-19 lockdown: A mixed methods analysis. *Frontiers in Psychology*, *11*, 559114. https://doi.org/10.3389/fpsyg.2020.559114

Robichaud, M., & Dugas, M. J. (2006). A cognitive-behavioral treatment targeting intolerance of uncertainty. In C. L. Graham & A. W. Dawey (Eds.), *Worry and its psychological disorders: Theory, assessment and treatment* (pp. 289–304). Wiley Online Books. https://doi.org/10.1002/9780470713143

Runco, M. A., & Albert, R. S. (2010). *Creativity research: A historical view.* Cambridge University Press.

Satici, B., Saricali, M., Satici, S. A., & Griffiths, M. D. (2022). Intolerance of uncertainty and mental wellbeing: Serial mediation by rumination and fear of COVID-19. *International Journal of Mental Health and Addiction*, *20*(5), 2731–2742. https://doi.org/10.1007/s11469-020-00305-0

Schiltz, J., Vindevogel, S., Derluyn, I., & Vanderplasschen, W. (2019). Uncertainty in situations of forced displacement: A critical interpretative synthesis of refugee literature. *Population, Space and Place*, *25*(3), e2194. https://doi.org/10.1002/psp.2194

Schumpe, B. M., Bélanger, J. J., Moyano, M., & Nisa, C. F. (2020). The role of sensation seeking in political violence: An extension of the Significance Quest Theory. *Journal of Personality and Social Psychology, 118*(4), 743. https://doi.org/10.1037/pspp0000223

Seligman, M. E. (2006). *Learned optimism: How to change your mind and your life*. Vintage.

Sensales, G., Di Cicco, G., Molinario, E., Prislei, L., & Kruglanski, A. W. (2024). Representations of populism, pandemic, and war among Italian citizens of different political orientations. A psycho-linguistic analysis of their associative productions (2019–2022). In G. Sensales (Ed.), *Political psychology perspectives on populism*. Palgrave MacMillan [in press].

Sharkey, C. M., Bakula, D. M., Baraldi, A. N., Perez, M. N., Suorsa, K. I., Chaney, J. M., & Mullins, L. L. (2018). Grit, illness-related distress, and psychosocial outcomes in college students with a chronic medical condition: A path analysis. *Journal of Pediatric Psychology, 43*(5), 552–560. https://doi.org/10.1093/jpepsy/jsx145

Smith, B. M., Twohy, A. J., & Smith, G. S. (2020). Psychological inflexibility and intolerance of uncertainty moderate the relationship between social isolation and mental health outcomes during COVID-19. *Journal of Contextual Behavioral Science, 18*, 162–174. https://doi.org/10.1016/j.jcbs.2020.09.005

Smith, S. M., Fabrigar, L. R., & Norris, M. E. (2008). Reflecting on six decades of selective exposure research: Progress, challenges, and opportunities. *Social and Personality Psychology Compass, 2*(1), 464–493. https://doi.org/10.1111/j.1751-9004.2007.00060.x

Snyder, C. R. (1995). Hope: Theory, measurement, and interventions. *Journal of Counseling and Development, 73*, 355–360.

Sorokowski, P., Groyecka, A., Kowal, M., Sorokowska, A., Białek, M., Lebuda, I., ... & Karwowski, M. (2020). Can information about pandemics increase negative attitudes toward foreign groups? A case of COVID-19 outbreak. *Sustainability, 12*(12), 4912. https://doi.org/10.3390/su12124912

Sorrentino, R. M., Bobocel, D. R., Gitta, M. Z., Olson, J. M., & Hewitt, E. C. (1988). Uncertainty orientation and persuasion: Individual differences in the effects of personal relevance on social judgments. *Journal of Personality and social Psychology, 55*(3), 357. https://doi.org/10.1037/0022-3514.55.3.357

Sweeny, K., & Howell, J. L. (2025). Managing Acute Uncertainty about the Future. In P. J. Carroll, K. Rios, & K. C. Oleson (Eds.), *Handbook of the Uncertain Self*, Second Edition. Routledge.

Szumowska, E., & Kruglanski, A. W. (2020). Curiosity as end and means. *Current Opinion in Behavioral Sciences, 35*, 35–39. https://doi.org/10.1016/j.cobeha.2020.06.008

Tanner, A., Voon, D., Hasking, P., & Martin, G. (2013). Underlying structure of ruminative thinking: Factor analysis of the ruminative thought style questionnaire. *Cognitive Therapy and Research, 37*, 633–646. https://doi.org/10.1007/s10608-012-9492-1

Tarhani, M., Goudarzi, F., Hasanvand, S., Ebrahimzadeh, F., & Rassouli, M. (2020). Uncertainty, anxiety, depression and the quality of life in patients with cancer. *Oncology and Radiotherapy, 46*(1), 20–27.

Thartori, E., Pastorelli, C., Cirimele, F., Remondi, C., Gerbino, M., Basili, E., ... & Caprara, G. V. (2021). Exploring the protective function of positivity and regulatory emotional self-efficacy in time of pandemic COVID-19. *International Journal of Environmental Research and Public Health, 18*(24), 13171. https://doi.org/10.3390/ijerph182413171

Thorisdottir, I. E., Agustsson, G., Oskarsdottir, S. Y., Kristjansson, A. L., Asgeirsdottir, B. B., Sigfusdottir, I. D., ... & Halldorsdottir, T. (2023). Effect of the COVID-19 pandemic on adolescent mental health and substance use up to March, 2022, in Iceland: A repeated, cross-sectional, population-based study. *The Lancet Child & Adolescent Health, 7*(5), 347–357. https://doi.org/10.1016/S2352-4642(23)00022-6

Van Bavel, J. J.., Baicker, K., Boggio, P. S., Capraro, V., Cichocka, A., Cikara, M., ... & Willer, R. (2020). Using social and behavioural science to support COVID-19 pandemic response. *Nature Human Behaviour, 4*(5), 460–471. https://doi.org/10.1037/0096-3445.136.2.289

Van Boven, L., & Ashworth, L. (2007). Looking forward, looking back: Anticipation is more evocative than retrospection. *Journal of Experimental Psychology: General, 136*(2), 289.

van den Bos, K. (2009). Making sense of life: The existential self trying to deal with personal uncertainty. *Psychological Inquiry, 20*(4), 197–217. https://doi.org/10.1080/10478400903333411

Van Lissa, C. J., Stroebe, W., Leander, N. P., Agostini, M., Draws, T., Grygoryshyn, A., ... & Bélanger, J. J. (2022). Using machine learning to identify important predictors of COVID-19 infection prevention behaviors during the early phase of the pandemic. *Patterns, 3*(4), 100482. https://doi.org/10.1016/j.patter.2022.100482

Yamagata, M., Teraguchi, T., & Miura, A. (2020). The relationship between infection-avoidance tendency and exclusionary attitudes towards foreigners: A case study of the COVID-19 outbreak in Japan. PsyArXiv. https:// doi.org/10.31234/osf.io/vhrqn

Yates, J. F. (Ed.) (1992). *Risk-taking behavior.* John Wiley & Sons.

Yıldırım, M., & Arslan, G. (2020). Exploring the associations between resilience, dispositional hope, subjective well-being, and psychological health among adults during early stage of COVID-19. *Current Psychology*, *39*, 1–11. https://doi.org/10.1007/s12144-020-01177-2

Waugh, C. E., Wager, T. D., Fredrickson, B. L., Noll, D. C., & Taylor, S. F. (2008). The neural correlates of trait resilience when anticipating and recovering from threat. *Social Cognitive and Affective Neuroscience*, *3*(4), 322–332. https://doi.org/10.1093/scan/nsn024

Webber, D., Babush, M., Schori-Eyal, N., Vazeou-Nieuwenhuis, A., Hettiarachchi, M., Bélanger, J. J., ... & Gelfand, M. J. (2018). The road to extremism: Field and experimental evidence that significance loss-induced need for closure fosters radicalization. *Journal of Personality and Social Psychology*, *114*(2), 270. https://doi.org/10.1037/pspi0000111

Whitehead, R., Bates, G., Elphinstone, B., Yang, Y., & Murray, G. (2019). Nonattachment mediates the relationship between mindfulness and psychological well-being, subjective well-being, and depression, anxiety and stress. *Journal of Happiness Studies*, *20*, 2141–2158. https://doi.org/10.1007/s10902-018-0041-9

WHO. (2020). *Mental health and COVID-19*. World Health Organization. Retrieved from: https://www.who.int/teams/mental-health-and-substance-use/mental-health-and-covid-19

WHO. (2022). *World Health Statistics 2022.* World Health Organization. Retrieved from: https://www.who.int/publications/i/item/9789240051157

Wilson, T. D., & Gilbert, D. T. (2003). Affective forecasting. In M. P. Zanna (Ed.), *Advances in experimental social psychology* (Vol. 35, pp. 345–411). Elsevier Academic Press. https://doi.org/10.1016/S0065-2601(03)01006-2

Wilson, W., Raj, J. P., Rao, S., Ghiya, M., Nedungalaparambil, N. M., Mundra, H., & Mathew, R. (2020). Prevalence and predictors of stress, anxiety, and depression among healthcare workers managing COVID-19 pandemic in India: A nationwide observational study. *Indian Journal of Psychological Medicine*, *42*(4), 353–358. https://doi.org/10.1177/0253717620933992

Zhou, M., & Guo, W. (2021). Social factors and worry associated with COVID-19: Evidence from a large survey in China. *Social Science & Medicine*, *277*, 113934. https://doi.org/10.1016/j.socscimed.2021.113934

Zuckerman, M. (2009). Sensation seeking. In M. R. Leary & R. H. Hoyle (Eds.), *Handbook of Individual differences in social behavior* (pp. 455–465). The Guilford Press.

18

CONFLICT BETWEEN BELIEF SYSTEMS AND CONSEQUENCES OF SELF-UNCERTAINTY

Kimberly Rios and Alexis T. Morales

People's self-concepts and social identities are multifaceted and consist of individual characteristics, values, and beliefs; social roles and relationships; and group memberships (Brewer & Gardner, 1996). Throughout the 21st century, social scientists have paid increasing attention to how different components of the self and identity interact with one another. Research on intersectionality suggests that belonging to multiple social categories can lead to unique and nuanced outcomes, beyond any additive effects of membership in each category alone (Purdie-Vaughns & Eibach, 2008; Rosenthal, 2016). For example, Black women in leadership contexts sometimes face double jeopardy (i.e., race- and gender-based penalties) due to negative stereotypes of both Black people and women (Rosette & Livingston, 2012), but at other times face "intersectional invisibility" (i.e., being overlooked or mischaracterized) due to being seen as less representative of the category "Black" than Black men and less representative of the category "women" than White women (Livingston et al., 2012).

Occasionally, people may perceive certain aspects of their identities as conflicting with one another, especially when each identity is associated with different social and behavioral norms (Hirsh & Kang, 2016). These perceptions of identity conflict have been studied quite extensively in the context of belonging to multiple groups (Kang & Bodenhausen, 2015). Espousing two or more social identities that are considered incompatible can activate the behavioral inhibition system—in other words, motivation to avoid negative outcomes—which in turn predicts feelings of anxiety, threat, and uncertainty (Hirsh & Kang, 2016). Below, we review some of the literature on social identity conflicts and their consequences. Our goal is not to provide a comprehensive review of all possible conflicts one might experience, but rather to introduce a few examples of how identity conflict can manifest.

Social Identity Conflicts

Research on biculturalism provides a useful framework through which to understand the antecedents and consequences of perceived identity conflict. According to this research, individuals who identify with more than one culture—for example, Chinese and American, or Mexican and American—may see these cultures as either in conflict or compatible, which reflects low or high bicultural identity integration, respectively. An example of a statement suggesting perceived conflict or low

DOI: 10.4324/9781003363385-21

bicultural identity integration is "I am conflicted between the American and Chinese ways of doing things" (Benet-Martínez & Haritatos, 2005). This distinction between bicultural identity conflict and integration parallels the integration dimension of cognitive complexity (i.e., the extent of reconciliation between different viewpoints) introduced by Paulhus and Suedfeld (1988). However, we focus on reconciliation versus conflict between entire belief systems (e.g., religion, politics, and science), rather than on reconciliation between viewpoints on specific issues (e.g., abortion, evolution).

In general, people low in bicultural identity integration (i.e., who perceive a conflict between their cultural identities) tend to have lower psychological well-being than do people high in bicultural identity integration. Additionally, emotional instability and related variables (e.g., anxiety), as well as contextual stressors such as experiences of discrimination, predict lower bicultural identity integration (Benet-Martínez & Haritatos, 2005; Manzi & Benet-Martinez, 2022). Benet-Martínez and colleagues have recently begun examining "identity integration" more broadly, which need not be specific to biculturalism and involves any two or more identities that may be viewed as incompatible. For instance, people who worked remotely during COVID-19 may have perceived their "work" and "family" identities as clashing with one another (low identity integration), or as relatively harmonious (high identity integration). Again, high identity integration in this context was associated with more positive psychological outcomes (Manzi et al., 2022).

A separate body of work focuses on women's feelings of threat in science, technology, engineering, and mathematics (STEM) fields (e.g., Cheryan et al., 2009; Diekman et al., 2017; Murphy et al., 2007; Spencer et al., 1999). There are many potential reasons that women are underrepresented in STEM, but most relevant to the present chapter, women may perceive the social roles and goals associated with being female as incompatible with the social roles and goals associated with pursuing a STEM career. For example, whereas STEM disciplines are often portrayed as involving solitary work and self-interest, women are often stereotyped as collaborative and motivated to help others (Diekman et al., 2011). This discrepancy may deter women from STEM fields, as they believe such fields are "not for people like them" (Belanger et al., 2020). Alternatively, women who see STEM as central to their self-concepts may disavow stereotypically female characteristics (e.g., gossipy, flirtatious, emotional) to attempt to fit in with their peers (Pronin et al., 2004).

Relatedly, Black students in the US face barriers to achievement in higher education, including the lack of available role models who self-identify as Black (Oyserman & Lewis, 2017; Pietri et al., 2018). These barriers can engender a perception that one must "act White" to succeed in academic contexts (Fordham & Ogbu, 1986; Ogbu, 2004). As a result, even Black students who are motivated toward academic achievement may experience a conflict between their Black identity and their academic identity. Supporting this possibility, Black undergraduates at Stanford University who were assigned to take a standardized test under threatening (versus non-threatening) conditions subsequently distanced themselves from stereotypically African American traits and activities (e.g., basketball, rap music) (Steele & Aronson, 1995).

Many of the documented outcomes of identity conflict relate to identification with the social groups or roles under question (e.g., Pronin et al., 2004; Steele & Aronson, 1995) or psychological well-being (e.g., Benet-Martínez & Haritatos, 2005; Manzi et al., 2022). It is also plausible, however, that experiences of identity conflict predict meta-cognitive variables (i.e., beliefs about one's beliefs), such as self-uncertainty. In other words, feeling conflicted between two or more identities may elicit doubts about "who one really is" and reduce the sense of having a consistent, coherent self-concept (Campbell et al., 1996). Perceptions of self-uncertainty are negatively correlated with self-esteem (DeMarree & Rios, 2014) and subjective well-being (Campbell et al., 1996). Although no research to date has examined the relationship between identity conflict and felt self-uncertainty, doing so is important for advancing understanding of ways to reduce identity conflict in the first place.

Some work has shown that exiting a social role can increase self-uncertainty. For example, people who deconvert from a religion, retire from a job, graduate school, or leave a group to which they previously belonged (e.g., a social club) tend to report greater uncertainty about themselves, even after controlling for self-esteem and demographic variables (Light & Visser, 2013). Similarly, the dissolution of a romantic relationship, be it through a breakup, divorce, or the death of a spouse/partner, can heighten one's feelings of self-uncertainty (Slotter & Emery, 2017; Slotter et al., 2010). Social role exits entail moving from one identity to another, rather than simultaneously holding and experiencing conflicts between both identities. However, the fact that social role exits predict self-uncertainty suggests it is feasible for identity conflicts to contribute to uncertainty about the self as well.

Belief-Based Conflicts

The existing research on identity conflict has highlighted perceptions of incompatibility between social groups or roles. We propose, though, that people may also experience conflicts between or within their cherished belief systems. The notion of belief conflict is rooted in cognitive dissonance theory, which postulates that holding two or more discrepant attitudes, beliefs, or behaviors can elicit psychological discomfort (Festinger, 1962). For example, somebody might regularly smoke cigarettes but realize that smoking is unhealthy. In this case, they would attempt to reduce any feelings of discomfort by either smoking less or changing their beliefs about smoking (e.g., smoking in moderation is fine). However, cognitive dissonance theory does not take into account the fact that some belief systems are closely intertwined with social identities. Conflicts between and within these types of belief systems may have unique antecedents and consequences, beyond what cognitive dissonance theory alone would predict.

In this section, we review our work on conflicts among three belief systems that implicate social identities: religion, political ideology, and science. Religion has long been construed as both a set of beliefs that provide explanatory power and a social group with which people strongly identify across time and in many societies (for review, see Ysseldyk et al., 2010). Although political ideology was initially studied in the context of research on attitudes, beliefs, and values (Allport, 1929; Feldman, 2003; Holbrook et al., 2001), more recent work has highlighted the growing tendency for polarization between political parties—that is, political intergroup biases (Balinhas, 2023; Jost et al., 2022; Morrison & Ybarra, 2009; Stewart et al., 2019). Regarding science, the past decade has seen an explosion within social psychology and adjacent fields (e.g., communication, political science) of research about how science-related attitudes and beliefs can create fissures between groups. For example, "faith in science" has been compared to religious fundamentalism in that both involve extremity and adherence to a particular worldview (Farias et al., 2013). Further, the onset of the COVID-19 pandemic exacerbated divisions in attitudes toward science (e.g., vaccine hesitancy) among political parties (Pink et al., 2021), religious groups (Chu et al., 2021), and racial and ethnic groups (Nguyen et al., 2022; Willis et al., 2021).

Conflict between Religion and Science

Since the mid-19th century, Western scientists and philosophers have written about the notion that religion and science are inherently incompatible (Draper, 1875; White, 1877). This "conflict narrative" is exemplified in research on the differences between System 1 processing, which involves using intuition and making spontaneous decisions, and System 2 processing, which involves rational thought and deliberative decision-making (Stanovich & West, 2000). Because religious belief is faith-based and science is characterized by analytical thinking, one potential extension of the System 1 versus System 2 dichotomy is that religion and science also implicate opposing schools of thought (Rios et al., 2023). Indeed, some studies point to a negative correlation between religiosity and a tendency to think analytically (Pennycook et al., 2016; Zuckerman et al., 2020).

Regardless of whether religion and science actually clash, the *perception* of a religion-science conflict persists in many societies. In 2009, the appointment of Dr. Francis Collins as head of the National Institutes of Health in the US garnered substantial backlash from people who believed Collins, an evangelical Christian, could not possibly reconcile his faith with science (Scheitle & Ecklund, 2017). Meanwhile, Harvard University professor Steven Pinker expressed widely publicized disdain for a proposal that would require undergraduate students to take a course in "Reason and Faith" (Miller, 2010) and has continued to argue that religion cannot be part of intellectual life (Clooney, 2018).

Beyond these examples of religion-science conflict perceptions in the public sphere, an initial set of studies demonstrated that North American college students automatically see religion and science as opposing belief systems. For instance, reading a strong (versus weak) scientific explanation for the origin of human life resulted in more negative implicit evaluations of God, and thinking about God's capacity to exert influence (versus a control topic) resulted in more negative implicit evaluations of science (Preston & Epley, 2009). Follow-up research has uncovered the different forms that perceived religion-science conflict can take. In addition to seeing scientific and religious explanations for events (e.g., evolution versus creation, the age of the Earth) as being at odds, people may view science- and religion-based beliefs about humans' interactions with the world (e.g., how humans should behave toward one another or toward the environment, how to treat physical or mental illness) as contradictory (Leicht et al., 2022). Notably, non-religious people generally perceive a greater religion-science conflict than do religious people (Leicht et al., 2022; Rios, 2021), perhaps because non-religious people are less motivated to reconcile their personal faith with science and thus feel more comfortable claiming that there is a fundamental clash between religious and scientific belief systems. However, to the extent that religious people do perceive a religion-science conflict (or simply believe that most others perceive such a conflict), negative consequences can ensue, as we detail in the "Consequences of Belief System Conflict" section below.

Conflict between Religion and Politics

In contrast to the religion-science conflict narrative, which has existed for over 150 years, perceptions of conflict between religious beliefs and political views are relatively recent and may be specific to the United States. Although church and state are formally separate in the US according to the Constitution, religious beliefs and political views still intersect (and sometimes clash) in many ways. For example, every state-level constitution includes at least one reference to God or the divine (Sandstrom, 2017), and students and staff at public schools in 47 states are required to recite the Pledge of Allegiance, which includes the line "One nation, under God" (Dress, 2022). Additionally, roughly half of US Americans consider it important for the President to have strong religious beliefs and for laws to reflect the Bible (Fahmy, 2020).

Within the United States, there is a tendency for religious people to be more politically conservative (Van der Toorn et al., 2017). However, the positive correlation between religiosity and conservatism is strongest among those who are highly engaged with politics, and hence who have more exposure to narratives implying that religiosity and conservatism go together (Malka et al., 2012). This finding suggests that religious and political belief systems may sometimes conflict in similar ways as do religion and science. Specifically, religion may be seen as less compatible with political liberalism than conservatism, whereas non-religion may be seen as less compatible with political conservatism than liberalism.

Some preliminary work from our lab indicates that religious and political identity conflicts can manifest at the individual level. In two correlational studies—one conducted with college undergraduates, and another conducted with a sample of US adults—we asked participants if they generally identified as religious or non-religious, as well as how they would describe their political views on a seven-point scale from "very liberal" to "very conservative." Using a five-item measure adapted from research on bicultural identity conflict and religion-science conflict (Benet-Martínez & Haritatos, 2005; Rios, 2021), we also had participants indicate the extent to which they saw their religious (or non-religious) beliefs as compatible versus incompatible with their political views. Example items included "I feel caught between my religious [non-religious] beliefs and my political views" and "How similar do you think your religious [non-religious] beliefs are to your political views?" (reverse coded). Across both studies, religious participants reported more subjective conflict between their religious beliefs and political views the more politically liberal they were, whereas non-religious participants reported more subjective conflict between their non-religious beliefs and political views the more politically conservative they were (Morales & Rios, 2023).

Antecedents of Belief System Conflict

As we explain in the following section, perceptions of both religion-science conflict and religion-politics conflict can vary according to situational factors, such as geographic location and whether a conflict (versus compatibility) mindset is made salient.

Religion and Science

Perceptions of conflict between religious and scientific belief systems can fluctuate as a function of the social context. A study of biologists and physicists at universities and research institutes across eight countries revealed that scientists in Western countries (the US, the United Kingdom, France, and Italy) were less likely to see religion and science as compatible than were scientists in non-Western countries (India, Hong Kong, Taiwan, and Turkey). Furthermore, scientists in the US, the UK, and France were especially prone to view religion and science as conflicting, and to side with science in this conflict (Ecklund et al., 2016). Consistent with these results, university students in the United Arab Emirates, a predominantly Muslim country, perceived a greater conflict between religion and science the more time they reported spending per year in the West (Rios & Aveyard, 2019).

Recent research suggests that perceptions of religion-science conflict can be experimentally manipulated. In one study, US Americans who read a passage about Francis Collins (who as noted earlier, is the former director of the National Institutes of Health and an evangelical Christian) subsequently reported believing that religion and science were more compatible than did those in a control group who did not read the passage. Interestingly, US Americans who read a passage about Richard Dawkins (an evolutionary biologist and outspoken atheist) did not differ from a control (no passage) group in religion-science compatibility beliefs (Scheitle & Ecklund). A potential explanation is that the conflict narrative was the "default" in this sample, whereas the Collins passage describing a religious scientist may have been more surprising and hence more likely to spark attitude change (Scheitle & Ecklund, 2017; Sharp et al., 2022). In additional work, US Christian participants reported perceiving more religion-science conflict after reading that religion and science are opposing (versus compatible) schools of thought, or after reading that most other people endorse (versus reject) the conflict narrative (Rios, 2021; see also Mackey et al., 2023).

Religion and Politics

It is likely that social-contextual factors influence perceptions of conflict between religious beliefs and political views, as well as between religion and science. For instance, people may experience greater subjective conflict in geographic areas that are either highly liberal and secular (e.g., the Northeastern US) or highly conservative and religious (e.g., the Southern US). This possibility remains to be investigated, though prior research on the role of geography in political identity provides precedent to do so (Feinberg et al., 2017).

We have begun to test manipulations of perceived conflict between religious beliefs and political views; however, this work is still in its infancy. In two experiments, we randomly assigned participants to recall a time during which their religious (or non-religious) beliefs either conflicted or coincided with their political views. We reasoned that even though religious liberals and non-religious conservatives tend to report greater belief conflict than do religious conservatives and non-religious liberals, most if not all people have had at least one experience of such conflict. For example, a politically conservative Catholic might see Pope Francis's welcoming of LGBTQ+ people into the church as conflicting with their political views, or a politically liberal atheist might feel conflicted about whether to support an organization that helps unhoused individuals but is religiously affiliated. The results of these two studies revealed that participants who recalled a past instance of religion-politics conflict were more likely to see their religious beliefs as clashing with their political views in general, relative to participants who recalled a past instance of religion-politics compatibility. Our findings held regardless of participants' personal religious beliefs and political views (Morales & Rios, 2023).

Consequences of Belief System Conflict for Self-Uncertainty

In this section, we review some documented and potential consequences of conflicts between belief systems. We focus on how belief system conflicts can affect self-uncertainty, whereas other chapters in this volume highlight how self-uncertainty evoked by threats can affect attitude extremity (Briñol & Petty, this volume), political polarization (Landau et al., this volume), and ingroup-serving behaviors (Paredes et al., this volume). That is, we call special attention to how self-uncertainty arises in the first place. However, we also discuss research on other relevant outcomes, such as feelings of threat and group identification.

Religion and Science

Research on the effects of perceived religion-science conflicts has focused primarily on the conflict between *Christianity* and science, as the conflict narrative is most prevalent in the majority Christian nations (Ecklund et al., 2016; Johnson et al., 2016). One set of effects involves Christians' identification with science. In a representative study, US Christian and non-Christian participants were randomly assigned to read an article suggesting that most other people thought Christianity was either compatible or incompatible with science; a third (control) group of participants did not read an article. Participants then completed a measure of their personal identification with scientific traits and abilities (e.g., problem-solving, mathematics). Christians exhibited lower science identification than did non-Christians in both the incompatible and control conditions. However, in the compatible condition, Christians and non-Christians did not differ in their identification with science, suggesting that reading about others' compatibility perceptions can bolster Christians' scientific engagement (Rios et al., 2015, Study 2).

In a more recent experiment, participants again read an article about others' perceptions of either religion-science compatibility or incompatibility. The results demonstrated that US Christians reported greater subjective feelings of threat in science (e.g., anticipation that their scientific ability would be negatively evaluated based on their religious [non-religious] beliefs) than did US non-Christians in the incompatible condition. Furthermore, Christians in the incompatible condition underperformed on a purported measure of scientific reasoning relative to non-Christians. By contrast, feelings of threat and performance did not differ between Christian and non-Christian participants who were induced to believe most people thought Christianity and science were compatible (Rios, 2021, Study 2). This experiment focused on participants' reactions to others' perceptions of conflict, rather than on their own perceptions of conflict, between Christianity and science. However, a correlational study in the same paper showed that Christians felt more threatened and performed worse on a science task than did non-Christians when they personally believed Christianity and science were incompatible, but not when they personally believed Christianity and science were compatible (Rios, 2021, Study 1).

Although religion-science conflict perceptions have been found to affect Christians' science identification, feelings of threat in science, and scientific task performance, little is known about how these conflict perceptions impact self-related outcomes outside science contexts. For example, do Christians who perceive religion and science as incompatible report greater self-uncertainty than those who perceive religion and science as compatible? Can reading about others' perceptions that religion and science are in conflict also heighten self-uncertainty? These questions are important for investigators to pursue in the future, given the psychological consequences of self-uncertainty for self-esteem and general well-being (Campbell et al., 1996; DeMarree & Rios, 2014).

Religion and Politics

As noted earlier, we have found that politically liberal religious people and politically conservative non-religious people experience greater conflict between their political views and religious beliefs than do politically conservative religious people and politically liberal non-religious people. These subjective feelings of conflict in turn predict weaker identification with both one's political views and one's religious (or non-religious) beliefs—that is, lower importance of one's political views and religious [non-religious] beliefs to the self-concept. In our experimental studies, having participants recall a personal instance of political-religious conflict (versus compatibility) results in weaker political identification, but does not significantly affect religious identification (Morales & Rios, 2023). It is possible that, because people are often raised with a religious (or non-religious) affiliation but do not vote in political elections until they are of legal age, religious identification is less easily influenced by our experimental manipulation than is political identification.

Critically, we have also begun examining the relationship between political-religious identity conflict and self-uncertainty—specifically, self-concept clarity (Campbell et al., 1996). In one of our two experiments, though there was no direct effect of condition on self-concept clarity, participants' weaker political identification in the conflict condition indirectly predicted lower self-concept clarity. That is, participants who recalled an instance of political-religious conflict subsequently disidentified with their political views and in turn, exhibited greater self-uncertainty. In our other experiment, we found a direct effect of condition on self-concept clarity that approached statistical significance, such that participants in the conflict condition tended to have lower self-concept clarity than participants in the compatibility condition (Morales & Rios, 2023). Thus, our results provide preliminary evidence that conflict between political and religious belief systems can heighten feelings of uncertainty about the self in general.

Future Research Directions

Perceptions of conflict between belief systems may have other downstream effects that are associated with self-uncertainty. For example, people who believe their belief systems are in conflict might choose to conceal their adherence to one or more of these belief systems when interacting with others. Some work has suggested this is the case for religious graduate students in science disciplines. Specifically, among these students, religiosity predicts greater tendencies to conceal one's religious identity, which in turn predicts weaker identification with science (Scheitle & Dabbs, 2021). It is also plausible that politically liberal religious or politically conservative non-religious individuals will conceal either their political or (non-)religious identities in contexts where it may be useful to do so (e.g., a religious person might avoid mentioning their religion when in a group of political liberals, just as a non-religious person might avoid mentioning their lack of religion when in a group of political conservatives). Another possible predictor of concealment is anticipated belief system conflict. For example, someone of a religious background applying to a politically liberal college may expect conflicts to arise between their current belief system and that of most other students at their prospective future institution, and as a result, may conceal their religious identity in their application materials. The relationship between identity concealment and self-uncertainty has yet to be tested. However, we suspect that belief concealment would predict higher self-uncertainty because someone who conceals their beliefs might question how important those beliefs—and related aspects of the self—are to them.

A second fruitful avenue for future research would be to examine what makes some subjective experiences of belief or identity conflict more impactful—for instance, predictive of greater self-uncertainty—than others. Belief-based conflicts can differ from one another, and from identity-based conflicts that do not explicitly involve beliefs, on several dimensions. For instance, whereas certain sources of conflict (e.g., political ideology) are relatively concealable, other sources (e.g., being bicultural, being a woman in STEM) are less so. Further, non-religious identities tend to be more concealable than many religious identities (e.g., Judaism and Islam, which involve wearing religious attire) (Mackey & Rios, 2023). On one hand, the conflict between concealable identities or belief systems may be especially prone to increasing self-uncertainty if the concealment results in more internal rumination, a correlate of uncertainty about the self (Campbell et al., 1996). On the other hand, conflict between less concealable identities or belief systems may produce greater self-uncertainty, due to the heightened potential to be confronted with others' perceptions of conflict as well as one's own perceptions of conflict. Supporting this possibility, research on identity denial suggests that multicultural individuals whose identities are consistently questioned (e.g., a Chinese American individual who is told they are both "not Chinese enough" and "not American enough") experience feelings of threat, which can be closely tied to self-uncertainty (McGregor et al., 2001; McGregor & Marigold, this volume). Thus, there is reason to predict that the concealability of belief systems or identities may either mitigate or exacerbate self-uncertainty and perhaps the answer depends on the context.

Somewhat relatedly, we have discussed both personal perceptions of conflict (e.g., people experiencing discord between their own religious beliefs and political identities) and others' perceptions of conflict (e.g., people believing that others think religion and science cannot coexist, even if they themselves view religion and science as compatible). We are not aware of any research that has examined whether personal perceptions of conflict or others' perceptions of conflict have stronger associations with self-uncertainty. However, one possibility is that perceiving conflict between one's own belief systems is more closely linked to self-uncertainty than knowing that other people perceive conflict between one's belief systems, given that self-perceptions of conflict (like self-uncertainty) are relatively intrapersonal. By contrast, knowing about others' perceptions of conflict may be more predictive of interpersonal outcomes, such as group identification. For example, some studies on identity denial have shown that Asian American individuals whose American identity is questioned will subsequently strive to demonstrate their "American-ness" to others (e.g., eating more stereotypically American foods, claiming more knowledge of American sitcoms) (Cheryan & Monin, 2005; Guendelman et al., 2011).

Another aspect of belief-based conflicts that may be more likely to cultivate self-uncertainty is the extent to which these beliefs are linked to one's morals (Luttrell et al., 2016). Religion (Simpson et al., 2016), science (Luttrell & Petty, 2021), and politics (Graham et al., 2012) have become increasingly moralized in many societies. Thus, it is perhaps not surprising that extant research on belief-based conflicts has focused on these three belief systems. Less is known about belief-based conflicts in other, potentially less moralized domains. For example, being "spiritual but not religious" is an increasingly common identity (Johnson et al., 2018), but may not be as closely tied to morality as being religious. Relatedly, paranormal beliefs resemble religious beliefs in some ways but are arguably less often characterized as "moral" or "immoral." It would be interesting to test, for instance, whether conflict between different spiritual or paranormal views is as likely to induce self-uncertainty as a conflict between religious and political, or religious and scientific, views.

Although we have focused in this chapter on conflict across belief dimensions (e.g., religion versus science, religion versus politics), it is also possible to experience conflict *within* belief dimensions. Similar to how people's beliefs about who they actually are may diverge from their beliefs about who they would ideally like to or think they ought to be (Higgins, 1989; see also DeMarree & Rios, 2014), people might feel a discrepancy from their actual religious beliefs and the religious beliefs they wish they had. For example, an individual who was raised in a highly religious community and is feeling doubts about their faith may wish they believed in God or a higher power more than they do. Furthermore, espousing multiple (non-)religious identities (e.g., having one Christian parent and one Muslim parent, identifying as Jewish but not believing in God; Corcoran et al., 2021) might sometimes trigger feelings of conflict and self-uncertainty. Finally, recent research on the religious residue effect has demonstrated that formerly religious people are psychologically "caught between" currently religious people and people who were never religious, in terms of attitudes toward religion (Van Tongeren et al., 2021) and consumer behavior (DeWall & Van Tongeren, 2022). Given that formerly religious people tend to conceal their (non-)religious identities more than do people who were never religious within majority religious contexts (Mackey et al., 2023), the formerly religious may be especially prone to internal conflict and self-uncertainty.

Finally, it will be important in future research to determine whether the effects of belief-based conflicts can generalize to contexts outside the US and Christianity. For instance, prior studies have demonstrated that the religion-science conflict narrative is less pronounced in non-Western than in Western societies (Ecklund et al., 2016; Johnson et al., 2016; Rios & Aveyard, 2019). One possible consequence is that religious people who value science in Western countries exhibit higher self-uncertainty than their counterparts in non-Western countries. Alternatively, conflicts between *any* belief systems may be less pronounced in societies where, and among individuals for whom, dialecticism (i.e., tolerance for contradiction) is high (Chen et al., 2013). As a final possibility, we have extensively discussed religious *beliefs* throughout this chapter, but some religions (e.g., Judaism) are more practice- and behavior-based than belief-based (Cohen & Hill, 2007; Cohen & Rozin, 2001). Perhaps within relatively practice-based religions, conflicts between religion and other belief systems are less likely to result in self-uncertainty. Again, however, this remains to be seen.

Conclusion

In sum, our preliminary research and suggestions for future work extend previous studies on conflict between identities. Specifically, we move from examining the possibility that people's social roles or group memberships can be viewed as discrepant from one another (e.g., Benet-Martínez & Haritatos, 2005; Diekman et al., 2011, 2017; Manzi et al., 2022; Pronin et al., 2004) to the possibility that people's *belief systems* may also clash. Here, we have focused on potential conflicts between religion and science, and between religious beliefs and political ideology. However, as we note in our "Future Research Directions" section, the opportunities for more work on belief-based conflicts are plentiful. We particularly look forward to seeing additional tests of whether, to what extent, and under what conditions conflicts between belief systems result in self-uncertainty and other negative outcomes.

References

Allport, G. W. (1929). The composition of political attitudes. *American Journal of Sociology*, *35*(2), 220–238.

Balinhas, D. (2023). Bringing critical social psychology to the study of political polarization. *Social and Personality Psychology Compass*, *17*(1), e12721

Belanger, A. L., Joshi, M. P., Fuesting, M. A., Weisgram, E. S., Claypool, H. M., & Diekman, A. B. (2020). Putting belonging in context: Communal affordances signal belonging in STEM. *Personality and Social Psychology Bulletin*, *46*(8), 1186–1204.

Benet-Martínez, V., & Haritatos, J. (2005). Bicultural identity integration (BII): Components and psychosocial antecedents. *Journal of Personality*, *73*(4), 1015–1050.

Brewer, M. B., & Gardner, W. (1996). Who is this" We"? Levels of collective identity and self representations. *Journal of Personality and Social Psychology*, *71*(1), 83–93.

Briñol, P., & Petty (2025). Multiple effects of discarding thoughts through invalidation: Attenuation, Elimination, Reversals, and Compensation. In P. J. Carroll, K. Rios, & K. C. Oleson (Eds.), *Handbook of the Uncertain Self*, Second Edition. Routledge.

Campbell, J. D., Trapnell, P. D., Heine, S. J., Katz, I. M., Lavallee, L. F., & Lehman, D. R. (1996). Self-concept clarity: Measurement, personality correlates, and cultural boundaries. *Journal of Personality and Social Psychology*, *70*(1), 141–156.

Chen, S. X., Benet-Martínez, V., Wu, W. C., Lam, B. C., & Bond, M. H. (2013). The role of dialectical self and bicultural identity integration in psychological adjustment. *Journal of Personality*, *81*(1), 61–75.

Cheryan, S., & Monin, B. (2005). Where are you really from?: Asian Americans and identity denial. *Journal of Personality and Social Psychology*, *89*(5), 717–730.

Cheryan, S., Plaut, V. C., Davies, P. G., & Steele, C. M. (2009). Ambient belonging: How stereotypical cues impact gender participation in computer science. *Journal of Personality and Social Psychology*, *97*(6), 1045–1060.

Chu, J., Pink, S. L., & Willer, R. (2021). Religious identity cues increase vaccination intentions and trust in medical experts among American Christians. *Proceedings of the National Academy of Sciences*, *118*(49), e2106481118.

Clooney, F. X. (2018, March 29). *Enlightenment here: Steven Pinker's myth of a secular Harvard*. Retrieved from: https://projects.iq.harvard.edu/francisclooney/blog/enlightenment-here-steven-pinkers-myth-secular-harvard

Cohen, A. B., & Hill, P. C. (2007). Religion as culture: Religious individualism and collectivism among American Catholics, Jews, and Protestants. *Journal of Personality*, *75*(4), 709–742.

Cohen, A. B., & Rozin, P. (2001). Religion and the morality of mentality. *Journal of Personality and Social Psychology*, *81*(4), 697–710.

Corcoran, K. E., Scheitle, C. P., & Dabbs, E. (2021). Multiple (non) religious identities leads to undercounting religious nones and Asian religious identities. *Journal for the Scientific Study of Religion*, *60*(2), 424–441.

DeMarree, K. G., & Rios, K. (2014). Understanding the relationship between self-esteem and self-clarity: The role of desired self-esteem. *Journal of Experimental Social Psychology*, *50*, 202–209.

DeWall, C. N., & Van Tongeren, D. R. (2022). No longer religious, but still spending money religiously: Religious rituals and community influence consumer behavior among religious dones. *The International Journal for the Psychology of Religion*, *32*(1), 53–70.

Diekman, A. B., Clark, E. K., Johnston, A. M., Brown, E. R., & Steinberg, M. (2011). Malleability in communal goals and beliefs influences attraction to stem careers: Evidence for a goal congruity perspective. *Journal of Personality and Social Psychology*, *101*(5), 902–918.

Diekman, A. B., Steinberg, M., Brown, E. R., Belanger, A. L., & Clark, E. K. (2017). A goal congruity model of role entry, engagement, and exit: Understanding communal goal processes in STEM gender gaps. *Personality and Social Psychology Review*, *21*(2), 142- 175.

Draper, J. W. (1875). *History of the conflict between religion and science* (Vol. 13). Henry S. King & Co.

Dress, B. (2022, April 2). *Here is a breakdown of laws in 47 states that require reciting the Pledge of Allegiance*. Retrieved from: https://thehill.com/homenews/3256719-47-states-require-the- pledge-of-allegiance-be-recited-in-schools-here-is-a-breakdown-of-each-states-laws/

Ecklund, E. H., Johnson, D. R., Scheitle, C. P., Matthews, K. R., & Lewis, S. W. (2016). Religion among scientists in international context: A new study of scientists in eight regions. *Socius*, *2*, 2378023116664353.

Fahmy, D. (2020, March 3). With religion-related rulings on the horizon, U.S. *Christians see Supreme Court Favorably*. Retrieved from: https://www.pewresearch.org/short-reads/2020/03/03/with- religion-related-rulings-on-the-horizon-u-s-christians-see-supreme-court-favorably/

Farias, M., Newheiser, A. K., Kahane, G., & de Toledo, Z. (2013). Scientific faith: Belief in science increases in the face of stress and existential anxiety. *Journal of Experimental Social Psychology*, 49(6), 1210–1213.

Feinberg, M., Tullett, A. M., Mensch, Z., Hart, W., & Gottlieb, S. (2017). The political reference point: How geography shapes political identity. *PLoS One*, *12*(2), e0171497.

Feldman, S. (2003). Values, ideology, and the structure of political attitudes. In D. O. Sears, L. Huddy, & R. Jervis (Eds.), *Oxford handbook of political psychology* (pp. 477–508). Oxford University Press.

Festinger, L. (1962). Cognitive dissonance. *Scientific American*, *207*(4), 93–106.

Fordham, S., & Ogbu, J. U. (1986). Black students' school success: Coping with the "burden of 'acting white'". *The Urban Review*, *18*(3), 176–206.

Graham, J., Nosek, B. A., & Haidt, J. (2012). The moral stereotypes of liberals and conservatives: Exaggeration of differences across the political spectrum. *PLoS One*, *7*(12), e50092.

Guendelman, M. D., Cheryan, S., & Monin, B. (2011). Fitting in but getting fat: Identity threat and dietary choices among US immigrant groups. *Psychological Science*, *22*(7), 959–967.

Higgins, E. T. (1989). Self-discrepancy theory: What patterns of self-beliefs cause people to suffer? In L. Berkowitz (Ed.), *Advances in experimental social psychology* (Vol. 22, pp. 93–136). New York: Academic Press.

Hirsh, J. B., & Kang, S. K. (2016). Mechanisms of identity conflict: Uncertainty, anxiety, and the behavioral inhibition system. *Personality and Social Psychology Review*, *20*(3), 223–244.

Holbrook, A. L., Krosnick, J. A., Visser, P. S., Gardner, W. L., & Cacioppo, J. T. (2001). Attitudes toward presidential candidates and political parties: Initial optimism, inertial first impressions, and a focus on flaws. *American Journal of Political Science*, 930–950.

Johnson, K. A., Sharp, C. A., Okun, M. A., Shariff, A. F., & Cohen, A. B. (2018). SBNR identity: The role of impersonal God representations, individualistic spirituality, and dissimilarity with religious groups. *The International Journal for the Psychology of Religion*, *28*(2), 121–140.

Jost, J. T., Baldassarri, D. S., & Druckman, J. N. (2022). Cognitive–motivational mechanisms of political polarization in social-communicative contexts. *Nature Reviews Psychology*, *1*(10), 560–576.

Kang, S. K., & Bodenhausen, G. V. (2015). Multiple identities in social perception and interaction: Challenges and opportunities. *Annual Review of Psychology*, 66, 547–574.

Landau, M. J., Ryu, Y. J., Greenberg, J., Chur, M., & Pyszczynski, T., (2025). A terror management perspective on life's "big" uncertainties. In P. J. Carroll, K. Rios, & K. C. Oleson (Eds.), *Handbook of the Uncertain Self*, Second Edition. Routledge.

Leicht, C., Sharp, C. A., LaBouff, J. P., Zarzeczna, N., & Elsdon-Baker, F. (2022). Content matters: Perceptions of the science-religion relationship. *The International Journal for the Psychology of Religion*, *32*(3), 232–255.

Light, A. E., & Visser, P. S. (2013). The ins and outs of the self: Contrasting role exits and role entries as predictors of self-concept clarity. *Self and Identity*, *12*(3), 291–306.

Livingston, R. W., Rosette, A. S., & Washington, E. F. (2012). Can an agentic Black woman get ahead? The impact of race and interpersonal dominance on perceptions of female leaders. *Psychological Science*, *23*(4), 354–358.

Luttrell, A., Petty, R. E., Briñol, P., & Wagner, B. C. (2016). Making it moral: Merely labeling an attitude as moral increases its strength. *Journal of Experimental Social Psychology*, *65*, 82–93.

Luttrell, A., & Petty, R. E. (2021). Evaluations of self-focused versus other-focused arguments for social distancing: An extension of moral matching effects. Social Psychological and Personality Science, 12(6), 946–954.

Mackey, C. D., & Rios, K. (2023). Identity centrality, social identity threat, and differences in concealment between religious minorities and nonreligious individuals. *The International Journal for the Psychology of Religion*, *33*(1), 52–68.

Mackey, C. D., Van Tongeren, D. R., & Rios, K. (2023). The social pain of religious deidentification: Religious dones conceal their identity and feel less belonging in religious cultures. *Psychology of Religion and Spirituality*. Advance online publication.

Malka, A., Lelkes, Y., Srivastava, S., Cohen, A. B., & Miller, D. T. (2012). The association of religiosity and political conservatism: The role of political engagement. *Political Psychology*, *33*(2), 275–299.

Manzi, C., & Benet-Martinez, V. (2022). Multiple identities juggling game: Types of identity integration and their outcomes. *Self and Identity*, *21*(5), 501–505.

Manzi, C., Koc, Y., Benet-Martínez, V., & Reverberi, E. (2022). Identity integration matters: The case of parents working from home during the COVID-19 health emergency. *Self and Identity*, *21*(8), 914–938.

McGregor, I., & Marigold, D. (2025). Reactive approach motivation: From personal uncertainty to love or hate, and meaning in life. In P. J. Carroll, K. Rios, & K. C. Oleson (Eds.), *Handbook of the Uncertain Self*, Second Edition. Routledge.

McGregor, I., Zanna, M. P., Holmes, J. G., & Spencer, S. J. (2001). Compensatory conviction in the face of personal uncertainty: Going to extremes and being oneself. *Journal of Personality and Social Psychology*, *80*(3), 472–488.

Miller, L. (2010, February 10). Why Harvard students should study more religion. Retrieved from: https://www.newsweek.com/why-harvard-students-should-study-more-religion-75231

Morales, A. T., & Rios, K. (2023). *Political and religious identity conflict.* Unpublished manuscript, University of Illinois Urbana-Champaign.

Morrison, K. R., & Ybarra, O. (2009). Symbolic threat and social dominance among liberals and conservatives: SDO reflects conformity to political values. *European Journal of Social Psychology*, *39*(6), 1039–1052.

Murphy, M. C., Steele, C. M., & Gross, J. J. (2007). Signaling threat: How situational cues affect women in math, science, and engineering settings. *Psychological Science*, *18*(10), 879- 885.

Nguyen, K. H., Anneser, E., Toppo, A., Allen, J. D., Parott, J. S., & Corlin, L. (2022). Disparities in national and state estimates of COVID-19 vaccination receipt and intent to vaccinate by race/ethnicity, income, and age group among adults≥ 18 years, United States. *Vaccine*, *40*(1), 107–113.

Ogbu, J. U. (2004). Collective identity and the burden of "acting White" in Black history, community, and education. *The Urban Review*, *36*(1), 1–35.

Oyserman, D., & Lewis Jr, N. A. (2017). Seeing the destination AND the path: Using identity-based motivation to understand and reduce racial disparities in academic achievement. *Social Issues and Policy Review*, *11*(1), 159–194.

Paredes, B., Briñol, P., & Petty, R. E. (2025). Identity fusion and doubt: Implications for pro-group behavior. In P.J. Carroll, K. Rios, & K.C. Oleson (Eds), *Handbook of the Uncertain Self*, Second Edition. Routledge.

Paulhus, D. L., & Suedfeld, P. (1988). Self-deception: A dynamic complexity model. In J. S. Lockard & D. L. Paulhus (Eds.), *Self-deception: An adoptive mechanism?* Prentice-Hall.

Pennycook, G., Ross, R. M., Koehler, D. J., & Fugelsang, J. A. (2016). Atheists and agnostics are more reflective than religious believers: Four empirical studies and a meta-analysis. *PLoS One*, *11*(4), e0153039.

Pietri, E. S., Johnson, I. R., & Ozgumus, E. (2018). One size may not fit all: Exploring how the intersection of race and gender and stigma consciousness predict effective identity-safe cues for Black women. *Journal of Experimental Social Psychology*, *74*, 291–306.

Pink, S. L., Chu, J., Druckman, J. N., Rand, D. G., & Willer, R. (2021). Elite party cues increase vaccination intentions among Republicans. *Proceedings of the National Academy of Sciences*, *118*(32), e2106559118.

Preston, J., & Epley, N. (2009). Science and God: An automatic opposition between ultimate explanations. *Journal of Experimental Social Psychology*, *45*(1), 238–241.

Pronin, E., Steele, C. M., & Ross, L. (2004). Identity bifurcation in response to stereotype threat: Women and mathematics. *Journal of Experimental Social Psychology*, *40*(2), 152–168.
Purdie-Vaughns, V., & Eibach, R. P. (2008). Intersectional invisibility: The distinctive advantages and disadvantages of multiple subordinate-group identities. *Sex Roles*, *59*, 377–391.
Rios, K. (2021). Examining Christians' reactions to reminders of religion–science conflict: Stereotype threat versus disengagement. *Personality and Social Psychology Bulletin*, *47*(3), 441–454.
Rios, K., & Aveyard, M. (2019). Science-religion compatibility beliefs across Middle Eastern and American young adult samples: The role of cross-cultural exposure. *Public Understanding of Science*, *28*(8), 949–957.
Rios, K., Cheng, Z. H., Totton, R. R., & Shariff, A. F. (2015). Negative stereotypes cause Christians to underperform in and disidentify with science. *Social Psychological and Personality Science*, *6*(8), 959–967.
Rios, K., Mackey, C. D., & Cheng, Z. H. (2023). Understanding Christians' underrepresentation in STEM and why it matters. *Frontiers in Social Psychology*. Advance online publication.
Rosenthal, L. (2016). Incorporating intersectionality into psychology: An opportunity to promote social justice and equity. *American Psychologist*, *71*(6), 474–485.
Rosette, A. S., & Livingston, R. W. (2012). Failure is not an option for Black women: Effects of organizational performance on leaders with single versus dual-subordinate identities. *Journal of Experimental Social Psychology*, *48*(5), 1162–1167.
Sandstrom, A. (2017, August 17). *God or the divine is referenced in every state constitution*. Retrieved from: https://www.pewresearch.org/short-reads/2017/08/17/god-or-the-divine-is-referenced-in- every-state-constitution/
Scheitle, C. P., & Dabbs, E. (2021). Religiosity and identity interference among graduate students in the sciences. *Social Science Research*, *93*, 102503.
Scheitle, C. P., & Ecklund, E. H. (2017). The influence of science popularizers on the public's view of religion and science: An experimental assessment. *Public Understanding of q Science*, *26*(1), 25–39.
Sharp, C. A., Leicht, C., Rios, K., Zarzeczna, N., & Elsdon-Baker, F. (2022). Religious diversity in science: Stereotypical and counter-stereotypical social identities. *Group Processes & Intergroup Relations*, *25*(7), 1836–1860.
Simpson, A., Piazza, J., & Rios, K. (2016). Belief in divine moral authority: Validation of a shortened scale with implications for social attitudes and moral cognition. *Personality and Individual Differences*, *94*, 256–265.
Slotter, E. B., & Emery, L. F. (2017). Self-concept clarity and social role transitions. In J. Lodi-Smith & K. G. DeMarree (Eds.), *Self-concept clarity: Perspectives on assessment, research, and applications* (pp. 85–106). Springer International Publishing.
Slotter, E. B., Gardner, W. L., & Finkel, E. J. (2010). Who am I without you? The influence of romantic breakup on the self-concept. *Personality and Social Psychology Bulletin*, *36*(2), 147–160.
Spencer, S. J., Steele, C. M., & Quinn, D. M. (1999). Stereotype threat and women's math performance. *Journal of Experimental Social Psychology*, *35*(1), 4–28.
Stanovich, K. E., & West, R. F. (2000). Advancing the rationality debate. *Behavioral and Brain Sciences*, *23*(5), 701–717.
Steele, C. M., & Aronson, J. (1995). Stereotype threat and the intellectual test performance of African Americans. *Journal of Personality and Social Psychology*, *69*(5), 797–811.
Stewart, B. D., Gulzaib, F., & Morris, D. S. (2019). Bridging political divides: Perceived threat and uncertainty avoidance help explain the relationship between political ideology and immigrant attitudes within diverse intergroup contexts. *Frontiers in Psychology*, *10*, 1236.
Van der Toorn, J., Jost, J. T., Packer, D. J., Noorbaloochi, S., & Van Bavel, J. J. (2017). In defense of tradition: Religiosity, conservatism, and opposition to same-sex marriage in North America. *Personality and Social Psychology Bulletin*, *43*(10), 1455–1468.
Van Tongeren, D. R., DeWall, C. N., Chen, Z., Sibley, C. G., & Bulbulia, J. (2021). Religious residue: Cross-cultural evidence that religious psychology and behavior persist following deidentification. *Journal of Personality and Social Psychology*, *120*(2), 484–503.
White, A. D. (1877). *The warfare of science*. Henry S. King & Company.
Willis, D. E., Andersen, J. A., Bryant-Moore, K., Selig, J. P., Long, C. R., Felix, H. C., … & McElfish, P. A. (2021). COVID-19 vaccine hesitancy: Race/ethnicity, trust, and fear. *Clinical and Translational Science*, *14*(6), 2200–2207.
Ysseldyk, R., Matheson, K., & Anisman, H. (2010). Religiosity as identity: Toward an understanding of religion from a social identity perspective. *Personality and Social Psychology Review*, *14*(1), 60–71.
Zuckerman, M., Li, C., Lin, S., & Hall, J. A. (2020). The negative intelligence–religiosity relation: New and confirming evidence. *Personality and Social Psychology Bulletin*, *46*(6), 856–868.

19

MANAGING ACUTE UNCERTAINTY

Kate Sweeny and Jennifer L. Howell

Life is full of uncertainty. Some uncertainty is stressful and anxiety-provoking, some is comforting and protective, and some can even be pleasurable. Various types of uncertainty also differ significantly in the amount of empirical attention researchers have paid to them. In this edited volume, chapters address well-studied types of uncertainty including causal uncertainty (i.e., not knowing why something happened; Chapter 12), self-uncertainty (i.e., a lack of clarity about one's self-concept or aspects of one's life; Chapters 5, 6, 7, 8, 10, and 14), relational uncertainty (i.e., feeling unsure about one's connections to others or their safety in relation to others; Chapters 15 and 20), and existential uncertainty (i.e., uncertainty about the meaning of life; Chapters 11 and 21). Perhaps surprisingly, one intuitive form of uncertainty has received relatively little attention in psychological science: acute uncertainty, or not knowing a specific piece of information that might be beneficial to know.

This chapter addresses the various ways people manage acute uncertainty. We first consider situations in which acute uncertainty is aversive, namely during stressful waiting periods. People regularly wait for feedback about their academic, professional, personal, and financial prospects, and most people find these waiting periods to be unpleasantly fraught with worry and uncertainty about the future. Two theoretical models, the *uncertainty navigation model* (Sweeny & Cavanaugh, 2012) and the new and improved *emotion-motivation-obstruction (EMO) model*, guide our coverage of aversive uncertainty and provide a roadmap to the subjective experiences, health consequences, and coping efforts such situations entail.

We then turn to situations in which uncertainty is desirable. People regularly avoid information to which they have ready access, even when acquiring the information may benefit them in various ways. We outline the evidence for this type of information avoidance and consider the motivations that trigger it, the situations that make it more likely, and the strategies interventionists can use to reduce its likelihood. We close by identifying links between these two seemingly contradictory phenomena, providing a complete picture of the who, what, when, and why of acute uncertainty management.

When We Want to Know

In *The Cobbler of Preston* (1716), Christopher Bullock famously noted that "'tis impossible to be sure of any thing but Death and Taxes." With due respect to Mr. Bullock, a third experience

 DOI: 10.4324/9781003363385-22

is nearly as assured: waiting for uncertain news. As noted above, people frequently encounter periods of not knowing when they wish, sometimes desperately, to know how the future will unfold. For example, the authors of this chapter remember all too well their search for an academic job at the end of graduate school, a time of deep personal and professional uncertainty that entailed repeated waiting periods as they each applied to jobs, awaited invitations to interview (or to hear through the grapevine that no invitation was forthcoming), and later awaited hoped-for job offers.

Despite the ubiquity of such waiting periods, relatively little research investigated these experiences of acute uncertainty prior to the 2010s. Before that time, research on waiting largely focused on the experience of queuing, or waiting in line. Queuing typically entails uncertainty about the timeframe in which one will reach a goal (namely, the front of the line) but little to no uncertainty about how the wait will resolve. Nonetheless, these relatively benign waiting experiences proved enticing as a research topic for the fields of consumer behavior, marketing, management and operations, retail, and even tourism, due to the age-old adage that "time is money" (of uncertain origin, appropriately). Several decades of research identified the situational factors that make queuing more or less unpleasant, what makes people more or less likely to keep waiting in line, and the various consequences of unpleasant queues for consumer behavior (e.g., Maister, 1984; Zhou & Soman, 2003). Other work went deeper, identifying the ways in which queues create mini social systems with concomitant norms, along with consequences for violating those norms (e.g., cutting in line; see Helweg-Larsen & LoMonaco, 2008 for an example with concertgoers; see also Schmitt et al., 1992).

Despite the consequences of queuing for corporations' (and bands') bottom line, the uncertainty that arises in those situations is typically not the type of acute uncertainty of particular interest in this chapter. Even when an overly lengthy queue has personal significance (e.g., waiting in line to be rebooked after a canceled flight, or waiting in line at a food bank), the emotional heft of those experiences is not in the queue itself but rather in the uncertainty of the outcome (will I make the wedding? Will I have food for my family tonight?). Those uncertainties, like the uncertainty the authors of this chapter experienced on the job market, are what we will call *high-stakes waiting*: waiting to learn some information that will alter the course of one's life, however small or large that change in trajectory might be.

High-Stakes Waiting in Healthcare

Much of the earliest research on high-stakes waiting focused on a particularly high-stakes context: healthcare. Specifically, a number of studies examined uncertainty in the context of breast cancer, investigating the experience of (primarily) women undergoing diagnostic testing (see Montgomery & McCrone, 2010; Poole, 1997 for reviews). One notable finding from these studies is that many women suffer intense distress during the diagnostic phase of a breast cancer journey, so much so that 83% of patients who had undergone a mastectomy identified the diagnostic phase as the most stressful part of the process (compared to the treatment and adaptation phases; Northouse, 1989; see also Lebel et al., 2003).

Most studies have interviewed patients either prior to a breast biopsy (typically following an abnormal mammogram) or much later, following diagnosis and even treatment; relatively few studies directly address the waiting period for diagnosis (Poole, 1997). In a rare exception, one study observed patients' experiences during the three-day wait for biopsy results and found that women who were particularly anxious at the start of the wait reported very high levels of distress during the waiting period—so high, in fact, that their levels of distress exceeded those of typical psychiatric outpatients (Poole et al., 1999). In a pattern to which we will return later in the chapter, even patients with relatively low anxiety at baseline showed a significant rise in anxiety as the "moment of truth" approached.

A smaller research literature has examined high-stakes waiting in the context of fertility treatment. For example, one study collected surveys from women undergoing in vitro fertilization (IVF) just before an embryo transfer, in the middle of the wait for a pregnancy test, and six weeks later. Much like women awaiting breast biopsy results, these women reported considerably greater anxiety during the wait for test results compared to the period prior to the embryo transfer (Ockhuijsen et al., 2014). Another study of women undergoing IVF found a similar pattern and further showed a decrease in anxiety following a negative pregnancy test, documenting the relief that accompanies the end of uncertainty (albeit often replaced with other forms of distress; Boivin & Lancastle, 2010).

Finally, a newer area of research addresses a particular form of high-stakes waiting that a 2010 Time Magazine article termed "scanxiety," namely the negative emotional experience that often arises around the time of a cancer-related medical test (i.e., a scan; Derry-Vick et al., 2023). Two recent scoping reviews (i.e., a "map" of the existing research literature on a given topic) reveal a small but growing literature (57 studies in one case, Bui, Liang et al., 2021; 36 studies in the other, Derry-Vick et al., 2023) that has documented low overall levels of scanxiety but a particularly difficult period (and an understudied point in time) during the wait between the scan and results (Bui, Blinman et al., 2021; Bui, Kiely et al., 2022; Derry-Vick et al., 2023; Mannion et al., 2023). Some patients with cancer have noted that the wait for scan results brought back unpleasant memories of the wait for their initial diagnosis (Brandzel et al., 2017).

Other Early Work on Waiting: Bracing for the Worst

Turning to psychology, our primary field of interest, one waiting-related topic received considerable empirical attention prior to 2010. As early as the 1970s, studies documented a curious pattern in outcome expectations, such that people seemed to turn from optimists into pessimists when they were relatively close to learning their outcome (e.g., becoming pessimistic in expectations of a test grade; e.g., Nisan, 1972). Several decades later, James Shepperd termed this pattern *bracing for the worst*, capturing the emotional preparation that such declines in optimism provide (Shepperd et al., 1996).

Dozens of studies followed Shepperd's landmark paper, establishing this downward trend in expectations as robust across performance domains, personality traits, and other situational and individual characteristics (see Sweeny & Krizan, 2013 for a meta-analysis; see also Carroll et al., 2006 and Sweeny et al., 2006 for early reviews). Although people brace for a number of reasons, the dominant cause seems to be a desire to avoid or minimize disappointment in the face of bad news by closing the gap between one's expectations and the outcome (e.g., Zeelenberg et al., 2000). This deep-dive into how people manage their expectations during waiting periods provided initial insight into the emotionally dynamic experience of high-stakes waiting. It was limited in scope, only addressing a single cognitive and affective aspect of waiting, but it served as a launching point for the next stage of waiting research.

The Uncertainty Navigation Model

The *uncertainty navigation model* was the first comprehensive theoretical approach to understanding the experience of high-stakes waiting (Sweeny & Cavanaugh, 2012). Although the first iteration of the model focused on the context of health-related news, its theoretical reach was intended to cover all domains in which people face stressful periods of acute uncertainty.

The uncertainty navigation model had three primary goals. First, it delineated the nature of distress during high-stakes waiting, an experience that creates a combination of anxiety and repetitive thought, referred to in later iterations of the model simply as *worry* (Sweeny, 2018). Second, the model described three categories of strategies that people use in an effort to mitigate or manage this distress: consequence mitigation, reappraisal, and direct emotion management. Finally, it identified predictors of distress during such waiting periods: proximity to the news, importance of the news, controllability of the outcome, risk of an undesirable outcome, and trait-like individual differences.

In contrast to approaches to understanding stress and coping in the face of a known stressor (e.g., Carver & Connor-Smith, 2010; Carver & Scheier, 1999; Folkman & Moskowitz, 2004), the uncertainty navigation model captured processes that are unique to or heightened during periods of uncertainty. For example, where much of the earlier literature on stress and coping implicated depression as a core affective response, the uncertainty navigation model identifies anxiety as a key affective response to waiting (Boivin & Lancastle, 2010; Sweeny & Falkenstein, 2015). The model also highlighted the future-focused, rather than past- or current-focused, nature of coping during high-stakes waiting periods with the inclusion of future-focused strategies such as preventive action, proactive coping, expectation management, and preemptive benefit finding.

The uncertainty navigation model generated numerous studies and research questions addressing stressful waiting periods. These studies provided broad and novel insight into the experience of high-stakes waiting, including associations between psychological distress and decrements in subjective health outcomes (Howell & Sweeny, 2016, 2020), the ineffectiveness of many strategies people spontaneously use to manage feelings of uncertainty and the consequences of waiting experiences on responses to good and bad news (Sweeny et al., 2016), the role of social support during uncertain waiting periods (Dooley et al., 2018, 2019, 2023), and individual differences in waiting experiences (Sweeny & Andrews, 2014; Sweeny et al., 2015).

This array of findings began to paint a more complete picture of the experience of acute uncertainty. However, despite its utility as an initial theoretical effort to bring together the various elements of a high-stakes waiting period, the uncertainty navigation model was not designed to reveal why acute uncertainty is so persistently and pervasively distressing. Instead, the model provided an important outline of when people are most likely to suffer during waiting periods and the set of coping strategies that people are most likely to use in response. It did not provide insight into why those coping strategies are particularly useful during waiting periods, nor the particular function they serve beyond reducing distress. It also identified a set of predictors of worry without articulating the mechanisms through which those situational and individual characteristics influence the waiting experience. In short, a need remained for a "2.0" theoretical approach to understanding high-stakes waiting periods. To that end, the authors of this chapter propose a novel theoretical model that provides insights into worry and waiting, but also extends to other emotional and coping experiences: *the emotion-motivation-obstruction (EMO)* model.[1]

The Emotion-Obstruction-Motivation (EMO) Model

The (EMO) model brings together research on the action readiness theory of emotions (Frijda, 1986; Zeelenberg et al., 2008), and the literature on coping processes (e.g., Folkman & Moskowitz, 2004) to propose a novel theoretical account of the relationship between emotions, coping, and well-being (Figure 19.1). The primary emotional pathways in the model are based on action-

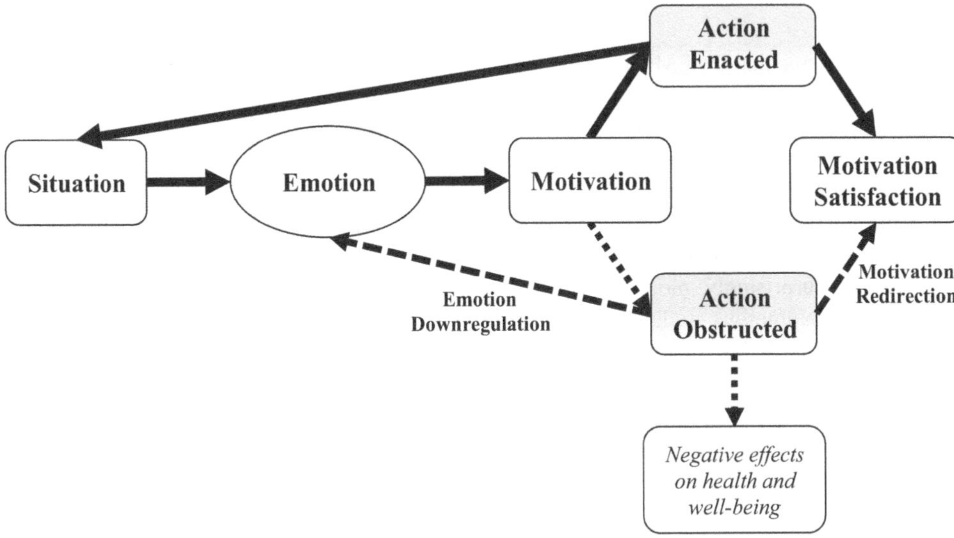

Figure 19.1 The emotion-motivation-obstruction (EMO) model.

readiness theory, also known as the feeling-is-for-doing approach. The action-readiness model extends the traditional focus on emotions' valence to suggest that specific emotions serve specific motivational purposes; that is, different emotions motivate different behaviors. For instance, although they are both negative emotions associated with experiencing an undesired outcome, regret and disappointment are distinct in that they inspire different subsequent behaviors. Feeling regret motivates people to pursue opportunities to rectify personal errors by returning to situations like the one that caused the undesired outcome. By contrast, disappointment motivates people to avoid the same situations in the future (Zeelenberg et al., 1998). In the EMO model, we adopt this action-based understanding of emotions and propose that situations (broadly defined) lead to discrete emotional states, which in turn generate discrete motivations and behaviors.

The EMO model then builds on action-readiness theory in several ways. First, the EMO model posits that action relevant to an emotion's concomitant motivation both satisfies that motivation (the solid path from "action enacted" to "motivation satisfaction" in Figure 19.1) and alters the emotion-generating situation, thus downregulating the emotion (i.e., the solid path from "action enacted" to "situation"). The pathway just described, represented by the solid lines in Figure 19.1, represents the typical and evolutionarily adaptive process following emotion generation. However, people often cannot engage in emotion-motivated behaviors for one reason or another. The EMO model suggests that an inability to realize an emotion's action tendency is an *obstruction* to that motivational tendency (the dotted path from "motivation" to "action obstructed"). We predict that when people cannot satisfy their emotion-relevant motivation, they will experience greater deterioration of their health and well-being (the dotted path from "action obstructed" to "negative effects on health and well-being").

So, what can a person do when they hit an emotion-motivational roadblock? We propose two routes that people take in these situations to resolve the tension created by an unsatisfied motivation. First, they can attempt to *downregulate* the emotion (the dashed path from "action obstructed" to "emotion"). Alternatively, they can attempt to *redirect* the motivation (the dashed path from "action obstructed" to "motivation satisfaction").

The EMO Model of Waiting

Although we argue that the EMO model applies to all emotional states (presuming that all discrete emotions have a concomitant motivational state), initial tests of the model have focused on the context of high-stakes waiting. Essential to our updated approach to waiting is an intrapsychic response at the center of this experience: worry. Although researchers debate the precise definition of worry (see McCaul & Mullens, 2003), we embrace a quasi-emotional understanding of worry that pairs the aversive emotional experience of anxiety with the tendency toward perseverative, unpleasant thoughts about the future (McCaul et al., 2021).

Perhaps unsurprisingly, most research on worry has focused on its unpleasant qualities and consequences. Numerous studies link the tendency to worry to poor psychological and physical health, and worry is implicated in the clinical psychology literature in psychopathology (e.g., Borkovec & Hu, 1990; Borkovec et al., 1993; Segerstrom et al., 1999; for a review, see Watkins, 2008). However, below psychopathological thresholds, worry is a typical experience for people that serves an important motivational purpose: It motivates people to prevent specific undesirable future outcomes (hereafter referred to as *prevention motivation*). Substantial evidence from health psychology research supports worry's motivational effects, suggesting that people who worry more about a given health outcome are more likely to engage in preventive health behavior (e.g., seatbelt use, Sutton & Eiser, 1990; safe sex practices, van der Pligt et al., 1993; vaccination, Brewer et al., 2004; Cuite et al., 2000; cancer screening, Hay et al., 2006; Portnoy et al., 2015; McCaul et al., 1996; skin protection, Kiviniemi & Ellis, 2014; Mermelstein et al., 1999).

McCaul and Mullens (2003) elucidated a three-step process by which worry motivates prevention. First, worry serves as a cue that an emerging situation requires attention. Second, worry keeps the situation at the center of one's attention via the repetitive, negative, perseverative thoughts that are intrinsic to worry. Finally, the very fact that worry is highly unpleasant motivates people to take action to reduce or eliminate it (e.g., Frijda et al., 1989). In sum, worry motivates people in uncertain situations to take action to avoid negative future outcomes.

Unfortunately, worry cannot always serve its full motivational function; in some contexts, the motivational process of worry is thwarted. High-stakes waiting is one such context. When awaiting news (e.g., a grade on an important exam), the time to exert control over the worry-causing outcome (e.g., one's performance on the exam) has passed. Thus, although uncertainty about one's outcome prompts rising worry, which in turn prompts prevention motivation (e.g., avoiding a poor grade on the exam), preventive action is obstructed by the constraints of the situation. Put another way, a lack of personal control obstructs the action that worry motivates. The EMO model is thus well-suited to provide theoretical guidance to understand the distress that the acute uncertainty of high-stakes waiting provokes.

Applying the EMO model to waiting expands beyond the prediction of the uncertainty navigation model in two notable ways. First, it moves beyond thinking primarily about the uncertainty inherent in waiting to include the lack of control that is fundamental to most high-stakes waiting periods (Howell et al., 2023). Second, it accounts for when and why people use the various strategies outlined in the uncertainty navigation model. Finally, it makes clear predictions about when health and well-being are most likely to suffer as a result of worry, namely when prevention motivation is obstructed.

Figure 19.2 depicts the EMO model in the context of worry. At the heart of this framework is the pseudo-emotion of worry. On the far left is the circumstance that typically provokes worry, namely *threatening uncertainty*. That is, uncertainty about the future is a necessary but insufficient condition to provoke worry—the possibility of threat must be salient. For example, healthy

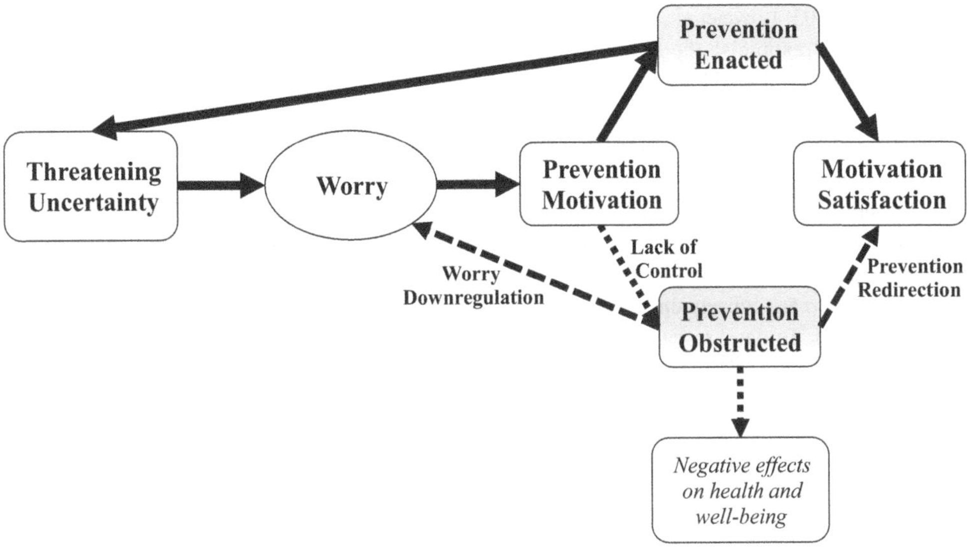

Figure 19.2 The EMO model of waiting.

individuals are persistently uncertain about whether they will develop cancer in their lifetime, but most people do not worry about developing cancer until the possibility becomes salient (e.g., following an abnormal mammogram or colonoscopy). As the intensity of this threatening uncertainty increases, worry rises. Increased worry, in turn, increases the motivation to prevent a bad outcome. In most cases, this prevention motivation would lead to exercising control over the future to enact prevention efforts (e.g., undergoing regular screenings and adopting a healthy lifestyle). If prevention is successfully enacted, the threat is mitigated and worry subsides for the moment (the solid path).

However, in the context of awaiting news, a lack of control obstructs the prevention motivation (the dotted arrow labeled "lack of control"); during the wait, one typically cannot change their outcome. Because the motivational function of worry is obstructed, it creates a metaphorical build-up that spills over and disrupts functioning. That is, persistent anxiety and perseverative negative thoughts lead to the negative consequences of worry: a fog of negative emotionality descends, psychological well-being declines, and sleep and health are disrupted (e.g., Howell & Sweeny, 2016).

To address this undesirable build-up, when prevention is obstructed during a high-stakes waiting period, people should adopt strategies aimed at (1) downregulating worry (thus downregulating the concomitant prevention motivation), and/or (2) redirecting the prevention motivation to achieve a sense of motivation satisfaction via an alternative route (dashed upward-pointing arrows).

Downregulating Worry

People can downregulate unpleasant emotional experiences in a variety of ways (see Webb et al., 2012), but the uncertainty navigation model outlines several coping strategies that should serve the function of downregulating worry in the context of high-stakes waiting. First, people can attempt to reduce the salience of threatening uncertainty by attempting to suppress relevant thoughts and emotions (suppression) or by distracting themselves from thoughts about the stressor (distraction;

Lebel et al., 2003; Lowe et al., 2003; Rankin et al., 2019; Stanton & Snider, 1993). Second, people can attempt to reappraise the severity of the threatening uncertainty by preemptively finding the silver lining in the feared bad outcome (preemptive benefit finding; Rankin et al., 2019; Rankin & Sweeny, 2022) or downplaying the personal relevance of feedback (psychological distancing; Sweeny & Cavanaugh, 2012). Third, people can reappraise the likelihood of the threat by embracing hope and optimism (positive expectation management; Sweeny et al., 2006).

Although research demonstrates that people use all of these coping strategies when awaiting uncertain news (e.g., Sweeny & Andrews, 2014; Sweeny et al., 2016), the best available evidence suggests that these strategies do little to reduce worry (Sweeny et al., 2016) or to mitigate the deleterious downstream consequences of worry for physical and psychological well-being (Howell & Sweeny, 2016). To date, research has failed to answer exactly why these strategies do not work. However, considering them in the context of the EMO model, we can provide a novel explanation: They do not always effectively downregulate worry. Studies are underway to test whether these strategies can, if deployed effectively, reduce worry during high-stakes waiting periods and in turn its pernicious effects on well-being.

Prevention Redirection

In most high-stakes waiting periods, preventive action is obstructed to some extent—the exam is completed, the interview is over, or the biopsy has been conducted. In these cases, people cannot directly exert control in an effort to prevent the feared outcome. However, people can exert various forms of secondary control (Rothbaum et al., 1982), thus redirecting their motivation toward preventing various consequences of a bad outcome in lieu of preventing the outcome itself.

The uncertainty navigation model points to three ways people might redirect their prevention motivation. First, they can take action to mitigate consequences that would occur in the case of bad news (preparative action). Second, they can spend time psychologically preparing to cope with bad news (proactive coping). For instance, some patients report using the waiting period following a diagnostic test to prepare for bad news (Poole et al., 1999; Montgomery & McCrone, 2010), and evidence suggests that longer waiting periods might benefit patients who ultimately face a dire diagnosis because the time allows patients to prepare (Harcourt, 2010). Third, as discussed earlier, they can attempt to prevent the shock of disappointment and unpleasant surprise by lowering their expectations and assuming the worst (bracing for the worst; Sweeny et al., 2006; Sweeny & Krizan, 2013).

When We Want to Know: Pulling it All Together

Any good theory should be able to explain existing findings as well or better than previous or competing theories. We argue that applying the EMO model to high-stakes waiting compellingly fits prior findings on waiting experiences and thus makes coherent literature that is dispersed across many decades and several fields.

The uncertainty navigation model, though generative, was limited to explaining simple links between worry and coping strategies. In contrast, the EMO model provides a comprehensive framework for understanding various waiting dynamics. For example, why do health and sleep suffer during waiting periods, particularly when worry is high? The EMO model argues that when worry is intense and control is low or nonexistent, health and sleep will suffer because of the obstruction of worry's preventive motivation. Why might coping strategies be ineffective, even when directed at waiting distress? For many people, these coping strategies may not successfully downregulate their worry or redirect their prevention motivation. Why do people worry more and engage more in coping efforts at the start and end of the wait? Threatening uncertainty is most salient at these points. Why are engaging distractions (e.g., flow states, or states of complete absorption in an activity) effective for reducing distress during waiting periods (Rankin et al., 2019; Sweeny et al., 2020)? Flow experiences reduce the salience of threatening uncertainty. Finally, why do some people (e.g., defensive pessimists, those intolerant of uncertainty, or those high in neuroticism) have a harder time waiting (Sweeny & Andrews, 2014; Sweeny et al., 2015)? Although the EMO model does not explicitly address individual differences, we suspect that people with these characteristics more readily perceive uncertainty to be threatening and have a harder time downregulating worry.

In sum, research on acute uncertainty in the context of high-stakes waiting has come a long way in less than 50 years: from early observations of bracing for the worst, through the lower-stakes focus on queuing, into the ultimate high-stakes context of healthcare, and finally to a place of theoretical cohesion and generativity. The first set of studies testing key tenets of the EMO model of waiting was published in 2023 (Howell et al., 2023); many more are in the pipeline. Suffice it to say, the study of acute uncertainty, particularly during high-stakes waiting periods in which people deeply wish to resolve that uncertainty, is alive and well.

When We Do Not Want to Know

In addition to adding "awaiting uncertain news" to Bullock's (1716) famous statement that "'tis impossible to be sure of any thing but Death and Taxes," we would also observe that these things that are supposedly so certain—death and taxes—are much more uncertain than they might seem. Indeed, both can be shrouded in a cloud of uncertainty prior to their arrival. For instance, taxation is often so complicated that people can be entirely surprised by their tax bills (Austin, 2019). Most relevant to the present discussion, people rarely know *when* they are going to die. And, in fact, most people actively *do not want to know* when they will die: In one representative survey of German and, separately, Spanish adults, about 85% responded "no" to the questions, "Would you want to know today when you will die?" and "Would you want to know today what will cause you to die?" (Gigerenzer & Garcia-Retamero, 2017). This preference not to learn when one will die suggests that, in contrast to their preference to escape acute uncertainty discussed thus far, people sometimes do *not* want to know specific information.

Information Avoidance

The decision to actively and deliberately not know information has gone by many names including information avoidance (Golman et al., 2017; Sweeny et al., 2010), deliberate ignorance (Hertwig & Engel, 2016), selective exposure (as a more narrow phenomenon; Frey, 1986), and the ostrich effect—named for the myth that ostriches bury their head underground in the face of danger (Karlsson et al., 2009). In this chapter, we will use the term *information avoidance*, as it is most frequently used in psychology and, we believe, the most accurate and inclusive term.

The broader literature addressing information avoidance literature is truly interdisciplinary, stemming from a variety of fields including psychology, communication, economics, information science, and healthcare, among others. Drawing on all of these approaches, we define information avoidance as behavior directed at preventing oneself from learning available information. There is evidence that information avoidance occurs in a wide variety of domains. For instance, people will avoid information about their romantic partners (Hussain et al., 2020), their physical health (Howell et al., 2020), their financial risk (Blajer-Gołębiewska et al., 2018), the stories they read (Maxwell,

2022), and their intergroup biases and privileges (Conway et al., 2017; Howell et al., 2013). Truly, in any domain in which people experience acute uncertainty, there are likely to be at least some people who actively avoid learning information.

Information avoidance has two key ingredients that distinguish it from simply *not knowing* information. First, information must be available. In the case of high-stakes waiting (e.g., for biopsy results), there is often no information to learn or avoid, so not knowing is not avoidance. Second, there must be specific behavior directed at avoiding information. The world is full of information that one might not know. For example, some readers might not know the answer to these questions: Where was cream cheese invented?[2] How far away is the moon?[3] Who won Season 42 of the reality television program Survivor?[4] Simply not knowing available information does not constitute avoidance—instead, it might simply represent not seeking information due to apathy or disinterest. Indeed, there exists nearly boundless information that one is neither actively seeking nor actively avoiding. Thus, information avoidance is not merely the opposite of information seeking. Instead, information avoidance is a unique construct that, while orthogonal to information seeking, requires behaviorally rejecting the option to learn information. As such, models for information seeking are often ill-suited to understanding avoidance.

When we say "behavior" we do not mean to imply that avoidance requires a person to specifically carry out an action. Indeed, avoiding information can be achieved through actions—for example, deleting an email containing one's medical test results—and inactions—*not* opening an email containing one's medical test results. Additionally, it might be a thoughtful, intentional decision—for example, actively choosing not to visit a specific website—or may seem more like an automatic reaction—for example, closing one's eyes when exposed to something one does not wish to see. However, in all cases, the goal of the behavior is identical: preventing oneself from learning available information. In other words, information avoidance behavior is classified primarily by the goal at which it is directed, rather than any specific type of behavior.

Motives for Avoiding Information

Broadly speaking, information avoidance serves a self-protective function (Howell et al., 2020). That is, people are motivated to avoid information to avoid the psychosocial threats that can stem from learning that information. Specifically, people will avoid information to the extent that learning that information might threaten their desired thoughts, feelings, or behaviors (Howell et al., 2020; Sweeny et al., 2010).

First, people will avoid information that will undermine their desired view of themselves or the world. For example, research suggests that people will avoid learning how attractive their peers find them, particularly to the extent that they feel learning that information might threaten their own view of their attractiveness (Howell et al., 2019). Similarly, people who have egalitarian self-views will avoid receiving feedback that they believe will indicate they are racist, but are open to feedback from an identical source if they believe it will confirm that they are egalitarian (Howell et al., 2013).

Second, people avoid information if they believe learning that information will make them do something they would rather not do. For example, people will avoid receiving feedback about their risk for a disease if learning that risk might obligate them to undergo invasive follow-up testing (e.g., a cervical swab) compared to less-invasive follow-up testing (e.g., a cheek swab) or if the treatment for the disease has unpleasant side-effects compared to no side effects (Howell & Shepperd, 2012a).

Third, people will avoid information if they believe learning that information will cause undesired emotions, including a reduction in positive emotions or an increase in negative emotions.

For instance, people often avoid information that could ruin surprises such as avoiding learning the end of stories, movies, and books (i.e., spoilers; Maxwell, 2022) or avoiding learning the sex of their child prior to their child's birth (Shipp et al., 2004). Similarly, people report that concern about experiencing negative emotions prompts them to avoid doctors (Persoskie et al., 2014; Taber, Leyva et al., 2015) and health risk information/diagnoses (Cutler & Hodgson, 2003; Orom et al., 2023; van der Steenstraten et al., 1994).

Most research and theorizing has focused on individual predictors of information avoidance (see Foust & Taber, 2023; Golman et al., 2017; Howell et al., 2020; Sweeny et al., 2010). Nevertheless, the social circumstances surrounding information avoidance are receiving increasing empirical attention. Research broadly suggests that, for example, people's social networks and the social norms of their close others influence their information avoidance decisions (Howell et al., 2014; Qu et al., 2023). Further, avoidance is often stigmatized if it is perceived as harmful to others (Heck & Meyer, 2019).

Relevant to the personal motives for avoidance discussed prior, an emerging body of research suggests that people will avoid information that might change how others think about them or behave toward them. For instance, people will avoid receiving medical feedback if they worry a diagnosis might result in social stigma (Hann et al., 2017; Lipsey & Shepperd, 2019a; Price et al., 2019). Similarly, people will avoid information if they believe it will change how powerful others such as insurance companies (Lipsey & Shepperd, 2019b, 2019a) and employers (Hoffman et al., 2023) treat them, especially if they expect that they will experience harm at the hands of those powerful audiences. While more research is needed to understand interpersonal and social influences on avoidance, it is clear that avoidance decisions are often made with social consequences in mind.

Coping With Threat and Information Avoidance

Although there is clear evidence that people are more likely to avoid learning information in situations that threaten their affect, cognitions, and behaviors, people do not always avoid information in these circumstances. Indeed, in every study cited thus far, some people want and often choose to learn the relevant information. Research into the individual differences that affect avoidance suggests an overarching concept that predicts lower avoidance: perceived threat-management resources (Howell et al., 2014).

When a person feels like they can cope with information, even if it is bad news, they are less likely to avoid that information (Hua & Howell, 2022). These perceptions of resources are derived from a variety of personal and interpersonal factors. For example, people who report less social support, or who recently experienced social exclusion, are more likely to avoid information about their health (Howell et al., 2014; Howell & Shepperd, 2017). Similarly, individual differences in factors such as optimism, self-esteem, and spontaneous self-affirmation—all of which serve a protective function against psychological threats—are associated with lower levels of information avoidance (Ferrer et al., 2014; Howell & Shepperd, 2016; Taber et al., 2014). In one study, when people were prompted to focus on their coping resources prior to making their decision to learn or avoid feedback about a health risk, they were subsequently less likely to avoid that feedback (Hua & Howell, 2022).

Reducing Problematic Information Avoidance

Information avoidance can be essential in protecting oneself from psychological threats, and it makes quite a bit of sense in many cases. For example, avoiding narrative spoilers can help prolong a person's enjoyment of a story (B. K. Johnson & Rosenbaum, 2018; Levine et al., 2016; Maxwell, 2022), whereas avoiding information about a romantic partner's prior relationship might prevent uncontrolled negative affect for which there no recourse (Hussain et al., 2020). Nevertheless, there are times when avoiding information might undermine physical health (Foust & Taber, 2023; Howell et al., 2020), financial well-being (Blajer-Gołębiewska et al., 2018), and performance attainment (Reb & Connolly, 2009). For instance, despite the fact that knowing one's HIV status can help prevent transmission of the sometimes-deadly disease and can improve the likelihood of personal survival (Prabhu et al., 2019), people will sometimes avoid testing for HIV or avoid learning their results in order to protect themselves from psychosocial threats (Price et al., 2019).

Several lines of research have examined strategies for reducing avoidance. Most have focused on the domain of health information avoidance, given the obvious problematic consequences of delayed diagnosis and misunderstanding of risk. These interventions fall into three broad categories of interventions that aim to (1) make people more rational, (2) reduce the threat of information, or (3) emphasize/enhance the utility of information.

First, researchers have aimed to reduce problematic information avoidance by promoting rational decision-making. The logic underlying these types of interventions is that people often make the decision to learn or avoid information as a gut reaction (Howell et al., 2016), focused myopically on the immediate affective, cognitive, and behavioral consequences of information avoidance (Howell & Shepperd, 2013; Reb & Connolly, 2009). Thus, these interventionists assume, and show, that prompting people to think more rationally about their decisions will reduce avoidance. For example, prompting people to make a pro/con list about their reasons for learning versus avoiding information can reduce avoidance (Howell & Shepperd, 2013), in part because it draws one's focus from their automatic preferences to a more rational decision (Howell et al., 2016). Similarly, focusing people on the long-term regret they might feel about avoiding information can reduce avoidance (e.g., A. E. Johnson & Howell, 2020; O'Carroll et al., 2015; Reb & Connolly, 2009; Sandberg & Conner, 2009; Zajac et al., 2017). Nevertheless, interventions aimed at prompting people to think more rationally and about the long-term consequences of avoidance only work when information avoidance is the rationally inferior decision (Howell & Shepperd, 2013). As a result, other work has focused on reducing the threat associated with information and increasing the utility of the information.

Example work aiming to reduce the threat associated with information are several studies showing that self-affirmation—a process that bolsters people's self-integrity against a psychological threat—can reduce information avoidance (Howell & Shepperd, 2012b, 2017; Taber et al., 2014). Indeed, prompting people to affirm their values prior to providing them the opportunity to learn their risk for disease reduces avoidance of that risk feedback, even in circumstances known to prompt avoidance (e.g., social exclusion, high behavioral obligation; Howell & Shepperd, 2012b, 2017). Similarly, prompting people to think about ways they have successfully coped with bad news in the past can reduce avoidance (Hua & Howell, 2022). Researchers theorize that this is because focusing on past successful coping can put the threat in perspective and show people that they will be able to cope with it (Hua & Howell, 2022).

Other research has aimed to emphasize the utility of information as a way to reduce avoidance. Specifically, research suggests that people find health information more useful and are less likely to avoid it if they believe that it provides them with some control over their health (Barbour et al., 2012; Emanuel et al., 2015; Orom et al., 2021; Woolley & Risen, 2018). As a result, emphasizing controllable predictors of a disease (Melnyk & Shepperd, 2012) or describing it as treatable (Yaniv et al., 2004) can reduce avoidance.

In sum, to reduce avoidance, interventionists have generally aimed at one of three processes: (1) making people's decision about whether to avoid information more rational, (2) reducing the threat associated with information, or (3) increasing the perceived utility of the information.

Connections and Conclusions

Earlier, we discussed the pain that comes with uncertainty, noting the toll it takes on physical and mental well-being. The consistent finding that people avoid information might, therefore, seem antithetical to our earlier assertions. If uncertainty is so distressing, why would people ever not want information?

Theoretically, the times we do and do not want to know information are linked in several important ways. First, information avoidance can be a strategy to avoid threatening uncertainty altogether. Although many of the acute pieces of information we discussed in the context of waiting have definitive outcomes—one either passes or fails the bar exam, one does or does not get a job—information often contains some degree of ambiguity or uncertainty. For example, learning that one is at risk for a disease does not tell a person whether they will or will not get the disease, only that they are at an increased likelihood. As a result, risk feedback can actually exacerbate feelings of uncertainty and reduce feelings of control (Hong, 2020; Simonovic et al., 2023). As such, avoiding risk feedback can be a way to avoid threatening uncertainty altogether. Consistent with this idea is evidence that people avoid genome sequencing results to the extent that they believe the results will be ambiguous (Taber, Klein et al., 2015). In other words, information avoidance can be used as a strategy to prevent a person from learning new information that will, somewhat paradoxically, serve to increase threatening uncertainty.

Second, the strategies used to manage acute uncertainty share a goal with information avoidance: they are aimed toward threat regulation. Information avoidance can be used within the context of uncertainty to provide a sense of control and downregulate worry. For example, people sometimes experience increased worry when they encounter news coverage of world events when outcomes are uncertain, such as coverage of pandemics, wars, and looming financial recessions. As suggested by the EMO model, seeing these stories upregulates uncertainty and worry, but typically people have very little control over the situation, undermining the expression of prevention motivation. As a result, people sometimes become stuck in a loop of attempting to gain more information in an effort to reduce uncertainty, even though receiving that information exacerbates uncertainty and worry (Rettie & Daniels, 2021), a phenomenon sometimes called *doomsurfing* or *doomscrolling* (Anand et al., 2022; Ytre-Arne & Moe, 2021). In this case, avoiding information, such as avoiding social media or the news, can be an effective strategy to prevent the upregulation of both uncertainty and worry (Mannell & Meese, 2022; Schäfer et al., 2023; Ytre-Arne & Moe, 2021).

Regardless of whether people want to avoid some piece of news or find themselves desperate to learn something, the literature points to an internal information-management system that prevents exposure to psychological threats and protects well-being. This system is sensitive to perceptions of control over a threat and involves clear emotion-motivation links. Nevertheless, there are situations when the system is unable to function properly, which can lead to negative consequences for health and well-being.

So what are people to do if they find themselves with conflicting feelings about some uncertainty in their lives? Figure 19.3 pulls together the various lines of research presented in this

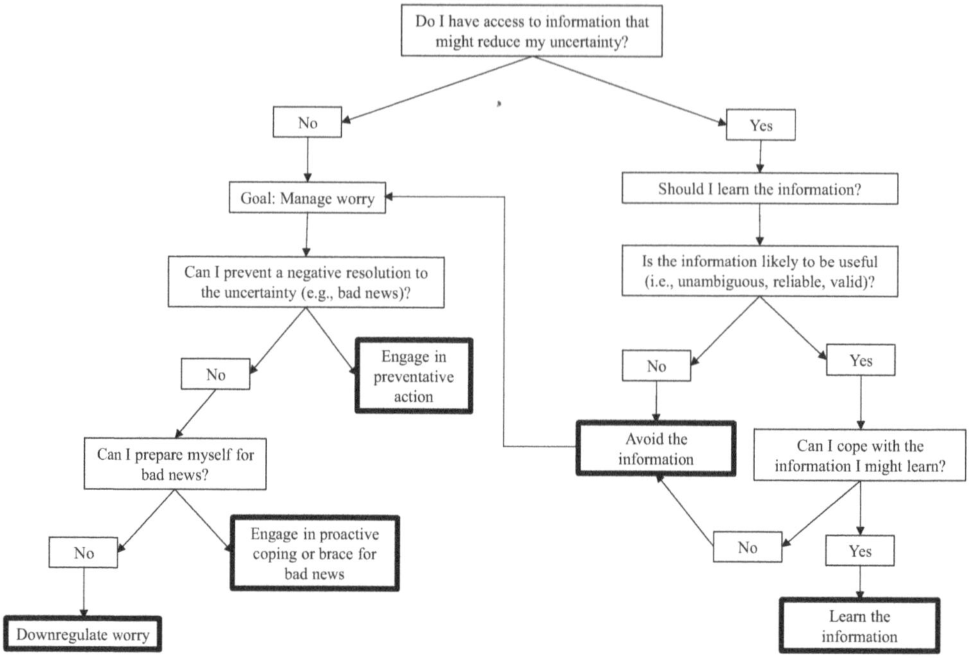

Figure 19.3 A decision tree for uncertainty navigation.

chapter to provide a decision tree for uncertainty navigation. The left side of the figure depicts the current state of the field when it comes to worry and waiting; the right side of the figure depicts the current state of the field when it comes to information avoidance. When the information that could resolve uncertainty is unavailable or unreliable, one's goal is generally to manage feelings of worry that often arise in the face of intractable uncertainty. How best to manage that worry depends on the available options at the time. Can the worrisome outcome be prevented? Then prevention is typically the best option. If prevention is not possible or would be too costly, can the blow of the worrisome outcome be softened in advance through proactive coping or expectation management? If so, preparation is a great option; if not, all that is left is to downregulate one's worry as much as possible to reduce consequences for health and well-being.

On the other hand, if useful information is available, one decision still remains: Might the information be too much or too unpleasant to handle? Is so, avoidance may be the preferable option, and managing worry once more becomes the goal. Although this decision tree is likely incomplete and certainly imperfect, it demonstrates the usefulness of the research outlined in this chapter—not only for understanding human experience but for bettering it.

Notes

1 The model was first articulated in a funded grant proposal to the National Science Foundation (PIs: Sweeny and Howell).
2 New York City (Marx, 2012).
3 On average, 384,400 km/238,855 miles (Battat et al., 2009).
4 Maryanne Oketch (Ross, 2022).

References

Anand, N., Sharma, M. K., Thakur, P. C., Mondal, I., Sahu, M., Singh, P., Kande, J. S., Ms, N., & Singh, R. (2022). Doomsurfing and doomscrolling mediate psychological distress in COVID-19 lockdown: Implications for awareness of cognitive biases. *Perspectives in Psychiatric Care*, *58*(1), 170–172.

Austin, C. R. (2019). The potential of tax surprises to affect measures of tax avoidance and researchers' inferences. *The Journal of the American Taxation Association*, *41*(1), 1–30.

Barbour, J. B., Rintamaki, L. S., Ramsey, J. A., & Brashers, D. E. (2012). Avoiding health information. *Journal of Health Communication*, *17*(2), 212–229.

Battat, J. B., Murphy, T., Adelberger, E. G., Gillespie, B., Hoyle, C., McMillan, R., Michelsen, E. L., Nordtvedt, K., Orin, A. E., & Stubbs, C. W. (2009). The Apache Point Observatory Lunar Laser-ranging Operation (APOLLO): Two years of millimeter-precision measurements of the Earth-Moon Range. *Publications of the Astronomical Society of the Pacific*, *121*(875), 29–40.

Blajer-Gołębiewska, A., Wach, D., & Kos, M. (2018). Financial risk information avoidance. *Economic Research*, *31*(1), 521–536.

Boivin, J., & Lancastle, L. D. (2010). Medical waiting periods: Imminence, emotions and coping. *Women's Health*, *6*, 59–69.

Borkovec, T. D., & Hu, S. (1990). The effect of worry on cardiovascular response to phobic imagery. *Behaviour Research and Therapy*, *28*, 69–73.

Borkovec, T. D., Lyonfields, J. D., Wiser, S. L., & Deihl, L. (1993). The role of worrisome thinking in the suppression of cardiovascular response to phobic imagery. *Behaviour Research and Therapy*, *31*, 321–324.

Brandzel, S., Rosenberg, D. E., Johnson, D., Bush, M., Kerlikowske, K., Onega, T., Henderson, L., Nekhlyudov, L., DeMartini, W., & Wernli, K. J. (2017). Women's experiences and preferences regarding breast imaging after completing breast cancer treatment. *Patient Preference and Adherence*, *11*, 199–204.

Brewer, N. T., Weinstein, N. D., Cuite, C. L., & Herrington Jr, J. E. (2004). Risk perceptions and their relation to risk behavior. *Annals of Behavioral Medicine*, *27*, 125–130.

Bui, K. T., Blinman, P., Kiely, B. E., Brown, C., & Dhillon, H. M. (2021). Experiences with scans and scanxiety in people with advanced cancer: A qualitative study. *Supportive Care in Cancer*, *29*, 7441–7449.

Bui, K. T., Kiely, B. E., Dhillon, H. M., Brown, C., Xu, K., Shafiei, M., & Blinman, P. (2022). Prevalence and severity of scanxiety in people with advanced cancers: A multicentre survey. *Supportive Care in Cancer*, *30*, 511–519.

Bui, K. T., Liang, R., Kiely, B. E., Brown, C., Dhillon, H. M., & Blinman, P. (2021). Scanxiety: A scoping review about scan-associated anxiety. *BMJ Open*, *11*, e043215.

Carroll, P., Sweeny, K., & Shepperd, J. A. (2006). Forsaking optimism. *Review of General Psychology*, *10*, 56–73.

Carver, C. S., & Connor-Smith, J. (2010). Personality and coping. *Annual Review of Psychology*, *61*, 679–704.

Carver, C. S., & Scheier, M. F. (1999). *Stress, coping, and self-regulatory processes.* : Guilford Press.

Conway, J. G., Lipsey, N. P., Pogge, G., & Ratliff, K. A. (2017). Racial prejudice predicts less desire to learn about white privilege. *Social Psychology*, *48*(5), 310–319.

Cuite, C. L., Brewer, N., Weinstein, N., Herrington, J., & Hayes, N. (2000). Illness-specific worry as a predictor of intentions to vaccinate against Lyme disease. *Annals of Behavioral Medicine*, *22*, S12.

Cutler, S. J., & Hodgson, L. G. (2003). To test or not to test: Interest in genetic testing for Alzheimer's disease among middle-aged adults. *American Journal of Alzheimer's Disease and Other Dementias*, *18*(1), 9–20.

Derry-Vick, H. M., Heathcote, L. C., Glesby, N., Stribling, J., Luebke, M., Epstein, A. S., & Prigerson, H. G. (2023). Scanxiety among adults with cancer: A scoping review to guide research and interventions. *Cancers*, *15*, 1381.

Dooley, M. D., Sweeny, K., Howell, J. L., & Reynolds, C. (2018). Perceptions of romantic partners' responsiveness during a period of stressful uncertainty. *Journal of Personality and Social Psychology*, *115*, 677–687.

Dooley, M., Sweeny, K., & Howell, J. L. (2023). Strategy specific support during uncertain waiting periods. *Journal of Social and Personal Relationships*, *40*, 2400–2421.

Dooley, M. D., Wilkinson, D., & Sweeny, K. (2019). Social support during stressful waiting periods: An inductive analysis. *Qualitative Psychology*, *7*(3), 228–244. https://doi.org/10.1037/qup0000143

Emanuel, A. S., Kiviniemi, M. T., Howell, J. L., Hay, J. L., Waters, E. A., Orom, H., & Shepperd, J. A. (2015). Avoiding cancer risk information. *Social Science & Medicine*, *147*, 113–120.

Ferrer, R. A., Taber, J. M., Klein, W. M., Harris, P. R., Lewis, K. L., & Biesecker, L. G. (2014). The role of current affect, anticipated affect and spontaneous self-affirmation in decisions to receive self-threatening genetic risk information. *Cognition and Emotion, 29,* 1456–1465.
Folkman, S., & Moskowitz, J. T. (2004). Coping: Pitfalls and promise. *Annual Review of Psychology, 45,* 745–774.
Foust, J. L., & Taber, J. M. (2023). Information avoidance: Past perspectives and future directions. *Perspectives on Psychological Science.* Published online ahead of print. https://doi.org/10.1177/17456916231197668
Frey, D. (1986). Recent research on selective exposure to information. *Advances in Experimental Psychology, 19,* 41–80.
Frijda, N. H. (1986). *The emotions.* Cambridge: Cambridge University Press.
Frijda, N. H., Kuipers, P., & ter Schure, E. (1989). Relations among emotion, appraisal, and emotion action readiness. *Journal of Personality and Social Psychology, 57,* 212–228.
Gigerenzer, G., & Garcia-Retamero, R. (2017). Cassandra's regret: The psychology of not wanting to know. *Psychological Review, 124*(2), 179.
Golman, R., Hagmann, D., & Loewenstein, G. (2017). Information avoidance. *Journal of Economic Literature, 55*(1), 96–135.
Hann, K. E., Freeman, M., Fraser, L., Waller, J., Sanderson, S. C., Rahman, B., Side, L., Gessler, S., Lanceley, A., & PROMISE Study Team. (2017). Awareness, knowledge, perceptions, and attitudes towards genetic testing for cancer risk among ethnic minority groups: A systematic review. *BMC Public Health, 17,* 1–30.
Harcourt, D. (2010). Same-day diagnosis of symptomatic breast problems: Psychological impact and coping strategies. *Psychology, Health, & Medicine, 4,* 57–71.
Hay, J. L., McCaul, K. D., & Magnan, R. E. (2006). Does worry about breast cancer predict screening behaviors? A meta-analysis of the prospective evidence. *Preventive Medicine, 42,* 401–408.
Heck, P. R., & Meyer, M. N. (2019). Information avoidance in genetic health: Perceptions, norms, and preferences. *Social Cognition, 37*(3), 266–293.
Helweg-Larsen, M., & LoMonaco, B. L. (2008). Queuing among U2 fans: Reactions to social norm violations. *Journal of Applied Social Psychology, 38*(9), 2378–2393.
Hertwig, R., & Engel, C. (2016). Homo ignorans: Deliberately choosing not to know. *Perspectives on Psychological Science, 11*(3), 359–372.
Hoffman, W. R., Aden, J. K., Barbera, D., & Tvaryanas, A. (2023). Self-reported health care avoidance behavior in US military pilots related to fear for loss of flying status. *Military Medicine, 188*(3–4), e446–e450.
Hong, S. J. (2020). Uncertainty in the process of communicating cancer-related genetic risk information with patients: A scoping review. *Journal of Health Communication, 25*(3), 251–270.
Howell, J. L., Collisson, B., Crysel, L., Garrido, C. O., Newell, S. M., Cottrell, C. A., Smith, C. T., & Shepperd, J. A. (2013). Managing the threat of impending implicit attitude feedback. *Social Psychological and Personality Science, 4*(6), 714–720.
Howell, J. L., Crosier, B. S., & Shepperd, J. A. (2014). Does lacking threat-management resources increase information avoidance? A multi-sample, multi-method investigation. *Journal of Research in Personality, 50,* 102–109.
Howell, J. L., Lipsey, N. P., & Shepperd, J. A. (2020). Health information avoidance. The Wiley Encyclopedia of Health Psychology In K. Sweeny, M.L. Robbins and L.M. Cohen (Eds.), *The Wiley Encyclopedia of Health Psychology* (pp. 279–286). https://doi.org/10.1002/9781119057840.ch77
Howell, J. L., Ratliff, K. A., & Shepperd, J. A. (2016). Automatic attitudes and health information avoidance. *Health Psychology, 35*(8), 816–823.
Howell, J. L., & Shepperd, J. A. (2012a). Behavioral obligation and information avoidance. *Annals of Behavioral Medicine, 45*(2), 258–263.
Howell, J. L., & Shepperd, J. A. (2012b). Reducing information avoidance through affirmation. *Psychological Science, 23*(2), 141–145.
Howell, J. L., & Shepperd, J. A. (2013). Reducing health-information avoidance through contemplation. *Psychological Science, 24*(9), 1696–1703.
Howell, J. L., & Shepperd, J. A. (2016). Establishing an information avoidance scale. *Psychological Assessment, 28*(12), 1695–1708.
Howell, J. L., & Shepperd, J. A. (2017). Social exclusion, self-affirmation, and health information avoidance. *Journal of Experimental Social Psychology, 68,* 21–26.
Howell, J. L., & Sweeny, K. (2016). Is waiting bad for subjective health? *Journal of Behavioral Medicine, 39,* 652–664.

Howell, J. L., Sweeny, K., Miller, W., & Shepperd, J. A. (2019). Hot or not? How self-view threat influences avoidance of attractiveness feedback. *Self and Identity*, *18*(2), 144–158.

Howell, J. L., & Sweeny, K. (2020). Health behavior during periods of stressful uncertainty: Associations with emotions, cognitions, and expectation management. *Psychology & Health, 35,* 1163–1183.

Howell, J. L., Sweeny, K., Hua, J., Werntz, A., Hussain, M., Hinojosa, B., Johnson, A., Lindgren, K., Meese, W., O'Shea, B., & Campbell, S. A. (2023). Uncertainty is worse when one lacks control: Physical, mental, and social well-being in China during the COVID-19 outbreak. *Emotion, 23,* 1458–1471.

Hua, J., & Howell, J. L. (2022). Coping self-efficacy influences health information avoidance. *Journal of Health Psychology*, *27*(3), 713–725.

Hussain, M., Price, D. M., Gesselman, A. N., Shepperd, J. A., & Howell, J. L. (2020). Avoiding information about one's romantic partner. *Journal of Social and Personal Relationships*, *38*(2), 626–647.

Johnson, A. E., & Howell, J. L. (2020). The role of anticipated affect in health risk information avoidance. *Annals of Behavioral Medicine, 54,* S562–S562.

Johnson, B. K., & Rosenbaum, J. E. (2018). (Don't) Tell me how it ends: Spoilers, enjoyment, and involvement in television and film. *Media Psychology*, *21*(4), 582–612.

Karlsson, N., Loewenstein, G., & Seppi, D. (2009). The ostrich effect: Selective attention to information. *Journal of Risk and Uncertainty*, *38*(2), 95–115.

Kiviniemi, M. T., & Ellis, E. M. (2014). Worry about skin cancer mediates the relation of perceived cancer risk and sunscreen use. *Journal of Behavioral Medicine, 37,* 1069–1074.

Lebel, S., Jakubovits, G., Rosberger, Z., Loiselle, C., Seguin, C., Cornaz, C., Ingram, J., August, L., & Lisbona, A. (2003). Waiting for a breast biopsy: Psychosocial consequences and coping strategies. *Journal of Psychosomatic Research, 55,* 437–443.

Levine, W. H., Betzner, M., & Autry, K. S. (2016). The effect of spoilers on the enjoyment of short stories. *Discourse Processes*, *53*(7), 513–531.

Lipsey, N. P., & Shepperd, J. A. (2019a). Powerful audiences are linked to health information avoidance: Results from two surveys. *Social Science & Medicine*, *225*, 51–59.

Lipsey, N. P., & Shepperd, J. A. (2019b). The role of powerful audiences in health information avoidance. *Social Science & Medicine*, *220*, 430–439.

Lowe, R., Vedhara, K., Bennett, P., Brookes, E., Gale, L., Munnoch, K., Schreiber-Kounine, C., Fowler, C., Rayter, Z., Sammon, A., & Farndon, J. (2003). Emotion-related primary and secondary appraisals, adjustment, and coping: Associations in women awaiting breast disease diagnosis. *British Journal of Health Psychology, 8,* 377–391.

Maister, D. H. (1984). *The psychology of waiting lines* (pp. 71–78). Harvard Business School.

Mannell, K., & Meese, J. (2022). From doom-scrolling to news avoidance: Limiting news as a wellbeing strategy during COVID lockdown. *Journalism Studies*, *23*(3), 302–319.

Mannion, S., Martin, N. A., O'Connor, J., Wieland, J., & Jatoi, A. (2023). In their own words, "waiting sucks": A qualitative study of medical testing-related anxiety in patients with cancer. *American Journal of Hospice and Palliative Medicine, 40*, 468–474.

Marx, J. A. (2012). "The days had come of curds and cream": The origins and development of cream cheese in America, 1870–1880. *Food, Culture & Society*, *15*(2), 177–195.

Maxwell, L. C. (2022). Spoilers ahead, proceed with caution: How engagement, enjoyment, and FoMO predict avoidance of spoilers. *Psychology of Popular Media*, *11*(2), 163–172.

McCaul, K. D., Magnan, R. E., & Mead, M. P. (2021). Disease-specific worry. In K. Sweeny & M. L. Robbins (Eds.), *The Wiley encyclopedia of health psychology: The social bases of health behavior* (Vol. 2, pp. 97–104). Wiley. https://doi.org/10.1002/9781119057840.ch55

McCaul, K. D., & Mullens, A. B. (2003). Affect, thoughts, and self-protective health behavior: The case of worry and cancer screening. In J. Suls & K. A. Wallston (Eds.), *Social psychological foundations of health and illness* (pp. 137–168). Oxford: Blackwell.

McCaul, K. D., Schroeder, D. M., & Reid, P. A. (1996). Breast cancer worry and screening: Some prospective data. *Health Psychology, 15,* 430–433.

Melnyk, D., & Shepperd, J. A. (2012). Avoiding risk information about breast cancer. *Annals of Behavioral Medicine*, *44*(2), 216–224.

Mermelstein, R. J., Weeks, K., Turner, L., & Cobb, J. (1999). When tailored feedback backfires. *Cancer Research Therapy and Control, 8,* 69–79.

Montgomery, M., & McCrone, S. H. (2010). Psychological distress associated with the diagnostic phase for suspected breast cancer: Systematic review. *Journal of Advanced Nursing, 66,* 2372–2390.

Nisan, M. (1972). Dimension of time in relation to choice behavior and achievement orientation. *Journal of Personality and Social Psychology, 21*(2), 175–182.

Northouse, L. L. (1989). The impact of breast cancer on patients and husbands. *Cancer Nursing, 12,* 278–284.

O'Carroll, R. E., Chambers, J. A., Brownlee, L., Libby, G., & Steele, R. J. (2015). Anticipated regret to increase uptake of colorectal cancer screening (ARTICS): A randomised controlled trial. *Social Science & Medicine, 142,* 118–127.

Ockhuijsen, H., van den Hoogen, A., Eijkemans, M., Macklon, N., & Boivin, J. (2014). The impact of a self-administered coping intervention on emotional well-being in women awaiting the outcome of IVF treatment: A randomized controlled trial. *Human Reproduction, 29,* 1459–1470.

Orom, H., Schofield, E., Kiviniemi, M. T., Waters, E. A., & Hay, J. L. (2021). Agency beliefs are associated with lower health information avoidance. *Health Education Journal, 80*(3), 272–286.

Orom, H., Stanar, S., Allard, N. C., Hay, J. L., Waters, E. A., Kiviniemi, M. T., & Lewicka, M. (2023). Reasons people avoid colorectal cancer information: A mixed-methods study. *Psychology & Health,* 1–23. https://doi.org/10.1080/08870446.2023.2280177

Persoskie, A., Ferrer, R. A., & Klein, W. M. (2014). Association of cancer worry and perceived risk with doctor avoidance: An analysis of information avoidance in a nationally representative US sample. *Journal of Behavioral Medicine, 37,* 977–987.

Poole, K. (1997). The emergence of the 'waiting game': A critical examination of the psychosocial issues in diagnosing breast cancer. *Journal of Advanced Nursing, 25,* 273–281.

Poole, K., Hood, K., Davis, B. D., Monypenny, I. J., Sweetland, H., Webster, D. J. T, Lyons, K., & Mansel, R. E. (1999). Psychological distress associated with waiting for results of diagnostic investigations for breast disease. *The Breast, 8,* 334–338.

Portnoy, D. B., Loud, J. T., Han, P. K., Mai, P. L., & Greene, M. H. (2015). Effects of false-positive cancer screenings and cancer worry on risk-reducing surgery among BRCA1/2 carriers. *Health Psychology, 34,* 709–717.

Prabhu, S., Harwell, J. I., & Kumarasamy, N. (2019). Advanced HIV: Diagnosis, treatment, and prevention. *The Lancet HIV, 6*(8), e540–e551.

Price, D. M., Howell, J. L., Gesselman, A. N., Finneran, S., Quinn, D. M., & Eaton, L. A. (2019). Psychological threat avoidance as a barrier to HIV testing in gay/bisexual men. *Journal of Behavioral Medicine, 42*(3), 534–544. https://doi.org/10.1007/s10865-018-0003-z

Qu, Y., Saffer, A. J., & Austin, L. (2023). What drives people away from COVID-19 information?: Uncovering the influences of personal networks on information avoidance. *Health Communication, 38*(2), 216–227.

Rankin, K., & Sweeny, K. (2022). Preparing silver linings for a cloudy day: The consequences of preemptive benefit finding. *Personality & Social Psychology Bulletin, 55,* 1255–1268.

Rankin, K., Walsh, L., & Sweeny, K. (2019). A better distraction: Exploring the benefits of flow during uncertain waiting periods. *Emotion, 19,* 818–828.

Reb, J., & Connolly, T. (2009). Myopic regret avoidance: Feedback avoidance and learning in repeated decision making. *Organizational Behavior and Human Decision Processes, 109*(2), 182–189.

Rettie, H., & Daniels, J. (2021). Coping and tolerance of uncertainty: Predictors and mediators of mental health during the COVID-19 pandemic. *American Psychologist, 76*(3), 427–437.

Ross, D. (2022). *Maryanne Oketch was "an emotional wreck crying every day" after "Survivor."* EW.Com. Retrieved from: https://ew.com/tv/survivor-42-maryanne-oketch-winner-finale-interview/

Rothbaum, F., Weisz, J. R., & Snyder, S. S. (1982). Changing the world and changing the self: A two-process model of perceived control. *Journal of Personality and Social Psychology, 42,* 5–37.

Sandberg, T., & Conner, M. (2009). A mere measurement effect for anticipated regret: Impacts on cervical screening attendance. *British Journal of Social Psychology, 48*(2), 221–236.

Schäfer, S., Aaldering, L., & Lecheler, S. (2023). "Give me a break!" Prevalence and predictors of intentional news avoidance during the COVID-19 pandemic. *Mass Communication and Society, 26*(4), 671–694.

Schmitt, B. H., Dubé, L., & Leclerc, F. (1992). Intrusions into waiting lines: Does the queue constitute a social system? *Journal of Personality and Social Psychology, 63*(5), 806–815.

Segerstrom, S. C., Glover, D. A., Craske, M. G., & Fahey, J. L. (1999). Worry affects the immune response to phobic fear. *Brain, Behavior, and Immunity, 13,* 80–92.

Shepperd, J. A., Ouellette, J. A., & Fernandez, J. K. (1996). Abandoning unrealistic optimism: Performance estimates and the temporal proximity of self-relevant feedback. *Journal of Personality and Social Psychology, 70,* 844–855.

Shipp, T. D., Shipp, D. Z., Bromley, B., Sheahan, R., Cohen, A., Lieberman, E., & Benacerraf, B. (2004). What factors are associated with parents' desire to know the sex of their unborn child? *Birth, 31*(4), 272–279.

Simonovic, N., Taber, J. M., Scherr, C. L., Dean, M., Hua, J., Howell, J. L., Chaudhry, B. M., Wain, K. E., & Politi, M. C. (2023). Uncertainty in healthcare and health decision making: Five methodological and conceptual research recommendations from an interdisciplinary team. *Journal of Behavioral Medicine, 46*(4), 541–555.

Stanton, A. L., & Snider, P. R. (1993). Coping with a breast cancer diagnosis: A prospective study. *Health Psychology, 12,* 16–23.

Sutton, S. R., & Eiser, J. R. (1990). The decision to wear a seat belt: The role of cognitive factors, fear and prior behavior. *Psychology and Health, 4,* 111–123.

Sweeny, K. (2018). On the experience of awaiting uncertain news. *Current Directions in Psychological Science, 27,* 281–285.

Sweeny, K., & Andrews, S. E. (2014). Mapping individual differences in the experience of a waiting period. *Journal of Personality & Social Psychology, 106,* 1015–1030.

Sweeny, K., Andrews, S. E., Nelson, S. K., & Robbins, M. L. (2015). Waiting for a baby: Navigating uncertainty while trying to conceive. *Social Science & Medicine, 141,* 123–132.

Sweeny, K., Carroll, P. J., & Shepperd, J. A. (2006). Thinking about the future: Is optimism always best? *Current Directions in Psychological Science, 15,* 302–306.

Sweeny, K., & Cavanaugh, A. G. (2012). Waiting is the hardest part: A model of uncertainty navigation in the context of health news. *Health Psychology Review, 6*(2), 147–164.

Sweeny, K., & Howell, J. L. (2017). Bracing later and coping better: Benefits of mindfulness during a stressful waiting period. *Personality and Social Psychology Bulletin, 43,* 1399–1414.

Sweeny, K., & Krizan, Z. (2013). Sobering up: A quantitative review of temporal declines in expectations. *Psychological Bulletin, 139,* 702–724.

Sweeny, K., Melnyk, D., Miller, W., & Shepperd, J. A. (2010). Information avoidance: Who, what, when, and why. *Review of General Psychology, 14*(4), 340–353.

Sweeny, K., Rankin, K., Cheng, X., Hou, L., Long, F., Meng, Y., Azer, L., Zhou, R., & Zhang, W. (2020). Flow in the time of COVID-19: Findings from China. *PLoS ONE, 15,* e0242043.

Sweeny, K., Reynolds, C., Falkenstein, A., Andrews, S. E., & Dooley, M. D. (2016). Two definitions of waiting well. *Emotion, 16,* 129–143.

Taber, J. M., Klein, W. M., Ferrer, R. A., Harris, P. R., Shepperd, J. A., & Biesecker, L. G. (2014). Information avoidance tendencies, spontaneous self-affirmation, and interest in genetic sequencing feedback. *Annals of Behavioral Medicine, 49,* 616–621.

Taber, J. M., Klein, W. M., Ferrer, R. A., Han, P. K., Lewis, K. L., Biesecker, L. G., & Biesecker, B. B. (2015). Perceived ambiguity as a barrier to intentions to learn genome sequencing results. *Journal of Behavioral Medicine, 38,* 715–726.

Taber, J. M., Leyva, B., & Persoskie, A. (2015). Why do people avoid medical care? A qualitative study using national data. *Journal of General Internal Medicine, 30,* 290–297.

van der Pligt, J., Otten, W., Richard, R., & van der Velde, F. W. (1993). Perceived risk of AIDS: Unrealistic optimism and self-protective action. In J. B. Prior & G. D. Reeder (Eds.), *The social psychology of HIV infection,* (pp. 39–58). Hillsdale, NJ: Erlbaum.

van der Steenstraten, I. M., Tibben, A., Roos, R., Van de Kamp, J., & Niermeijer, M. F. (1994). Predictive testing for Huntington disease: Nonparticipants compared with participants in the Dutch program. *American Journal of Human Genetics, 55*(4), 618–625.

Watkins, E. R. (2008). Constructive and unconstructive repetitive thought. *Psychological Bulletin, 134,* 163–206.

Webb, T. L., Miles, E., & Sheeran, P. (2012). Dealing with feeling: A meta-analysis of the effectiveness of strategies derived from the process model of emotion regulation. *Psychological Bulletin, 138,* 775–808.

Woolley, K., & Risen, J. L. (2018). Closing your eyes to follow your heart: Avoiding information to protect a strong intuitive preference. *Journal of Personality and Social Psychology, 114*(2), 230–245.

Yaniv, I., Benador, D., & Sagi, M. (2004). On not wanting to know and not wanting to inform others: Choices regarding predictive genetic testing. *Risk Decision and Policy, 9*(4), 317–336.

Ytre-Arne, B., & Moe, H. (2021). Doomscrolling, monitoring and avoiding: News use in COVID-19 pandemic lockdown. *Journalism Studies, 22*(13), 1739–1755.

Zajac, I. T., Duncan, A., Freegard, S., Wilson, C., Flight, I., & Turnbull, D. (2017). Exploring the potential of anticipated regret as an emotional cue to improve bowel cancer screening uptake. *BioMed Research International,* https://doi.org/10.1155/2017/2949020.

Zeelenberg, M., Nelissen, R. M., Breugelmans, S. M., & Pieters, R. (2008). On emotion specificity in decision making: Why feeling is for doing. *Judgment and Decision Making, 3,* 18–27.

Zeelenberg, M., van Dijk, W. W., Van der Pligt, J., Manstead, A. S., Van Empelen, P., & Reinderman, D. (1998). Emotional reactions to the outcomes of decisions: The role of counterfactual thought in the experience of regret and disappointment. *Organizational Behavior and Human Decision Processes, 75,* 117–141.

Zeelenberg, M., van Dijk, W. W., Manstead, A. S. R., & van der Pligt, J. (2000). On bad decisions and disconfirmed expectancies: The psychology of regret and disappointment. *Cognition & Emotion, 14,* 521–541.

Zhou, R., & Soman, D. (2003). Looking back: Exploring the psychology of queuing and the effect of the number of people behind. *Journal of Consumer Research, 29*(4), 517–530.

20

THE UNSETTLED QUESTIONS OF BELONGING UNCERTAINTY

Shannon T. Brady, Gregg A. Muragishi and Rebecca Getu

The Unsettled Questions of Belonging Uncertainty

People desire to belong with the people and in the places that structure their lives. The desire for belonging is a human need (Baumeister & Leary, 1995)—not just something we want, but something we need to flourish. However, our feelings of belonging are not always settled. They are tentative, they fluctuate, they are contingent. It is this flavor of belonging—belonging uncertainty—that we concern ourselves with here. We first define it, distinguish it from belonging, and address measurement issues. Then, we discuss antecedents, consequences, and interventions, and future directions for the research on belonging uncertainty. Throughout our discussion, we rely primarily on research and examples from educational settings and, to a lesser extent, the workplace, as these are the domains in which nearly all of the research on belonging uncertainty has taken place.

Defining Belonging Uncertainty

"A sense of belonging" has been defined in various ways by different scholars (Allen et al., 2021; Covarrubias, 2023). Here, we use the definition by Walton and Brady (2021) that positions belonging as a person's perception of the quality of their relationship with a valued context. There are three notable aspects of this definition that distinguish it from other possible conceptions. First, belonging is a perception, a feeling. As such, it is inherently subjective and likely to vary not only from person to person but also from moment to moment for a given person. Second, belonging is gestalt. It is informed by particulars—the number and quality of one's social relationships, and one's performance—but it also transcends these. It is possible to have very high performance and still not feel like you belong. It is possible to have many friends in a context and still not feel like you belong—or to have few friends but feel like you do belong. Third, belonging is about the relation between oneself and one's context. This is sometimes referred to as fit, or person-environment fit, where belonging is informed by whether a person perceives that their individual goals, needs, and values do (or do not) match their current context (for reviews see van Vianen, 2018; Schmader & Sedikides, 2018). For example, in organizations, employees are more likely to feel a sense of fit with their company if they believe their roles allow them to use their skills (Cable & DeRue, 2002) or if they believe they match the demographics, personality, and values of their team (Flynn & Chatman, 2001).

DOI: 10.4324/9781003363385-23

While belonging indexes one's overall *level* of connection to a particular environment or setting, belonging uncertainty indexes the *stability* or *lability* of that sense of connection[1]. Belonging uncertainty, then, is the extent to which a person feels secure about their level of belonging in a particular environment. The concept was originally introduced by Walton and Cohen (2007). They wrote,

> We suggest that, in academic and professional settings, members of socially stigmatized groups are more uncertain of the quality of their social bonds and thus more sensitive to issues of social belonging. We call this state *belonging uncertainty*, and suggest that it contributes to racial disparities in achievement.
>
> (p. 82)

Subsequently, Cohen and Garcia (2008) defined it as "doubt to whether one will be accepted or rejected by key figures in the social environment" (p. 365). More recently, Walton and Brady have described it as involving persistent doubts about whether oneself or people like oneself can belong in a context (2017) or, more simply, as feeling worried or unsettled about one's sense of belonging (2021).

To illustrate the difference between belonging and belonging uncertainty, imagine two people, both of whom generally feel like they belong at their workplace. One person feels secure in their belonging at work—in fact, they rarely think about their belonging and, when they do, it is from a place of confidence. But the other person thinks about their belonging frequently; even small events can lead them to worry or wonder about whether they (or people like them) really belong at this workplace. Though both are moderately high in belonging, the first person is low in belonging uncertainty while the second person is high in belonging uncertainty. Indeed, Walton and Cohen (2007) found exactly this pattern in a pilot study. Both White college students and minoritized college students (i.e., Black and Latinx) reported similar levels of belonging, but minoritized students reported greater belonging uncertainty. Recent correlational studies have also found empirical support for the independence of the two constructs (Edwards et al., 2022; Fink et al., 2023).

Of course, it is worth noting that although belonging and belonging uncertainty are distinguishable constructs, they are inversely correlated. It does tend to be the case that people lower in belonging are higher in belonging uncertainty. For example, in a sample of four-year college students ($N = 839$) from six universities in the United States, Gilbertson and colleagues (2022) found a correlation of $r = -0.71$ between students' sense of belonging and belonging uncertainty at their college. In a sample of four-year college students enrolled in chemistry courses, Edwards and colleagues (2022) found correlations of $r = -0.74$ and $r = -0.79$ at the beginning and end of a semester, respectively. Harackiewicz and colleagues (2014) found a correlation of $r = -0.45$. In our own unpublished data, we have often found correlations between $r = -.45$ and $r = -.70$ (Kaplan et al., 2024; Brady et al., 2024).

From its inception, belonging uncertainty has been situated within work on identity threat and attributional ambiguity. This literature suggests that people are motivated to view themselves as fundamentally good and capable and to maintain this sense of self-integrity (Steele, 1988; Walton & Wilson, 2018). Thus, when people enter new settings, they are often vigilant to cues or signals that convey whether any part of their social identity (e.g., gender, race, socioeconomic status, sexual orientation) is at risk of being devalued (Abrams & Hogg, 1999; Crocker et al., 1998).

This vigilance process is heightened among people whose identity is or may be marginalized in the setting, for example, people who are worried about being viewed through the lens of a negative stereotype (Steele, 1997) or that their group may be underrepresented (Murphy & Taylor,

2012). This "threat in the air" (Steele, 2010) can seed ambiguity in the meaning behind how they are treated and viewed by others, including peers and authority figures. Belonging uncertainty and identity threat can be mutually reinforcing. Identity threat can contribute to belonging uncertainty, as people concerned about mistreatment due to their social identity are more likely to question their acceptance within a particular group or setting. Conversely, belonging uncertainty can exacerbate social identity threat. When individuals are uncertain about their belonging, they may be more attuned to potential threats related to their social identity, amplifying the impact of social identity threat.

Consider the example in education where students receive critical feedback on their assignments from their teachers. While critical feedback is intended to scaffold and help facilitate students' learning, there can sometimes be ambiguity around the purpose of the feedback for students (Cohen et al., 1999; Griffiths et al., 2023). This ambiguity may particularly be true for African American students who may be unsure of whether feedback from their teachers reflects their teacher's motivations to help them learn and become successful, or if the critical feedback is reflective of the teacher's belief in the negative stereotype about African Americans' abilities in school (Yeager et al., 2014). Consider another example in work settings. Even though both men and women want their contributions to matter at work (Lombard & Cheryan, 2024; Muragishi et al., 2024), women working in technology companies may be unsure of whether being interrupted in a meeting represents others' beliefs in the negative stereotype about women's abilities to contribute to science and engineering or something more innocuous (Muragishi et al., 2024). Belonging uncertainty follows this same pattern. Even as all people may be uncertain of their belonging and seek out evidence to remedy that uncertainty, marginalization can exacerbate that process.

"A Concept Not Yet Well Understood"

Despite growing interest in belonging uncertainty, our empirical understanding of it remains markedly modest. Zander and Ertl (2023) aptly note that it is still "a concept not yet well understood" (p. 1).

One reason for this is that definitions of belonging and belonging uncertainty are often conflated. For example, Deiglmayr and colleagues (2019) write, "belonging uncertainty, to specify the term, is an individual's perception that 'people like me do not belong here,'" citing Walton and Cohen (2007, p. 83) for the quoted section. Similarly, Smith and Lucena (2016) write that it is "when underrepresented students believe that people like them do not belong in a particular institutional or social setting" (p. 3). We believe that this is a misinterpretation of the concept. The full quote from Walton and Cohen (2007) reads, "Belonging uncertainty may take the form of a broad-based hypothesis that "people like me do not belong here" (p. 83). In this conceptualization, belonging uncertainty is *not* a belief or perception but rather a *working hypothesis*, a worry, a concern—an unsettled question that people are seeking answers to (Walton & Brady, 2017). As such, it may be more pernicious than a belief. Ambiguous information relevant to one's potentially marginalized identity is more likely to consume working memory than unambiguous information (Dardenne et al., 2007; Dumont et al., 2010; Salvatore & Shelton, 2007).

A second issue is a lack of clarity on whether there is a distinction between "social belonging" and "ability belonging" and thus should be a similar distinction for belonging uncertainty. As originally conceptualized by Walton and Cohen (2007, 2011), one's belonging in school—and thus, by extension, one's worries or uncertainty about that belonging—is comprised of both social and academic/ability elements. However, other scholars have argued that they are separable (Banchefsky et al., 2019), even developing a scale designed specifically to measure the ability component

(Lewis & Hodges, 2015). A theory paper by Schmader and Sedikides (2018) outlines three kinds of "fit": social fit (wherein they locate belonging), goal fit (which might align, at least partially, with ability fit), and self-concept fit. One possibility may be that in certain academic environments—perhaps even many academic environments—these three types of fit are tightly coupled, but in other academic environments, they may be more loosely connected (Guo & Schmader, Chapter 10).

A third issue is that researchers often conceptualize their research in terms of belonging uncertainty, but ultimately measure belonging. Then, they take low belonging, measured cross-sectionally at a single point in time, as evidence of high belonging uncertainty (e.g., J. L. Smith et al., 2014). As noted above, the high correlation between belonging and belonging uncertainty makes such choices understandable. And yet this approach, coupled with the sparsity of data specifically on belonging uncertainty (Edwards et al., 2022), impedes our ability to develop clear and nuanced conceptual understandings.

This points to a fourth issue: there is not yet a well-accepted conceptual model of belonging uncertainty. However, two recent models may help fill this void (see also Cohen & Garcia, 2008). Schmader and Sedikides (2018) recently introduced the *state authenticity as fit to environment (SAFE)* model (see also Guo & Schmader, Chapter 10). The central organizing concept of the model is authenticity, which they argue is experienced when people feel three kinds of fit in an environment or domain: social fit (akin to belonging), goal fit, and self-concept fit. In their conceptualization, each kind of fit contributes to a person's experience of fluency, which then drives approach or avoidance behavior in the environment or domain (see also Aday & Schmader, 2019). They contend that cues in a setting signal which social identities "fit" and which do not, often leading to feelings of authenticity for people from non-marginalized identities and feelings of inauthenticity for people from marginalized identities. Although this model does not explicitly distinguish between belonging and belonging uncertainty, it may have utility in establishing the landscape in which belonging uncertainty functions.

Drawing considerably on the SAFE model, Zander and Ertl (2023) recently introduced the *belonging uncertainty as incongruency of communion and agency perceptions* (BICAP) model in a chapter about women in the natural sciences. Central to this model is the idea that students engage in social comparison in evaluative contexts, assessing the extent to which their skills, interests, and goals are aligned with others in their environment. When students experience or anticipate incongruence, they experience belonging uncertainty, which leads them to exert behavioral or psychological strategies to increase congruence. Depending on whether cues in the environment signal the malleability or stability of the incongruence, students are likely to engage in approach-oriented (malleability) strategies or avoidance-oriented (stability) strategies.

Finally, how belonging uncertainty relates to many other similar phenomena has not been clearly delineated. Take the imposter phenomenon, also known as imposter syndrome or, simply, imposterism (Chrousos & Mentis, 2020; Clance & Imes, 1978; Slank, 2019). The imposter phenomenon is when, despite clear skill and achievement, someone doubts their abilities or fears being exposed as a fraud. Doubt is central to both belonging uncertainty and the imposter phenomenon, and the experiencer is likely left feeling inauthentic (see Guo & Schmader, Chapter 10; Schmader & Sedikides, 2018). However, belonging uncertainty does not require a past track record of outstanding accomplishments and is typically broader than a pure performance concern. However, it is likely that belonging uncertainty mediates the effects of feeling like an imposter on performance outcomes, much like it does in cases of solo status or tokenism (Dasgupta, 2011).

Measuring Belonging Uncertainty

In their initial paper introducing belonging uncertainty, Walton and Cohen (2007) experimentally demonstrated belonging uncertainty by showing that belonging can be sensitive to threats. They asked both Black and White college students to list friends who would fit in well in the university's computer science department. They manipulated whether the task was easy (list two friends) or challenging (list eight friends). For Black students who contend with the specter of negative stereotypes about their ability, the more difficult task subsequently led them to report lower feelings of belonging. Another experimental demonstration of belonging uncertainty asked students to report their racial-ethnic identity or to reflect on experiences of discrimination either before or after reporting on their belonging. When students of color were first reminded of their race or their experiences of discrimination, they reported lower belonging than when they had not yet had these reminders (Mallett et al., 2011). White students' belonging was unaffected by such reminders. In both of these examples, however, belonging uncertainty was not explicitly assessed.

Given belonging uncertainty's focus on lability, a dramatic (and labor-intensive) way to assess belonging uncertainty is to measure belonging *over time*. Note that this is different from a single cross-sectional assessment of belonging, which we critique above because the longitudinal nature of the data can reveal *fluctuations* in belonging—a key feature of belonging uncertainty. In a few instances, researchers have done just this. For example, Walton and Cohen (2011) asked students to report their feelings of belonging at college in daily diaries twice a day for one week. Similar measures have been used in other studies (Murphy et al., 2020; Walton et al., 2015). Researchers have found that adversity predicts fluctuations in the belonging of students likely to be experiencing identity threat.

While these daily diary measures can capture feelings of belonging uncertainty dynamically, they are impractical in many studies due to the need for repeated measurement over time. Therefore, researchers have developed scales designed to assess belonging uncertainty that require only a single administration. The most common of these, designed to be used with students, was introduced by Walton and Cohen (2007). The scale consists of three items (scale: 1 = strongly disagree, 7 = strongly agree): "Sometimes I feel that I belong at [School Name], and sometimes I feel that I don't belong at [School Name]," "When something good happens, I feel that I really belong at [School Name]" (reverse-scored), and "When something bad happens, I feel that maybe I don't belong at [School Name]." The first item clearly highlights the lability of belonging uncertainty, while the second and third items capture the contingency of belonging uncertainty. That said, the second item inconsistently loads with the other two and is sometimes dropped (e.g., Brady et al., 2020) or is not assessed (Fink et al., 2020). In some cases, only one of the items is assessed (McPartlan et al., 2020) or retained (Totonchi et al., 2023).

More recently, Yeager and colleagues (2013) have developed a face-valid single-item measure: "When you think about [setting/context], how often, if ever, do you wonder: 'Maybe I don't belong here?" (scale: 1 = never, 5 = always). As the scale has primarily been used in education, the setting or context has typically been a particular course, a discipline or major, or the school as a whole, but it could be adapted for other situations. A slightly longer scale is also currently under development (Zander & Höhne, personal communication, September 12, 2023), aimed at addressing the somewhat lower internal consistency often found for the original scale.

As we will discuss later, a number of studies informed by theoretical understandings of belonging uncertainty do not measure belonging uncertainty as an outcome. Rather, they posit belonging uncertainty as a mediating psychological process and measure the hypothesized downstream outcomes of that process. While this might seem curious, it is consistent with a tradition in social psychology that relies on manipulating a proposed mediating psychological process in order to clearly establish the causal role of the mediator (Spencer et al., 2005).

What Makes Us Uncertain about Our Belonging?

People, regardless of their identity or personal background, can be uncertain about their belonging. Indeed, there may be particular moments that leave us all vulnerable to wondering about whether we belong. For example, the transition to middle school may be one such time (Borman et al., 2019). But we are not ahistorical, and our backgrounds often matter for how we feel about our belonging in a particular context. We often know that one of our identities has been historically and/or contemporaneously devalued.

In general, people from backgrounds that have been stigmatized, negatively stereotyped, or marginalized in a particular domain often report greater uncertainty about their belonging in that domain. For example, women in science and technology domains report greater belonging uncertainty than men, including in computer science (Höhne & Zander, 2019), chemistry (Fink et al., 2020), physics (Edwards et al., 2022), and biology (Harackiewicz et al., 2014). Black students and first-generation college students at four-year colleges report greater belonging uncertainty than their White and continuing-generation counterparts (Edwards et al., 2022; Gopalan et al., 2022; Harackiewicz et al., 2016). For bisexual people, the more often they experience identity denial (that is, being told their bisexual identity is a phase or otherwise not real), the greater their concerns about whether others would accept them (Maimon et al., 2021). In cases where people's devalued sociodemographic characteristics are more visible, experiences of ostracism due to that devalued characteristic may compound the direct effects of belonging uncertainty (Janke et al., 2024); ostracism is less prevalent for people whose devalued characteristic is more concealable, like parental education.

In addition to the stigma associated with sociodemographic identities, people can also experience stigma due to their personal circumstances. For example, students who transferred from community colleges described considerable doubt about their belonging at four-year universities due, in part, to the way in which community colleges were viewed by their four-year college peers as inferior institutions (Shaw et al., 2019). Relatedly, the less chemistry content knowledge a student had before beginning introductory chemistry, and the less college-preparatory experience, the greater their belonging uncertainty.

What unites these disparate experiences—negative stereotypes, stigma, identity denial—is that they position people lower on the social hierarchy. With regard to physical resources, being lower on the social hierarchy makes one's access to those resources less certain. It is the same with the psychological resource of belonging. Of course, not all people with a shared sociodemographic identity or personal circumstance will experience belonging uncertainty in the same way or to the same extent. People's own past experiences are likely to color how they respond to challenges. To illustrate, Offidani-Bertrand and colleagues (2022) compared the college transition experiences of Black and Latinx students at a predominantly White college who had attended high schools where the other students were predominantly of the same race or were predominantly White. They found that when students interpreted racial-ethnic tension as evidence of their inadequacy—a tendency that was more common for students who had attended predominantly same-race high schools—they reported greater belonging uncertainty. In contrast, when students viewed these tensions as evidence of structural inequalities on campus—a tendency more common among students who had attended predominantly White high schools—they reported less belonging uncertainty, even as they were more critical of their institution.

In closing, we wish to underscore the dynamic nature of belonging uncertainty (Chaudhari, 2022). Belonging uncertainty is not a personal trait that is carried and felt from place to place. Rather, it manifests from an ongoing assessment of how one might be viewed or treated in a particular setting or domain and, as such, can be sensitive to minor cues that others might not notice. When there are identity-threatening cues (e.g., low numerical group representation) that suggest that a person's identity is at risk of being marginalized, belonging uncertainty increases. When there are identity-safety cues (e.g., higher numerical group representation) that suggest a person's identity is safe, and not at risk of marginalization, belonging uncertainty subsides. Of course, cues interact with a person's past and ongoing experiences and construals. This is illustrated in the study above where the extent of belonging uncertainty among Black and Latinx students attending a predominantly White college (and, therefore, experiencing low numerical group representation) was dependent on their interpretation of the meaning of racial-ethnic tension they experienced, which was itself correlated with features of the school they had attended during high school.

Consequences of Belonging Uncertainty

A key short-term consequence of belonging uncertainty is heightened vigilance (Cohen & Garcia, 2008). People in a state of belonging uncertainty are more sensitive to information in their environment, perhaps especially as it relates to the self and one's sense of fit. Then, as people assimilate the information they find, two other processes may shape the meaning they make (Brands & Fernandez-Mateo, 2017). First, people experiencing greater belonging uncertainty may give greater weight to information about their sense of fit in the environment (Murphy & Zirkel, 2015). If you have been marginalized in a domain before, you are likely to be more attuned and sensitive to the potential for marginalization when you enter that space again. Second, because they are walking around with the hypothesis "maybe I don't belong here" bedeviling their minds, people experiencing belonging uncertainty may engage in confirmation processes (Nickerson, 1998; Snyder & Swann, 1978)—interpreting even ambiguous information in light of that hypothesis. Importantly, people need not personally experience marginalization for these processes to feed a negative recursive cycle. Even viewing or hearing how others who are like you have been treated could engage these processes (Cohen & Garcia, 2005; Shapiro & Neuberg, 2007).

In academic domains, belonging uncertainty predicts feelings of stress, lower expectations for success, and higher perceived costs (Höhne et al., 2022; Totonchi et al., 2023). In some cases, these relationships are found only for students more likely to be experiencing identity threat (e.g., minoritized students, Murphy & Zirkel, 2015; first-generation students, Totonchi et al., 2023) and sometimes they are more general (Höhne et al., 2022).

If a person questions whether they belong in an environment, it can be difficult to fully commit to the behaviors necessary to succeed or feel comfortable in that environment. This includes, ironically, the actions necessary to develop positive relationships, which could help cultivate a sense of belonging (Brady et al., 2020; Walton et al., 2015). Similarly, feeling a lack of belonging promotes feelings of inauthenticity (Slepian & Jacoby-Senghor, 2020), which may lead a person to disengage from the domain. In college, belonging uncertainty can predict students' intentions to drop out of a course, over and above previous academic performance, self-efficacy, and perceived value of the subject (Höhne & Zander, 2019) as well as actual course persistence (Manai et al., 2016). In fact, in a study of community college students, belonging uncertainty assessed four weeks into the semester was the best predictor of course completion in a developmental math course, even after controlling for prior content knowledge and personal-demographic factors (Yeager et al., 2013). It was also the best predictor of whether students met the performance benchmark to be considered "prepared" for subsequent courses.

A rich qualitative study illustrates some of these findings (Fink et al., 2023). In it, students were first asked to complete a question about the extent to which they felt like they belonged in a science course and then to explain why. In their belonging explanations, marginalized students were more likely to discuss social interactions with their peers and to compare themselves with their peers. They were more likely to mention their ability and learning in the course and less likely to mention positive feelings of interest and enjoyment. They were also more likely to discuss their interpretations of themselves and how their performance in the course affected those interpretations. Of note, however, some of those evaluations were positive: in fact, more Black students said positive things about their learning or performance than did White students. For example, a Black student wrote, "At the beginning of the semester, I was afraid I would be unable to grasp a lot of the concepts…However, I am doing better than expected and I understand a large portion of the material" (p. 336). Marginalized students' concerns about belonging may have led them to expend greater time and attention on evaluating their fit in the course, or vice versa.

Outside of the academic domain, researchers have found that students' feelings of belonging uncertainty are correlated with their mental health (Gopalan et al., 2022). Students higher in belonging uncertainty reported higher depression and greater anxiety. Notably, within-person decreases in belonging uncertainty over the course of a year buffered students against depression, with the largest effects for Black, Latinx, Indigenous, first-generation college, and first-year college students. Similar effects have been found for bisexual people: low belonging uncertainty reduces the link between experiences of identity denial from others and depression (Maimon et al., 2021).

However, most of our understanding regarding the consequences of belonging uncertainty comes from experimental studies designed to mitigate it. This is consistent with a long tradition in social psychology of demonstrating the consequences of a hypothesized mediator by manipulating it (Spencer et al., 2005). Walton and Cohen (2007, 2011) introduced the social belonging intervention in the same manuscript as they introduced belonging uncertainty. The intervention is a reading -and-writing exercise designed to contextualize common challenges in an academic transition like earning lower-than-expected grades or feeling lonely or intimidated (Walton & Brady, 2021). Students first read survey results, ostensibly from other students at their school or schools like theirs, that report that most students experienced challenges and worries at first in their transition to the new social and academic environment at their school. The results then explain that with time, most students became more comfortable at school, and their feelings of belonging increased. These survey results are followed by stories, attributed to fellow students, that share these same insights in narrative form. Afterward, students are invited to reflect on their own experiences in writing and forecast a positive trajectory in their own belonging.

The intervention has been tested in numerous randomized controlled trials in which students either complete the intervention or an active control exercise similar in structure but focused on more mundane aspects of the school environment, like the physical space and the weather (see Walton & Brady, 2021, for a review). In the first study (Walton & Cohen, 2007, 2011), the intervention was delivered individually, in person to college students in the middle of their first year of college. However, subsequent studies have delivered the intervention in classes (Goyer et al., 2019; Murphy et al., 2020; Walton et al., 2015) or via online orientation modules (Walton et al., 2023; Yeager et al., 2016) and to students making the transition to middle school (Borman et al., 2019; Goyer et al., 2019; Pyne & Borman, 2020), high school (Williams et al., 2020), and college (Walton et al., 2023; Yeager et al., 2016).

In the short term, the intervention reduces belonging uncertainty by uncoupling the association between adversity and belonging—making students' belonging more stable over time (Walton & Cohen, 2007, 2011). It also increases students' academic engagement, like going to a professor's office hours, and opens them up to embracing academic challenges. In the longer term, the intervention has yielded benefits on academic persistence and performance, well-being, and the formation of social bonds (see Brady et al., 2020; and Walton et al., 2023 for process models). For example, Black students in the original trial of the social-belonging intervention had higher grades, higher happiness, and better self-reported health than their control counterparts at the end of college, more than three years after they had participated in the intervention (Walton & Cohen, 2011). The academic benefits were mediated by the uncoupling described above. When these same Black students were young adults (~age 27), those who had been in the intervention condition reported better self-perceived psychological well-being and career outcomes (Brady et al., 2020). These longer-term effects were not mediated by their college grades, but rather by the presence and quality of college mentors.

A large-scale study involving more than 29,000 students at 22 U.S. colleges and generalizing to more than 1 million first-year students at 749 colleges offered insight into when and for whom belonging interventions are best poised to yield benefits (Walton et al., 2023). In contrast to past work that had often grouped together students from different marginalized backgrounds, this study analyzed students in terms of "local identity groups"— students of a given race-ethnicity, with a given first-generation status, at a given college, in a given year of the study. This was done to recognize that identities are always contextual: what it means to be, for instance, a first-generation student is different in different college contexts and even across time. The study found that the intervention increased first-year full-time persistence for students, especially those from local identity groups that historically had lower college persistence rates. However, this was only the case when the college environment provided moderate or high opportunities for people from their group to belong. This research underscores that belonging uncertainty is importantly affected by the context.

Key to understanding the consequences of belonging uncertainty is the notion of recursion (Walton & Cohen, 2007). Belonging uncertainty undermines outcomes, and these worsened outcomes can then heighten belonging uncertainty, further undermining outcomes, in an interminable feedback loop. Using longitudinal data, Edwards and colleagues (2022) found evidence of just such a recursive process for women in general chemistry. The social belonging intervention can break this cycle, by reducing the likelihood that adversity gets translated into subsequent worsened belonging (Walton & Cohen, 2011).

Interventions

It seems that institutions and companies have caught a bit of 'belonging fever': everywhere you look, institutions and companies are trying to assure you that "you belong here." The San Mateo California County Fair wants you to know this. So does the 2023 American Psychological Association Convention. And PepsiCo. Same with Montgomery College (Maryland), Lewis & Clark College (Oregon), Asbury University (Kentucky), Michigan State University, and many other colleges and universities.

While these efforts may be well-intentioned, they may also be misguided. Efforts to simply "pump people up" about belonging may not work well for those who are uncertain. For example, encouraging messaging from university administrators, accompanied by university swag, improved the belonging of White—but not Black—college students and, presumably, reduced their belonging uncertainty (Hausmann et al., 2009). As a consequence, an intervention designed to enhance belonging exacerbated inequalities in it.

If platitudes are ineffective, what should organizations do to address concerns about belonging, especially for people from marginalized groups? Backed by considerable empirical evidence (Brannon, 2023; Brannon & Lin, 2021), Tiffany Brannon and her colleagues advocate for a "pride and prejudice" approach, whereby efforts are made both to affirm identity-based strengths (pride) and to mitigate sources of negative difference (prejudice). This approach is consistent with the idea that a marginalized identity is often tied to both risks and resilience.

Affirming identity-based strengths goes beyond decontextualized slogans. Rather, the crux of the "pride" approach to supporting people's belonging involves direct acknowledgment of specific strengths related to one's marginalized identity or identities. This could involve offering physical spaces that include ideas and practices associated with one's identity, highlighting identity-relevant role models (Ahn et al., 2020; Covarrubias & Fryberg, 2015; Dasgupta, 2011; Laiduc et al., 2021; Morgenroth et al., 2015), or offering culturally relevant curricula (Sleeter & Zavala, 2020; see also Bonilla et al., 2021). It could involve creating opportunities for people to reflect on their personal values (Cohen & Sherman, 2014; Manke et al., 2021). The goal of these strategies is to affirm individuals that their identities are welcomed and valued in the context and that they belong.

While creating experiences, spaces, and messages that value the perspectives and identities of marginalized people is an important component of reducing belonging uncertainty, institutions and organizations also need to focus on reducing experiences of negative difference and improving intergroup relationships. As with the pride approach, there are diverse ways in which this "prejudice" approach can be accomplished. To start, organizations can communicate positive social norms about inclusion—that the vast majority of people within the organization hold pro-diversity attitudes and seek to be inclusive in their behavior (Murrar et al., 2020). When the context is evaluative, the organization or institution can offer structured support, which may both improve performance and support belonging. For example, academic courses or programs that offer greater structure, feedback, and support can reduce inequalities in performance and persistence and also lead to increased feelings of belonging (Casey et al., 2023; Mendoza-Denton et al., 2017, 2018). When the City University of New York implemented the Accelerated Study in Associate Programs (ASAP) initiative, which provided students with a comprehensive package of structural supports including tuition waivers, transportation vouchers, and access to in-depth advising and enhanced career services, the proportion of students who reported low belonging at college dropped substantially (Scrivener et al., 2015). In addition, efforts to proactively contextualize common difficulties and forecast positive growth—as the social belonging intervention described earlier does—can disrupt the link between experiencing challenges and questioning one's belonging (Walton & Brady, 2021).

In their model of belonging uncertainty, Zander and Ertl (2023) emphasize that people experiencing belonging uncertainty look to their environments to determine whether the disconnect they are experiencing is stable or malleable. Their assessment, then, shapes how people choose to respond—by strengthening their identification or engagement with the domain or by disidentifying and disengaging. This highlights another means to alleviate deleterious consequences of belonging uncertainty: encourage people to see their abilities as malleable and ensure that that message is indeed true in the local context (Carroll et al., 2023; Guo & Schmader, Chapter 10; Hecht, Bryan, et al., 2023; Hecht, Dweck, et al., 2023; Yeager et al., 2019).

With regard to education, Greg Walton noted, (2022), "It's not our job to tell students how they feel. It is our job to create ways of thinking, cultures, and personal relationships that make school a place of genuine belonging for every child." The same can be said for institutions beyond schools as well. In creating these places of genuine belonging, institutional gatekeepers must bear in mind that the seemingly "same" action can feel very different to someone based on the specific, and sometimes seemingly minor, details of how it is executed (Walton & Brady, 2020). Institutional efforts that come across as marketing or pandering or otherwise inauthentic are unlikely to be effective.

Future Directions

Given that belonging uncertainty is "not yet well understood," many open questions, even seemingly basic ones, remain unaddressed. We outline four here.

Who feels uncertain about their belonging? So far, research has identified that people facing marginalization and negative stereotypes about their group's abilities are more susceptible to belonging uncertainty (Walton & Cohen, 2007). But there may be other personal qualities that heighten belonging uncertainty or serve as a buffer. For example, people high in neuroticism, low in extraversion or agreeableness, and with low self-esteem may all be more likely to experience belonging uncertainty (Hernández et al., 2017; Stubblebine et al., 2024). In contrast, personal qualities that can buffer against threat—such as having a strong purpose in life (Burrow & Rainone, 2017)—may serve as a protective factor against worries about one's belonging. There may be differences not only in peoples' *levels* of belonging uncertainty but also in the *consequences* of belonging uncertainty for their outcomes. Extrapolating from Guo and Schmader's chapter on authenticity in this volume (Chapter 10), people with certain personal qualities, such as higher openness to experience or greater value for diversity and inclusion, may be better able to tolerate belonging uncertainty without having it undermine their performance, commitment, or well-being because they are more likely to view it as a transient state.

How does belonging uncertainty unfold over time? Much of the research on belonging uncertainty has focused on students at transition points (Edwards et al., 2022; Walton & Brady, 2021), with the idea that one's uncertainty about belonging may be greatest as one enters a new context. Some (Zander & Ertl) have suggested that a person's belonging uncertainty should go down over time in a context. But, so far, longitudinal examinations of belonging uncertainty are limited and we do not yet know normative patterns of how belonging uncertainty unfolds over time in a context.

How does belonging uncertainty function outside of evaluative contexts? To date, research on belonging uncertainty has largely taken place in academic and, to a lesser extent, workplace contexts. A valuable research direction is to study belonging uncertainty in contexts that place less of a premium on performance. For example, to what extent do people experience belonging uncertainty in their church or faith/spiritual community? In the queer community? In their neighborhood? What are the consequences of this uncertainty for the person and the other people in the community? In thinking about how more of us are bowling—and doing so many other things—alone (Putnam, 2001), how does a person's anticipated belonging uncertainty possibly prevent them from joining a community (Kraus & Crul, 2022; see also Jansen et al., 2015) or taking other actions that they'd like to? In one promising illustration of work aligned with these questions, Pathakis (2020) has introduced the concept of political belonging uncertainty. Supported by both correlational and experimental evidence, she argues that political belonging uncertainty contributes to the lower political expression engagement of women and people from minoritized racial-ethnic backgrounds.

What features of a context heighten belonging uncertainty and how can institutions and organizations change those features to be more welcoming? Often, institutions and organizations focus on changing the explicit and tangible features of their context that may elicit identity threat and the risk of marginalization for people. Indeed, empirically supported strategies such as increasing the numerical representation of people from underrepresented groups (Murphy et al., 2007), adopting more inclusive diversity philosophies (Purdie-Vaughns et al., 2008), changing physical decor (Cheryan et al., 2009), or improving interpersonal interactions (Muragishi et al., 2024; see also Moser & Branscombe, 2022) have been found to support people from marginalized identities' belonging. It will be important for future research, however, also to examine the default cultural beliefs at an institution or in a domain about who belongs, such as masculine defaults in Science, Technology, Engineering, Mathematics (STEM). Masculine defaults in STEM exist when institutions view characteristics and behaviors typically associated with masculinity as necessary for success and viewed as the standard (Cheryan & Markus, 2020). For example, if the default belief that is only brilliant people are able to belong in STEM and men are considered more brilliant than women (Bian et al., 2017), it could be grounds for women to experience greater belonging uncertainty if they do not, or others treat them as if they do not, fit that default of brilliance (Garr-Schultz et al., 2023; see also Pronin et al., 2004). As such, future research may focus its efforts on first directly testing the relationship between defaults (e.g., masculine, White, straight, and/or able-bodied) and belonging uncertainty. If defaults of who belongs do positively predict belonging uncertainty for individuals who do not fit those defaults, then research could examine ways to either dismantle those defaults or expand those defaults to reflect a more diverse definition of who can belong.

Conclusion

We end on a hopeful note. Despite the current messiness in conceptualization and measurement, belonging uncertainty captures something important about our relationship with valued contexts. As researchers continue to refine our understanding of belonging uncertainty, what we already know has informed practices and approaches that improve well-being and mitigate inequality.

Acknowledgment

G. A. Muragishi was supported by an NSF STEM Education Postdoctoral Research Fellowship #2222381.

Note

1 These definitions parallel ones from the attitude literature, where attitudes index a general positive or negative evaluation of an object while attitude certainty describes one's sense of confidence or conviction in that evaluation (Tormala, 2016).

References

Abrams, D., & Hogg, M. A. (1999). *Social identity and social cognition*. Blackwell Oxford.

Aday, A., & Schmader, T. (2019). Seeking authenticity in diverse contexts: How identities and environments constrain "free" choice. *Social and Personality Compass*, *16*(6), Article e12450. https://doi.org/10.1111/spc3.12450

Ahn, J. N., Hu, D., & Vega, M. (2020). "Do as I do, not as I say": Using social learning theory to unpack the impact of role models on students' outcomes in education. *Social and Personality Psychology Compass*, *14*(2), Article e12517. https://doi.org/10.1111/spc3.12517

Allen, K.-A., Kern, M. L., Rozek, C. S., McInerney, D. M., & Slavich, G. M. (2021). Belonging: A review of conceptual issues, an integrative framework, and directions for future research. *Australian Journal of Psychology*, *73*(1), 87–102. https://doi.org/10.1080/00049530.2021.1883409

Banchefsky, S., Lewis, K. L., & Ito, T. A. (2019). The role of social and ability belonging in men's and women's pSTEM persistence. *Frontiers in Psychology*, *10*, Article 02386. https://doi.org/10.3389/fpsyg.2019.02386

Baumeister, R. F., & Leary, M. R. (1995). The need to belong: Desire for interpersonal attachments as a fundamental human motivation. *Psychological Bulletin*, *117*(3), 497–529. https://doi.org/10.1037/0033-2909.117.3.497

Bian, L., Leslie, S.-J., & Cimpian, A. (2017). Gender stereotypes about intellectual ability emerge early and influence children's interests. *Science*, *355*(6323), 389–391. https://doi.org/10.1126/science.aah6524

Bonilla, S., Dee, T. S., & Penner, E. K. (2021). Ethnic studies increases longer-run academic engagement and attainment. *Proceedings of the National Academy of Sciences*, *118*(37), e2026386118. https://doi.org/10.1073/pnas.2026386118

Borman, G. D., Rozek, C. S., Pyne, J., & Hanselman, P. (2019). Reappraising academic and social adversity improves middle school students' academic achievement, behavior, and well-being. *Proceedings of the National Academy of Sciences*, *116*(33), 16286–16291. https://doi.org/10.1073/pnas.1820317116

Brady, S. T., Cohen, G. L., Jarvis, S. N., & Walton, G. M. (2020). A brief social-belonging intervention in college improves adult outcomes for black Americans. *Science Advances*, *6*(18), eaay3689. https://doi.org/10.1126/sciadv.aay3689

Brady, S. T., Ospina, J. P., & Walton, G. M. (2024). Social and academic life study [Unpublished raw data]. Wake Forest University.

Brands, R. A., & Fernandez-Mateo, I. (2017). Leaning out: How negative recruitment experiences shape women's decisions to compete for executive roles. *Administrative Science Quarterly*, *62*(3), 405–442. https://doi.org/10.1177/0001839216682728

Brannon, T. N. (2023). Pride-and-prejudice perspectives of marginalization can advance science and society. *Current Directions in Psychological Science*, *32*(1), 73–80. https://doi.org/10.1177/09637214221121818

Brannon, T. N., & Lin, A. (2021). "Pride and prejudice" pathways to belonging: Implications for inclusive diversity practices within mainstream institutions. *American Psychologist*, *76*(3), 488–501. https://doi.org/10.1037/amp0000643

Burrow, A. L., & Rainone, N. (2017). How many likes did I get?: Purpose moderates links between positive social media feedback and self-esteem. *Journal of Experimental Social Psychology*, *69*, 232–236. https://doi.org/10.1016/j.jesp.2016.09.005

Cable, D. M., & DeRue, D. S. (2002). The convergent and discriminant validity of subjective fit perceptions. *Journal of Applied Psychology*, 87(5), 875–884. https://doi.org/10.1037/0021-9010.87.5.875

Carroll, J. M., Yeager, D. S., Buontempo, J., Hecht, C., Cimpian, A., Mhatre, P., Muller, C., & Crosnoe, R. (2023). Mindset × Context: Schools, classrooms, and the unequal translation of expectations into math achievement. *Monographs of the Society for Research in Child Development*, *88*(2), 7–109. https://doi.org/10.1111/mono.12471

Casey, J. R., Supriya, K., Shaked, S., Caram, J. R., Russell, A., & Courey, A. J. (2023). Participation in a high-structure general chemistry course increases student sense of belonging and persistence to organic chemistry. *Journal of Chemical Education*, *100*(8), 2860–2872. https://doi.org/10.1021/acs.jchemed.2c01253

Chaudhari, P. (2022). A mixed sense of belonging: Fluid experiences for multiracial and multiethnic college students. In M. P. Johnston-Guerrero, L. D. Combs, & V. K. Malaney-Brown (Eds.), *Preparing for higher education's mixed race future: Why multiraciality matters* (pp. 105–124). Springer International Publishing. https://doi.org/10.1007/978-3-030-88821-3_6

Cheryan, S., Plaut, V. C., Davies, P. G., & Steele, C. M. (2009). Ambient belonging: How stereotypical cues impact gender participation in computer science. *Journal of Personality and Social Psychology*, *97*, 1045–1060. https://doi.org/10.1037/a0016239

Chrousos, G. P., & Mentis, A.-F. A. (2020). Imposter syndrome threatens diversity. *Science*, *367*(6479), 749–750. https://doi.org/10.1126/science.aba8039

Clance, P. R., & Imes, S. A. (1978). The imposter phenomenon in high achieving women: Dynamics and therapeutic intervention. *Psychotherapy: Theory, Research & Practice*, *15*(3), 241. https://doi.org/10.1037/h0086006

Cohen, G. L., & Garcia, J. (2005). "I am us": Negative stereotypes as collective threats. *Journal of Personality and Social Psychology*, *89*(4), 566–582. https://doi.org/10.1037/0022-3514.89.4.566

Cohen, G. L., & Garcia, J. (2008). Identity, belonging, and achievement: A model, interventions, implications. *Current Directions in Psychological Science, 17*(6), 365–369.

Cohen, G. L., & Sherman, D. K. (2014). The psychology of change: Self-affirmation and social psychological intervention. *Annual Review of Psychology, 65*(1), 333–371. https://doi.org/10.1146/annurev-psych-010213-115137

Cohen, G. L., Steele, C. M., & Ross, L. D. (1999). The mentor's dilemma: Providing critical feedback across the racial divide. *Personality and Social Psychology Bulletin, 25*(10), 1302–1318. https://doi.org/10.1177/0146167299258011

Covarrubias, R. (2023). What does it mean to belong? An interdisciplinary integration of theory and research on belonging. *Social and Personality Psychology Compass, 18*(1), Article e12858. https://doi.org/10.1111/spc3.12858

Covarrubias, R., & Fryberg, S. A. (2015). The impact of self-relevant representations on school belonging for Native American students. *Cultural Diversity and Ethnic Minority Psychology, 21*(1), 10–18. https://doi.org/10.1037/a0037819

Crocker, J., Major, B., & Steele, C. (1998). Social stigma. In D. T. Gilbert, S. T. Fiske, & G. Lindzey (Eds.), *The handbook of social psychology* (4th ed., Vol 1-2, pp. 504–553). McGraw-Hill.

Dardenne, B., Dumont, M., & Bollier, T. (2007). Insidious dangers of benevolent sexism: Consequences for women's performance. *Journal of Personality and Social Psychology, 93*(5), 764–779. https://doi.org/10.1037/0022-3514.93.5.764

Dasgupta, N. (2011). Ingroup experts and peers as social vaccines who inoculate the self-concept: The stereotype inoculation model. *Psychological Inquiry, 22*(4), 231–246. https://doi.org/10.1080/1047840X.2011.607313

Deiglmayr, A., Stern, E., & Schubert, R. (2019). Beliefs in "brilliance" and belonging uncertainty in male and female STEM students. *Frontiers in Psychology, 10*, Article 01114. https://doi.org/10.3389/fpsyg.2019.01114

Dumont, M., Sarlet, M., & Dardenne, B. (2010). Be too kind to a woman, she'll feel incompetent: Benevolent sexism shifts self-construal and autobiographical memories toward incompetence. *Sex Roles, 62*(7), 545–553. https://doi.org/10.1007/s11199-008-9582-4

Edwards, J. D., Barthelemy, R. S., & Frey, R. F. (2022). Relationship between course-level social belonging (sense of belonging and belonging uncertainty) and academic performance in general chemistry 1. *Journal of Chemical Education, 99*(1), 71–82. https://doi.org/10.1021/acs.jchemed.1c00405

Fink, A. F., Frey, R., & D. Solomon, E. (2020). Belonging in general chemistry predicts first-year undergraduates' performance and attrition. *Chemistry Education Research and Practice, 21*(4), 1042–1062. https://doi.org/10.1039/D0RP00053A

Fink, A., Young, J. D., Vuppala, N. K., & Frey, R. F. (2023). Mixed-methods exploration of students' written belonging explanations from general chemistry at a selective institution. *Chemistry Education Research and Practice, 24*(1), 327–352 https://doi.org/10.1039/D2RP00166G

Flynn, F. J., & Chatman, J. A. (2001). Strong cultures and innovation: Oxymoron or opportunity? In S. Cartwright, C. Cooper, & P. C. Earley (Eds.), *International handbook of organizational culture and climate* (pp. 263–287). Wiley.

Garr-Schultz, A., Muragishi, G. A., Mortejo, T. A., & Cheryan, S. (2023). Masculine defaults in academic science, technology, engineering, and mathematics (STEM) fields. *Psychological Science in the Public Interest, 24*(1), 1–9. https://doi.org/10.1177/15291006231170829

Gilbertson, M. K., Brady, S. T., Ablorh, T., Logel, C., & Schnitker, S. A. (2022). Closeness to god, spiritual struggles, and wellbeing in the first year of college. *Frontiers in Psychology, 13*, Article 742265. https://doi.org/10.3389/fpsyg.2022.742265

Gopalan, M., Linden-Carmichael, A., & Lanza, S. (2022). College students' sense of belonging and mental health amidst the COVID-19 pandemic. *Journal of Adolescent Health, 70*(2), 228–233. https://doi.org/10.1016/j.jadohealth.2021.10.010

Goyer, J. P., Cohen, G. L., Cook, J. E., Master, A., Apfel, N., Lee, W., Henderson, A. G., Reeves, S. L., Okonofua, J. A., & Walton, G. M. (2019). Targeted identity-safety interventions cause lasting reductions in discipline citations among negatively stereotyped boys. *Journal of Personality and Social Psychology, 117*(2), 229–259. https://doi.org/10.1037/pspa0000152

Griffiths, C. M., Murdock-Perriera, L., & Eberhardt, J. L. (2023). "Can you tell me more about this?": Agentic written feedback, teacher expectations, and student learning. *Contemporary Educational Psychology, 73*, Article 102145. https://doi.org/10.1016/j.cedpsych.2022.102145

Guo, Y., & Schmader, T. (2025). Inauthentic or merely uncertain: When do people tolerate situations of identity misfit? In P. J. Carroll, K. Rios, & K. C. Oleson (Eds.), *Handbook of the uncertain self* (2nd ed.). Routledge.

Harackiewicz, J. M., Canning, E. A., Tibbetts, Y., Giffen, C. J., Blair, S. S., Rouse, D. I., & Hyde, J. S. (2014). Closing the social class achievement gap for first-generation students in undergraduate biology. *Journal of Educational Psychology*, *106*(2), 375–389. https://doi.org/10.1037/a0034679

Harackiewicz, J. M., Canning, E. A., Tibbetts, Y., Priniski, S. J., & Hyde, J. S. (2016). Closing achievement gaps with a utility-value intervention: Disentangling race and social class. *Journal of Personality and Social Psychology*, *111*(5), 745–765. https://doi.org/10.1037/pspp0000075

Hausmann, L. R. M., Ye, F., Schofield, J. W., & Woods, R. L. (2009). Sense of belonging and persistence in White and African American first-year students. *Research in Higher Education*, *50*(7), 649–669. https://doi.org/10.1007/s11162-009-9137-8

Hecht, C. A., Bryan, C. J., & Yeager, D. S. (2023). A values-aligned intervention fosters growth mindset–supportive teaching and reduces inequality in educational outcomes. *Proceedings of the National Academy of Sciences*, *120*(25), e2210704120. https://doi.org/10.1073/pnas.2210704120

Hecht, C. A., Dweck, C. S., Murphy, M. C., Kroeper, K. M., & Yeager, D. S. (2023). Efficiently exploring the causal role of contextual moderators in behavioral science. *Proceedings of the National Academy of Sciences*, *120*(1), e2216315120. https://doi.org/10.1073/pnas.2216315120

Hernández, M. M., Robins, R. W., Widaman, K. F., & Conger, R. D. (2017). Ethnic pride, self-esteem, and school belonging: A reciprocal analysis over time. *Developmental Psychology*, *53*(12), 2384. https://doi.org/10.1037/dev0000434

Höhne, E., Fekete, S. P., Schild, J., & Zander, L. (2022). Perceived stress, individual psychological resources, and social resources among computer science students during the covid-19 pandemic. *Frontiers in Education*, *7*. Retrieved from: https://www.frontiersin.org/articles/10.3389/feduc.2022.840216

Höhne, E., & Zander, L. (2019). Belonging uncertainty as predictor of dropout intentions among first-semester students of the computer sciences. *Zeitschrift Für Erziehungswissenschaft*, *22*(5), 1099–1119. https://doi.org/10.1007/s11618-019-00907-y

Janke, S., Messerer, L. A., Merkle, B., & Rudert, S. C. (2024). Why do minority students feel they don't fit in? Migration background and parental education differentially predict social ostracism and belongingness. *Group Processes & Intergroup Relations*, *27*(2) 278–299. https://doi.org/10.1177/13684302221142781

Jansen, W. S., Otten, S., & van der Zee, K. I. (2015). Being part of diversity: The effects of an all-inclusive multicultural diversity approach on majority members' perceived inclusion and support for organizational diversity efforts. *Group Processes & Intergroup Relations*, *18*(6), 817–832. https://doi.org/10.1177/1368430214566892

Kaplan, C. A, Griffiths, C. M., Hoxie, A.-M., Martin, S. E., & Brady, S. T. (2024). Teacher well-being and teacher race [Unpublished raw data]. Wake Forest University.

Kraus, L.-M., & Crul, M. (2022). Signalling inclusion, increasing belonging: People without a migration background in ethnically diverse neighbourhoods. *City, Culture and Society*, *30*, 100461. https://doi.org/10.1016/j.ccs.2022.100461

Laiduc, G., Herrmann, S., & Covarrubias, R. (2021). Relatable role models: An online intervention highlighting first-generation faculty benefits first-generation students. *Journal of First-Generation Student Success*, *1*(3), 159–186. https://doi.org/10.1080/26906015.2021.1983402

Lewis, K. L., & Hodges, S. D. (2015). Expanding the concept of belonging in academic domains: Development and validation of the ability uncertainty scale. *Learning and Individual Differences*, *37*, 197–202. https://doi.org/10.1016/j.lindif.2014.12.002

Lombard, E. J., & Cheryan, S. (2024). Does my work matter? Reduced sense of mattering as a source of gender disparities. *Social and Personality Psychology Compass*, *18*(1), Article e12907. https://doi.org/10.1111/spc3.12907

Maimon, M. R., Sanchez, D. T., Albuja, A. F., & Howansky, K. (2021). Bisexual identity denial and health: Exploring the role of societal meta-perceptions and belonging threats among bisexual adults. *Self and Identity*, *20*(4), 515–527. https://doi.org/10.1080/15298868.2019.1624275

Mallett, R. K., Mello, Z. R., Wagner, D. E., Worrell, F., Burrow, R. N., & Andretta, J. R. (2011). Do I belong? It depends on when you ask. *Cultural Diversity and Ethnic Minority Psychology*, *17*(4), 432–436. https://doi.org/10.1037/a0025455

Manai, O., Yamada, H., & Thorn, C. (2016). Real-time indicators and targeted supports: Using online platform data to accelerate student learning. *Proceedings of the Sixth International Conference on Learning Analytics & Knowledge*, 183–187. https://doi.org/10.1145/2883851.2883942

Manke, K. J., Brady, S. T., Baker, M. D., & Cohen, G. L. (2021). Affirmation on the go: A proof-of-concept for text message delivery of values affirmation in education. *Journal of Social Issues*, *77*(3), 888–910. https://doi.org/10.1111/josi.12435

Cheryan, S., & Markus, H. R. (2020). Masculine defaults: Identifying and mitigating hidden cultural biases. *Psychological Review*, *127*(6), 1022–1052. https://doi.org/10.1037/rev0000209

McPartlan, P., Solanki, S., Xu, D., & Sato, B. (2020). Testing basic assumptions reveals when (not) to expect mindset and belonging interventions to succeed. *AERA Open*, *6*(4), 233285842096699. https://doi.org/10.1177/2332858420966994

Mendoza-Denton, R., Patt, C., Fisher, A., Eppig, A., Young, I., Smith, A., & Richards, M. A. (2017). Differences in STEM doctoral publication by ethnicity, gender and academic field at a large public research university. *PLOS ONE*, *12*(4), e0174296. https://doi.org/10.1371/journal.pone.0174296

Mendoza-Denton, R., Patt, C., & Richards, M. (2018). Go beyond bias training. *Nature*, *557*(7705), 299–301. https://doi.org/10.1038/d41586-018-05144-7

Morgenroth, T., Ryan, M. K., & Peters, K. (2015). The motivational theory of role modeling: How role models influence role aspirants' goals. *Review of General Psychology*, *19*(4), 465–483. https://doi.org/10.1037/gpr0000059

Moser, C. E., & Branscombe, N. R. (2022). Male allies at work: Gender-equality supportive men reduce negative underrepresentation effects among women. *Social Psychological and Personality Science*, *13*(2), 372–381. https://doi.org/10.1177/19485506211033748

Muragishi, G. A., Aguilar, L., Carr, P. B., & Walton, G. M. (2024). Microinclusions: Treating women as respected work partners increases a sense of fit in technology companies. *Journal of Personality and Social Psychology*. *126*(3), 431–460. https://doi.org/10.1037/pspi0000430

Murphy, M. C., & Taylor, V. J. (2012). The role of situational cues in signaling and maintaining stereotype threat. In M. Inzlicht & T. Schmader (Eds.), *Stereotype threat: Theory, process, and application* (pp. 17–33). Oxford University Press.

Murphy, M. C., Gopalan, M., Carter, E. R., Emerson, K. T., Bottoms, B. L., & Walton, G. M. (2020). A customized belonging intervention improves retention of socially disadvantaged students at a broad-access university. *Science Advances*, *6*(29), eaba4677. https://doi.org/10.1126/sciadv.aba4677

Murphy, M. C., Steele, C. M., & Gross, J. J. (2007). Signaling threat: How situational cues affect women in math, science, and engineering settings. *Psychological Science*, *18*, 879–885. https://doi.org/10.1111/j.1467-9280.2007.01995.x

Murphy, M. C., & Zirkel, S. (2015). Race and belonging in school: How anticipated and experienced belonging affect choice, persistence, and performance. *Teachers College Record*, *117*(12), 1–40. https://doi.org/10.1177/016146811511701204

Murrar, S., Campbell, M. R., & Brauer, M. (2020). Exposure to peers' pro-diversity attitudes increases inclusion and reduces the achievement gap. *Nature Human Behaviour*, *4*(9), 889–897. https://doi.org/10.1038/s41562-020-0899-5

Nickerson, R. S. (1998). Confirmation bias: A ubiquitous phenomenon in many guises. *Review of General Psychology*, *2*(2), 175–220. https://doi.org/10.1037/1089-2680.2.2.175

Offidani-Bertrand, C., Velez, G., Benz, C., & Keels, M. (2022). "I wasn't expecting it": High school experiences and navigating belonging in the transition to college. *Emerging Adulthood*, *10*(1), 212–224. https://doi.org/10.1177/2167696819882117

Pathakis, K. M. (2020). *Who belongs in American democracy? The importance of belonging to political engagement for underrepresented groups*. University of California, San Diego.

Pronin, E., Steele, C. M., & Ross, L. (2004). Identity bifurcation in response to stereotype threat: Women and mathematics. *Journal of Experimental Social Psychology*, *40*(2), 152–168. https://doi.org/10.1016/S0022-1031(03)00088-X

Purdie-Vaughns, V., Steele, C. M., Davies, P. G., Ditlmann, R., & Crosby, J. R. (2008). Social identity contingencies: How diversity cues signal threat or safety for African Americans in mainstream institutions. *Journal of Personality and Social Psychology*, *94*(4), 615.

Putnam, R. D. (2001). *Bowling alone*. Simon & Schuster.

Pyne, J., & Borman, G. D. (2020). Replicating a scalable intervention that helps students reappraise academic and social adversity during the transition to middle school. *Journal of Research on Educational Effectiveness*, *13*(4), 652–678. https://doi.org/10.1080/19345747.2020.1784330

Salvatore, J., & Shelton, J. N. (2007). Cognitive costs of exposure to racial prejudice. *Psychological Science*, *18*(9), 810–815. https://doi.org/10.1111/j.1467-9280.2007.01984.x

Schmader, T., & Sedikides, C. (2018). State authenticity as fit to environment: The implications of social identity for fit, authenticity, and self-segregation. *Personality and Social Psychology Review*, *22*(3), 228–259. https://doi.org/10.1177/1088868317734080

Scrivener, S., Weiss, M. J., Ratledge, A., Rudd, T., Sommo, C., & Fresques, H. (2015). *Doubling graduation rates: Three-year effects of CUNY's accelerated study in associate programs (ASAP) for developmental education students.* New York: MDRC. https://files.eric.ed.gov/fulltext/ED558511.pdf

Shapiro, J. R., & Neuberg, S. L. (2007). From stereotype threat to stereotype threats: Implications of a multi-threat framework for causes, moderators, mediators, consequences, and interventions. *Personality and Social Psychology Review*, *11*(2), 107–130. https://doi.org/10.1177/1088868306294790

Shaw, S. T., Spink, K., & Chin-Newman, C. (2019). "Do I really belong here?": The stigma of being a community college transfer student at a four-year university. *Community College Journal of Research and Practice*, *43*(9), 657–660.

Slank, S. (2019). Rethinking the imposter phenomenon. *Ethical Theory and Moral Practice*, *22*(1), 205–218. https://doi.org/10.1007/s10677-019-09984-8

Sleeter, C. E., & Zavala, M. (2020). *Transformative ethnic studies in schools: Curriculum, pedagogy, and research.* Teachers College Press.

Slepian, M. L., & Jacoby-Senghor, D. S. (2020). Identity threats in everyday life: Distinguishing belonging from inclusion. *Social Psychological and Personality Science, 12*(3), 392–405. https://doi.org/10.1177/1948550619895008

Smith, J. L., Cech, E., Metz, A., Huntoon, M., & Moyer, C. (2014). Giving back or giving up: Native American student experiences in science and engineering. *Cultural Diversity and Ethnic Minority Psychology*, *20*(3), 413–429.

Smith, J. M., & Lucena, J. C. (2016). Invisible innovators: How low-income, first-generation students use their funds of knowledge to belong in engineering. *Engineering Studies*, *8*(1), 1–26. https://doi.org/10.1080/19378629.2016.1155593

Snyder, M., & Swann, W. B. (1978). Hypothesis-testing processes in social interaction. *Journal of Personality and Social Psychology*, *36*(11), 1202–1212. https://doi.org/10.1037/0022-3514.36.11.1202

Spencer, S. J., Zanna, M. P., & Fong, G. T. (2005). Establishing a causal chain: Why experiments are often more effective than mediational analyses in examining psychological processes. *Journal of Personality and Social Psychology*, *89*(6), 845–851. https://doi.org/10.1037/0022-3514.89.6.845

Steele, C. M. (1988). The psychology of self-affirmation: Sustaining the integrity of the self. *Advances in Experimental Social Psychology*, *21*, 261–302. https://doi.org/10.1016/S0065-2601(08)60229-4

Steele, C. M. (1997). A threat in the air: How stereotypes shape intellectual identity and performance. *American Psychologist*, *52*(6), 613–629. https://doi.org/10.1037/0003-066X.52.6.613

Steele, C. (2011). *Whistling Vivaldi: How stereotypes affect us and what we can do*. Norton.

Stubblebine, A. M., Gopalan, M., & Brady, S. T. (2024). Who feels like they belong? Personality and belonging in college. *PLOS ONE, 19*(1), Aritcle e0295436. https://doi.org/10.1371/journal.pone.0295436

Tormala, Z. L. (2016). The role of certainty (and uncertainty) in attitudes and persuasion. *Current Opinion in Psychology*, *10*, 6–11. https://doi.org/10.1016/j.copsyc.2015.10.017

Totonchi, D. A., Tibbetts, Y., Williams, C. L., Francis, M. K., DeCoster, J., Lee, G. A., Hull, J. W., & Hulleman, C. S. (2023). The cost of being first: Belonging uncertainty predicts math motivation and achievement for first-generation, but not continuing-generation, students. *Learning and Individual Differences*, *107*, Article 102365. https://doi.org/10.1016/j.lindif.2023.102365

van Vianen, A. E. M. (2018). Person–environment fit: A review of its basic tenets. *Annual Review of Organizational Psychology and Organizational Behavior*, *5*(1), 75–101. https://doi.org/10.1146/annurev-orgpsych-032117-104702

Walton, G. M., & Brady, S. T. (2017). The many questions of belonging. In A. J. Elliot, C. S. Dweck, & D. S. Yeager (Eds.), *Handbook of competence and motivation: Theory and application* (2nd ed., pp. 272–293). Guilford Press.

Walton, G. M., & Brady, S. T. (2020). "Bad" things reconsidered. In J. P. Forgas, W. D. Crano, & K. Fielder (Eds.), *Applications of social psychology: How social psychology can contribute to the solution of real-world problems* (pp. 58–81). Routledge.

Walton, G. M., & Brady, S. T. (2021). The social-belonging intervention. In G. M. Walton & A. J. Crum (Eds.), *Handbook of wise interventions: How social psychology can help people change* (pp. 36–62). Guilford Press.

Walton, G. M., & Cohen, G. L. (2007). A question of belonging: Race, social fit, and achievement. *Journal of Personality and Social Psychology*, *92*(1), 82–96. https://doi.org/10.1037/0022-3514.92.1.82

Walton, G. M., & Cohen, G. L. (2011). A brief social-belonging intervention improves academic and health outcomes of minority students. *Science*, *331*(6023), 1447–1451. https://doi.org/10.1126/science.1198364

Walton, G. M., & Wilson, T. D. (2018). Wise interventions: Psychological remedies for social and personal problems. *Psychological Bulletin*, 125(5), 617–655. https://doi.org/10.1037/rev0000115

Walton, G. M., Logel, C., Peach, J. M., Spencer, S. J., & Zanna, M. P. (2015). Two brief interventions to mitigate a "chilly climate" transform women's experience, relationships, and achievement in engineering. *Journal of Educational Psychology*, *107*(2), 468–485. https://doi.org/10.1037/a0037461

Walton, G. M., Murphy, M. C., Logel, C., Yeager, D. S., Goyer, J. P., Brady, S. T., Emerson, K. T. U., Paunesku, D., Fotuhi, O., Blodorn, A., Boucher, K. L., Carter, E. R., Gopalan, M., Henderson, A., Kroeper, K. M., Murdock-Perriera, L. A., Reeves, S. L., Ablorh, T. T., Ansari, S., … Krol, N. (2023). Where and with whom does a brief social-belonging intervention promote progress in college? *Science*, *380*(6644), 499–505. https://doi.org/10.1126/science.ade4420

Williams, C. L., Hirschi, Q., Sublett, K. V., Hulleman, C. S., & Wilson, T. D. (2020). A brief social belonging intervention improves academic outcomes for minoritized high school students. *Motivation Science*, *6*(4), 423–437. https://doi.org/10.1037/mot0000175

Yeager, D. S., Bryk, A., Muhich, J., Hausman, H., & Morales, L. (2013). *Practical measurement.* Palo Alto, CA: Carnegie Foundation for the Advancement of Teaching, 78712. Retrieved from: https://www.carnegiefoundation.org/wp-content/uploads/2013/12/*Practical_Measurement*.pdf

Yeager, D. S., Hanselman, P., Walton, G. M., Murray, J. S., Crosnoe, R., Muller, C., Tipton, E., Schneider, B., Hulleman, C. S., Hinojosa, C. P., Paunesku, D., Romero, C., Flint, K., Roberts, A., Trott, J., Iachan, R., Buontempo, J., Yang, S. M., Carvalho, C. M., … Dweck, C. S. (2019). A national experiment reveals where a growth mindset improves achievement. *Nature*, *573*(7774), Article 7774. https://doi.org/10.1038/s41586-019-1466-y

Yeager, D. S., Purdie-Vaughns, V., Garcia, J., Apfel, N., Brzustoski, P., Master, A., Hessert, W. T., Williams, M. E., & Cohen, G. L. (2014). Breaking the cycle of mistrust: Wise interventions to provide critical feedback across the racial divide. *Journal of Experimental Psychology: General*, *143*(2), 804–824. https://doi.org/10.1037/a0033906

Yeager, D. S., Walton, G. M., Brady, S. T., Akcinar, E. N., Paunesku, D., Keane, L., Kamentz, D., Ritter, G., Duckworth, A. L., Urstein, R., Gomez, E. M., Markus, H. R., Cohen, G. L., & Dweck, C. S. (2016). Teaching a lay theory before college narrows achievement gaps at scale. *Proceedings of the National Academy of Sciences*, *113*(24), E3341–E3348. https://doi.org/10.1073/pnas.1524360113

Zander, L., & Ertl, B. (2023). Female students' belonging uncertainty in higher education STEM environments: Explanations and indications. In P. Watson, D. Rubie-Davies, & B. Ertl (Eds.), *The international handbook of gender beliefs, stereotype threat, and teacher expectations: Sharing solutions for safer spaces* (pp. 61–78). Routledge.

21
DOUBT AS A FORM OF SPIRITUAL STRUGGLE

Julie J. Exline, Yehudis Keller, Andrew C. Moffitt and Kenneth I. Pargament

For many people, religion helps to address big existential questions around the nature of ultimate reality. Religious teachings can provide believers with a sense of security (Granqvist et al., 2010) and meaning (Park, 2013) by helping to answer these core questions. However, religion does not always provide satisfying answers. Religion can also introduce new sources of strain or doubt. In this chapter, we will explore these doubt-related struggles around religion, including those relevant to the uncertain self. In line with the definition given in Chapter 1, we use the term *uncertain self* to refer to a subjective sense of doubt or instability in self-views, world-views, and the interrelation between the two (Rios, Oleson, & Carroll, this volume). We will consider ways that doubt might creep in to challenge religious beliefs, and we will conclude by reflecting on how doubts might lead to both distress and growth.

Before we discuss religious doubt, we will take a step back to consider a basic question: What functions do religious beliefs serve, especially in terms of meaning-making and security? Reflecting on this question should make it easy to see how challenges to foundational beliefs could indeed make people feel "shaken to the core" (Pargament & Exline, 2022, 2023).

The Quest for Meaning: How Might Religion Play in?

Human beings are meaning-making creatures. We want to feel like our lives have purpose and value, as reflected in constructs such as meaning in life (George & Park, 2016; Steger et al., 2006), global meaning (Park, 2010), and the personal orienting systems that help people make sense of the world (Pargament, 1997). In comparison with those who lack a strong sense of meaning in their lives, people who find an overarching sense of meaning tend to do better psychologically, reporting less distress and greater well-being (Steger et al., 2006). Many people continue to search for a deep sense of meaning in life (Steger et al., 2006), which relates to the idea of a *quest orientation* to religion—a mindset in which people hold their religious beliefs loosely, embrace uncertainty, and expect beliefs to continue shifting over time (Batson & Schoenrade, 1991; Beck & Jessup, 2004).

Sometimes the search for meaning leads people toward *spirituality*, which we define as a search for the sacred (Pargament et al., 2013). Spirituality involves, in part, a quest for answers to ultimate questions, and it often includes a sense of tapping into something transcendent or divine. Although

 DOI: 10.4324/9781003363385-24

people may experience spirituality in ways that are entirely personal and private, spirituality often takes place in a religious context. Religion takes this search for the sacred to a group level, where people join together around shared beliefs or practices (Pargament et al., 2013). Religious beliefs and identities can be a major part of a person's global meaning system (Park, 2013) or the orienting system that helps guide them through their lives (Pargament, 1997). So it makes sense that when life stressors or crises arise, many people turn to religion to help them cope (Pargament, 1997, 2011).

What core questions does religion try to answer? Granted, not all religions address all of the questions below. But by sketching out this list, we hope to provide a clearer sense of why people turn to religion–and why doubts around core religious beliefs could upset people.

Who/What Else Is Out There?

Many religions speak of an enchanted world, one populated by supernatural agents: deities, devils, angels, human spirits—or powerful forces such as karma, fate, destiny, or luck. (See Exline & Wilt, 2023, for a review of supernatural attributions.) Religions often provide information about the supernatural operating rules (Exline et al., 2023) of these entities: Do supernatural beings intervene in our daily lives? How can we please the gods, or ward off evil influences? Is two-way communication possible?

How Our World Began

Many religions offer foundational stories to explain the origins of life on our planet (Smith, 1958). They might explain how the Earth fits into the broader universe: Are humans indeed at the center of everything? Their narratives might try to explain why human beings are here, as well as our level of significance: Do we have a specific purpose? How much do our lives and efforts matter? What happens when we die?

People who lack a strong sense of identity might find it especially comforting to find a compelling narrative about where they came from, why they are here, and where they belong. But tough questions can arise: When people suffer from chronic physical or psychological challenges, or if their sexual orientations or gender identities go against religious norms (Anderton et al., 2011; Herek & McLemore, 2013), they might wonder, "Did God make me this way? And if so, why?" (Etengoff et al., 2023; Grubbs & Exline, 2014).

What People Are Like

Religious origin stories may also give clues about people's basic qualities (Barbour, 2002): Are we fundamentally good or bad? Do we have free will, or are we mere pawns of the gods or victims of fate? Are we simply animals, or do we occupy a special category (perhaps even the very pinnacle of creation)? Of course, there is no guarantee that religions will provide comforting answers to these questions; on the contrary, some might portray humans as weak, foolish, or morally corrupt. But regardless, religions often do make claims about what people are like and what we can expect from them. Again, there are many connections to the uncertain self here: People who struggle with chronic self-doubt may seek reassurance that they are valuable, morally good, agentic beings who can also count on supernatural assistance.

How Things Should Be

Religions often take the form of moral communities, where people join together around shared values (Graham & Haidt, 2010). Most religions convey some set of ideals that describe what a good, well-lived life looks like—as well as ideal visions of human relationships and society. They often create a shared moral code: Which behaviors are right vs. wrong? Which offenses are most serious? What happens to rule-breakers? By addressing such questions, religious teachings may appeal to those seeking moral guidance—and perhaps especially those feeling unsure that they can trust their own moral compass (Schutt & Exline, 2023).

How Things Will Be

Religious traditions often provide a vision of the future of humanity: Are we evolving in a positive direction, or are we heading toward an apocalypse or cosmic abyss (Stewart & Harding, 1999)? Over the centuries, humans have turned to prophecies, oracles, and fortune-telling to pursue glimpses of future events (Ashe, 2001). Many religions also speak of an afterlife (Johnson, 2018), whether in the form of heaven, hell, a spirit realm, or reincarnation. People may turn to their faith for guidance about how to ensure a good afterlife—perhaps via correct beliefs, transformative experiences, good deeds, or sacred rituals.

Who's in Charge?

Religions often provide guidance about the ultimate, most trustworthy sources of authority: Who is qualified to make religious truth claims? Who can generate, change, or enforce the tradition's rules? Even if they see deities as their ultimate guides, people still need to receive and transmit these divine messages somehow. To accomplish this goal, religions might turn to charismatic leaders, prophecies, sacred texts, or oral traditions. Especially when people feel unsure of their own decision-making abilities, they may find great comfort in having a clear, external source of authority to follow. Depending on their moral foundations (Graham et al., 2011), believers may see obedience to this authority as a moral imperative. If so, they may frame challenges to religious leaders, texts, or teachings as acts of rebellion against the divine.

Who's on My Team?

Religion's communal aspects can help to meet the powerful human need to belong (Baumeister & Leary, 1995) while clarifying ingroup/outgroup boundaries: Who is part of my tribe, and who is not? How should I treat outgroup members? People with high levels of self-uncertainty might value groups that boost a sense of belonging (Brady, in press; Saroglou, 2011) and identity (Ysseldyk et al., 2010).

In short, religion can offer answers to deep human and existential questions, many of which are directly relevant to the uncertain self. These meaning-making and security-building functions can build on other benefits of religion, such as social support and spiritual practices (Saroglou, 2011). As such, it makes sense that many people turn to religion for meaning-making (Park, 2013) or as a coping resource (Pargament, 1997). But it doesn't always work. Sometimes religion actually becomes a source of stress.

Religious and Spiritual Struggles, Including Struggles with Doubt

We use the term *religious and spiritual struggles* (or simply *spiritual struggles*) to refer to experiences of tension, strain, or conflict that people encounter around religion and spirituality (Pargament & Exline, 2022). We developed the Religious and Spiritual Struggles (RSS) Scale (Exline et al., 2014) and the shorter RSS-14 (Exline et al., 2022) to assess several common types of spiritual struggles. Both measures assess six types of struggles, one of which involves doubts and questions about religious beliefs. The other five struggle types include: *interpersonal* (conflicts or hurts involving religious people or communities), *divine* (negative thoughts or emotions involving beliefs about God), *demonic* (feeling attacked or tempted by the devil or evil spirits), *ultimate meaning* (questioning whether there is a deeper purpose to life), and *moral* (struggling to do what's right or feeling guilty about moral failures). Although these six types of spiritual struggle are conceptually and empirically distinct, they correlate positively with each other (Exline, Pargament et al., 2014, 2022). As we examine doubt struggles in this chapter, it should be easy to see many common threads that they share with other spiritual struggles.

Why should researchers study spiritual struggles? One reason is that many people experience them. In a survey of over 17,000 U.S. adults (Exline, Pargament, & Grubbs, 2014), 70% reported some type of spiritual struggle in the past few weeks. Spiritual struggles also show consistent links with indicators of psychological distress, such as anxiety and depression (e.g., Abu-Raiya et al. 2015; see Pargament & Exline, 2022, for a recent review). Pargament and Lomax (2013) suggested that spiritual struggles can be *primary* (spiritual struggles predict psychological distress), *secondary* (psychological problems lead to spiritual struggles), or *complex* (psychological distress predicts increased spiritual struggle and vice versa). Longitudinal studies have shown evidence for all three patterns (e.g., primary: meta-analysis by Bockrath et al., 2021; secondary: Wilt et al., 2017; complex: Cowden et al., 2022). In short, there is abundant evidence that spiritual struggles are linked with distress.

This chapter will focus on doubt-related struggles. Here are the four items from the RSS Doubt subscale (Exline, Pargament et al., 2014): (Those marked by* are on the RSS-14 (Exline et al., 2022).)

- Struggled to figure out what I really believe about religion/spirituality.
- Felt confused about my religious/spiritual beliefs.*
- Felt troubled by doubts or questions about religion or spirituality.*
- Worried about whether my beliefs about religion/spirituality were correct.

Many people experience these doubt-related struggles around religion. In our study of over 17,000 U.S. adults (Exline et al., 2014), 35% reported some level of doubt-related struggle in the past few weeks. People who disengage from organized religion often show elevated levels of doubt-related struggles (Exline et al., 2020) and religious doubt more broadly (Fisher, 2016; Hunsberger et al., 2002; see also Gull, 2022; McLaughlin et al., 2020). Importantly, doubt-related struggles are not limited to people who identify as religious. Nonreligious people, including atheists and those identifying as "spiritual but not religious," can also experience doubt (Exline et al., 2020; Sedlar et al., 2018). In cases like these, people might doubt their earlier religious beliefs, or they might question their nonbelief itself. On average, people who have left religion (religious "dones" or the religiously disengaged) report more doubt-related struggles than those who were never religious (religious "nones" or "nevers"; Exline et al., 2020). This finding is consistent with the idea of a *religious residue effect* (cf. Van Tongeren et al., 2021), in which individuals who have left religion continue to think and behave more like religious people vs. people who were never religious.

Both religious doubts and doubt-related struggles show consistent links with distress (for reviews, see Flannelly, 2017; Pargament & Exline, 2022) and psychiatric symptoms (Galek et al., 2007), including depression (Moffitt et al., 2024; Upenieks et al., 2023; Willis et al., 2019), anxiety (Moffitt et al., 2022; Galek et al., 2007; Wilt et al., 2017), and death anxiety (Henrie & Patrick, 2014; Willis et al., 2019), along with insecure attachment (Love et al., 2022) and lower self-esteem and life satisfaction (Krause, 2008; Moffitt et al., 2022). But doubt also has a hopeful side: When controlling for overlap with other spiritual struggles, doubt struggles can flip direction and become predictive of less depression (Exline, Pargament et al., 2014; Exline et al., 2022; Wong & Pargament, 2019). We will take a closer look at these links with distress later. For now, we will start with origins: What exactly is doubt, and how might it find its way into religious beliefs?

Doubt: Basic Concepts and Application to Religion

Before getting into the specifics of religious doubt, we should clarify what we mean by the term *doubt.* We have found Sayre's (1997) philosophical work helpful here. According to Sayre, doubt arises when people are considering *propositions.* Propositions are ideas that a person could evaluate as true or false—or maybe somewhere in between, like "a little bit true" or "mostly false." Beliefs are attitudes about propositions: When people form a belief, they are taking a stand on the correctness of the proposition concerned. When people believe in things, they have decided (or affirmed) that a proposition is true. They might also disaffirm the belief, deciding that the proposition is not true. But there can be a big middle ground because often people simply are not sure whether a proposition is true; and this is where doubt comes in. According to Sayre (1997), when people doubt, they lack confidence or certainty about whether a certain belief is true or untrue. We have also framed doubt as a middle ground between belief and unbelief (Pargament & Exline, 2022).

Of course, people might immediately doubt new claims that they hear. For instance, a person might hear something that they immediately evaluate as false–perhaps even as a lie or manipulation attempt. Here, doubt would be a quick stop on the way to dismissing the information, and the idea never makes its way into a person's belief system. Such cases might not prompt much doubt-related struggle—although there could be conflict with the person introducing the idea, as in reactions to proselytizing.

In other cases, new ideas might seem more persuasive, and a person might start to evaluate and compare ideas. But what if they cannot settle on a satisfying belief? Some might set the decision aside for later, whereas others might relegate it to a realm of mystery. For some people, this sense of indecision, or the effort put into the exploration and evaluation, could be stressful. Such indecision could be reflected in an uncertain sense of self, as people struggle with issues of identity, core beliefs, values, and life purpose (Rios & Morales, in press). If people feel unsure about their beliefs, or if their beliefs are weakly held, they may find it difficult to focus their energies.

In the sections below, we will focus mainly on challenges to existing beliefs—in this case, religious beliefs. So we will be emphasizing beliefs around the big questions raised above, and we will assume that people have already considered these beliefs to some degree. Hunsberger and his colleagues (1993, p. 28) have defined *religious doubt* as "… a feeling of uncertainty toward, or questioning of, religious teachings and beliefs." In some cases, people might experience religious doubt as a gray area, an error term, or a sense of "fuzziness" around a specific belief. Some people may feel chronically confused about which beliefs are correct, while others may feel as though the certainty of their beliefs is eroding, declining, or weakening. Our next aim is to consider some potential sources of religious doubt: What factors might create challenges to religious beliefs—forming holes or cracks in their foundations?

Seeds of Religious Doubt

Religions generate a wealth of propositions, as we described above. They include claims about origins, supernatural beings, and the future, along with moral codes, authority structures, and ingroup/outgroup boundaries. What are the odds that a person will fully embrace every single claim from a given tradition? There are many opportunities for doubt to creep in.

Scholars have begun to pinpoint sources of religious doubt. For example, Kooistra (1990) identified several sources of doubt among Christian high school students: problems of evil, violations of self-interest, hypocrisy, conflicting evidence, failures of ritual, the problem of relativism, and questions about whether humans invented the idea of God to serve personal needs. Later, Kooistra and Pargament (1999) assessed the degree of uncertainty and wondering that people experienced around specific Christian beliefs (e.g., the existence of God, heaven, and hell). Altemeyer and Hunsberger (1997) made a measure including 20 reasons for religious doubt, ranging from intellectual reasons (e.g., God's existence; evolution vs. creation; Bible is God's word) to interpersonal concerns (e.g., intolerance; hypocrisy; harms committed in the name of religion). Krause and Ellison (2009) asked participants to indicate how often they experienced doubts focused on four domains; their faith, what they had learned in church, whether prayers make a difference, and whether God was directly involved in their lives). More recently, Henrie and Patrick (2014) listed reasons for religious doubt that echoed many of the above themes. Although our measurement discussion here is necessarily brief, we hope to at least give a sense of the tools scholars have used to assess reasons for doubt.

How might we integrate these diverse ideas about sources of religious doubt? Given the huge array of claims that religions can make, it would be overwhelming to try to catalog all of the specific sources of doubt. So we take a different approach here. Below, we organize our ideas around three broad sources of doubt: cognitive, emotional/motivational, and social. (For brevity, this section focuses on broad themes. Although we do not repeat citations to specific measures or studies, we note that most studies mentioned above tapped one or more of these sources of doubt).

Cognitive Sources of Doubt

Although people may be willing to take certain things "on faith," this tendency should have limits. Truth claims should need to surpass some bar of reasonable plausibility before people will believe them (Exline & Wilt, 2023). In their attempts to answer so many core questions, religious systems cover a lot of ground as they try to shed light on topics often shrouded in mystery. Many cognitive sources of doubt could creep in as people consider these religious truth claims, and we will review a few of these next.

Problems of Logical Consistency and Coherence

Do the basic beliefs and claims of a tradition make sense? Whether they are listening to religious stories or learning about the moral teachings of a given tradition, people may be troubled by logical inconsistencies. Some might center on historical claims within a text. For example, the Christian Bible includes some discrepancies in accounts of key events (e.g., differing Gospel accounts of Jesus' birth, death, and resurrection). Moral directives might also seem to contradict one another (e.g., "Are we supposed to love our enemies or fight against them?" "Is sex sacred or impure?") Such inconsistencies could easily become a source of doubt.

Problems of Evidence

Doubt may arise if a person does not see strong evidence supporting key claims of a tradition. For example, people might not see evidence suggesting the existence of a deity, evil spirits, or an afterlife; not only have they not had relevant personal experiences, but they are not persuaded by other people's accounts. What if a religious conversion is expected to lead to a dramatic life transformation, but the person feels or acts the same as before? Religions might also offer people prophecies about the future, which could range from election winners to the end of the world: But what happens when these prophecies fail (cf. Festinger et al., 1956)?

In other cases, evidence from trusted sources might directly contradict religious teachings. For example, people raised to believe literally in the biblical account of a seven-day creation (Genesis 1) may learn about scientific theories (e.g., evolution; quantum theory) or evidence (e.g., from geology, archaeology, or biology) that challenge this explanation (Rios & Morales, in press). Or consider a case in which someone has a spiritually transformative experience that is "off the grid" of their faith tradition. For example, imagine a person who believes that people go straight to heaven or hell after they die, and how these beliefs might be profoundly shaken by a near-death experience or memories that seem to suggest a past life.

Questioning Religious Leaders

Religions often promote certain people, texts, or methods (e.g., prophecy) as sources of authority. But here, too, doubts could creep in. People might begin to question the expertise of leaders: Do they have the tools to evaluate scientific claims, for instance? And what if leaders show their own moral failings–perhaps in the form of hypocrisy, abuse, or financial exploitation?

Of course, when religious leaders or communities misbehave, people may react not only with reduced trust in their judgment, but with anger and distaste: They want to distance themselves from the group, and they could develop an associated distaste for the group's beliefs. This point leads directly into the next section.

Emotional/Motivational Sources of Doubt

On its surface, the topic of doubt might seem to focus entirely on analytical reasoning and rational thought. But emotions and motivations could also fuel doubt. Negative emotions such as anxiety can fuel doubt-related struggles, as shown in longitudinal work (Wilt et al., 2017). People might also be motivated to reject religious truth claims that they see as distasteful, using the argument that Kunda (1990) developed in her classic article on motivated reasoning: At some level, people believe what they want to believe. Terror management research also suggests that people will revise their attitudes in order to defend their worldviews (Arndt et al., 1997), and people may also shift their beliefs to resolve uncomfortable states of dissonance (Festinger, 1957; for an application to LGBTQ+ identities, see Anderton et al., 2011). As applied to religious beliefs, it makes sense that people will hold on tightly to beliefs that feel good, whereas they tend to doubt or dismiss beliefs associated with fear, guilt, or sadness. Along these lines, we have found that when people reflect on their belief in supernatural entities (e.g., God; karma; spirits), desires to believe correlate strongly with actual levels of belief (Wilt et al., 2022).

Taken together, this body of work raises the possibility that emotion and motivation could feed into religious doubt: People might simply not want to believe certain teachings. Why? We will consider a few examples here.

Negative Emotions Focused on Religion or Religious People

As mentioned above, sometimes religious leaders or community members behave badly—by manipulating, abusing, or cheating people, for instance. When others learn about these offenses, their trust in the leaders may erode; but they may also feel strong negative emotions such as anger, contempt, disgust, or even hatred toward religion or religious people. As such, they might begin to seriously doubt and oppose any claims or positions of the group (McGraw et al., 2018). These negative emotions should be even more powerful if the group caused direct harm to them or to close others, making the offense more personal.

Moral Codes Seem Wrong or Oppressive

Sometimes problems arise from religious beliefs themselves, rather than religious people. Many of these issues stem from the moral codes that religions typically produce. What if a particular religious teaching directly contradicts a person's deeply held personal values? For example, how might a pacifist struggle when reading a religious text that promotes violence against outgroup members (cf. Bushman et al., 2007)? What about a parent who believes strongly that they need to support their young adult child's gender transition, knowing that their faith tradition only accepts cisgender identities and behaviors (cf. Exline, Przeworski et al., 2021)? Or consider the person who sees religion's focus on the afterlife as a distraction from vital concerns in this world, such as environmental or human rights crises. In cases like these, doubts arise from the person's own conscience: The religion's moral codes simply seem wrong.

People might also hesitate to adopt or follow religious codes that seem oppressive. Religious rules may prohibit people from doing things they really want to do (e.g., drink alcohol; have sex). Some religious teachings also promote grim views of human nature, suggesting that people are fundamentally corrupt, weak, or helpless. It would make sense for people to try to avoid these depressing and confidence-stripping thoughts about themselves and others. In addition, a strong focus on sin and its punishing consequences could amplify fear and guilt around moral failures. Religions may create moral standards that seem impossible to reach, feeding perfectionistic strivings (Allen & Wang, 2014) or a sense of hopelessness.

Supernatural Beliefs Are Disturbing

Some supernatural beliefs are scary. People could find it terrifying to think of the world in the hands of an angry, punitive God or under demonic control. They might also have fears about an afterlife: What if ghosts start haunting them? What if their misdeeds in this life will lead to karmic retribution in some future life (White & Norenzayan, 2019)? What if they or their loved ones end up in hell forever? Some people with secular worldviews might find even benevolent supernatural beliefs to be upsetting because the idea that a supernatural or spiritual world exists would require a dramatic shift in their orienting systems. Along these lines, we did a study in which we asked atheists and agnostics how they might feel if they saw compelling evidence that God existed (Exline et al., 2015). Confusion was, by far, the predominant response, and some participants also expected to feel afraid, ashamed, or angry.

Social Influence as a Source of Religious Doubt

Our own writing has framed doubt-related struggles as being *intrapersonal*–within the person (Pargament & Exline, 2022). But religious doubts could also stem from social sources, in which case doubt struggles and interpersonal religious struggles would go hand in hand.

Dissenters Raise Questions

As discussed above, people could doubt religious teachings if they question the skill or character of their leaders. Social influence processes could also play a major role here. Like participants in classic obedience and conformity studies (Asch, 1956; Milgram, 1974), those who observe others challenging religious authorities may feel more free to ask questions themselves. They may also begin to question whether they actually belong in the group (cf. Brady, in press).

Religion Actively Promotes Self-Doubt

A final twist is worth considering, one directly related to the uncertain self: Some religious doctrines may encourage people to doubt themselves. Religious teachings on human sinfulness, frailty, or susceptibility to dark influences could cause people to doubt their basic goodness or decision-making abilities. For example, the King James Bible states: "The heart is deceitful above all things, and desperately wicked: who can know it?" (Jeremiah 17:9) and "…the wisdom of this world is foolishness with God" (I Corinthians 3:19a). One of our recent studies (Schutt & Exline, 2023) showed that people trust their consciences less if they see them as vulnerable to demonic influence. In some cases, teachings that undercut self-reliance may reflect well-intentioned attempts to encourage humility or healthy interdependence. But in other cases, power-seeking religious leaders might follow the leads of corrupt advertisers or political despots: They could intentionally sow seeds of fear, uncertainty, and doubt (Lidwell, 2020; Tannenbaum et al., 2015) in hopes that frightened, disoriented people will turn to them for safety or guidance.

What Might Make Doubts Especially Distressing?

Given the many ways that doubt could infiltrate religious (or nonreligious) beliefs, as well as the potential of religion to create doubts about the self, it is easy to understand why so many people struggle with religious doubt. We noted earlier that doubt-related struggles are linked with distress, such as higher levels of anxiety, stress, and depression. In this section, we will speculate about a few factors that might make religious doubts especially upsetting.

Doubt Shakes Core Parts of Orienting System

Questions about peripheral religious teachings (e.g., rarely-emphasized rules, details of historical events) might not be very upsetting. But, as we discussed earlier, religions often address core existential questions about human identities, purpose, and ultimate destinations. Doubts should be most frightening when they disorient people in terms of these big questions, and perhaps especially when they threaten to undermine people's main sources of security. These are the cases we have described as being "shaken to the core" (Pargament & Exline, 2021, 2022). For example, theistic traditions might teach people that they have a personal relationship with a caring God—a belief that can serve basic attachment needs (Granqvist et al., 2010). Questions about God's benevolence or existence could be terrifying for those who have viewed God as a primary attachment figure. Doubts about an afterlife could make life seem bleak and meaningless for some, and they could greatly intensify feelings of loss after a loved one dies.

Given the stressful consequences of losing faith, it is easy to see why people may hold on tightly to cherished beliefs. When facing threats to these beliefs, people might suppress their doubts (Krause & Ellison, 2009). They might also "double down," intensifying threatened core beliefs (e.g., Arndt et al., 1997; Batson, 1975), or they might add qualifications to make the beliefs seem more plausible and less dissonant (Festinger et al., 1956).

Pressure to Hold Correct Beliefs

Some religions focus heavily on shared rituals and practices (Saroglou, 2011). Others invite dialogue and questioning within the constraints of a broader belief system, such as the Rabbinic tradition within Judaism. Mystical sides of religious and spiritual traditions often encourage an embrace of wonder and mystery. In contrast, religious fundamentalism places a heavy emphasis on holding the one set of correct beliefs (Hood et al., 2005). Some faiths, such as fundamentalist strains of Christianity and Islam, even hold out the threat of eternal punishment for those who fail to "see the truth." Pressure to hold correct beliefs, coupled with drastic consequences for incorrect ones, could make religious doubts very threatening indeed.

Doubt Threatens Religious Authorities or Group Members

Expressions of religious doubt might pose a threat to the authority of the religious leaders who espouse the beliefs. Questioning might also threaten religious community members by raising doubts about whether their own beliefs are correct, and it might cause ruptures in family relationships. (For applications to "coming out" as atheist, see Hammer et al., 2012; Zimmerman et al., 2015). Questioning might also make a person seem disloyal to the group and raise concern about a possible exit. Under threat, religious leaders or community members might respond to doubters and dissenters with social judgment (e.g., being labeled an apostate or infidel), spiritual abuse (cf. Koch & Edstrom, 2022), punishment, rejection, or even aggression. (For applications to Orthodox Judaism, see Fader, 2017, 2020; Kali & Romi, 2022, Miles et al., 2023; for applications to LGBTQ+ issues, see Herek & McLemore, 2013; Hoffarth et al., 2018; LeFevor et al., 2021). Given these social threats, it makes sense that some members of religious communities will suppress their doubts in response (Krause & Ellison, 2009).

Religious Seekers Cannot Find Satisfying Answers

We have been framing doubts mainly as challenges to existing beliefs. But for some people, doubt might prevent them from choosing a belief system, and the resulting confusion could be stressful. Some people might seek answers to deep existential questions outside religion, and others might feel comfortable without answers. But those who seek answers to ultimate questions through religion might feel existentially adrift or purposeless if they cannot find good solutions. Whether they are searching within a single tradition or evaluating multiple traditions, an ongoing quest might make a person feel frustrated or fatigued—especially if they believe that there is a single true religion that remains outside their reach.

What's Good about Doubt? The Potential for Growth

Broadly speaking, the question of whether spiritual struggles lead to growth has been a challenging one (Pargament & Exline, 2022). It can be hard to define what growth is because ideas of having grown are tied to specific values. Which is growth: Staying in a tradition or leaving? Focusing on the afterlife or on life here on earth? Becoming more independent or fostering healthy dependence? Retrospective, subjective reports of growth may also reflect biases, such as attempts to make meaning or resolve dissonance (Jayawickreme & Infurna, 2021). Another challenge, especially in cross-sectional studies, is that people may not see growth while they are in the throes of a struggle; they only see their suffering.

Perhaps as a result of these issues, research findings to date do not suggest a clear link between spiritual struggles and growth. But despite these caveats, we would like to suggest several ways that doubt—even if it brings struggle--could also open the door for growth. (For more discussion on doubt and growth, see Krause & Ellison, 2009; Pargament & Exline, 2022.)

Deeper Evaluation of Core Beliefs

People may adopt religious beliefs because of parental or peer socialization, or by following group leaders or norms. If they fully trust their leaders or sacred texts, they might not spend much energy reflecting on the basis of their beliefs. In such cases, doubt could have value by encouraging people to reflect more deeply on religious teachings. For example, consider a young adult who begins to doubt the religious beliefs she learned in childhood, based on simplified stories from a religious curriculum. As she looks back on how her beliefs were formed, she might recognize strong sources of social influence. If she chooses to evaluate her beliefs more thoroughly and critically, she may eventually find herself on better footing to make a thoughtful decision about whether to stay within her tradition, to leave, or one of the many shades in between (Exline et al., 2020; Van Tongeren & DeWall, 2023).

Greater Trust of One's Own Instincts

Doubts sometimes reflect reduced trust in religious authorities, including sacred texts and religious leaders. In some cases, a questioning process might lead people to a greater trust of our own instincts. In cases where religion has led to greater dependency, reduced self-esteem, a lower sense of authenticity (Schmader & Guo, in press), and more self-uncertainty, doubt could serve a useful function by helping people to attune more to their own values, desires, reasoning, and discernment processes. Even if people ultimately retain some trust in religious leaders, texts, or communities, they can balance this external input with other sources and with their own ideas, priorities, and values.

Wakeup Call to Leave Toxic Religious Systems or Leaders

The value of doubt becomes especially clear when we consider people who suffer abuse or other harms within toxic religious systems (Koch & Edstrom, 2022). Consider a cult in which the leader is taking control of people's lives, time, and finances. Or perhaps a religious community member is suffering ongoing sexual or emotional abuse from a religious leader. In order to protect themselves, people suffering harm in religious communities need to see the danger and damage that they (and perhaps others) are facing. But even in a religious environment where leaders and community members are doing their best to follow religious teachings, the beliefs themselves may cause harm: What if a person lives daily in fear of hell, feels ashamed of their sexual orientation or gender identity, or is told to stay in an abusive marriage, all because of religious beliefs? Allowing oneself to doubt, in situations like these, might be seen as an act of courage: Through doubt, the person takes the risks of going against the group, the tradition's leaders, and perhaps even their own prior views about ultimate reality. But taking these risks might be vital for the person's longer-term safety and healing.

Openness to Change and Growth

Doubt might also open doors toward higher levels of moral/spiritual development (Fowler, 1995) or identity development (Ebaugh, 1988; Gull, 2022). For example, a person whose religious beliefs were based on fear of punishment might start to care more about restorative justice. Or perhaps a person who has scrupulously followed rules or group norms begins to see cases where it seems more ethical to bend the rules or disagree with the group. Granted, the developmental transitions represented by such doubts could be destabilizing while they are occurring. As suggested in popular writing about life transitions (Bridges & Bridges, 2019), the unsettled time between leaving one belief and embracing a new one could create a sense of disorientation, anxiety, or loss. Questioners might also feel foolish for having held the prior belief—or, in contrast, to see their doubts or religious disengagement as a failure. But as they leave outgrown beliefs behind, they may open up space for new ones that might serve them better psychologically. In cases like these, doubt might be seen as a "growing edge."

Greater Humility, Flexibility, and Tolerance

Doubt is closely tied to a quest orientation around religion (e.g., Keller et al., 2023; Love et al., 2022; see also Hunsberger et al., 1993)—a perspective that suggests openness, flexibility, and ongoing change around religious beliefs (Batson & Schoenrade, 1991; Beck & Jessup, 2004). Not only does a quest orientation reflect personal flexibility around beliefs, but it consistently shows negative links with prejudice against outgroup members (e.g., Duck & Hunsberger, 1999). Thus, a willingness to tolerate doubt might help people to tolerate interpersonal differences as well—including differences in beliefs. Doubt-related struggles also show links with intellectual humility (Keller et al., 2023), which involves holding one's beliefs loosely, and recognizing that they might be wrong or limited (Leary, 2018). Some people might actively embrace uncertainty—even deep uncertainty about themselves or which identities or choices are most authentic for them (cf. Rios & Morales, in press; Schmader & Guo, in press), in the service of personal growth. In terms of virtues, some people might also cultivate courage and patience by finding themselves able to say, "I don't have all of the information, so I'm not going to make a firm decision about what I believe on this issue—or at least not yet."

Conclusion

Although religions try to address many core human questions, doubts can slip in through a number of avenues: intellectual, motivational, and social. These doubts, despite being a common part of the human condition, can be profoundly distressing: Not only might doubt itself be confusing and unsettling, but religious doubts have the potential to shake foundational, security-related beliefs and put people at odds with religious authorities and communities. Yet religious doubts might also foster growth in some cases. They might help people to critically evaluate their beliefs (or, in some cases, their religious nonbelief) and the systems of authority behind them, which could open the door for healthier options and openness to new possibilities. In some sense, then, a willingness to face religious doubts could represent a form of courage: Doubts could create both personal struggle and social risks, but they might ultimately lead a person to greater wholeness through a better reasoned, more intrinsically guided, and more flexible set of core beliefs.

References

Abu-Raiya, H., Pargament, K. I., Krause, N., & Ironson, G. (2015). Robust links between religious/spiritual struggles, psychological distress, and well-being in a national sample of American adults. *American Journal of Orthopsychiatry, 85*(6), 565–575. https://doi.org/10.1037/ort0000084

Allen, G. E. K., & Wang, K. T. (2014). Examining religious commitment, perfectionism, scrupulosity, and well-being among LDS individuals. *Psychology of Religion and Spirituality, 6*(3), 257–264. https://doi.org/10.1037/a0035197

Altemeyer, B., & Hunsberger, B. (1997). *Amazing conversions: Why some turn to faith and others abandon religion.* Prometheus.

Anderton, C. L., Pender, D. A., & Asner-Self, K. K. (2011). A review of the religious identity/sexual orientation identity conflict literature: Revisiting Festinger's cognitive dissonance theory. *Journal of LGBT Issues in Counseling, 5*(3–4), 259–281.

Arndt, J., Greenberg, J., Pyszczynski, T., & Solomon, S. (1997). Subliminal exposure to death-related stimuli increases defense of the cultural worldview. *Psychological Science, 8*(5), 379–385. https://doi.org/10.1111/j.1467-9280.1997.tb00429.x

Asch, S. E. (1956). Studies of independence and conformity: A minority of one against a unanimous majority. *Psychological Monographs, 70*(9): 1–70. https://doi.org/10.1037/h0093718

Ashe, G. (2001). *Encyclopedia of prophecy.* Bloomsbury.

Barbour, I. G. (2002). *Nature, human nature, and God.* Fortress.

Batson, C. D. (1975). Rational processing or rationalization? The effect of disconfirming information on a stated religious belief. *Journal of Personality and Social Psychology, 32*(1), 176–184. https://doi.org/10.1037/h0076771

Batson, C. D., & Schoenrade, P. A. (1991). Measuring religion as Quest: 1) Validity concerns. *Journal for the Scientific Study of Religion, 30*(4), 416–429. https://doi.org/10.2307/1387277

Baumeister, R. F., & Leary, M. R. (1995). The need to belong: Desire for interpersonal attachments as a fundamental human motivation. *Psychological Bulletin, 117*(3), 497–529. https://doi.org/10.1037/0033-2909.117.3.497

Beck, R., & Jessup, R. K. (2004). The multidimensional nature of quest motivation. *Journal of Psychology and Theology, 32*(4), 283–294. https://doi.org/10.1177/009164710403200401

Bockrath, M. F., Pargament, K. I., Wong, S., Harriott, V. A., Pomerleau, J., M. Homolka, S., Chaudhary, Z. B., & Exline, J. J. (2021). Religious and spiritual struggles and their links to psychological adjustment: A meta-analysis of longitudinal studies. *Psychology of Religion & Spirituality, 14*(3), 283–299. https://doi.org/10.1037/rel0000400

Brady, S. (2025). Belonging uncertainty. In K. Rios, P. Carroll, & K. Olesen (Eds.), *Handbook of the uncertain self* (2nd ed.). Routledge.

Bridges, W., & Bridges, S. (2019). *Transitions: Making sense of life's changes.* Da Capo Lifelong Books.

Bushman, B. J., Ridge, R. D., Das, E., Key, C. W., & Busath, G. L. (2007). When God sanctions killing: Effect of scriptural violence on aggression. *Psychological Science, 18*(3), 204–207. https://doi.org/10.1111/j.1467-9280.2007.01873.x

Cowden, R. G., Pargament, K. I., Chen, Z. J., Davis, E. B., Lemke, A. W., Glowiak, K. J., Rueger, S. Y., & Worthington, E. L., Jr. (2022). Religious/spiritual struggles and psychological distress: A test of three models in a longitudinal study of adults with chronic health conditions. *Journal of Clinical Psychology, 78*(4), 544–558. https://doi.org/10.1002/jclp.23232

Duck, R. J., & Hunsberger, B. (1999). Religious orientation and prejudice: The role of religious proscription, right-wing authoritarianism and social desirability. *International Journal for the Psychology of Religion, 9*(3), 157–179. https://doi.org/10.1207/s15327582ijpr0903_1

Ebaugh, H. R. F. (1988). *Becoming an EX: The process of role exit.* University of Chicago Press.

Etengoff, C., Lefevor, G. T., Huynh, K. D., Rodriguez, E. M., & Luong, E. (2023). Development and validation of the Sexual Minority and Religious Identity Integration (SMRII) scale. *Journal of Homosexuality*. Advance online publication. https://doi.org/10.1080/00918369.2023.2201870

Exline, J. J., Pargament, K. I., & Grubbs, J. B. (2014). [Longitudinal study of religious/spiritual struggles among U.S. adults using Qualtrics panels]. Unpublished raw data.

Exline, J. J., Pargament, K. I., Grubbs, J. B., & Yali, A. M. (2014). The Religious and Spiritual Struggles Scale: Development and initial validation. *Psychology of Religion and Spirituality, 6*(3), 208–222. https://doi.org/10.1037/a0036465

Exline, J. J., Pargament, K. I., Wilt, J. A., Grubbs, J. G., & Yali, A. M. (2022). The RSS-14: Development and preliminary validation of a 14-item form of the Religious and Spiritual Struggles Scale. *Psychology of Religion and Spirituality, 14*(3), 300–311. https://doi.org/10.1037/rel0000472

Exline, J. J., Przeworski, A., Peterson, E., Turnamian, M. R., Stauner, N., & Uzdavines, A. (2021). Religious and spiritual struggles among transgender and gender non-conforming (TGNC) adults. *Psychology of Religion and Spirituality, 13*(3), 276–286. https://doi.org/10.1037/rel0000404

Exline, J. J., Uzdavines, A., & Bradley, D. F. (2015, March). *If given clear evidence for the existence of a god, how do atheists and agnostics think they would respond?* Presentation at the annual Midyear Research Conference on Religion and Spirituality, Provo, UT.

Exline, J. J., Van Tongeren, D. R., Bradley, D. F., Wilt, J. A., Stauner, N., Pargament, K. I., & DeWall, C. N. (2020). Pulling away from religion: Religious/spiritual struggles and religious disengagement among college students. *Psychology of Religion and Spirituality*, *14*(3), 300–311. https://doi.org/10.1037/rel0000375

Exline, J. J., Wilt, J. A., Stauner, N., Schutt, W. A., Pargament, K. I., Fincham, F., & May, R. W. (2023). Supernatural operating rules: How people envision and experience God, the devil, ghosts/spirits, fate/destiny, karma, and luck. *Psychology of Religion and Spirituality,* 15(4), 504–514. https://doi.org/10.1037/rel0000444

Exline, J. J., & Wilt, J. A. (2023). Supernatural attributions: Seeing God, the devil, demons, spirits, fate, and karma as causes of events. *Annual Review of Clinical Psychology, 19*(1), 461–487. https://doi.org/10.1146/annurev-clinpsy-080921-081114

Fader, A. (2017). Ultra-Orthodox Jewish interiority, the Internet, and the crisis of faith. *HAU: Journal of Ethnographic Theory*, *7*(1), 185–206. https://doi.org/10.14318/hau7.1.016

Fader, A. (2020). *Hidden heretics: Jewish doubt in the digital age*. Princeton University Press. https://doi.org/10.1515/9780691201481

Festinger, L. (1957). *A theory of cognitive dissonance.* Stanford University Press. https://doi.org/10.1515/9781503620766

Festinger, L., Riecken, H. W., & Schachter, S. (1956). *When prophecy fails.* Harper & Row.

Fisher, A. R. (2016). A review and conceptual model of the research on doubt, disaffiliation, and related religious changes. *Psychology of Religion and Spirituality*, *9*(4), 358–367. https://doi.org/10.1037/rel0000088

Flannelly, K. J. (2017). Religious doubt and mental health. In K. J. Flannelly (Ed.), *Religious beliefs, evolutionary psychiatry, and mental health in America: Evolutionary threat assessment systems theory* (pp. 233–242). Springer International. https://doi.org/10.1007/978-3-319-52488-7_23

Fowler, J. W. (1995). *Stages of faith: The psychology of human development and the quest for meaning.* HarperOne.

Galek, K., Krause, N., Ellison, C. G., Kudler, T., & Flannelly, K. J. (2007). Religious doubt and mental health across the lifespan. *Journal of Adult Development, 14*(1–2), 16–25. https://doi.org/10.1007/s10804-007-9027-2

George, L. S., & Park, C. L. (2016). Meaning in life as comprehension, purpose, and mattering: Toward integration and new research questions. *Review of General Psychology, 20*(3), 205–220. https://doi.org/10.1037/gpr0000077

Graham, J., & Haidt, J. (2010). Beyond beliefs: Religions bind individuals into moral communities. *Personality and Social Psychology Review, 14*(1), 140–150. https://doi.org/10.1177/1088868309353415

Graham, J., Nosek, B. A., Haidt, J., Iyer, R., Koleva, S., & Ditto, P. H. (2011). Mapping the moral domain. *Journal of Personality and Social Psychology, 101*(2), 366–385. https://doi.org/10.1037/a0021847

Granqvist, P., Mikulincer, M., & Shaver, P. R. (2010). Religion as attachment: Normative processes and individual differences. *Personality and Social Psychology Review*, *14*(1), 49–59. https://doi.org/10.1177/1088868309348618

Grubbs, J. B., & Exline, J. J. (2014). Why did God make me this way? Anger at God in the context of personal transgressions. *Journal of Psychology and Theology, 42*(4), 315–325. https://doi.org/10.1177/009164711404200401

Gull, B. (2022). "We are the women our parents warned us against:" Identity reconstruction and the re-imagining of gender after high-cost religious disaffiliation. *Symbolic Interaction*, *45*(1), 97–122. https://doi.org/10.1002/symb.541

Hammer, J. H., Cragun, R. T., Hwang, K., & Smith, J. M. (2012). Forms, frequency, and correlates of perceived anti-atheist discrimination. *Secularism and Nonreligion*, *1*, 43. https://doi.org/10.5334/snr.ad

Henrie, J., & Patrick, J. H. (2014). Religiousness, religious doubt, and death anxiety. *International Journal of Aging & Human Development*, *78*(3), 203–227. https://doi.org/10.2190/AG.78.3.a

Herek, G. M., & McLemore, K. A. (2013). Sexual prejudice. *Annual Review of Psychology*, *64*, 309–333. https://doi.org/10.1146/annurev-psych-113011-143826

Hoffarth, M. R., Hodson, G., & Molnar, D. S. (2018). When and why is religious attendance associated with antigay bias and gay rights opposition? A justification-suppression model approach. *Journal of Personality and Social Psychology*, *115*(3), 526–563. https://doi.org/10.1037/pspp0000146

Hood, R. W., Hill, P. C., & Williamson, W. P. (2005). *The psychology of religious fundamentalism.* Guilford.

Hunsberger, B., McKenzie, B., Pratt, M., & Pancer, S. M. (1993). Religious doubt: A social psychological analysis. *Research in the Social Scientific Study of Religion*, *5*(1), 27–51.

Hunsberger, B., Pratt, M., & Pancer, S. M. (2002). A longitudinal study of religious doubts in high school and beyond: Relationships, stability, and searching for answers. *Journal for the Scientific Study of Religion*, *41*(2), 255–266. https://doi.org/10.1111/1468-5906.00115

Jayawickreme, E., & Infurna, F. J. (2021). Toward a more credible understanding of post-traumatic growth. *Journal of Personality*, *89*(1), 5–8. https://doi.org/10.1111/jopy.12575

Johnson, C. J. (Ed.) (2018). *How different religions view death and afterlife.* XanEdu.

Kali, A., & Romi, S. (2022). Social re-evaluation model: A mechanism for evaluating the social capital of at-risk adolescents in an ultra-Orthodox collective society. *Child & Youth Services*, *43*(4), 366–390. https://doi.org/10.1080/0145935X.2021.1996226

Keller, Y., Exline, J. J., Moffitt, D., Wilt, J. A., & Pargament, K. I. (2023). *Religious doubt and disengagement among college students: Connections with quest orientation, search for meaning, intellectual humility, and openness to experience.* Manuscript in preparation.

Koch, D., & Edstrom, L. (2022). Development of the spiritual harm and abuse scale. *Journal for the Scientific Study of Religion*, *61*(2), 476–506. https://doi.org/10.1111/jssr.12792

Kooistra, W. (1990). *An empirical examination of religious doubt among Christian adolescents.* Unpublished doctoral dissertation, Bowling Green State University.

Kooistra, W., & Pargament, K. (1999). Religious doubting in parochial school adolescents. *Journal of Psychology and Theology*, *27*(1), 33–42. https://doi.org/10.1177/009164719902700103

Krause, N. (2008). Religious doubt and psychological well-being: A longitudinal investigation. *Review of Religious Research*, *50*(Special Issue), 94–110. https://www.jstor.org/stable/20447552

Krause, N., & Ellison, C. G. (2009). The doubting process: A longitudinal study of the precipitants and consequences of religious doubt. *Journal for the Scientific Study of Religion*, *48*(2), 293–312. https://doi.org/10.1111/j.1468-5906.2009.01448.x

Kunda, Z. (1990). The case for motivated reasoning. *Psychological Bulletin*, *108*(3), 480–498. https://doi.org/10.1037/0033-2909.108.3.480

Leary, M. R. (2018, September). *The psychology of intellectual humility.* Report for the John Templeton Foundation. https://www.templeton.org/wp-content/uploads/2020/08/JTF_Intellectual_Humility_final.pdf

Lefevor, G. T., Huffman, C. E., & Blaber, I. P. (2021). Navigating potentially traumatic conservative religious environments as a sexual/gender minority. In E. M. Lund, C. Burgess, & A. J. Johnson (Eds.), *Violence against LGBTQ+ persons: Research, practice, and advocacy* (pp. 317–329). Springer Nature Switzerland AG. https://doi.org/10.1007/978-3-030-52612-2_25

Lidwell, W. (2020). *FUD: The 37 power tactics of fear, uncertainty, and doubt.* Wiley.

Love, N. S., Merlo, C. A., Hall, M. E. L., & Hill, P. C. (2022). Attachment to God and quest as moderators of the relationship between religious doubt and mental health. *Journal of Psychology and Theology*, *50*(2), 174–191. https://doi.org/10.1177/0091647121992409

McGraw, J. S., Peer, S. O., & Draper, M. R. (2018). Reactionary deconversion from Mormonism: Polarization of ideological and behavioral religiosity among active and former Mormons. *Review of Religious Research*, *60*(4), 535–553. https://doi.org/10.1007/s13644-018-0343-8

McLaughlin, A. T., Van Tongeren, D. R., Teahan, K., Davis, D. E., Rice, K. G., & DeWall, C. N. (2020). Who are the religious "dones?": A cross-cultural latent profile analysis of formerly religious individuals. *Psychology of Religion and Spirituality*, *14*(4), 512–524. https://doi.org/10.1037/rel0000376

Miles, R., Chavarga, A., Hirsch, E., Eisen, P., & Keller, Y. (2023). Reasons for leaving: Causes and initial triggers for disaffiliation from Orthodox Judaism. *Journal for the Scientific Study of Religion*. Advance online publication. https://doi.org/10.1111/jssr.12840

Milgram, S. (1974). *Obedience to authority: An experimental view*. Tavistock Publications.

Moffitt, A. C., Exline, J. J., Keller, Y., Wilt, J. A., & Pargament, K. I. (2024). *Sources of religious doubt: Links with doubt-related spiritual struggles and mental health*. Manuscript in preparation.

Pargament, K. I. (1997). *The psychology of religion and coping: Theory, research, practice*. Guilford.

Pargament, K. I. (2011). Religion and coping: The current state of knowledge. In S. Folkman (Ed.), *Oxford handbook of stress, health, and coping* (pp. 269–288). Oxford.

Pargament, K. I., & Exline, J. J. (2021). *The psychology of spiritual struggle*. Report prepared for the John Templeton Foundation. https://www.templeton.org/wp-content/uploads/2021/10/Spiritual-Struggle-Whitepaper_FINAL-10.5.pdf

Pargament, K. I., & Exline, J. J. (2022). *Working with spiritual struggles in psychotherapy: From research to practice*. Guilford.

Pargament, K. I., & Exline, J. J. (2023). Shaken to the core: Understanding and addressing spiritual struggles in psychotherapy. In P. S. Richards, G. E. K. Allen, & D. K. Judd (Eds.), *Handbook of spiritually integrated psychotherapies* (pp. 119–134). American Psychological Association.

Pargament, K. I., & Lomax, J. W. (2013). Understanding and addressing religion among people with mental illness. *World Psychiatry*, *12*(1), 26–32. https://doi.org/10.1002/wps.20005

Pargament, K. I., & Mahoney, A., & Exline, J. J., Jones, J. W., & Shafranske, E. P. (2013). Envisioning an integrative paradigm for the psychology of religion and spirituality. In K. I. Pargament, J. J. Exline, & J. W. Jones (Eds.), *APA handbook of psychology, religion, and spirituality (Vol. 1): Context, theory, and research* (pp. 3–19). American Psychological Association.

Park, C. L. (2010). Making sense of the meaning literature: An integrative review of meaning making and its effects on adjustment to stressful life events. *Psychological Bulletin*, *136*(2), 257–301. https://doi.org/10.1037/a0018301

Park, C. L. (2013). Religion and meaning. In R. F. Paloutzian & C. L. Park (Eds.), *Handbook of the psychology of religion and spirituality* (2nd ed., pp. 357–379). Guilford.

Rios, K., & Morales, A. (in press). Conflicts between identities and belief systems. In K. Rios, P. Carroll, & K. Olesen (Eds.), *Handbook of the uncertain self* (2nd ed.). Routledge.

Saroglou, V. (2011). Believing, bonding, behaving, and belonging: The big four religious dimensions and cultural variation. *Journal of Cross-Cultural Psychology*, *42*(8), 1320–1340. https://doi.org/10.1177/0022022111412267

Sayre, K. M. (1997). *Belief and knowledge: Mapping the cognitive landscape*. Rowman & Littlefield.

Schmader, T., & Guo, Y. (in press). Navigating inauthenticity: When do people embrace self-uncertainty? In K. Rios, P. Carroll, & K. Olesen (Eds.), *Handbook of the uncertain self* (2nd ed.). Routledge.

Schutt, W. A., & Exline, J. J. (2023). Can God or the devil influence the conscience? Links between religion/spirituality, beliefs about the conscience, and attempts to follow the conscience. Advance online publication. *Spirituality in Clinical Practice*. https://doi.org/10.1037/scp0000320

Sedlar, A. E., Stauner, N., Pargament, K. I., Exline, J. J., Grubbs, J. B., & Bradley, D. F. (2018). Spiritual struggles among atheists: Links to psychological distress and well-being. *Religions, 9*(8), 242. https://doi.org/10.3390/rel9080242

Smith, H. (1958). *The religions of man*. Harper and Row.

Steger, M. F., Frazier, P., Oishi, S., & Kaler, M. (2006). The meaning in life questionnaire: Assessing the presence of and search for meaning in life. *Journal of Counseling Psychology*, *53*(1), 80–93. https://doi.org/10.1037/0022-0167.53.1.80

Stewart, K., & Harding, S. (1999). Bad endings: American apocalypsis. *Annual Review of Anthropology*, *28*(1), 285–310. https://doi.org/10.1146/annurev.anthro.28.1.285

Tannenbaum, M. B., Hepler, J., Zimmerman, R. S., Saul, L., Jacobs, S., Wilson, K., & Albarracín, D. (2015). Appealing to fear: A meta-analysis of fear appeal effectiveness and theories. *Psychological Bulletin*, *141*(6), 1178–1204. https://doi.org/10.1037/a0039729.

Upenieks, L., Bonhag, R., & McGowan, A. C. (2023). Religious doubt and depression in later life: Gender differences in the buffering role of supportive pastoral relationships. *International Psychogeriatrics*. Advance online publication. https://doi.org/10.1017/S1041610222000448

Van Tongeren, D. R., & DeWall, C. N. (2023). Disbelief, disengagement, discontinuance, and disaffiliation: An integrative framework for the study of religious deidentification. *Psychology of Religion and Spirituality*, *15*(4), 515–524. https://doi.org/10.1037/rel0000434

Van Tongeren, D. R., DeWall, C. N., Chen, Z., Sibley, C. G., & Bulbulia, J. (2021). Religious residue: Cross-cultural evidence that religious psychology and behavior persist following deidentification. *Journal of Personality and Social Psychology*, *120*(2), 484–503. https://doi.org/10.1037/pspp0000288

White, C. J. M., & Norenzayan, A. (2019). Belief in karma: How cultural evolution, cognition, and motivations shape belief in supernatural justice. In J. M. Olson (Ed.), *Advances in experimental social psychology* (Vol. 60, pp. 1–63). Elsevier.

Willis, K. D., Nelson, T., & Moreno, O. (2019). Death anxiety, religious doubt, and depressive symptoms across race in older adults. *International Journal of Environmental Research and Public Health*, *16*(19), 3645. https://doi.org/10.3390/ijerph16193645

Wilt, J. A., Grubbs, J. B., Lindberg, M. J., Exline, J. J., & Pargament, K. I. (2017). Anxiety predicts increases in religious/spiritual doubt over two weeks, one month, and one year. *International Journal for the Psychology of Religion*, *27*(1), 26–34. https://doi.org/10.1080/10508619.2015.1098820

Wilt, J. A., Stauner, N., & Exline, J. J. (2022). Beliefs and experiences involving God, the devil, human spirits, and fate: Social, motivational, and cognitive predictors. *International Journal for the Psychology of Religion*, *33*(1), 19–35. https://doi.org/10.1080/10508619.2022.2061151

Wong, S., & Pargament, K. (2019). Meaning, "maker," and morality: Spiritual struggles as predictors of distress and growth in family caregivers. *International Journal of Existential Positive Psychology*, *8*(2), 1–17.

Ysseldyk, R., Matheson, K., & Anisman, H. (2010). Religiosity as identity: Toward an understanding of religion from a social identity perspective. *Personality and Social Psychology Review*, *14*(1), 60–71. https://doi.org/10.1177/1088868309349693

Zimmerman, K. J., Smith, J. M., Simonson, K., & Myers, W. B. (2015). Familial relationship outcomes of coming out as an atheist. *Secularism and Nonreligion*, *4*(1), Article 1. https://doi.org/10.5334/snr.aw

General Commentary

22

A BIGGER PICTURE

Self-Uncertainty, Social Identity, and Intergroup Relations

Michael Hogg

Social and personality psychologists have long viewed uncertainty as playing a significant role in human behavior, and they have been intrigued by the question of what is the self and what role does it play in human behavior. In this book these two foci, uncertainty and the self, come together in the study of the uncertain self. The first edition of this book, edited by Arkin, Oleson and Carroll was published in 2010. One of the striking features of that volume was the sheer quantity and diversity of research on uncertainty that had been conducted and was underway. There were 20 substantive chapters from leading research teams that covered cognitive, motivational, and clinical dimensions of the uncertain self. It appeared that we already knew a great deal about the uncertain self, and that there was enormous and growing excitement in the topic. The future looked bright.

My own chapter in that 2010 book (Hogg, 2010) noted that many separate themes threaded their way through the volume, some being more prominent than others in different chapters. I identified six major themes and emphases and mapped them onto chapters where they seemed to be more central. These themes included: (a) the cognitive architecture of uncertainty, (b) judgment and decision-making, (c) self-regulation, (d) individual differences, (e) health and well-being, and (f) academic achievement. However, I felt that one possible aspect of the uncertain self seemed to be significantly underemphasized – the self as a collective "we" self and its relationship to group identity, and group and intergroup processes and phenomena.

I went on to discuss the multifaceted self and its relationship to groups and explain why I believed that the group identity dimension of self-uncertainty was important. I then briefly introduced what at that time was a relatively embryonic line of research into the relationship between self-uncertainty, group identity, and group behavior—uncertainty-identity theory (Hogg, 2000, 2007). I then briefly suggested, by reflecting back on some of the more relevant chapters in the 2010 book, ways in which this analysis might inform and advance the study of the uncertain self.

A Second Edition of the Handbook of the Uncertain Self

The existence of this second edition of the *Handbook of the Uncertain Self* attests not only to the continued attention that the uncertain self attracts but also to the field's burgeoning development. In their introduction to this second edition Rios, Oleson and Carroll do a magnificent and complete job of describing the rationale, structure, and foci of the book, as well as the history of

DOI: 10.4324/9781003363385-26

self-uncertainty in social and personality psychology. They also echo a sentiment shared by many other contributors to this book; that although uncertainty may be part of the human condition, the world may actually have become a much more uncertain place in which the self may have become more uncertain, more often, and more extremely so. Self-uncertainty may have, in itself and in its consequences, become a significant social issue that attracts growing scientific interest in self-uncertainty.

Instead of revisiting Rios and colleagues' introduction, what I would like to do in this closing commentary chapter is pick up on Rios and colleagues' observation that one development in this second edition of the handbook is that there is a greater representation of chapters focused on self-uncertainty within group contexts (especially the chapters by Schmader and colleagues, Kuljian and Hohman, and Paredes and colleagues)—a development that directly addresses the social identity and intergroup relations lacuna I had noted in the first edition. Rios and colleagues observe that these chapters exemplify the social psychological emphasis on situating and understanding self-uncertainty within the context of social groups and intergroup relations.

Since the 2010 book uncertainty-identity theory and research has developed and expanded very significantly (Hogg, 2021a), most notably in its application to radicalization and societal extremism (Hogg, 2021b), and its more nuanced and balanced view of the identity-contingent positive and negative societal consequences of self-uncertainty (e.g., Hogg, 2024). The present chapter very briefly overviews the current state of uncertainty-identity theory, and thus the role played by the uncertain self in an uncertain world.

Uncertainty and Self-Uncertainty

Because uncertainty is part of daily life, and an enduring feature of the wider world we live in, it is no surprise that uncertainty has been a significant focus of psychological research and has been considered a key motivator of human behavior. For example, Fromm (1947) proposed that people need a clear sense of identity, social connection, and place in the world, and Tajfel (1969) considered stereotyping and prejudice to partially reflect a cognitive drive for mental coherence. Others have focused on the role of uncertainty in decision-making (e.g., Kahneman et al., 1982) and social comparison (e.g., Festinger, 1954; see, Križan, & Gibbons, 2014).

However, people can experience and react to uncertainty in different ways, as a function of their individual attributes and the nature and context of the uncertainty. And so, a key question is how might uncertainty and one's experience of uncertainty shape and drive what we do, what we think and how we feel, and ultimately affect the world we live in? How might uncertainty influence people and how they might feel about and respond to uncertainty?

Scholars generally agree that people can never *feel* completely certain, only less uncertain (Pollock, 2003), so they strive to reduce uncertainty in order to *feel* less uncertain. And because reducing uncertainty can be cognitively demanding, and people are strategic in how they allocate their limited cognitive resources (e.g., Fiske & Taylor, 2021), they expend cognitive energy resolving only those uncertainties that they feel are important to them. When they feel "sufficiently" certain and that there is "adequate" cognitive closure (cf. Kruglanski & Fishman, 2009; Kruglanski & Webster, 1996) they move on to invest cognitive effort elsewhere.

And this is where *self*-uncertainty comes in. Because the self is an organizing and planning mechanism for how we represent and act within the world (e.g., Sedikides et al., 2021; Swann & Bosson, 2010), many of our most psychologically important and impactful uncertainties are those that involve self-conception. Thus, whether an uncertainty "matters" enough to warrant resolution rests on the extent to which self is involved.

Uncertainty-identity theory (e.g., Hogg, 2021a) focuses specifically on self-uncertainty, uncertainty about who we are and about our self-related perceptions, attitudes, feelings, and behaviors, as a significant motivator (e.g., Brown et al., 2021; Jonas, McGregor, Klackl et al., 2014) that drive us to reduce such uncertainties so we feel less uncertain about ourselves and the world we live in. Self-uncertainty reduction makes the world and our own behavior and expectations within it appear more predictable and controllable and allows us to feel we know ourselves, anticipate how others will perceive and treat us, and plan how we should act. Uncertainty-identity theory theorizes about the motivational role of *self*-uncertainty, not uncertainties that do not reflect on or involve self-conception. And, as we shall now see, in arguing that self-uncertainty is resolved by group identification, uncertainty-identity theory specifically and explicitly theorizes the causal link between self-uncertainty and social identity and group and intergroup processes.

Self-Uncertainty and Group Identification

Group identification is a highly effective way to reduce uncertainty about one's self, particularly one's collective self that has attributes that are shared among fellow members of a group one belongs to. This core premise draws on social identity theory's analysis of the role of social categorization of self and others in constructing and expressing social identity and associated group and intergroup behaviors (Tajfel & Turner, 1986; Turner et al., 1987; also see Abrams & Hogg, 2010; Hogg, 2016, 2018).

Groups define who we are. They provide us with a social identity, and associated identity-defining attributes, which prescribe how we ought to view the world, other people, and ourselves, and how we ought to act as group members. When we categorize ourselves and others as group members we transform the way we act and view ourselves and others to conform to the relevant group identity. Social categorization depersonalizes perception and action, and accentuates identity-relevant similarities within groups and identity-relevant differences between groups (between "us" and "them").

According to uncertainty-identity theory, self-uncertainty reduction is a key motivation for social identity processes and associated group and intergroup phenomena. Feelings of uncertainty about who one is and how one should behave motivate uncertainty-reduction; and group identification, particularly with distinctive groups that have clearly defined identities, is effective at reducing self-uncertainty. It provides us with an identity and sense of who we are that prescribes what we should think, feel, and do; it regulates social interaction; and it reduces uncertainty about how others, both ingroup and outgroup members, will behave and about how social interactions will unfold.

Group identification also provides consensual validation of our worldview and sense of self, which further reduces self-uncertainty. This is because people in our group share the same prototype of "us" and share the same prototype of "them," and therefore our own expectations about the identity-based behavior of others are usually confirmed, by our fellow group members, who agree with our perceptions, beliefs, attitudes, and values and approve of how we behave. People in a group have a shared social identity and a shared reality (Echterhoff et al., 2009; Hogg & Rinella, 2018). Indeed, a discovery that fellow ingroup members do not see the world as we do (they do not share our reality) can create significant uncertainty about the group's identity and thus one's self-conception (e.g., Wagoner et al., 2017).

Because identification reduces and protects people from self-uncertainty, the most basic prediction is that the more uncertain people are the more likely they are to identify, and to identify more strongly, with a self-inclusive social category. This prediction has been confirmed across numerous studies (see meta-analysis of 4,657 participants across 35 studies by Choi & Hogg, 2020).

There is even evidence that having a "certain" sense of self can take precedence over having a favorable sense of self. People confronted by feelings of self-uncertainty will identify with a group that confers undesirable status and thus lower self-esteem and an unfavorable sense of self if such a group is their only social identity option (Reid & Hogg, 2005).

Distinctive Groups with Unambiguous Identities

Identification reduces uncertainty. However, some groups and their associated social identities have properties that do a better job of reducing uncertainty through identification. One such property is *entitativity* (e.g., Hamilton & Sherman, 1996; Lickel et al., 2000).

An entitative group is a distinctive, coherent, and clearly structured unit with clearly delineated intergroup boundaries, within which members share attributes and goals, have a shared fate, and interact with one another in a climate of interdependence—such a group, which has a clear and unambiguous ingroup prototype, does an excellent job of reducing or fending off self-uncertainty. In contrast, a low entitativity group is unclearly structured with fuzzy boundaries, ambiguous membership criteria, limited shared goals, and little agreement on group attributes—it does not have a clear and unambiguous ingroup prototype, and thus is poorly equipped to reduce self-uncertainty.

In essence, highly entitative groups have a clear ingroup prototype (identity) that people can reference to reduce their uncertainty, whereas low entitativity groups have no such ingroup prototype (identity) that people can reference. Furthermore, group members who feel marginal and remote from a group's prototype and core identity attributes can find it particularly difficult to access the group's defining prototype, and thus they feel particularly self-uncertain (see Kuljian & Hohman's chapter in this volume; also see Hohman et al., 2017).

Identification reduces uncertainty because it internalizes a self and identity that prescribes how one ought to think, feel, and behave. It follows that ingroup identities that are simple, clear, unambiguous, prescriptive, focused and consensual are more effective than those that are vague, ambiguous, unfocused and dissensual. The former identities are more likely to be associated with highly entitative groups; and people are more likely to anchor such identities in invariant underlying group essences (e.g., Haslam et al., 2006) that provide further predictability and stability and make the group and its identity even better at reducing and fending off uncertainty. Uncertainty-identity theory predicts that people feeling self-uncertain (in the immediate situation or broader context) identify more strongly with high than low entitativity groups, and, if possible, dis-identify from low entitativity groups or work to make such groups appear more entitative. Numerous direct tests support this prediction (e.g., Hogg et al., 2010; Hogg et al., 2007).

Uncertainty-identity theory, in conjunction with the theory of subjective group dynamics (e.g., Pinto et al., 2010), notes that group members can pose a threat to group entitativity and identity clarity if they deviate from or fail to embody ingroup identity-defining norms, particularly if they deviate towards rather than away from an outgroup (e.g., Anjewierden et al., 2024). The existence of such identity deviants or defectors within a group (e.g., Mannetti et al., 2010), as much as the entry of new members (e.g., Theodorou et al., 2023), can blur intergroup boundaries and fray internal identity-related consensus and cohesion, which weakens entitativity and distinctiveness.

This can elevate identity uncertainty and self-uncertainty, which motivates people to restore entitativity by rejection, marginalization, and/or attempts to (re)socialize those who violate the group's identity defining attributes (Pinto et al., 2010), and under some circumstances motivates people to dis-identify from the group altogether and psychologically exit to join a more entitative group. People's drive to reject ingroup deviants (black sheep) is stronger when identification and group entitativity are high; because under these circumstances the motivation to protect identity and entitativity to fend off uncertainty is strongest (e.g., Rullo & Livi, 2019).

Factors Affecting how People Experience and React to Self-Uncertainty

In addition to group distinctiveness and identity clarity, there are other factors that significantly influence how people react to, self-uncertainty. Self-uncertainty can be experienced in different ways depending on (a) what aspect of self is most implicated, (b) how much overlap there is among different aspects of selves or different social identities, (c) the resources people feel they have to deal with self-uncertainty, and (d) the primary cause of the self-uncertainty. How people experience self-uncertainty may influence the dynamics and manifestation of uncertainty-reducing group identification.

Aspects of Self

Brewer and Gardner (1996; also see Sedikides & Brewer, 2001) propose three distinct aspects of self (a) *individual self,* based on personal traits that differentiate "me" from all others; (b) *relational self,* based on connections and role relationships with specific significant others, and (c) *collective self,* based on group membership that differentiates 'us' from 'them'. Self-uncertainty can be associated with any of these aspects. You can feel uncertain about your individual attributes, yourself in relation to specific other people, or yourself as a group member. Although these aspects are qualitatively different, uncertainty experienced in one domain can spread to other self-domains. For example, if you are primarily uncertain about your relational self, you may also become uncertain about your individual self. Relevant research shows that self-uncertainty strengthens group identification, particularly when people feel uncertain about their collective self (Hogg & Mahajan, 2018).

Overlapping Selves and Overlapping Identities

The degree to which self-uncertainty in one domain pervades other domains of self is influenced by self- and social identity-complexity—the extent that attributes that define one aspect of self (or one social identity) overlap with or are the same as those that define other aspects of self (or other social identities) (Brewer & Pierce, 2005; Roccas & Brewer, 2002). A person has a complex self-concept and social identity if they have many discrete and dissimilar identities that do not overlap; a person has a simple social identity if they have few identities and they are largely the same. A complex self-structure can quarantine identity-specific self-uncertainty, and allow people to compensate by identifying more strongly with other identities (or aspects of self) that they believe are central to their overall sense of self (Grant & Hogg, 2012).

For example, consider someone whose dominant social identities are their national, religious, and political identities, and they experience self-uncertainty primarily grounded in their national identity. If these three identities have such different attributes that they hardly overlap at all then such a person has a complex self-structure; national identity-grounded self-uncertainty is unlikely to contaminate one's religious and/or political identities, and one can reduce overall uncertainty by identifying more strongly in religious and/or political terms. However, if the three identities have such similar attributes that they are practically identical one has a simple self-structure; national identity uncertainty readily elevates religious and political identity uncertainty, leaving one with no other identities to reduce uncertainty, and creating a perfect storm of self-uncertainty that pervades the entire self-concept.

Resources to Reduce Self-Uncertainty

Self-uncertainty can be experienced differently depending on whether someone believes they have adequate cognitive, emotional, social, and material resources to reduce the uncertainty (cf., Blascovich et al., 2003; Blascovich & Tomaka, 1996). With adequate resources, uncertainty is an exhilarating challenge to embrace, even seek out, and resolve; without such resources, it is an anxiety-provoking and stressful threat to avoid and protect against.

Whether self-uncertainty is experienced as a challenge or a threat may influence the behaviors people adopt to reduce uncertainty—behaviors that can reflect a more promotive (e.g., self- and identity-promoting) or more preventative (e.g., self- and identity-protective) behavioral orientation (cf. Higgins's, 1998, regulatory focus theory). Uncertainty experienced as a challenge might encourage promotive behaviors (e.g., confident and proud assertion of one's identity). Uncertainty experienced as a threat might encourage more protective behaviors (e.g., retreat into polarized identity echo chambers)—behaviors that might rest on an identity that also legitimizes and supports "extremism".

As yet there is no research that directly or systematically explores how self-uncertainty and resource sufficiency (i.e., self-uncertainty experienced as a challenge or a threat) interact to affect regulatory focus (promotion versus prevention) and associated behavior (see Hogg, 2023; Hogg & Gaffney, 2023). Existing literature is only obliquely relevant—for example, studies of challenge and threat appraisals and intergroup relations (Scheepers, 2009), and studies of the interactive effect of regulatory focus (promotion/prevention) and challenge/threat on behavior (Sassenberg & Scholl, 2019).

Causes of Self-Uncertainty

There are many potential causes of self-uncertainty: new social contexts, life transitions, and crises, relationship changes, globalization, immigration and mass migration, climate change, automation, the reconfiguration of "work," socio-political instability, and the realignment of super-national entities and alliances. Although these causes differ in many ways, they all share the ability to create uncertainty about one's collective self and one's social identity.

Collective self-uncertainty can be especially triggered by uncertainty about the identity-defining attributes of a group that one identifies with (social identity clarity and distinctiveness are absent—Wagoner et al., 2017), about how well one fits into and is accepted by a group that is central to one sense of self (Goldman & Hogg, 2016; Hohman et al., 2017), and about how well one's group fits into a larger collective (for example a nation within the European Union – Wagoner et al., 2018; Wagoner & Hogg, 2016). But most importantly, people are motivated to reduce self-uncertainty only when exogenous conditions create a sense of self-uncertainty.

Consequences of Self-Uncertainty-Motivated Group Identification

Identification to reduce self-uncertainty has a number of consequences for group behavior and intergroup relations, some positive and some negative, which may be influenced by the extent to which uncertainty is mainly experienced as an exciting challenge or an aversive threat. Uncertainty-identity theory emphasizes both positive and negative consequences of the uncertainty-identification relationship (Hogg, 2007, 2021a, 2024), though in keeping with other literatures it has tended to focus more on the negative (Hogg, 2021b, 2023, in press).

The Bright Side: Positive Consequences of Uncertainty and the Uncertainty-Identification Relationship

Research highlighting the positive consequences of uncertainty and self-uncertainty emphasizes people's approach rather than avoidance of the uncertain and highlights people's positive feelings about novel and uncertain situations. For example, research on creativity (Sternberg & Kaufman, 2010) and on curiosity and exploration (Szumowska & Kruglanski, 2020)—for review see Kruglanski, Ellenberg, Molinario, Speckhard et al., 2023.

Focusing specifically on the self-uncertainty-identification relationship it is known that under normal circumstances the uncertainty-identity relationship strengthens group identification (Choi & Hogg, 2020). The relationship makes distinctive and cohesive groups and unambiguous identities attractive and thus delivers all the positive and desirable outcomes of group identification for individuals, groups, and society. These outcomes are numerous (see Hogg, 1993; Van Knippenberg & Hogg, 2018).

Identification motivates group members to express solidarity and work hard for the group to achieve its goals. People have a sense of attachment, commitment, belonging, and "fitting in," and feel they have efficacy and authorship of their own destiny in a predictable and navigable world. There is an atmosphere of interdependence, shared fate, and mutual loyalty within groups, and members place the group's interest ahead of self-interest and show a willingness to engage in extra-role behavior and to "go the extra mile" for the group. There is social identity-centered communication to establish, refine, and build consensus around the group's norms and identity that members conform to. Finally, there is trust in leadership and willingness to be led, particularly by group prototypical leaders (who are viewed as "one of us"), and members extend innovation credit to their leaders and, within limits, buy into leader-sponsored and group promotive identity reconfigurations.

The Dark Side: Negative Consequences of Uncertainty and the Uncertainty-Identification Relationship

There is, however, a dark side to the uncertainty-identification relationship, which is a significant focus of uncertainty research that emphasizes the tendency for people to avoid uncertainty and unpredictability, seek cognitive closure, crave security, and compensate for the aversive state associated with uncertainty (e.g., Brizi, Mannetti, & Kruglanski, 2016; Chirumbolo et al., 2004; De Grada et al., 1999; Frenkel-Brunswick, 1948; Kosic et al., 2004; Kruglanski, 2004; Kruglanski et al., 2006; Mannetti et al., 2002).

This dark side has also become a significant focus of uncertainty-identity theory (e.g., Hogg, 2014, 2021b, 2023; Hogg & Gaffney, 2023). Under some conditions the self-uncertainty-identification relationship becomes distorted, such that self-uncertainty-motivated identification can have toxic and destructive consequences for individuals, groups, and society. These consequences emerge when self-uncertainty is extreme and chronic, and experienced as a threat that people feel they do not have the resources to resolve; and when people have a simple identity structure with few discrete (and positive) identities (e.g., Roccas & Brewer, 2002), and their sense of self is grounded in a single social identity that saturates the self-concept (e.g., Swann et al., 2012).

Under these circumstances, people are desperate to identify and belong, and yearn for decisive leadership to resolve their uncertainty and make them feel included and validated. Distinctive groups with unambiguously defined identities and directive leadership are particularly attractive—more attractive than fuzzy groups with ambiguous non-consensual identities and laissez-faire leadership. The former provides members with a clear, unequivocal, and concrete sense of what the group is and therefore who they are, which is precisely what is sought when self-uncertainty is elevated.

Other group attributes are similarly attractive because they convey self-uncertainty-reducing identity information. For example, people develop a social identity and group-membership preference for partisan, xenophobic groups that are polarized, intolerant of internal dissent, and have demagogic leaders (e.g., Hogg et al., 2010). Group-centrism becomes entrenched (e.g., Kruglanski et al., 2006). People expose themselves primarily to the opinions of ingroup members; endorse central authority that dictates social identity; suppress dissent, shun diversity, and promote ingroup favoritism; and venerate and fiercely adhere to their group's norms and traditions. They embrace ethnocentrism (Brewer & Campbell, 1976), mistrust and fear outsiders (Stephan, 2014), view group attributes as fixed essences (Haslam et al., 2006), and harbor the potential to dehumanize outgroups (Haslam, 2006; Haslam et al., 2008). A sense of identity threat and societal disrespect can cause hatred, aggression, and violence to become a part of the group's identity (e.g., Belavadi et al., 2020; Rios et al., 2018).

Populist leaders and ideologies prevail because they strengthen the perceived ability of the group and its identity to reduce self-uncertainty (Hogg & Gøtzsche-Astrup, 2021). Conspiracy theories thrive (e.g., Douglas & Sutton, 2018), as does a sense of collective narcissism and under-appreciated superiority. There is a narrative of collective victimhood that unites the group, recruits third-party sympathy and support (e.g., Belavadi & Hogg, 2018), and raises the specter of an existential threat to the ingroup that invites and justifies violence against the outgroup (e.g., Belavadi et al., 2020).

Leadership and identity messaging play a significant role. They can fuel polarization, build barriers between groups, and sustain zero-sum intergroup conflict and hostility (e.g., Rast & Hogg, 2017). Self-uncertainty creates a need for leadership (Rast et al., 2012), particularly leadership that constructs, embodies, and communicates a simple and unambiguous ingroup identity (Gaffney et al., 2018). There is a preference for leaders who are dominant and autocratic (Rast et al., 2013) and who exemplify and promote a populist ideology (e.g., Hogg & Gøtzsche-Astrup, 2021). Self-uncertainty also creates an environment in which leaders who exhibit the Dark Triad attributes of Machiavellianism, narcissism, and psychopathy (a personality mix associated with autocratic, toxic, and dysfunctional leadership) secure and thrive in leadership positions (e.g., Guillén et al., 2023).

In our contemporary social media environment, "leadership" and identity-messaging often play out via influential online identity silos and echo-chambers (e.g., Cinelli et al., 2021). These platforms can take advantage of identity fault lines to satisfy people's need for identity confirmation, promote intergroup threat and hostility, and fan the flames of schism and social fragmentation (e.g. Wagoner et al., 2018).

Concluding Summary

This *Handbook of the uncertain self* is a second edition of the original book, edited by Arkin, Oleson, and Carroll, which was published over 15 years ago in 2010. The original book highlighted the growing research interest and activity shown by social and personality psychologists in the causes, manifestations, and consequences of self-uncertainty. The book contained 20 chapters covering a diverse range of perspectives on and approaches to the uncertain self.

One of those chapters (Hogg, 2010) noted a lacuna; an under-emphasis on the self as a collective "we" self, and its relationship to group identity, and group and intergroup processes and phenomena. The chapter argued that the group identity and intergroup relations dimension of self-uncertainty were important, and went on to briefly introduce what at that time was a relatively embryonic line of research into the relationship between self-uncertainty, group identity, and group behavior—uncertainty-identity theory (Hogg, 2000, 2007). It also suggested, by reflecting back on some of the more relevant chapters in the 2010 book, ways in which this analysis might inform and advance the study of the uncertain self.

This second edition of the handbook highlights a continuing, and growing, interest in the uncertain self. Of particular relevance is the observation by Rios, Oleson, and Carroll in their opening chapter that one notable development is a greater representation of chapters situating and understanding self-uncertainty within group and intergroup contexts (especially the chapters by Schmader and colleagues, Kuljian and Hohman, and Paredes and colleagues)—a development that directly addresses the social identity and intergroup relations lacuna I had noted in the first edition.

Since the 2010 book uncertainty-identity theory and research have developed very significantly (Hogg, 2021a), most notably in its application to radicalization and societal extremism (Hogg, 2021b, 2023, in press), and its more nuanced and balanced view of identity-contingent positive and negative societal consequences of self-uncertainty (e.g., Hogg, 2024). The present chapter provides a brief but completely updated overview of the current state of uncertainty-identity theory, and thus the role played by the uncertain self in social identity and group and intergroup phenomena in an uncertain world.

People are motivated to reduce uncertainty because uncertainty, which pervades everyday life and the wider world we live in, makes it difficult to predict what to expect and what to do. Successfully reducing uncertainty is satisfying because it delivers a sense of mastery and agency in a more predictable world. However, uncertainty reduction is cognitively effortful so people only invest their limited cognitive resources in reducing those uncertainties that really matter; and then only do as much as it takes to feel adequately certain. One significant determinant of how much uncertainty matters is the extent to which the uncertainty reflects on or is directly about one's sense of self and identity–about who one is.

Group identification can decisively reduce self-uncertainty because the process of identification provides one with a shared identity that prescribes how one should think and act and how others (as ingroup or outgroup members) will view and treat us. It also furnishes us with consensual validation of who we are and a sense of belonging. However, some groups and identities have properties that do a better job of reducing self-uncertainty through identification. Specifically, highly entitative groups that have distinctive, consensual, and clearly defined identities—such groups reduce self-uncertainty precisely because they provide an unambiguous and clearly defined sense of who one is. Thus, self-uncertainty motivates group identification and social identity processes and phenomena. And, because self-uncertainty motivates group identification, it can also deliver all the beneficial outcomes of group identification for individuals, groups, and society—attachment, commitment, cohesion, common purpose, shared vision, trust in leadership, and so forth.

However, the subjective experience and context of self-uncertainty can vary and affect how identification-contingent uncertainty reduction impacts group and intergroup phenomena. The aspect of self (individual, interpersonal, or collective) is most proximally implicated in uncertainty matters—collective self-uncertainty is most effectively reduced by identification. Self and identity complexity also matters—a complex identity structure (multiple, positive, discrete, non-overlapping identities) is more resilient in the face of self-uncertainty than a simple identity structure (few identities that overlap substantially). In addition, resources (cognitive, emotional, social, and material) to resolve self-uncertainty affect whether uncertainty is experienced as an exciting challenge to be sought out and resolved or an anxiety-provoking threat to be avoided. Self-uncertainty as a challenge may sponsor a promotive behavioral orientation that facilitates positive outcomes of identification, whereas self-uncertainty as threat may sponsor a preventative orientation that may generate undesirable outcomes associated with extremism, populism, autocratic leadership, echo chambers, suppression of diversity, and so forth.

Finally, many of the contributors to this book echo a shared sentiment that although uncertainty may be part of the human condition the world may have become a much more uncertain place in which the self may have become more uncertain, more often, and more extremely so. Self-uncertainty may have, in itself and in its consequences, become a significant social issue. From an uncertainty-identity perspective, one might speculate that in a world of overwhelming change and uncertainty that impacts people's sense of who they are (for example globalization that transforms society and marginalizes many - e.g., Ozer et al., 2023) self-uncertainty is all too often experienced as a crushing threat, not an exciting challenge. People can all too easily resolve this threatening uncertainty by living in identity echo chambers, walling out people who are "different," seeking homogeneity and the safety of like-minded others, turning to toxic and populist leaders, and feeling liberated by the internet to express hatred and vilify others.

References

Abrams, D., & Hogg, M. A. (2010). Social identity and self-categorization. In J. F. Dovidio, M. Hewstone, P. Glick & V. M. Esses (Eds.), *The Sage handbook of prejudice, stereotyping and discrimination* (pp. 179–193). Sage.

Anjewierden, B. J., Syfers, L., Pinto, I. R., Gaffney, A., M., & Hogg, M. A. (2024). Group responses to deviance: Disentangling the motivational roles of collective enhancement and self-uncertainty reduction. *Group Processes and Intergroup Relations*, *27*(5), 1170–1187. https://doi.org/10.1177/13684302241247030

Belavadi, S., & Hogg, M. A. (2018). We are victims! How observers evaluate a group's claim of collective victimhood. *Journal of Applied Social Psychology, 48*(12), 651–660. https://doi.org/10.1002/jts5.37

Belavadi, S., Rinella, M., & Hogg, M. A. (2020). When social identity-defining groups become violent: Collective responses to identity uncertainty, status erosion, and resource threat. In C. A. Ireland, M. Lewis, A. C. Lopez, & J. L. Ireland (Eds.), *The handbook of collective violence: Current developments and understanding* (pp. 17–30). Routledge.

Blascovich, J., Mendes, W. B., Tomaka, J., Salomon, K., & Seery, M. (2003). The robust nature of the biopsychosocial model of challenge and threat: A reply to Wright and Kirby. *Personality and Social Psychology Review, 7*(3), 234–243. https://doi.org/10.1207/s15327957pspr0703_03

Blascovich, J., & Tomaka, J. (1996). The biopsychosocial model of arousal regulation. *Advances in Experimental Social Psychology, 28*, 1–51. https://doi.org/10.1016/S0065-2601(08)60235-X

Brewer, M. B., & Campbell, D. T. (1976). *Ethnocentrism and intergroup attitudes: East African evidence*. New York: Sage.

Brewer, M. B., & Gardner, W. (1996). Who is this "we"? Levels of collective identity and self representations. *Journal of Personality and Social Psychology, 71*(1), 83–93. https://doi.org/10.1037/0022-3514.71.1.83

Brewer, M. B., & Pierce, K. P. (2005). Social identity complexity and outgroup tolerance. *Personality and Social Psychology Bulletin, 31*(3), 428–437. https://doi.org/10.1177/0146167204271710

Brizi, A., Mannetti, L., & Kruglanski, A. W. (2016). The closing of open minds: Need for closure moderates the impact of uncertainty salience on outgroup discrimination. *British Journal of Social Psychology, 55*(2), 244–262. https://doi.org/10.1111/bjso.12131

Brown, J. K., Hohman, Z. P., Niedbaka, E. M., & Stinnett, A. J (2021). Sweating the big stuff: Arousal and stress as functions of self-uncertainty and identification. *Psychophysiology, 00*, e13836. https://doi.org/10.1111/psyp.13836

Chirumbolo, A., Livi, S., Mannetti, L., Pierro, A., & Kruglanski, A. W. (2004). Effects of need for closure on creativity in small group interactions. *European Journal of Personality, 18*(4), 265–278. https://doi.org/10.1002/per.518

Choi, E. U., & Hogg, M. A. (2020). Self-uncertainty and group identification: A meta-analysis. *Group Processes and Intergroup Relations, 23*(4), 483–501. https://doi.org/10.1177/1368430219846990

Cinelli, M., De Francisci Morales, G., Galeazzi, A., Quattrociocchi, W., & Starnini, M. (2021). The echo chamber effect. *PNAS, 118*(9), e2023301118. https://doi.org/10.1073/pnas.2023301118

De Grada, E., Kruglanski, A. W., Mannetti, L., & Pierro, A. (1999). Motivated cognition and group interaction: Need for closure affects the contents and processes of collective negotiations. *Journal of Experimental Social Psychology, 35*(4), 346–365. https://doi.org/10.1006/jesp.1999.1376

Douglas, K. M., & Sutton, R. M. (2018). Why conspiracy theories matter: A social psychological analysis. *European Review of Social Psychology, 29*, 256–298. https://doi.org/10.1080/10463283.2018.1537428

Echterhoff, G., Higgins, E. T., & Levine J. M. (2009). Shared reality: Experiencing commonality with others' inner states about the world. *Perspectives on Psychological Science, 4*(5), 496–521. https//doi.org/10.1111/j.1745-6924.2009.01161.x

Festinger, L. (1954). A theory of social comparison processes. *Human Relations, 7*, 117–140. https://doi.org/10.1177/001872675400700202

Fiske, S. T., & Taylor, S. E. (2021). *Social cognition: From brains to culture* (4th ed.). Sage.

Frenkel-Brunswick, E. (1948). Intolerance of ambiguity as an emotional and perceptual personality variable. *Journal of Personality, 18*, 108–123. https://doi.org/10.1111/j.1467-6494.1949.tb01236.x

Fromm, E. (1947). *Man for himself: An inquiry into the psychology of ethics*. Rinehart.

Gaffney, A. M., Hackett, J. D., Rast, D. E III, Hohman, Z. P., & Jaurique, A. (2018). The state of American protest: Shared anger and populism. *Analyses of Social Issues and Public Policy, 18*(1), 11–33. https://doi.org/10.1111/asap.12145

Goldman, L., & Hogg, M. A. (2016). Going to extremes for one's group: The role of prototypicality and group acceptance. *Journal of Applied Social Psychology, 46*(9), 544–553. https://doi.org/10.1111/jasp.12382

Grant, F., & Hogg, M. A. (2012). Self-uncertainty, social identity prominence and group identification. *Journal of Experimental Social Psychology, 48*(2), 538–542. https://doi.org/10.1016/j.jesp.2011.11.006

Guillén, L., Jacquart, P., & Hogg, M. A. (2023). To lead, or to follow? How self-uncertainty and the dark triad of personality influence leadership motivation. *Personality and Social Psychology Bulletin, 49*(7), 1043–1057. https://doi.org/10.1177/01461672221086771

Hamilton, D. L., & Sherman, S. J. (1996). Perceiving persons and groups. *Psychological Review, 103*(2), 336–355. https://doi.org/10.1037/0033-295X.103.2.336

Haslam, N. (2006). Dehumanization: An integrative review. *Personality and Social Psychology Review, 10*(3), 252–264. https://doi.org/10.1207/s15327957pspr1003_4

Haslam, N., Bastian, B., Bain, P., & Kashima, Y. (2006). Psychological essentialism, implicit theories, and intergroup relations. *Group Processes and Intergroup Relations, 9*(1), 63–76. https://doi.org/10.1177/1368430206059861

Haslam, N., Loughnan, S., & Kashima, Y. (2008). Attributing and denying humanness to others. *European Review of Social Psychology, 19*, 55–85. https://doi.org/10.1080/10463280801981645

Higgins, E. T. (1998). Promotion and prevention: Regulatory focus as a motivational principle. *Advances in Experimental Social Psychology, 30*, 1–46. https://doi.org/10.1016/S0065-2601(08)60381-0

Hogg, M. A. (1993). Group cohesiveness: A critical review and some new directions. *European Review of Social Psychology, 4*(1), 85–111. https://doi.org/10.1080/14792779343000031

Hogg, M. A. (2000). Subjective uncertainty reduction through self-categorization: A motivational theory of social identity processes. *European Review of Social Psychology, 11*, 223–255. https://doi.org/10.1080/14792772043000040

Hogg, M. A. (2007). Uncertainty-identity theory. *Advances in Experimental Social Psychology, 39*, 69–126. https://doi.org/10.1016/s0065-2601(06)39002-8

Hogg, M. A. (2010). Human groups, social categories, and collective self: Social identity and the management of self-uncertainty. In R. M. Arkin, K. C. Oleson, & P. J. Carroll (Eds.), *Handbook of the uncertain self* (pp. 401–420). Psychology Press.

Hogg, M. A. (2014). From uncertainty to extremism: Social categorization and identity processes. *Current Directions in Psychological Science, 23*(5), 338–342. https://doi.org/10.1177/0963721414540168

Hogg, M. A. (2016). Social identity theory. In S. McKeown, R. Haji, & N. Ferguson (Eds.), *Understanding peace and conflict through social identity theory: Contemporary global perspectives* (pp. 3–17). Springer. https://doi.org/10.1007/978-3-319-29869-6_1

Hogg, M. A. (2018). Social identity theory. In P. J. Burke (Ed.), *Contemporary social psychological theories* (2nd ed., pp. 112–138). Stanford University Press.

Hogg, M. A. (2021a). Self-uncertainty and group identification: Consequences for social identity, group behavior, intergroup relations, and society. *Advances in Experimental Social Psychology, 64*, 263–316. https://doi.org/10.1016/bs.aesp.2021.04.004

Hogg, M. A. (2021b). Uncertain self in a changing world: A foundation for radicalization, populism and autocratic leadership. *European Review of Social Psychology, 32(*2), 235–268. https://doi.org/10.1080/10463283.2020.1827628

Hogg, M. A. (2023). Walls between groups: Self-uncertainty, social identity, and intergroup leadership. *Journal of Social Issues*, *79*, 825–840. https://doi.org/10.1111/josi.12584

Hogg, M. A. (2024). Uncertainty, group identification and intergroup behavior: Positive and negative outcomes of how people experience uncertainty. *Psychology Hub*, *41*, 63–72. https://doi.org/10.13133/2724-2943/18404

Hogg, M. A. (in press). Social identity, self-uncertainty, and violent extremism. In M. Obaidi, & J. R. Kunst (Eds.), *Cambridge handbook of the psychology of violent extremism*. Cambridge University Press.

Hogg, M. A., & Gaffney, A. M. (2023). Social identity dynamics in the face of overwhelming uncertainty. In J. P. Forgas, W. D. Crano, & K. Fiedler (Eds.), *The psychology of insecurity: Seeking certainty where none can be found* (pp. 244–264). Routledge. https://doi.org/10.4324/9781003317623-17

Hogg, M. A., & Gøtzsche-Astrup, O. (2021). Self-uncertainty and populism: Why we endorse populist ideologies, identify with populist groups, and support populist leaders. In J. P. Forgas, W. D. Crano, & K. Fiedler (Eds.), *The psychology of populism: The tribal challenge to liberal democracy* (pp. 197–218). Routledge.

Hogg, M. A., & Mahajan, N. (2018). Domains of self-uncertainty and their relationship to group identification. *Journal of Theoretical Social Psychology, 2*(3), 67–75. https://doi.org/10.1002/jts5.20

Hogg, M. A., Meehan, C., & Farquharson, J. (2010). The solace of radicalism: Self-uncertainty and group identification in the face of threat. *Journal of Experimental Social Psychology, 46*(6), 1061–1066. https://doi.org/10.1016/j.jesp.2010.05.005

Hogg, M. A., & Rinella, M. J. (2018). Social identities and shared realities. *Current Opinion in Psychology, 23*, 6–10. https://doi.org/10.1016/j.copsyc.2017.10.003

Hogg, M. A., Sherman, D. K., Dierselhuis, J., Maitner, A. T., & Moffitt, G. (2007). Uncertainty, entitativity, and group identification. *Journal of Experimental Social Psychology, 43*(1), 135–142. https://doi.org/10.1016/j.jesp.2005.12.008

Hohman, Z. P., Gaffney, A. M., & Hogg, M. A. (2017). Who am I if I am not like my group? Self-uncertainty and feeling peripheral in a group. *Journal of Experimental Social Psychology, 72*, 125–132. https://doi.org/10.1016/j.jesp.2017.05.002

Jonas, E., McGregor, I., Klackl, J., Agroskin, D., Fritsche, I., Holbrook, C., Nash, K., Proulx, T., & Quirin, M. (2014). Threat and defense: From anxiety to approach. *Advances in Experimental Social Psychology, 49*, 219–286. https://doi.org/10.1016/B978-0-12-800052-6.00004-4

Kahneman, D., Slovic, P., & Tversky, A. (Eds.) 1982. *Judgment under uncertainty: Heuristics and biases*. New York: Cambridge University Press.

Kosic, A., Kruglanski, A. W., Pierro, A., & Mannetti, L. (2004). The social cognition of immigrants' acculturation: Effects of the need for closure and the reference group at entry. *Journal of Personality and Social Psychology, 86*(6), 796–813. https://doi.org/10.1037/0022-3514.86.6.796

Križan, Z., & Gibbons, F. X. (Eds.) (2014). *Communal functions of social comparison.* Cambridge University Press.

Kruglanski, A. W. (2004). *The psychology of closed mindedness.* Psychology Press.

Kruglanski, A. W., Ellenberg, M., Szumowska, E., Molinario, E., Speckhard, A., et al. (2023). Frustration-aggression hypothesis reconsidered: The role of significance quest. *Aggressive Behavior, 49*(5), 445–468. https://doi.org/10.1002/ab.22092

Kruglanski, A. W., & Fishman, S. (2009). The need for cognitive closure. In M. R. Leary & R. H. Hoyle (Eds.), *Handbook of individual differences in social behavior* (pp. 343–353). Guilford Press.

Kruglanski, A. W., Pierro, A., Mannetti, L., & De Grada, E. (2006). Groups as epistemic providers: Need for closure and the unfolding of group-centrism. *Psychological Review, 113*(1), 84–100. https://doi.org/10.1037/0033-295X.113.1.84

Kruglanski, A. W., & Webster, D. M. (1996). Motivated closing of the mind: 'Seizing' and 'freezing'. *Psychological Review, 103*(2), 263–283. https://doi.org/10.1037/0033-295X.103.2.263

Lickel, B., Hamilton, D. L., Wieczorkowska, G., Lewis, A., Sherman, S. J., & Uhles, A. N. (2000). Varieties of groups and the perception of group entitativity. *Journal of Personality and Social Psychology, 78*(2), 223–246. https://doi.org/10.1037/0022-3514.78.2.223

Mannetti, L., Levine, J. M., Pierro, A., & Kruglanski, A. W. (2010). Group reaction to defection: The impact of shared reality. *Social Cognition, 28*(3), 447–464. https://doi.org/10.1521/soco.2010.28.3.447

Mannetti, L., Pierro, A., Kruglanski, A. W., Taris, T., & Bezinovic, P. (2002). A cross cultural study of the need for cognitive closure scale: Comparing its structure in Croatia, Italy, USA and the Netherlands. *British Journal of Social Psychology, 41*(1), 139–156. https://doi.org/10.1348/014466602165108

Ozer, S., Obaidi, M., & Anjum, G. (2023). Extreme reactions to globalization: Investigating indirect, longitudinal, and experimental effects of the globalization-radicalization nexus. *Personality and Social Psychology Bulletin, 0*(0), 1–26. https://doi.org/10.1177/01461672231167694

Pinto, I. R., Marques, J. M., Levine, J. M., & Abrams, D. (2010). Membership status and subjective group dynamics: Who triggers the black sheep effect? *Journal of Personality and Social Psychology, 99*(1), 107–119. https://doi.org/10.1037/a0018187

Pollock, H. N. (2003). *Uncertain science... uncertain world.* Cambridge University Press.

Rast, D. E. III, Gaffney, A. M., Hogg, M. A., & Crisp, R. J. (2012). Leadership under uncertainty: When Leaders who are non-prototypical group members can gain support. *Journal of Experimental Social Psychology, 48*(3), 646–653. https://doi.org/10.1016/j.jesp.2011.12.013

Rast, D. E. III, Hogg, M. A., & Giessner, S. R. (2013). Self-uncertainty and support for autocratic leadership. *Self and Identity, 12*(6), 635–649. https://doi.org/10.1080/15298868.2012.718864

Rast, D. E. III, & Hogg, M. A. (2017). Leadership in the face of crisis and uncertainty. In J. Storey, J. Hartley, J.- L. Denis, P. 't Hart, & D. Ulrich (Eds.), *The Routledge companion to leadership* (pp. 52–64). Routledge.

Reid, S. A., & Hogg, M. A. (2005). Uncertainty reduction, self-enhancement, and ingroup identification. *Personality and Social Psychology Bulletin, 31*(6), 804–817. https://doi.org/10.1177/0146167204271708

Rios, K., Sosa, N., & Osborn, H. (2018) An experimental approach to Intergroup Threat Theory: Manipulations, moderators, and consequences of realistic vs. symbolic threat. *European Review of Social Psychology, 29*, 212–255. https://doi.org/10.1080/10463283.2018.1537049

Roccas, S., & Brewer, M. B. (2002). Social identity complexity. *Personality and Social Psychology Review, 6*(2), 88–106. https://doi.org/10.1207/S15327957PSPR0602_01

Rullo, M., & Livi, S. (2019). Not every flock has its black sheep: The role of entitativity and identification on deviants' derogation. *Rassegna di Psicologia, 36*(2), 39–51.

Sassenberg, K., & Scholl, A. (2019). Linking regulatory focus and threat–challenge: Transitions between and outcomes of four motivational states. *European Review of Social Psychology, 30*(1), 174–215. https://doi.org/10.1080/10463283.2019.1647507

Scheepers, D. (2009). Turning social identity threat into challenge: Status stability and cardiovascular reactivity during inter-group competition. *Journal of Experimental Social Psychology, 45*(1), 228–233. https://doi.org/10.1016/j.jesp.2008.09.011

Sedikides, C., Alicke, M. D., & Skowronski, J. J. (2021). On the utility of the self in social perception: An egocentric tactician model. *Advances in Experimental Social Psychology, 63*, 247–298. https://doi.org/10.1016/bs.aesp.2020.11.005

Sedikides, C., & Brewer, M. B. (Eds.) (2001). *Individual self, relational self, and collective self.* Philadelphia, PA: Psychology Press.

Stephan, W. G. (2014). Intergroup anxiety: Theory, research, and practice. *Personality and Social Psychology Review, 18*(3), 239–255. https://doi.org/10.1177/1088868314530518

Sternberg, R. J., & Kaufman, J. C. (2010). Constraints on creativity: Obvious and not so obvious. In J. C. Kaufman & R. J. Sternberg (Eds.), *The Cambridge handbook of creativity* (pp. 467–482). New York: Cambridge University Press.

Swann, W. B., & Bosson, J. K. (2010). Self and identity. In S. T. Fiske, D. T. Gilbert, & G. Lindzey (Eds.), *Handbook of social psychology* (5th ed., Vol. 1, pp. 589–628). Wiley.

Swann, W. B., Jetten, J., Gomez, A., Whitehouse, H., & Bastian, B. (2012). When group membership gets personal: A theory of identity fusion. *Psychological Review, 119*(3), 441–456. https://doi.org/10.1037/a0028589

Szumowska, E., & Kruglanski, A. W. (2020). Curiosity as end and means. *Current Opinion in Behavioral Sciences, 35*, 35–39. https://doi.org/10.1016/j.cobeha.2020.06.008
Tajfel, H. (1969). Cognitive aspects of prejudice. *Journal of Social Issues, 25*(4), 79–97. https://doi.org/10.1111/j.1540-4560.1969.tb00620.x
Tajfel, H., & Turner, J. C. (1986). The social identity theory of intergroup behaviour. In S. Worchel & W. G. Austin (Eds.), *Psychology of intergroup relations* (2nd ed., pp. 7–24). Nelson-Hall.
Theodorou, A., Livi, S., Kruglanski, A. W., & Pierro, A. (2023). Motivated team innovation: Impact of need for closure and epistemic authority. *Group Processes and Intergroup Relations, 26*(2), 284–303. https://doi.org/10.1177/13684302211038055
Turner, J. C., Hogg, M. A., Oakes, P. J., Reicher, S. D., & Wetherell, M. S. (1987). *Rediscovering the social group: A self-categorization theory*. Blackwell.
Van Knippenberg, D., & Hogg, M. A. (2018). Social identifications in organizational behavior. In D. L. Ferris, R. E. Johnson, & C. Sedikides (Eds.), *The self at work: Fundamental theory and research* (pp. 72–90). Routledge.
Wagoner, J. A., Antonini, M., Hogg, M. A., Barbieri, B., & Talamo, A. (2018). Identity-centrality, dimensions of uncertainty, and pursuit of subgroup autonomy: The case of Sardinia within Italy. *Journal of Applied Social Psychology, 48*(10), 582–589. https://doi.org/10.1111/jasp.12549
Wagoner, J. A., Belavadi, S., & Jung, J. (2017). Social identity uncertainty: Conceptualization, measurement, and construct validity. *Self and Identity, 16*(5), 505–530. https://doi.org/10.1080/15298868.2016.1275762
Wagoner, J. A., & Hogg, M. A. (2016). Normative dissensus, identity-uncertainty, and subgroup autonomy. *Group Dynamics: Theory, Research, and Practice, 20*(4), 310–322. https://doi.org/10.1037/gdn0000057

INDEX

Note: *Italic* page numbers refer to figures.